MILITARY AIRCRAFT MARKINGS 2001

Peter R. March & Howard J. Curtis

Contents

Photographs by Peter R. March (PRM) unless otherwise credited

This twenty-second edition published 2001

ISBN 0 7110 2782 X

Published by Ian Allan Publishing

an imprint of Ian Allan Publishing Ltd,, Hersham, Surrey KT12 4RG.

Printed by Ian Allan Printing Ltd, Hersham, Surrey KT12 4RG.

Code: 0301/F2

Front cover: Eurofighter Typhoon ZH588, the Warton, Lancs based DA2. *BAE Systems*

Back cover: Army Air Corps WAH-64 Apache Longbow AH1 ZJ167 of No 651 Sqn, Middle Wallop. *PRM*

Introduction

Now in its twenty-second annual edition, the *abc Military Aircraft Markings*, jointly edited by Peter R. March and Howard J Curtis, lists in alphabetical and numerical order all of the aircraft that carry a United Kingdom military serial, and **which are based, or might be seen, in the UK**. It also includes airworthy and current RAF/RN/Army aircraft that are based permanently or temporarily overseas. The term *aircraft* used here covers powered, manned aeroplanes, helicopters, airships and gliders. Included are all the current Royal Air Force, Royal Navy, Army Air Corps, Defence Procurement Agency, Defence Evaluation & Research Agency, manufacturers' test aircraft and civilian-owned aircraft with military markings.

Aircraft withdrawn from operational use but which are retained in the UK for ground training purposes or otherwise preserved by the Services and in the numerous museums and collections are listed. The serials of some incomplete aircraft have been included, such as the cockpit sections of machines displayed by the RAF, aircraft used by airfield fire sections and for service battle damage repair training (BDRT), together with significant parts of aircraft held by preservation groups and societies. Where only part of the aircraft fuselage remains the abbreviation <ff> for front fuselage/cockpit section or <rf> for rear fuselage is shown after the type. Many of these aircraft are allocated, and sometimes wear, a secondary identity, such as an RAF Logistics Command 'M' maintenance number. These numbers are listed against those aircraft to which they have been allocated.

A serial 'missing' from a sequence is either because it was never issued as it formed part of a 'blackout block' (a practice that has now ceased) or because the aircraft is written off, scrapped, sold abroad or allocated an alternative marking. Aircraft used as targets on MoD ranges to which access is restricted, and un-manned target drones, are generally omitted, as are UK military aircraft that have been permanently grounded and are based overseas and unlikely to return to Britain.

In the main, the serials listed are those markings presently displayed on the aircraft. Where an aircraft carries a false serial it is quoted in *italic type*. Very often these serials are carried by replicas, that are denoted by <R> after the type. The manufacturer and aircraft type are given, together with recent alternative, previous, secondary or civil identity shown in round brackets. Complete records of multiple previous identities are only included where space permits. The operating unit and its based location, along with any known unit and base code markings in square brackets, are given as accurately as possible. The unit markings are normally carried boldly on the sides of the fuselage or on the aircraft's fin. In the case of RAF and AAC machines currently in service, they are usually one or two letters or numbers, while the RN continues to use a well-established system of three-figure codes between 000 and 999 together with a fin letter code denoting the aircraft's operational base. RN squadrons, units and bases are allocated blocks of numbers from which individual aircraft codes are issued. To help identification of RN bases and landing platforms on ships, a list of tail-letter codes with their appropriate name, helicopter code number, ship pennant number and type of vessel, is included; as is a helicopter code number/ships' tail-letter code grid cross-reference.

Codes change, for example when aircraft move between units, and therefore the markings currently painted on a particular aircraft might not be those shown in this edition because of subsequent events. Aircraft currently under manufacture or not yet delivered to the Service, such as GKN-Westland WAH-64D Apaches at Yeovil and the remaining C-130J Hercules temporarily stored at Cambridge, most of which carry civil registrations, are listed under their allocated RAF serial. Likewise there are a number of newly built aircraft for overseas air arms that carry British serials for their UK and delivery flights. The four C-17 Globemasters leased from the US government unusually carry out-of-sequence serials ZZ171-ZZ174. Those airframes which may not appear in the next edition because of sale, accident, etc, have their fates, where known, given in italic type in the *locations* column.

The Irish Army Air Corps fleet is listed, together with the serials of other overseas air arms whose aircraft might be seen visiting the UK from time to time. The serial numbers are as usually presented on the individual machine or as they are normally identified. Where possible, the aircraft's base and operating unit have been shown.

USAF, US Army and US Navy aircraft based in the UK and in Western Europe, and types that regularly visit the UK from the USA, are each listed in separate sections by aircraft type. The serial number actually displayed on the aircraft is shown in full, with additional Fiscal Year (FY) or full serial information also provided. Where appropriate, details of the operating wing, squadron allocation and base are added. The USAF is, like the RAF, in a continuing period of change, resulting in the adoption of new unit titles, squadron and equipment changes and the closure of bases. Only details that concern changes effected by January 2001 are shown.

Veteran and vintage aircraft which carry overseas military markings but which are based in the UK have been separately listed showing their principal means of identification. The growing list of aircraft in government or military service, often under contract to private operating companies, that carry civil registrations has again been included, at the end of the respective country.

With the use of the Internet now very well established as a rich source of information, the section listing a selection of military aviation 'world wide web' sites, has been further expanded and up-dated this year. Although only a few of these provide details of aircraft serials and markings, they do give interesting insights into air arms and their operating units, aircraft, museums and a broad range of associated topics.

Information shown is believed to be correct at 31 January 2001, and significant changes can be monitored through the monthly 'Military Markings' column in *Aircraft Illustrated* and for Internet up-dates the 'Airnet' column.

Acknowledgements

The compilers again wish to thank the many people who have taken trouble to send comments, additions, deletions and other useful information following the publication of the previous edition of *abc Military Aircraft Markings*. In particular the following individuals: Lucio Alfieri, Dave Almey, Dave Arkle, Allan Barley, Michael Barnes, Jeff Bell, Keith Blincow, Pavel Bondaryk, Oscar Bosman, Derek Bower, Damien Burke, Steve Buttriss, Ian Carroll, Richard Cawsey, Phil Charlton, Dougie Couch, Duncan Curtis, Gary Donnison, Anthony Doyle, Bob Dunn, Nigel Elliot, Chris Evans, Lorence Fizia, Graham Gaff, Wal Gandy, Alessandro Gasparini, Donald Gatt, Stefan Goossens, Dave Graham, Edwin de Greeuw, Jerry Gunner, Dave Haines, Stephen Halksworth, Kevin Hall, Hans en Hinke, Nigel Hitchman, Raymond Hoddinott, Frits van Hout, Nick Jackson, Thomas Kaminski, Paul Kendrick, Bob Kent, Christoph Kugler, Richard Laskewitz, Kevin Latham, Koen Leuvering, Alan Macey, Andrew March, Daniel March, Andy Marden, Bernard Martin, Joe McDermott, Tom McGhee, Eugene van der Meer, Jeff Middleton, Ed Miller, Gavin Mills, David Moore, Gary Morris, Coert Munk, Jeremy Parkin, Chris Parsons, Lindsay Peacock, Dave Peel, John Poxon, Keith Preen, Doug Pritchard, Fabrizio Pruneti, Stephen Rhymes, Mike Riach, Robby Robinson, David Rogers, Cristian Schrik, Pete Simmonds, James Simpson, Chris Slack, Tony Smith, Steve Speight, David Stretton, John Sullivan, Michael Tafel, Mervyn Thomas, Robert Thomas, David Thompson, John Tillett, Jurgen van Toor, Richard Tregear, Chris Vaughan, Hans van der Vlist, Colin Walford, Gary Watson, Anthony Williams, Dave Wilton, Sander Wittenaar and Mark Young.

The compilation has also relied heavily on the publications and aviation groups and societies as follows: *Air-Britain News* (Air-Britain), *Air Link* (Lincolnshire Aviation Society), Apache Research Group, East London Aviation Society, Friends of Leeming Aviation Group, *Irish Air Letter*, *Military Aviation Review* (MAP), Military Spotter's Forum, *Osprey* (Solent Aviation Society), *RAF News*, *Scramble* (Dutch Aviation Society), St Athan Aviation Group, *Stansted Aviation News* (Stansted Aviation Society), Top Spotters Mil Forum and the Wolverhampton Aviation Group.

PRM & HJC   **January 2001**

Abbreviations

AAC	Army Air Corps	Cav	Cavalry
AACS	Airborne Air Control Squadron	CC	County Council
AACTS	Airborne Air Control Training Squadron	CCF	Combined Cadet Force/Canadian Car & Foundry Company
AAS	Aeromedical Airlift Squadron		
ABS	Air Base Squadron	CDE	Chemical Defence Establishment
ACC	Air Combat Command	CEAM	Centre d'Expérimentation Aériennes Militaires (Military Air Experimental Centre)
ACCGS	Air Cadets Central Gliding School		
ACCS	Airborne Command and Control Squadron	CEV	Centre d'Essais en Vol (Flight Test Centre)
		CFS	Central Flying School
ACW	Airborne Control Wing	CGMF	Central Glider Maintenance Flight
AD&StA	Aberdeen, Dundee & St Andrews	CIFAS	Centre d'Instruction des Forces Aériennes Stratégiques (Air Strategic Training Centre)
AEF	Air Experience Flight		
AESS	Air Engineering & Survival School		
AEW	Airborne Early Warning	CinC	Commander in Chief
AF	Arméflyget (Army Air Battalion)	CinCLANT	Commander in Chief Atlantic
AFB	Air Force Base	CITac	Centre d'Instruction Tactique (Tactical Training Centre)
AFD	Air Fleet Department		
AFRC	Air Force Reserve Command	Co	Company
AFSC	Air Force Systems Command	Comp	Composite with
AFSK	Armeflygskolan (Army Flying School)	CT	College of Technology
AFWF	Advanced Fixed Wing Flight	CTE	Central Training Establishment
AG	Airlift Group	CV	Chance-Vought
AGA	Academia General del Aire (General Air Academy)	D-BA	Daimler-Benz Aerospace
		D-BD	Dassault-Breguet Dornier
AkG	Aufklärüngsgeschwader (Reconnaissance Wing)	D&G	Dumfries and Galloway
		DARA	Defence Aviation Repair Agency
AMC	Air Mobility Command	DEODS	Defence Explosives Ordnance Disposal School
AMD-BA	Avions Marcel Dassault-Breguet Aviation		
AMF	Aircraft Maintenance Flight	DERA	Defence Evaluation and Research Agency
AMG	Aircraft Maintenance Group	Det	Detachment
AMIF	Aircraft Maintenance Instruction Flight	DH	de Havilland
AMS	Air Movements School	DHC	de Havilland Canada
AMW	Air Mobility Wing	DHFS	Defence Helicopter Flying School
ANG	Air National Guard	dlt	dopravni letka (Transport Squadron)
APS	Aircraft Preservation Society	DPA	Defence Procurement Agency
ARS	Air Refuelling Squadron	DTI	Department of Trade and Industry
ARW	Air Refuelling Wing	EA	Escadron Aérien (Air Squadron)
ARWS	Advanced Rotary Wing Squadron	EAC	Ecole de l'Aviation de Chasse (Fighter Aviation School)
AS	Airlift Squadron/Air Squadron		
ASCW	Airborne Surveillance Control Wing	EAP	European Aircraft Project
ASF	Aircraft Servicing Flight	EAT	Ecole de l'Aviation de Transport (Transport Aviation School)
AS&RU	Aircraft Salvage and Repair Unit		
ATC	Air Training Corps	EC	Escadre de Chasse (Fighter Wing)
ATCC	Air Traffic Control Centre	ECS	Electronic Countermeasures Squadron
Avn	Aviation	EDA	Escadre de Detection Aéroportée (Air Detection Wing)
Avn Co	Aviation Company		
AW	Airlift Wing/Armstrong Whitworth Aircraft	EdC	Escadron de Convoyage
AWC	Air Warfare Centre	EDCA	Escadron de Détection et de Control Aéroportée (Airborne Detection & Control Sqn)
BAC	British Aircraft Corporation		
BAe	British Aerospace PLC		
BAPC	British Aviation Preservation Council	EE	English Electric/Escadrille Electronique
BATUS	British Army Training Unit Suffield	EET	Escadron Electronique Tactique (Tactical Electronics Flight)
BBMF	Battle of Britain Memorial Flight		
BDRF	Battle Damage Repair Flight	EH	Escadron d'Helicoptères (Helicopter Flight)
BDRT	Battle Damage Repair Training		
Be	Beech	EHI	European Helicopter Industries
Bf	Bayerische Flugzeugwerke	EL	Escadre de Liaison (Liaison Wing)
BFWF	Basic Fixed Wing Flight	EMA	East Midlands Airport
BG	Bomber Group	EMVO	Elementaire Militaire Vlieg Opleiding (Elementary Flying Training)
BGA	British Gliding & Soaring Association		
bk	black (squadron colours and markings)	ENOSA	Ecole des Navigateurs Operationales Systemes d'Armees (Navigation School)
bl	blue (squadron colours and markings)		
BNFL	British Nuclear Fuels Ltd	EoN	Elliot's of Newbury
BnHATk	Helicopter Attack Battalion	EPAA	Ecole de Pilotage Elementaire de l'Armée de l'Air (Air Force Elementary Flying School)
BnHLn	Liaison Battalion		
BP	Boulton & Paul		
br	brown (squadron colours and markings)	EPE	Ecole de Pilotage Elementaire (Elementary Flying School)
BS	Bomber Squadron		
B-V	Boeing-Vertol	EPNER	Ecole du Personnel Navigant d'Essais et de Reception
BW	Bomber Wing		
CAC	Commonwealth Aircraft Corporation	EPTT	Exhibition, Production & Transportation Team
CAM	College of Aviation Medicine		
CARG	Cotswold Aircraft Restoration Group	ER	Escadre de Reconnaissance (Reconnaissance Wing)
CASA	Construcciones Aeronautics SA		

7

ERS	Escadron de Reconnaissance Stratégique (Strategic Reconnaissance Squadron)
ERV	Escadre de Ravitaillement en Vol (Air Refuelling Wing)
ES	Escadrille de Servitude
Esc	Escuadron (Squadron)
Esk	Eskadrille (Squadron)
Eslla	Escuadrilla (Squadron)
Esq	Esquadra (Squadron)
ET	Escadre de Transport (Transport Squadron)
ETE	Escadron de Transport et Entrainment (Transport Training Squadron)
ETEC	Escadron de Transport d'Entrainement et de Calibration (Transport Training & Calibration Sqn)
ETL	Escadron de Transport Légère (Light Transport Squadron)
ETO	Escadron de Transition Operationnelle
ETOM	Escadron de Transport Outre Mer (Overseas Transport Squadron)
ETPS	Empire Test Pilots' School
ETS	Engineering Training School
FAA	Fleet Air Arm/Federal Aviation Administration
FACF	Forward Air Control Flight
FBS	Flugbereitschaftsstaffel
FBW	Fly by wire
FC	Forskokcentralen (Flight Centre)
FE	Further Education
FETC	Fire and Emergency Training Centre
ff	Front fuselage
FG	Fighter Group
FH	Fairchild-Hiller
FI	Falkland Islands
FISt	Flieger Staffel (Flight Squadron)
Flt	Flight
FMA	Fabrica Militar de Aviones
FMT	Flotila Militara de Transport (Transport Regiment)
FMV	Forsvarets Materielwerk
FONA	Flag Officer Naval Aviation
FRADU	Fleet Requirements and Air Direction Unit
FRA	FR Aviation
FS	Fighter Squadron
FSAIU	Flight Safety & Accident Investigation Unit
FSCTE	Fire Services Central Training Establishment
FTS	Flying Training School
FTW	Flying Training Wing
Fw	Focke Wulf
FW	Fighter Wing/Foster Wickner
FWTS	Fixed Wing Test Squadron
FY	Fiscal Year
F3 OCU	Tornado F3 Operational Conversion Unit
GAL	General Aircraft Ltd
GAM	Groupe Aerien Mixte (Composite Air Group)
gd	gold (squadron colours and markings)
GD	General Dynamics
GHL	Groupe d'Helicopteres Legeres (Light Helicopter Group)
GI	Ground Instruction/Groupement d'Instruction (Instructional Group)
GKNW	GKN Westland
gn	green (squadron colours and markings)
GRD	Gruppe fur Rustunggdienste (Group for Service Preparation)
GT	Grupo de Transporte (Transport Wing)
GTT	Grupo de Transporte de Tropos (Troop Carrier Wing)
gy	grey (squadron colours and markings)
H&W	Hereford and Worcester
HAF	Historic Aircraft Flight
HC	Helicopter Combat Support Squadron
HF	Historic Flying Ltd
HFR	Heeresfliegerregiment (Army Air Regiment)
HFWS	Heeresflieger Waffenschule (Army Air Weapons School)
Hkp Div	Helikopterdivisionen (Helicopter Division)
HMA	Helicopter Maritime Attack
HMF	Harrier Maintenance Flight/Helicopter Maintenance Flight
HMS	Her Majesty's Ship
HOCU	Harrier OCU
HP	Handley-Page
HQ	Headquarters
HS	Hawker Siddeley
HSF	Harrier Servicing Flight
IAF	Israeli Air Force
INTA	Instituto Nacional de Tecnica Aerospacial
IOW	Isle Of Wight
IWM	Imperial War Museum
JATE	Joint Air Transport Establishment
JbG	Jagdbombergeschwader (Fighter Bomber Wing)
JFACSTU	Joint Forward Air Control Students Training Unit
JG	Jagdgeschwader (Fighter Wing)
Kridlo	Wing
Letka	Squadron
ltBVr	letka Bitevnich Vrtulníkù (Attack Helicopter Squadron)
LTG	Lufttransportgeschwader (Air Transport Wing)
LTV	Ling-Temco-Vought
LVG	Luftwaffen Versorgungs Geschwader (Air Force Maintenance Wing)/Luft Verkehrs Gesellschaft
LZO	Letecky Zku_ební Odbor (Aviation Test Department)
m	multi-coloured (squadron colours and markings)
MAPK	Mira Anachestisis Pantos Kerou (All Weather Interception Sqn)
MARPAT	Maritime Patrouillegroep (Maritime Patrol Group)
MBB	Messerschmitt Bolkow-Blohm
MCAS	Marine Corps Air Station
McD	McDonnell Douglas
Med	Medical
MFG	Marine Flieger Geschwader (Naval Air Wing)
MH	Max Holste
MIB	Military Intelligence Battalion
MiG	Mikoyan – Gurevich
Mod	Modified
MR	Maritime Reconnaissance
MRF	Meteorological Research Flight
MS	Morane-Saulnier
MTM	Mira Taktikis Metaforon (Tactical Transport Sqn)
MU	Maintenance Unit
Mus'm	Museum
NA	North American
NACDS	Naval Air Command Driving School
NAEWF	NATO Airborne Early Warning Force
NAF	Naval Air Facility
NAS	Naval Air Station
NASU	Naval Air Support Unit
NATO	North Atlantic Treaty Organisation
NAWC	Naval Air Warfare Center
NAWC-AD	Naval Air Warfare Center Aircraft Division
NBC	Nuclear, Biological and Chemical
NE	North-East
NFATS	Naval Force Aircraft Test Squadron
NI	Northern Ireland
NMSU	Nimrod Major Servicing Unit
NYARC	North Yorks Aircraft Restoration Centre
OCU	Operational Conversion Unit
OEU	Operation Evaluation Unit
OFMC	Old Flying Machine Company

or	orange (squadron colours and markings)
OSAC	Operational Support Airlift Command
OVH Kmp	Observations-Helicopter Kompagni
PASF	Puma Aircraft Servicing Flight
PAT	Priority Air Transport Detachment
PBN	Pilatus Britten-Norman
PLM	Pulk Lotnictwa Mysliwskiego (Fighter Regiment)
pr	purple (squadron colours and markings)
PRU	Photographic Reconnaissance Unit
PVH Kmp	Panservaerns-Helicopter Kompagni
pzdlt	pruzkumná dopravni letka (Reconnaissance & Transport Squadron)
r	red (squadron colours and markings)
R	Replica
RAeS	Royal Aeronautical Society
RAF	Royal Aircraft Factory/Royal Air Force
RAFC	Royal Air Force College
RAFM	Royal Air Force Museum
RAFGSA	Royal Air Force Gliding and Soaring Association
RCAF	Royal Canadian Air Force
RE	Royal Engineers
Regt	Regiment
REME	Royal Electrical & Mechanical Engineers
rf	Rear fuselage
RJAF	Royal Jordanian Air Force
RM	Royal Marines
RMB	Royal Marines Base
RMC of S	Royal Military College of Science
RN	Royal Navy
RNAS	Royal Naval Air Station
RNAW	Royal Naval Aircraft Workshop
RNAY	Royal Naval Aircraft Yard
RNGSA	Royal Navy Gliding and Soaring Association
ROF	Royal Ordnance Factory
RQS	Rescue Squadron
R-R	Rolls-Royce
RS	Reid & Sigrist/Reconnaissance Squadron
RSV	Reparto Sperimentale Volo (Experimental Flight School)
RW	Reconnaissance Wing
SA	Scottish Aviation
Saab	Svenska Aeroplan Aktieboleg
SAH	School of Air Handling
SAL	Scottish Aviation Limited
SAOEU	Strike/Attack Operational Evaluation Unit
SAR	Search and Rescue
Saro	Saunders-Roe
SARTU	Search and Rescue Training Unit
SBoLK	Stíhacie Bombardovacie Letecké Kridlo (Fighter Bomber Air Wing)
SCW	Strategic Communications Wing
SEAE	School of Electrical & Aeronautical Engineering
SEPECAT	Société Européenne de Production de l'avion Ecole de Combat et d'Appui Tactique
SFDO	School of Flight Deck Operations
SHAPE	Supreme Headquarters Allied Forces Europe
si	silver (squadron colours and markings)
SIET	Section d'Instruction et d'Etude du Tir
SKTU	Sea King Training Unit
Skv	Skvadron (Squadron)
SLK	Stíhacie Letecké Kridlo (Fighter Air Wing)
slt	stíhací letka (Fighter Squadron)
SLV	School Licht Vliegwezen (Flying School)
Sm	Smaldeel (Squadron)
SNCAN	Société Nationale de Constructions Aéronautiques du Nord
SOES	Station Operations & Engineering Squadron
SOG	Special Operations Group
SOS	Special Operations Squadron
SoTT	School of Technical Training
SOW	Special Operations Wing
SPAD	Société Pour les Appareils Deperdussin
Sqn	Squadron
SSF	Station Servicing Flight
SWWAPS	Second World War Aircraft Preservation Society
TA	Territorial Army
TAP	Transporten Avio Polk (Air Transport Regiment)
T&EE	Test & Evaluation Establishment
TFC	The Fighter Collection
TGp	Test Groep
TIARA	Tornado Integrated Avionics Research Aircraft
tlt	taktická letka (Tactical Squadron)
TMF	Tornado Maintenance Flight
TMTS	Trade Management Training School
tpzlt	taktická a pruzkumná letka (Tactical & Reconnaissance Squadron)
TS	Test Squadron
TsAGI	Tsentral'ny Aerogidrodinamicheski Instut (Central Aero & Hydrodynamics Institute)
TsLw	Technische Schule der Luftwaffe (Luftwaffe Technical School)
TSW	Tactical Supply Wing
TW	Test Wing
UAS	University Air Squadron
Uberwg	Uberwachunggeschwader (Surveillance Wing)
UK	United Kingdom
UKAEA	United Kingdom Atomic Energy Authority
UNFICYP	United Nations' Forces in Cyprus
US	United States
USAF	United States Air Force
USAFE	United States Air Forces in Europe
USAREUR	US Army Europe
USCGS	US Coast Guard Station
USEUCOM	United States European Command
USMC	United States Marine Corps
USN	United States Navy
NWTSPM	United States Navy Test Pilots School
VAAC	Vectored thrust Advanced Aircraft flight Control
VFW	Vereinigte Flugtechnische Werke
VGS	Volunteer Gliding School
vlt	vycviková letka (Training Squadron)
VMGR	Marine Aerial Refuelling/Transport Squadron
VMGRT	Marine Aerial Refuelling/Transport Training Squadron
VQ	Fleet Air Reconnaissance Squadron
VR	Fleet Logistic Support Squadron
VS	Vickers-Supermarine
VSD	Vegyes Szàllitorepülő Dandàr (Aircraft Transport Brigade)
VSL	Vycvikové Stredisko Letectva (Flying Training Centre)
w	white (squadron colours and markings)
Wg	Wing
WLT	Weapons Loading Training
WRS	Weather Reconnaissance Squadron
WS	Westland
WTD	Wehrtechnische Dienstelle (Technical Support Unit)
WW2	World War II
y	yellow (squadron colours and markings)
zDL	základna Dopravního Letectva (Air Transport Base)
ZmDK	Zmie_an_ Dopravn_ Kridlo (Mixed Transport Wing)
zSL	základna _kolního Letectva (Training Air Base)
zTL	základna Taktického Letectva (Tactical Air Base)
zVrL	základna Vrtulníkového Letectva (Helicopter Air Base)

A Guide to the Location of Operational Military Bases in the UK

This section is to assist the reader to locate the places in the United Kingdom where operational military aircraft are based. The term *aircraft* also includes helicopters and gliders.

The alphabetical order listing gives each location in relation to its county and to its nearest classified road(s) (*by* means adjoining; *of* means proximate to), together with its approximate direction and mileage from the centre of a nearby major town or city. Some civil airports are included where active military units are also based, but **excluded** are MoD sites with non-operational aircraft (eg *gate guardians*), the bases of privately-owned civil aircraft that wear military markings and museums.

User	Base name	County/Region	Location	Distance/direction from (town)
DERA	Aberporth	Dyfed	N of A487	6m ENE of Cardigan
Army	Abingdon	Oxfordshire	W by B4017, W of A34	5m SSW of Oxford
RAF	Aldergrove/Belfast Airport	Co Antrim	W by A26	13m W of Belfast
RM	Arbroath	Angus	E of A933	2m NW of Arbroath
RAF/ Hunting	Barkston Heath	Lincolnshire	W by B6404, S of A153	5m NNE of Grantham
RAF	Benson	Oxfordshire	E by A423	1m NE of Wallingford
DERA/ RAF	Boscombe Down	Wiltshire	S by A303, W of A338	6m N of Salisbury
RAF	Boulmer	Northumberland	E of B1339	4m E of Alnwick
RAF	Brize Norton	Oxfordshire	W of A4095	5m SW of Witney
Marshall	Cambridge Airport/ Teversham	Cambridgeshire	S by A1303	2m E of Cambridge
RM/RAF	Chivenor	Devon	S of A361	4m WNW of Barnstaple
RAF	Church Fenton	Yorkshire North	S of B1223	7m WNW of Selby
RAF	Colerne	Wiltshire	S of A420, E of Fosse Way	5m NE of Bath
RAF	Coltishall	Norfolk	W of B1150	9m NNE of Norwich
RAF	Coningsby	Lincolnshire	S of A153, W by B1192	10m NW of Boston
RAF	Cosford	Shropshire	W of A41, N of A464	9m WNW of Wolverhampton
RAF	Cottesmore	Leicestershire	W of A1, N of B668	9m NW of Stamford
RAF	Cranwell	Lincolnshire	N by A17, S by B1429	5m WNW of Sleaford
RN	Culdrose	Cornwall	E by A3083	1m SE of Helston
Army	Dishforth	Yorkshire North	E by A1	4m E of Ripon
USAF	Fairford	Gloucestershire	S of A417	9m ESE of Cirencester
RN	Fleetlands	Hampshire	E by A32	2m SE of Fareham
RAF	Glasgow Airport	Strathclyde	N by M8 jn 28	7m W of city
RAF	Halton	Buckinghamshire	N of A4011, S of B4544	4m ESE of Aylesbury
RAF	Henlow	Bedfordshire	E of A600, W of A6001	1m SW of Henlow
RAF	Honington	Suffolk	E of A134, W of A1088	6m S of Thetford
Army	Hullavington	Wiltshire	W of A429	1m N of M4 jn 17
RAF	Kenley	Greater London	W of A22	1m W of Warlingham
RAF	Kinloss	Grampian	E of B9011, N of B9089	3m NE of Forres
RAF	Kirknewton	Lothian	E by B7031, N by A70	8m SW of Edinburgh
USAF	Lakenheath	Suffolk	W by A1065	8m W of Thetford
RAF	Leeming	Yorkshire North	E by A1	5m SW of Northallerton
RAF	Leuchars	Fife	E of A919	7m SE of Dundee
RAF	Linton-on-Ouse	Yorkshire North	E of B6265	10m NW of York
DERA	Llanbedr	Gwynedd	W of A496	7m NNW of Barmouth
RAF	Lossiemouth	Grampian	W of B9135, S of B9040	4m N of Elgin
RAF	Lyneham	Wiltshire	W of A3102, S of A420	10m WSW of Swindon
RAF	Marham	Norfolk	N by A1122	6m W of Swaffham
Army	Middle Wallop	Hampshire	S by A343	6m SW of Andover
USAF	Mildenhall	Suffolk	S by A1101	9m NNE of Newmarket
RAF	Northolt	Greater London	N by A40	3m E of M40 jn 1
RAF	Odiham	Hampshire	E of A32	2m S of M3 jn 5
RN	Predannack	Cornwall	W by A3083	7m S of Helston
RN	Prestwick Airport	Strathclyde	E by A79	3m N of Ayr
RAF	St Athan	South Glamorgan	N of B4265	13m WSW of Cardiff
RAF	St Mawgan/Newquay	Cornwall	N of A3059	4m ENE of Newquay
RAF	Scampton	Lincolnshire	W by A15	6m N of Lincoln

User	Base name	County/Region	Location	Distance/direction from (town)
RAF	Sealand	Flint	W by A550	6m WNW of Chester
RAF	Shawbury	Shropshire	W of B5063	7m NNE of Shrewsbury
RAF	Syerston	Nottinghamshire	W by A46	5m SW of Newark
RAF	Ternhill	Shropshire	SW by A41	3m SW of Market Drayton
RAF/ Army	Topcliffe	Yorkshire North	E of A167, W of A168	3m SW of Thirsk
RAF	Valley	Gwynedd	S of A5 on Anglesey	5m SE of Holyhead
RAF	Waddington	Lincolnshire	E by A607, W by A15	5m S of Lincoln
BAe	Warton	Lancashire	S by A584	8m SE of Blackpool
Army/ RAF	Wattisham	Suffolk	N of B1078	5m SSW of Stowmarket
DERA	West Freugh	Dumfries & Galloway	S by A757, W by A715	5m SE of Stranraer
RAF	Weston-on-the-Green	Oxfordshire	E by A43	9m N of Oxford
RAF	Wittering	Cambridgeshire	W by A1, N of A47	3m S of Stamford
RAF	Woodvale	Merseyside	W by A565	5m SSW of Southport
RAF	Wyton	Cambridgeshire	E of A141, N of B1090	3m NE of Huntingdon
WS	Yeovil	Somerset	N of A30, S of A3088	1m W of Yeovil
RN	Yeovilton	Somerset	S by B3151, S of A303	5m N of Yeovil

Canberra PR9 XH168 (AD), one of five still operated by No 39 (1PRU) Squadron RAF. *Daniel March*

British Military Aircraft Serials

The Committee of Imperial Defence through its Air Committee introduced a standardised system of numbering aircraft in November 1912. The Air Department of the Admiralty was allocated the first batch 1-200 and used these to cover aircraft already in use and those on order. The Army was issued with the next block from 201-800, which included the number 304 which was given to the Cody Biplane now preserved in the Science Museum. By the outbreak of World War 1 the Royal Navy was on its second batch of serials 801-1600 and this system continued with alternating allocations between the Army and Navy until 1916 when number 10000, a Royal Flying Corps BE2C, was reached.

It was decided not to continue with five digit numbers but instead to start again from 1, prefixing RFC aircraft with the letter A and RNAS aircraft with the prefix N. The RFC allocations commenced with A1 an FE2D and before the end of the year had reached A9999 an Armstrong Whitworth FK8. The next group commenced with B1 and continued in logical sequence through the C, D, E and F prefixes. G was used on a limited basis to identify captured German aircraft, while H was the last block of wartime-ordered aircraft. To avoid confusion I was not used, so the new postwar machines were allocated serials in the J range. A further minor change was made in the serial numbering system in August 1929 when it was decided to maintain four numerals after the prefix letter, thus omitting numbers 1 to 999. The new K series therefore commenced at K1000, which was allocated to an AW Atlas.

The Naval N prefix was not used in such a logical way. Blocks of numbers were allocated for specific types of aircraft such as seaplanes or flying-boats. By the late 1920s the sequence had largely been used up and a new series using the prefix S was commenced. In 1930 separate naval allocations were stopped and subsequent serials were issued in the 'military' range which had by this time reached the K series. A further change in the pattern of allocations came in the L range. Commencing with L7272 numbers were issued in blocks with smaller blocks of serials between not used. These were known as blackout blocks. As M had already been used as a suffix for Maintenance Command instructional airframes it was not used as a prefix. Although N had previously been used for naval aircraft it was used again for serials allocated from 1937.

With the build-up to World War 2 the rate of allocations quickly accelerated and the prefix R was being used when war was declared. The letters O and Q were not allotted, and nor was S which had been used up to S1865 for naval aircraft before integration into the RAF series. By 1940 the serial Z9999 had been reached, as part of a blackout block, with the letters U and Y not used to avoid confusion. The option to recommence serial allocation at A1000 was not taken up; instead it was decided to use an alphabetical two-letter prefix with three numerals running from 100 to 999. Thus AA100 was allocated to a Blenheim IV.

This two-letter, three-numeral serial system which started in 1940 continues today. The letters C, I, O, Q, U and Y were, with the exception of NC, not used. For various reasons the following letter combinations were not issued: DA, DB, DH, EA, GA to GZ, HA, HT, JE, JH, JJ, KR to KT, MR, NW, NZ, SA to SK, SV, TN, TR and VE. The first postwar serials issued were in the VP range while the end of the WZs had been reached by the Korean War. The current new issues are in the latter part of the ZJ range and there are now no blackout blocks of unallocated serials. This being so, and at the current rate of issue, the Z range will last for many years. Occasionally an 'out-of-sequence' serial is issued to a manufacturer's prototype or development aircraft viz ZK101 and ZT800. However, a break in the established sequence has come with the four Boeing C-17 Globemasters leased from the US government, that have been allocated the serials ZZ171-ZZ174.

Note: Whilst every effort has been made to ensure the accuracy of this publication, no part of the contents has been obtained from official sources. The compilers will be pleased to receive comments, corrections and further information for inclusion in subsequent editions of *Military Aircraft Markings* and the monthly up-date of additions and amendments that is published in *Aircraft Illustrated*. Please send your information to Military Aircraft Markings, PO Box 46, Westbury-on-Trym, Bristol BS9 1TF; fax to 0117 968 3928 or e-mail to HJCurtis@cwcom.net.

British Military Aircraft Markings

A serial in *italics* denotes that it is not the genuine marking for that airframe.

Serial	Type (other identity) [code]	Owner/operator, location or fate	Notes
168	Sopwith Tabloid Scout <R> (G-BFDE)	RAF Museum, Hendon	
304	Cody Biplane (BAPC 62)	Science Museum, South Kensington	
687	RAF BE2b <R> (BAPC 181)	RAF Museum, Hendon	
1701	RAF BE2c <R> (BAPC 117)	Privately owned, Orpington	
2345	Vickers FB5 Gunbus <R> (G-ATVP)	RAF Museum, Hendon	
2699	RAF BE2c	Imperial War Museum, Lambeth	
2882	Vickers FB5 Gunbus <R> (BAPC 234)	Barton Aviation Heritage Society, Barton	
3066	Caudron GIII (G-AETA/9203M)	RAF Museum, Hendon	
5964	DH2 <R> (BAPC 112)	Museum of Army Flying, stored Middle Wallop	
5964	DH2 <R> (G-BFVH)	Privately owned, Withybush	
6232	RAF BE2c <R> (BAPC 41)	Yorkshire Air Museum, stored Elvington	
8359	Short 184 <ff>	FAA Museum, RNAS Yeovilton	
A301	Morane BB (frame)	RAF Museum, stored Wyton	
A1325	RAF BE2e (G-BVGR)	Privately owned, Milden	
A1742	Bristol Scout D <R> (BAPC 38)	Privately owned, Solihull	
A4850	RAF SE5a <R> (BAPC 176)	Bygone Times Antique Warehouse, Ecclestone, Lancs	
A7317	Sopwith Pup <R> (BAPC 179)	Midland Air Museum, Coventry	
A8226	Sopwith 1½ Strutter <R> (G-BIDW)	RAF Museum, Hendon	
B1807	Sopwith Pup (G-EAVX) [A7]	Privately owned, Keynsham, Avon	
B2458	Sopwith 1F.1 Camel <R> (G-BPOB/F542) [R]	Privately owned, Booker	
B3459	Nieuport Scout 17/23 <R> (G-BWMJ) [21]	Privately owned, Fairoaks	
B6401	Sopwith 1F.1 Camel <R> (G-AWYY/C1701)	FAA Museum, RNAS Yeovilton	
B7270	Sopwith 1F.1 Camel <R> (G-BFCZ)	Brooklands Museum, Weybridge	
C1904	RAF SE5a <R> (G-PFAP) [Z]	Privately owned, Syerston	
C3011	Phoenix Currie Super Wot (G-SWOT) [S]	The Real Aeroplane Company, Breighton	
C3988	Sopwith 5F.1 Dolphin	RAF Museum, stored Wyton	
C4451	Avro 504J <R> (BAPC 210)	Southampton Hall of Aviation	
C4918	Bristol M1C <R> (G-BWJM)	The Shuttleworth Collection, Old Warden	
C4940	Bristol M1C <R>	Currently not known	
C4994	Bristol M1C <R> (G-BLWM)	RAF Museum, Hendon	
C9533	RAF SE5a <R> (G-BUWE) [M]	Privately owned, DERA Boscombe Down	
D276	RAF SE5a <R> (BAPC 208) [A]	Prince's Mead Shopping Centre, Farnborough	
D3419	Sopwith 1F.1 Camel <R> (F1921/BAPC 59)	RAF Museum, Cosford	
D7560	Avro 504K	Museum of Army Flying, Middle Wallop	
D7889	Bristol F2b Fighter (G-AANM/ BAPC 166)	Privately owned, stored Sandown	
D8084	Bristol F2b Fighter (G-ACAA/ F4516) [S]	The Fighter Collection, Duxford	
D8096	Bristol F2b Fighter (G-AEPH) [D]	The Shuttleworth Collection, Old Warden	
D8781	Avro 504K <R> (G-ECKE)	The Aircraft Restoration Company, Duxford	
E373	Avro 504K <R> (BAPC 178)	Privately owned,	
E449	Avro 504K (G-EBJE/9205M)	RAF Museum, Hendon	
E2466	Bristol F2b Fighter (BAPC 165) [I]	RAF Museum, Hendon	
E2581	Bristol F2b Fighter [13]	Imperial War Museum, Duxford	
F141	RAF SE5a <R> (G-SEVA) [G]	Privately owned, DERA Boscombe Down	
F235	RAF SE5a <R> (G-BMDB) [B]	Privately owned, Boscombe Down	

Notes	Serial	Type (other identity) [code]	Owner/operator, location or fate
	F760	SE5a Microlight <R> [A]	Privately owned, Redhill
	F904	RAF SE5a (G-EBIA)	The Shuttleworth Collection, Old Warden
	F938	RAF SE5a (G-EBIC/9208M)	RAF Museum, Hendon
F943	RAF SE5a <R> (G-BIHF) [S]	Museum of Army Flying, Middle Wallop
F943	RAF SE5a <R> (G-BKDT)	Yorkshire Air Museum, Elvington
	F1010	Airco DH9A [C]	RAF Museum, Hendon
	F3556	RAF RE8	Imperial War Museum, Duxford
F4013	Sopwith 1F.1 Camel <R>	Privately owned, Coventry
F5447	RAF SE5a <R> (G-BKER) [N]	Privately owned, Cumbernauld
F5459	RAF SE5a <R> (G-INNY) [Y]	Privately owned, Goodwood
F5475	RAF SE5a <R> (BAPC 250)	Brooklands Museum, Weybridge
	F6314	Sopwith 1F.1 Camel (9206M) [B]	RAF Museum, Hendon
F8010	RAF SE5a <R> (G-BDWJ) [Z]	Privately owned, Graveley
	F8614	Vickers FB27A Vimy IV <R> (G-AWAU)	RAF Museum, Hendon
H1968	Avro 504K <R> (BAPC 42)	Yorkshire Air Museum, stored Elvington
	H2311	Avro 504K (G-ABAA)	Gr Manchester Mus of Science & Industry
H3426	Hawker Hurricane <R> (BAPC 68)	Privately owned,
	H5199	Avro 504K (BK892/3118M/ G-ACNB/G-ADEV)	The Shuttleworth Collection, Old Warden
	J7326	DH53 Humming Bird (G-EBQP)	Privately owned, Audley End
	J8067	Westland Pterodactyl 1a	Science Museum, South Kensington
J9941	Hawker Hart 2 (G-ABMR)	RAF Museum, Hendon
	K1786	Hawker Tomtit (G-AFTA)	The Shuttleworth Collection, Old Warden
K2050	Isaacs Fury II (G-ASCM)	Privately owned, Brize Norton
K2059	Isaacs Fury II (G-PFAR)	Privately owned, Dunkeswell
K2060	Isaacs Fury II (G-BKZM)	Privately owned, Haverfordwest
K2075	Isaacs Fury II (G-BEER)	Privately owned, Temple Bruer
K2227	Bristol 105 Bulldog IIA (G-ABBB)	RAF Museum, Hendon
K2567	DH82A Tiger Moth (DE306/7035M/ G-MOTH)	Privately owned, Tadlow
K2572	DH82A Tiger Moth (NM129/ G-AOZH)	Privately owned, Shoreham
K2572	DH82A Tiger Moth <R>	The Aircraft Restoration Company, Duxford
K2587	DH82A Tiger Moth <R> (G-BJAP)	Privately owned, Shobdon
	K3215	Avro 621 Tutor (G-AHSA)	The Shuttleworth Collection, Old Warden
	K3661	Hawker Nimrod II (G-BURZ)	Aero Vintage, St Leonards-on-Sea
K3731	Isaacs Fury <R> (G-RODI)	Privately owned, Hailsham
	K4259	DH82A Tiger Moth (G-ANMO) [71]	Privately owned, White Waltham
	K4972	Hawker Hart Trainer IIA (1764M)	RAF Museum, Cosford
K5054	Supermarine Spitfire <R> (BAPC 190/*EN398*)	Privately owned, Sevenoaks, Kent
K5054	Supermarine Spitfire <R> (BAPC 214)	Tangmere Military Aviation Museum
K5054	Supermarine Spitfire <R> (G-BRDV)	Southampton Hall of Aviation
K5054	Supermarine Spitfire <R>	Kent Battle of Britain Museum, Hawkinge
K5414	Hawker Hind (G-AENP/BAPC 78) [XV]	The Shuttleworth Collection, Old Warden
	K5600	Hawker Audax I (2015M/G-BVVI)	Aero Vintage, St Leonards-on-Sea
K5673	Isaacs Fury II (G-BZAS)	Privately owned, Bournemouth
K5673	Hawker Fury I <R> (BAPC 249)	Brooklands Museum, Weybridge
	K6035	Westland Wallace II (2361M)	RAF Museum, Hendon
K7271	Hawker Fury II <R> (BAPC 148)	Shropshire Wartime Aircraft Recovery Grp Mus, Sleap
	K8042	Gloster Gladiator II (8372M)	RAF Museum, Hendon
	K8203	Hawker Demon I (G-BTVE/2292M)	Demon Displays, Hatch
K8303	Isaacs Fury II (G-BWWN) [D]	Privately owned, Lower Upham
K9926	VS300 Spitfire I <R> (BAPC 217) [JH-C]	RAF Bentley Priory, on display
	K9942	VS300 Spitfire I (8383M) [SD-D]	RAF Museum, Hendon
K9962	VS300 Spitfire I <R> [JH-C]	Privately owned, Greenford, W London
	L1070	VS300 Spitfire I <R> (BAPC 227) [XT-A]	Edinburgh airport, on display
	L1592	Hawker Hurricane I [KW-Z]	Science Museum, South Kensington
L1679	Hawker Hurricane I <R> (BAPC 241) [JX-G]	Tangmere Military Aviation Museum
L1710	Hawker Hurricane I <R> (BAPC 219) [AL-D]	RAF Biggin Hill, on display

Serial	Type (other identity) [code]	Owner/operator, location or fate	Notes
L2301	VS Walrus I (G-AIZG)	FAA Museum, RNAS Yeovilton	
L2940	Blackburn Skua I	FAA Museum, RNAS Yeovilton	
L5343	Fairey Battle I [VO-S]	RAF Museum, Hendon	
L6906	Miles M14A Magister I (G-AKKY/ T9841/BAPC 44)	Museum of Berkshire Aviation, Woodley	
L8756	Bristol 149 Bolingbroke IVT (RCAF 10001) [XD-E]	RAF Museum, Hendon	
L8841	Bristol 149 Bolingbroke IVT (G-BPIV/R3821) [QY-C]	The Aircraft Restoration Company, Duxford	
N248	Supermarine S6A (S1596)	Southampton Hall of Aviation	
N500	Sopwith LC-1T Triplane <R> (G-PENY/G-BWRA)	FAA Museum, RNAS Yeovilton	
N546	Wright Quadruplane 1 <R> (BAPC 164)	Southampton Hall of Aviation	
N1671	Boulton Paul P82 Defiant I (8370M) [EW-D]	RAF Museum, Hendon	
N1854	Fairey Fulmar II (G-AIBE)	FAA Museum, RNAS Yeovilton	
N2078	Sopwith Baby (8214/8215)	FAA Museum, RNAS Yeovilton	
N2532	Hawker Hurricane I <R> (BAPC ..) [GZ-H]	Kent Battle of Britain Museum, Hawkinge	
N2980	Vickers Wellington IA [R]	Brooklands Museum, Weybridge	
N3177	RAF BE2e <R>	Barton Aviation Heritage Society, Barton	
N3194	VS300 Spitfire I <R> (BAPC 220) [GR-Z]	RAF Biggin Hill, on display	
N3289	VS300 Spitfire I <R> (BAPC 65) [DW-K]	Kent Battle of Britain Museum, Hawkinge	
N3313	VS300 Spitfire I <R> (MH314/ BAPC 69) [KL-B]	Kent Battle of Britain Museum, Hawkinge	
N3317	VS361 Spitfire IX <R>	Imperial War Museum, Duxford	
N3320	VS361 Spitfire IX <R>	Newark Air Museum, Winthorpe	
N3378	Boulton Paul P82 Defiant I	Boulton Paul Association, Wolverhampton	
N4389	Fairey Albacore (N4172) [4M]	FAA Museum, RNAS Yeovilton	
N4877	Avro 652A Anson I (G-AMDA) [VX-F]	Imperial War Museum, Duxford	
N5177	Sopwith 1½ Strutter <R>	Botany Bay Village, Chorley, Lancs	
N5182	Sopwith Pup <R> (G-APUP/ 9213M)	RAF Museum, Hendon	
N5195	Sopwith Pup (G-ABOX)	Museum of Army Flying, Middle Wallop	
N5492	Sopwith Triplane <R> (BAPC 111)	FAA Museum, RNAS Yeovilton	
N5628	Gloster Gladiator II	RAF Museum, Hendon	
N5903	Gloster Sea Gladiator II (N2276/ G-GLAD) [H]	The Fighter Collection, Duxford	
N5912	Sopwith Triplane (8385M)	RAF Museum, Hendon	
N6181	Sopwith Pup (G-EBKY/N5180)	The Shuttleworth Collection, Old Warden	
N6290	Sopwith Triplane <R> (G-BOCK)	The Shuttleworth Collection, Old Warden	
N6452	Sopwith Pup <R> (G-BIAU)	FAA Museum, RNAS Yeovilton	
N6466	DH82A Tiger Moth (G-ANKZ)	Privately owned, Sywell	
N6537	DH82A Tiger Moth (G-AOHY)	AAC Historic Aircraft Flt, Middle Wallop	
N6720	DH82A Tiger Moth (G-BYTN/ 7014M) [RUO-B]	Privately owned, Hatch	
N6797	DH82A Tiger Moth (G-ANEH)	Privately owned, Goodwood	
N6812	Sopwith 2F.1 Camel	Imperial War Museum, Lambeth	
N6847	DH82A Tiger Moth (G-APAL)	Privately owned, Little Gransden	
N6965	DH82A Tiger Moth (G-AJTW) [FL-J] (wreck)	Privately owned, Tibenham	
N6985	DH82A Tiger Moth (G-AHMN)	Crashed 29 May 2000, Middle Wallop	
N9191	DH82A Tiger Moth (G-ALND)	Privately owned, Abergavenny	
N9192	DH82A Tiger Moth (G-DHZF) [RCO-N]	Privately owned, Sywell	
N9389	DH82A Tiger Moth (G-ANJA)	Privately owned, Seething	
N9899	Supermarine Southampton I (fuselage)	RAF Museum, Hendon	
P1344	HP52 Hampden I (9175M) [PL-K]	RAF Museum, stored Wyton	
P1344	HP52 Hampden I <rf> (parts Hereford L6012)	RAF Museum, Hendon	
P2617	Hawker Hurricane I (8373M) [AF-A]	RAF Museum, Hendon	
P2793	Hawker Hurricane I <R> (BAPC 236) [SD-M]	Eden Camp Theme Park, Malton, North Yorkshire	
P2902	Hawker Hurricane I (G-ROBT) [DX-X]	Privately owned, Milden	

Notes	Serial	Type (other identity) [code]	Owner/operator, location or fate
	P2921	Hawker Hurricane I <R> (BAPC ..) [GZ-L]	Kent Battle of Britain Museum, Hawkinge
	P3059	Hawker Hurricane I <R> (BAPC 64) [SD-N]	Kent Battle of Britain Museum, Hawkinge
	P3175	Hawker Hurricane I (wreck)	RAF Museum, Hendon
	P3208	Hawker Hurricane I <R> (BAPC 63/ L1592) [SD-T]	Kent Battle of Britain Museum, Hawkinge
	P3386	Hawker Hurricane I <R> (BAPC 218) [FT-A]	RAF Bentley Priory, on display
	P3395	Hawker Hurricane IV (KX829) [JX-B]	Birmingham Mus of Science & Industry, stored
	P3554	Hawker Hurricane I (composite)	The Air Defence Collection, Salisbury
	P3717	Hawker Hurricane I (composite) (DR348)	Privately owned, Hinckley, Leics
	P3873	Hawker Hurricane I <R> [YO-H]	Yorkshire Air Museum, Elvington
	P4139	Fairey Swordfish II (HS618) [5H]	FAA Museum, RNAS Yeovilton
	P6382	Miles M14A Hawk Trainer 3 (G-AJRS) [C]	The Shuttleworth Collection, Old Warden
	P7350	VS329 Spitfire IIA (G-AWIJ) [XT-D]	RAF BBMF, Coningsby
	P7540	VS329 Spitfire IIA (DU-W)	Dumfries & Galloway Avn Mus, Dumfries
	P7966	VS329 Spitfire II <R> [D-B]	Wonderland Pleasure Pk, Farnsfield, Notts
	P8140	VS329 Spitfire II <R> (P9390/ BAPC 71) [ZF-K]	Norfolk & Suffolk Avn Museum, Flixton
	P8448	VS329 Spitfire II <R> (BAPC 225) [UM-D]	RAF Cranwell, on display
	P9374	VS300 Spitfire IA (G-MKIA)	Privately owned, Sandown
	P9444	VS300 Spitfire IA [RN-D]	Science Museum, South Kensington
	R1914	Miles M14A Magister (G-AHUJ)	Privately owned, Strathallan
	R3821	Bristol 149 Bolingbroke IVT (G-BPIV/Z5722) [UX-N]	Repainted as L8841, 1999
	R4115	Hawker Hurricane I <R> [LE-X]	Imperial War Museum, Duxford
	R4959	DH82A Tiger Moth II (G-ARAZ) [59]	Privately owned, Temple Bruer
	R5136	DH82A Tiger Moth II (G-APAP)	The Aircraft Restoration Co, Duxford
	R5172	DH82A Tiger Moth II (G-AOIS) [FIJ-E]	Privately owned, Sherburn-in-Elmet
	R5250	DH82A Tiger Moth II (G-AODT)	Privately owned, Tibenham
	R5868	Avro 683 Lancaster I (7325M) [PO-S]	RAF Museum, Hendon
	R6690	VS300 Spitfire I <R> (BAPC 254) [PR-A]	Yorkshire Air Museum, Elvington
	R6915	VS300 Spitfire I	Imperial War Museum, Lambeth
	R9125	Westland Lysander III (8377M) [LX-L]	RAF Museum, Hendon
	R9371	HP59 Halifax II <ff>	Cotswold Aircraft Rest'n Grp, Innsworth
	S1287	Fairey Flycatcher <R> (G-BEYB)	FAA Museum, RNAS Yeovilton
	S1579	Hawker Nimrod I <R> (G-BBVO) [571]	Privately owned, Basingstoke
	S1581	Hawker Nimrod I (G-BWWK) [573]	The Fighter Collection, Duxford
	S1595	Supermarine S6B	Science Museum, South Kensington
	T5298	Bristol 156 Beaufighter I (4552M) <ff>	Midland Air Museum, Coventry
	T5424	DH82A Tiger Moth II (G-AJOA)	Privately owned, Chiseldon
	T5672	DH82A Tiger Moth II (G-ALRI)	Privately owned, Chalmington
	T5854	DH82A Tiger Moth II (G-ANKK)	Privately owned, Welshpool
	T5879	DH82A Tiger Moth II (G-AXBW) [RUC-W]	Privately owned, Frensham
	T6296	DH82A Tiger Moth II (8387M)	RAF Museum, Hendon
	T6313	DH82A Tiger Moth II (G-AHVU)	Privately owned, Liphook
	T6562	DH82A Tiger Moth II (G-ANTE)	Privately owned, Sywell
	T6818	DH82A Tiger Moth II (G-ANKT) [91]	The Shuttleworth Collection, Old Warden
	T6953	DH82A Tiger Moth II (G-ANNI)	Privately owned, Little Gransden
	T6991	DH82A Tiger Moth II (G-ANOR/ DE694)	Privately owned, Paddock Wood
	T7230	DH82A Tiger Moth II (G-AFVE)	Privately owned, Boscombe Down
	T7281	DH82A Tiger Moth II (G-ARTL)	Privately owned, Egton, nr Whitby
	T7404	DH82A Tiger Moth II (G-ANMV) [04]	Privately owned, Booker
	T7793	DH82A Tiger Moth II (G-ANKV)	Privately owned, Croydon, on display
	T7842	DH82A Tiger Moth II (G-AMTF)	Privately owned, Boughton, Suffolk

Serial	Type (other identity) [code]	Owner/operator, location or fate	Notes
T7909	DH82A Tiger Moth II (G-ANON)	Privately owned, Sherburn-in-Elmet	
T7997	DH82A Tiger Moth II (NL750/ G-AHUF)	Privately owned, Edburton	
T8191	DH82A Tiger Moth II (G-BWMK)	Privately owned, Welshpool	
T9707	Miles M14A Magister I (G-AKKR/ 8378M/T9708)	Museum of Army Flying, Middle Wallop	
T9738	Miles M14A Magister I (G-AKAT)	Privately owned, Breighton	
V1075	Miles M14A Magister I (G-AKPF)	Privately owned, stored Sandown	
V3388	Airspeed AS10 Oxford I (G-AHTW)	Imperial War Museum, Duxford	
V6028	Bristol 149 Bolingbroke IVT (G-MKIV) [GB-D] <rf>	The Aircraft Restoration Co, stored Duxford	
V6799	Hawker Hurricane I <R> (BAPC 72/V7767) [SD-X]	Gloucestershire Av'n Coll, stored Glos	
V7350	Hawker Hurricane I (fuselage)	Brenzett Aeronautical Museum	
V7467	Hawker Hurricane I <R> (BAPC 223) [LE-D]	RAF Coltishall, on display	
V7767	Hawker Hurricane I <R> (BAPC 72)	Repainted as V6799 by January 2000	
V9441	Westland Lysander IIIA (G-AZWT) [AR-A]	The Shuttleworth Collection, Old Warden	
V9673	Westland Lysander IIIA (V9300/ G-LIZY) [MA-J]	Imperial War Museum, Duxford	
V9723	Westland Lysander IIIA (2442/ OO-SOT) [MA-D]	SABENA Old Timers, Brussels, Belgium	
W1048	HP59 Halifax II (8465M) [TL-S]	RAF Museum, Hendon	
W2068	Avro 652A Anson I (VH-ASM) [68]	RAF Museum, Hendon	
W2718	VS Walrus I (G-RNLI)	Dick Melton Aviation, Great Yarmouth	
W4041	Gloster E28/39 [G]	Science Museum, South Kensington	
W4050	DH98 Mosquito	Mosquito Aircraft Museum, London Colney	
W5856	Fairey Swordfish II (G-BMGC) [A2A]	RN Historic Flight, Yeovilton	
W9385	DH87B Hornet Moth (G-ADND) [YG-L,3]	The Shuttleworth Collection, Old Warden	
X4590	VS300 Spitfire I (8384M) [PR-F]	RAF Museum, Hendon	
X7688	Bristol 156 Beaufighter I (3858M/ G-DINT)	Privately owned, Hatch	
Z2033	Fairey Firefly I (G-ASTL) [275]	FAA Museum, stored RNAS Yeovilton	
Z2315	Hawker Hurricane IIA [JU-E]	Imperial War Museum, Duxford	
Z2389	Hawker Hurricane IIA	Brooklands Museum, Weybridge	
Z5207	Hawker Hurricane IIB (G-BYDL)	Privately owned, Billingshurst	
Z5252	Hawker Hurricane IIB (G-BWHA/ Z5053) [GO-B]	Privately owned, Dursley, Glos	
Z7015	Hawker Sea Hurricane IB (G-BKTH) [7-L]	The Shuttleworth Collection, Old Warden	
Z7197	Percival P30 Proctor III (G-AKZN/ 8380M)	RAF Museum, Hendon	
Z7258	DH89A Dragon Rapide (NR786/ G-AHGD)	Privately owned, Membury (wreck)	
Z7381	Hawker Hurricane XIIA (G-HURI) [XR-T]	Historic Aircraft Collection, Audley End	
AA550	VS349 Spitfire VB <R> (BAPC 230/ AA908) [GE-P]	Eden Camp Theme Park, Malton, North Yorkshire	
AB130	VS349 Spitfire VA (parts)	Privately owned,	
AB910	VS349 Spitfire VB (G-AISU) [ZD-C]	RAF BBMF, Coningsby	
AD540	VS349 Spitfire VB (wreck)	Dumfries & Galloway Avn Mus, Dumfries	
AE436	HP52 Hampden I [PL-J] (parts)	Lincolnshire Avn Heritage Centre, E Kirkby	
AE977	Hawker Sea Hurricane X (G-TWTD) [LE–D]	Hawker Restorations Ltd, Milden	
AL246	Grumman Martlet I	FAA Museum, RNAS Yeovilton	
AM561	Lockheed Hudson V (parts)	Cornwall Aero Park, Helston	
AP506	Cierva C30A (G-ACWM)	The Helicopter Museum, Weston-super-Mare	
AP507	Cierva C30A (G-ACWP) [KX-P]	Science Museum, South Kensington	
AR213	VS300 Spitfire IA (K9853/G-AIST) [PR-D]	Privately owned, Booker	
AR501	VS349 Spitfire LF VC (G-AWII/ AR4474) [NN-A]	The Shuttleworth Collection, Old Warden	
AR614	VS349 Spitfire VC (5378M/7555M/ G-BUWA) [DU-Z]	Sold to the US as N614VC, Spring 2000	

BB807 – FE992

Notes	Serial	Type (other identity) [code]	Owner/operator, location or fate
	BB807	DH82A Tiger Moth (G-ADWO)	Southampton Hall of Aviation
	BE417	Hawker Hurricane XIIB (G-HURR) [LK-A]	The Real Aeroplane Company, Breighton
	BE421	Hawker Hurricane IIC <R> (BAPC 205) [XP-G]	RAF Museum, Hendon
	BL614	VS349 Spitfire VB (4354M) [ZD-F]	RAF Museum, Hendon
	BL655	VS349 Spitfire VB (wreck)	Lincolnshire Avn Heritage Centre, East Kirkby
	BL924	VS349 Spitfire VB <R> (BAPC 242) [AZ-G]	Tangmere Military Aviation Museum
	BM361	VS349 Spitfire VB <R> [XR-C]	RAF Lakenheath, on display
	BM597	VS349 Spitfire LF VB (5718M/ G-MKVB) [JH-C]	Historic Aircraft Collection, Duxford
	BN230	Hawker Hurricane IIC (LF751/ 5466M) [FT-A]	RAF Manston, Memorial Pavilion
	BR600	VS361 Spitfire IX <R> (BAPC 222) [SH-V]	RAF Uxbridge, on display
	BR600	VS361 Spitfire IX <R> (fuselage)	Privately owned, Dunkeswell, derelict
	BW881	Hawker Hurricane XIIA (G-KAMM)	Privately owned, Milden
	CB733	SA122 Bulldog (G-BCUV/G-112)	Privately owned, Old Sarum
	DD931	Bristol 152 Beaufort VIII (9131M) [L]	RAF Museum, Hendon
	DE208	DH82A Tiger Moth II (G-AGYU)	Privately owned, Ronaldsway
	DE470	DH82A Tiger Moth II (G-ANMY)	Privately owned, Oaksey Park, Wilts
	DE623	DH82A Tiger Moth II (G-ANFI)	Privately owned, Cardiff
	DE673	DH82A Tiger Moth II (6948M/ G-ADNZ)	Privately owned, Swanton Morley
	DE992	DH82A Tiger Moth II (G-AXXV)	Privately owned, Upavon
	DF112	DH82A Tiger Moth II (G-ANRM)	Privately owned, Clacton
	DF128	DH82A Tiger Moth II (G-AOJJ) [RCO-U]	Privately owned, White Waltham
	DF155	DH82A Tiger Moth II (G-ANFV)	Privately owned, Shempston Fm, Lossiemouth
	DF198	DH82A Tiger Moth II (G-BBRB)	Privately owned, Biggin Hill
	DG202	Gloster F9/40 (5758M) [G]	RAF Museum, Cosford
	DG590	Miles M2H Hawk Major (8379M/ G-ADMW)	RAF Museum, stored Wyton
	DP872	Fairey Barracuda II (fuselage)	FAA Museum, stored Yeovilton
	DR613	Foster-Wikner GM1 Wicko (G-AFJB)	Privately owned, Southampton
	DV372	Avro 683 Lancaster I <ff>	Imperial War Museum, Lambeth
	EE416	Gloster Meteor F3 <ff>	Martin Baker Aircraft, Chalgrove
	EE425	Gloster Meteor F3 <ff>	Gloucestershire Av'n Coll, stored Glos
	EE531	Gloster Meteor F4 (7090M)	Midland Air Museum, Coventry
	EE549	Gloster Meteor F4 (7008M) [A]	Tangmere Military Aviation Museum
	EF545	VS349 Spitfire VC <ff>	Privately owned, High Wycombe
	EJ693	Hawker Tempest V (N7027E) [SA-J]	Privately owned, Booker
	EJ922	Hawker Typhoon IB <ff>	Privately owned, Hawkinge
	EM720	DH82A Tiger Moth II (G-AXAN)	Privately owned, Little Gransden
	EM727	DH82A Tiger Moth II (G-AOXN)	Privately owned, Yeovil
	EN224	VS366 Spitfire F XII (G-FXII)	Privately owned, Newport Pagnell
	EN343	VS365 Spitfire PR XI <R> (BAPC 226)	RAF Benson, on display
	EN398	VS361 Spitfire F IX <R> (BAPC 184) [WO-A]	Shropshire Wartime Aircraft Recovery Grp Mus, Sleap
	EP120	VS349 Spitfire LF VB (5377M/ 8070M/G-LFVB) [AE-A]	The Fighter Collection, Duxford
	EX976	NA AT-6D Harvard III (FAP.1657)	FAA Museum, RNAS Yeovilton
	EZ259	NA AT-6D Harvard III (G-BMJW) <ff>	Privately owned, Wakefield, West Yorkshire
	FB226	Bonsall Mustang <R> (G-BDWM) [MT-A]	Privately owned, Gamston
	FE695	Noorduyn AT-16 Harvard IIB (G-BTXI) [94]	The Fighter Collection, Duxford
	FE905	Noorduyn AT-16 Harvard IIB (LN-BNM)	RAF Museum, Hendon
	FE992	Noorduyn AT-16 Harvard IIB (G-BDAM) [K-T]	Privately owned, Duxford

Serial	Type (other identity) [code]	Owner/operator, location or fate	Notes
FH153	Noorduyn AT-16 Harvard IIB (G-BBHK) [GW-A]	Privately owned, stored Cardiff	
FJ992	Boeing-Stearman PT-17 Kaydet (442/OO-JEH)	Privately owned, Wevelgem, Belgium	
FL586	Douglas Dakota III (N147DC) [AI]	Privately owned, North Weald	
FM118	Avro 683 Lancaster B X <ff>	Privately owned, Gosport, Hants	
FR886	Piper L-4J Cub (G-BDMS)	Privately owned, Old Sarum	
FS628	Fairchild Argus 2 (43-14601/ G-AIZE)	RAF Museum, Cosford	
FS668	Noorduyn AT-16 Harvard IIB (PH-TBR)	Privately owned, The Netherlands	
FT323	NA AT-6D Harvard III (FAP 1513)	Air Engineering Services, Swansea	
FT391	Noorduyn AT-16 Harvard IIB (G-AZBN)	Privately owned, Shoreham	
FX301	NA AT-6D Harvard III (EX915/ G-JUDI) [FD-NQ]	Privately owned, Bryngwyn Bach, Clwyd	
FX360	Noorduyn AT-16 Harvard IIB (KF435)	Booker Aircraft Museum	
FX442	Noorduyn AT-16 Harvard IIB	Kent Battle of Britain Museum, Hawkinge	
FX760	Curtiss P-40N Kittyhawk IV (9150M) [GA-?]	RAF Museum, stored Wyton	
HB275	Beech C-45 Expeditor II (G-BKGM)	Privately owned, North Weald	
HB751	Fairchild Argus III (G-BCBL)	Privately owned, Little Gransden	
HH379	GAL48 Hotspur II (BAPC 261)	Museum of Army Flying, Middle Wallop	
HJ711	DH98 Mosquito NF II [VI-C]	Night-Fighter Preservation Tm, Elvington	
HM354	Percival P34 Proctor III (G-ANPP)	Privately owned, Stansted	
HM503	Miles M12 Mohawk (G-AEKW)	RAF Museum, stored Wyton	
HM580	Cierva C-30A (G-ACUU) [KX-K]	Imperial War Museum, Duxford	
HS503	Fairey Swordfish IV (BAPC 108)	RAF Museum, stored Wyton	
JG891	VS349 Spitfire LF VC (A58-178/ G-LFVC)	Historic Flying Ltd, Audley End	
JR505	Hawker Typhoon IB <ff>	Midland Air Museum, Coventry	
JV482	Grumman Wildcat V	Ulster Aviation Society, Langford Lodge	
JV579	Grumman FM-2 Wildcat (N4845V/ G-RUMW) [F]	The Fighter Collection, Duxford	
KB889	Avro 683 Lancaster B X (G-LANC) [NA-I]	Imperial War Museum, Duxford	
KB994	Avro 683 Lancaster B X (G-BVBP)	Privately owned, Sandtoft	
KD345	Goodyear FG-1D Corsair (88297/ G-FGID) [130-A]	The Fighter Collection, Duxford	
KD431	CV Corsair IV [E2-M]	FAA Museum, RNAS Yeovilton	
KE209	Grumman Hellcat II	FAA Museum, RNAS Yeovilton	
KE418	Hawker Tempest <rf>	RAF Museum, stored Wyton	
KF183	Noorduyn AT-16 Harvard IIB [3]	DPA/AFD, DERA Boscombe Down	
KF435	Noorduyn AT-16 Harvard IIB <ff>	Privately owned, Swindon	
KF487	Noorduyn AT-16 Harvard IIB	The Aircraft Restoration Co, Duxford, spares use	
KF488	Noorduyn AT-16 Harvard IIB	Bournemouth Aviation Museum	
KF532	Noorduyn AT-16 Harvard IIB <ff>	Newark Air Museum, Winthorpe	
KF584	CCF T-6J Texan (FT239/G-BIWX/ G-RAIX) [RAI-X]	Privately owned, North Weald	
KG374	Douglas Dakota IV (KN645/8355M) [YS]	RAF Museum, Cosford	
KJ351	Airspeed AS58 Horsa II (TL659/ BAPC 80) [23]	Museum of Army Flying, Middle Wallop	
KK995	Sikorsky Hoverfly I [E]	RAF Museum, Hendon	
KL216	Republic P-47D Thunderbolt (45-49295/9212M) [RS-L]	RAF Museum, Cosford	
KN442	Douglas Dakota C4 (G-AMPZ)	Atlantic Airlines, Coventry	
KN448	Douglas Dakota C4 <ff>	Science Museum, South Kensington	
KN751	Consolidated Liberator C VI (IAF HE807) [F]	RAF Museum, Cosford	
KP208	Douglas Dakota IV [YS]	Airborne Forces Museum, Aldershot	
KZ191	Hawker Hurricane IV (frame only)	Privately owned, North Weald	
KZ321	Hawker Hurricane IV (G-HURY) (frame only)	The Fighter Collection, stored Duxford	
LA198	VS356 Spitfire F21 (7118M) [RAI-G]	Royal Scottish Mus'm of Flight, E Fortune	
LA226	VS356 Spitfire F21 (7119M)	RAF Museum, stored Wyton	

Notes	Serial	Type (other identity) [code]	Owner/operator, location or fate
	LA255	VS356 Spitfire F21 (6490M) [JX-U]	RAF No 1 Sqn, Cottesmore (preserved)
	LB264	Taylorcraft Plus D (G-AIXA)	Privately owned, Loughborough
	LB294	Taylorcraft Plus D (G-AHWJ)	Museum of Army Flying, Whitchurch, Hants
	LB312	Taylorcraft Plus D (HH982/ G-AHXE)	Privately owned, Old Sarum
	LB367	Taylorcraft Plus D (G-AHGZ)	Privately owned, Netheravon
	LB375	Taylorcraft Plus D (G-AHGW)	Privately owned, Edge Hill
	LF363	Hawker Hurricane IIC [US-C]	RAF BBMF, Coningsby
	LF738	Hawker Hurricane IIC (5405M) [UH-A]	RAF Museum, Cosford
	LF789	DH82 Queen Bee (K3584/ BAPC 186) [R2-K]	Mosquito Aircraft Museum, London Colney
	LF858	DH82 Queen Bee (G-BLUZ)	Privately owned, Rush Green
	LS326	Fairey Swordfish II (G-AJVH) [L2]	RN Historic Flight, Yeovilton
	LV907	HP59 Halifax III (HR792) [NP-F]	Yorkshire Air Museum, Elvington
	LZ551	DH100 Vampire	FAA Museum, RNAS Yeovilton
	LZ766	Percival P34 Proctor III (G-ALCK)	Imperial War Museum, Duxford
	MA863	VS349 Spitfire VC	To the US, April 2000
	MF628	Vickers Wellington T10 (9210M)	RAF Museum, Hendon
	MH434	VS361 Spitfire LF IXB (G-ASJV) [ZD-B]	The Old Flying Machine Company, Duxford
	MH486	VS361 Spitfire LF IX <R> (BAPC 206) [FF-A]	RAF Museum, Hendon
	MH777	VS361 Spitfire IX <R> (BAPC 221) [RF-N]	RAF Northolt, on display
	MJ147	VS361 Spitfire LF IX	Privately owned, Kent
	MJ627	VS509 Spitfire T9 (G-BMSB) [9G-P]	Privately owned, Coventry
	MJ730	VS361 Spitfire HF IXE (G-HFIX) [GZ-?]	Sold as N730MJ, January 2000
	MJ751	VS361 Spitfire IX <R> (BAPC 209) [DU-V]	D-Day Museum, Shoreham Airport
	MJ832	VS361 Spitfire IX <R> (L1096/ BAPC 229) [DN-Y]	RAF Digby, on display
	MK178	VS361 Spitfire LF XVIE (TE311/ X4474/7241M) [LZ-V]	RAF BBMF, stored Coningsby
	MK356	VS361 Spitfire LF IXC (5690M) [2I-V]	RAF BBMF, Coningsby
	MK356	VS361 Spitfire LF IXC <R> [2I-V]	Kent Battle of Britain Museum, Hawkinge
	MK673	VS361 Spitfire LF XVIE (TB382/ X4277/7244M) [SK-E]	RAF BBMF, stored Coningsby
	MK732	VS361 Spitfire LF IXC (8633M/ G-HVDM/PH-???) [OU-U]	Repainted in Dutch markings by March 2000
	MK805	VS361 Spitfire LF IX <R> [SH-B]	Privately owned, Chiseldon
	MK912	VS361 Spitfire LF IXE (G-BRRA) [SH-L]	Historic Flying Ltd, Duxford
	ML407	VS509 Spitfire T9 (G-LFIX) [OU-V]	Privately owned, Duxford
	ML411	VS361 Spitfire LF IXE	Privately owned, Kent
	ML417	VS361 Spitfire LF IXE (G-BJSG) [2I-T]	The Old Flying Machine Company, Duxford
	ML427	VS361 Spitfire IX (6457M) [ST-I]	Skysport Ltd, Hatch
	ML796	Short S25 Sunderland V	Imperial War Museum, Duxford
	ML824	Short S25 Sunderland V [NS-Z]	RAF Museum, Hendon
	MN235	Hawker Typhoon IB	RAF Museum, Hendon
	MP425	Airspeed AS10 Oxford I (G-AITB) [G]	RAF Museum, Hendon
	MS902	Miles M25 Martinet TT1 (TF-SHC)	Museum of Berkshire Aviation, Woodley
	MT197	Auster IV (G-ANHS)	Repainted as G-ANHS
	MT438	Auster III (G-AREI)	Privately owned, Petersfield
	MT847	VS379 Spitfire FR XIVE (6960M) [AX-H]	Gr Manchester Mus of Science & Industry
	MT928	VS359 Spitfire HF VIIIC (G-BKMI/ MV154/AR654) [ZX-M]	Privately owned, Filton
	MV262	VS379 Spitfire FR XIV (G-CCVV)	Privately owned, Catfield
	MV268	VS379 Spitfire FR XIV (MV293/ G-SPIT) [JE-J]	The Fighter Collection, Duxford
	MV293	VS379 Spitfire FR XIV (G-SPIT) [OI-C]	Repainted as MV268 by July 2000
	MW401	Hawker Tempest II (IAF HA604/ G-PEST)	Privately owned, Hemswell, Lincs
	MW404	Hawker Tempest II (IAF HA557)	Privately owned
	MW758	Hawker Tempest II (IAF HA580)	Privately owned

Serial	Type (other identity) [code]	Owner/operator, location or fate	Notes
MW763	Hawker Tempest II (IAF HA586/ G-TEMT) [HF-A]	Privately owned, Hemswell, Lincs	
MW810	Hawker Tempest II (IAF HA591)	Privately owned, Hibaldstow, Lincs	
NF370	Fairey Swordfish III	Imperial War Museum, Duxford	
NF389	Fairey Swordfish III [D]	RN Historic Flight, Yeovilton	
NJ673	Auster 5D (G-AOCR)	Privately owned, Canterbury	
NJ695	Auster 4 (G-AJXV)	Privately owned, Newark	
NJ703	Auster 5 (G-AKPI)	Privately owned, Croft, Lincs	
NJ719	Auster 5 (TW385/G-ANFU)	Privately owned, Newcastle	
NL750	DH82A Tiger Moth II (T7997/ G-AOBH)	Privately owned, Thruxton	
NL772	DH82A Tiger Moth II (G-BXMN)	Crashed 25 May 1999, near Blackburn	
NL846	DH82A Tiger Moth II (F-BGEQ)	Brooklands Museum, Weybridge	
NL985	DH82A Tiger Moth I (7015M/ G-BWIK)	Privately owned, Sywell	
NM181	DH82A Tiger Moth I (G-AZGZ)	Privately owned, Dunkeswell	
NP294	Percival P31 Proctor IV [TB-M]	Lincolnshire Avn Heritage Centre, E Kirkby	
NP303	Percival P31 Proctor IV (G-ANZJ)	Privately owned, Byfleet, Surrey	
NV778	Hawker Tempest TT5 (8386M)	RAF Museum, stored Wyton	
NX534	Auster III (G-BUDL)	Privately owned, Netheravon	
NX611	Avro 683 Lancaster B VII (8375M/ G-ASXX) [DE-C, LE-C]	Lincolnshire Avn Heritage Centre, E Kirkby	
PA474	Avro 683 Lancaster B I [QR-M]	RAF BBMF, Coningsby	
PF179	HS Gnat T1 (XR541/8602M)	Privately owned, Binbrook	
PK624	VS356 Spitfire F22 (8072M) [RAU-T]	The Fighter Collection, Duxford	
PK664	VS356 Spitfire F22 (7759M) [V6-B]	RAF Museum, stored Wyton	
PK683	VS356 Spitfire F24 (7150M)	Southampton Hall of Aviation	
PK724	VS356 Spitfire F24 (7288M)	RAF Museum, Hendon	
PL344	VS361 Spitfire LF IXE (G-IXCC) [Y2-P]	Privately owned, Booker	
PL965	VS365 Spitfire PR XI (G-MKXI) [R]	The Real Aeroplane Company, Breighton	
PL983	VS365 Spitfire PR XI (G-PRXI) [JV-F]	Privately owned, Goudhurst, Kent	
PM631	VS390 Spitfire PR XIX [S]	RAF BBMF, Coningsby	
PM651	VS390 Spitfire PR XIX (7758M) [X]	RAF Museum, stored Wyton	
PN323	HP Halifax VII <ff>	Imperial War Museum, Lambeth	
PP566	Fairey Firefly I (fuselage)	South Yorkshire Avn Museum, Firbeck	
PP972	VS358 Seafire LF IIIC (G-BUAR)	Flying A Services, Earls Colne	
PR536	Hawker Tempest II (IAF HA457) [OQ-H]	RAF Museum, Hendon	
PS853	VS390 Spitfire PR XIX (G-MXIX/ G-RRGN) [C]	Rolls-Royce, Filton	
PS915	VS390 Spitfire PR XIX (7548M/ 7711M) [UM-G]	RAF BBMF, Coningsby	
PT462	VS509 Spitfire T9 (G-CTIX/ N462JC) [SW-A]	Privately owned, Caernarfon/Duxford	
PV202	VS509 Spitfire T9 (G-TRIX) [5R-Q] (on rebuild	Historic Flying Limited, Audley End	
PZ865	Hawker Hurricane IIC (G-AMAU) [Q]	RAF BBMF, Coningsby	
RA848	Slingsby Cadet TX1	The Aeroplane Collection, stored Wigan	
RA854	Slingsby Cadet TX1	Privately owned, Wigan	
RA897	Slingsby Cadet TX1	Newark Air Museum store, Hucknall	
RD220	Bristol 156 Beaufighter TF X	Royal Scottish Mus'm of Flight, E Fortune	
RD253	Bristol 156 Beaufighter TF X (7931M)	RAF Museum, Hendon	
RF342	Avro 694 Lincoln B II (G-29-1/ G-APRJ)	Privately owned, Sandtoft	
RF398	Avro 694 Lincoln B II (8376M)	RAF Museum, Cosford	
RG333	Miles M38 Messenger IIA (G-AIEK)	Privately owned, Felton, Bristol	
RH377	Miles M38 Messenger 4A (G-ALAH)	Privately owned, Stretton, Cheshire	
RH746	Bristol 164 Brigand TF1 (fuselage)	North-East Aircraft Museum, stored Usworth	
RL962	DH89A Dominie II (G-AHED)	RAF Museum, stored Wyton	
RM221	Percival P31 Proctor IV (G-ANXR)	Privately owned, Biggin Hill	
RM689	VS379 Spitfire F XIV (G-ALGT) (remains)	Rolls-Royce, Derby	
RM694	VS379 Spitfire F XIV (6640M)	Privately owned, High Wycombe	

21

Notes	Serial	Type (other identity) [code]	Owner/operator, location or fate
	RM927	VS379 Spitfire F XIV	Privately owned, High Wycombe
	RN218	Isaacs Spitfire <R> (G-BBJI) [N]	Privately owned, Langham
	RR232	VS361 Spitfire HF IXC (G-BRSF)	Sussex Spraying Services, Lancing, W Sussex
	RT486	Auster 5 (G-AJGJ) [PF-A]	Bournemouth Aviation Museum
	RT520	Auster 5 (G-ALYB)	Aeroventure, Doncaster
	RT610	Auster 5A-160 (G-AKWS)	Privately owned, Crowfield
	RW388	VS361 Spitfire LF XVIE (6946M) [U4-U]	Stoke-on-Trent City Museum, Hanley
	RW393	VS361 Spitfire LF XVIE (7293M) [XT-A]	RAF Museum, Cosford
	RX168	VS358 Seafire L IIIC (IAC 157/ G-BWEM)	Privately owned, Bourne Park, Hants
	SL611	VS361 Spitfire LF XVIE	Supermarine Aero Engineering, Stoke-on-Trent
	SL674	VS361 Spitfire LF IX (8392M) [RAS-H]	RAF Museum, stored Wyton
	SM520	VS361 Spitfire LF IX (G-BXHZ)	Privately owned, Oxford
	SM832	VS379 Spitfire F XIVE (G-WWII/ F-AZSJ) [YB-A]	Privately owned, Dijon, France
	SM845	VS394 Spitfire FR XVIII (G-BUOS)	Historic Flying Limited, Duxford
	SX137	VS384 Seafire F XVII	FAA Museum, RNAS Yeovilton
	SX336	VS384 Seafire F XVII (G-BRMG)	Privately owned, Twyford, Bucks
	TA122	DH98 Mosquito FB VI [UP-G]	Mosquito Aircraft Museum, London Colney
	TA634	DH98 Mosquito TT35 (G-AWJV) [8K-K]	Mosquito Aircraft Museum, London Colney
	TA639	DH98 Mosquito TT35 (7806M) [AZ-E]	RAF Museum, Cosford
	TA719	DH98 Mosquito TT35 (G-ASKC)	Imperial War Museum, Duxford
	TA805	VS361 Spitfire HF IX (G-PMNF)	Privately owned, Sandown
	TB252	VS361 Spitfire LF XVIE (G-XVIE) [GW-H]	Historic Flying Ltd, Audley End
	TB752	VS361 Spitfire LF XVIE (8086M) [KH-Z]	RAF Manston, Memorial Pavilion
	TD248	VS361 Spitfire LF XVIE (7246M/ G-OXVI) [D]	Historic Flying Limited, Duxford
	TD314	VS361 Spitfire LF IX (N601DA)	Privately owned, Norwich
	TE184	VS361 Spitfire LF XVIE (6850M/ G-MXVI)	Repainted in French marks, July 2000
	TE462	VS361 Spitfire LF XVIE (7243M)	Royal Scottish Mus'm of Flight, E Fortune
	TE517	VS361 Spitfire LF IXE (G-CCIX) [HL-K]	Privately owned, stored Booker
	TG263	Saro SR A1 (G-12-1)	Southampton Hall of Aviation
	TG511	HP67 Hastings C1 (8554M)	RAF Museum, Cosford
	TG517	HP67 Hastings T5	Newark Air Museum, Winthorpe
	TG528	HP67 Hastings C1A	Imperial War Museum, Duxford
	TJ118	DH98 Mosquito TT35 <ff>	Mosquito Aircraft Museum, stored London Colney
	TJ138	DH98 Mosquito B35 (7607M) [VO-L]	RAF Museum, Hendon
	TJ324	Auster 5 (G-APAH)	Privately owned, Cumbernauld
	TJ343	Auster 5 (G-AJXC)	Privately owned, stored Hook
	TJ398	Auster AOP6 (BAPC 70)	Aircraft Pres'n Soc of Scotland, E Fortune
	TJ569	Auster 5 (G-AKOW)	Museum of Army Flying, Middle Wallop
	TJ672	Auster 5D (G-ANIJ) [TS-D]	Privately owned, Whitchurch, Hants
	TJ704	Beagle A61 Terrier 2 (VW993/ G-ASCD) [JA]	Yorkshire Air Museum, Elvington
	TJ707	Auster 5 (frame)	Boscombe Down Museum
	TK718	GAL59 Hamilcar I	National Tank Museum, Bovington
	TK777	GAL59 Hamilcar I (fuselage)	Museum of Army Flying, Middle Wallop
	TL615	Airspeed AS58 Horsa II	Robertsbridge Aviation Society, Mayfield
	TS291	Slingsby Cadet TX1 (BGA852)	Royal Scottish Mus'm of Flight, E Fortune
	TS423	Douglas C-47A Dakota C3 (G-DAKS/N147DC) [A]	Privately owned, North Weald
	TS798	Avro 685 York C1 (G-AGNV)	RAF Museum, Cosford
	TV959	DH98 Mosquito T III [AF-V]	The Fighter Collection, stored Duxford
	TV959	DH98 Mosquito T III <R>	Privately owned, Heald Green, Cheshire
	TW439	Auster 5 (G-ANRP)	The Real Aeroplane Company, Breighton
	TW467	Auster 5 (G-ANIE) [ROD-F]	Privately owned, Bassingbourn
	TW511	Auster 5 (G-APAF)	Privately owned, North Coates
	TW533	Beagle A61 Terrier 2 (G-ASAX)	Privately owned, Netherley, Grampian

Serial	Type (other identity) [code]	Owner/operator, location or fate	Notes
TW536	Auster AOP6 (7704M/G-BNGE) [TS-V]	Privately owned, Netheravon	
TW591	Auster 6A (G-ARIH) [N]	Privately owned, Abbots Bromley	
TW641	Beagle A61 Terrier 2 (G-ATDN)	Privately owned, Biggin Hill	
TX183	Avro 652A Anson C19 (G-BSMF)	Privately owned, Arbroath	
TX213	Avro 652A Anson C19 (G-AWRS)	North-East Aircraft Museum, Usworth	
TX214	Avro 652A Anson C19 (7817M)	RAF Museum, Cosford	
TX226	Avro 652A Anson C19 (7865M)	Air Atlantique Historic Flight, Coventry	
TX235	Avro 652A Anson C19	Air Atlantique Historic Flight, Coventry	
VF301	DH100 Vampire F1 (7060M) [RAL-G]	Midland Air Museum, Coventry	
VF512	Auster 6A (G-ARRX) [PF-M]	Privately owned, White Waltham	
VF516	Beagle A61 Terrier 2 (G-ASMZ) [T]	Privately owned, Bagby	
VF526	Auster 6A (G-ARXU) [T]	Privately owned, Netheravon	
VF548	Beagle A61 Terrier 1 (G-ASEG)	Privately owned, Dunkeswell	
VF560	Auster 6A (frame)	Aeroventure, Doncaster	
VF611	Beagle A61 Terrier 2 (G-ATBU)	Privately owned, Hucknall	
VH127	Fairey Firefly TT4 [200/R]	FAA Museum, RNAS Yeovilton	
VL348	Avro 652A Anson C19 (G-AVVO)	Newark Air Museum, Winthorpe	
VL349	Avro 652A Anson C19 (G-AWSA) [V7-Q]	Norfolk & Suffolk Avn Mus'm, Flixton	
VM325	Avro 652A Anson C19	Gloucestershire Av'n Coll, stored Glos	
VM360	Avro 652A Anson C19 (G-APHV)	Royal Scottish Mus'm of Flight, E Fortune	
VM791	Slingsby Cadet TX3 (XA312/ 8876M)	RAF Manston History Museum	
VN148	Grunau Baby IIb (BAPC 33/ BGA2400)	Privately owned, Dunstable	
VN485	VS356 Spitfire F24 (7326M)	Imperial War Museum, Duxford	
VN799	EE Canberra T4 (WJ874)	RAF No 39(1 PRU) Sqn, Marham	
VP293	Avro 696 Shackleton T4 [A] <ff>	Avro Aircraft Heritage Society, Coventry	
VP519	Avro 652A Anson C19 (G-AVVR) <ff>	Privately owned, Wolverhampton	
VP952	DH104 Devon C2 (8820M)	RAF Museum, Cosford	
VP955	DH104 Devon C2 (G-DVON)	Privately owned, Kemble	
VP957	DH104 Devon C2 (8822M) <ff>	No 1137 Sqn ATC, Belfast	
VP975	DH104 Devon C2 [M]	Science Museum, Wroughton	
VP978	DH104 Devon C2 (8553M)	Scrapped	
VP981	DH104 Devon C2 (G-DHDV)	Air Atlantique Historic Flight, Coventry	
VR137	Westland Wyvern TF1	FAA Museum, RNAS Yeovilton	
VR192	Percival P40 Prentice T1 (G-APIT)	SWWAPS, Lasham	
VR249	Percival P40 Prentice T1 (G-APIY) [FA-EL]	Newark Air Museum, Winthorpe	
VR259	Percival P40 Prentice T1 (G-APJB) [M]	Air Atlantique Historic Flight, Coventry	
VR930	Hawker Sea Fury FB11 (8382M) [110/O]	RN Historic Flight, Yeovilton	
VS356	Percival P40 Prentice T1 (G-AOLU)	Privately owned, Montrose	
VS562	Avro 652A Anson T21 (8012M)	Privately owned, Llanbedr	
VS610	Percival P40 Prentice T1 (G-AOKL) [K-L]	The Shuttleworth Collection, stored Old Warden	
VS623	Percival P40 Prentice T1 (G-AOKZ) [KQ-F]	Midland Air Museum, Coventry	
VT409	Fairey Firefly AS5 <rf>	North-East Aircraft Museum, stored Usworth	
VT812	DH100 Vampire F3 (7200M) [N]	RAF Museum, stored Wyton	
VT871	DH100 Vampire FB6 (J-1173/ LZ551/G-DHXX) [G]	Source Classic Jet Flight, Bournemouth	
VT935	Boulton Paul P111A (VT769)	Midland Air Museum, Coventry	
VT987	Auster AOP6 (G-BKXP)	Aerobuild Ltd, Little Gransden, Cambs	
VV106	Supermarine 510 (7175M)	FAA Museum, stored RNAS Yeovilton	
VV217	DH100 Vampire FB5 (7323M)	North-East Aircraft Museum, stored Usworth	
VV612	DH112 Venom FB50 (J-1523/ WE402/G-VENI)	Source Classic Jet Flight, Bournemouth	
VV901	Avro 652A Anson T21	Yorkshire Air Museum, Elvington	
VW238	Hawker Fury FB10 (Iraqi AF 243/ PR772/G-BTTA) [107/Q]	Sold to South Africa, September 2000	
VW453	Gloster Meteor T7 (8703M) [Z]	RAF Innsworth, on display	
VW985	Auster AOP6 (G-ASEF)	Privately owned, Upper Arncott, Oxon	
VX118	Auster AOP6 (G-ASNB)	Vliegend Museum, Seppe, The Netherlands	
VX147	Alon A2 Aircoupe (G-AVIL)	Privately owned, Monewdon	

Notes	Serial	Type (other identity) [code]	Owner/operator, location or fate
	VX185	EE Canberra B(I)8 (7631M) <ff>	Royal Scottish Mus'm of Flight, E Fortune
	VX250	DH103 Sea Hornet 21 [48] <rf>	Mosquito Aircraft Museum, London Colney
	VX272	Hawker P.1052 (7174M)	FAA Museum, stored RNAS Yeovilton
	VX275	Slingsby T21B Sedbergh TX1 (8884M/BGA 572)	RAF Museum, stored Wyton
	VX461	DH100 Vampire FB5 (7646M)	RAF Museum, stored Wyton
	VX573	Vickers Valetta C2 (8389M)	RAF Museum, stored Cosford
	VX580	Vickers Valetta C2	Norfolk & Suffolk Avn Museum, Flixton
	VX595	WS51 Dragonfly HR1	FAA Museum, RNAS Yeovilton
	VX665	Hawker Sea Fury FB11 <rf>	RN Historic Flight, at BAE Systems Brough
	VX926	Auster T7 (G-ASKJ)	Privately owned, Little Gransden
	VZ345	Hawker Sea Fury T20S	RN Historic Flight, stored Yeovilton
	VZ467	Gloster Meteor F8 (G-METE) [01]	Kennet Aviation, Cranfield
	VZ477	Gloster Meteor F8 (7741M) <ff>	Midland Air Museum, Coventry
	VZ608	Gloster Meteor FR9	Newark Air Museum, Winthorpe
	VZ634	Gloster Meteor T7 (8657M)	Newark Air Museum, Winthorpe
	VZ638	Gloster Meteor T7 (G-JETM) [HF]	Gatwick Aviation Museum, Charlwood, Surrey
	VZ728	RS4 Desford Trainer (G-AGOS)	Snibston Discovery Park, stored Coalville
	VZ962	WS51 Dragonfly HR1 [904]	The Helicopter Museum, Weston-super-Mare
	WA473	VS Attacker F1 [102/J]	FAA Museum, RNAS Yeovilton
	WA576	Bristol 171 Sycamore 3 (7900M/ G-ALSS)	Dumfries & Galloway Avn Mus, Dumfries
	WA577	Bristol 171 Sycamore 3 (7718M/ G-ALST)	North-East Aircraft Museum, Usworth
	WA591	Gloster Meteor T7 (7917M/ G-BWMF) [W]	Meteor Flight, Yatesbury
	WA630	Gloster Meteor T7 [69] <ff>	Robertsbridge Aviation Society, Newhaven
	WA634	Gloster Meteor T7/8	RAF Museum, Cosford
	WA638	Gloster Meteor T7(mod)	Martin Baker Aircraft, Chalgrove, spares use
	WA662	Gloster Meteor T7	Aeroventure, Doncaster
	WA829	Gloster Meteor F8 (WA984) [A]	Tangmere Military Aviation Museum
	WB188	Hawker Hunter F3 (7154M)	Tangmere Military Aviation Museum
	WB271	Fairey Firefly AS5 [204/R]	RN Historic Flight, RNAS Yeovilton
	WB440	Fairey Firefly AS6 <ff>	Privately owned, Newton-le-Willows
	WB491	Avro 706 Ashton 2 (TS897/ G-AJJW) <ff>	Avro Aircraft Heritage Society, BAE Systems Woodford
	WB556	DHC1 Chipmunk T10	RAFGSA, Bicester
	WB560	DHC1 Chipmunk T10	South Yorkshire Avn Museum, Firbeck
	WB565	DHC1 Chipmunk T10 (G-PVET) [X]	Privately owned, Kemble
	WB569	DHC1 Chipmunk T10 (G-BYSJ) [R]	Privately owned, Duxford
	WB584	DHC1 Chipmunk T10 (7706M) <ff>	Royal Scottish Mus'm of Flight, E Fortune
	WB585	DHC1 Chipmunk T10 (G-AOSY) [M]	Privately owned, Blackbushe
	WB588	DHC1 Chipmunk T10 (G-AOTD) [D]	Privately owned, Biggin Hill
	WB615	DHC1 Chipmunk T10 (G-BXIA) [E]	Privately owned, Blackpool
	WB624	DHC1 Chipmunk T10 <ff>	Newark Air Museum, Winthorpe
	WB626	DHC1 Chipmunk T10 <ff>	Privately owned, South Molton, Devon
	WB627	DHC1 Chipmunk T10 (9248M) [N]	Dulwich College CCF
	WB645	DHC1 Chipmunk T10 (8218M)	RAFGSA, Bicester, spares use
	WB652	DHC1 Chipmunk T10 (G-CHPY) [V]	Privately owned, Cardiff
	WB654	DHC1 Chipmunk T10 (G-BXGO) [U]	Privately owned, Booker
	WB657	DHC1 Chipmunk T10 [908]	RN Historic Flight, Yeovilton
	WB660	DHC1 Chipmunk T10 (G-ARMB)	Privately owned, Shipdham
	WB670	DHC1 Chipmunk T10 (8361M) <ff>	Privately owned, Currie, Lothian
	WB671	DHC1 Chipmunk T10 (G-BWTG) [910]	Privately owned, Epse, The Netherlands
	WB685	DHC1 Chipmunk T10 (comp WP969/G-ATHC)	North-East Aircraft Museum, Usworth
	WB697	DHC1 Chipmunk T10 (G-BXCT) [95]	Privately owned, Wickenby
	WB702	DHC1 Chipmunk T10 (G-AOFE)	Privately owned, Goodwood
	WB703	DHC1 Chipmunk T10 (G-ARMC)	Privately owned, White Waltham
	WB711	DHC1 Chipmunk T10 (G-APPM)	Privately owned, Crowfield
	WB726	DHC1 Chipmunk T10 (G-AOSK) [E]	Privately owned, Audley End
	WB733	DHC1 Chipmunk T10 (comp WG422)	Aeroventure, Doncaster
	WB758	DHC1 Chipmunk T10 (7729M) [P]	Privately owned, Torbay
	WB763	DHC1 Chipmunk T10 (G-BBMR) [14]	Privately owned, Twyford, Bucks

Serial	Type (other identity) [code]	Owner/operator, location or fate	Notes
WB922	Slingsby T21B Sedbergh TX1 (BGA 4366)	Privately owned, Kingston Deverill	
WB924	Slingsby T21B Sedbergh TX1 (BGA 3901)	Privately owned, Dunstable	
WB938	Slingsby T21B Sedbergh TX1	Privately owned, Halton	
WB943	Slingsby T21B Sedbergh TX1 (BGA 2941)	Privately owned, Rufforth	
WB971	Slingsby T21B Sedbergh TX1 (BGA 3324)	Privately owned, Tibenham	
WB975	Slingsby T21B Sedbergh TX1 (BGA 3288)	Privately owned, Drumshade, Fife	
WB981	Slingsby T21B Sedbergh TX1 (BGA 1218)	Privately owned, Aston Down	
WD286	DHC1 Chipmunk T10 (G-BBND)	Privately owned, Croydon, Cambs	
WD288	DHC1 Chipmunk T10 (G-AOSO) [38]	Privately owned, Charlton Park, Wilts	
WD292	DHC1 Chipmunk T10 (G-BCRX)	Privately owned, White Waltham	
WD293	DHC1 Chipmunk T10 (7645M) <ff>	No 210 Sqn ATC, Newport, Gwent	
WD305	DHC1 Chipmunk T10 (G-ARGG)	Privately owned, Coventry	
WD310	DHC1 Chipmunk T10 (G-BWUN) [B]	Privately owned, Ringmer, E Sussex	
WD318	DHC1 Chipmunk T10 (8207M) <ff>	No 145 Sqn ATC, Timperley, Gr Manchester	
WD325	DHC1 Chipmunk T10 [N]	AAC Historic Aircraft Flight, Middle Wallop	
WD331	DHC1 Chipmunk T10 (G-BXDH) [J]	Privately owned, Kemble	
WD347	DHC1 Chipmunk T10 (G-BBRV)	Privately owned, Liverpool	
WD355	DHC1 Chipmunk T10 (WD335) <ff>	No 1955 Sqn ATC, Wells, Somerset	
WD356	DHC1 Chipmunk T10 (7625M)	Sold to Canada, 1999	
WD363	DHC1 Chipmunk T10 (G-BCIH) [5]	Privately owned, Andrewsfield	
WD370	DHC1 Chipmunk T10 <ff>	Privately owned, Brighton	
WD373	DHC1 Chipmunk T10 (G-BXDI) [12]	Privately owned, Perth	
WD377	DHC1 Chipmunk T10 <ff>	RAF Millom Museum, Haverigg	
WD379	DHC1 Chipmunk T10 (WB696/ G-APLO) [K]	Privately owned, Jersey	
WD386	DHC1 Chipmunk T10 (comp WD377)	Dumfries & Galloway Avn Mus, Dumfries	
WD390	DHC1 Chipmunk T10 (G-BWNK) [68]	Privately owned, Breighton	
WD413	Avro 652A Anson T21 (7881M/ G-BFIR/G-VROE)	Repainted as G-VROE	
WD615	Gloster Meteor TT20 (WD646/ [R]	RAF Manston History Museum	
WD646	Gloster Meteor TT20 (8189M) [R]	Repainted as WD615 by November 2000	
WD686	Gloster Meteor NF11	Muckleburgh Collection, Weybourne	
WD790	Gloster Meteor NF11 (8743M)<ff>	North-East Aircraft Museum, Usworth	
WD889	Fairey Firefly AS5 <ff>	North-East Aircraft Museum, Usworth	
WD931	EE Canberra B2 <ff>	RAF Museum, stored Cosford	
WD935	EE Canberra B2 (8440M) <ff>	Privately owned, Alveley, Shropshire	
WD954	EE Canberra B2 <ff>	Privately owned, Rayleigh, Essex	
WE113	EE Canberra T4 <ff>	Privately owned, Woodhurst, Cambridgeshire	
WE122	EE Canberra TT18 [845] <ff>	Blyth Valley Aviation Collection, Walpole, Suffolk	
WE139	EE Canberra PR3 (8369M)	RAF Museum, Hendon	
WE168	EE Canberra PR3 (8049M) <ff>	Privately owned, Colchester	
WE173	EE Canberra PR3 (8740M) <ff>	Robertsbridge Aviation Society, Mayfield	
WE188	EE Canberra T4	Solway Aviation Society, Carlisle	
WE192	EE Canberra T4 <ff>	Blyth Valley Aviation Collection, Walpole, Suffolk	
WE275	DH112 Venom FB50 (J-1601/ G-VIDI)	BAE Systems Hawarden, Fire Section	
WE569	Auster T7 (G-ASAJ)	Privately owned, Sandy, Beds	
WE591	Auster T7 (G-ASAK) [Y]	Privately owned, Biggin Hill	
WE600	Auster T7 Antarctic (7602M)	RAF Museum, Cosford	
WE724	Hawker Sea Fury FB11 (VX653/ G-BUCM) [062]	The Fighter Collection, Duxford	
WE925	Gloster Meteor F8	Classic Jet Aircraft Group, Loughborough	
WE982	Slingsby T30B Prefect TX1 (8781M)	RAF Museum, stored Cosford	
WE990	Slingsby T30B Prefect TX1 (BGA 2583)	Privately owned, stored Beds	

Notes	Serial	Type (other identity) [code]	Owner/operator, location or fate
	WF118	Percival P57 Sea Prince T1 (G-DACA)	Gatwick Aviation Museum, Charlwood, Surrey
	WF122	Percival P57 Sea Prince T1 [575/CU]	Flambards Village Theme Park, Helston
	WF128	Percival P57 Sea Prince T1 (8611M)	Norfolk & Suffolk Avn Museum, Flixton
	WF137	Percival P57 Sea Prince C1	SWWAPS, Lasham
	WF145	Hawker Sea Hawk F1 <ff>	Privately owned, Welshpool
	WF225	Hawker Sea Hawk F1 [CU]	RNAS Culdrose, at main gate
	WF259	Hawker Sea Hawk F2 (171/A)	Royal Scottish Mus'm of Flight,E Fortune
	WF369	Vickers Varsity T1 [F]	Newark Air Museum, Winthorpe
	WF372	Vickers Varsity T1 [A]	Brooklands Museum, Weybridge
	WF376	Vickers Varsity T1	Bristol Airport Fire Section
	WF408	Vickers Varsity T1 (8395M)	Privately owned, East Grinstead
	WF410	Vickers Varsity T1 [F]	Brunel Technical College, Lulsgate
	WF643	Gloster Meteor F8 [X]	Norfolk & Suffolk Avn Museum, Flixton
	WF714	Gloster Meteor F8 (WK914)	Privately owned, stored Scampton
	WF784	Gloster Meteor T7 (7895M)	Gloucestershire Avn Coll, stored Glos
	WF825	Gloster Meteor T7 (8359M) [A]	Avon Air Museum, stored Malmesbury
	WF877	Gloster Meteor T7 (G-BPOA)	Privately owned, Kemble
	WF911	EE Canberra B2 [CO] <ff>	The Griffin Trust, Hooton Park, Cheshire
	WF922	EE Canberra PR3	Midland Air Museum, Coventry
	WG300	DHC1 Chipmunk T10 <ff>	RAFGSA, Bicester
	WG303	DHC1 Chipmunk T10 (8208M) <ff>	RAFGSA, Bicester
	WG307	DHC1 Chipmunk T10 (G-BCYJ)	Privately owned, Shempston Fm, Lossiemouth
	WG308	DHC1 Chipmunk T10 (G-BYHL) [71]	Privately owned, Newton
	WG316	DHC1 Chipmunk T10 (G-BCAH)	Privately owned, Shoreham
	WG321	DHC1 Chipmunk T10 (G-DHCC)	Privately owned, Wevelgem, Belgium
	WG348	DHC1 Chipmunk T10 (G-BBMV)	Privately owned, Sywell
	WG350	DHC1 Chipmunk T10 (G-BPAL)	Privately owned, Thruxton
	WG362	DHC1 Chipmunk T10 (8437M/ 8630M/*WX643*) <ff>	RAF Newton, instructional use
	WG407	DHC1 Chipmunk T10 (G-BWMX)	Privately owned, Spanhoe Lodge
	WG418	DHC1 Chipmunk T10 (8209M/ G-ATDY) <ff>	No 1940 Sqn ATC, Levenshulme, Gr Manchester
	WG419	DHC1 Chipmunk T10 (8206M) <ff>	No 1053 Sqn ATC, Armthorpe
	WG422	DHC1 Chipmunk T10 (8394M/ G-BFAX) [116]	The Aircraft Restoration Co, Duxford
	WG432	DHC1 Chipmunk T10 [L]	Museum of Army Flying, Middle Wallop
	WG465	DHC1 Chipmunk T10 (G-BCEY)	Privately owned, White Waltham
	WG469	DHC1 Chipmunk T10 (G-BWJY) [72]	Privately owned, Newtownards
	WG471	DHC1 Chipmunk T10 (8210M) <ff>	No 863 Sqn ATC, Thurston
	WG472	DHC1 Chipmunk T10 (G-AOTY)	Privately owned, Bryngwyn Bach, Clwyd
	WG477	DHC1 Chipmunk T10 (8362M/ G-ATDP) <ff>	No 281 Sqn ATC, Birkdale, Merseyside
	WG482	DHC1 Chipmunk T10 (VH-ZOT) [01]	Privately owned, Duxford
	WG483	DHC1 Chipmunk T10 (WG393/ VH-ZIT)	Privately owned, Duxford
	WG486	DHC1 Chipmunk T10	RAF BBMF, Coningsby
	WG498	Slingsby Sedbergh TX1 (BGS3245)	Privately owned, Aston Down
	WG511	Avro 696 Shackleton T4 (fuselage)	Flambards Village Theme Park, Helston
	WG718	WS51 Dragonfly HR3 [934]	Privately owned, Elvington
	WG719	WS51 Dragonfly HR5 (G-BRMA)	The Helicopter Museum, Weston-super-Mare
	WG724	WS51 Dragonfly HR5 [932]	North-East Aircraft Museum, Usworth
	WG751	WS51 Dragonfly HR5 [710/GJ]	World Naval Base, Chatham
	WG754	WS51 Dragonfly HR3 (WG725/ 7703M) [912/CU]	*To Australia, February 2000*
	WG760	EE P1A (7755M)	RAF Museum, Cosford
	WG763	EE P1A (7816M)	Gr Manchester Mus of Science & Industry
	WG768	Short SB5 (8005M)	RAF Museum, Cosford
	WG774	BAC 221	Science Museum, at FAA Museum, RNAS Yeovilton
	WG777	Fairey FD2 (7986M)	RAF Museum, Cosford
	WG789	EE Canberra B2/6 <ff>	Privately owned, Mendlesham, Suffolk
	WH132	Gloster Meteor T7 (7906M) [J]	No 276 Sqn ATC, Chelmsford
	WH166	Gloster Meteor T7 (8052M) [A]	Privately owned, Birlingham, Worcs

Serial	Type (other identity) [code]	Owner/operator, location or fate	Notes
WH291	Gloster Meteor F8	SWWAPS, Lasham	
WH301	Gloster Meteor F8 (7930M) [T]	RAF Museum, Hendon	
WH364	Gloster Meteor F8 (8169M)	Privately owned, Kemble	
WH453	Gloster Meteor D16 [L]	DPA, stored DERA Llanbedr	
WH646	EE Canberra T17A <ff>	Midland Air Museum, Coventry	
WH657	EE Canberra B2	Brenzett Aeronautical Museum	
WH665	EE Canberra T17 (8763M) [J]	BAE Systems Filton, Fire Section	
WH725	EE Canberra B2	Imperial War Museum, Duxford	
WH734	EE Canberra B2(mod)	DPA, DERA Llanbedr	
WH739	EE Canberra B2 <ff>	No 2475 Sqn ATC, Ammanford, Dyfed	
WH740	EE Canberra T17 (8762M) [K]	East Midlands Airport Aeropark	
WH773	EE Canberra PR7 (8696M)	Gatwick Aviation Museum, Charlwood, Surrey	
WH775	EE Canberra PR7 (8128M/8868M) <ff>	Privately owned, Welshpool	
WH779	EE Canberra PR7 [BP]	RAF, stored Marham	
WH780	EE Canberra T22 <rf>	RAF St Athan, Fire Section	
WH791	EE Canberra PR7 (8165M/8176M/ 8187M)	Newark Air Museum, Winthorpe	
WH796	EE Canberra PR7 <ff>	*Scrapped at Stock*	
WH797	EE Canberra T22 <rf>	RAF St Athan, Fire Section	
WH803	EE Canberra T22 <ff>	Privately owned, Stock, Essex	
WH840	EE Canberra T4 (8350M) <ff>	Privately owned, Flixton	
WH846	EE Canberra T4	Yorkshire Air Museum, Elvington	
WH849	EE Canberra T4	RAF No 39(1 PRU) Sqn, Marham	
WH850	EE Canberra T4 <ff>	Barton Aviation Heritage Society, Barton	
WH854	EE Canberra T4 <ff>	*Scrapped at Chalgrove*	
WH863	EE Canberra T17 (8693M) [CP] <ff>	Newark Air Museum, Winthorpe	
WH876	EE Canberra B2(mod)	DERA Aberporth, instructional use	
WH887	EE Canberra TT18 [847]	DPA, stored DERA Llanbedr	
WH903	EE Canberra B2 <ff>	Yorkshire Air Museum, Elvington	
WH903	EE Canberra B2 (8584M) <ff>	Gatwick Aviation Museum, Charlwood, Surrey	
WH904	EE Canberra T19	Newark Air Museum, Winthorpe	
WH946	EE Canberra B6(mod) (8185M) <ff>	Privately owned, Tetney, Grimsby	
WH953	EE Canberra B6(mod) <ff>	Blyth Valley Aviation Collection, Walpole, Suffolk	
WH957	EE Canberra E15 (8869M) <ff>	Lincolnshire Avn Heritage Centre, East Kirkby	
WH960	EE Canberra B15 (8344M) <ff>	Privately owned, Nottingham	
WH964	EE Canberra E15 (8870M) <ff>	Privately owned, Southampton	
WH984	EE Canberra B15 (8101M) <ff>	RAF Sealand	
WH991	WS51 Dragonfly HR3	Privately owned, Elvington	
WJ231	Hawker Sea Fury FB11 (*WE726*) [115/O]	FAA Museum, Yeovilton	
WJ358	Auster AOP6 (G-ARYD)	Museum of Army Flying, stored Middle Wallop	
WJ565	EE Canberra T17 (8871M) <ff>	Privately owned, Binbrook	
WJ567	EE Canberra B2 <ff>	Privately owned, Houghton, Cambs	
WJ576	EE Canberra T17 <ff>	Boulton Paul Association, Wolverhampton	
WJ581	EE Canberra PR7 <ff>	Privately owned, Canterbury	
WJ603	EE Canberra B2 (8664M) <ff>	Privately owned, Stock, Essex	
WJ630	EE Canberra T17 [ED]	*Currently not known*	
WJ633	EE Canberra T17 [EF] <ff>	RAF Wyton	
WJ639	EE Canberra TT18 [39]	North-East Aircraft Museum, Usworth	
WJ640	EE Canberra B2 (8722M) <ff>	Pinewood Studios, Bucks	
WJ676	EE Canberra B2 (7796M) <ff>	Privately owned, Heswall, Merseyside	
WJ677	EE Canberra B2 <ff>	Privately owned, Redruth	
WJ680	EE Canberra TT18 (G-BURM) [CT]	Canberra Flight, Bournemouth	
WJ717	EE Canberra TT18 (9052M) <ff>	RAF St Athan, Fire Section	
WJ721	EE Canberra TT18 [21] <ff>	Dundonald Aviation Centre, Strathclyde	
WJ731	EE Canberra B2T [BK] <ff>	Privately owned, Luton	
WJ775	EE Canberra B6 (8581M) [J] (fuselage)	*Scrapped at Bodney Camp, Norfolk*	
WJ821	EE Canberra PR7 (8668M)	Army, Bassingbourn, on display	
WJ863	EE Canberra T4 <ff>	Cambridge Airport Fire Section	
WJ865	EE Canberra T4	Privately owned, Bromsgrove	
WJ866	EE Canberra T4 [AV]	RAF No 39(1 PRU) Sqn, Marham	
WJ872	EE Canberra T4 (8492M) <ff>	No 327 Sqn ATC, Kilmarnock	
WJ876	EE Canberra T4 <ff>	RAF EPTT, St Athan	
WJ880	EE Canberra T4 (8491M) <ff>	South Yorkshire Avn Museum, Firbeck	

Notes	Serial	Type (other identity) [code]	Owner/operator, location or fate
	WJ893	Vickers Varsity T1	*Scrapped at Aberporth*
	WJ903	Vickers Varsity T1 <ff>	Aeroventure, Doncaster
	WJ945	Vickers Varsity T1 (G-BEDV) [21]	Imperial War Museum, Duxford
	WJ975	EE Canberra T19	Bomber County Aviation Museum, Hemswell
	WJ992	EE Canberra T4	Bournemouth Int'l Airport, Fire Section
	WK102	EE Canberra T17 (8780M) <ff>	Privately owned, Welshpool
	WK118	EE Canberra TT18 <ff>	Privately owned, Worcester
	WK122	EE Canberra TT18 [22]	Flambards Village Theme Park, Helston
	WK124	EE Canberra TT18 (9093M) [CR]	MoD FSCTE, Manston
	WK126	EE Canberra TT18 (N2138J) [843]	Gloucestershire Avn /Coll, stored Glos
	WK127	EE Canberra TT18 (8985M) <ff>	No 2484 Sqn ATC, Bassingbourn
	WK128	EE Canberra B2	DPA, DERA Llanbedr
	WK163	EE Canberra B6(mod) (G-BVWC)	Classic Aviation Projects, Bruntingthorpe
	WK198	VS Swift F4 (7428M) (fuselage)	North-East Aircraft Museum, Usworth
	WK275	VS Swift F4	Privately owned, Upper Hill, nr Leominster
	WK277	VS Swift FR5 (7719M) [N]	Newark Air Museum, Winthorpe
	WK281	VS Swift FR5 (7712M) [S]	Tangmere Military Aviation Museum
	WK393	DH112 Venom FB1 <ff>	Aeroventure, Doncaster
	WK511	DHC1 Chipmunk T10 (G-BVBT) [905]	Kennet Aviation, Cranfield
	WK512	DHC1 Chipmunk T10 (G-BXIM) [A]	Privately owned, Brize Norton
	WK517	DHC1 Chipmunk T10 (G-ULAS) [84]	Privately owned, Booker
	WK518	DHC1 Chipmunk T10 [K]	RAF BBMF, Coningsby
	WK522	DHC1 Chipmunk T10 (G-BCOU)	Privately owned,
	WK549	DHC1 Chipmunk T10 (G-BTWF)	Privately owned, Rufforth
	WK570	DHC1 Chipmunk T10 (8211M) <ff>	No 424 Sqn ATC, Southampton Hall of Aviation
	WK576	DHC1 Chipmunk T10 (8357M) <ff>	No 1206 Sqn ATC, Lichfield
	WK584	DHC1 Chipmunk T10 (7556M) <ff>	No 216 Sqn ATC, Bawtry
	WK585	DHC1 Chipmunk T10 (G-BZGA)	The Aircraft Restoration Co, Duxford
	WK586	DHC1 Chipmunk T10 (G-BXGX) [V]	Privately owned, Shoreham
	WK590	DHC1 Chipmunk T10 (G-BWVZ) [69]	Privately owned, Spanhoe
	WK608	DHC1 Chipmunk T10 [906]	RN Historic Flight, Yeovilton
	WK609	DHC1 Chipmunk T10 (G-BXDN) [B]	Privately owned, Halton
	WK611	DHC1 Chipmunk T10 (G-ARWB)	Privately owned, Thruxton
	WK613	DHC1 Chipmunk T10 [P]	*Currently not known*
	WK620	DHC1 Chipmunk T10 [T] (fuselage)	Privately owned, Twyford, Bucks
	WK622	DHC1 Chipmunk T10 (G-BCZH)	Privately owned, Horsford
	WK624	DHC1 Chipmunk T10 (G-BWHI)	The Aircraft Restoration Co, Duxford
	WK626	DHC1 Chipmunk T10 (8213M) <ff>	South Yorkshire Avn Museum, Firbeck
	WK628	DHC1 Chipmunk T10 (G-BBMW)	Privately owned, Shoreham
	WK630	DHC1 Chipmunk T10 (G-BXDG) [11]	Privately owned, Swanton Morley
	WK633	DHC1 Chipmunk T10 (G-BXEC) [A]	Privately owned, Seething
	WK638	DHC1 Chipmunk T10 (G-BWJZ) [83]	*Crashed 22 August 1999, Bagby*
	WK640	DHC1 Chipmunk T10 (G-BWUV) [C]	Privately owned, Bagby
	WK642	DHC1 Chipmunk T10 (G-BXDP) [94]	Privately owned, Eire
	WK654	Gloster Meteor F8 (8092M) [B]	City of Norwich Aviation Museum
	WK800	Gloster Meteor D16 [Z]	DPA, DERA Llanbedr
	WK864	Gloster Meteor F8 (WL168/7750M) [C]	Yorkshire Air Museum, Elvington
	WK935	Gloster Meteor Prone Pilot (7869M)	RAF Museum, Cosford
	WK991	Gloster Meteor F8 (7825M)	Imperial War Museum, Duxford
	WL131	Gloster Meteor F8 (7751M) <ff>	Aeroventure, Doncaster
	WL181	Gloster Meteor F8 [X]	North-East Aircraft Museum, Usworth
	WL332	Gloster Meteor T7 [888]	Privately owned, Long Marston
	WL345	Gloster Meteor T7	St Leonard's Motors, Hollington, E Sussex
	WL349	Gloster Meteor T7 [Z]	Staverton, Glos, stored
	WL360	Gloster Meteor T7 (7920M) [G]	Meteor Flight, Yatesbury
	WL375	Gloster Meteor T7(mod)	Dumfries & Galloway Avn Mus, Dumfries
	WL405	Gloster Meteor T7	Martin Baker Aircraft, Chalgrove
	WL419	Gloster Meteor T7	Martin Baker Aircraft, Chalgrove
	WL505	DH100 Vampire FB9 (7705M/ G-FBIX)	De Havilland Aviation, Swansea

Serial	Type (other identity) [code]	Owner/operator, location or fate	Notes
WL505	DH100 Vampire FB6 (J-1167/ VZ304/G-MKVI)	De Havilland Aviation, Swansea	
WL626	Vickers Varsity T1 (G-BHDD) [P]	East Midlands Airport Aeropark	
WL627	Vickers Varsity T1 (8488M) [D] <ff>	Privately owned, Preston, E Yorkshire	
WL679	Vickers Varsity T1 (9155M)	RAF Museum, Cosford	
WL732	BP P108 Sea Balliol T21	RAF Museum, Cosford	
WL795	Avro 696 Shackleton MR2C (8753M) [T]	RAF St Mawgan, on display	
WL798	Avro 696 Shackleton MR2C (8114M) <ff>	Privately owned, Elgin	
WL925	Slingsby T31B Cadet TX3 (WV925) <ff>	RAF No 633 VGS, Cosford	
WM145	AW Meteor NF11 <ff>	N Yorks Aircraft Recovery Centre, Chop Gate	
WM167	AW Meteor NF11 (G-LOSM)	Privately owned, Bournemouth	
WM267	Gloster Meteor NF11 <ff>	Blyth Valley Aviation Collection, Walpole, Suffolk	
WM292	AW Meteor TT20 [841]	FAA Museum, stored RNAS Yeovilton	
WM311	AW Meteor TT20 (WM224/8177M)	Privately owned, North Weald	
WM366	AW Meteor NF13 (4X-FNA) comp VZ462)	SWWAPS, Lasham	
WM367	AW Meteor NF13 <ff>	Jet Avn Preservation Grp, Long Marston	
WM571	DH112 Sea Venom FAW21 [VL]	Southampton Hall of Aviation	
WM729	DH113 Vampire NF10 [A] <ff>	Mosquito Aircraft Museum, stored Glos	
WM913	Hawker Sea Hawk FB5 (8162M) [456/J]	Newark Air Museum, Winthorpe	
WM961	Hawker Sea Hawk FB5 [J]	Caernarfon Air World	
WM969	Hawker Sea Hawk FB5 [10/Z]	Imperial War Museum, Duxford	
WM993	Hawker Sea Hawk FB5 [034]	Privately owned, Peasedown St John, Avon	
WN105	Hawker Sea Hawk FB3 (WF299/ 8164M)	Privately owned, Birlingham, Worcs	
WN108	Hawker Sea Hawk FB5 [033]	Ulster Aviation Society, Langford Lodge	
WN149	BP P108 Balliol T2	Boulton Paul Association, Wolverhampton	
WN411	Fairey Gannet AS1 (fuselage)	Privately owned, Southampton	
WN493	WS51 Dragonfly HR5	FAA Museum, RNAS Yeovilton	
WN499	WS51 Dragonfly HR5 [Y]	Caernarfon Air World	
WN516	BP P108 Balliol T2 <ff>	North-East Aircraft Museum, Usworth	
WN534	BP P108 Balliol T2 <ff>	Boulton Paul Association, Wolverhampton	
WN890	Hawker Hunter F2 <ff>	Aeroventure, Doncaster	
WN904	Hawker Hunter F2 (7544M) [3]	RE 39 Regt, Waterbeach, on display	
WN907	Hawker Hunter F2 (7416M) <ff>	Blyth Valley Aviation Collection, Walpole, Suffolk	
WP185	Hawker Hunter F5 (7583M)	Privately owned, Great Dunmow, Essex	
WP190	Hawker Hunter F5 (7582M/8473M/ WP180) [K]	Privately owned, Quedgeley, Glos.	
WP250	DH113 Vampire NF10 <ff>	*Currently not known*	
WP255	DH113 Vampire NF10 <ff>	Aeroventure, Doncaster	
WP270	EoN Eton TX1 (8598M)	Gr Manchester Mus of Science & Industry, stored	
WP271	EoN Eton TX1	Privately owned, stored Keevil	
WP308	Percival P57 Sea Prince T1 (G-GACA) [572/CU]	Gatwick Aviation Museum, Charlwood, Surrey	
WP313	Percival P57 Sea Prince T1 [568/CU]	FAA Museum, stored RNAS Yeovilton	
WP314	Percival P57 Sea Prince T1 (8634M) [573/CU]	Privately owned, Carlisle Airport	
WP321	Percival P57 Sea Prince T1 (G-BRFC/N7SY)	Bournemouth Aviation Museum	
WP503	WS51 Dragonfly HR3 [901]	*Sunk at Capernwray, Lancs*	
WP515	EE Canberra B2 <ff>	Privately owned, Welshpool	
WP772	DHC1 Chipmunk T10 [Q] (wreck)	RAF Manston History Museum	
WP784	DHC1 Chipmunk T10 <ff>	Jet Avn Preservation Grp, Long Marston	
WP788	DHC1 Chipmunk T10 (G-BCHL)	Privately owned, Sleap	
WP790	DHC1 Chipmunk T10 (G-BBNC) [T]	Mosquito Aircraft Museum, London Colney	
WP795	DHC1 Chipmunk T10 (G-BVZZ) [901]	Privately owned, Lee-on-Solent	
WP800	DHC1 Chipmunk T10 (G-BCXN) [2]	Privately owned, Halton	
WP803	DHC1 Chipmunk T10 (G-HAPY) [G]	Privately owned, Booker	

Notes	Serial	Type (other identity) [code]	Owner/operator, location or fate
	WP805	DHC1 Chipmunk T10 (G-MAJR) [D]	Privately owned, Fareham
	WP808	DHC1 Chipmunk T10 (G-BDEU)	Privately owned, Binham
	WP809	DHC1 Chipmunk T10 (G-BVTX) [78]	Privately owned, Husbands Bosworth
	WP833	DHC1 Chipmunk T10 (G-BZDU) [H]	Privately owned, Duxford
	WP839	DHC1 Chipmunk T10 [A]	Privately owned, Thornton-Cleveleys, Lancs
	WP840	DHC1 Chipmunk T10 (G-BXDM) [9]	Privately owned, Halton
	WP843	DHC1 Chipmunk T10 (G-BDBP) [F]	Sold to South Africa, August 2000
	WP844	DHC1 Chipmunk T10 (G-BWOX) [85]	Privately owned, King's Coughton
	WP845	DHC1 Chipmunk T10 <ff>	Privately owned, Leicestershire
	WP856	DHC1 Chipmunk T10 (G-BVWP) [904]	Privately owned, Horsham
	WP857	DHC1 Chipmunk T10 (G-BDRJ) [24]	Privately owned, Elstree
	WP859	DHC1 Chipmunk T10 (G-BXCP) [E]	Privately owned, Eire
	WP860	DHC1 Chipmunk T10 (G-BXDA) [6]	Privately owned, Cumbernauld
	WP863	DHC1 Chipmunk T10 (8360M/ G-ATJI) <ff>	No ...Sqn ATC, DERA Boscombe Down
	WP864	DHC1 Chipmunk T10 (8214M) <ff>	Sold to the USA
	WP871	DHC1 Chipmunk T10 [W]	AAC, Middle Wallop, for display
	WP896	DHC1 Chipmunk T10 (G-BWVY) [M]	Privately owned, London
	WP901	DHC1 Chipmunk T10 (G-BWNT) [B]	Privately owned, East Midlands Airport
	WP903	DHC1 Chipmunk T10 (G-BCGC)	Privately owned, Shoreham
	WP907	DHC1 Chipmunk T10 <ff> (7970M)	Privately owned, Reading
	WP912	DHC1 Chipmunk T10 (8467M)	RAF Museum, Cosford
	WP921	DHC1 Chipmunk T10 (G-ATJJ) <ff>	Privately owned, Brooklands
	WP925	DHC1 Chipmunk T10 (G-BXHA) [C]	Privately owned, Camberley
	WP927	DHC1 Chipmunk T10 (8216M/ G-ATJK) <ff>	No 1343 Sqn ATC, Odiham
	WP928	DHC1 Chipmunk T10 (G-BXGM) [D]	Privately owned, Shoreham
	WP929	DHC1 Chipmunk T10 (G-BXCV) [F]	Privately owned, Duxford
	WP930	DHC1 Chipmunk T10 (G-BXHF) [J]	Privately owned, Redhill
	WP962	DHC1 Chipmunk T10 [C]	RAF Museum, Hendon
	WP964	DHC1 Chipmunk T10 [Y]	AAC Historic Aircraft Flight, Middle Wallop
	WP971	DHC1 Chipmunk T10 (G-ATHD)	Privately owned, Denham
	WP978	DHC1 Chipmunk T10 (7467M) <ff>	Privately owned, Bournemouth
	WP983	DHC1 Chipmunk T10 (G-BXNN) [B]	Privately owned, Old Sarum
	WP984	DHC1 Chipmunk T10 (G-BWTO) [H]	Privately owned, Duxford
	WR360	DH112 Venom FB50 (J-1626/ G-DHSS)	Source Classic Jet Flight, Bournemouth
	WR410	DH112 Venom FB50 (J-1539/ G-DHUU/WE410)	Source Classic Jet Flight, Bournemouth
	WR410	DH112 Venom FB54 (J-1790/ G-BLKA) [N]	Source Classic Jet Flight, stored Bournemouth
	WR421	DH112 Venom FB50 (J-1611/ G-DHTT)	Source Classic Jet Flight, Bournemouth
	WR539	DH112 Venom FB4 (8399M) [F]	Mosquito Aircraft Museum, stored Glos
	WR960	Avro 696 Shackleton AEW2 (8772M)	Gr Manchester Mus of Science & Industry
	WR963	Avro 696 Shackleton AEW2	Air Atlantique Historic Flight, Coventry
	WR971	Avro 696 Shackleton MR3 (8119M) [Q]	Fenland & W Norfolk Aviation Museum, Wisbech
	WR974	Avro 696 Shackleton MR3 (8117M) [K]	Gatwick Aviation Museum, Charlwood, Surrey
	WR977	Avro 696 Shackleton MR3 (8186M) [B]	Newark Air Museum, Winthorpe
	WR982	Avro 696 Shackleton MR3 (8106M) [J]	Gatwick Aviation Museum, Charlwood, Surrey
	WR985	Avro 696 Shackleton MR3 (8103M) [H]	Privately owned, Long Marston
	WS103	Gloster Meteor T7 [709/VL]	FAA Museum, stored RNAS Yeovilton
	WS692	Gloster Meteor NF12 (7605M) [C]	Newark Air Museum, Winthorpe
	WS726	Gloster Meteor NF14 (7960M) [G]	No 1855 Sqn ATC, Royton, Gr Manchester
	WS739	Gloster Meteor NF14 (7961M)	Newark Air Museum, Winthorpe
	WS760	Gloster Meteor NF14 (7964M)	Meteor Flight, stored Yatesbury

Serial	Type (other identity) [code]	Owner/operator, location or fate	Notes
WS774	Gloster Meteor NF14 (7959M)	Privately owned, Quedgeley, Glos	
WS776	Gloster Meteor NF14 (7716M) [K]	Privately owned, Sandtoft	
WS788	Gloster Meteor NF14 (7967M) [Z]	Yorkshire Air Museum, Elvington	
WS792	Gloster Meteor NF14 (7965M) [K]	Brighouse Bay Caravan Park, Borgue, D&G	
WS807	Gloster Meteor NF14 (7973M) [N]	Gloucestershire Avn Colln, stored Glos	
WS832	Gloster Meteor NF14 [W]	Solway Aviation Society, Carlisle	
WS838	Gloster Meteor NF14	Midland Air Museum, Coventry	
WS843	Gloster Meteor NF14 (7937M) [Y]	RAF Museum, stored Cosford	
WT121	Douglas Skyraider AEW1 (WT983) [415/CU]	FAA Museum, stored RNAS Yeovilton	
WT205	EE Canberra B15	No 2431 Sqn ATC, Eastwood, Essex	
WT308	EE Canberra B(I)6	RN, Predannack Fire School	
WT309	EE Canberra B(I)6 <ff>	Privately owned, Farnborough	
WT319	EE Canberra B(I)6 <ff>	Privately owned, Bedford	
WT333	EE Canberra B6(mod) (G-BVXC)	Privately owned, Bruntingthorpe	
WT339	EE Canberra B(I)8 (8198M)	RAF Barkston Heath Fire Section	
WT480	EE Canberra T4 [AT]	RAF, stored Shawbury	
WT482	EE Canberra T4 <ff>	Privately owned	
WT483	EE Canberra T4 [83]	Privately owned, Long Marston	
WT486	EE Canberra T4 (8102M) <ff>	Flight Experience Workshop, Belfast	
WT507	EE Canberra PR7 (8131M/8548M) [44] <ff>	No 384 Sqn ATC, Mansfield	
WT509	EE Canberra PR7 [BR]	RAF, stored Marham	
WT510	EE Canberra T22 <ff>	Privately owned, Stock, Essex	
WT519	EE Canberra PR7 [CH]	RAF Wyton, Fire Section	
WT520	EE Canberra PR7 (8094M/8184M) <ff>	No 967 Sqn ATC, Warton	
WT525	EE Canberra T22 <ff>	Privately owned, South Woodham Ferrers	
WT532	EE Canberra PR7 (8728M/8890M) <ff>	Bournemouth Aviation Museum	
WT534	EE Canberra PR7 (8549M) [43] <ff>	No 492 Sqn ATC, Shirley, W. Midlands	
WT536	EE Canberra PR7 (8063M) <ff>	Privately owned, Portsmouth	
WT537	EE Canberra PR7	BAE Systems Samlesbury, on display	
WT538	EE Canberra PR7 [CJ] <ff>	RAF St Athan Fire Section	
WT555	Hawker Hunter F1 (7499M)	Vanguard Haulage, Greenford, London	
WT569	Hawker Hunter F1 (7491M)	No 2117 Sqn ATC, Kenfig Hill, Mid-Glamorgan	
WT612	Hawker Hunter F1 (7496M)	RAF Henlow on display	
WT619	Hawker Hunter F1 (7525M)	Gr Manchester Mus of Science & Industry	
WT648	Hawker Hunter F1 (7530M) <ff>	The Air Defence Collection, Salisbury	
WT651	Hawker Hunter F1 (7532M) [C]	Newark Air Museum, Winthorpe	
WT660	Hawker Hunter F1 (7421M) [C]	Highland Aircraft Preservation Society, Inverness	
WT680	Hawker Hunter F1 (7533M) [J]	No 1429 Sqn ATC, at DERA Aberporth	
WT684	Hawker Hunter F1 (7422M) <ff>	South Yorkshire Avn Museum, Firbeck	
WT694	Hawker Hunter F1 (7510M)	Caernarfon Air World	
WT711	Hawker Hunter GA11 [833/DD]	Air Atlantique, Coventry	
WT720	Hawker Hunter F51 (RDAF E-408/ 8565M) [B]	RAF Sealand, on display	
WT722	Hawker Hunter T8C (G-BWGN) [878/VL]	Classic Jet Aircraft Co, Exeter	
WT723	Hawker Hunter PR11 (G-PRII) [866/VL,3]	Classic Jets, Brustem, Belgium	
WT744	Hawker Hunter GA11 [868/VL]	South West Aviation Heritage, Eaglescott	
WT746	Hawker Hunter F4 (7770M) [A]	Dumfries & Galloway Avn Mus, Dumfries	
WT799	Hawker Hunter T8C [879]	Privately owned, North Weald	
WT804	Hawker Hunter GA11 [831/DD]	FETC, Moreton-in-Marsh, Glos	
WT806	Hawker Hunter GA11	Privately owned, Sproughton	
WT859	Supermarine 544 <ff>	Brooklands Museum, Weybridge	
WT867	Slingsby T31B Cadet TX3	Privately owned, Eaglescott	
WT898	Slingsby T31B Cadet TX3 (BGA 3284/BGA 4412)	Privately owned, Rufforth	
WT899	Slingsby T31B Cadet TX3	Privately owned, stored Swindon	
WT901	Slingsby T31B Cadet TX3	Privately owned, stored Rothwell, Northants	
WT902	Slingsby T31B Cadet TX3 (BGA 3147)	Privately owned, Lleweni Parc, Clwyd	
WT905	Slingsby T31B Cadet TX3	*Currently not known*	
WT908	Slingsby T31B Cadet TX3 (BGA 3487)	Privately owned, Dunstable	

Notes	Serial	Type (other identity) [code]	Owner/operator, location or fate
	WT910	Slingsby T31B Cadet TX3 (BGA 3953)	Privately owned, Challock
	WT933	Bristol 171 Sycamore 3 (G-ALSW /7709M)	Newark Air Museum, Winthorpe
	WV106	Douglas Skyraider AEW1 [427/C]	FAA Museum, at RNAS Culdrose
	WV198	Sikorsky S55 Whirlwind HAR21 (G-BJWY) [K]	Solway Aviation Society, Carlisle
	WV256	Hawker Hunter GA11 [862/VL]	Classic Jet Aircraft Co, Exeter
	WV276	Hawker Hunter F4 (7847M) [D]	Privately owned, stored Scampton
	WV318	Hawker Hunter T7B (G-FFOX)	Delta Jets, Kemble
	WV322	Hawker Hunter T8C (9096M) [Y]	Privately owned, Kemble
	WV332	Hawker Hunter F4 (7673M) <ff>	No 1254 Sqn ATC, Godalming
	WV372	Hawker Hunter T7 (G-BXFI) [R]	Privately owned, Kemble
	WV381	Hawker Hunter GA11 [732/VL] (fuselage)	UKAEA, Culham, Oxon
	WV382	Hawker Hunter GA11 [830/VL]	Jet Avn Preservation Grp, Long Marston
	WV383	Hawker Hunter T7	DERA Farnborough, on display
	WV396	Hawker Hunter T8C (9249M) [91]	RAF Valley, at main gate
	WV483	Percival P56 Provost T1 (7693M) [N-E]	Currently not known
	WV493	Percival P56 Provost T1 (G-BDYG/ 7696M) [29]	Royal Scottish Mus'm of Flight, stored E Fortune
	WV499	Percival P56 Provost T1 (7698M) [P-S]	Privately owned, Sandtoft
	WV562	Percival P56 Provost T1 (7606M) [P-C]	RAF Museum, Cosford
	WV605	Percival P56 Provost T1 [T-B]	Norfolk & Suffolk Avn Museum, Flixton
	WV606	Percival P56 Provost T1 (7622M) [P-B]	Newark Air Museum, Winthorpe
	WV666	Percival P56 Provost T1 (7925M/ G-BTDH) [O-D]	Crashed 28 March 1999 near Lasham
	WV679	Percival P56 Provost T1 (7615M) [O-J]	Wellesbourne Wartime Museum
	WV703	Percival P66 Pembroke C1 (8108M/G-IIIM)	Privately owned, Tattershall Thorpe
	WV705	Percival P66 Pembroke C1 <ff>	Southampton Hall of Aviation, stored
	WV740	Percival P66 Pembroke C1 (G-BNPH)	Privately owned, Jersey
	WV746	Percival P66 Pembroke C1 (8938M)	RAF Museum, Cosford
	WV781	Bristol 171 Sycamore HR12 (G-ALTD/7839M)	Caernarfon Air World
	WV783	Bristol 171 Sycamore HR12 (G-ALSP/7841M)	RAF Museum, stored Wyton
	WV787	EE Canberra B2/8 (8799M)	Newark Air Museum, Winthorpe
	WV795	Hawker Sea Hawk FGA6 (8151M)	Kennet Aviation, Cranfield
	WV797	Hawker Sea Hawk FGA6 (8155M) [491/J]	Midland Air Museum, Coventry
	WV798	Hawker Sea Hawk FGA6 [026/CU]	SWWAPS, Lasham
	WV838	Hawker Sea Hawk FGA4 <ff>	RNAY Fleetlands Museum
	WV856	Hawker Sea Hawk FGA6 [163]	FAA Museum, RNAS Yeovilton
	WV903	Hawker Sea Hawk FGA4 (8153M) [128/C]	RN Historic Flight, stored Yeovilton
	WV908	Hawker Sea Hawk FGA6 (8154M) [188/A]	RN Historic Flight, Yeovilton
	WV910	Hawker Sea Hawk FGA6 <ff>	Boscombe Down Museum
	WV911	Hawker Sea Hawk FGA4 [115/C]	RN Historic Flight, Yeovilton
	WW138	DH112 Sea Venom FAW22 [227/Z]	FAA Museum, RNAS Yeovilton
	WW145	DH112 Sea Venom FAW22 [680/LM]	Royal Scottish Mus'm of Flight, E Fortune
	WW217	DH112 Sea Venom FAW22 [351]	Newark Air Museum, Winthorpe
	WW388	Percival P56 Provost T1 (7616M) [O-F]	Bomber County Aviation Museum, Hemswell
	WW421	Percival P56 Provost T1 (7688M) [P-B]	Privately owned, Sandtoft
	WW442	Percival P56 Provost T1 (7618M) [N]	Gatwick Aviation Museum, Charlwood, Surrey
	WW444	Percival P56 Provost T1 [D]	Privately owned, Rugeley, Staffs
	WW447	Percival P56 Provost T1	Privately owned, Grazeley, Berks
	WW453	Percival P56 Provost T1 (G-TMKI) [W-S]	Privately owned, RNAS Yeovilton

Serial	Type (other identity) [code]	Owner/operator, location or fate	Notes
WW654	Hawker Hunter GA11 [834/DD]	Privately owned, Ford, W Sussex	
WX788	DH112 Venom NF3	Night-Fighter Preservation Team, Elvington	
WX853	DH112 Venom NF3 (7443M)	Mosquito Aircraft Museum, London Colney	
WX905	DH112 Venom NF3 (7458M)	Newark Air Museum, Winthorpe	
WZ425	DH115 Vampire T11	Privately owned, Birlingham, Worcs	
WZ450	DH115 Vampire T11 <ff>	Lashenden Air Warfare Museum, Headcorn	
WZ458	DH115 Vampire T11 (7728M) [31] <ff>	Blyth Valley Aviation Collection, Walpole, Suffolk	
WZ464	DH115 Vampire T11 (N62430) [40]	Vintage Aircraft Team, Bruntingthorpe	
WZ507	DH115 Vampire T11 (G-VTII)	De Havilland Aviation, Swansea	
WZ515	DH115 Vampire T11 [60]	Solway Aviation Society, Carlisle	
WZ518	DH115 Vampire T11	North-East Aircraft Museum, Usworth	
WZ549	DH115 Vampire T11 (8118M) [F]	Ulster Aviation Society, Langford Lodge	
WZ553	DH115 Vampire T11 (G-DHYY) [40]	Source Classic Jet Flight, stored Bournemouth	
WZ557	DH115 Vampire T11	N Yorks Aircraft Recovery Centre, Chop Gate	
WZ581	DH115 Vampire T11 <ff>	The Vampire Collection, Hemel Hempstead	
WZ584	DH115 Vampire T11 [K] <ff>	Privately owned, Sandtoft	
WZ589	DH115 Vampire T11 [19]	Lashenden Air Warfare Museum, Headcorn	
WZ589	DH115 Vampire T55 (U-1230/ G-DHZZ)	Source Classic Jet Flight, Bournemouth	
WZ590	DH115 Vampire T11 [19]	Imperial War Museum, Duxford	
WZ608	DH115 Vampire T11 [56] <ff>	Privately owned,	
WZ620	DH115 Vampire T11 [68]	Avon Aviation Museum, Yatesbury	
WZ662	Auster AOP9 (G-BKVK)	Privately owned, Middle Wallop	
WZ706	Auster AOP9 (7851M/G-BURR)	Privately owned, Middle Wallop	
WZ711	Auster AOP9/Beagle E3 (G-AVHT)	Privately owned, Middle Wallop	
WZ721	Auster AOP9	Museum of Army Flying, Middle Wallop	
WZ724	Auster AOP9 (7432M)	AAC Middle Wallop, at main gate	
WZ729	Auster AOP9 (G-BXON)	Privately owned, Newark-on-Trent	
WZ736	Avro 707A (7868M)	Gr Manchester Mus of Science & Industry	
WZ744	Avro 707C (7932M)	RAF Museum, Cosford	
WZ753	Slingsby T38 Grasshopper TX1	Southampton Hall of Aviation	
WZ767	Slingsby T38 Grasshopper TX1	North-East Aircraft Museum, stored Usworth	
WZ768	Slingsby T38 Grasshopper TX1 (comp XK820)	Privately owned, Kirton-in-Lindsey, Lincs	
WZ769	Slingsby T38 Grasshopper TX1	*Currently not known*	
WZ772	Slingsby T38 Grasshopper TX1	Museum of Army Flying, Middle Wallop	
WZ779	Slingsby T38 Grasshopper TX1	Privately owned, Old Sarum	
WZ784	Slingsby T38 Grasshopper TX1	Privately owned, Thurrock College	
WZ791	Slingsby T38 Grasshopper TX1 (8944M)	RAF Museum, Hendon	
WZ792	Slingsby T38 Grasshopper TX1	Privately owned, Sproughton	
WZ793	Slingsby T38 Grasshopper TX1	Whitgift School, Croydon	
WZ796	Slingsby T38 Grasshopper TX1	Privately owned, stored Nympsfield, Glos	
WZ816	Slingsby T38 Grasshopper TX1 (BGA 3979)	Privately owned, stored Ashford, Kent	
WZ819	Slingsby T38 Grasshopper TX1 (BGA 3498)	Privately owned, Halton	
WZ820	Slingsby T38 Grasshopper TX1	Shoreham Airport, on display	
WZ822	Slingsby T38 Grasshopper TX1	South Yorkshire Avn Museum, Firbeck	
WZ824	Slingsby T38 Grasshopper TX1	Privately owned, stored Strathaven, Strathclyde	
WZ825	Slingsby T38 Grasshopper TX1	RAF Museum, stored Cosford	
WZ826	Vickers Valiant B(K)1 (XD826/ 7872M) <ff>	Privately owned, Foulness	
WZ827	Slingsby T38 Grasshopper TX1	RAFGSA, stored Bicester	
WZ828	Slingsby T38 Grasshopper TX1 (BGA 4421)	Privately owned, Bicester	
WZ829	Slingsby T38 Grasshopper TX1	*Sold to Germany*	
WZ831	Slingsby T38 Grasshopper TX1	Privately owned, stored Nympsfield, Glos	
WZ846	DHC1 Chipmunk T10 (G-BCSC/ 8439M)	No 1404 Sqn ATC, Chatham	
WZ847	DHC1 Chipmunk T10 (G-CPMK) [F]	Privately owned, Sleap	

Notes	Serial	Type (other identity) [code]	Owner/operator, location or fate
	WZ866	DHC1 Chipmunk T10 (8217M/ G-ATEB) <ff>	South Yorkshire Avn Museum, Firbeck
	WZ868	DHC1 Chipmunk T10 (G-BCIW) [H]	Privately owned, Sandtoft
	WZ869	DHC1 Chipmunk T10 (8019M) [R] <ff>	Currently not known
	WZ872	DHC1 Chipmunk T10 (G-BZGB) [E]	Privately owned, Newcastle
	WZ876	DHC1 Chipmunk T10 (G-BBWN) <ff>	Privately owned, Twyford, Bucks
	WZ879	DHC1 Chipmunk T10 (G-BWUT) [73]	Privately owned, Earls Colne
	WZ882	DHC1 Chipmunk T10 (G-BXGP) [K]	Privately owned, Eaglescott
	XA109	DH115 Sea Vampire T22	Royal Scottish Mus'm of Flight, E Fortune
	XA127	DH115 Sea Vampire T22 <ff>	FAA Museum, stored RNAS Yeovilton
	XA129	DH115 Sea Vampire T22	FAA Museum, stored RNAS Yeovilton
	XA225	Slingsby T38 Grasshopper TX1	Churchers College, Petersfield, Hants
	XA228	Slingsby T38 Grasshopper TX1	Royal Scottish Mus'm of Flight, E Fortune
	XA230	Slingsby T38 Grasshopper TX1 (BGA 4098)	Privately owned, Henlow
	XA231	Slingsby T38 Grasshopper TX1 (8888M)	RAF Manston History Museum
	XA240	Slingsby T38 Grasshopper TX1 (BGA 4556)	Privately owned, Keevil
	XA241	Slingsby T38 Grasshopper TX1	Shuttleworth Collection, Old Warden
	XA243	Slingsby T38 Grasshopper TX1 (8886M)	Privately owned, Gransden Lodge, Cambs
	XA244	Slingsby T38 Grasshopper TX1	RAF, stored Cosford
	XA282	Slingsby T31B Cadet TX3	Caernarfon Air World
	XA286	Slingsby T31B Cadet TX3	Privately owned, stored Rufforth
	XA289	Slingsby T31B Cadet TX3	Privately owned, Eaglescott
	XA290	Slingsby T31B Cadet TX3	Privately owned, stored Rufforth
	XA293	Slingsby T31B Cadet TX3	Privately owned, Breighton
	XA302	Slingsby T31B Cadet TX3 (BGA3786)	Privately owned, Syerston
	XA454	Fairey Gannet COD4	Scrapped at Yeovilton
	XA459	Fairey Gannet ECM6 [E]	Privately owned, Lambourn, Berks
	XA460	Fairey Gannet ECM6 [768/BY]	Deeside College, Connah's Quay, Clwyd
	XA466	Fairey Gannet COD4 [777/LM]	FAA Museum, stored Yeovilton
	XA508	Fairey Gannet T2 [627/GN]	FAA Museum, at Midland Air Museum, Coventry
	XA564	Gloster Javelin FAW1 (7464M)	RAF Museum, Cosford
	XA634	Gloster Javelin FAW4 (7641M)	RAF Leeming, on display
	XA699	Gloster Javelin FAW5 (7809M)	Midland Air Museum, Coventry
	XA847	EE P1B (8371M)	Privately owned, Stowmarket, Suffolk
	XA862	WS55 Whirlwind HAR1 (G-AMJT) [9]	The Helicopter Museum, Weston-super-Mare
	XA864	WS55 Whirlwind HAR1	FAA Museum, stored Yeovilton
	XA870	WS55 Whirlwind HAR1	Flambards Village Theme Park, Helston
	XA880	DH104 Devon C2 (G-BVXR)	Privately owned, Kemble
	XA893	Avro 698 Vulcan B1 (8591M) <ff>	RAF Museum, Cosford
	XA903	Avro 698 Vulcan B1 <ff>	Privately owned, Wellesbourne Mountford
	XA917	HP80 Victor B1 (7827M) <ff>	Privately owned, Guardbridge, Fife
	XB259	Blackburn B101 Beverley C1 (G-AOAI)	Museum of Army Transport, Beverley
	XB261	Blackburn B101 Beverley C1 <ff>	Duxford Aviation Society, Duxford
	XB446	Grumman TBM-3 Avenger ECM6B	FAA Museum, Yeovilton
	XB480	Hiller HT1 [537]	FAA Museum, stored Yeovilton
	XB812	Canadair CL-13 Sabre F4 (9227M) [U]	RAF Museum, Hendon
	XD145	Saro SR53	RAF Museum, Cosford
	XD163	WS55 Whirlwind HAR10 (8645M) [X]	The Helicopter Museum, Weston-super-Mare
	XD165	WS55 Whirlwind HAR10 (8673M) [B]	AAC Wattisham, instructional use
	XD215	VS Scimitar F1 <ff>	Privately owned, Cheltenham
	XD235	VS Scimitar F1 <ff>	Privately owned, Welshpool
	XD317	VS Scimitar F1 [112/R]	FAA Museum, RNAS Yeovilton
	XD332	VS Scimitar F1 [194/C]	Southampton Hall of Aviation
	XD375	DH115 Vampire T11 (7887M) [72]	Scrapped
	XD377	DH115 Vampire T11 (8203M) <ff>	South Yorkshire Avn Museum, Firbeck
	XD382	DH115 Vampire T11 (8033M)	Anchor Surplus, Ripley, Derbys

Serial	Type (other identity) [code]	Owner/operator, location or fate	Notes
XD425	DH115 Vampire T11 <ff>	RAF Millom Museum, Haverigg	
XD434	DH115 Vampire T11 [25]	Fenland & W Norfolk Aviation Museum, Wisbech	
XD445	DH115 Vampire T11	Bomber County Aviation Museum, Hemswell	
XD447	DH115 Vampire T11 [50]	Jet Avn Preservation Grp, Long Marston	
XD452	DH115 Vampire T11 (7990M) [66] <ff>	Vampire Support Team, RAF Sealand	
XD459	DH115 Vampire T11 [63] <ff>	East Midlands Airport Aeropark	
XD463	DH115 Vampire T11 (8023M)	Privately owned, Nottingham	
XD506	DH115 Vampire T11 (7983M)	Gloucestershire Avn Coll, stored Glos	
XD515	DH115 Vampire T11 (7998M/ XM515)	Privately owned, Rugeley, Staffs	
XD525	DH115 Vampire T11 (7882M) <ff>	Kinegar Camp, Hollywood, Northern Ireland	
XD528	DH115 Vampire T11 (8159M) <ff>	Gamston Aerodrome Fire Section	
XD534	DH115 Vampire T11 [41]	Military Aircraft Pres'n Grp, Barton	
XD535	DH115 Vampire T11 <ff>	Destroyed	
XD536	DH115 Vampire T11 (7734M) [H]	Alleyn's School CCF, Northolt	
XD542	DH115 Vampire T11 (7604M) [N]	Montrose Air Station Museum	
XD547	DH115 Vampire T11 [Z] (composite)	Dumfries & Galloway Avn Mus, Dumfries	
XD593	DH115 Vampire T11 [50]	Newark Air Museum, Winthorpe	
XD595	DH115 Vampire T11 <ff>	Privately owned, Glentham, Lincs	
XD596	DH115 Vampire T11 (7939M)	Southampton Hall of Aviation	
XD599	DH115 Vampire T11 <ff>	Privately owned, Welshpool	
XD602	DH115 Vampire T11 (7737M) (composite)	Dundonald Aviation Centre	
XD614	DH115 Vampire T11 (8124M) <ff>	Privately owned, Southampton	
XD616	DH115 Vampire T11 [56]	Mosquito Aircraft Museum, stored Glos	
XD622	DH115 Vampire T11 (8160M)	No 2214 Sqn ATC, Usworth	
XD624	DH115 Vampire T11 [O]	Macclesfield Technical College	
XD626	DH115 Vampire T11 [Q]	Midland Air Museum, Coventry	
XD674	Hunting Jet Provost T1 (7570M) [T]	RAF Museum, stored Cosford	
XD693	Hunting Jet Provost T1 (XM129/ G-AOBU) [Z-Q]	Kennet Aviation, Cranfield	
XD816	Vickers Valiant B(K)1 <ff>	Brooklands Museum, Weybridge	
XD818	Vickers Valiant B(K)1 (7894M)	RAF Museum, Hendon	
XD857	Vickers Valiant B(K)1 <ff>	RAF Manston History Museum	
XD875	Vickers Valiant B(K)1 <ff>	British Aviation Heritage, Bruntingthorpe	
XE317	Bristol 171 Sycamore HR14 (G-AMWO) [S-N]	South Yorkshire Avn Museum, Firbeck	
XE327	Hawker Sea Hawk FGA6 [644/LH]	Privately owned, Bruntingthorpe	
XE339	Hawker Sea Hawk FGA6 (8156M) [149/E]	RN Historic Flight, stored Yeovilton	
XE340	Hawker Sea Hawk FGA6 [131/Z]	FAA Museum, at Montrose Air Station Museum	
XE368	Hawker Sea Hawk FGA6 [200/J]	Flambards Village Theme Park, Helston	
XE489	Hawker Sea Hawk FGA6 (G-JETH)	Gatwick Aviation Museum, Charlwood, Surrey	
XE521	Fairey Rotodyne Y (parts)	The Helicopter Museum, Weston-super-Mare	
XE584	Hawker Hunter FGA9 <ff>	Avro Aircraft Heritage Society, Woodford	
XE601	Hawker Hunter FGA9	Boscombe Down Museum	
XE606	Hawker Hunter F6A (XJ673/ 8841M)	RAF Cottesmore	
XE624	Hawker Hunter FGA9 (8875M) [G]	Army, Cawdor Barracks, Brawdy, on display	
XE627	Hawker Hunter F6A [T]	Imperial War Museum, Duxford	
XE643	Hawker Hunter FGA9 (8586M) <ff>	RAF EPTT, Aldergrove	
XE664	Hawker Hunter F4 <ff>	Gloucestershire Avn Coll, stored Glos	
XE665	Hawker Hunter T8C (G-BWGM) [876/VL]	Classic Jet Aircraft Co, Exeter	
XE668	Hawker Hunter GA11 [832/DD]	RN, Predannack Fire School	
XE670	Hawker Hunter F4 (7762M/8585M) <ff>	RAF Museum, Cosford	
XE685	Hawker Hunter GA11 (G-GAII) [861/VL]	Privately owned, Exeter	
XE689	Hawker Hunter GA11 (G-BWGK) [864/VL]	Privately owned, Exeter	
XE786	Slingsby T31B Cadet TX3	RAF, stored Arbroath	
XE793	Slingsby T31B Cadet TX3 (8666M)	Currently not known	

35

Notes	Serial	Type (other identity) [code]	Owner/operator, location or fate
	XE796	Slingsby T31B Cadet TX3	Privately owned, stored North Weald
	XE799	Slingsby T31B Cadet TX3 (8943M) [R]	RAFGSA, Syerston
	XE802	Slingsby T31B Cadet TX3	Privately owned, stored Cupar, Fife
	XE807	Slingsby T31B Cadet TX3 (BGA3545)	Privately owned, Halesland
	XE849	DH115 Vampire T11 (7928M) [V3]	Privately owned, Shobdon
	XE852	DH115 Vampire T11 [H]	No 2247 Sqn ATC, Hawarden
	XE855	DH115 Vampire T11	Midland Air Museum, Coventry
	XE856	DH115 Vampire T11 (G-DUSK)	Privately owned, Henlow
	XE864	DH115 Vampire T11(comp XD435) <ff>	Privately owned, Welshpool
	XE872	DH115 Vampire T11 [62]	Midland Air Museum, Coventry
	XE874	DH115 Vampire T11 (8582M)	Montrose Air Station Museum
	XE897	DH115 Vampire T11 (XD403)	Privately owned, Errol, Tayside
	XE897	DH115 Vampire T55 (U-1214/ G-DHVV)	Source Classic Jet Flight, Bournemouth
	XE920	DH115 Vampire T11 (8196M/ G-VMPR) [A]	Vampire Support Team, Swansea
	XE921	DH115 Vampire T11 [64] <ff>	Privately owned, Barton
	XE935	DH115 Vampire T11	Aeroventure, Doncaster
	XE946	DH115 Vampire T11 (7473M) <ff>	RAF Cranwell Aviation Heritage Centre
	XE956	DH115 Vampire T11 (G-OBLN)	De Havilland Aviation, Swansea
	XE979	DH115 Vampire T11 [54]	Privately owned, Birlingham, Worcs
	XE982	DH115 Vampire T11 (7564M) [01]	Privately owned, Dunkeswell
	XE985	DH115 Vampire T11 (*WZ476*)	De Havilland Aviation, Swansea
	XE993	DH115 Vampire T11 (8161M)	Privately owned, Cosford
	XE995	DH115 Vampire T11 [53]	Privately owned, High Halden, Kent
	XE998	DH115 Vampire T11 (*U-1215*)	Privately owned, Brooklands Museum, Weybridge
	XF113	VS Swift F7 [19] <ff>	Boscombe Down Museum
	XF114	VS Swift F7 (G-SWIF)	Privately owned, Scampton
	XF300	Hawker Hunter GA11 [860/VL]	Classic Jet Aircraft Co, Exeter
	XF303	Hawker Hunter F58A (J-4105/ G-BWOU) [105,A]	The Old Flying Machine Company, Scampton
	XF314	Hawker Hunter F51 (RDAF E-412) [N]	Privately owned, Booker
	XF321	Hawker Hunter T7	Classic Jet Aircraft Co, Exeter (spares use)
	XF324	Hawker Hunter F51 (RDAF E-427) [D]	British Aviation Heritage, Bruntingthorpe
	XF357	Hawker Hunter T8C (G-BWGL)	*Repainted as XJ615, May 2000*
	XF358	Hawker Hunter T8C [870/VL]	DERA Boscombe Down, Apprentice School
	XF368	Hawker Hunter GA11 [863/VL]	*Sold to South Africa, November 2000*
	XF375	Hawker Hunter F6A (8736M/ G-BUEZ) [05]	The Old Flying Machine Co, Duxford
	XF382	Hawker Hunter F6A [15]	Midland Air Museum, Coventry
	XF383	Hawker Hunter F6 (8706M) <ff>	Privately owned, Kidlington
	XF418	Hawker Hunter F51 (RDAF E-430)	Gatwick Aviation Museum, Charlwood, Surrey
	XF509	Hawker Hunter F6 (8708M)	Humbrol Paints, Marfleet, E Yorkshire
	XF515	Hawker Hunter F6A (8830M/ G-KAXF) [R]	Kennet Aviation, Cranfield
	XF516	Hawker Hunter F6A (8685M/ G-BVVC) [19]	Privately owned, Kemble
	XF519	Hawker Hunter FGA9 (8677M/ 8738M/9183M) (comp XJ695) [J]	MoD FSCTE, Manston
	XF522	Hawker Hunter F6 <ff>	No 1365 Sqn ATC, Aylesbury
	XF526	Hawker Hunter F6 (8679M) [78/E]	Privately owned, Birlingham, Worcs
	XF527	Hawker Hunter F6 (8680M)	RAF Halton, on display
	XF545	Percival P56 Provost T1 (7957M) [O-K]	Privately owned, Thatcham
	XF597	Percival P56 Provost T1 (G-BKFW) [AH]	Privately owned, Thatcham
	XF603	Percival P56 Provost T1 (G-KAPW)	Kennet Aviation, Cranfield
	XF690	Percival P56 Provost T1 (8041M/ G-MOOS)	Kennet Aviation, Cranfield
	XF708	Avro 716 Shackleton MR3 [203/C]	Imperial War Museum, Duxford
	XF785	Bristol 173 (7648M/G-ALBN)	RAF Museum, stored Cosford
	XF836	Percival P56 Provost T1 (8043M/ G-AWRY) [JG]	Privately owned, Thatcham

Serial	Type (other identity) [code]	Owner/operator, location or fate	Notes
XF844	Percival P56 Provost T1 [70]	British Aviation Heritage, Bruntingthorpe	
XF877	Percival P56 Provost T1 (G-AWVF) [JX]	Privately owned, Sandown	
XF926	Bristol 188 (8368M)	RAF Museum, Cosford	
XF967	Hawker Hunter T8C (9186M) [T]	Sold to South Africa, November 2000	
XF994	Hawker Hunter T8C [873/VL]	DERA Boscombe Down, Apprentice School	
XF995	Hawker Hunter T8B (9237M) [K]	Sold to South Africa, November 2000	
XG154	Hawker Hunter FGA9 (8863M) [54]	RAF Museum, Hendon	
XG160	Hawker Hunter F6A (8831M/ G-BWAF)	Bournemouth Aviation Museum	
XG164	Hawker Hunter F6 (8681M)	Privately owned, Taunton	
XG172	Hawker Hunter F6A (8832M) [A]	Privately owned, North Weald	
XG190	Hawker Hunter F51 (RDAF E-425) [C]	Midland Air Museum, Coventry	
XG193	Hawker Hunter FGA9 (XG297) (comp with WT741)	Bomber County Aviation Museum, Hemswell	
XG195	Hawker Hunter FGA9 <ff>	Shropshire Wartime Aircraft Recovery Grp Mus, Sleap	
XG196	Hawker Hunter F6A (8702M) [31]	Army, Mytchett, Surrey, on display	
XG209	Hawker Hunter F6 (8709M) <ff>	Privately owned, Chelmsford	
XG210	Hawker Hunter F6	Privately owned, Beck Row, Suffolk	
XG225	Hawker Hunter F6A (8713M) [S]	RAF Cosford on display	
XG226	Hawker Hunter F6A (8800M) [28] <ff>	No 1242 Sqn ATC, Faversham, Kent	
XG252	Hawker Hunter FGA9 (8840M) [U]	Privately owned, Bosbury, Hereford	
XG254	Hawker Hunter FGA9 (8881M)	Privately owned, Clacton	
XG274	Hawker Hunter F6 (8710M) [71]	Privately owned, Sproughton	
XG290	Hawker Hunter F6 (8711M) <ff>	Boscombe Down Museum	
XG297	Hawker Hunter FGA9 <ff>	South Yorkshire Avn Museum, stored Firbeck	
XG325	EE Lightning F1 <ff>	No 1476 Sqn ATC, Southend	
XG329	EE Lightning F1 (8050M)	Privately owned, Flixton	
XG331	EE Lightning F1 <ff>	Gloucestershire Avn Coll, stored Glos	
XG337	EE Lightning F1 (8056M) [M]	RAF Museum, Cosford	
XG452	Bristol 192 Belvedere HC1 (7997M/G-BRMB)	The Helicopter Museum, Weston-super-Mare	
XG454	Bristol 192 Belvedere HC1 (8366M)	Gr Manchester Mus of Science & Industry	
XG462	Bristol 192 Belvedere HC1 <ff>	The Helicopter Museum, stored Weston-super-Mare	
XG474	Bristol 192 Belvedere HC1 (8367M) [O]	RAF Museum, Hendon	
XG502	Bristol 171 Sycamore HR14	Museum of Army Flying, Middle Wallop	
XG506	Bristol 171 Sycamore HR14 (7852M) [S-P]	Aeroventure, Doncaster	
XG518	Bristol 171 Sycamore HR14 (8009M) [S-E]	Norfolk & Suffolk Avn Museum, Flixton	
XG523	Bristol 171 Sycamore HR14 <ff> [K]	Norfolk & Suffolk Avn Museum, Flixton	
XG540	Bristol 171 Sycamore HR14 (7899M/8345M) [Y-S]	Scrapped at Chorley by Spring 2000	
XG544	Bristol 171 Sycamore HR14	Privately owned, Tremar, Cornwall	
XG547	Bristol 171 Sycamore HR14 (G-HAPR) [S-T]	The Helicopter Museum, Weston-super-Mare	
XG574	WS55 Whirlwind HAR3 [752/PO]	FAA Museum, RNAS Yeovilton	
XG577	WS55 Whirlwind HAR3 (9050M)	RAF Leconfield Crash Rescue Training	
XG588	WS55 Whirlwind HAR3 (G-BAMH/ VR-BEP)	East Midlands Airport Aeropark	
XG594	WS55 Whirlwind HAS7 [517/PO]	FAA Museum, at R. Scottish Mus'm of Flt, E Fortune	
XG596	WS55 Whirlwind HAS7 [66]	The Helicopter Museum, Weston-super-Mare	
XG597	WS55 Whirlwind HAS7	Privately owned, Siddal, West Yorkshire	
XG613	DH112 Sea Venom FAW21	Imperial War Museum, Duxford	
XG629	DH112 Sea Venom FAW22 <ff>	Privately owned, Fownhope, Worcester	
XG680	DH112 Sea Venom FAW22 [438]	North-East Aircraft Museum, Usworth	
XG691	DH112 Sea Venom FAW22 [93/J]	Gloucestershire Avn Coll, stored Glos	
XG692	DH112 Sea Venom FAW22 [668/ LM]	Privately owned, Stockport	
XG730	DH112 Sea Venom FAW22 [499/A]	Mosquito Aircraft Museum, London Colney	
XG736	DH112 Sea Venom FAW22	Ulster Aviation Society, Newtownards	

XG737 – XJ565

Notes	Serial	Type (other identity) [code]	Owner/operator, location or fate
	XG737	DH112 Sea Venom FAW22 [220/Z]	Jet Avn Preservation Grp, stored Long Marston
	XG743	DH115 Sea Vampire T22 [597/LM]	Imperial War Museum, Duxford
	XG775	DH115 Vampire T55 (U-1219/ G-DHWW) [VL]	Source Classic Jet Flight, Bournemouth
	XG797	Fairey Gannet ECM6 [277]	Imperial War Museum, Duxford
	XG831	Fairey Gannet ECM6 [396]	Flambards Village Theme Park, Helston
	XG882	Fairey Gannet T5 (8754M) [771/LM]	Privately owned, Errol, Tayside
	XG883	Fairey Gannet T5 [773/BY]	FAA Museum, at Museum of Berkshire Aviation, Woodley
	XG900	Short SC1	Science Museum, stored Wroughton
	XG905	Short SC1	Ulster Folk & Transpt Mus, Holywood, Co Down
	XH131	EE Canberra PR9 [AA]	RAF No 39(1 PRU) Sqn, Marham
	XH134	EE Canberra PR9 [AB]	RAF No 39(1 PRU) Sqn, Marham
	XH135	EE Canberra PR9 [AC]	RAF No 39(1 PRU) Sqn, Marham
	XH136	EE Canberra PR9 (8782M) <ff>	Phoenix Aviation, Bruntingthorpe
	XH165	EE Canberra PR9 <ff>	Blyth Valley Aviation Collection, Walpole
	XH168	EE Canberra PR9 [AD]	RAF No 39(1 PRU) Sqn, Marham
	XH169	EE Canberra PR9	RAF No 39(1 PRU) Sqn, Marham
	XH170	EE Canberra PR9 (8739M)	RAF Wyton, on display
	XH171	EE Canberra PR9 (8746M) [U]	RAF Museum, Cosford
	XH174	EE Canberra PR9 <ff>	RAF, stored Shawbury
	XH175	EE Canberra PR9 <ff>	Privately owned, Stock, Essex
	XH177	EE Canberra PR9 <ff>	Newark Air Museum, Winthorpe (on loan)
	XH278	DH115 Vampire T11 (8595M/ 7866M) [42]	Privately owned, Felton, Northumberland
	XH312	DH115 Vampire T11 [18]	Privately owned, Dodleston, Cheshire
	XH313	DH115 Vampire T11 [E] <ff>	Privately owned, Sandtoft
	XH318	DH115 Vampire T11 (7761M) [64]	Privately owned, Southampton
	XH328	DH115 Vampire T11 <ff>	Privately owned, Duxford
	XH330	DH115 Vampire T11 [73]	Privately owned, Camberley, Surrey
	XH537	Avro 698 Vulcan B2MRR (8749M) <ff>	Privately owned, Bruntingthorpe
	XH558	Avro 698 Vulcan B2 (G-VLCN)	British Aviation Heritage, Bruntingthorpe
	XH560	Avro 698 Vulcan K2 <ff>	Privately owned, Foulness
	XH563	Avro 698 Vulcan B2MRR <ff>	Privately owned, Banchory, Fife
	XH568	EE Canberra B6(mod) (G-BVIC)	Classic Aviation Projects, Bruntingthorpe
	XH584	EE Canberra T4 (G-27-374) <ff>	Aeroventure, Doncaster
	XH592	HP80 Victor K1A (8429M) <ff>	Phoenix Aviation, Bruntingthorpe
	XH648	HP80 Victor K1A	Imperial War Museum, Duxford
	XH669	HP80 Victor K2 (9092M) <ff>	Privately owned, Foulness
	XH670	HP80 Victor SR2 <ff>	Privately owned, Foulness
	XH672	HP80 Victor K2	RAF Museum, Cosford
	XH673	HP80 Victor K2 (8911M)	RAF Marham, on display
	XH767	Gloster Javelin FAW9 (7955M) [A]	City of Norwich Aviation Museum
	XH783	Gloster Javelin FAW7 (7798M) <ff>	Privately owned, Catford
	XH837	Gloster Javelin FAW7 (8032M) <ff>	Caernarfon Air World
	XH892	Gloster Javelin FAW9R (7982M) [J]	Norfolk & Suffolk Avn Museum, Flixton
	XH897	Gloster Javelin FAW9	Imperial War Museum, Duxford
	XH903	Gloster Javelin FAW9 (7938M) <ff>	Gloucestershire Avn Coll, stored Glos
	XH992	Gloster Javelin FAW8 (7829M) [P]	Newark Air Museum, Winthorpe
	XJ314	RR Thrust Measuring Rig	Science Museum, stored Wroughton
	XJ380	Bristol 171 Sycamore HR14 (8628M)	Montrose Air Station Museum
	XJ389	Fairey Jet Gyrodyne (XD759/ G-AJJP)	Museum of Berkshire Aviation, Woodley
	XJ409	WS55 Whirlwind HAR10 (XD779)	Privately owned, Llanbedr
	XJ435	WS55 Whirlwind HAR10 (XB804/ 8671M) [V]	RAF Manston History Museum, spares use
	XJ476	DH110 Sea Vixen FAW1 <ff>	No 424 Sqn ATC, Southampton Hall of Avn
	XJ481	DH110 Sea Vixen FAW1 [VL]	FAA Museum, at RNAY Fleetlands Museum
	XJ482	DH110 Sea Vixen FAW1 [713/VL]	Norfolk & Suffolk Avn Museum, Flixton
	XJ488	DH110 Sea Vixen FAW1 <ff>	Robertsbridge Aviation Society, Mayfield
	XJ494	DH110 Sea Vixen FAW2	Privately owned, Bruntingthorpe
	XJ560	DH110 Sea Vixen FAW2 (8142M) [242]	Newark Air Museum, Winthorpe
	XJ565	DH110 Sea Vixen FAW2 [127/E]	Mosquito Aircraft Museum, London Colney

Serial	Type (other identity) [code]	Owner/operator, location or fate	Notes
XJ571	DH110 Sea Vixen FAW2 (8140M) [242/R]	Privately owned, Brooklands Museum, Weybridge	
XJ575	DH110 Sea Vixen FAW2 <ff> [SAH-13]	Wellesbourne Wartime Museum	
XJ579	DH110 Sea Vixen FAW2 <ff>	Midland Air Museum, Coventry	
XJ580	DH110 Sea Vixen FAW2 [131/E]	Tangmere Military Aviation Museum	
XJ615	Hawker Hunter T8C(mod) (XF357/ G-BWGL)	The Old Flying Machine Co, Duxford	
XJ639	Hawker Hunter F6A (8687M) [H]	Privately owned, Sproughton	
XJ676	Hawker Hunter F6A (8844M) <ff>	Privately owned, Leavesden	
XJ714	Hawker Hunter FR10 (comp XG226)	Jet Avn Preservation Grp, Long Marston	
XJ723	WS55 Whirlwind HAR10	Montrose Air Station Museum	
XJ726	WS55 Whirlwind HAR10 [F]	Caernarfon Air World	
XJ727	WS55 Whirlwind HAR10 (8661M) [L]	RAF Manston History Museum	
XJ729	WS55 Whirlwind HAR10 (8732M/ G-BVGE)	Repainted as G-BVGE	
XJ758	WS55 Whirlwind HAR10 (8464M) <ff>	Privately owned, Welshpool	
XJ771	DH115 Vampire T55 (U-1215/ G-HELV)	Privately owned, Bournemouth	
XJ772	DH115 Vampire T11 [H]	Mosquito Aircraft Museum, London Colney	
XJ823	Avro 698 Vulcan B2A	Solway Aviation Society, Carlisle	
XJ824	Avro 698 Vulcan B2A	Imperial War Museum, Duxford	
XJ917	Bristol 171 Sycamore HR14 [H-S]	Bristol Sycamore Group, stored Kemble	
XJ918	Bristol 171 Sycamore HR14 (8190M)	RAF Museum, Cosford	
XK149	Hawker Hunter F6A (8714M) [L]	Privately owned, Bruntingthorpe	
XK378	Auster AOP9 (TAD200/XS238)	Privately owned, Dale, Dyfed	
XK416	Auster AOP9 (7855M/G-AYUA)	De Havilland Aviation, Swansea	
XK417	Auster AOP9 (G-AVXY)	Auster 9 Group, Melton Mowbray	
XK418	Auster AOP9 (7976M)	SWWAPS, Lasham	
XK421	Auster AOP9 (8365M) (frame)	South Yorkshire Avn Museum, Firbeck	
XK482	Saro Skeeter AOP12 (7840M/ G-BJWC) [C]	Privately owned, Ongar	
XK488	Blackburn NA39 Buccaneer S1	FAA Museum, RNAS Yeovilton	
XK526	Blackburn NA39 Buccaneer S2 (8648M)	RAF Honington, at main gate	
XK527	Blackburn NA39 Buccaneer S2D (8818M) <ff>	RNAY Fleetlands Museum	
XK532	Blackburn NA39 Buccaneer S1 (8867M) [632/LM]	The Fresson Trust, Inverness Airport	
XK533	Blackburn NA39 Buccaneer S1 <ff>	Royal Scottish Mus'm of Flight, E Fortune	
XK590	DH115 Vampire T11 [V]	Wellesbourne Wartime Museum	
XK623	DH115 Vampire T11 (G-VAMP) [56]	Caernarfon Air World	
XK624	DH115 Vampire T11 [32]	Norfolk & Suffolk Avn Museum, Flixton	
XK625	DH115 Vampire T11 [12]	Brenzett Aeronautical Museum	
XK627	DH115 Vampire T11	Privately owned, Barton	
XK632	DH115 Vampire T11 [67]	No 2370 Sqn ATC, Denham	
XK637	DH115 Vampire T11 [56]	RAF Millom Museum, Haverigg	
XK655	DH106 Comet C2(RC) (G-AMXA) <ff>	Gatwick Airport, on display (BOAC colours)	
XK659	DH106 Comet C2(RC) (G-AMXC) <ff>	Scrapped	
XK695	DH106 Comet C2(RC) (G-AMXH/ 9164M) <ff>	Mosquito Aircraft Museum, London Colney	
XK699	DH106 Comet C2 (7971M)	RAF Lyneham on display	
XK724	Folland Gnat F1 (7715M)	RAF Museum, Cosford	
XK740	Folland Gnat F1 (8396M)	Southampton Hall of Aviation	
XK741	Folland Gnat F1 (fuselage)	Midland Air Museum, Coventry	
XK776	ML Utility 1	Museum of Army Flying, Middle Wallop	
XK788	Slingsby T38 Grasshopper TX1	Privately owned, Sproughton	
XK789	Slingsby T38 Grasshopper TX1	Midland Air Museum, stored Coventry	
XK790	Slingsby T38 Grasshopper TX1	Privately owned, stored Husbands Bosworth	
XK819	Slingsby T38 Grasshopper TX1	Privately owned, Selby	
XK822	Slingsby T38 Grasshopper TX1	Privately owned, Kenley	
XK895	DH104 Sea Devon C20 (G-SDEV) [19/CU]	Privately owned, Shoreham	

Notes	Serial	Type (other identity) [code]	Owner/operator, location or fate
	XK896	DH104 Sea Devon C20 (G-RNAS) (fuselage)	Privately owned, Filton (spares use)
	XK907	WS55 Whirlwind HAS7 [U]	Midland Air Museum, Coventry
	XK911	WS55 Whirlwind HAS7 [519/PO]	Privately owned, Adlington, Lancs
	XK936	WS55 Whirlwind HAS7 [62]	Imperial War Museum, Duxford
	XK940	WS55 Whirlwind HAS7 (G-AYXT) [911]	The Helicopter Museum, Weston-super-Mare
	XK944	WS55 Whirlwind HAS7	No 617 Sqn ATC, Malpas, Cheshire
	XK970	WS55 Whirlwind HAR10 (8789M)	Army, Bramley, Hants
	XK988	WS55 Whirlwind HAR10 [D]	Burnt at Middle Wallop
	XL149	Blackburn B101 Beverley C1 (7988M) <ff>	Newark Air Museum, Winthorpe
	XL160	HP80 Victor K2 (8910M) <ff>	HP Victor Association, Walpole
	XL164	HP80 Victor K2 (9215M) <ff>	Gatwick Aviation Museum, Charlwood, Surrey
	XL188	HP80 Victor K2 (9100M) (fuselage)	RAF Kinloss Fire Section
	XL190	HP80 Victor K2 (9216M) <ff>	RAF Manston History Museum
	XL231	HP80 Victor K2	Yorkshire Air Museum, Elvington
	XL318	Avro 698 Vulcan B2 (8733M)	RAF Museum, Hendon
	XL319	Avro 698 Vulcan B2	North-East Aircraft Museum, Usworth
	XL360	Avro 698 Vulcan B2A	Midland Air Museum, Coventry
	XL388	Avro 698 Vulcan B2 <ff>	Blyth Valley Aviation Collection, Walpole
	XL391	Avro 698 Vulcan B2	Privately owned, Blackpool
	XL426	Avro 698 Vulcan B2 (G-VJET)	Vulcan Restoration Trust, Southend
	XL445	Avro 698 Vulcan K2 (8811M) <ff>	Blyth Valley Aviation Collection, Walpole
	XL449	Fairey Gannet AEW3 <ff>	Privately owned, Camberley, Surrey
	XL472	Fairey Gannet AEW3 [044/R]	Gatwick Aviation Museum, Charlwood, Surrey
	XL497	Fairey Gannet AEW3 [041/R]	RN, Prestwick, on display
	XL500	Fairey Gannet AEW3 [CU]	World Naval Base, Chatham
	XL502	Fairey Gannet AEW3 (8610M/ G-BMYP)	Privately owned, Sandtoft
	XL503	Fairey Gannet AEW3 [070/E]	FAA Museum, RNAS Yeovilton
	XL563	Hawker Hunter T7 (9218M)	Privately owned, Bosbury, Hereford
	XL565	Hawker Hunter T7 (parts of WT745)	Delta Jets, Kemble
	XL567	Hawker Hunter T7 (8723M) [84]	Privately owned, Exeter
	XL568	Hawker Hunter T7A (9224M) [C]	AMIF, RAFC Cranwell
	XL569	Hawker Hunter T7 (8833M) [SC]	East Midlands Airport Aeropark
	XL571	Hawker Hunter T7 (XL572/8834M/ G-HNTR) [V]	Yorkshire Air Museum, Elvington
	XL573	Hawker Hunter T7 (G-BVGH)	Privately owned, Plymouth
	XL577	Hawker Hunter T7 (G-BXKF/ 8676M)	Delta Jets, Kemble
	XL578	Hawker Hunter T7 (fuselage)	Privately owned, Kemble
	XL580	Hawker Hunter T8M [723]	FAA Museum, RNAS Yeovilton
	XL586	Hawker Hunter T7 <rf>	Delta Jets, Kemble
	XL587	Hawker Hunter T7 (8807M/ G-HPUX) [Z]	The Old Flying Machine Company, Duxford
	XL591	Hawker Hunter T7	Delta Jets, Kemble
	XL592	Hawker Hunter T7 (8836M) [Y]	Classic Jet Aircraft Co, Exeter
	XL601	Hawker Hunter T7 [874/VL]	Classic Jets, Brustem, Belgium
	XL602	Hawker Hunter T8M (G-BWFT)	South West Aviation Heritage, Exeter
	XL603	Hawker Hunter T8M [724]	Sold as N603XL, June 2000
	XL612	Hawker Hunter T7 [2]	DPA/AFD/ETPS, DERA Boscombe Down
	XL613	Hawker Hunter T7 (G-BVMB)	Classic Jet Aircraft Co, Exeter
	XL618	Hawker Hunter T7 (8892M) [05]	Caernarfon Air World
	XL621	Hawker Hunter T7 (G-BNCX)	Privately owned, Brooklands Museum
	XL623	Hawker Hunter T7 (8770M)	The Planets Leisure Centre, Woking
	XL629	EE Lightning T4	DERA Boscombe Down, at main gate
	XL703	SAL Pioneer CC1 (8034M)	RAF Museum, Cosford
	XL714	DH82A Tiger Moth II (T6099/ G-AOGR)	Privately owned, Swanton Morley
	XL716	DH82A Tiger Moth II (T7363/ G-AOIL)	Privately owned, Chandlers Ford
	XL735	Saro Skeeter AOP12	Privately owned, Tattershall Thorpe
	XL738	Saro Skeeter AOP12 (7860M)	Privately owned, Ivybridge, Devon
	XL739	Saro Skeeter AOP12	AAC Wattisham, instructional use
	XL762	Saro Skeeter AOP12 (8017M)	Royal Scottish Mus'm of Flight, E Fortune
	XL763	Saro Skeeter AOP12	Privately owned, Ivybridge, Devon
	XL764	Saro Skeeter AOP12 (7940M) [J]	Newark Air Museum, Winthorpe
	XL765	Saro Skeeter AOP12	Privately owned, Clapham, Beds
	XL770	Saro Skeeter AOP12 (8046M)	Southampton Hall of Aviation

Serial	Type (other identity) [code]	Owner/operator, location or fate	Notes
XL809	Saro Skeeter AOP12 (G-BLIX)	Privately owned, Wilden, Beds	
XL811	Saro Skeeter AOP12	The Helicopter Museum, Weston-super-Mare	
XL812	Saro Skeeter AOP12 (G-SARO)	Privately owned, Old Buckenham	
XL813	Saro Skeeter AOP12	Museum of Army Flying, Middle Wallop	
XL814	Saro Skeeter AOP12	AAC Historic Aircraft Flight, Middle Wallop	
XL824	Bristol 171 Sycamore HR14 (8021M)	Gr Manchester Mus of Science & Industry	
XL829	Bristol 171 Sycamore HR14	Bristol Industrial Museum	
XL840	WS55 Whirlwind HAS7	Privately owned, Long Marston	
XL847	WS55 Whirlwind HAS7 [83]	AAC Middle Wallop Fire Section	
XL853	WS55 Whirlwind HAS7 [PO]	FAA Museum, stored RNAS Yeovilton	
XL875	WS55 Whirlwind HAR9	Perth Technical College	
XL929	Percival P66 Pembroke C1 (G-BNPU)	D-Day Museum, Shoreham Airport	
XL954	Percival P66 Pembroke C1 (9042M/N4234C/G-BXES)	Air Atlantique Historic Flight, Coventry	
XL993	SAL Twin Pioneer CC1 (8388M)	RAF Museum, Cosford	
XM135	BAC Lightning F1 [B]	Imperial War Museum, Duxford	
XM144	BAC Lightning F1 (8417M) <ff>	Privately owned, Booker	
XM169	BAC Lightning F1A (8422M) <ff>	N Yorks Aircraft Recovery Centre, Chop Gate	
XM172	BAC Lightning F1A (8427M)	Privately owned, Booker	
XM173	BAC Lightning F1A (8414M) [A]	RAF Bentley Priory, at main gate	
XM191	BAC Lightning F1A (7854M/ 8590M) <ff>	RAF EPTT, St Athan	
XM192	BAC Lightning F1A (8413M) [K]	Bomber County Aviation Museum, Hemswell	
XM223	DH104 Devon C2 (G-BWWC) [J]	Air Atlantique, Coventry	
XM279	EE Canberra B(I)8 <ff>	Privately owned, Flixton	
XM300	WS58 Wessex HAS1	Welsh Industrial & Maritime Mus'm, stored Cardiff	
XM328	WS58 Wessex HAS3 [653/PO]	SFDO, RNAS Culdrose	
XM330	WS58 Wessex HAS1	The Helicopter Museum, Weston-super-Mare	
XM349	Hunting Jet Provost T3A (9046M) [T]	Global Aviation, Binbrook	
XM350	Hunting Jet Provost T3A (9036M)	Aeroventure, Doncaster	
XM351	Hunting Jet Provost T3 (8078M) [Y]	RAF Museum, Cosford	
XM355	Hunting Jet Provost T3 (8229M) [D]	Privately owned, Shobdon	
XM358	Hunting Jet Provost T3A (8987M) [53]	Privately owned, Llanwrtyd Wells, Powys	
XM362	Hunting Jet Provost T3 (8230M)	RAF No 1 SoTT, Cosford	
XM363	Hunting Jet Provost T3 <ff>	RAF Cranwell	
XM365	Hunting Jet Provost T3A (G-BXBH) [37]	Privately owned, Little Snoring	
XM369	Hunting Jet Provost T3A (8084M) [C]	Privately owned, Portsmouth	
XM370	Hunting Jet Provost T3A (G-BVSP) [10]	Privately owned, Norwich	
XM372	Hunting Jet Provost T3A (8917M) [55]	RAF Linton-on-Ouse Fire Section	
XM375	Hunting Jet Provost T3 (8231M) [B]	RAF Cottesmore Fire Section	
XM378	Hunting Jet Provost T3A (G-BWZE) [34]	Crashed Lelystad, The Netherlands, 16 October 2000	
XM383	Hunting Jet Provost T3A [90]	Newark Air Museum, Winthorpe	
XM402	Hunting Jet Provost T3 (8055AM) [J]	Fenland & W Norfolk Aviation Museum, Wisbech	
XM404	Hunting Jet Provost T3 (8055BM)	FETC, Moreton-in-Marsh, Glos	
XM409	Hunting Jet Provost T3 (8082M) <rf>	Air Scouts, Guernsey Airport	
XM410	Hunting Jet Provost T3 (8054AM) [B]	RAF North Luffenham Training Area	
XM411	Hunting Jet Provost T3 (8434M) <ff>	South Yorkshire Avn Museum, Firbeck	
XM412	Hunting Jet Provost T3A (9011M) [41]	Privately owned, Sproughton	
XM414	Hunting Jet Provost T3A (8996M)	Flight Experience Workshop, Belfast	
XM417	Hunting Jet Provost T3 (8054BM) [D] <ff>	Privately owned, Hednesford, Staffs	
XM419	Hunting Jet Provost T3A (8990M) [102]	DARA Training School, RAF St Athan	
XM424	Hunting Jet Provost T3A (G-BWDS)	Privately owned, North Weald	

Notes	Serial	Type (other identity) [code]	Owner/operator, location or fate
	XM425	Hunting Jet Provost T3A (8995M) [88]	Privately owned, Longton, Staffs
	XM426	Hunting Jet Provost T3 [64] <ff>	Aeroventure, Doncaster
	XM459	Hunting Jet Provost T3A [F]	Global Aviation, Binbrook
	XM463	Hunting Jet Provost T3A [38] (fuselage)	RAF Museum, Hendon
	XM468	Hunting Jet Provost T3 (8081M)	Privately owned, Terrington St Clement
	XM470	Hunting Jet Provost T3A (G-BWZZ) [12]	Privately owned, Lincs
	XM473	Hunting Jet Provost T3A (8974M/ G-TINY)	Bedford College, instructional use
	XM474	Hunting Jet Provost T3 (8121M) <ff>	Aeroventure, Doncaster
	XM475	Hunting Jet Provost T3A (9112M) [44]	Burnt at Manston, 1999
	XM478	Hunting Jet Provost T3A (8983M/ G-BXDL)	Transair(UK) Ltd, North Weald
	XM479	Hunting Jet Provost T3A (G-BVEZ) [54]	Privately owned, Newcastle
	XM480	Hunting Jet Provost T3 (8080M)	4x4 Car Centre, Chesterfield
	XM496	Bristol 253 Britannia C1 (EL-WXA)	Britannia Preservation Society, Kemble
	XM529	Saro Skeeter AOP12 (7979M/ G-BDNS)	Privately owned, Handforth
	XM553	Saro Skeeter AOP12 (G-AWSV)	Privately owned, Middle Wallop
	XM555	Saro Skeeter AOP12 (8027M)	RAF Museum, Cosford
	XM561	Saro Skeeter AOP12 (7980M)	South Yorkshire Avn Museum, Firbeck
	XM564	Saro Skeeter AOP12	National Tank Museum, Bovington
	XM569	Avro 698 Vulcan B2 <ff>	Gloucestershire Avn Coll, stored Glos
	XM575	Avro 698 Vulcan B2A (G-BLMC)	East Midlands Airport Aeropark
	XM594	Avro 698 Vulcan B2	Newark Air Museum, Winthorpe
	XM597	Avro 698 Vulcan B2	Royal Scottish Mus'm of Flight, E Fortune
	XM598	Avro 698 Vulcan B2 (8778M)	RAF Museum, Cosford
	XM602	Avro 698 Vulcan B2 (8771M) <ff>	Avro Aircraft Heritage Society, Woodford
	XM603	Avro 698 Vulcan B2	Avro Aircraft Heritage Society, Woodford
	XM607	Avro 698 Vulcan B2 (8779M)	RAF Waddington, on display
	XM612	Avro 698 Vulcan B2	City of Norwich Aviation Museum
	XM652	Avro 698 Vulcan B2 <ff>	Privately owned, Welshpool
	XM655	Avro 698 Vulcan B2 (G-VULC)	Privately owned, Wellesbourne Mountford
	XM660	WS55 Whirlwind HAS7 [78]	RAF Millom Museum, Haverigg
	XM685	WS55 Whirlwind HAS7 (G-AYZJ) [513/PO]	Newark Air Museum, Winthorpe
	XM692	HS Gnat T1 <ff>	Boscombe Down Museum
	XM693	HS Gnat T1 (7891M)	BAE Systems Hamble, on display
	XM693	HS Gnat T1 (8618M/XP504/ G-TIMM) [04]	Kennet Aviation, Cranfield
	XM697	HS Gnat T1 (G-NAAT)	Bournemouth Aviation Museum
	XM708	HS Gnat T1 (8573M)	Privately owned, Kings Langley, Herts
	XM709	HS Gnat T1 (8617M) [67]	Currently not known
	XM715	HP80 Victor K2	British Aviation Heritage, Bruntingthorpe
	XM717	HP80 Victor K2 <ff>	RAF Museum, Hendon
	XM819	Lancashire EP9 Prospector (G-APXW)	Museum of Army Flying, Middle Wallop
	XM833	WS58 Wessex HAS3	SWWAPS, Lasham
	XM868	WS58 Wessex HAS1 [517]	RN, Predannack Fire School
	XM870	WS58 Wessex HAS3 [PO]	RN, Predannack Fire School
	XM874	WS58 Wessex HAS1 [521/CU]	RN, Predannack Fire School
	XM927	WS58 Wessex HAS3 (8814M) [660/PO]	RAF Shawbury Fire Section
	XN126	WS55 Whirlwind HAR10 (8655M) [S]	Pinewood Studios, Elstree
	XN157	Slingsby T21B Sedbergh TX1	Privately owned, stored Long Mynd
	XN185	Slingsby T21B Sedbergh TX1 (8942M/BGA 4077)	RAFGSA, Syerston
	XN187	Slingsby T21B Sedbergh TX1 (BGA 3903)	Privately owned, Seighford
	XN198	Slingsby T31B Cadet TX3	Privately owned, Challock Lees
	XN238	Slingsby T31B Cadet TX3 <ff>	South Yorkshire Avn Museum, Firbeck
	XN239	Slingsby T31B Cadet TX3 (8889M) [G]	Imperial War Museum, Duxford
	XN243	Slingsby T31B Cadet TX3 (BGA 3145)	Privately owned, Bicester
	XN246	Slingsby T31B Cadet TX3	Southampton Hall of Aviation

Serial	Type (other identity) [code]	Owner/operator, location or fate	Notes
XN258	WS55 Whirlwind HAR9 [589/CU]	North-East Aircraft Museum, Usworth	
XN263	WS55 Whirlwind HAS7	Privately owned, Bosham, W Sussex	
XN297	WS55 Whirlwind HAR9 (XN311) [12]	Privately owned, Hull	
XN298	WS55 Whirlwind HAR9 [810/LS]	International Fire Training Centre, Chorley	
XN299	WS55 Whirlwind HAS7 [ZZ]	Tangmere Military Aviation Museum	
XN304	WS55 Whirlwind HAS7 [64]	Norfolk & Suffolk Avn Museum, Flixton	
XN332	Saro P531 (G-APNV) [759]	FAA Museum, RNAS Yeovilton	
XN334	Saro P531	FAA Museum, stored RNAS Yeovilton	
XN341	Saro Skeeter AOP12 (8022M)	Stondon Transport Mus & Garden Centre, Beds	
XN344	Saro Skeeter AOP12 (8018M)	Science Museum, South Kensington	
XN351	Saro Skeeter AOP12 (G-BKSC)	Privately owned, Ipswich	
XN380	WS55 Whirlwind HAS7	Lashenden Air Warfare Museum, Headcorn	
XN385	WS55 Whirlwind HAS7	Botany Bay Villages, Chorley, Lancs	
XN386	WS55 Whirlwind HAR9 [435/ED]	Aeroventure, Doncaster	
XN412	Auster AOP9	Auster 9 Group, Melton Mowbray	
XN435	Auster AOP9 (G-BGBU)	Privately owned, Egham	
XN437	Auster AOP9 (G-AXWA)	Privately owned, North Weald	
XN441	Auster AOP9 (G-BGKT)	Auster 9 Group, Melton Mowbray	
XN459	Hunting Jet Provost T3A (G-BWOT)	Transair(UK) Ltd, North Weald	
XN462	Hunting Jet Provost T3A [17]	FAA Museum, stored RNAS Yeovilton	
XN466	Hunting Jet Provost T3A [29] <ff>	No 1005 Sqn ATC, Radcliffe, Gtr Manchester	
XN492	Hunting Jet Provost T3 (8079M) <ff>	South Yorkshire Avn Museum, Firbeck	
XN493	Hunting Jet Provost T3 (XN137) <ff>	Privately owned, Camberley	
XN494	Hunting Jet Provost T3A (9012M) [43]	Crawley Technical College	
XN497	Hunting Jet Provost T3A [52]	DARA, RAF St Athan	
XN500	Hunting Jet Provost T3A [48]	Oxford Avn Services Ltd, Oxford, ground instruction	
XN501	Hunting Jet Provost T3A (8958M) [G]	Privately owned, Billockby, Norfolk	
XN503	Hunting Jet Provost T3 <ff>	No 1284 Sqn ATC, Milford Haven	
XN505	Hunting Jet Provost T3A [25]	Privately owned, Binbrook	
XN508	Hunting Jet Provost T3A [47]	DARA, RAF St Athan	
XN510	Hunting Jet Provost T3A (G-BXBI) [40]	Privately owned, Sproughton	
XN549	Hunting Jet Provost T3 (8235M) [32,P]	RAF Shawbury Fire Section	
XN551	Hunting Jet Provost T3A (8984M)	DARA Training School, RAF St Athan	
XN554	Hunting Jet Provost T3 (8436M) [K]	RAF North Luffenham Training Area	
XN573	Hunting Jet Provost T3 [E] <ff>	Newark Air Museum, Winthorpe	
XN577	Hunting Jet Provost T3A (8956M) [89,F]	Privately owned, Billockby, Norfolk	
XN579	Hunting Jet Provost T3A (9137M) [14]	RAF North Luffenham Training Area	
XN582	Hunting Jet Provost T3A (8957M) [95,H]	Arbury College, Cambridge	
XN584	Hunting Jet Provost T3A (9014M) [E]	Phoenix Aviation, Bruntingthorpe	
XN586	Hunting Jet Provost T3A (9039M) [91,S]	Brooklands Technical College	
XN589	Hunting Jet Provost T3A (9143M) [46]	RAF Linton-on-Ouse, on display	
XN592	Hunting Jet Provost T3 <ff>	No 1105 Sqn ATC, Winchester	
XN593	Hunting Jet Provost T3A (8988M) [97,Q]	Privately owned, Billockby, Norfolk	
XN594	Hunting Jet Provost T3 (8234M/XN458)	Privately owned, Ashington, W Sussex	
XN597	Hunting Jet Provost T3 (7984M) <ff>	RAF Millom Museum, Haverigg	
XN607	Hunting Jet Provost T3 <ff>	N Yorks Aircraft Recovery Centre, Chop Gate	
XN629	Hunting Jet Provost T3A (G-BVEG/G-KNOT) [49]	Transair (UK) Ltd, North Weald	
XN632	Hunting Jet Provost T3 (8352M)	Privately owned, Birlingham, Worcs	
XN634	Hunting Jet Provost T3A <ff>	Privately owned, Sproughton	
XN634	Hunting Jet Provost T3A [53] <rf>	BAE Systems Warton Fire Section	

XN636 – XP350

Notes	Serial	Type (other identity) [code]	Owner/operator, location or fate
	XN636	Hunting Jet Provost T3A (9045M)	*Currently not known*
	XN637	Hunting Jet Provost T3 (G-BKOU) [03]	Phoenix Aviation, stored Bruntingthorpe
	XN647	DH110 Sea Vixen FAW2 [707/VL]	Flambards Village Theme Park, Helston
	XN649	DH110 Sea Vixen FAW2 [126]	*Scrapped at Farnborough*
	XN650	DH110 Sea Vixen FAW2 <ff>	Privately owned, Welshpool
	XN651	DH110 Sea Vixen FAW2 <ff>	Communications & Electronics Museum, Bletchley Park
	XN657	DH110 Sea Vixen D3 [TR-1]	Privately owned, Stock, Essex
	XN685	DH110 Sea Vixen FAW2 (8173M) [03/VL]	Midland Air Museum, Coventry
	XN688	DH110 Sea Vixen FAW2 (8141M) [511]	*Scrapped at Farnborough*
	XN691	DH110 Sea Vixen FAW2 (8143M) [247/H]	Privately owned, North Weald
	XN696	DH110 Sea Vixen FAW2 <ff>	Blyth Valley Aviation Collection, Walpole
	XN714	Hunting H126	RAF Museum, Cosford
	XN724	EE Lightning F2A (8513M) [F]	Privately owned, Newcastle-upon-Tyne
	XN726	EE Lightning F2A (8545M) <ff>	Boscombe Down Museum
	XN728	EE Lightning F2A (8546M) [V]	Privately owned, Balderton, Notts
	XN734	EE Lightning F3A (8346M/ G-BNCA) <ff>	Privately owned, Cranfield
	XN769	EE Lightning F2 (8402M) <ff>	Privately owned, Sidcup, Kent
	XN776	EE Lightning F2A (8535M) [C]	Royal Scottish Mus'm of Flight, E Fortune
	XN795	EE Lightning F2A <ff>	Privately owned, Foulness
	XN817	AW660 Argosy C1	DERA West Freugh Fire Section
	XN819	AW660 Argosy C1 (8205M) <ff>	Newark Air Museum, Winthorpe
	XN923	HS Buccaneer S1 [13]	Gatwick Aviation Museum, Charlwood, Surrey
	XN928	HS Buccaneer S1 (8179M) <ff>	RAF Manston History Museum
	XN957	HS Buccaneer S1	FAA Museum, RNAS Yeovilton
	XN964	HS Buccaneer S1 [613/LM]	Newark Air Museum, Winthorpe
	XN967	HS Buccaneer S1 <ff>	Muckleburgh Collection, Weybourne, Norfolk
	XN972	HS Buccaneer S1 (8183M/XN962) <ff>	RAF Museum, Hendon
	XN974	HS Buccaneer S2A	Yorkshire Air Museum, Elvington
	XN983	HS Buccaneer S2B <ff>	Fenland & W Norfolk Aviation Museum,
	XP110	WS58 Wessex HAS3 [55/FL]	RN AESS, *HMS Sultan*, Gosport, BDRT
	XP137	WS58 Wessex HAS3 [711/DD]	SFDO, RNAS Culdrose
	XP142	WS58 Wessex HAS3	FAA Museum, stored Yeovilton
	XP150	WS58 Wessex HAS3 [LS]	FETC, Moreton-in-Marsh, Glos
	XP157	WS58 Wessex HAS1 [AN]	*Scrapped at Yeovilton, July 2000*
	XP159	WS58 Wessex HAS1 (8877M) [047/R]	Privately owned, Brands Hatch
	XP160	WS58 Wessex HAS1	RN, Predannack Fire School
	XP165	WS Scout AH1	The Helicopter Museum, Weston-super-Mare
	XP166	WS Scout AH1 (G-APVL)	Privately owned, East Dereham, Norfolk
	XP190	WS Scout AH1	Aeroventure, Doncaster
	XP191	WS Scout AH1	Army, Bramley, Hants
	XP226	Fairey Gannet AEW3 [073/E]	Newark Air Museum, Winthorpe
	XP241	Auster AOP9	Privately owned, Eggesford (on rebuild)
	XP242	Auster AOP9 (G-BUCI)	AAC Historic Aircraft Flight, Middle Wallop
	XP244	Auster AOP9 (7864M/*M7922*)	Army SEAE, Arborfield
	XP248	Auster AOP9 (7863M/WZ679)	Privately owned, Sandy, Beds
	XP254	Auster AOP11 (G-ASCC)	Privately owned, Tollerton
	XP279	Auster AOP9 (G-BWKK)	Privately owned, Popham
	XP280	Auster AOP9	Snibston Discovery Park, Coalville
	XP281	Auster AOP9	Imperial War Museum, Duxford
	XP283	Auster AOP9 (7859M) (frame)	*Currently not known*
	XP299	WS55 Whirlwind HAR10 (8726M)	RAF Museum, Cosford
	XP329	WS55 Whirlwind HAR10 (8791M) [V]	Privately owned, Tattershall Thorpe
	XP330	WS55 Whirlwind HAR10	CAA Fire School, Tees-side Airport
	XP344	WS55 Whirlwind HAR10 (8764M) [H723]	RAF North Luffenham Training Area
	XP345	WS55 Whirlwind HAR10 (8792M) [UN]	York Helicopter Preservation Group, Elvington
	XP346	WS55 Whirlwind HAR10 (8793M)	Privately owned, Long Marston
	XP350	WS55 Whirlwind HAR10	Flambards Village Theme Park, Helston

Serial	Type (other identity) [code]	Owner/operator, location or fate	Notes
XP351	WS55 Whirlwind HAR10 (8672M) [Z]	RAF Shawbury, on display	
XP353	WS55 Whirlwind HAR10 (8720M)	Privately owned, Brands Hatch	
XP354	WS55 Whirlwind HAR10 (8721M)	Scrapped at Cricklade, 1999	
XP355	WS55 Whirlwind HAR10 (8463M/ G-BEBC)	City of Norwich Aviation Museum	
XP359	WS55 Whirlwind HAR10 (8447M)	Dundonald Aviation Centre, Strathclyde	
XP360	WS55 Whirlwind HAR10 [V]	Privately owned, Upper Hill, nr Leominster	
XP395	WS55 Whirlwind HAR10 (8674M) [A]	Privately owned, Tattershall Thorpe	
XP398	WS55 Whirlwind HAR10 (8794M)	Gatwick Aviation Museum, Charlwood, Surrey	
XP399	WS55 Whirlwind HAR10	Privately owned, Wickford, Essex	
XP404	WS55 Whirlwind HAR10 (8682M)	The Helicopter Museum, Weston-super-Mare	
XP411	AW660 Argosy C1 (8442M) [C]	RAF Museum, Cosford	
XP454	Slingsby T38 Grasshopper TX1	Wellingborough School, Wellingborough	
XP458	Slingsby T38 Grasshopper TX1	City of Norwich Aviation Museum	
XP488	Slingsby T38 Grasshopper TX1	Fenland & W Norfolk Aviation Museum, stored Wisbech	
XP493	Slingsby T38 Grasshopper TX1	Privately owned, stored Aston Down	
XP494	Slingsby T38 Grasshopper TX1	Privately owned, Rattlesden, Suffolk	
XP502	HS Gnat T1 (8576M)	Privately owned, Sproughton	
XP503	HS Gnat T1 (8568M) [73]	Sold to the US, January 2000	
XP505	HS Gnat T1	Science Museum, Wroughton	
XP516	HS Gnat T1 (8580M) [16]	DERA Structures Dept, Farnborough	
XP540	HS Gnat T1 (8608M) [62]	Arbury College, Cambridge	
XP542	HS Gnat T1 (8575M) [42]	R. Military College of Science, Shrivenham	
XP556	Hunting Jet Provost T4 (9027M) [B]	RAF Cranwell Aviation Heritage Centre	
XP557	Hunting Jet Provost T4 (8494M) [72]	Bomber County Aviation Museum, Hemswell	
XP558	Hunting Jet Provost T4 (8627M) [20]	Privately owned, Norwich Airport	
XP563	Hunting Jet Provost T4 (9028M) [C]	Privately owned, Sproughton	
XP568	Hunting Jet Provost T4	Jet Avn Preservation Grp, Long Marston	
XP573	Hunting Jet Provost T4 (8236M) [19]	Jersey Airport Fire Section	
XP585	Hunting Jet Provost T4 (8407M) [24]	NE Wales Institute, Wrexham	
XP627	Hunting Jet Provost T4	North-East Aircraft Museum, Usworth	
XP629	Hunting Jet Provost T4 (9026M) [P]	RAF North Luffenham Training Area	
XP638	Hunting Jet Provost T4 (9034M) [A]	RAF Waddington, BDRT	
XP640	Hunting Jet Provost T4 (8501M) [27]	Yorkshire Air Museum, Elvington	
XP642	Hunting Jet Provost T4 <ff>	Privately owned, Luton	
XP672	Hunting Jet Provost T4 (8458M/ G-RAFI) [03]	Privately owned, North Weald	
XP677	Hunting Jet Provost T4 (8587M) <ff>	No 1343 Sqn ATC, East Grinstead	
XP680	Hunting Jet Provost T4 (8460M)	FETC, Moreton-in-Marsh, Glos	
XP686	Hunting Jet Provost T4 (8401M/ 8502M) [G]	RAF North Luffenham Training Area	
XP688	Hunting Jet Provost T4 (9031M)	Botany Bay Villages, Chorley, Lancs	
XP701	BAC Lightning F3 (8924M) <ff>	Robertsbridge Aviation Society, Mayfield	
XP703	BAC Lightning F3 <ff>	Lightning Preservation Grp, RAF Coltishall	
XP706	BAC Lightning F3 (8925M)	Lincs Lightning Pres'n Society, Hemswell	
XP745	BAC Lightning F3 (8453M) <ff>	Greenford Haulage, West London	
XP772	DHC2 Beaver AL1 (G-BUCJ)	AAC Historic Aircraft Flight, stored Duxford	
XP775	DHC2 Beaver AL1	Privately owned	
XP806	DHC2 Beaver AL1	Privately owned, Cumbernauld	
XP820	DHC2 Beaver AL1	AAC Historic Aircraft Flight, Middle Wallop	
XP821	DHC2 Beaver AL1 [MCO]	Museum of Army Flying, Middle Wallop	
XP822	DHC2 Beaver AL1	Museum of Army Flying, Middle Wallop	
XP831	Hawker P.1127 (8406M)	Science Museum, South Kensington	
XP841	Handley-Page HP115	FAA Museum, RNAS Yeovilton	
XP846	WS Scout AH1 [B,H] (fuselage)	RE 39 Regt, Waterbeach, instructional use	
XP847	WS Scout AH1	Museum of Army Flying, Middle Wallop	
XP848	WS Scout AH1	AAC Arborfield, on display	
XP849	WS Scout AH1	Privately owned, East Dereham, Norfolk	
XP853	WS Scout AH1	Army, Bramley, Hants	
XP854	WS Scout AH1 (7898M/TAD043)	AAC Wattisham, instructional use	
XP855	WS Scout AH1	Army SEAE, Arborfield	

Notes	Serial	Type (other identity) [code]	Owner/operator, location or fate
	XP856	WS Scout AH1	Army, Bramley, Hants
	XP883	WS Scout AH1	DERA Boscombe Down, Apprentice School
	XP884	WS Scout AH1	AAC Middle Wallop, instructional use
	XP885	WS Scout AH1	AAC Wattisham, instructional use
	XP886	WS Scout AH1	Yeovil College
	XP888	WS Scout AH1	Army SEAE, Arborfield
	XP890	WS Scout AH1 [G] (fuselage)	Privately owned, Ipswich
	XP893	WS Scout AH1	AAC Middle Wallop, BDRT
	XP899	WS Scout AH1 [D]	Army SEAE, Arborfield
	XP900	WS Scout AH1	AAC Wattisham, instructional use
	XP902	WS Scout AH1 <ff>	South Yorkshire Avn Museum, Firbeck
	XP905	WS Scout AH1	Army SEAE, Arborfield
	XP907	WS Scout AH1 (G-SROE)	Privately owned, Wattisham
	XP910	WS Scout AH1	Museum of Army Flying, Middle Wallop
	XP919	DH110 Sea Vixen FAW2 (8163M) [706/VL]	Blyth Valley Aviation Collection, Walpole
	XP924	DH110 Sea Vixen D3 (G-CVIX)	De Havilland Aviation, Bournemouth
	XP925	DH110 Sea Vixen FAW2 [752] <ff>	No 1268 Sqn ATC, Haslemere, Surrey
	XP956	DH110 Sea Vixen FAW2	*Currently not known*
	XP980	Hawker P.1127	FAA Museum, RNAS Yeovilton
	XP984	Hawker P.1127	Brooklands Museum, Weybridge
	XR220	BAC TSR2 (7933M)	RAF Museum, Cosford
	XR222	BAC TSR2	Imperial War Museum, Duxford
	XR232	Sud Alouette AH2 (F-WEIP)	Museum of Army Flying, Middle Wallop
	XR240	Auster AOP9 (G-BDFH)	Privately owned, Booker
	XR241	Auster AOP9 (G-AXRR)	The Aircraft Restoration Co, Duxford
	XR244	Auster AOP9	AAC Historic Aircraft Flight, Middle Wallop
	XR246	Auster AOP9 (7862M/G-AZBU)	Auster 9 Group, Melton Mowbray
	XR267	Auster AOP9 (G-BJXR)	Cotswold Aircraft Rest'n Grp, Innsworth
	XR271	Auster AOP9	Museum of Artillery, Woolwich
	XR371	SC5 Belfast C1	RAF Museum, Cosford
	XR379	Sud Alouette AH2	AAC Historic Aircraft Flight, Middle Wallop
	XR453	WS55 Whirlwind HAR10 (8873M) [A]	RAF Odiham, on gate
	XR458	WS55 Whirlwind HAR10 (8662M) [H]	Museum of Army Flying, Middle Wallop
	XR485	WS55 Whirlwind HAR10 [Q]	Norfolk & Suffolk Avn Museum, Flixton
	XR486	WS55 Whirlwind HCC12 (8727M/ G-RWWW)	The Helicopter Museum, Weston-super-Mare
	XR497	WS58 Wessex HC2 [F]	RAF No 72 Sqn, Aldergrove
	XR498	WS58 Wessex HC2 [X]	RAF No 72 Sqn, Aldergrove
	XR499	WS58 Wessex HC2 [W]	RN AESS, *HMS Sultan*, Gosport
	XR501	WS58 Wessex HC2	RN AESS, *HMS Sultan*, Gosport
	XR502	WS58 Wessex HC2 [Z]	Privately owned, Colsterworth
	XR503	WS58 Wessex HC2	RN AESS, *HMS Sultan*, Gosport
	XR504	WS58 Wessex HC2 [*Joker*]	*Withdrawn from use at Akrotiri, 2000*
	XR506	WS58 Wessex HC2 [V]	RAF No 72 Sqn, Aldergrove
	XR507	WS58 Wessex HC2	*Scrapped, 2000*
	XR508	WS58 Wessex HC2 [B]	RN AESS, *HMS Sultan*, Gosport
	XR511	WS58 Wessex HC2 [L]	RAF No 72 Sqn, Aldergrove
	XR516	WS58 Wessex HC2 [WB]	RN AESS, *HMS Sultan*, Gosport
	XR517	WS58 Wessex HC2 [N]	Privately owned, Sproughton
	XR518	WS58 Wessex HC2 [O]	RAF, stored Shawbury
	XR520	WS58 Wessex HC2	RN AESS, *HMS Sultan*, Gosport
	XR523	WS58 Wessex HC2 [M]	RAF, stored RNAY Fleetlands
	XR525	WS58 Wessex HC2 [G]	RAF No 72 Sqn, Aldergrove
	XR526	WS58 Wessex HC2 (8147M)	The Helicopter Museum, Weston-super-Mare
	XR528	WS58 Wessex HC2	SFDO, RNAS Culdrose
	XR529	WS58 Wessex HC2 [E]	RAF No 72 Sqn, Aldergrove
	XR534	HS Gnat T1 (8578M) [65]	Newark Air Museum, Winthorpe
	XR537	HS Gnat T1 (8642M/G-NATY) [T]	Bournemouth Aviation Museum
	XR569	HS Gnat T1 (8560M) [08]	Phoenix Aviation, Bruntingthorpe
	XR571	HS Gnat T1 (8493M)	RAF *Red Arrows*, Cranwell, on display
	XR574	HS Gnat T1 (8631M) [72]	RAF No 1 SoTT, Cosford
	XR588	WS58 Wessex HC2 [*Hearts*]	RAF No 84 Sqn, Akrotiri
	XR595	WS Scout AH1 (G-BWHU) [M]	Privately owned, Glenrothes
	XR597	WS Scout AH1 (fuselage)	Army, Wattisham, BDRT
	XR601	WS Scout AH1	Army SEAE, Arborfield
	XR625	WS Scout AH1 (XR633/*XR777*)	Privately owned, Sproughton
	XR627	WS Scout AH1 [X]	AAC Wattisham, BDRT

Serial	Type (other identity) [code]	Owner/operator, location or fate	Notes
XR628	WS Scout AH1	Privately owned, Ipswich	
XR629	WS Scout AH1 (fuselage)	Privately owned, Ipswich	
XR630	WS Scout AH1	*Burnt at Middle Wallop*	
XR635	WS Scout AH1	Army SEAE, Arborfield	
XR650	Hunting Jet Provost T4 (8459M) [28]	Boscombe Down Museum	
XR654	Hunting Jet Provost T4 <ff>	Privately owned, Sealand	
XR658	Hunting Jet Provost T4 (8192M)	Deeside College, Connah's Quay, Clwyd	
XR662	Hunting Jet Provost T4 (8410M) [25]	Boulton Paul Association, Wolverhampton	
XR672	Hunting Jet Provost T4 (8495M) [50]	RAF Halton, Fire Section	
XR673	Hunting Jet Provost T4 (G-BXLO/ 9032M) [L]	Privately owned, North Weald	
XR681	Hunting Jet Provost T4 (8588M) <ff>	No 1216 Sqn ATC, Newhaven, E Sussex	
XR700	Hunting Jet Provost T4 (8589M) <ff>	RAF EPTT, Aldergrove	
XR713	BAC Lightning F3 (8935M) [C]	RAF Leuchars, on display	
XR718	BAC Lightning F6 (8932M) [DA]	Blyth Valley Aviation Collection, Walpole	
XR724	BAC Lightning F6 (G-BTSY)	The Lightning Association, Binbrook	
XR725	BAC Lightning F6	Privately owned, Binbrook	
XR726	BAC Lightning F6 <ff>	Privately owned, Harrogate	
XR728	BAC Lightning F6 [JS]	Lightning Preservation Grp, Bruntingthorpe	
XR747	BAC Lightning F6 <ff>	Privately owned, Booker	
XR749	BAC Lightning F3 (8934M) [DA]	Tees-side Airport, on display	
XR751	BAC Lightning F3	Privately owned, Tremar, Cornwall	
XR753	BAC Lightning F6 (8969M) [BP]	RAF Leeming on display	
XR754	BAC Lightning F6 (8972M) <ff>	Aeroventure, Doncaster	
XR755	BAC Lightning F6	Privately owned, Callington, Cornwall	
XR757	BAC Lightning F6 <ff>	Privately owned, Grainthorpe, Lincs	
XR759	BAC Lightning F6 <ff>	Privately owned, Haxey, Lincs	
XR770	BAC Lightning F6 [AA]	Privately owned, Grainthorpe, Lincs	
XR771	BAC Lightning F6 [BM]	Midland Air Museum, Coventry	
XR806	BAC VC10 C1K <ff>	RAF Brize Norton, BDRT	
XR807	BAC VC10 C1K	DARA, stored RAF St Athan	
XR808	BAC VC10 C1K	RAF No 10 Sqn, Brize Norton	
XR810	BAC VC10 C1K	RAF No 10 Sqn, Brize Norton	
XR944	Wallis WA116 (G-ATTB)	RAF Museum, Hendon	
XR954	HS Gnat T1 (8570M) [30]	Privately owned, Bournemouth	
XR955	HS Gnat T1 [SAH-2]	Privately owned, Leavesden	
XR977	HS Gnat T1 (8640M) [3]	RAF Museum, Cosford	
XR985	HS Gnat T1 (7886M)	Vintage Aircraft Team, Bruntingthorpe	
XR991	HS Gnat T1 (8624M/XS102/ G-MOUR)	Privately owned, Kemble	
XR993	HS Gnat T1 (8620M/XP534/ G-BVPP)	Kennet Aviation, Cranfield	
XS100	HS Gnat T1 (8561M) [57]	Privately owned, Ongar	
XS101	HS Gnat T1 (8638M) (G-GNAT)	Privately owned, Cranfield	
XS122	WS58 Wessex HAS3 (655/PO]	RN AESS, *HMS Sultan*, Gosport	
XS128	WS58 Wessex HAS1 [37]	RNAS Yeovilton Fire Section	
XS149	WS58 Wessex HAS3 (661/GL]	The Helicopter Museum, Weston-super-Mare	
XS165	Hiller UH12E (G-ASAZ) [37]	Privately owned, North Weald	
XS176	Hunting Jet Provost T4 (8514M)	Privately owned, Solihull	
XS177	Hunting Jet Provost T4 (9044M) [N]	RAF Valley Fire Section	
XS179	Hunting Jet Provost T4 (8237M) [20]	University of Salford, Manchester	
XS180	Hunting Jet Provost T4 (8238M) [21]	RAF St Athan Fire Section	
XS181	Hunting Jet Provost T4 (9033M) <ff>	Communications & Electronics Museum, Bletchley Park	
XS183	Hunting Jet Provost T4 <ff>	Privately owned, Plymouth	
XS186	Hunting Jet Provost T4 (8408M) [M]	RAF North Luffenham Training Area	
XS209	Hunting Jet Provost T4 (8409M)	Privately owned, Kemble	
XS215	Hunting Jet Provost T4 (8507M) [17]	RAF Halton	
XS216	Hunting Jet Provost T4 <ff>	No 2357 Sqn ATC, Goole	
XS217	Hunting Jet Provost T4 (9029M) [O]	Privately owned, Bruntingthorpe	

Notes	Serial	Type (other identity) [code]	Owner/operator, location or fate
	XS218	Hunting Jet Provost T4 (8508M) <ff>	No 447 Sqn ATC, Henley-on-Thames, Berks
	XS231	BAC Jet Provost T5 (G-ATAJ)	Privately owned, Sproughton
	XS235	DH106 Comet 4C (G-CPDA)	British Aviation Heritage, Bruntingthorpe
	XS416	BAC Lightning T5 <ff>	Privately owned, Grainthorpe, Lincs
	XS417	BAC Lightning T5 [DZ]	Newark Air Museum, Winthorpe
	XS420	BAC Lightning T5	Privately owned, Norfolk
	XS421	BAC Lightning T5 <ff>	Privately owned, Foulness
	XS456	BAC Lightning T5 [DX]	Privately owned, Wainfleet
	XS457	BAC Lightning T5 <ff>	Privately owned, North Coates
	XS458	BAC Lightning T5	T5 Projects, Cranfield
	XS459	BAC Lightning T5 [AW]	Fenland & W Norfolk Aviation Museum, Wisbech
	XS463	WS Wasp HAS1 (XT431)	Privately owned, Ipswich
	XS479	WS58 Wessex HU5 (8819M) [XF]	Privately owned, Stock, Essex
	XS481	WS58 Wessex HU5	Aeroventure, Doncaster
	XS482	WS58 Wessex HU5 [A/D]	RAF Manston History Museum
	XS485	WS58 Wessex HC5C (comp XR503) [*Hearts*]	RN AESS, *HMS Sultan*, Gosport
	XS486	WS58 Wessex HU5 (9272M) [524/CU,F]	No 93 Sqn ATC, Bath
	XS488	WS58 Wessex HU5 (9056M) [XK]	AAC Wattisham, instructional use
	XS489	WS58 Wessex HU5 [R]	RN AESS, *HMS Sultan*, Gosport
	XS491	WS58 Wessex HU5 [XM]	Sunk at Capernwray, Lancs
	XS492	WS58 Wessex HU5 [623]	RN, stored RNAY Fleetlands
	XS493	WS58 Wessex HU5	RN, stored RNAY Fleetlands
	XS496	WS58 Wessex HU5 [625/PO]	RN AESS, *HMS Sultan*, Gosport
	XS498	WS58 Wessex HC5C (comp XS677) [WK]	Privately owned, Hixon, Staffs
	XS507	WS58 Wessex HU5	RN AESS, *HMS Sultan*, Gosport
	XS508	WS58 Wessex HU5	FAA Museum, stored RNAS Yeovilton
	XS510	WS58 Wessex HU5 [626/PO]	RN AESS, *HMS Sultan*, Gosport
	XS511	WS58 Wessex HU5 [M]	RN AESS, *HMS Sultan*, Gosport
	XS513	WS58 Wessex HU5 [419/CU]	RN AESS, *HMS Sultan*, Gosport
	XS514	WS58 Wessex HU5 [L]	RN AESS, *HMS Sultan*, Gosport
	XS515	WS58 Wessex HU5 [N]	RN AESS, *HMS Sultan*, Gosport
	XS516	WS58 Wessex HU5 [Q]	RN, Predannack Fire School
	XS517	WS58 Wessex HC5C (comp XS679) [*Diamonds*]	RN AESS, *HMS Sultan*, Gosport, BDRT
	XS520	WS58 Wessex HU5 [F]	RN AESS, *HMS Sultan*, Gosport
	XS522	WS58 Wessex HU5 [ZL]	RN, Predannack Fire School
	XS527	WS Wasp HAS1	FAA Museum, stored RNAS Yeovilton
	XS529	WS Wasp HAS1	RN, Predannack Fire School
	XS539	WS Wasp HAS1 [435]	RNAY Fleetlands Apprentice School
	XS567	WS Wasp HAS1 [434/E]	Imperial War Museum, Duxford
	XS568	WS Wasp HAS1 [441]	RN AESS, *HMS Sultan*, Gosport
	XS569	WS Wasp HAS1	RNAY Fleetlands Apprentice School
	XS570	WS Wasp HAS1 [445/P]	Warship Preservation Trust, Birkenhead
	XS576	DH110 Sea Vixen FAW2 [125/E]	Imperial War Museum, Duxford
	XS587	DH110 Sea Vixen FAW(TT)2 (8828M/G-VIXN)	Gatwick Aviation Museum, Charlwood, Surrey
	XS590	DH110 Sea Vixen FAW2 [131/E]	FAA Museum, RNAS Yeovilton
	XS596	HS Andover C1(PR)	DPA/AFD/*Open Skies*, DERA Boscombe Down
	XS598	HS Andover C1 (fuselage)	FETC, Moreton-in-Marsh, Glos
	XS606	HS Andover C1	DPA/AFD/ETPS, DERA Boscombe Down
	XS639	HS Andover E3A	RAF Museum, Cosford
	XS641	HS Andover C1(PR) (9198M) [Z]	RAF No 1 SoTT, Cosford
	XS643	HS Andover E3A (9278M)	MoD FSCTE, Manston
	XS646	HS Andover C1(mod)	DPA/AFD, DERA Boscombe Down
	XS652	Slingsby T45 Swallow TX1 (BGA 1107)	Privately owned, Rufforth
	XS674	WS58 Wessex HC2 [R]	Privately owned, Sproughton
	XS675	WS58 Wessex HC2 [*Spades*]	RAF No 84 Sqn, Akrotiri
	XS677	WS58 Wessex HC2 [WK]	RAF, stored Shawbury
	XS695	HS Kestrel FGA1	RAF Museum, stored Wyton
	XS709	HS125 Dominie T1 [M]	RAF No 3 FTS/55(R) Sqn, Cranwell
	XS710	HS125 Dominie T1 (9259M) [O]	RAF No 1 SoTT, Cosford
	XS711	HS125 Dominie T1 [L]	RAF No 3 FTS/55(R) Sqn, Cranwell
	XS712	HS125 Dominie T1 [A]	RAF No 3 FTS/55(R) Sqn, Cranwell
	XS713	HS125 Dominie T1 [C]	RAF No 3 FTS/55(R) Sqn, Cranwell
	XS714	HS125 Dominie T1 (9246M) [P]	MoD FSCTE, Manston
	XS726	HS125 Dominie T1 (9273M) [T]	RAF No 1 SoTT, Cosford

Serial	Type (other identity) [code]	Owner/operator, location or fate	Notes
XS727	HS125 Dominie T1 [D]	RAF No 3 FTS/55(R) Sqn, Cranwell	
XS728	HS125 Dominie T1 [E]	RAF No 3 FTS/55(R) Sqn, Cranwell	
XS729	HS125 Dominie T1 (9275M) [G]	RAF No 1 SoTT, Cosford	
XS730	HS125 Dominie T1 [H]	RAF No 3 FTS/55(R) Sqn, Cranwell	
XS731	HS125 Dominie T1 [J]	RAF No 3 FTS/55(R) Sqn, Cranwell	
XS732	HS125 Dominie T1 [B] (fuselage)	*Burnt at Manston by July 1998*	
XS733	HS125 Dominie T1 (9276M) [Q]	RAF No 1 SoTT, Cosford	
XS734	HS125 Dominie T1 (9260M) [N]	RAF No 1 SoTT, Cosford	
XS735	HS125 Dominie T1 [R]	RAF Sealand, instructional use	
XS736	HS125 Dominie T1 [S]	RAF No 3 FTS/55(R) Sqn, Cranwell	
XS737	HS125 Dominie T1 [K]	RAF No 3 FTS/55(R) Sqn, Cranwell	
XS738	HS125 Dominie T1 (9274M) [U]	RAF No 1 SoTT, Cosford	
XS739	HS125 Dominie T1 [F]	RAF No 3 FTS/55(R) Sqn, Cranwell	
XS743	Beagle B206Z Basset CC1	DPA/AFD/ETPS, DERA Boscombe Down	
XS765	Beagle B206Z Basset CC1 (G-BSET)	Privately owned, Cranfield	
XS770	Beagle B206Z Basset CC1 (G-HRHI)	Privately owned, Cranfield	
XS790	HS748 Andover CC2 <ff>	Boscombe Down Museum	
XS791	HS748 Andover CC2	Phoenix Aviation, Bruntingthorpe	
XS862	WS58 Wessex HAS3	Privately owned, Hixon, Staffs	
XS863	WS58 Wessex HAS1	Imperial War Museum, Duxford	
XS866	WS58 Wessex HAS1 [520/CU]	RN, Predannack Fire School	
XS868	WS58 Wessex HAS1	RN, Predannack Fire School	
XS871	WS58 Wessex HAS1 (8457M) [265]	Privately owned, Chippenham, Wilts	
XS876	WS58 Wessex HAS1 [523/PO]	SFDO, RNAS Culdrose	
XS881	WS58 Wessex HAS1	RN, Predannack Fire School	
XS885	WS58 Wessex HAS1 [512/DD]	SFDO, RNAS Culdrose	
XS886	WS58 Wessex HAS1 [527/CU]	Sea Scouts, Evesham, Worcs	
XS887	WS58 Wessex HAS1 [403/FI]	Flambards Village Theme Park, Helston	
XS888	WS58 Wessex HAS1 [521]	Guernsey Airport Fire Section	
XS897	BAC Lightning F6	Aeroventure, Doncaster	
XS898	BAC Lightning F6 <ff>	Privately owned, Lavendon, Bucks	
XS899	BAC Lightning F6 <ff>	RAF Coltishall	
XS903	BAC Lightning F6 [BA]	Yorkshire Air Museum, Elvington	
XS904	BAC Lightning F6 [BQ]	Lightning Preservation Grp, Bruntingthorpe	
XS919	BAC Lightning F6	Wonderland Pleasure Park, Farnsfield, Notts	
XS922	BAC Lightning F6 (8973M) <ff>	The Air Defence Collection, Salisbury	
XS923	BAC Lightning F6 <ff>	Privately owned, Welshpool	
XS925	BAC Lightning F6 (8961M) [BA]	RAF Museum, Hendon	
XS928	BAC Lightning F6 [D]	BAE Systems Warton, on display	
XS932	BAC Lightning F6 <ff>	D-Day Museum, Shoreham	
XS933	BAC Lightning F6 <ff>	Privately owned, Terrington St Clement	
XS936	BAC Lightning F6	Castle Motors, Liskeard, Cornwall	
XT108	Agusta-Bell 47G-3 Sioux AH1 [U]	Museum of Army Flying, Middle Wallop	
XT123	WS Sioux AH1 (XT827) [D]	AAC Middle Wallop, at main gate	
XT131	Agusta-Bell 47G-3 Sioux AH1 [B]	AAC Historic Aircraft Flight, Middle Wallop	
XT133	Agusta-Bell 47G-3 Sioux AH1 (7923M)	Royal Engineers' Museum, stored Chattenden	
XT140	Agusta-Bell 47G-3 Sioux AH1	Perth Technical College	
XT148	Agusta-Bell 47G-3 Sioux AH1	The Helicopter Museum, stored Weston-super-Mare	
XT150	Agusta-Bell 47G-3 Sioux AH1 (7883M) [R]	AAC Netheravon, at main gate	
XT151	WS Sioux AH1 [W]	Museum of Army Flying, stored Middle Wallop	
XT175	WS Sioux AH1 (TAD175)	Privately owned, Cambs	
XT176	WS Sioux AH1 [U]	FAA Museum, stored Yeovilton	
XT190	WS Sioux AH1	The Helicopter Museum, Weston-super-Mare	
XT200	WS Sioux AH1 [F]	Newark Air Museum, Winthorpe	
XT223	WS Sioux AH1 (G-BGZK/G-XTUN)	Privately owned, North Weald	
XT236	WS Sioux AH1 (frame only)	North-East Aircraft Museum, stored Usworth	
XT242	WS Sioux AH1 (composite) [12]	Aeroventure, Doncaster	
XT257	WS58 Wessex HAS3 (8719M)	Privately owned, East Grinstead	
XT277	HS Buccaneer S2A (8853M) <ff>	Privately owned, Welshpool	
XT280	HS Buccaneer S2A <ff>	Dundonald Aviation Centre, Strathclyde	
XT284	HS Buccaneer S2A (8855M) <ff>	Privately owned, Felixstowe	

Notes	Serial	Type (other identity) [code]	Owner/operator, location or fate
	XT288	HS Buccaneer S2B (9134M)	Royal Scottish Museum of Flight, stored E Fortune
	XT420	WS Wasp HAS1 [606]	Privately owned, East Dereham, Norfolk
	XT422	WS Wasp HAS1 [324]	Privately owned, Burgess Hill
	XT427	WS Wasp HAS1 [606]	FAA Museum, stored RNAS Yeovilton
	XT434	WS Wasp HAS1 [455]	RNAY Fleetlands Apprentice School
	XT439	WS Wasp HAS1 [605]	Privately owned, King's Lynn
	XT443	WS Wasp HAS1 [422/AU]	The Helicopter Museum, Weston-super-Mare
	XT453	WS58 Wessex HU5 [A/B]	RN AESS, *HMS Sultan*, Gosport
	XT455	WS58 Wessex HU5 [U]	RN AESS, *HMS Sultan*, Gosport
	XT456	WS58 Wessex HU5 (8941M) [XZ]	RAF Aldergrove, BDRT
	XT458	WS58 Wessex HU5 [622]	RN AESS, *HMS Sultan*, Gosport
	XT460	WS58 Wessex HU5	RN AESS, *HMS Sultan*, Gosport, BDRT
	XT463	WS58 Wessex HC5C (comp XR508) [*Clubs*]	Privately owned, Hixon, Staffs
	XT466	WS58 Wessex HU5 (8921M) [XV]	RNAY Fleetlands
	XT467	WS58 Wessex HU5 (8922M) [BF]	Army, Bramley, Hants
	XT468	WS58 Wessex HU5 (comp XT460) [628]	RN, Predannack Fire School
	XT469	WS58 Wessex HU5 (8920M)	RAF No 16 MU, Stafford, ground instruction
	XT472	WS58 Wessex HU5 [XC]	The Helicopter Museum, Weston-super-Mare
	XT474	WS58 Wessex HU5 [820]	RN AESS, *HMS Sultan*, Gosport
	XT480	WS58 Wessex HU5 [468/RG]	RNAY Fleetlands, on display
	XT482	WS58 Wessex HU5 [ZM/VL]	FAA Museum, RNAS Yeovilton
	XT484	WS58 Wessex HU5 [H]	RN AESS, *HMS Sultan*, Gosport
	XT485	WS58 Wessex HU5	RN AESS, *HMS Sultan*, Gosport
	XT575	Vickers Viscount 837 <ff>	Brooklands Museum, Weybridge
	XT595	McD F-4K Phantom FG1 (8851M) <ff>	*Currently not known*
	XT596	McD F-4K Phantom FG1	FAA Museum, RNAS Yeovilton
	XT597	McD F-4K Phantom FG1	Boscombe Down Museum
	XT601	WS58 Wessex HC2 (9277M) (composite)	RAF Odiham, BDRT
	XT602	WS58 Wessex HC2	RN AESS, *HMS Sultan*, Gosport, BDRT
	XT604	WS58 Wessex HC2	Privately owned, Colsterworth
	XT606	WS58 Wessex HC2 [WL]	RAF, stored Shawbury
	XT607	WS58 Wessex HC2 [P]	RAF, stored RNAY Fleetlands
	XT617	WS Scout AH1	AAC Wattisham, on display
	XT620	WS Scout AH1	*Scrapped at Dishforth*
	XT621	WS Scout AH1	R. Military College of Science, Shrivenham
	XT623	WS Scout AH1	Army SEAE, Arborfield
	XT626	WS Scout AH1 [Q]	AAC Historic Aircraft Flt, Middle Wallop
	XT630	WS Scout AH1 (G-BXRL) [X]	Privately owned, Thruxton (spares use)
	XT631	WS Scout AH1 [D]	Privately owned, Ipswich
	XT632	WS Scout AH1 (G-BZBD)	Privately owned, Thruxton (spares use)
	XT633	WS Scout AH1	Army SEAE, Arborfield
	XT634	WS Scout AH1 (G-BYRX) [T]	Privately owned, Thruxton
	XT638	WS Scout AH1 [N]	AAC Middle Wallop, at gate
	XT640	WS Scout AH1	Army SEAE, Arborfield
	XT643	WS Scout AH1 [Z]	Army, Thorpe Camp, East Wretham
	XT645	WS Scout AH1 (fuselage)	Privately owned, Ipswich
	XT668	WS58 Wessex HC2 [S]	RAF No 72 Sqn, Aldergrove
	XT670	WS58 Wessex HC2	RN AESS, *HMS Sultan*, Gosport, BDRT
	XT671	WS58 Wessex HC2 (G-BYRC) [D]	Privately owned, Redhill
	XT672	WS58 Wessex HC2 [WE]	*Scrapped, 2000*
	XT676	WS58 Wessex HC2 [I]	RAF No 72 Sqn, Aldergrove
	XT677	WS58 Wessex HC2 (8016M)	Privately owned, Stock, Essex
	XT680	WS58 Wessex HC2 [*Diamonds*]	RAF No 84 Sqn, Akrotiri
	XT681	WS58 Wessex HC2 (9279M) [U]	RAF Benson, BDRT
	XT761	WS58 Wessex HU5	RN AESS, *HMS Sultan*, Gosport
	XT762	WS58 Wessex HU5	RN, Predannack Fire School
	XT764	WS58 Wessex HU5 [G]	RN AESS, *HMS Sultan*, Gosport
	XT765	WS58 Wessex HU5 [J]	RN AESS, *HMS Sultan*, Gosport
	XT766	WS58 Wessex HU5 (9054M) [822/CU]	RN AESS, *HMS Sultan*, Gosport, BDRT
	XT769	WS58 Wessex HU5 [823]	FAA Museum, RNAS Yeovilton
	XT770	WS58 Wessex HU5 (9055M) [P]	Privately owned, Shawell, Leics
	XT771	WS58 Wessex HU5 [620/PO]	RN AESS, *HMS Sultan*, Gosport
	XT772	WS58 Wessex HU5 (8805M)	SARTU RAF Valley, ground instruction

Serial	Type (other identity) [code]	Owner/operator, location or fate	Notes
XT773	WS58 Wessex HU5 (9123M) [822/CU]	DARA, RAF St Athan, BDRT	
XT778	WS Wasp HAS1 [430]	FAA Museum, stored Yeovilton	
XT780	WS Wasp HAS1 [636]	RNAY Fleetlands Apprentice School	
XT781	WS Wasp HAS1 (NZ3908/ G-KAWW) [426]	Kennet Aviation, Cranfield	
XT788	WS Wasp HAS1 (G-BMIR) [316] (painted as XT78?)	Privately owned, Dunkeswell	
XT793	WS Wasp HAS1 [456]	Privately owned, East Dereham, Norfolk	
XT803	WS Sioux AH1 [Y]	Privately owned, Panshanger	
XT852	McD YF-4M Phantom FGR2	DERA West Freugh Fire Section	
XT863	McD F-4K Phantom FG1 <ff>	Privately owned, Cowes, IOW	
XT864	McD F-4K Phantom FG1 (8998M/ XT684) [BJ]	RAF Leuchars on display	
XT867	McD F-4K Phantom FG1 (9064M) [BH]	RAF Leuchars BDRT	
XT891	McD F-4M Phantom FGR2 (9136M) [Z]	RAF Coningsby, at main gate	
XT903	McD F-4M Phantom FGR2 <ff>	RAF Museum, stored Wyton	
XT905	McD F-4M Phantom FGR2 [P]	RAF North Luffenham Training Area	
XT907	McD F-4M Phantom FGR2 (9151M) [W]	DEODS, Chattenden, Kent	
XT914	McD F-4M Phantom FGR2	RAF Brampton, Cambs, on display	
XV101	BAC VC10 C1K	RAF No 10 Sqn, Brize Norton	
XV102	BAC VC10 C1K	RAF No 10 Sqn, Brize Norton	
XV103	BAC VC10 C1K	RAF St Athan, stored	
XV104	BAC VC10 C1K	RAF No 10 Sqn, Brize Norton	
XV105	BAC VC10 C1K	RAF No 10 Sqn, Brize Norton	
XV106	BAC VC10 C1K	RAF No 10 Sqn, Brize Norton	
XV107	BAC VC10 C1K	RAF No 10 Sqn, Brize Norton	
XV108	BAC VC10 C1K	RAF No 10 Sqn, Brize Norton	
XV109	BAC VC10 C1K	RAF No 10 Sqn, Brize Norton	
XV118	WS Scout AH1 (9141M)	RAF Air Movements School, Brize Norton	
XV121	WS Scout AH1 (G-BYKJ)	Privately owned, Thruxton	
XV122	WS Scout AH1 [D]	R. Military College of Science, Shrivenham	
XV123	WS Scout AH1	Privately owned, Ipswich	
XV124	WS Scout AH1 [W]	Army SEAE, Arborfield	
XV126	WS Scout AH1 (G-SCTA) [X]	Privately owned, Thruxton	
XV127	WS Scout AH1	Museum of Army Flying, Middle Wallop	
XV130	WS Scout AH1 (G-BWJW) [R]	Privately owned, Redhill	
XV131	WS Scout AH1 [Y]	AAC 70 Aircraft Workshops, Middle Wallop, BDRT	
XV134	WS Scout AH1 (G-BWLX) [P]	Privately owned, East Dereham, Norfolk	
XV136	WS Scout AH1 [X]	AAC Netheravon, on display	
XV137	WS Scout AH1 (G-CRUM)	Privately owned, Glenrothes	
XV138	WS Scout AH1	Privately owned, East Dereham, Norfolk	
XV139	WS Scout AH1	Yeovil College	
XV140	WS Scout AH1 (G-KAXL) [K]	Kennet Aviation, Cranfield	
XV141	WS Scout AH1	REME Museum, Arborfield	
XV147	HS Nimrod MR1(mod) (fuselage)	BAE Systems, Warton	
XV148	HS Nimrod MR1(mod) <ff>	Privately owned, Guildford	
XV161	HS Buccaneer S2B (9117M) <ff>	Privately owned, Birtley, Tyne & Wear	
XV165	HS Buccaneer S2B <ff>	Gloucestershire Avn Coll, stored Glos	
XV168	HS Buccaneer S2B	BAE Systems Brough, on display	
XV176	Lockheed C-130K Hercules C3	RAF Lyneham Transport Wing	
XV177	Lockheed C-130K Hercules C3	RAF Lyneham Transport Wing	
XV178	Lockheed C-130K Hercules C1	To LMASC, USA, 26 November 2000	
XV179	Lockheed C-130K Hercules C1	RAF Lyneham Transport Wing	
XV181	Lockheed C-130K Hercules C1	RAF Lyneham Transport Wing	
XV182	Lockheed C-130K Hercules C1	To LMASC, USA, 12 November 2000	
XV183	Lockheed C-130K Hercules C3	RAF Lyneham Transport Wing	
XV184	Lockheed C-130K Hercules C1	RAF Lyneham Transport Wing	
XV185	Lockheed C-130K Hercules C1	RAF Lyneham Transport Wing	
XV186	Lockheed C-130K Hercules C1	RAF Lyneham Transport Wing	
XV187	Lockheed C-130K Hercules C1	RAF Lyneham Transport Wing	
XV188	Lockheed C-130K Hercules C3	RAF Lyneham Transport Wing	
XV189	Lockheed C-130K Hercules C3	To LMASC, USA, 10 December 2000	
XV190	Lockheed C-130K Hercules C3	RAF Lyneham Transport Wing	
XV191	Lockheed C-130K Hercules C1	RAF Lyneham Transport Wing	
XV192	Lockheed C-130K Hercules C1	RAF Lyneham Transport Wing	
XV195	Lockheed C-130K Hercules C1	RAF Lyneham Transport Wing	
XV196	Lockheed C-130K Hercules C1	RAF Lyneham Transport Wing	

Notes	Serial	Type (other identity) [code]	Owner/operator, location or fate
	XV197	Lockheed C-130K Hercules C3	RAF Lyneham Transport Wing
	XV199	Lockheed C-130K Hercules C3	RAF Lyneham Transport Wing
	XV200	Lockheed C-130K Hercules C1	RAF Lyneham Transport Wing
	XV201	Lockheed C-130K Hercules C1K	RAF, stored Cambridge
	XV202	Lockheed C-130K Hercules C3	RAF Lyneham Transport Wing
	XV203	Lockheed C-130K Hercules C1K	*To Sri Lanka as CR-880,*
			6 September 2000
	XV205	Lockheed C-130K Hercules C1	RAF Lyneham Transport Wing
	XV206	Lockheed C-130K Hercules C1	RAF Lyneham Transport Wing
	XV207	Lockheed C-130K Hercules C3	*To LMASC, USA, 26 November 2000*
	XV208	Lockheed C-130K Hercules W2	DPA/MRF, DERA Boscombe Down
	XV209	Lockheed C-130K Hercules C3	RAF Lyneham Transport Wing
	XV210	Lockheed C-130K Hercules C1	*To LMASC, USA, 10 December 2000*
	XV211	Lockheed C-130K Hercules C1	RAF Lyneham Transport Wing
	XV212	Lockheed C-130K Hercules C3	RAF Lyneham Transport Wing
	XV213	Lockheed C-130K Hercules C1K	*To Sri Lanka as CR-881, 15 March 2000*
	XV214	Lockheed C-130K Hercules C3	RAF Lyneham Transport Wing
	XV215	Lockheed C-130K Hercules C1	*To LMASC, USA, 12 November 2000*
	XV217	Lockheed C-130K Hercules C3	RAF Lyneham Transport Wing
	XV218	Lockheed C-130K Hercules C1	*To LMASC, USA, 10 December 2000*
	XV219	Lockheed C-130K Hercules C3	*To LMASC, USA, 26 November 2000*
	XV220	Lockheed C-130K Hercules C3	RAF Lyneham Transport Wing
	XV221	Lockheed C-130K Hercules C3	RAF Lyneham Transport Wing
	XV222	Lockheed C-130K Hercules C3	RAF Lyneham Transport Wing
	XV223	Lockheed C-130K Hercules C3	*To LMASC, USA, 12 November 2000*
	XV226	HS Nimrod MR2	RAF Kinloss MR Wing
	XV227	HS Nimrod MR2	RAF Kinloss MR Wing
	XV228	HS Nimrod MR2	RAF Kinloss MR Wing
	XV229	HS Nimrod MR2	RAF Kinloss MR Wing
	XV230	HS Nimrod MR2	RAF Kinloss MR Wing
	XV231	HS Nimrod MR2	RAF Kinloss MR Wing
	XV232	HS Nimrod MR2	RAF Kinloss MR Wing
	XV233	HS Nimrod MR2	*To be converted to Nimrod MRA4 ZJ520*
	XV235	HS Nimrod MR2	RAF Kinloss MR Wing
	XV236	HS Nimrod MR2	RAF Kinloss MR Wing
	XV237	HS Nimrod MR2 <ff>	Privately owned, St Austell
	XV238	HS Nimrod <R> (parts of G-ALYW)	RAF EPTT, St Athan
	XV240	HS Nimrod MR2 [CXX]	RAF Kinloss MR Wing
	XV241	HS Nimrod MR2	RAF Kinloss MR Wing
	XV243	HS Nimrod MR2	RAF Kinloss MR Wing
	XV244	HS Nimrod MR2	RAF Kinloss MR Wing
	XV245	HS Nimrod MR2	RAF Kinloss MR Wing
	XV246	HS Nimrod MR2	RAF Kinloss MR Wing
	XV248	HS Nimrod MR2	RAF Kinloss MR Wing
	XV249	HS Nimrod R1	RAF No 51 Sqn, Waddington
	XV250	HS Nimrod MR2	RAF Kinloss MR Wing
	XV252	HS Nimrod MR2	RAF Kinloss MR Wing
	XV253	HS Nimrod MR2 (9118M)	RAF Kinloss, instructional use
	XV254	HS Nimrod MR2	RAF Kinloss MR Wing
	XV255	HS Nimrod MR2	RAF Kinloss MR Wing
	XV259	BAe Nimrod AEW3 <ff>	Privately owned, Carlisle
	XV260	HS Nimrod MR2	RAF Kinloss MR Wing
	XV263	BAe Nimrod AEW3P (8967M) <ff>	BAE Systems, Warton, instructional use
	XV263	BAe Nimrod AEW3P (8967M) <rf>	FR Aviation, Bournemouth
	XV268	DHC2 Beaver AL1 (G-BVER)	Privately owned
	XV277	HS P.1127(RAF)	Royal Scottish Mus'm of Flight, E Fortune
	XV279	HS P.1127(RAF) (8566M)	RAF Harrier Maintenance School,
			Wittering
	XV280	HS P.1127(RAF) <ff>	RNAS Yeovilton Fire Section
	XV290	Lockheed C-130K Hercules C3	RAF Lyneham Transport Wing
	XV291	Lockheed C-130K Hercules C1	RAF Lyneham Transport Wing
	XV292	Lockheed C-130K Hercules C1	RAF Lyneham Transport Wing
	XV293	Lockheed C-130K Hercules C1	RAF Lyneham Transport Wing
	XV294	Lockheed C-130K Hercules C3	RAF Lyneham Transport Wing
	XV295	Lockheed C-130K Hercules C1	RAF Lyneham Transport Wing
	XV296	Lockheed C-130K Hercules C1K	RAF, stored Cambridge
	XV297	Lockheed C-130K Hercules C1	RAF Lyneham Transport Wing
	XV299	Lockheed C-130K Hercules C3	RAF Lyneham Transport Wing
	XV300	Lockheed C-130K Hercules C1	RAF Lyneham Transport Wing
	XV301	Lockheed C-130K Hercules C3	RAF Lyneham Transport Wing
	XV302	Lockheed C-130K Hercules C3	RAF Lyneham Transport Wing
	XV303	Lockheed C-130K Hercules C3	RAF Lyneham Transport Wing
	XV304	Lockheed C-130K Hercules C3	RAF Lyneham Transport Wing

Serial	Type (other identity) [code]	Owner/operator, location or fate	Notes
XV305	Lockheed C-130K Hercules C3	RAF Lyneham Transport Wing	
XV306	Lockheed C-130K Hercules C1	RAF Lyneham Transport Wing	
XV307	Lockheed C-130K Hercules C3	RAF Lyneham Transport Wing	
XV328	BAC Lightning T5 <ff>	Phoenix Aviation, Bruntingthorpe	
XV332	HS Buccaneer S2B (9232M)	RAF Marham Fire Section	
XV333	HS Buccaneer S2B [234/H]	FAA Museum, RNAS Yeovilton	
XV337	HS Buccaneer S2C (8852M) <ff>	Privately owned, Diseworth, Leics	
XV344	HS Buccaneer S2C	DERA Farnborough, on display	
XV350	HS Buccaneer S2B	East Midlands Airport Aeropark	
XV352	HS Buccaneer S2B <ff>	RAF Manston History Museum	
XV353	HS Buccaneer S2B (9144M) <ff>	*Currently not known*	
XV359	HS Buccaneer S2B [035/R]	RNAS Culdrose, on display	
XV361	HS Buccaneer S2B	Ulster Aviation Society, Langford Lodge	
XV370	Sikorsky SH-3D [260]	RN AESS, *HMS Sultan*, Gosport	
XV371	WS61 Sea King HAS1(DB) [261]	RN AESS, *HMS Sultan*, Gosport	
XV372	WS61 Sea King HAS1	RAF St Mawgan, instructional use	
XV399	McD F-4M Phantom FGR2 <ff>	Privately owned, Stock, Essex	
XV401	McD F-4M Phantom FGR2 [I]	Boscombe Down Museum	
XV406	McD F-4M Phantom FGR2 (9098M) [CK]	Solway Aviation Society, Carlisle Airport	
XV408	McD F-4M Phantom FGR2 (9165M) [Z]	RAF Halton	
XV411	McD F-4M Phantom FGR2 (9103M) [L]	MoD FSCTE, Manston	
XV415	McD F-4M Phantom FGR2 (9163M) [E]	RAF Boulmer, on display	
XV420	McD F-4M Phantom FGR2 (9247M) [BT]	RAF Neatishead, at main gate	
XV423	McD F-4M Phantom FGR2 [Y]	RAF Leeming, BDRT	
XV424	McD F-4M Phantom FGR2 (9152M) [I]	RAF Museum, Hendon	
XV426	McD F-4M Phantom FGR2 <ff>	Privately owned, RAF Coltishall	
XV426	McD F-4M Phantom FGR2 [P] <ff>	RAF Coningsby, BDRT	
XV435	McD F-4M Phantom FGR2 [R]	DERA Llanbedr Fire Section	
XV460	McD F-4M Phantom FGR2 <ff>	No 2214 Sqn ATC, Usworth	
XV465	McD F-4M Phantom FGR2 [S]	RAF Leeming, decoy	
XV467	McD F-4M Phantom FGR2 (9158M) [F]	*Scrapped at Benbecula, April 2000*	
XV468	McD F-4M Phantom FGR2 (9159M) [H]	RAF Woodvale, on display	
XV474	McD F-4M Phantom FGR2 [T]	The Old Flying Machine Company, Duxford	
XV490	McD F-4M Phantom FGR2 <ff>	Privately owned, Nantwich	
XV497	McD F-4M Phantom FGR2 [W]	RAF Coningsby, decoy	
XV498	McD F-4M Phantom FGR2 (XV500/9113M) [U]	RAF St Athan, on display	
XV499	McD F-4M Phantom FGR2	RAF Leeming, WLT	
XV577	McD F-4K Phantom FG1 (9065M) [AM]	RAF Leuchars, BDRT	
XV581	McD F-4K Phantom FG1 (9070M) <ff>	No 2481 Sqn ATC, Bridge of Don	
XV582	McD F-4K Phantom FG1 (9066M) [M]	RAF Leuchars, on display	
XV586	McD F-4K Phantom FG1 (9067M) [AJ]	RAF Leuchars, on display	
XV591	McD F-4K Phantom FG1 <ff>	RAF Museum, Cosford	
XV625	WS Wasp HAS1 [471]	RN, Prestwick	
XV629	WS Wasp HAS1	AAC Middle Wallop, BDRT	
XV631	WS Wasp HAS1 (fuselage)	DERA Acoustics Dept, Farnborough	
XV642	WS61 Sea King HAS2A [259]	RN AESS, *HMS Sultan*, Gosport	
XV643	WS61 Sea King HAS6 [262]	RN AESS, *HMS Sultan*, Gosport	
XV647	WS61 Sea King HU5 [820/CU]	DARA, RNAY Fleetlands	
XV648	WS61 Sea King HU5 [708/PW]	RN No 819 Sqn, Prestwick	
XV649	WS61 Sea King AEW2 [184/L]	RN No 849 Sqn, B Flt, Culdrose	
XV650	WS61 Sea King AEW2 [185/N]	RN No 849 Sqn, A Flt, Culdrose	
XV651	WS61 Sea King HU5 [599/CU]	DARA, RNAY Fleetlands	
XV653	WS61 Sea King HAS6 [513/CU]	RN No 810 Sqn, Culdrose	
XV654	WS61 Sea King HAS6 [705] (wreck)	RN AESS, *HMS Sultan*, Gosport	
XV655	WS61 Sea King HAS6 [270/N]	RN, stored, *HMS Sultan*, Gosport	
XV656	WS61 Sea King AEW2 [187]	RN No 849 Sqn, A Flt, Culdrose	
XV657	WS61 Sea King HAS5 (*ZA135*) [32/DD]	SFDO, RNAS Culdrose	

Notes	Serial	Type (other identity) [code]	Owner/operator, location or fate
	XV659	WS61 Sea King HAS6 [510/CU]	RN, stored, *HMS Sultan*, Gosport
	XV660	WS61 Sea King HAS6 [269/N]	RN, stored, *HMS Sultan*, Gosport
	XV661	WS61 Sea King HU5 [821]	RN No 771 Sqn, Culdrose
	XV663	WS61 Sea King HAS6	RN, stored, *HMS Sultan*, Gosport
	XV664	WS61 Sea King AEW2 [186/N]	RN No 849 Sqn, A Flt, Culdrose
	XV665	WS61 Sea King HAS6 [507/CU]	RN No 849 Sqn, A Flt, Culdrose
	XV666	WS61 Sea King HU5 [823/CU]	RN AMG, Culdrose
	XV669	WS61 Sea King HAS1 [10]	Privately owned, Gosport
	XV670	WS61 Sea King HU5 [588]	DARA, RNAY Fleetlands
	XV671	WS61 Sea King AEW2 [188/N]	RN No 849 Sqn, A Flt, Culdrose
	XV672	WS61 Sea King AEW7 [182/L]	DPA/GKN Westland, Weston-super-Mare (conversion)
	XV673	WS61 Sea King HU5 [597]	DARA, RNAY Fleetlands
	XV674	WS61 Sea King HAS6 [015/L]	RN No 820 Sqn, Culdrose
	XV675	WS61 Sea King HAS6 [701/PW]	DARA, RNAY Fleetlands
	XV676	WS61 Sea King HAS6 [506]	RN No 810 Sqn, Culdrose
	XV677	WS61 Sea King HAS6 [269]	RN, stored, *HMS Sultan*, Gosportt
	XV696	WS61 Sea King HAS6 [267/N]	RN AMG, Culdrose
	XV697	WS61 Sea King AEW2 [187]	RN AMG, Culdrose
	XV699	WS61 Sea King HU5	RN No 819 Sqn, Prestwick
	XV700	WS61 Sea King HAS6 [505/CU]	RN No 810 Sqn, Culdrose
	XV701	WS61 Sea King HAS6 [268/N]	RN, stored, *HMS Sultan*, Gosport
	XV703	WS61 Sea King HAS6 [706/PW]	RN No 819 Sqn, Prestwick
	XV704	WS61 Sea King AEW2 [181/CU]	RN No 849 Sqn, HQ Flt, Culdrose
	XV705	WS61 Sea King HU5 [821/CU]	RN, stored, *HMS Sultan*, Gosport
	XV706	WS61 Sea King HAS6 [011/L]	RN No 820 Sqn, Culdrose
	XV707	WS61 Sea King AEW7	DPA/GKN Westland, Weston-super-Mare (conversion)
	XV708	WS61 Sea King HAS6 [501/CU]	RN No 810 Sqn, Culdrose
	XV709	WS61 Sea King HAS6 [505/CU]	RN, stored, *HMS Sultan*, Gosportt
	XV710	WS61 Sea King HAS6 [264]	RN AESS, *HMS Sultan*, Gosport
	XV711	WS61 Sea King HAS6 [515/CT]	RN No 810 Sqn, B Flt, Culdrose
	XV712	WS61 Sea King HAS6 [266]	RN AESS, *HMS Sultan*, Gosport
	XV713	WS61 Sea King HAS6 [018]	RN, stored, *HMS Sultan*, Gosport
	XV714	WS61 Sea King AEW2 [180]	RN No 849 Sqn, HQ Flt, Culdrose
	XV720	WS58 Wessex HC2	RN AESS, *HMS Sultan*, Gosport
	XV721	WS58 Wessex HC2 [H]	RAF No 72 Sqn, Aldergrove
	XV722	WS58 Wessex HC2 [WH]	*Scrapped, 2000*
	XV723	WS58 Wessex HC2 [Q]	RAF No 72 Sqn, Aldergrove
	XV724	WS58 Wessex HC2	RAF, stored RNAY Fleetlands
	XV725	WS58 Wessex HC2 [C]	RN AESS, *HMS Sultan*, Gosport
	XV726	WS58 Wessex HC2 [J]	RAF No 72 Sqn, Aldergrove
	XV728	WS58 Wessex HC2 [A]	Newark Air Museum, Winthorpe
	XV729	WS58 Wessex HC2	Privately owned, Redhill
	XV730	WS58 Wessex HC2 [*Clubs*]	RAF No 84 Sqn, Akrotiri
	XV731	WS58 Wessex HC2 [Y]	Privately owned, Redhill
	XV732	WS58 Wessex HCC4	RAF, stored Shawbury
	XV733	WS58 Wessex HCC4	RAF, stored Shawbury
	XV741	HS Harrier GR3 [1]	SFDO, RNAS Culdrose
	XV744	HS Harrier GR3 (9167M) [3K]	R. Military College of Science, Shrivenham
	XV747	HS Harrier GR3 (8979M) (fuselage)	*Destroyed at Hucknall, 1998*
	XV748	HS Harrier GR3 [3D]	Yorkshire Air Museum, Elvington
	XV751	HS Harrier GR3	Gatwick Aviation Museum, Charlwood, Surrey
	XV752	HS Harrier GR3 (9078M) [B,HF]	RAF No 1 SoTT, Cosford
	XV753	HS Harrier GR3 (9075M) [53]	SFDO, RNAS Culdrose
	XV755	HS Harrier GR3 [M]	RNAS Yeovilton Fire Section
	XV759	HS Harrier GR3 [O] <ff>	Privately owned, Luton, Beds
	XV779	HS Harrier GR3 (8931M) [01,A]	RAF Wittering on display
	XV783	HS Harrier GR3 [83]	SFDO, RNAS Culdrose
	XV784	HS Harrier GR3 (8909M) <ff>	Boscombe Down Museum
	XV786	HS Harrier GR3 <ff>	RNAS Culdrose
	XV786	HS Harrier GR3 [S] <rf>	RN, Predannack Fire School
	XV798	HS Harrier GR1(mod)	Bristol Aero Collection, stored Kemble
	XV804	HS Harrier GR3 (9280M) [O]	RAF North Luffenham Training Area
	XV808	HS Harrier GR3 (9076M) [08]	SFDO, RNAS Culdrose
	XV810	HS Harrier GR3 (9038M) [K]	Privately owned, Bruntingthorpe
	XV814	DH106 Comet 4 (G-APDF) <ff>	Privately owned, Chipping Campden
	XV863	HS Buccaneer S2B (9115M/ 9139M/9145M) [S]	RAF Lossiemouth, on display
	XV864	HS Buccaneer S2B (9234M)	MoD FSCTE, Manston
	XV865	HS Buccaneer S2B (9226M)	Privately owned, Duxford

Serial	Type (other identity) [code]	Owner/operator, location or fate	Notes
XV867	HS Buccaneer S2B <ff>	N Yorks Aircraft Recovery Centre, Chop Gate	
XW175	HS Harrier T4(VAAC)	DPA/AFD, DERA Boscombe Down	
XW198	WS Puma HC1	RAF No 72 Sqn, Aldergrove	
XW199	WS Puma HC1	DPA/GKN Westland, Weston-super-Mare (on repair)	
XW200	WS Puma HC1	RAF No 33 Sqn, Benson	
XW201	WS Puma HC1	RAF No 230 Sqn, Aldergrove	
XW202	WS Puma HC1	RAF No 33 Sqn, Benson	
XW204	WS Puma HC1	RAF No 33 Sqn, Benson	
XW206	WS Puma HC1	RAF No 72 Sqn, Aldergrove	
XW207	WS Puma HC1	*Crashed 19 April 2000, Hipswell Moor*	
XW208	WS Puma HC1	RAF No 230 Sqn, Aldergrove	
XW209	WS Puma HC1 [AE]	RAF No 72 Sqn, Aldergrove	
XW210	WS Puma HC1 (comp XW215)	RAF No 33 Sqn, Benson	
XW211	WS Puma HC1	RAF No 33 Sqn, Benson	
XW212	WS Puma HC1	RAF No 230 Sqn, Aldergrove	
XW213	WS Puma HC1	RAF No 230 Sqn, Aldergrove	
XW214	WS Puma HC1	RAF No 33 Sqn, Benson	
XW216	WS Puma HC1	RAF No 33 Sqn, Benson	
XW217	WS Puma HC1	RAF No 33 Sqn, Benson	
XW218	WS Puma HC1	RAF No 33 Sqn, Benson	
XW219	WS Puma HC1	RAF No 230 Sqn, Aldergrove	
XW220	WS Puma HC1	RAF No 230 Sqn, Aldergrove	
XW221	WS Puma HC1	RAF No 72 Sqn, Aldergrove	
XW222	WS Puma HC1	RAF No 33 Sqn, Benson	
XW223	WS Puma HC1	RAF No 33 Sqn, Benson	
XW224	WS Puma HC1	RAF No 230 Sqn, Aldergrove	
XW225	WS Puma HC1	RAF	
XW226	WS Puma HC1	RAF No 230 Sqn, Aldergrove	
XW227	WS Puma HC1	RAF No 230 Sqn, Aldergrove	
XW229	WS Puma HC1	RAF No 33 Sqn, Benson	
XW231	WS Puma HC1	RAF No 230 Sqn, Aldergrove	
XW232	WS Puma HC1	RAF No 33 Sqn, Benson	
XW234	WS Puma HC1	RAF No 230 Sqn, Aldergrove	
XW235	WS Puma HC1	RAF No 33 Sqn, Benson	
XW236	WS Puma HC1	RAF No 33 Sqn, Benson	
XW237	WS Puma HC1	RAF No 33 Sqn, Benson	
XW241	Sud SA330E Puma	DERA Avionics & Sensors Dept, Farnborough	
XW264	HS Harrier T2 <ff>	Gloucestershire Avn Coll, stored Glos	
XW265	HS Harrier T4A [W]	RAF No 1 SoTT, Cosford	
XW267	HS Harrier T4 [SA]	Territorial Army, Beeston, Notts	
XW269	HS Harrier T4 [BD]	RAF, stored DERA Boscombe Down	
XW270	HS Harrier T4 (fuselage)	Phoenix Aviation, Bruntingthorpe	
XW271	HS Harrier T4 [71]	SFDO, RNAS Culdrose	
XW272	HS Harrier T4 (8783M) (fuselage) (comp XV281)	BAE Systems Samlesbury, GI use	
XW276	Aérospatiale SA341 Gazelle (F-ZWRI)	Newark Air Museum, Winthorpe	
XW281	WS Scout AH1 (G-BYNZ) [U]	Privately owned, Thruxton (wreck)	
XW283	WS Scout AH1 [U]	RM, stored Yeovilton	
XW284	WS Scout AH1 [A] (fuselage)	Privately owned, Ipswich	
XW289	BAC Jet Provost T5A (G-BVXT/ G-JPVA) [73]	Kennet Aviation, Cranfield	
XW290	BAC Jet Provost T5A (9199M) [41,MA]	RAF No 1 SoTT, Cosford	
XW292	BAC Jet Provost T5A (9128M) [32]	RAF No 1 SoTT, Cosford	
XW293	BAC Jet Provost T5 (G-BWCS) [Z]	Privately owned, Sandtoft	
XW294	BAC Jet Provost T5A (9129M) [45]	RAF No 1 SoTT, Cosford	
XW299	BAC Jet Provost T5A (9146M) [60,MB]	RAF No 1 SoTT, Cosford	
XW301	BAC Jet Provost T5A (9147M) [63,MC]	RAF No 1 SoTT, Cosford	
XW302	BAC Jet Provost T5B (N166A/ G-BYED)	*Repainted as G-BYED*	
XW303	BAC Jet Provost T5A (9119M) [127]	RAF No 1 SoTT, Cosford	
XW304	BAC Jet Provost T5 (9172M) [MD]	RAF No 1 SoTT, Cosford	
XW309	BAC Jet Provost T5 (9179M) [V,ME]	RAF No 1 SoTT, Cosford	

Notes	Serial	Type (other identity) [code]	Owner/operator, location or fate
	XW311	BAC Jet Provost T5 (9180M) [W,MF]	RAF No 1 SoTT, Cosford
	XW312	BAC Jet Provost T5A (9109M) [64]	RAF No 1 SoTT, Cosford
	XW315	BAC Jet Provost T5A <ff>	Privately owned, Wolverhampton
	XW318	BAC Jet Provost T5A (9190M) [78,MG]	RAF No 1 SoTT, Cosford
	XW320	BAC Jet Provost T5A (9015M) [71]	RAF No 1 SoTT, Cosford
	XW321	BAC Jet Provost T5A (9154M) [62,MH]	RAF No 1 SoTT, Cosford
	XW323	BAC Jet Provost T5A (9166M) [86]	RAF Museum, Hendon
	XW324	BAC Jet Provost T5 (G-BWSG)	Privately owned, North Weald
	XW325	BAC Jet Provost T5B (G-BWGF) [E]	Privately owned, Woodford
	XW327	BAC Jet Provost T5A (9130M) [62]	RAF No 1 SoTT, Cosford
	XW328	BAC Jet Provost T5A (9177M) [75,MI]	RAF No 1 SoTT, Cosford
	XW330	BAC Jet Provost T5A (9195M) [82,MJ]	RAF No 1 SoTT, Cosford
	XW333	BAC Jet Provost T5A (G-BVTC)	Global Aviation, Humberside]
	XW335	BAC Jet Provost T5A (9061M) [74]	RAF No 1 SoTT, Cosford
	XW351	BAC Jet Provost T5A (9062M) [31]	RAF No 1 SoTT, Cosford
	XW353	BAC Jet Provost T5A (9090M) [3]	RAF Cranwell, on display
	XW358	BAC Jet Provost T5A (9181M) [59,MK]	RAF No 1 SoTT, Cosford
	XW360	BAC Jet Provost T5A (9153M) [61,ML]	RAF No 1 SoTT, Cosford
	XW361	BAC Jet Provost T5A (9192M) [81,MM]	RAF No 1 SoTT, Cosford
	XW363	BAC Jet Provost T5A [36]	No .... Sqn ATC, Samlesbury
	XW364	BAC Jet Provost T5A (9188M) [35,MN]	RAF No 1 SoTT, Cosford
	XW365	BAC Jet Provost T5A (9018M) [73]	RAF No 1 SoTT, Cosford
	XW366	BAC Jet Provost T5A (9097M) [75]	RAF No 1 SoTT, Cosford
	XW367	BAC Jet Provost T5A (9193M) [64,MO]	RAF No 1 SoTT, Cosford
	XW370	BAC Jet Provost T5A (9196M) [72,MP]	RAF No 1 SoTT, Cosford
	XW375	BAC Jet Provost T5A (9149M) [52]	RAF No 1 SoTT, Cosford
	XW404	BAC Jet Provost T5A (9049M)	DARA Training School, RAF St Athan
	XW405	BAC Jet Provost T5A (9187M) [J,MQ]	RAF No 1 SoTT, Cosford
	XW409	BAC Jet Provost T5A (9047M)	DARA Training School, RAF St Athan
	XW410	BAC Jet Provost T5A (9125M) [80,MR]	RAF No 1 SoTT, Cosford
	XW413	BAC Jet Provost T5A (9126M) [69]	RAF No 1 SoTT, Cosford
	XW416	BAC Jet Provost T5A (9191M) [84,MS]	RAF No 1 SoTT, Cosford
	XW418	BAC Jet Provost T5A (9173M) [MT]	RAF No 1 SoTT, Cosford
	XW419	BAC Jet Provost T5A (9120M) [125]	RAF No 1 SoTT, Cosford
	XW420	BAC Jet Provost T5A (9194M) [83,MU]	RAF No 1 SoTT, Cosford
	XW421	BAC Jet Provost T5A (9111M) [60]	RAF No 1 SoTT, Cosford
	XW423	BAC Jet Provost T5A (G-BWUW) [14]	Privately owned, Norwich
	XW425	BAC Jet Provost T5A (9200M) [H,MV]	RAF No 1 SoTT, Cosford
	XW427	BAC Jet Provost T5A (9124M) [67]	RAF No 1 SoTT, Cosford
	XW430	BAC Jet Provost T5A (9176M) [77,MW]	RAF No 1 SoTT, Cosford
	XW432	BAC Jet Provost T5A (9127M) [76,MX]	RAF No 1 SoTT, Cosford
	XW433	BAC Jet Provost T5A (G-JPRO)	Global Aviation, Humberside]
	XW434	BAC Jet Provost T5A (9091M) [78,MY]	RAF No 1 SoTT, Cosford
	XW436	BAC Jet Provost T5A (9148M) [68]	RAF No 1 SoTT, Cosford
	XW527	HS Buccaneer S2B <ff>	Privately owned, Wittering
	XW528	HS Buccaneer S2B (8861M) [C]	RAF Coningsby Fire Section
	XW530	HS Buccaneer S2B	Buccaneer Service Station, Elgin
	XW544	HS Buccaneer S2B (8857M) [Y]	Privately owned, Shawbury
	XW547	HS Buccaneer S2B (9095M/ 9169M) [R]	RAF Museum, Cosford

Serial	Type (other identity) [code]	Owner/operator, location or fate	Notes
XW549	HS Buccaneer S2B (8860M) (fuselage)	RAF Kinloss, BDRT	
XW550	HS Buccaneer S2B <ff>	Privately owned, West Horndon, Essex	
XW566	SEPECAT Jaguar T2	DERA Avionics & Sensors Dept, Farnborough	
XW613	WS Scout AH1 (G-BXRS) [W]	Privately owned, Thruxton	
XW616	WS Scout AH1	AAC Dishforth, instructional use	
XW630	HS Harrier GR3	RNAS Yeovilton, Fire Section	
XW635	Beagle D5/180 (G-AWSW)	Privately owned, Spanhoe Lodge	
XW664	HS Nimrod R1	RAF No 51 Sqn, Waddington	
XW665	HS Nimrod R1	RAF No 51 Sqn, Waddington	
XW666	HS Nimrod R1 <ff>	Jet Avn Preservation Grp, Long Marston	
XW750	HS748 Series 107	DPA/AFD, DERA Boscombe Down	
XW763	HS Harrier GR3 (9002M/9041M) <ff>	Privately owned, Bruntingthorpe	
XW768	HS Harrier GR3 (9072M) [N]	RAF No 1 SoTT, Cosford	
XW784	Mitchell-Procter Kittiwake I (G-BBRN) [VL]	Privately owned, Compton Abbas	
XW795	WS Scout AH1	Blessingbourne Museum, Fivemiletown, Co Tyrone, NI	
XW796	WS Scout AH1	AAC Wattisham, BDRT	
XW799	WS Scout AH1 (G-BXSL)	Repainted as G-BXSL	
XW835	WS Lynx	AAC Wattisham, instructional use	
XW837	WS Lynx (fuselage)	RNAS Yeovilton Fire Section	
XW838	WS Lynx (TAD 009)	Army SEAE, Arborfield	
XW839	WS Lynx	The Helicopter Museum, Weston-super-Mare	
XW844	WS Gazelle AH1	RNAY Fleetlands Apprentice School	
XW845	WS Gazelle HT2 [47/CU]	RN, stored Shawbury	
XW846	WS Gazelle AH1 [M]	AAC No 671 Sqn/2 Regt, Middle Wallop	
XW847	WS Gazelle AH1	AAC No 665 Sqn/5 Regt, Aldergrove	
XW848	WS Gazelle AH1 [D]	AAC No 671 Sqn/2 Regt, Middle Wallop	
XW849	WS Gazelle AH1 [G]	RM No 847 Sqn, Yeovilton	
XW851	WS Gazelle AH1 [H]	RM No 847 Sqn, Yeovilton	
XW852	WS Gazelle HCC4	RAF, stored RNAY Fleetlands	
XW853	WS Gazelle HT2 [53/CU]	RN, stored Shawbury	
XW854	WS Gazelle HT2 [46/CU]	RN, stored Shawbury	
XW855	WS Gazelle HCC4	RAF, stored RNAY Fleetlands	
XW856	WS Gazelle HT2 [49/CU]	RN, stored Shawbury	
XW857	WS Gazelle HT2 [55/CU]	RN, stored Shawbury	
XW858	WS Gazelle HT3 [C]	RAF, stored Shawbury	
XW860	WS Gazelle HT2 (TAD021)	Army SEAE, Arborfield	
XW861	WS Gazelle HT2 (G-BZFJ) [52/CU]	Privately owned, Redhill	
XW862	WS Gazelle HT3 [D]	RAF, stored Shawbury	
XW863	WS Gazelle HT2 (TAD022) [42/CU]	Army SEAE, Arborfield	
XW864	WS Gazelle HT2 [54/CU]	RN, stored Shawbury	
XW865	WS Gazelle AH1 [C]	AAC No 671 Sqn/2 Regt, Middle Wallop	
XW866	WS Gazelle HT3 (G-BXTH) [E]	Flightline Ltd, Southend	
XW868	WS Gazelle HT2 [50/CU]	RN, stored Shawbury	
XW870	WS Gazelle HT3 [F]	RAF, stored Shawbury (damaged)	
XW871	WS Gazelle HT2 [44/CU]	RN, stored Shawbury	
XW884	WS Gazelle HT2 (G-BZDV) [41/CU]	Privately owned, Stapleford Tawney	
XW885	WS Gazelle AH1	AAC, stored Shawbury	
XW887	WS Gazelle HT2 [FL]	RN, stored Shawbury	
XW888	WS Gazelle AH1 (TAD017)	Army SEAE, Arborfield	
XW889	WS Gazelle AH1 (TAD018)	Army SEAE, Arborfield	
XW890	WS Gazelle HT2	RNAS Yeovilton, on display	
XW892	WS Gazelle AH1 [C]	AAC, stored Shawbury	
XW893	WS Gazelle AH1 <ff>	AAC, stored Shawbury	
XW894	WS Gazelle HT2 [37/CU]	RN, stored Shawbury	
XW895	WS Gazelle HT2 (G-BXZD) [51/CU]	Privately owned, Redhill	
XW897	WS Gazelle AH1 [Y]	AAC No 658 Sqn/7 Regt, Netheravon	
XW898	WS Gazelle HT3 [G]	RAF, stored Shawbury	
XW899	WS Gazelle AH1 [Z]	AAC No 658 Sqn/7 Regt, Netheravon	
XW900	WS Gazelle AH1 (TAD900)	Army SEAE, Arborfield	
XW902	WS Gazelle HT3 [H]	RAF, stored Shawbury	
XW903	WS Gazelle AH1	AAC, stored Shawbury	
XW904	WS Gazelle AH1 [H]	AAC No 666(V) Sqn/7 Regt, Netheravon	
XW906	WS Gazelle HT3 [J]	DERA Boscombe Down, Apprentice School	
XW907	WS Gazelle HT2 [48/CU]	RN, stored Shawbury	
XW908	WS Gazelle AH1 [A]	AAC No 666(V) Sqn/7 Regt, Netheravon	
XW909	WS Gazelle AH1	AAC No 656 Sqn/9 Regt, Dishforth	

Notes	Serial	Type (other identity) [code]	Owner/operator, location or fate
	XW910	WS Gazelle HT3 (G-BXZE) [K]	Privately owned, Redhill
	XW911	WS Gazelle AH1 [H]	AAC, stored Shawbury
	XW912	WS Gazelle AH1 (TAD019)	Army SEAE, Arborfield
	XW913	WS Gazelle AH1	AAC No 662 Sqn/3 Regt, Wattisham
	XW917	HS Harrier GR3 (8975M)	RAF Cottesmore, at main gate
	XW919	HS Harrier GR3 [W]	R. Military College of Science, Shrivenham
	XW922	HS Harrier GR3 (8885M)	MoD FSCTE, Manston
	XW923	HS Harrier GR3 (8724M) <ff>	RAF Wittering, Fire Section
	XW924	HS Harrier GR3 (9073M) [G]	RAF Cottesmore, on display
	XW934	HS Harrier T4 [Y]	DPA, DERA Farnborough (wfu)
	XW986	HS Buccaneer S2B	Delta Jets, Kemble
	XX105	BAC 1-11/201AC (G-ASJD)	DPA/AFD, DERA Boscombe Down
	XX108	SEPECAT Jaguar GR1A	DPA/BAE Systems, Warton
	XX109	SEPECAT Jaguar GR1 (8918M) [US]	RAF Coltishall, ground instruction
	XX110	SEPECAT Jaguar GR1 (8955M) [EP]	RAF No 1 SoTT, Cosford
	XX110	SEPECAT Jaguar GR1 <R> (BAPC 169)	RAF No 1 SoTT, Cosford
	XX112	SEPECAT Jaguar GR3 [EA]	RAF No 6 Sqn, Coltishall
	XX115	SEPECAT Jaguar GR1 (8821M) (fuselage)	RAF No 1 SoTT, Cosford
	XX116	SEPECAT Jaguar GR3A	RAF AWC/SAOEU, DERA Boscombe Down
	XX117	SEPECAT Jaguar GR3 [A]	RAF No 16(R) Sqn, Coltishall
	XX119	SEPECAT Jaguar GR3A (8898M) [GD]	RAF No 54 Sqn, Coltishall
	XX121	SEPECAT Jaguar GR1 (92..M) [EQ]	Privately owned, Charlwood, Surrey
	XX139	SEPECAT Jaguar T4 [PT]	RAF No 16(R) Sqn, Coltishall
	XX140	SEPECAT Jaguar T2 (9008M) [D,JJ]	*Scrapped at Faygate, 2000*
	XX141	SEPECAT Jaguar T2A [T]	AMIF, RAFC Cranwell
	XX143	SEPECAT Jaguar T2A [X] (wreck)	Privately owned, Charlwood, Surrey
	XX144	SEPECAT Jaguar T2A [U]	RAF, stored Shawbury
	XX145	SEPECAT Jaguar T2A	DPA/AFD/ETPS, DERA Boscombe Down
	XX146	SEPECAT Jaguar T4 [GT]	RAF AMF, Coltishall
	XX150	SEPECAT Jaguar T4 [W]	RAF No 16(R) Sqn, Coltishall
	XX153	WS Lynx AH1	AAC Wattisham, instructional use
	XX154	HS Hawk T1	DPA, DERA Llanbedr
	XX156	HS Hawk T1	RAF No 4 FTS/*208(R) Sqn*, Valley
	XX157	HS Hawk T1A	RN FRADU, Culdrose
	XX158	HS Hawk T1A	RAF No 4 FTS, Valley
	XX159	HS Hawk T1A	RAF No 4 FTS/*208(R) Sqn*, Valley
	XX160	HS Hawk T1	RAF No 4 FTS/*208(R) Sqn*, Valley
	XX161	HS Hawk T1W	RAF No 4 FTS/*208(R) Sqn*, Valley
	XX162	HS Hawk T1	RAF CAM, DERA Boscombe Down
	XX163	HS Hawk T1 (9243M) [PH] (wreck)	Phoenix Aviation, Bruntingthorpe
	XX165	HS Hawk T1	RAF No 4 FTS/*208(R) Sqn*, Valley
	XX167	HS Hawk T1W	RAF No 4 FTS/*208(R) Sqn*, Valley
	XX168	HS Hawk T1	RAF No 4 FTS/*208(R) Sqn*, Valley
	XX169	HS Hawk T1	RAF No 4 FTS/*208(R) Sqn*, Valley
	XX170	HS Hawk T1	RN FRADU, Culdrose
	XX171	HS Hawk T1	RN FRADU, Culdrose
	XX172	HS Hawk T1	RAF No 4 FTS/*208(R) Sqn*, Valley
	XX173	HS Hawk T1	RAF No 4 FTS, Valley
	XX174	HS Hawk T1	RAF No 4 FTS/*208(R) Sqn*, Valley
	XX175	HS Hawk T1	RAF No 4 FTS/*208(R) Sqn*, Valley
	XX176	HS Hawk T1W	RAF No 4 FTS, Valley
	XX177	HS Hawk T1	RAF No 4 FTS/*208(R) Sqn*, Valley
	XX178	HS Hawk T1W	RAF No 4 FTS, Valley
	XX179	HS Hawk T1W	RAF No 4 FTS, Valley
	XX181	HS Hawk T1W	RAF No 4 FTS, Valley
	XX183	HS Hawk T1	RAF No 4 FTS/*208(R) Sqn*, Valley
	XX184	HS Hawk T1	RAF No 4 FTS/*19(R) Sqn*, Valley
	XX185	HS Hawk T1	RAF No 4 FTS, Valley
	XX187	HS Hawk T1A	RN FRADU, Culdrose
	XX188	HS Hawk T1A	RAF No 4 FTS, Valley
	XX189	HS Hawk T1A	RAF No 4 FTS, Valley
	XX190	HS Hawk T1A	RAF No 4 FTS/*19(R) Sqn*, Valley
	XX191	HS Hawk T1A	RAF No 4 FTS/*19(R) Sqn*, Valley
	XX194	HS Hawk T1A [CO]	RAF No 100 Sqn/JFACSTU, Leeming

Serial	Type (other identity) [code]	Owner/operator, location or fate	Notes
XX195	HS Hawk T1W	RAF No 4 FTS, Valley	
XX196	HS Hawk T1A	RAF No 4 FTS, Valley	
XX198	HS Hawk T1A	RAF No 4 FTS, Valley	
XX199	HS Hawk T1A	RAF No 4 FTS, Valley	
XX200	HS Hawk T1A [CF]	RAF No 100 Sqn, Leeming	
XX201	HS Hawk T1A	RN FRADU, Culdrose	
XX202	HS Hawk T1A	DARA, RAF St Athan	
XX203	HS Hawk T1A	RAF No 4 FTS, Valley	
XX204	HS Hawk T1A	RAF No 4 FTS/208(R) Sqn, Valley	
XX205	HS Hawk T1A	RAF No 4 FTS, Valley	
XX217	HS Hawk T1A [CC]	RAF No 100 Sqn, Leeming	
XX218	HS Hawk T1A	RAF No 4 FTS/19(R) Sqn, Valley	
XX219	HS Hawk T1A [CT]	RAF No 100 Sqn/JFACSTU, Leeming	
XX220	HS Hawk T1A	RN FRADU, Culdrose	
XX221	HS Hawk T1A	RAF No 4 FTS, Valley	
XX222	HS Hawk T1A [CA]	RAF No 100 Sqn, Leeming	
XX223	HS Hawk T1 (fuselage)	Privately owned, Charlwood, Surrey	
XX224	HS Hawk T1W	RN FRADU, Culdrose	
XX225	HS Hawk T1	RAF No 4 FTS, Valley	
XX226	HS Hawk T1 [CR]	RAF No 100 Sqn, Leeming	
XX226	HS Hawk T1 <R> (XX263/ BAPC 152)	RAF EPTT, St Athan	
XX227	HS Hawk T1A	RAF Red Arrows, Scampton	
XX228	HS Hawk T1A	RAF No 4 FTS/208(R) Sqn, Valley	
XX230	HS Hawk T1A	RN FRADU, Culdrose	
XX231	HS Hawk T1W	RN FRADU, Culdrose	
XX232	HS Hawk T1	RAF No 4 FTS/19(R) Sqn, Valley	
XX233	HS Hawk T1	RAF Red Arrows, Scampton	
XX234	HS Hawk T1	RAF No 4 FTS/208(R) Sqn, Valley	
XX235	HS Hawk T1W	RAF No 4 FTS/19(R) Sqn, Valley	
XX236	HS Hawk T1W	RAF No 4 FTS, Valley	
XX237	HS Hawk T1	RAF Red Arrows, Scampton	
XX238	HS Hawk T1	RAF No 4 FTS/208(R) Sqn, Valley	
XX239	HS Hawk T1W	RAF No 4 FTS, Valley	
XX240	HS Hawk T1	RAF No 4 FTS/208(R) Sqn, Valley	
XX242	HS Hawk T1	RAF No 4 FTS, Valley	
XX244	HS Hawk T1	RAF No 4 FTS/208(R) Sqn, Valley	
XX245	HS Hawk T1	RAF No 4 FTS/208(R) Sqn, Valley	
XX246	HS Hawk T1A	RAF No 4 FTS, Valley	
XX246	HS Hawk T1A <rf>	RAF CTTS, St Athan	
XX247	HS Hawk T1A [CM]	RAF No 100 Sqn, Leeming	
XX248	HS Hawk T1A [CJ]	RAF No 100 Sqn, Leeming	
XX249	HS Hawk T1W	RAF No 4 FTS, Valley	
XX250	HS Hawk T1	RAF No 4 FTS/19(R) Sqn, Valley	
XX252	HS Hawk T1A (fuselage)	Privately owned, Charlwood	
XX253	HS Hawk T1A	RAF Red Arrows, Scampton	
XX253	HS Hawk T1 <R> (XX297/ BAPC 171)	RAF EPTT, St Athan	
XX254	HS Hawk T1A	DPA/BAE Systems, Brough	
XX254	HS Hawk T1A <R>	Privately owned, Marlow, Bucks	
XX255	HS Hawk T1A	RN FRADU, Culdrose	
XX256	HS Hawk T1A	DARA, RAF St Athan	
XX258	HS Hawk T1A	RAF No 4 FTS, Valley	
XX260	HS Hawk T1A	RAF Red Arrows, Scampton	
XX261	HS Hawk T1A	RAF No 4 FTS/208(R) Sqn, Valley	
XX263	HS Hawk T1A	RAF No 4 FTS, Valley	
XX264	HS Hawk T1A	RAF Red Arrows, Scampton	
XX265	HS Hawk T1A [CN]	RAF No 100 Sqn, Leeming	
XX266	HS Hawk T1A	RAF Red Arrows, Scampton	
XX278	HS Hawk T1A [CC]	RAF No 100 Sqn, Leeming	
XX280	HS Hawk T1A	RAF No 4 FTS, Valley	
XX281	HS Hawk T1A	RAF No 4 FTS/19(R) Sqn, Valley	
XX282	HS Hawk T1A [CQ]	Crashed, Lowick, Northumberland, 18 October 2000	
XX283	HS Hawk T1W	RAF No 4 FTS/208(R) Sqn, Valley	
XX284	HS Hawk T1A	RAF No 4 FTS, Valley	
XX285	HS Hawk T1A	RAF No 4 FTS, Valley	
XX286	HS Hawk T1A	RN FRADU, Culdrose	
XX287	HS Hawk T1A	RAF No 4 FTS/208(R) Sqn, Valley	
XX289	HS Hawk T1A [CI]	RAF No 100 Sqn, Leeming	
XX290	HS Hawk T1W	RAF No 4 FTS/208(R) Sqn, Valley	
XX292	HS Hawk T1W	RAF Red Arrows, Scampton	
XX294	HS Hawk T1	RAF Red Arrows, Scampton	

Notes	Serial	Type (other identity) [code]	Owner/operator, location or fate
	XX295	HS Hawk T1W [DA]	RAF No 4 FTS/208(R) Sqn, Valley
	XX296	HS Hawk T1	RAF No 4 FTS/19(R) Sqn, Valley
	XX299	HS Hawk T1W [CS]	RAF No 100 Sqn, Leeming
	XX301	HS Hawk T1A	RN FRADU, Culdrose
	XX303	HS Hawk T1A	RAF No 4 FTS/19(R) Sqn, Valley
	XX304	HS Hawk T1A (fuselage)	DARA, RAF St Athan
	XX306	HS Hawk T1A	RAF Red Arrows, Scampton
	XX307	HS Hawk T1	RAF Red Arrows, Scampton
	XX308	HS Hawk T1	RAF Red Arrows, Scampton
	XX309	HS Hawk T1	RAF No 4 FTS/208(R) Sqn, Valley
	XX310	HS Hawk T1W	RAF No 4 FTS/208(R) Sqn, Valley
	XX311	HS Hawk T1	RN FRADU, Culdrose
	XX312	HS Hawk T1W	DARA, RAF St Athan
	XX313	HS Hawk T1W	RAF No 4 FTS/208(R) Sqn, Valley
	XX314	HS Hawk T1W	RAF No 4 FTS/208(R) Sqn, Valley
	XX315	HS Hawk T1A	RN FRADU, Culdrose
	XX316	HS Hawk T1A	RAF No 4 FTS/19(R) Sqn, Valley
	XX317	HS Hawk T1A [CH]	RAF No 100 Sqn, Leeming
	XX318	HS Hawk T1A	DARA, RAF St Athan
	XX319	HS Hawk T1A	RAF No 100 Sqn, Leeming
	XX320	HS Hawk T1A	RAF No 4 FTS, Valley
	XX321	HS Hawk T1A [CG]	RAF No 100 Sqn, Leeming
	XX322	HS Hawk T1A	RN FRADU, Culdrose
	XX323	HS Hawk T1A	RAF No 4 FTS, Valley
	XX324	HS Hawk T1A	DPA/BAE Systems, Warton
	XX325	HS Hawk T1A [CE]	RAF No 100 Sqn, Leeming
	XX326	HS Hawk T1A	DPA/BAE Systems, Brough (on rebuild)
	XX327	HS Hawk T1	RAF CAM, DERA Boscombe Down
	XX329	HS Hawk T1A	DARA, RAF St Athan
	XX330	HS Hawk T1A [CL]	RAF No 100 Sqn, Leeming
	XX331	HS Hawk T1A [CK]	RAF No 100 Sqn, Leeming
	XX332	HS Hawk T1A	RAF No 4 FTS/19(R) Sqn, Valley
	XX335	HS Hawk T1A [CD]	RAF No 100 Sqn, Leeming
	XX337	HS Hawk T1A	RN FRADU, Culdrose
	XX338	HS Hawk T1W	RAF No 4 FTS/19(R) Sqn, Valley
	XX339	HS Hawk T1A	RAF No 4 FTS/208(R) Sqn, Valley
	XX341	HS Hawk T1 ASTRA [1]	DPA/AFD/ETPS, DERA Boscombe Down
	XX342	HS Hawk T1 [2]	DPA/AFD/ETPS, DERA Boscombe Down
	XX343	HS Hawk T1 [3] (wreck)	Boscombe Down Museum
	XX344	HS Hawk T1 (8847M) (fuselage)	DERA Farnborough Fire Section
	XX345	HS Hawk T1A	RAF No 4 FTS, Valley
	XX346	HS Hawk T1A	RAF No 4 FTS, Valley
	XX348	HS Hawk T1A	RAF No 4 FTS/19(R) Sqn, Valley
	XX349	HS Hawk T1W [CE]	RAF No 100 Sqn, Leeming
	XX350	HS Hawk T1A	RAF No 4 FTS, Valley
	XX351	HS Hawk T1A [CQ]	RAF No 100 Sqn, Leeming
	XX352	HS Hawk T1A [CP]	RAF No 100 Sqn/JFACSTU, Leeming
	XX370	WS Gazelle AH1	AAC No 665 Sqn/5 Regt, Aldergrove
	XX371	WS Gazelle AH1	AAC No 12 Flt, Brüggen
	XX372	WS Gazelle AH1	AAC No 9 Regt, Dishforth
	XX375	WS Gazelle AH1	AAC No 663 Sqn/3 Regt, Wattisham
	XX378	WS Gazelle AH1 [Q]	AAC No 671 Sqn/2 Regt, Middle Wallop
	XX379	WS Gazelle AH1	AAC No 8 Flt, Middle Wallop
	XX380	WS Gazelle AH1 [A]	RM No 847 Sqn, Yeovilton
	XX381	WS Gazelle AH1	AAC No 662 Sqn/3 Regt, Wattisham
	XX382	WS Gazelle HT3 [M]	RAF, stored Shawbury
	XX383	WS Gazelle AH1 [D]	AAC No 666(V) Sqn/7 Regt, Netheravon
	XX384	WS Gazelle AH1	AAC No 9 Regt, Dishforth
	XX385	WS Gazelle AH1	AAC No 663 Sqn/3 Regt, Wattisham
	XX386	WS Gazelle AH1	AAC No 12 Flt, Brüggen
	XX387	WS Gazelle AH1 (TAD 014)	Army SEAE, Arborfield
	XX388	WS Gazelle AH1	AAC, stored Shawbury
	XX389	WS Gazelle AH1	AAC No 656 Sqn/9 Regt, Dishforth
	XX391	WS Gazelle HT2 [56/CU]	RN, stored Shawbury
	XX392	WS Gazelle AH1	AAC No 3(V) Flt/7 Regt, Leuchars
	XX393	WS Gazelle AH1 (fuselage)	AAC, stored Shawbury
	XX394	WS Gazelle AH1 [X]	AAC No 654 Sqn/4 Regt, Wattisham
	XX396	WS Gazelle HT3 (8718M) [N]	RAFC Cranwell, on display
	XX398	WS Gazelle AH1	AAC No 654 Sqn/4 Regt, Wattisham
	XX399	WS Gazelle AH1	RM No 847 Sqn, Yeovilton
	XX403	WS Gazelle AH1	AAC No 671 Sqn/2 Regt, Middle Wallop
	XX405	WS Gazelle AH1	AAC No 665 Sqn/5 Regt, Aldergrove
	XX406	WS Gazelle HT3 [P]	RAF No 7 Sqn, Odiham

Serial	Type (other identity) [code]	Owner/operator, location or fate	Notes
XX409	WS Gazelle AH1	AAC No 669 Sqn/4 Regt, Wattisham	
XX411	WS Gazelle AH1 <rf>	FAA Museum, RNAS Yeovilton	
XX412	WS Gazelle AH1 [B]	RM No 847 Sqn, Yeovilton	
XX413	WS Gazelle AH1 [C]	RM, stored Shawbury	
XX414	WS Gazelle AH1	AAC, stored RNAY Fleetlands	
XX416	WS Gazelle AH1	AAC No 9 Regt, Dishforth	
XX417	WS Gazelle AH1	AAC No 667 Sqn, Middle Wallop	
XX418	WS Gazelle AH1	AAC, stored Shawbury	
XX419	WS Gazelle AH1	AAC No 662 Sqn/3 Regt, Wattisham	
XX431	WS Gazelle HT2 [43/CU]	RN, stored Shawbury	
XX432	WS Gazelle AH1	AAC No 665 Sqn/5 Regt, Aldergrove	
XX433	WS Gazelle AH1 [F]	AAC, stored Shawbury	
XX435	WS Gazelle AH1 [V]	AAC No 658 Sqn/7 Regt, Netheravon	
XX436	WS Gazelle HT2 [39/CU]	RN, stored Shawbury	
XX437	WS Gazelle AH1	AAC	
XX438	WS Gazelle AH1	AAC No 657 Sqn/9 Regt, Dishforth	
XX439	WS Gazelle AH1	AAC No 9 Regt, Dishforth	
XX440	WS Gazelle AH1 (G-BCHN)	RNAY Fleetlands Apprentice School	
XX441	WS Gazelle HT2 [38/CU]	RN, stored Shawbury	
XX442	WS Gazelle AH1 [E]	AAC No 666(V) Sqn/7 Regt, Netheravon	
XX443	WS Gazelle AH1 [Y]	AAC Stockwell Hall, Middle Wallop, instructional use	
XX444	WS Gazelle AH1	AAC No 25 Flt, Belize	
XX445	WS Gazelle AH1 [T]	AAC No 658 Sqn/7 Regt, Netheravon	
XX446	WS Gazelle HT2 [57/CU]	RN, stored Shawbury	
XX447	WS Gazelle AH1 [D1]	AAC No 671 Sqn/2 Regt, Middle Wallop	
XX448	WS Gazelle AH1	AAC No 664 Sqn/9 Regt, Dishforth	
XX449	WS Gazelle AH1	AAC No 664 Sqn/9 Regt, Dishforth	
XX450	WS Gazelle AH1 [D]	RM, stored Shawbury	
XX453	WS Gazelle AH1	AAC No 669 Sqn/4 Regt, Wattisham	
XX454	WS Gazelle AH1 (fuselage)	RAF Waddington, instructional use	
XX455	WS Gazelle AH1	AAC No 652 Sqn/1 Regt, Brüggen	
XX456	WS Gazelle AH1	AAC No 3(V) Flt/7 Regt, Leuchars	
XX457	WS Gazelle AH1 <ff>	Jet Avn Preservation Grp, Long Marston	
XX460	WS Gazelle AH1	AAC No 662 Sqn/3 Regt, Wattisham	
XX462	WS Gazelle AH1 [W]	AAC No 658 Sqn/7 Regt, Netheravon	
XX467	HS Hunter T66B/T7 (XL605/ G-TVII) [86]	Privately owned, Kemble	
XX475	HP137 Jetstream T2 (N1036S)	DPA, DERA West Freugh	
XX476	HP137 Jetstream T2 (N1037S) [561/CU]	RN No 750 Sqn, Culdrose	
XX477	HP137 Jetstream T1 (G-AXXS/ 8462M) <ff>	RAF Cranwell, instructional use	
XX478	HP137 Jetstream T2 (G-AXXT) [564/CU]	RN No 750 Sqn, Culdrose	
XX479	HP137 Jetstream T2 (G-AXUR)	RN, Predannack Fire School	
XX481	HP137 Jetstream T2 (G-AXUP) [560/CU]	RN, stored Culdrose	
XX482	SA Jetstream T1 [J]	RAF No 3 FTS/45(R) Sqn, Cranwell	
XX484	SA Jetstream T2 [566/CU]	RN No 750 Sqn, Culdrose	
XX486	SA Jetstream T2 [569/CU]	RN No 750 Sqn, Culdrose	
XX487	SA Jetstream T2 [568/CU]	RN No 750 Sqn, Culdrose	
XX488	SA Jetstream T2 [562/CU]	RN No 750 Sqn, Culdrose	
XX491	SA Jetstream T1 [K]	RAF No 3 FTS/45(R) Sqn, Cranwell	
XX492	SA Jetstream T1 [A]	RAF No 3 FTS/45(R) Sqn, Cranwell	
XX493	SA Jetstream T1 [L]	RAF No 3 FTS/45(R) Sqn, Cranwell	
XX494	SA Jetstream T1 [B]	RAF No 3 FTS/45(R) Sqn, Cranwell	
XX495	SA Jetstream T1 [C]	RAF No 3 FTS/45(R) Sqn, Cranwell	
XX496	SA Jetstream T1 [D]	RAF No 3 FTS/45(R) Sqn, Cranwell	
XX497	SA Jetstream T1 [E]	RAF No 3 FTS/45(R) Sqn, Cranwell	
XX498	SA Jetstream T1 [F]	RAF No 3 FTS/45(R) Sqn, Cranwell	
XX499	SA Jetstream T1 [G]	RAF No 3 FTS/45(R) Sqn, Cranwell	
XX500	SA Jetstream T1 [H]	RAF No 3 FTS/45(R) Sqn, Cranwell	
XX510	WS Lynx HAS2 [69/LS]	SFDO, RNAS Culdrose	
XX513	SA Bulldog T1 [10]	RAF, stored Shawbury	
XX514	SA122 Bulldog (G-BCUS)	Privately owned, Leicester	
XX515	SA Bulldog T1 [4]	RAF Manchester & Salford Universities AS/No 10 AEF, Woodvale	
XX516	SA Bulldog T1 [A]	RAF, stored Shawbury	
XX518	SA Bulldog T1 [S]	RAF Liverpool UAS, Woodvale	
XX519	SA Bulldog T1 [14]	Sold to the USA, August 2000	
XX520	SA Bulldog T1 [A]	No . . . . Sqn ATC, Haywards Heath	
XX521	SA Bulldog T1 [H]	RAF, stored Shawbury	

XX522 – XX630

Notes	Serial	Type (other identity) [code]	Owner/operator, location or fate
	XX522	SA Bulldog T1 [06]	RAF, stored Shawbury
	XX523	SA Bulldog T1 (G-BZFM) [X]	Privately owned, Ashbourne, Derbyshire
	XX524	SA Bulldog T1 [04]	RAF, stored Shawbury
	XX525	SA Bulldog T1	RAF Southampton UAS/No 2 AEF, DERA Boscombe Down
	XX526	SA Bulldog T1 [C]	RAF, stored Shawbury
	XX527	SA Bulldog T1 [05]	Sold to the USA, as N527BD, August 2000
	XX528	SA Bulldog T1 [D]	Privately owned, Cardiff
	XX529	SA Bulldog T1 [08]	Privately owned, Sproughton
	XX530	SA Bulldog T1 (XX637/9197M) [F]	No 327 Sqn ATC, Kilmarnock
	XX531	SA Bulldog T1 [G]	RAF University of Birmingham AS/ No 8 AEF, Cosford
	XX532	SA Bulldog T1 [1]	RAF stored Shawbury
	XX533	SA Bulldog T1 [U]	RAF Northumbrian Universities AS/ No 11 AEF, Leeming
	XX534	SA Bulldog T1 [B]	RAF University of Birmingham AS/ No 8 AEF, Cosford
	XX535	SA Bulldog T1 [S]	RAF CFS, Cranwell
	XX536	SA Bulldog T1 [6]	RAF Manchester & Salford Universities AS/No 10 AEF, Woodvale
	XX537	SA Bulldog T1 [C]	RAF, stored Shawbury
	XX538	SA Bulldog T1 [O]	RAF Manchester & Salford Universities AS/No 10 AEF, Woodvale
	XX539	SA Bulldog T1 [L]	RAF, stored Shawbury
	XX540	SA Bulldog T1 [15]	Sold to the USA, as N540BD, August 2000
	XX541	SA Bulldog T1 [F]	RAF, stored Shawbury
	XX543	SA Bulldog T1 [F]	RAF, stored Shawbury
	XX544	SA Bulldog T1 (G-BZLR) [01]	Sold to the USA, as N544BD, August 2000
	XX545	SA Bulldog T1 [02]	Scrapped at Leuchars
	XX546	SA Bulldog T1 [03]	RAF, stored Shawbury
	XX547	SA Bulldog T1	RAF Woodvale
	XX548	SA Bulldog T1 [06]	RAF, stored Shawbury
	XX549	SA Bulldog T1 [6]	RAF Southampton UAS/No 2 AEF, DERA Boscombe Down
	XX550	SA Bulldog T1 [Z]	RAF Northumbrian Universities AS/ No 11 AEF, Leeming
	XX551	SA Bulldog T1 (G-BZDP) [E]	Privately owned, Wellesbourne Mountford
	XX552	SA Bulldog T1 [08]	RAF, stored Shawbury
	XX553	SA Bulldog T1 [07]	RAF, stored Shawbury
	XX554	SA Bulldog T1 (G-BZMD) [09]	Privately owned, Grantham
	XX555	SA Bulldog T1 [U]	RAF, stored Shawbury
	XX556	SA Bulldog T1 [M]	RAF, stored Shawbury
	XX558	SA Bulldog T1 [A]	RAF University of Birmingham AS/ No 8 AEF, Cosford
	XX559	SA Bulldog T1 [F]	RAF University of Birmingham AS/ No 8 AEF, Cosford
	XX560	SA Bulldog T1 [F]	RAF, stored Shawbury
	XX561	SA Bulldog T1 (G-BZEP) [7]	Privately owned, Biggin Hill
	XX562	SA Bulldog T1 [18]	RAF Northumbrian Universities AS/ No 11 AEF, Leeming
	XX611	SA Bulldog T1 [7]	RAF Southampton UAS/No 2 AEF, DERA Boscombe Down
	XX612	SA Bulldog T1 [A,03]	RAF, stored Shawbury
	XX614	SA Bulldog T1 [V]	RAF, stored Shawbury
	XX615	SA Bulldog T1 [2]	RAF, stored Shawbury
	XX616	SA Bulldog T1	Sold as F-AZRM, April 2000
	XX617	SA Bulldog T1 [2]	RAF, stored Shawbury
	XX619	SA Bulldog T1 [T]	RAF Northumbrian Universities AS/ No 11 AEF, Leeming
	XX620	SA Bulldog T1 [02]	RAF, stored Shawbury
	XX621	SA Bulldog T1 [H]	RAF University of Birmingham AS/ No 8 AEF, Cosford
	XX622	SA Bulldog T1 [B]	RAF, stored Shawbury
	XX623	SA Bulldog T1 [M]	Sold to the USA, ,August 2000
	XX624	SA Bulldog T1 [E]	RAF, stored Shawbury
	XX625	SA Bulldog T1 [U,01]	RAF Northumbrian Universities AS/ No 11 AEF, Leeming
	XX626	SA Bulldog T1 [W,02]	RAF CTTS, St Athan
	XX627	SA Bulldog T1 [7]	RAF, stored Shawbury
	XX628	SA Bulldog T1 [9]	RAF Southampton UAS/No 2 AEF, DERA Boscombe Down
	XX629	SA Bulldog T1 [V]	RAF, stored Shawbury
	XX630	SA Bulldog T1 (G-SIJW) [5]	Privately owned, Sleap

Serial	Type (other identity) [code]	Owner/operator, location or fate	Notes
XX631	SA Bulldog T1 [W]	RAF, stored Shawbury	
XX632	SA Bulldog T1 [A]	*Sold to the USA, as N632BD, August 2000*	
XX633	SA Bulldog T1 [X]	RAF, stored Shawbury	
XX634	SA Bulldog T1 [T]	RAF, Woodvale	
XX635	SA Bulldog T1 (8767M)	DARA Training School, RAF St Athan	
XX636	SA Bulldog T1 [Y]	RAF Northumbrian Universities AS/ No 11 AEF, Leeming	
XX638	SA Bulldog T1	RAF, stored Shawbury	
XX639	SA Bulldog T1 [D]	RAF Northumbrian Universities AS/ No 11 AEF, Leeming	
XX640	SA Bulldog T1 [K]	RAF, stored Shawbury	
XX653	SA Bulldog T1 [E]	Apprentice School, DERA Boscombe Down	
XX654	SA Bulldog T1 [3]	RAF, stored Shawbury	
XX655	SA Bulldog T1 [B]	RAF, Coterne (wfu)	
XX656	SA Bulldog T1 [C]	RAF, Woodvale	
XX657	SA Bulldog T1 [U]	*Sold to the USA, August 2000*	
XX658	SA Bulldog T1 [07]	RAF East Lowlands UAS, Leuchars	
XX659	SA Bulldog T1 [E]	RAF, stored Shawbury	
XX661	SA Bulldog T1 [6]	RAF, stored Shawbury	
XX663	SA Bulldog T1 [01]	RAF, stored Shawbury	
XX664	SA Bulldog T1 [04]	RAF Northumbrian Universities AS/ No 11 AEF, Leeming	
XX665	SA Bulldog T1	No 2409 Sqn ATC, Halton	
XX666	SA Bulldog T1 [08]	*Sold to the USA, August 2000*	
XX667	SA Bulldog T1 (G-BZFN) [16]	Privately owned, Ashbourne, Derbyshire	
XX668	SA Bulldog T1 [1]	RAF Manchester & Salford Universities AS/No 10 AEF, Woodvale	
XX669	SA Bulldog T1 (8997M) [B]	Privately owned, Llantrisant	
XX670	SA Bulldog T1 [C]	RAF University of Birmingham AS/ No 8 AEF, Cosford	
XX671	SA Bulldog T1 [D]	RAF University of Birmingham AS/ No 8 AEF, Cosford	
XX672	SA Bulldog T1 [E]	RAF University of Birmingham AS/ No 8 AEF, Cosford	
XX685	SA Bulldog T1 (G-BZLB) [11]	Privately owned, Hurstbourne Tarrant	
XX686	SA Bulldog T1 [5]	RAF CTTS, St Athan	
XX687	SA Bulldog T1	RAF Northumbrian Universities AS/ No 11 AEF, Leeming	
XX688	SA Bulldog T1 [8]	RAF, stored Shawburyl	
XX689	SA Bulldog T1 [D]	RAF, stored Shawbury	
XX690	SA Bulldog T1 [A]	RAF, stored Shawbury	
XX691	SA Bulldog T1 [10]	*To Maltese Armed Forces as 9H-ADQ, 13 February 2000*	
XX692	SA Bulldog T1 (G-BZMH) [A]	Privately owned, Harbourne	
XX693	SA Bulldog T1 (G-BZML) [07]	Privately owned, Colchester	
XX694	SA Bulldog T1 [E]	RAF, stored Shawbury	
XX695	SA Bulldog T1 [3]	RAF Manchester & Salford Universities AS/No 10 AEF, Woodvale	
XX696	SA Bulldog T1 [S]	*To Maltese Armed Forces as 9H-ADR, 13 February 2000*	
XX697	SA Bulldog T1 [H]	RAF, stored Shawbury	
XX698	SA Bulldog T1 (G-BZME) [9]	Privately owned, Grantham	
XX699	SA Bulldog T1 [F]	RAF, stored Shawbury	
XX700	SA Bulldog T1	RAF Southampton UAS/No 2 AEF, DERA Boscombe Downl	
XX701	SA Bulldog T1 [2]	RAF, stored Shawbury	
XX702	SA Bulldog T1	RAF, Woodvale	
XX704	SA Bulldog T1 [U]	*Sold to the USA, August 2000*	
XX705	SA Bulldog T1 [5]	RAF Southampton UAS/No 2 AEF, DERA Boscombe Down	
XX706	SA Bulldog T1 [1]	RAF Southampton UAS/No 2 AEF, DERA Boscombe Down	
XX707	SA Bulldog T1 [4]	RAF Southampton UAS/No 2 AEF, DERA Boscombe Down	
XX708	SA Bulldog T1 [3]	RAF Southampton UAS/No 2 AEF, DERA Boscombe Down	
XX709	SA Bulldog T1 [E]	*To Maltese Armed Forces as 9H-ADS, 13 February 2000*	
XX711	SA Bulldog T1 [X]	RAF Liverpool UAS, Woodvale	
XX713	SA Bulldog T1 [G]	RAF, stored Shawbury	
XX714	SA Bulldog T1 [D]	*To Maltese Armed Forces as 9H-ADT, 13 February 2000*	

Notes	Serial	Type (other identity) [code]	Owner/operator, location or fate
	XX720	SEPECAT Jaguar GR3 [GB]	RAF No 54 Sqn, Coltishall
	XX722	SEPECAT Jaguar GR1 [EF]	RAF, stored St Athan
	XX723	SEPECAT Jaguar GR3A [GQ]	RAF No 54 Sqn, Coltishall
	XX724	SEPECAT Jaguar GR3A [GA]	RAF, St Athan (conversion)
	XX725	SEPECAT Jaguar GR3A [GU]	RAF No 54 Sqn, Coltishall
	XX725	SEPECAT Jaguar GR1 <R> (BAPC 150/*XX718*) [GU]	RAF EPTT, St Athan
	XX726	SEPECAT Jaguar GR1 (8947M) [EB]	RAF No 1 SoTT, Cosford
	XX727	SEPECAT Jaguar GR1 (8951M) [ER]	RAF No 1 SoTT, Cosford
	XX729	SEPECAT Jaguar GR3 [EL]	RAF No 6 Sqn, Coltishall
	XX730	SEPECAT Jaguar GR1 (8952M) [EC]	RAF No 1 SoTT, Cosford
	XX733	SEPECAT Jaguar GR1B [ER]	*Currently not known*
	XX734	SEPECAT Jaguar GR1 (8816M) (fuselage)	Gatwick Aviation Museum, Charlwood
	XX736	SEPECAT Jaguar GR1 (9110M) <ff>	BAE Systems Brough
	XX737	SEPECAT Jaguar GR3 [EE]	RAF No 6 Sqn, Coltishall
	XX738	SEPECAT Jaguar GR3 [GG]	RAF No 54 Sqn, Coltishall
	XX739	SEPECAT Jaguar GR1 (8902M) [I]	RAF No 1 SoTT, Cosford
	XX741	SEPECAT Jaguar GR1A [04]	RAF, stored Shawbury
	XX743	SEPECAT Jaguar GR1 (8949M) [EG]	RAF No 1 SoTT, Cosford
	XX744	SEPECAT Jaguar GR1	RAF Coltishall, instructional use
	XX745	SEPECAT Jaguar GR1A [GV]	RAF No 54 Sqn, Coltishall
	XX746	SEPECAT Jaguar GR1A (8895M) [09]	RAF No 1 SoTT, Cosford
	XX747	SEPECAT Jaguar GR1 (8903M)	AMIF, RAFC Cranwell
	XX748	SEPECAT Jaguar GR3A [GK]	RAF No 54 Sqn, Coltishall
	XX751	SEPECAT Jaguar GR1 (8937M) [10]	RAF No 1 SoTT, Cosford
	XX752	SEPECAT Jaguar GR3A [D]	RAF No 16(R) Sqn, Coltishall
	XX753	SEPECAT Jaguar GR1 (9087M) <ff>	RAF EPTT, St Athan
	XX756	SEPECAT Jaguar GR1 (8899M) [AM]	RAF No 1 SoTT, Cosford
	XX757	SEPECAT Jaguar GR1 (8948M) [CU]	RAF No 1 SoTT, Cosford
	XX761	SEPECAT Jaguar GR1 (8600M) <ff>	Boscombe Down Museum
	XX763	SEPECAT Jaguar GR1 (9009M)	DARA Training School, RAF St Athan
	XX764	SEPECAT Jaguar GR1 (9010M)	DARA Training School, RAF St Athan
	XX765	SEPECAT Jaguar ACT	RAF Museum, Cosford
	XX766	SEPECAT Jaguar GR1A [EA]	RAF, stored St Athan
	XX767	SEPECAT Jaguar GR3 [GE]	RAF No 54 Sqn, Coltishall
	XX818	SEPECAT Jaguar GR1 (8945M) [DE]	RAF No 1 SoTT, Cosford
	XX819	SEPECAT Jaguar GR1 (8923M) [CE]	RAF No 1 SoTT, Cosford
	XX821	SEPECAT Jaguar GR1 (8896M) [P]	AMIF, RAFC Cranwell
	XX824	SEPECAT Jaguar GR1 (9019M) [AD]	RAF No 1 SoTT, Cosford
	XX825	SEPECAT Jaguar GR1 (9020M) [BN]	RAF No 1 SoTT, Cosford
	XX826	SEPECAT Jaguar GR1 (9021M) [34,JH]	RAF No 1 SoTT, Cosford
	XX829	SEPECAT Jaguar T2A [GZ]	RAF, stored St Athan
	XX830	SEPECAT Jaguar T2	RAF Coltishall, GI use
	XX832	SEPECAT Jaguar T2A [EZ]	RAF No 6 Sqn, Coltishall
	XX833	SEPECAT Jaguar T2B	RAF AWC/SAOEU, DERA Boscombe Down
	XX835	SEPECAT Jaguar T4 [FY]	RAF No 41 Sqn, Coltishall
	XX836	SEPECAT Jaguar T2A [X]	RAF, stored Shawbury
	XX837	SEPECAT Jaguar T2 (8978M) [Z]	RAF No 1 SoTT, Cosford
	XX838	SEPECAT Jaguar T4 [PR]	RAF No 16(R) Sqn, Coltishall
	XX839	SEPECAT Jaguar T2A (9256M)	RAF, stored St Athan
	XX840	SEPECAT Jaguar T4 [S]	RAF No 16(R) Sqn, Coltishall
	XX841	SEPECAT Jaguar T4 [ES]	RAF No 6 Sqn, Coltishall
	XX842	SEPECAT Jaguar T2A [X]	DPA/BAE Systems, Warton
	XX845	SEPECAT Jaguar T4	RAF No 6 Sqn, Coltishall

Serial	Type (other identity) [code]	Owner/operator, location or fate	Notes
XX846	SEPECAT Jaguar T4 [V]	RAF No 16(R) Sqn, Coltishall	
XX847	SEPECAT Jaguar T2A	RAF, stored St Athan	
XX885	HS Buccaneer S2B (9225M)	The Old Flying Machine Company, Scampton	
XX888	HS Buccaneer S2B <ff>	Dundonald Aviation Centre, Strathclyde	
XX889	HS Buccaneer S2B	Gloucestershire Avn Coll, stored Glos	
XX892	HS Buccaneer S2B <ff>	Christies Garden Centre, Forres, Grampian	
XX893	HS Buccaneer S2B <ff>	Privately owned, Birtley, Tyne & Wear	
XX894	HS Buccaneer S2B [020/R]	Buccaneer Preservation Society, Kemble	
XX895	HS Buccaneer S2B <ff>	Privately owned, Oxford	
XX897	HS Buccaneer S2B(mod)	Privately owned, Bournemouth	
XX899	HS Buccaneer S2B <ff>	Midland Air Museum, Coventry	
XX900	HS Buccaneer S2B	British Aviation Heritage, Bruntingthorpe	
XX901	HS Buccaneer S2B	Yorkshire Air Museum, Elvington	
XX907	WS Lynx AH1	DERA Structures Dept, Farnborough	
XX910	WS Lynx HAS2	DERA Structures Dept, Farnborough	
XX914	BAC VC10/1103 (8777M) <rf>	RAF AMS, Brize Norton	
XX919	BAC 1-11/402AP (PI-C1121) <ff>	Boscombe Down Museum	
XX946	Panavia Tornado (P02) (8883M)	RAF Museum, Hendon	
XX947	Panavia Tornado (P03) (8797M)	DARA, RAF St Athan, BDRT	
XX948	Panavia Tornado (P06) (8879M) [P]	RAF No 1 SoTT, Cosford	
XX955	SEPECAT Jaguar GR1A [GK]	RAF, stored Shawbury	
XX956	SEPECAT Jaguar GR1 (8950M) [BE]	RAF No 1 SoTT, Cosford	
XX958	SEPECAT Jaguar GR1 (9022M) [BK,JG]	RAF No 1 SoTT, Cosford	
XX959	SEPECAT Jaguar GR1 (8953M) [CJ]	RAF No 1 SoTT, Cosford	
XX962	SEPECAT Jaguar GR1B [E]	AMIF, RAFC Cranwell	
XX965	SEPECAT Jaguar GR1A [C]	AMIF, RAFC Cranwell	
XX966	SEPECAT Jaguar GR1A (8904M) [EL]	RAF No 1 SoTT, Cosford	
XX967	SEPECAT Jaguar GR1 (9006M) [AC,JD]	RAF No 1 SoTT, Cosford	
XX968	SEPECAT Jaguar GR1 (9007M) [AJ,JE]	RAF No 1 SoTT, Cosford	
XX969	SEPECAT Jaguar GR1A (8897M) [01]	RAF No 1 SoTT, Cosford	
XX970	SEPECAT Jaguar GR3 [EH]	RAF No 6 Sqn, Coltishall	
XX974	SEPECAT Jaguar GR3 [B]	RAF No 16(R) Sqn, Coltishall	
XX975	SEPECAT Jaguar GR1 (8905M) [07]	RAF No 1 SoTT, Cosford	
XX976	SEPECAT Jaguar GR1 (8906M) [BD]	RAF No 1 SoTT, Cosford	
XX977	SEPECAT Jaguar GR1 (9132M) [DL,05]	DARA, RAF St Athan, BDRT	
XX979	SEPECAT Jaguar GR1A	DARA, RAF St Athan	
XZ101	SEPECAT Jaguar GR1A (9282M) [D]	DERA Boscombe Down, GI use	
XZ103	SEPECAT Jaguar GR3 [FP]	RAF No 41 Sqn, Coltishall	
XZ104	SEPECAT Jaguar GR3 [FM]	RAF No 41 Sqn, Coltishall	
XZ106	SEPECAT Jaguar GR3 [FR]	RAF No 41 Sqn, Coltishall	
XZ107	SEPECAT Jaguar GR3 [FH]	RAF No 41 Sqn, Coltishall	
XZ109	SEPECAT Jaguar GR3 [EN]	RAF No 6 Sqn, Coltishall	
XZ111	SEPECAT Jaguar GR1A [GO]	Crashed near Dumfries, 27 October 2000	
XZ112	SEPECAT Jaguar GR3A [GA]	RAF No 54 Sqn, Coltishall	
XZ113	SEPECAT Jaguar GR3 [FD]	RAF No 41 Sqn, Coltishall	
XZ114	SEPECAT Jaguar GR1A [FB]	RAF, stored Shawbury	
XZ115	SEPECAT Jaguar GR3 [FC]	RAF No 41 Sqn, Coltishall	
XZ117	SEPECAT Jaguar GR3	RAF No 16(R) Sqn, Coltishall	
XZ118	SEPECAT Jaguar GR3 [FF]	RAF AMF, Coltishall	
XZ119	SEPECAT Jaguar GR1A [F]	AMIF, RAFC Cranwell	
XZ129	HS Harrier GR3 [ETS]	RN ETS, Yeovilton	
XZ130	HS Harrier GR3 (9079M) [A,HE]	RAF No 1 SoTT, Cosford	
XZ131	HS Harrier GR3 (9174M) <ff>	No 2156 Sqn ATC, Brierley Hill, W Midlands	
XZ132	HS Harrier GR3 (9168M) [C]	ATF, RAFC Cranwell	
XZ133	HS Harrier GR3 [10]	Imperial War Museum, Duxford	
XZ135	HS Harrier GR3 (8848M) <ff>	RAF EPTT, St Athan	
XZ138	HS Harrier GR3 (9040M) <ff>	RAFC Cranwell, Trenchard Hall	

Notes	Serial	Type (other identity) [code]	Owner/operator, location or fate
	XZ145	HS Harrier T4 [45]	SFDO, RNAS Culdrose
	XZ146	HS Harrier T4 (9281M) [S]	RAF Wittering, for display
	XZ170	WS Lynx AH9	DPA/GKN Westland, Yeovil
	XZ171	WS Lynx AH7	AAC No 654 Sqn/4 Regt, Wattisham
	XZ172	WS Lynx AH7	AAC No 655 Sqn/5 Regt, Aldergrove
	XZ173	WS Lynx AH7	AAC No 661 Sqn/1 Regt, Brüggen
	XZ174	WS Lynx AH7	AAC No 662 Sqn/3 Regt, Wattisham
	XZ175	WS Lynx AH7	AAC No 664 Sqn/9 Regt, Dishforth
	XZ176	WS Lynx AH7	AAC, stored RNAY Fleetlands
	XZ177	WS Lynx AH7	DARA, RNAY Fleetlands
	XZ178	WS Lynx AH7	AAC No 661 Sqn/1 Regt, Brüggen
	XZ179	WS Lynx AH7	AAC No 652 Sqn/1 Regt, Brüggen
	XZ180	WS Lynx AH7	RM No 847 Sqn, Yeovilton
	XZ181	WS Lynx AH1	GKN Westland, Yeovil, wfu
	XZ182	WS Lynx AH7 [M]	RM No 847 Sqn, Yeovilton
	XZ183	WS Lynx AH7	AAC No 656 Sqn/9 Regt, Dishforth
	XZ184	WS Lynx AH7 [Z]	AAC, stored RNAY Fleetlands
	XZ185	WS Lynx AH7	AAC, stored RNAY Fleetlands
	XZ186	WS Lynx AH7 (wreckage)	DARA, RNAY Fleetlands
	XZ187	WS Lynx AH7	AAC No 655 Sqn/5 Regt, Aldergrove
	XZ188	WS Lynx AH7	Army SEAE, Arborfield
	XZ190	WS Lynx AH7	AAC No 663 Sqn/3 Regt, Wattisham
	XZ191	WS Lynx AH7 [A]	AAC No 671 Sqn/2 Regt, Middle Wallop
	XZ192	WS Lynx AH7	DPA/GKN Westland, Weston-super-Mare (on rebuild)
	XZ193	WS Lynx AH7 [I]	AAC No 671 Sqn/2 Regt, Middle Wallop
	XZ194	WS Lynx AH7	AAC No 664 Sqn/9 Regt, Dishforth
	XZ195	WS Lynx AH7	AAC, stored RNAY Fleetlands
	XZ196	WS Lynx AH7	AAC No 664 Sqn/9 Regt, Dishforth
	XZ197	WS Lynx AH7	AAC No 1 Regt, Brüggen
	XZ198	WS Lynx AH7	DARA, RNAY Fleetlands
	XZ203	WS Lynx AH7 [L]	AAC No 671 Sqn/2 Regt, Middle Wallop
	XZ205	WS Lynx AH7	AAC No 655 Sqn/5 Regt, Aldergrove
	XZ206	WS Lynx AH7	AAC No 25 Flt, Belize
	XZ207	WS Lynx AH7	DARA, RNAY Fleetlands (damaged)
	XZ208	WS Lynx AH7	AAC No 669 Sqn/4 Regt, Wattisham
	XZ209	WS Lynx AH7	AAC No 655 Sqn/5 Regt, Aldergrove
	XZ210	WS Lynx AH7	AAC No 1 Regt, Brüggen
	XZ211	WS Lynx AH7	AAC, stored RNAY Fleetlands
	XZ212	WS Lynx AH7	AAC No 656 Sqn/9 Regt, Dishforth
	XZ213	WS Lynx AH1 (TAD 213)	RNAY Fleetlands Apprentice School
	XZ214	WS Lynx AH7	AAC No 657 Sqn, Odiham
	XZ215	WS Lynx AH7 [4]	AAC No 655 Sqn/5 Regt, Aldergrove
	XZ216	WS Lynx AH7	AAC No 661 Sqn/1 Regt, Brüggen
	XZ217	WS Lynx AH7	AAC No 654 Sqn/4 Regt, Wattisham
	XZ218	WS Lynx AH7	AAC No 655 Sqn/5 Regt, Aldergrove
	XZ219	WS Lynx AH7	AAC No 656 Sqn/9 Regt, Dishforth
	XZ220	WS Lynx AH7	Currently not known
	XZ221	WS Lynx AH7	AAC No 654 Sqn/4 Regt, Wattisham
	XZ222	WS Lynx AH7	AAC No 657 Sqn, Odiham
	XZ228	WS Lynx HAS3S [335/CF]	RN No 815 Sqn, Cardiff Flt, Yeovilton
	XZ229	WS Lynx HAS3S [457/LA]	RN No 815 Sqn, Lancaster Flt, Yeovilton
	XZ230	WS Lynx HAS3S [302]	DARA, RNAY Fleetlands
	XZ232	WS Lynx HAS3S [411/EB]	RN No 815 Sqn, Edinburgh Flt, Yeovilton
	XZ233	WS Lynx HAS3(ICE) [645]	RN No 702 Sqn, Yeovilton
	XZ234	WS Lynx HAS3S [633]	RN No 702 Sqn, Yeovilton
	XZ235	WS Lynx HAS3S [635]	RN No 702 Sqn, Yeovilton
	XZ236	WS Lynx HMA8	DPA/AFD, DERA Boscombe Down
	XZ237	WS Lynx HAS3S [630]	RN No 702 Sqn, Yeovilton
	XZ238	WS Lynx HAS3S(ICE) [435/EE]	RN No 815 Sqn, Endurance Flt, Yeovilton
	XZ239	WS Lynx HAS3S [345/NC]	RN No 815 Sqn, Newcastle Flt, Yeovilton
	XZ241	WS Lynx HAS3S(ICE)	DARA, RNAY Fleetlands
	XZ243	WS Lynx HAS3 <ff>	RNAS Culdrose, Fire Section
	XZ245	WS Lynx HAS3S [410/GC]	RN No 815 Sqn, Gloucester Flt, Yeovilton
	XZ246	WS Lynx HAS3S [434/EE]	RN No 815 Sqn, Endurance Flt, Yeovilton
	XZ248	WS Lynx HAS3S [638]	RN No 702 Sqn, Yeovilton
	XZ250	WS Lynx HAS3S [631]	RN No 702 Sqn, Yeovilton
	XZ252	WS Lynx HAS3S	RN, stored RNAY Fleetlands
	XZ254	WS Lynx HAS3S [355/SM]	RN No 815 Sqn, Somerset Flt, Yeovilton
	XZ255	WS Lynx HMA8 [462/WM]	RN No 815 Sqn, Westminster Flt, Yeovilton
	XZ256	WS Lynx HMA8 [352/SD]	RN No 815 Sqn, Sheffield Flt, Yeovilton
	XZ257	WS Lynx HMA8 [644]	DARA, RNAY Fleetlands (conversion)

Serial	Type (other identity) [code]	Owner/operator, location or fate	Notes
XZ284	HS Nimrod MR2	*To be converted to Nimrod MRA4 ZJ519*	
XZ286	BAe Nimrod AEW3 <rf>	RAF Kinloss Fire Section	
XZ287	BAe Nimrod AEW3 (9140M) (fuselage)	RAF TSW, Stafford	
XZ290	WS Gazelle AH1	AAC No 665 Sqn/5 Regt, Aldergrove	
XZ291	WS Gazelle AH1	AAC No 12 Flt, Brüggen	
XZ292	WS Gazelle AH1	AAC No 669 Sqn/4 Regt, Wattisham	
XZ294	WS Gazelle AH1 [X]	AAC No 658 Sqn/7 Regt, Netheravon	
XZ295	WS Gazelle AH1	AAC No 12 Flt, Brüggen	
XZ296	WS Gazelle AH1	AAC, stored RNAY Fleetlands	
XZ298	WS Gazelle AH1	AAC No 656 Sqn/9 Regt, Dishforth	
XZ299	WS Gazelle AH1	AAC No 665 Sqn/5 Regt, Aldergrove	
XZ300	WS Gazelle AH1 [L] (wreck)	Army, Bramley, Hants	
XZ301	WS Gazelle AH1 [U]	AAC, stored RNAY Fleetlands	
XZ302	WS Gazelle AH1 (fuselage)	*Scrapped at Fleetlands*	
XZ303	WS Gazelle AH1	AAC No 663 Sqn/3 Regt, Wattisham	
XZ304	WS Gazelle AH1	AAC No 6(V) Flt/7 Regt, Shawbury	
XZ305	WS Gazelle AH1 (TAD 020)	Army SEAE, Arborfield	
XZ307	WS Gazelle AH1	RNAY Fleetlands Apprentice School	
XZ308	WS Gazelle AH1 [V]	AAC No 9 Regt, Dishforth	
XZ309	WS Gazelle AH1	AAC No 6(V) Flt/7 Regt, Shawbury	
XZ311	WS Gazelle AH1	AAC No 6(V) Flt/7 Regt, Shawbury	
XZ312	WS Gazelle AH1	DARA, RNAY Fleetlands	
XZ313	WS Gazelle AH1	AAC No 667 Sqn, Middle Wallop	
XZ314	WS Gazelle AH1	AAC No 8 Flt, Middle Wallop	
XZ315	WS Gazelle AH1	AAC No 665 Sqn/5 Regt, Aldergrove	
XZ316	WS Gazelle AH1 [B]	AAC No 666(V) Sqn/7 Regt, Netheravon	
XZ317	WS Gazelle AH1 [R]	AAC, stored Shawbury	
XZ318	WS Gazelle AH1 (fuselage)	AAC, stored RNAY Fleetlands	
XZ320	WS Gazelle AH1	AAC No 669 Sqn/4 Regt, Wattisham	
XZ321	WS Gazelle AH1	AAC No 665 Sqn/5 Regt, Aldergrove	
XZ322	WS Gazelle AH1 (9283M) [N]	DARA, RAF St Athan, BDRT	
XZ323	WS Gazelle AH1	AAC No 16 Flt, Dhekelia, Cyprus	
XZ324	WS Gazelle AH1	AAC No 3(V) Flt/7 Regt, Leuchars	
XZ325	WS Gazelle AH1 [T]	Army SEAE, Arborfield	
XZ326	WS Gazelle AH1	AAC No 664 Sqn/9 Regt, Dishforth	
XZ327	WS Gazelle AH1	DARA, RNAY Fleetlands	
XZ328	WS Gazelle AH1	AAC No 662 Sqn/3 Regt, Wattisham	
XZ329	WS Gazelle AH1	AAC, stored Shawbury	
XZ330	WS Gazelle AH1 [Y]	AAC No 671 Sqn/2 Regt, Middle Wallop	
XZ331	WS Gazelle AH1	AAC No 654 Sqn/4 Regt, Wattisham	
XZ332	WS Gazelle AH1 [O]	Army SEAE, Arborfield	
XZ333	WS Gazelle AH1 [A]	Army SEAE, Arborfield	
XZ334	WS Gazelle AH1 [S]	DARA, RNAY Fleetlands	
XZ335	WS Gazelle AH1	AAC No 6(V) Flt/7 Regt, Shawbury	
XZ337	WS Gazelle AH1	AAC No 662 Sqn/3 Regt, Wattisham	
XZ338	WS Gazelle AH1	AAC, stored RNAY Fleetlands	
XZ339	WS Gazelle AH1	AAC No 654 Sqn/4 Regt, Wattisham	
XZ340	WS Gazelle AH1 [5A]	AAC No 29 Flt, BATUS, Suffield, Canada	
XZ341	WS Gazelle AH1	AAC No 3(V) Flt/7 Regt, Leuchars	
XZ342	WS Gazelle AH1	AAC No 8 Flt, Credenhill	
XZ343	WS Gazelle AH1	AAC, stored RNAY Fleetlands	
XZ344	WS Gazelle AH1	AAC No 9 Regt, Dishforth	
XZ345	WS Gazelle AH1	AAC No 656 Sqn/9 Regt, Dishforth	
XZ346	WS Gazelle AH1	REME, Middle Wallop, instructional use	
XZ347	WS Gazelle AH1	AAC No 9 Regt, Dishforth	
XZ348	WS Gazelle AH1 (wreck)	AAC, stored RNAY Fleetlands	
XZ349	WS Gazelle AH1 [G1]	AAC No 671 Sqn/2 Regt, Middle Wallop	
XZ355	SEPECAT Jaguar GR3A [FJ]	RAF No 41 Sqn, Coltishall	
XZ356	SEPECAT Jaguar GR1A [EP]	RAF, stored Shawbury	
XZ357	SEPECAT Jaguar GR3 [FK]	RAF No 41 Sqn, Coltishall	
XZ358	SEPECAT Jaguar GR1A [L]	AMIF, RAFC Cranwell	
XZ360	SEPECAT Jaguar GR3 [FN]	RAF No 41 Sqn, Coltishall	
XZ361	SEPECAT Jaguar GR1A [FT]	RAF No 41 Sqn, Coltishall	
XZ363	SEPECAT Jaguar GR3 [FO]	RAF No 41 Sqn, Coltishall	
XZ363	SEPECAT Jaguar GR1A <R> (*XX824*/BAPC 151) [A]	RAF EPTT, St Athan	
XZ364	SEPECAT Jaguar GR3	RAF No 54 Sqn, Coltishall	
XZ366	SEPECAT Jaguar GR3 [FS]	RAF No 41 Sqn, Coltishall	
XZ367	SEPECAT Jaguar GR3A [GP]	RAF, stored Shawbury	
XZ368	SEPECAT Jaguar GR1 [8900M] [AG]	RAF No 1 SoTT, Cosford	
XZ369	SEPECAT Jaguar GR3 [EF]	RAF No 6 Sqn, Coltishall	

XZ370 – XZ614

Notes	Serial	Type (other identity) [code]	Owner/operator, location or fate
	XZ370	SEPECAT Jaguar GR1 (9004M) [JB]	RAF No 1 SoTT, Cosford
	XZ371	SEPECAT Jaguar GR1 (8907M) [AP]	RAF No 1 SoTT, Cosford
	XZ372	SEPECAT Jaguar GR3	RAF No 6 Sqn, Coltishall
	XZ374	SEPECAT Jaguar GR1 (9005M) [JC]	RAF No 1 SoTT, Cosford
	XZ375	SEPECAT Jaguar GR1A (9255M)	RAF, stored St Athan
	XZ377	SEPECAT Jaguar GR3 [EG]	RAF No 6 Sqn, Coltishall
	XZ378	SEPECAT Jaguar GR1A [EP]	RAF, stored Shawbury
	XZ382	SEPECAT Jaguar GR1 (8908M)	Privately owned, Bruntingthorpe
	XZ383	SEPECAT Jaguar GR1 (8901M) [AF]	RAF No 1 SoTT, Cosford
	XZ384	SEPECAT Jaguar GR1 (8954M) [BC]	RAF No 1 SoTT, Cosford
	XZ385	SEPECAT Jaguar GR1A [C]	RAF No 16(R) Sqn, Coltishall
	XZ389	SEPECAT Jaguar GR1 (8946M) [BL]	RAF No 1 SoTT, Cosford
	XZ390	SEPECAT Jaguar GR1A (9003M) [35,JA]	RAF No 1 SoTT, Cosford
	XZ391	SEPECAT Jaguar GR3 [EB]	RAF No 6 Sqn, Coltishall
	XZ392	SEPECAT Jaguar GR3	DARA, RAF St Athan
	XZ394	SEPECAT Jaguar GR3 [GN]	RAF No 54 Sqn, Coltishall
	XZ396	SEPECAT Jaguar GR1A [EM]	RAF No 6 Sqn, Coltishall
	XZ398	SEPECAT Jaguar GR3 [FA]	RAF No 41 Sqn, Coltishall
	XZ399	SEPECAT Jaguar GR3A [EJ]	RAF No 6 Sqn, Coltishall
	XZ400	SEPECAT Jaguar GR3 [GR]	DPA/BAE Systems, Warton
	XZ431	HS Buccaneer S2B (9233M)	*Sold to Belgium, August 2000*
	XZ439	BAe Sea Harrier FA2	DPA/BAE Systems, Warton
	XZ440	BAe Sea Harrier FA2 [127]	RN No 800 Sqn, Yeovilton
	XZ455	BAe Sea Harrier FA2 [001]	RN FSAIU, Yeovilton (wreck)
	XZ459	BAe Sea Harrier FA2]	RN AMG, Yeovilton
	XZ493	BAe Sea Harrier FRS1 [001/N] (comp XV760)	FAA Museum, RNAS Yeovilton
	XZ493	BAe Sea Harrier FRS1 <ff>	RN Yeovilton, Fire Section
	XZ494	BAe Sea Harrier FA2 [128]	DPA/BAE Systems, Warton
	XZ497	BAe Sea Harrier FA2 [001]	RN No 801 Sqn, Yeovilton
	XZ499	BAe Sea Harrier FA2	RN No 899 Sqn, Yeovilton
	XZ559	Slingsby T61F Venture T2 (G-BUEK)	Privately owned, Tibenham
	XZ570	WS61 Sea King HAS5(mod)	DPA/GKN Westland, Yeovil
	XZ571	WS61 Sea King HAS6 [016/L]	RN No 820 Sqn, Culdrose
	XZ574	WS61 Sea King HAS6 [512]	RN No 810 Sqn, Culdrose
	XZ575	WS61 Sea King HU5	DPA/AFD, DERA Boscombe Down
	XZ576	WS61 Sea King HAS6	DPA/AFD, DERA Boscombe Down
	XZ578	WS61 Sea King HU5 [709/PW]	RN No 819 Sqn, Prestwick
	XZ579	WS61 Sea King HAS6 [707/PW]	RN No 819 Sqn, Prestwick
	XZ580	WS61 Sea King HAS6 [704/PW]	RN No 819 Sqn, Prestwick
	XZ581	WS61 Sea King HAS6 [69/CU]	RN, stored *HMS Sultan*, Gosport
	XZ585	WS61 Sea King HAR3	RAF No 202 Sqn, E Flt, Leconfield
	XZ586	WS61 Sea King HAR3 [S]	RAF HMF, St Mawgan
	XZ587	WS61 Sea King HAR3	RAF No 202 Sqn, E Flt, Leconfield
	XZ588	WS61 Sea King HAR3	RAF No 202 Sqn, E Flt, Leconfield
	XZ589	WS61 Sea King HAR3	RAF No 22 Sqn, C Flt, Valley
	XZ590	WS61 Sea King HAR3	RAF No 78 Sqn, Mount Pleasant, FI
	XZ591	WS61 Sea King HAR3	RAF HMF, St Mawgan
	XZ592	WS61 Sea King HAR3 [S]	RAF No 203(R) Sqn, St Mawgan
	XZ593	WS61 Sea King HAR3	RAF No 203(R) Sqn, St Mawgan
	XZ594	WS61 Sea King HAR3	RAF HMF, St Mawgan
	XZ595	WS61 Sea King HAR3	RAF No 22 Sqn, C Flt, Valley
	XZ596	WS61 Sea King HAR3	RAF No 78 Sqn, Mount Pleasant, FI
	XZ597	WS61 Sea King HAR3	RAF No 202 Sqn, D Flt, Lossiemouth
	XZ598	WS61 Sea King HAR3	DARA, RNAY Fleetlands
	XZ599	WS61 Sea King HAR3	RAF No 202 Sqn, D Flt, Lossiemouth
	XZ605	WS Lynx AH7 [Y]	RM No 847 Sqn, Yeovilton
	XZ606	WS Lynx AH7	DARA, RNAY Fleetlands
	XZ607	WS Lynx AH7	DARA, RNAY Fleetlands
	XZ608	WS Lynx AH7	AAC No 657 Sqn, Odiham
	XZ609	WS Lynx AH7	AAC No 652 Sqn/1 Regt, Brüggen
	XZ611	WS Lynx AH7	AAC No 661 Sqn/1 Regt, Brüggen
	XZ612	WS Lynx AH7	RM No 847 Sqn, Yeovilton
	XZ613	WS Lynx AH7 [F]	Army SEAE, Arborfield
	XZ614	WS Lynx AH7 [X]	RM No 847 Sqn, Yeovilton

Serial	Type (other identity) [code]	Owner/operator, location or fate	Notes
XZ615	WS Lynx AH7	AAC No 655 Sqn/5 Regt, Aldergrove	
XZ616	WS Lynx AH7	DARA, RNAY Fleetlands	
XZ617	WS Lynx AH7	AAC No 662 Sqn/3 Regt, Wattisham	
XZ630	Panavia Tornado GR1 (8976M)	DARA, RAF St Athan, BDRT	
XZ631	Panavia Tornado GR1	DPA/BAE Systems, Warton	
XZ641	WS Lynx AH7	AAC No 25 Flt, Belize	
XZ642	WS Lynx AH7	AAC No 663 Sqn/3 Regt, Wattisham	
XZ643	WS Lynx AH7	AAC No 654 Sqn/4 Regt, Wattisham	
XZ645	WS Lynx AH7	AAC No 4 Regt, Wattisham	
XZ646	WS Lynx AH7	AAC No 657 Sqn, Odiham	
XZ647	WS Lynx AH7	AAC No 667 Sqn, Middle Wallop	
XZ648	WS Lynx AH7	AAC No 664 Sqn/9 Regt, Dishforth	
XZ649	WS Lynx AH7	AAC, stored RNAY Fleetlands	
XZ651	WS Lynx AH7	AAC No 657 Sqn, Odiham	
XZ652	WS Lynx AH7 [T]	AAC No 671 Sqn/2 Regt, Middle Wallop	
XZ653	WS Lynx AH7	AAC No 663 Sqn/3 Regt, Wattisham	
XZ654	WS Lynx AH7	DARA, RNAY Fleetlands	
XZ655	WS Lynx AH7	AAC No 655 Sqn/5 Regt, Aldergrove	
XZ661	WS Lynx AH1	AAC No 655 Sqn/5 Regt, Aldergrove	
XZ662	WS Lynx AH7	*Crashed 2 March 2000, Mullaghbawn, N Ireland*	
XZ663	WS Lynx AH7	AAC No 655 Sqn/5 Regt, Aldergrove	
XZ664	WS Lynx AH7	AAC No 663 Sqn/3 Regt, Wattisham	
XZ665	WS Lynx AH7	AAC, stored RNAY Fleetlands	
XZ666	WS Lynx AH7	Army SEAE, Arborfield	
XZ668	WS Lynx AH7 [UN] (wreckage)	AAC Middle Wallop, instructional use	
XZ669	WS Lynx AH7	AAC No 663 Sqn/3 Regt, Wattisham	
XZ670	WS Lynx AH7	AAC, stored RNAY Fleetlands	
XZ671	WS Lynx AH7 <ff>	GKN Westland, Yeovil, instructional use	
XZ672	WS Lynx AH7	AAC No 655 Sqn/5 Regt, Aldergrove	
XZ673	WS Lynx AH7	AAC No 655 Sqn/5 Regt, Aldergrove	
XZ674	WS Lynx AH7	AAC No 656 Sqn/9 Regt, Dishforth	
XZ675	WS Lynx AH7 [E]	AAC No 671 Sqn/2 Regt, Middle Wallop	
XZ676	WS Lynx AH7 [N]	AAC No 671 Sqn/2 Regt, Middle Wallop	
XZ677	WS Lynx AH7	AAC, stored RNAY Fleetlands	
XZ678	WS Lynx AH7	DARA, RNAY Fleetlands	
XZ679	WS Lynx AH7	DARA, RNAY Fleetlands	
XZ680	WS Lynx AH7	DARA, RNAY Fleetlands	
XZ681	WS Lynx AH1	*Scrapped at Middle Wallop*	
XZ689	WS Lynx HMA8 [674]	RN No 702 Sqn, Yeovilton	
XZ690	WS Lynx HMA8 [412/CW]	RN No 815 Sqn, *Cornwall* Flt, Yeovilton	
XZ691	WS Lynx HMA8 [670]	RN No 702 Sqn, Yeovilton	
XZ692	WS Lynx HMA8 [365/AY]	DARA, RNAY Fleetlands	
XZ693	WS Lynx HAS3S [644]	RN No 702 Sqn, Yeovilton	
XZ694	WS Lynx HAS3S [420/EX]	RN AMG, Yeovilton	
XZ695	WS Lynx HMA8	DARA, RNAY Fleetlands (conversion)	
XZ696	WS Lynx HAS3S [363/MA]	RN No 815 Sqn, *Marlborough* Flt, Yeovilton	
XZ697	WS Lynx HMA8 [308]	RN AMG, Yeovilton	
XZ698	WS Lynx HMA8 [672]	RN No 702 Sqn, Yeovilton	
XZ699	WS Lynx HAS3S [303]	DARA, RNAY Fleetlands	
XZ719	WS Lynx HMA8	RN No 815 Sqn OEU, Yeovilton	
XZ720	WS Lynx HAS3S [360/MC]	RN No 815 Sqn, *Manchester* Flt, Yeovilton	
XZ721	WS Lynx HMA8 [350/CL]	RN No 815 Sqn, *Cumberland* Flt, Yeovilton	
XZ722	WS Lynx HMA8	RN AMG, Yeovilton	
XZ723	WS Lynx HMA8	DARA, RNAY Fleetlands	
XZ724	WS Lynx HAS3S [415/MM]	RN AMG, Yeovilton	
XZ725	WS Lynx HMA8 [633]	DARA, RNAY Fleetlands (conversion)	
XZ726	WS Lynx HMA8 [404/IR]	RN No 815 Sqn, *Iron Duke* Flt, Yeovilton	
XZ727	WS Lynx HAS3S [303]	RN AMG, Yeovilton	
XZ728	WS Lynx HMA8 [415/MM]	RN, stored RNAY Fleetlands	
XZ729	WS Lynx HMA8 [632]	DARA, RNAY Fleetlands (conversion)	
XZ730	WS Lynx HAS3CTS [632]	RN No 702 Sqn, Yeovilton	
XZ731	WS Lynx HMA8 [307]	RN No 815 Sqn, HQ Flt, Yeovilton	
XZ732	WS Lynx HMA8 [318]	RN No 815 Sqn OEU, Yeovilton	
XZ733	WS Lynx HAS3S [344/GW]	RN No 815 Sqn, *Glasgow* Flt, Yeovilton	
XZ735	WS Lynx HAS3S [437/GT]	RN No 815 Sqn, *Grafton* Flt, Yeovilton	
XZ736	WS Lynx HMA8 [352/SD]	RN No 815 Sqn, *Sheffield* Flt, Yeovilton	
XZ920	WS61 Sea King HU5 [822/CU]	RN, stored RNAY Fleetlands	
XZ921	WS61 Sea King HAS6 [269]	RN ETS, Culdrose	
XZ922	WS61 Sea King HAS6 [701]	RN No 819 Sqn, Prestwick	
XZ930	WS Gazelle HT3 [Q]	RN AESS, *HMS Sultan*, Gosport	

Notes	Serial	Type (other identity) [code]	Owner/operator, location or fate
	XZ931	WS Gazelle HT3 [R]	RAF, stored Shawbury
	XZ932	WS Gazelle HT3 [S]	RAF, stored Shawbury
	XZ933	WS Gazelle HT3 [T]	RAF, stored Shawbury
	XZ934	WS Gazelle HT3 [U]	RAF, stored Shawbury
	XZ935	WS Gazelle HCC4	RAF, stored RNAY Fleetlands
	XZ936	WS Gazelle HT2 [6]	DPA/AFD/ETPS, DERA Boscombe Down
	XZ937	WS Gazelle HT2 [Y]	Privately owned, Stapleford Tawney
	XZ938	WS Gazelle HT2 [45/CU]	RN, stored Shawbury
	XZ939	WS Gazelle HT2 [9]	DPA/AFD/ETPS, DERA Boscombe Down
	XZ940	WS Gazelle HT2 [O]	RAF, stored Shawbury
	XZ941	WS Gazelle HT2 [B]	RAF, stored Shawbury
	XZ942	WS Gazelle HT2 [42/CU]	RN, stored Shawbury
	XZ964	BAe Harrier GR3 [D]	Royal Engineers Museum, Chatham
	XZ966	BAe Harrier GR3 (9221M) [G]	MoD FSCTE, Manston
	XZ968	BAe Harrier GR3 (9222M) [3G]	Muckleborough Collection, Weybourne
	XZ969	BAe Harrier GR3 [D]	SFDO, RNAS Culdrose
	XZ971	BAe Harrier GR3 (9219M) [G]	RAF, stored Shawbury
	XZ987	BAe Harrier GR3 (9185M) [C]	RAF Stafford, at main gate
	XZ990	BAe Harrier GR3 <ff>	No 1220 Sqn ATC, March, Cambs
	XZ990	BAe Harrier GR3 <rf>	RAF Wittering, derelict
	XZ991	BAe Harrier GR3 (9162M) [3A]	DARA, RAF St Athan, BDRT
	XZ993	BAe Harrier GR3 (9240M) (fuselage)	DARA, RAF St Athan, fire training
	XZ994	BAe Harrier GR3 (9170M) [U]	RAF Air Movements School, Brize Norton
	XZ995	BAe Harrier GR3 (9220M) [3G]	Shoreham Airport, on display
	XZ996	BAe Harrier GR3 [96]	SFDO, RNAS Culdrose
	XZ997	BAe Harrier GR3 (9122M) [V]	RAF Museum, Hendon
	ZA101	BAe Hawk 100 (G-HAWK)	DPA/BAE Systems, Warton
	ZA105	WS61 Sea King HAR3 [S]	RAF No 202 Sq, A Flt, Boulmer
	ZA110	BAe Jetstream T2 (F-BTMI) [563/CU]	RN No 750 Sqn, Culdrose
	ZA111	BAe Jetstream T2 (9Q-CTC) [565/CU]	RN No 750 Sqn, Culdrose
	ZA126	WS61 Sea King HAS6 [504/CU]	RN No 810 Sqn, Culdrose
	ZA127	WS61 Sea King HAS6 [509/CU]	RN No 810 Sqn, Culdrose
	ZA128	WS61 Sea King HAS6 [010]	RN No 810 Sqn, Culdrose
	ZA129	WS61 Sea King HAS6 [502/CU]	DARA, RNAY Fleetlands
	ZA130	WS61 Sea King HU5 [824]	RN No 771 Sqn, Culdrose
	ZA131	WS61 Sea King HAS6 [271/N]	RN stored, *HMS Sultan*, Gosport
	ZA133	WS61 Sea King HAS6 [013/L]	RN No 820 Sqn, Culdrose
	ZA134	WS61 Sea King HU5 [825]	RN No 771 Sqn, Culdrose
	ZA135	WS61 Sea King HAS6 [705/PW]	RN No 819 Sqn, Prestwick
	ZA135	*WS61 Sea King HAS5 [XV657]*	*Repainted as XV657 by May 2000*
	ZA136	WS61 Sea King HAS6 [018/L]	RN, AESS, *HMS Sultan*, Gosport (wreck)
	ZA137	WS61 Sea King HU5 [820]	RN No 771 Sqn, Culdrose
	ZA140	BAe VC10 K2 (G-ARVL) [A]	RAF, stored St Athan
	ZA141	BAe VC10 K2 (G-ARVG) [B]	*Scrapped St Athan, November 2000*
	ZA142	BAe VC10 K2 (G-ARVI) [C]	RAF, stored St Athan
	ZA143	BAe VC10 K2 (G-ARVK) [D]	*Scrapped St Athan, September 2000*
	ZA144	BAe VC10 K2 (G-ARVC) [E]	RAF, stored St Athan
	ZA147	BAe VC10 K3 (5H-MMT) [F]	RAF No 101 Sqn, Brize Norton
	ZA148	BAe VC10 K3 (5Y-ADA) [G]	RAF No 101 Sqn, Brize Norton
	ZA149	BAe VC10 K3 (5X-UVJ) [H]	RAF No 101 Sqn, Brize Norton
	ZA150	BAe VC10 K3 (5H-MOG) [J]	RAF No 101 Sqn, Brize Norton
	ZA166	WS61 Sea King HU5 [189/CU]	RN No 849 Sqn, Culdrose
	ZA167	WS61 Sea King HU5 [822/CU]	RN No 771 Sqn, Culdrose
	ZA168	WS61 Sea King HAS6 [512/CU]	RN AMG, Culdrose
	ZA169	WS61 Sea King HAS6 [500/CU]	RN No 810 Sqn, Culdrose
	ZA170	WS61 Sea King HU5	RN, stored *HMS Sultan*, Gosport
	ZA175	BAe Sea Harrier FA2 [126/N]	RN, St Athan
	ZA176	BAe Sea Harrier FA2 [128/N]	RN, St Athan
	ZA195	BAe Sea Harrier FA2	DPA/BAE Systems, Warton
	ZA250	BAe Harrier T52 (G-VTOL)	Brooklands Museum, Weybridge
	ZA254	Panavia Tornado F2 (fuselage)	RAF Coningsby, instructional use
	ZA267	Panavia Tornado F2	RAF Marham, instructional use
	ZA283	Panavia Tornado F2	RAF St Athan Fire Section
	ZA291	WS61 Sea King HC4 [ZX]	RN No 848 Sqn, Yeovilton
	ZA292	WS61 Sea King HC4 [ZR]	DPA/GKN Westland, Weston-super-Mare
	ZA293	WS61 Sea King HC4 [ZO]	RN No 848 Sqn, Yeovilton
	ZA295	WS61 Sea King HC4 [ZR]	RN No 848 Sqn, Yeovilton
	ZA296	WS61 Sea King HC4 [VO]	RN No 846 Sqn, Yeovilton
	ZA297	WS61 Sea King HC4 [C]	RN No 845 Sqn, Yeovilton

Serial	Type (other identity) [code]	Owner/operator, location or fate	Notes
ZA298	WS61 Sea King HC4 [G]	RN No 845 Sqn, Yeovilton	
ZA299	WS61 Sea King HC4 [ZT]	RN No 848 Sqn, Yeovilton	
ZA310	WS61 Sea King HC4 [ZY]	RN No 848 Sqn, Yeovilton	
ZA312	WS61 Sea King HC4 [ZS]	RN No 848 Sqn, Yeovilton	
ZA313	WS61 Sea King HC4 [M]	RN No 845 Sqn, Yeovilton	
ZA314	WS61 Sea King HC4 [F]	RN No 845 Sqn, Yeovilton	
ZA319	Panavia Tornado GR1 [TAV]	RAF No 15(R) Sqn, Lossiemouth	
ZA320	Panavia Tornado GR1 [TAW]	RAF No 15(R) Sqn, Lossiemouth	
ZA321	Panavia Tornado GR1 [TAB]	RAF No 15(R) Sqn, Lossiemouth	
ZA322	Panavia Tornado GR1 [TAC]	RAF No 15(R) Sqn, Lossiemouth	
ZA323	Panavia Tornado GR1 [TAZ]	RAF No 15(R) Sqn, Lossiemouth	
ZA324	Panavia Tornado GR1 [TAY]	RAF No 15(R) Sqn, Lossiemouth	
ZA325	Panavia Tornado GR1 [TAX]	RAF No 15(R) Sqn, Lossiemouth	
ZA326	Panavia Tornado GR1P	DPA/AFD, DERA Boscombe Down	
ZA327	Panavia Tornado GR1	DPA/BAE Systems, Warton	
ZA328	Panavia Tornado GR1	DPA/BAE Systems, Warton	
ZA352	Panavia Tornado GR1 [TAU]	RAF No 15(R) Sqn, Lossiemouth	
ZA353	Panavia Tornado GR1 [B-53]	DPA/AFD, DERA Boscombe Down	
ZA354	Panavia Tornado GR1	DPA/BAE Systems, Warton	
ZA355	Panavia Tornado GR1 [TAA]	RAF No 15(R) Sqn, Lossiemouth	
ZA356	Panavia Tornado GR1 [TP]	RAF No 15(R) Sqn, Lossiemouth	
ZA357	Panavia Tornado GR1 [TS]	RAF No 15(R) Sqn, Lossiemouth	
ZA358	Panavia Tornado GR1	DPA/BAE Systems, Warton	
ZA359	Panavia Tornado GR1	BAE Systems Warton, Overseas Customer Training Centre	
ZA360	Panavia Tornado GR1 [TC]	RAF No 15(R) Sqn, Lossiemouth	
ZA361	Panavia Tornado GR4 [B-57]	DPA/BAE Systems, Warton (conversion)	
ZA362	Panavia Tornado GR1 [TR]	RAF No 15(R) Sqn, Lossiemouth	
ZA365	Panavia Tornado GR4 [AJ-Y]	RAF No 617 Sqn, Lossiemouth	
ZA367	Panavia Tornado GR4 [II]	DARA, RAF St Athan	
ZA369	Panavia Tornado GR4A [U]	RAF No 13 Sqn, Marham	
ZA370	Panavia Tornado GR1A [A]	RAF No 2 Sqn, Marham	
ZA371	Panavia Tornado GR4A [C]	RAF No 2 Sqn, Marham	
ZA372	Panavia Tornado GR1A [E]	RAF No 2 Sqn, Marham	
ZA373	Panavia Tornado GR4A [H]	DPA/BAE Systems, Warton (conversion)	
ZA374	Panavia Tornado GR1B [AJ-L]	RAF No 617 Sqn, Lossiemouth	
ZA375	Panavia Tornado GR1B [AJ-W]	RAF No 617 Sqn, Lossiemouth	
ZA393	Panavia Tornado GR1 [BE]	RAF No 13 Sqn, Marham	
ZA395	Panavia Tornado GR4A [N]	DPA/BAE Systems, Warton (conversion)	
ZA398	Panavia Tornado GR4A [S]	RAF St Athan	
ZA399	Panavia Tornado GR1B [AJ-C]	RAF No 617 Sqn, Lossiemouth	
ZA400	Panavia Tornado GR4A	RAF No 2 Sqn, Marham	
ZA401	Panavia Tornado GR1A [R]	RAF No 2 Sqn, Marham	
ZA402	Panavia Tornado GR4A	DPA/BAE Systems, Warton (conversion)	
ZA404	Panavia Tornado GR4A [W]	RAF No 2 Sqn, Marham	
ZA405	Panavia Tornado GR4A [Y]	DPA/BAE Systems, Warton (conversion)	
ZA406	Panavia Tornado GR1 [CI]	RAF No 12 Sqn, Lossiemouth	
ZA407	Panavia Tornado GR1B [AJ-N]	RAF No 617 Sqn, Lossiemouth	
ZA409	Panavia Tornado GR1B [FQ]	RAF No 12 Sqn, Lossiemouth	
ZA410	Panavia Tornado GR4	RAF No 31 Sqn, Brüggen	
ZA411	Panavia Tornado GR1B [AJ-S]	RAF No 617 Sqn, Lossiemouth	
ZA412	Panavia Tornado GR1 [IV]	RAF No 15(R) Sqn, Lossiemouth	
ZA446	Panavia Tornado GR1B [U]	RAF AWC/SAOEU, DERA Boscombe Down	
ZA447	Panavia Tornado GR1B [FA]	RAF No 12 Sqn, Lossiemouth	
ZA449	Panavia Tornado GR4 [Q]	DPA/BAE Systems, Warton (conversion)	
ZA450	Panavia Tornado GR1B [FG]	RAF No 12 Sqn, Lossiemouth	
ZA452	Panavia Tornado GR1B [FC]	RAF No 12 Sqn, Lossiemouth	
ZA453	Panavia Tornado GR1B [AJ-M]	RAF No 617 Sqn, Lossiemouth	
ZA455	Panavia Tornado GR1B [F]	RAF No 15(R) Sqn, Lossiemouth	
ZA456	Panavia Tornado GR1B [AJ-Q]	RAF No 617 Sqn, Lossiemouth	
ZA457	Panavia Tornado GR1B [AJ-J]	RAF No 617 Sqn, Lossiemouth	
ZA458	Panavia Tornado GR4 [DG]	RAF No 31 Sqn, Brüggen	
ZA459	Panavia Tornado GR1B [AJ-B]	RAF No 617 Sqn, Lossiemouth	
ZA460	Panavia Tornado GR1B [AJ-A]	RAF, stored St Athan	
ZA461	Panavia Tornado GR1B [FD]	RAF No 12 Sqn, Lossiemouth	
ZA462	Panavia Tornado GR1 [BV]	RAF ASF, Lossiemouth	
ZA463	Panavia Tornado GR1 [FK]	RAF No 12 Sqn, Lossiemouth	
ZA465	Panavia Tornado GR1B [FF]	RAF No 12 Sqn, Lossiemouth	
ZA466	Panavia Tornado GR1 <ff>	DARA, RAF St Athan, BDRT	
ZA469	Panavia Tornado GR1B [TM]	RAF No 15(R) Sqn, Lossiemouth	
ZA470	Panavia Tornado GR1 [BQ]	RAF No 15(R) Sqn, Lossiemouth	
ZA471	Panavia Tornado GR1B [AJ-K]	DARA, St Athan (on repair)	

ZA472 – ZA682

Notes	Serial	Type (other identity) [code]	Owner/operator, location or fate
	ZA472	Panavia Tornado GR1 [FL]	RAF No 12 Sqn, Lossiemouth
	ZA473	Panavia Tornado GR1B [TK]	RAF No 15(R) Sqn, Lossiemouth
	ZA474	Panavia Tornado GR1B [AJ-F]	RAF No 617 Sqn, Lossiemouth
	ZA475	Panavia Tornado GR1B [FH]	RAF No 12 Sqn, Lossiemouth
	ZA490	Panavia Tornado GR1B [FJ]	RAF No 12 Sqn, Lossiemouth
	ZA491	Panavia Tornado GR1B [TI]	RAF No 15(R) Sqn, Lossiemouth
	ZA492	Panavia Tornado GR1B [TE]	RAF No 15(R) Sqn, Lossiemouth
	ZA541	Panavia Tornado GR4 [DZ]	RAF No 31 Sqn, Brüggen
	ZA542	Panavia Tornado GR4 [DM]	RAF No 31 Sqn, Brüggen
	ZA543	Panavia Tornado GR4	DPA/BAE Systems, Warton
	ZA544	Panavia Tornado GR4 [FZ]	RAF No 12 Sqn, Lossiemouth
	ZA546	Panavia Tornado GR1 [TB]	RAF No 15(R) Sqn, Lossiemouth
	ZA547	Panavia Tornado GR4 [DC]	RAF No 31 Sqn, Brüggen
	ZA548	Panavia Tornado GR4 [III]	RAF No 2 Sqn, Marham
	ZA549	Panavia Tornado GR4 [AJ-Z]	RAF No 617 Sqn, Lossiemouth
	ZA550	Panavia Tornado GR4 [DD]	RAF No 31 Sqn, Brüggen
	ZA551	Panavia Tornado GR4 [AX]	RAF No 9 Sqn, Brüggen
	ZA552	Panavia Tornado GR4 [IV]	RAF No 2 Sqn, Marham
	ZA553	Panavia Tornado GR4 [DI]	RAF No 31 Sqn, Brüggen
	ZA554	Panavia Tornado GR4 [DF]	RAF No 31 Sqn, Brüggen
	ZA556	Panavia Tornado GR4 [F]	RAF No 13 Sqn, Marham
ZA556	*ZA556*	Panavia Tornado GR1 <R> (ZA368/BAPC 155) [F]	RAF EPTT, St Athan
	ZA557	Panavia Tornado GR4 [AC]	RAF No 9 Sqn, Brüggen
	ZA559	Panavia Tornado GR4 [AD]	RAF No 9 Sqn, Brüggen
	ZA560	Panavia Tornado GR4 [BC]	RAF No 14 Sqn, Lossiemouth
	ZA562	Panavia Tornado GR4 [TT]	DPA/BAE Systems, Warton (conversion)
	ZA563	Panavia Tornado GR4 [AG]	RAF No 9 Sqn, Brüggen
	ZA564	Panavia Tornado GR1 [TJ]	RAF No 15(R) Sqn, Lossiemouth
	ZA585	Panavia Tornado GR4 [AH]	RAF No 9 Sqn, Brüggen
	ZA587	Panavia Tornado GR1 [F]	DARA, RAF St Athan
	ZA588	Panavia Tornado GR4 [TM]	DPA/BAE Systems, Warton (conversion)
	ZA589	Panavia Tornado GR4 [TE]	DPA/AFD, DERA Boscombe Down
	ZA590	Panavia Tornado GR1	RAF, stored St Athan
	ZA591	Panavia Tornado GR4 [DJ]	RAF No 31 Sqn, Brüggen
	ZA592	Panavia Tornado GR4 [C]	DPA/BAE Systems, Warton (conversion)
	ZA594	Panavia Tornado GR4 [XY]	RAF, St Athan
	ZA595	Panavia Tornado GR4 [VIII]	RAF No 13 Sqn, Marham
	ZA596	Panavia Tornado GR4	RAF No 14 Sqn, Lossiemouth
	ZA597	Panavia Tornado GR1 [TA]	RAF No 15(R) Sqn, Lossiemouth
	ZA598	Panavia Tornado GR4 [AY]	RAF No 9 Sqn, Brüggen
	ZA599	Panavia Tornado GR4 [TX]	RAF St Athan
	ZA600	Panavia Tornado GR4 [TH]	DPA/BAE Systems, Warton (conversion)
	ZA601	Panavia Tornado GR4 [AK]	RAF No 9 Sqn, Brüggen
	ZA602	Panavia Tornado GR4 [BY]	RAF No 14 Sqn, Lossiemouth
	ZA604	Panavia Tornado GR4 [TY]	RAF No 617 Sqn Lossiemouth
	ZA606	Panavia Tornado GR4	DPA/AFD, DERA Boscombe Down
	ZA607	Panavia Tornado GR4 [AB]	RAF No 9 Sqn, Brüggen
	ZA608	Panavia Tornado GR4 [TK]	DPA/BAE Systems, Warton (conversion)
	ZA609	Panavia Tornado GR4	RAF AWC/SAOEU DERA Boscombe Down
	ZA611	Panavia Tornado GR4 [TG]	DPA/BAE Systems, Warton (conversion)
	ZA612	Panavia Tornado GR4	RAF No 14 Sqn, Lossiemouth
	ZA613	Panavia Tornado GR1	RAF No 15(R) Sqn, Lossiemouth
	ZA614	Panavia Tornado GR4 [TB]	DPA/BAE Systems, Warton (conversion)
	ZA634	Slingsby T61F Venture T2 (G-BUHA) [C]	Privately owned, Rufforth
	ZA663	Slingsby T61F Venture T2 (G-BUFP)	*Crashed 12 May 2000, Markyate, Beds*
	ZA670	B-V Chinook HC2 (N37010) [EY]	RAF No 7 Sqn, Odiham
	ZA671	B-V Chinook HC2 (N37011) [BB]	RAF No 18 Sqn, Odiham
	ZA673	B-V Chinook HC2 (N37016) [NT]	RAF No 27 Sqn, Odiham
	ZA674	B-V Chinook HC2 (N37019)	RAF No 7 Sqn, Odiham
	ZA675	B-V Chinook HC2 (N37020) [EB]	RAF No 18 Sqn, Odiham
	ZA676	B-V Chinook HC1 (N37021/9230M) [FG] (wreck)	AAC, Wattisham
	ZA677	B-V Chinook HC2 (N37022) [EG]	RAF No 7 Sqn, Odiham
	ZA678	B-V Chinook HC1 (N37023/9229M) [EZ] (wreck)	RAF Odiham, BDRT
	ZA679	B-V Chinook HC2 (N37025) [BC]	RAF No 18 Sqn, Odiham
	ZA680	B-V Chinook HC2 (N37026) [NX]	DARA, RNAY Fleetlands
	ZA681	B-V Chinook HC2 (N37027) [ED]	RAF No 18 Sqn, Odiham
	ZA682	B-V Chinook HC2 (N37029) [EW]	RAF No 7 Sqn, Odiham

Serial	Type (other identity) [code]	Owner/operator, location or fate	Notes
ZA683	B-V Chinook HC2 (N37030)	DARA, RNAY Fleetlands	
ZA684	B-V Chinook HC2 (N37031) [U]	RAF No 7 Sqn, Odiham	
ZA704	B-V Chinook HC2 (N37033) [EJ]	DARA, RNAY Fleetlands (wreck)	
ZA705	B-V Chinook HC2 (N37035) [BE]	RAF No 18 Sqn, Odiham	
ZA707	B-V Chinook HC2 (N37040) [EV]	RAF No 7 Sqn, Odiham	
ZA708	B-V Chinook HC2 (N37042)	RAF No 27 Sqn, Odiham	
ZA709	B-V Chinook HC2 (N37043) [EQ]	DARA, RNAY Fleetlands	
ZA710	B-V Chinook HC2 (N37044) [NC]	RAF No 27 Sqn, Odiham	
ZA711	B-V Chinook HC2 (N37046) [ET]	RAF No 7 Sqn, Odiham	
ZA712	B-V Chinook HC2 (N37047) [ER]	RAF No 27 Sqn, Odiham	
ZA713	B-V Chinook HC2 (N37048) [EM]	RAF No 7 Sqn, Odiham	
ZA714	B-V Chinook HC2 (N37051) [NT]	RAF No 27 Sqn, Odiham	
ZA717	B-V Chinook HC1 (N37056/9238M) (wreck)	RAF Cranwell, BDRT	
ZA718	B-V Chinook HC2 (N37058) [BN]	RAF No 78 Sqn, Mount Pleasant, FI	
ZA720	B-V Chinook HC2 (N37060) [EP]	RAF No 7 Sqn, Odiham	
ZA726	WS Gazelle AH1 [F1]	AAC No 671 Sqn/2 Regt, Middle Wallop	
ZA728	WS Gazelle AH1	RM No 847 Sqn, Yeovilton	
ZA729	WS Gazelle AH1	AAC No 1 Regt, Brüggen	
ZA730	WS Gazelle AH1	AAC, stored Shawbury	
ZA731	WS Gazelle AH1 [5C]	AAC No 29 Flt, BATUS, Suffield, Canada	
ZA733	WS Gazelle AH1	RNAY Fleetlands Apprentice School	
ZA734	WS Gazelle AH1	AAC No 25 Flt, Belize	
ZA735	WS Gazelle AH1	AAC No 25 Flt, Belize	
ZA736	WS Gazelle AH1	AAC No 29 Flt, BATUS, Suffield, Canada	
ZA737	WS Gazelle AH1	Museum of Army Flying, Middle Wallop	
ZA766	WS Gazelle AH1	AAC, stored RNAY Fleetlands	
ZA768	WS Gazelle AH1 [F] (wreck)	AAC, stored RNAY Fleetlands	
ZA769	WS Gazelle AH1 [K]	Army SEAE, Arborfield	
ZA771	WS Gazelle AH1	AAC No 663 Sqn/3 Regt, Wattisham	
ZA772	WS Gazelle AH1	AAC No 665 Sqn/5 Regt, Aldergrove	
ZA773	WS Gazelle AH1 [F]	AAC No 666(V) Sqn/7 Regt, Netheravon	
ZA774	WS Gazelle AH1	AAC No 665 Sqn/5 Regt, Aldergrove	
ZA775	WS Gazelle AH1	AAC No 665 Sqn/5 Regt, Aldergrove	
ZA776	WS Gazelle AH1 [F]	RM No 847 Sqn, Yeovilton	
ZA777	WS Gazelle AH1 [B]	AAC No 671 Sqn/2 Regt, Middle Wallop	
ZA802	WS Gazelle HT3 [W]	RAF, stored Shawbury	
ZA803	WS Gazelle HT3 [X]	RAF, stored Shawbury	
ZA804	WS Gazelle HT3 [I]	RAF, stored Shawbury	
ZA934	WS Puma HC1	RAF No 72 Sqn, Aldergrove	
ZA935	WS Puma HC1	RAF No 33 Sqn, Benson	
ZA936	WS Puma HC1	RAF No 33 Sqn, Benson	
ZA937	WS Puma HC1	RAF No 72 Sqn, Aldergrove	
ZA938	WS Puma HC1	RAF No 72 Sqn, Aldergrove	
ZA939	WS Puma HC1	RAF No 230 Sqn, Aldergrove	
ZA940	WS Puma HC1	RAF No 230 Sqn, Algergrove	
ZA947	Douglas Dakota C3 [YS-H]	RAF BBMF, Coningsby	
ZB500	WS Lynx 800 (G-LYNX/ZA500)	The Helicopter Museum, Weston-super-Mare	
ZB506	WS61 Sea King Mk 4X	DPA/AFD, DERA Boscombe Down	
ZB507	WS61 Sea King HC4 [ZN]	RN No 848 Sqn, Yeovilton	
ZB600	BAe Harrier T4	BAE Systems RNAS Yeovilton, for Indian Navy	
ZB601	BAe Harrier T4 (fuselage)	RNAS Yeovilton, Fire Section	
ZB602	BAe Harrier T4	BAE Systems RNAS Yeovilton, for Indian Navy	
ZB603	BAe Harrier T8 [722/VL]	RN, St Athan	
ZB604	BAe Harrier T8 [722]	RN No 899 Sqn, Yeovilton	
ZB605	BAe Harrier T8 [720/VL]	RN No 899 Sqn, Yeovilton	
ZB615	SEPECAT Jaguar T2A	DPA/AFD, DERA Boscombe Down	
ZB625	WS Gazelle HT3 [N]	RAF, Odiham	
ZB626	WS Gazelle HT3 (G-BZDW) [L]	Privately owned, Stapleford Tawney	
ZB627	WS Gazelle HT3 [A]	RAF, stored Shawbury	
ZB629	WS Gazelle HCC4	AAC, Middle Wallop	
ZB646	WS Gazelle HT2 [59/CU]	RN, stored Shawbury	
ZB647	WS Gazelle HT2 [40/CU]	RN, stored Shawbury	
ZB649	WS Gazelle HT2 [VL]	RN, stored Shawbury	
ZB665	WS Gazelle AH1	AAC No 665 Sqn/5 Regt, Aldergrove	
ZB666	WS Gazelle AH1	Crashed 24 February 2000, Mount Kenya	
ZB667	WS Gazelle AH1	AAC No 16 Flt, Dhekelia, Cyprus	
ZB668	WS Gazelle AH1 (TAD 015)	AAC Stockwell Hall, Middle Wallop, instructional use	

Notes	Serial	Type (other identity) [code]	Owner/operator, location or fate
	ZB669	WS Gazelle AH1	AAC No 654 Sqn/4 Regt, Wattisham
	ZB670	WS Gazelle AH1	AAC No 665 Sqn/5 Regt, Aldergrove
	ZB671	WS Gazelle AH1 [5A]	AAC No 29 Flt, BATUS, Suffield, Canada
	ZB672	WS Gazelle AH1	Army Training Regiment, Winchester
	ZB673	WS Gazelle AH1 [P]	AAC No 671 Sqn/2 Regt, Middle Wallop
	ZB674	WS Gazelle AH1	AAC No 665 Sqn/5 Regt, Aldergrove
	ZB676	WS Gazelle AH1 [C]	RM No 847 Sqn, Yeovilton
	ZB677	WS Gazelle AH1 [3]	AAC No 29 Flt, BATUS, Suffield, Canada
	ZB678	WS Gazelle AH1	Army SEAE, Arborfield
	ZB679	WS Gazelle AH1	AAC No 16 Flt, Dhekelia, Cyprus
	ZB682	WS Gazelle AH1	AAC No 665 Sqn/5 Regt, Aldergrove
	ZB683	WS Gazelle AH1	AAC No 665 Sqn/5 Regt, Aldergrove
	ZB684	WS Gazelle AH1	AAC No 665 Sqn/5 Regt, Aldergrove
	ZB685	WS Gazelle AH1	AAC No 665 Sqn/5 Regt, Aldergrove
	ZB686	WS Gazelle AH1	AAC No 665 Sqn/5 Regt, Aldergrove
	ZB688	WS Gazelle AH1 [H]	AAC No 671 Sqn/2 Regt, Middle Wallop
	ZB689	WS Gazelle AH1	AAC No 665 Sqn/5 Regt, Aldergrove
	ZB690	WS Gazelle AH1	AAC No 16 Flt, Dhekelia, Cyprus
	ZB691	WS Gazelle AH1	AAC No 9 Regt, Dishforth
	ZB692	WS Gazelle AH1	AAC No 9 Regt, Dishforth
	ZB693	WS Gazelle AH1	AAC No 29 Flt, BATUS, Suffield, Canada
	ZD230	BAC Super VC10 K4 (G-ASGA) [K]	RAF No 101 Sqn, Brize Norton
	ZD234	BAC Super VC10 (G-ASGF/8700M)	RAF Brize Norton, tanker simulator
	ZD235	BAC Super VC10 K4 (G-ASGG) [L]	RAF No 101 Sqn, Brize Norton
	ZD239	BAC Super VC10 (G-ASGK)	*Burnt at Manston, 1999*
	ZD240	BAC Super VC10 K4 (G-ASGL) [M]	RAF No 101 Sqn, Brize Norton
	ZD241	BAC Super VC10 K4 (G-ASGM) [N]	RAF No 101 Sqn, Brize Norton
	ZD242	BAC Super VC10 K4 (G-ASGP)	RAF No 101 Sqn, Brize Norton
	ZD249	WS Lynx HAS3S [637]	RN No 702 Sqn, Yeovilton
	ZD250	WS Lynx HAS3S [302]	RN No 815 Sqn, HQ Flt, Yeovilton
	ZD251	WS Lynx HAS3S [636]	RN No 702 Sqn, Yeovilton
	ZD252	WS Lynx HMA8 [671]	RN No 702 Sqn, Yeovilton
	ZD253	WS Lynx HAS3S [410/GC]	RN AMG, Yeovilton
	ZD254	WS Lynx HAS3S [344/GW]	DARA, RNAY Fleetlands
	ZD255	WS Lynx HAS3S	RN No 815 Sqn, Yeovilton
	ZD257	WS Lynx HMA8 [474/RM]	RN No 815 Sqn, *Richmond* Flt, Yeovilton
	ZD258	WS Lynx HMA8 (*XZ258*) [319]	RN No 815 Sqn OEU, Yeovilton
	ZD259	WS Lynx HMA8 [635]	DARA, RNAY Fleetlands (conversion)
	ZD260	WS Lynx HMA8 [444/MR]	RN No 815 Sqn, *Montrose* Flt, Yeovilton
	ZD261	WS Lynx HMA8 [319]	RN No 815 Sqn OEU, Yeovilton
	ZD262	WS Lynx HMA8 [334/SN]	RN AMG, Yeovilton
	ZD263	WS Lynx HAS3S [306]	RN No 815 Sqn, HQ Flt, Yeovilton
	ZD264	WS Lynx HAS3S [457/LA]	RN No 815 Sqn, *Lancaster* Flt, Yeovilton
	ZD265	WS Lynx HMA8 [407/YK]	RN No 815 Sqn, *York* Flt, Yeovilton
	ZD266	WS Lynx HMA8	DPA/GKN Westland, Weston-super-Mare
	ZD267	WS Lynx HMA8	DPA/GKN Westland, Weston-super-Mare
	ZD268	WS Lynx HMA8 [372/NL]	RN No 815 Sqn, *Northumberland* Flt, Yeovilton
	ZD272	WS Lynx AH7 [H]	AAC No 671 Sqn/2 Regt, Middle Wallop
	ZD273	WS Lynx AH7	AAC No 655 Sqn/5 Regt, Aldergrove
	ZD274	WS Lynx AH7	AAC No 664 Sqn/9 Regt, Dishforth
	ZD276	WS Lynx AH7 [X]	AAC No 671 Sqn/2 Regt, Middle Wallop
	ZD277	WS Lynx AH7	DARA, RNAY Fleetlands
	ZD278	WS Lynx AH7 [A]	AAC No 655 Sqn/5 Regt, Aldergrove
	ZD279	WS Lynx AH7	AAC No 655 Sqn/5 Regt, Aldergrove
	ZD280	WS Lynx AH7	AAC No 661 Sqn/1 Regt, Brüggen
	ZD281	WS Lynx AH7 [K]	AAC No 671 Sqn/2 Regt, Middle Wallop
	ZD282	WS Lynx AH7 [L]	RM No 847 Sqn, Yeovilton
	ZD283	WS Lynx AH7 [P]	AAC No 671 Sqn/2 Regt, Middle Wallop
	ZD284	WS Lynx AH7 [H]	AAC No 1 Regt, Brüggen
	ZD285	WS Lynx AH7	DPA/AFD, DERA Boscombe Down
	ZD318	BAe Harrier GR7	DPA/BAE Systems, Warton
	ZD319	BAe Harrier GR7	DPA/AFD, DERA Boscombe Down
	ZD320	BAe Harrier GR7	DPA/AFD, DERA Boscombe Down
	ZD321	BAe Harrier GR7 [02]	RAF HOCU/No 20(R) Sqn, Wittering
	ZD322	BAe Harrier GR7 [03]	RAF No 1 Sqn, Cottesmore
	ZD323	BAe Harrier GR7 [04]	RAF No 1 Sqn, Cottesmore
	ZD327	BAe Harrier GR7 [08]	RAF HOCU/No 20(R) Sqn, Wittering
	ZD328	BAe Harrier GR7 [09]	RAF HOCU/No 20(R) Sqn, Wittering
	ZD329	BAe Harrier GR7 [10]	RAF No 3 Sqn, Cottesmore
	ZD330	BAe Harrier GR7 [11]	RAF HOCU/No 20(R) Sqn, Wittering
	ZD346	BAe Harrier GR7 [13]	RAF No 4 Sqn, Cottesmore

Serial	Type (other identity) [code]	Owner/operator, location or fate	Notes
ZD347	BAe Harrier GR7 [14]	RAF No 4 Sqn, Cottesmore	
ZD348	BAe Harrier GR7 [15]	DARA, RAF St Athan	
ZD350	BAe Harrier GR5 (9189M) <ff>	DARA, RAF St Athan, BDRT	
ZD351	BAe Harrier GR7 (fuselage)	RAF, stored St Athan	
ZD352	BAe Harrier GR7 [19]	DARA, RAF St Athan	
ZD353	BAe Harrier GR5 (fuselage)	BAE Systems, Brough	
ZD354	BAe Harrier GR7 [21]	RAF No 1 Sqn, Cottesmore	
ZD375	BAe Harrier GR7 [23]	RAF HOCU/No 20(R) Sqn, Wittering	
ZD376	BAe Harrier GR7 [24]	RAF No 1 Sqn, Cottesmore	
ZD378	BAe Harrier GR7 [26]	DARA, RAF St Athan	
ZD379	BAe Harrier GR7 [27]	RAF No 4 Sqn, Cottesmore	
ZD380	BAe Harrier GR7 [28]	RAF HOCU/No 20(R) Sqn, Wittering	
ZD401	BAe Harrier GR7 [30]	RAF No 1 Sqn, Cottesmore	
ZD402	BAe Harrier GR7 [31]	RAF HOCU/No 20(R) Sqn, Wittering	
ZD403	BAe Harrier GR7 [32]	RAF, stored St Athan	
ZD404	BAe Harrier GR7 [33]	RAF HOCU/No 20(R) Sqn, Wittering	
ZD405	BAe Harrier GR7 [34]	RAF AWC/SAOEU, DERA Boscombe Down	
ZD406	BAe Harrier GR7 [35]	DARA, RAF St Athan	
ZD407	BAe Harrier GR7 [36]	RAF HOCU/No 20(R) Sqn, Wittering	
ZD408	BAe Harrier GR7 [37]	RAF AWC/SAOEU, DERA Boscombe Down	
ZD409	BAe Harrier GR7 [38]	RAF No 4 Sqn, Cottesmore	
ZD410	BAe Harrier GR7 [39]	RAF No 3 Sqn, Cottesmore	
ZD411	BAe Harrier GR7	DARA, RAF St Athan	
ZD412	BAe Harrier GR5 (fuselage)	BAE Systems Brough, fatigue testing	
ZD431	BAe Harrier GR7 [43]	DARA, RAF St Athan	
ZD433	BAe Harrier GR7 [45]	RAF HOCU/No 20(R) Sqn, Wittering	
ZD435	BAe Harrier GR7 [47]	RAF No 1 Sqn, Cottesmore	
ZD436	BAe Harrier GR7 [48]	RAF No 3 Sqn, Cottesmore	
ZD437	BAe Harrier GR7 [49]	RAF HOCU/No 20(R) Sqn, Wittering	
ZD438	BAe Harrier GR7 [50]	RAF No 1 Sqn, Cottesmore	
ZD461	BAe Harrier GR7 [51]	RAF No 3 Sqn, Cottesmore	
ZD462	BAe Harrier GR7 [52]	DARA, RAF St Athan (damaged)	
ZD463	BAe Harrier GR7 [53]	RAF No 4 Sqn, Cottesmore	
ZD464	BAe Harrier GR7 [54]	RAF No 4 Sqn, Cottesmore	
ZD465	BAe Harrier GR7 [55]	RAF, stored St Athan	
ZD466	BAe Harrier GR7 [56]	RAF HOCU/No 20(R) Sqn, Wittering	
ZD467	BAe Harrier GR7 [57]	RAF No 1 Sqn, Cottesmore	
ZD468	BAe Harrier GR7 [58]	RAF, stored St Athan	
ZD469	BAe Harrier GR7 [59]	RAF No 4 Sqn, Cottesmore	
ZD470	BAe Harrier GR7 [60]	RAF No 3 Sqn, Cottesmore	
ZD476	WS61 Sea King HC4 [ZU]	RN No 848 Sqn, Yeovilton	
ZD477	WS61 Sea King HC4 [H]	RN No 845 Sqn, Yeovilton	
ZD478	WS61 Sea King HC4 [VX]	RN No 846 Sqn, Yeovilton	
ZD479	WS61 Sea King HC4 [ZV]	RN No 848 Sqn, Yeovilton	
ZD480	WS61 Sea King HC4 [E]	RN No 845 Sqn, Yeovilton	
ZD559	WS Lynx AH5X	DPA/AFD, DERA Boscombe Down	
ZD560	WS Lynx AH7	DPA/AFD/ETPS, DERA Boscombe Down	
ZD565	WS Lynx HMA8	RN AMG, Yeovilton	
ZD566	WS Lynx HMA8 [422/SU]	RN No 815 Sqn, *Sutherland* Flt, Yeovilton	
ZD574	B-V Chinook HC2 (N37077) [EH]	DARA, RNAY Fleetlands	
ZD575	B-V Chinook HC2 (N37078) [BW]	RAF No 27 Sqn, Odiham	
ZD578	BAe Sea Harrier FA2 [126]	RN No 800 Sqn, Yeovilton	
ZD579	BAe Sea Harrier FA2 [003/L]	DARA, RAF St Athan	
ZD580	BAe Sea Harrier FA2	RN, stored St Athan	
ZD581	BAe Sea Harrier FA2 [124]	RN No 800 Sqn, Yeovilton	
ZD582	BAe Sea Harrier FA2 [712]	DPA/BAE Systems, Warton	
ZD607	BAe Sea Harrier FA2 [125/N]	DPA/BAE Systems, Warton	
ZD608	BAe Sea Harrier FA2 [710]	RN No 899 Sqn, Yeovilton	
ZD610	BAe Sea Harrier FA2 [711]	DPA/BAE Systems, Warton	
ZD611	BAe Sea Harrier FA2	DPA/BAE Systems, Warton	
ZD612	BAe Sea Harrier FA2 [711]	RN, AMG Yeovilton	
ZD613	BAe Sea Harrier FA2	RN, stored St Athan	
ZD614	BAe Sea Harrier FA2 [122]	RN No 800 Sqn, Yeovilton	
ZD615	BAe Sea Harrier FA2	RN AMG, Yeovilton	
ZD620	BAe 125 CC3	RAF No 32(The Royal) Sqn, Northolt	
ZD621	BAe 125 CC3	RAF No 32(The Royal) Sqn, Northolt	
ZD625	WS61 Sea King HC4 [VZ]	RN No 846 Sqn, Yeovilton	
ZD626	WS61 Sea King HC4 [ZZ]	RN No 848 Sqn, Yeovilton	
ZD627	WS61 Sea King HC4 [VR]	RN No 846 Sqn, Yeovilton	
ZD630	WS61 Sea King HAS6 [012/L]	RN No 820 Sqn, Culdrose	

Notes	Serial	Type (other identity) [code]	Owner/operator, location or fate
	ZD631	WS61 Sea King HAS6 [66] (fuselage)	RN, Predannack Fire School
	ZD633	WS61 Sea King HAS6 [014/L]	RN, stored *HMS Sultan*, Gosport
	ZD634	WS61 Sea King HAS6 [503]	RN No 810 Sqn, Culdrose
	ZD636	WS61 Sea King AEW2 [183]	RN No 849 Sqn, B Flt, Culdrose
	ZD637	WS61 Sea King HAS6 [700/PW]	RN No 819 Sqn, Prestwick
	ZD657	Schleicher ASW-19B Valiant TX1	*Currently not known*
	ZD658	Schleicher ASW-19B Valiant TX1	*Currently not known*
	ZD659	Schleicher ASW-19B Valiant TX1	*Privately owned, Dunstable*
	ZD660	Schleicher ASW-19B Valiant TX1	*Currently not known*
	ZD667	BAe Harrier GR3 (9201M) [67]	SFDO, RNAS Culdrose
	ZD668	BAe Harrier GR3 [3E]	*Currently not known*
	ZD670	BAe Harrier GR3 [3A]	The Trocadero, Leicester Square, London
	ZD703	BAe 125 CC3	RAF No 32(The Royal) Sqn, Northolt
	ZD704	BAe 125 CC3	RAF No 32(The Royal) Sqn, Northolt
	ZD707	Panavia Tornado GR1 [BU]	RAF No 14 Sqn, Lossiemouth
	ZD708	Panavia Tornado GR4	DPA/BAE Systems, Warton
	ZD709	Panavia Tornado GR4	RAF No 12 Sqn, Lossiemouth
	ZD710	Panavia Tornado GR1 <ff>	Robertsbridge Aviation Society, Mayfield
	ZD711	Panavia Tornado GR4 [II]	RAF No 2 Sqn, Marham
	ZD712	Panavia Tornado GR4 [BX]	RAF No 14 Sqn, Lossiemouth
	ZD713	Panavia Tornado GR1 [TW]	RAF No 15(R) Sqn, Lossiemouth
	ZD714	Panavia Tornado GR4 [DL]	RAF No 31 Sqn, Brüggen
	ZD715	Panavia Tornado GR4 [AM]	RAF No 9 Sqn, Brüggen
	ZD716	Panavia Tornado GR1 [JM]	RAF, No 14 Sqn, Lossiemouth
	ZD719	Panavia Tornado GR4]	DPA/BAE Systems, Warton
	ZD720	Panavia Tornado GR4	RAF, stored St Athan
	ZD739	Panavia Tornado GR1	RAF, stored St Athan
	ZD740	Panavia Tornado GR4 [AF]	RAF No 9 Sqn, Brüggen
	ZD741	Panavia Tornado GR4 [BZ]	RAF No 14 Sqn, Lossiemouth
	ZD742	Panavia Tornado GR4	RAF No 12 Sqn, Lossiemouth
	ZD743	Panavia Tornado GR4	RAF No 2 Sqn, Marham
	ZD744	Panavia Tornado GR1 [FP]	RAF No 12 Sqn, Lossiemouth
	ZD745	Panavia Tornado GR4 [DA]	RAF No 31 Sqn, Brüggen
	ZD746	Panavia Tornado GR4	RAF AWC/SAOEU, DERA Boscombe Down
	ZD747	Panavia Tornado GR1 [AJ-P]	RAF No 617 Sqn, Lossiemouth
	ZD748	Panavia Tornado GR4 [AK]	DPA/BAE Systems, Warton (conversion)
	ZD749	Panavia Tornado GR1 [BG]	RAF No 13 Sqn, Marham
	ZD788	Panavia Tornado GR1 [BT]	RAF No 2 Sqn, Marham
	ZD789	Panavia Tornado GR1 <ff>	RAF, stored Shawbury
	ZD790	Panavia Tornado GR4	RAF No 617 Sqn, Lossiemouth
	ZD792	Panavia Tornado GR4 [DE]	RAF No 31 Sqn, Brüggen
	ZD793	Panavia Tornado GR1 [BA]	RAF No 14 Sqn, Lossiemouth
	ZD810	Panavia Tornado GR4 [DB]	DPA/BAE Systems, Warton (conversion)
	ZD811	Panavia Tornado GR4 [JJ]	RAF No 14 Sqn, Lossiemouth
	ZD812	Panavia Tornado GR4	RAF No 14 Sqn, Lossiemouth
	ZD842	Panavia Tornado GR4	DPA/BAE Systems, Warton (conversion)
	ZD843	Panavia Tornado GR1 [CJ]	RAF No 12 Sqn, Lossiemouth
	ZD844	Panavia Tornado GR4 [DH]	RAF, St Athan
	ZD847	Panavia Tornado GR4 [AA]	RAF No 9 Sqn, Brüggen
	ZD848	Panavia Tornado GR4	RAF, St Athan
	ZD849	Panavia Tornado GR1 [FE]	RAF No 12 Sqn, Lossiemouth
	ZD850	Panavia Tornado GR4 [AJ-T]	RAF No 617 Sqn, Lossiemouth
	ZD851	Panavia Tornado GR4 [BO]	DPA/BAE Systems, Warton (conversion)
	ZD890	Panavia Tornado GR4 [AE]	DARA, RAF St Athan
	ZD892	Panavia Tornado GR4	RAF St Athan)
	ZD895	Panavia Tornado GR1 [S]	RAF No 2 Sqn, Marham
	ZD899	Panavia Tornado F2	DPA/BAE Systems, Warton
	ZD900	Panavia Tornado F2 (comp ZE343)	RAF, stored St Athan (fuselage)
	ZD901	Panavia Tornado F2 (comp ZE154)	RAF, stored St Athan
	ZD902	Panavia Tornado F2A(TIARA)	DPA/AFD, DERA Boscombe Down
	ZD903	Panavia Tornado F2 (comp ZE728)	RAF, stored St Athan (fuselage)
	ZD904	Panavia Tornado F2 (comp ZE759)	RAF St Athan, Fire Section
	ZD905	Panavia Tornado F2 (comp ZE258)	RAF, stored St Athan
	ZD906	Panavia Tornado F2 (comp ZE294)	RAF St Athan, Fire Section
	ZD932	Panavia Tornado F2 (comp ZE255)	RAF, stored St Athan
	ZD933	Panavia Tornado F2 (comp ZE729)	RAF, stored St Athan
	ZD934	Panavia Tornado F2 (comp ZE786) <ff>	RAF, St Athan Fire Section
	ZD935	Panavia Tornado F2 (comp ZE793) <ff>	RAF, stored Shawbury
	ZD936	Panavia Tornado F2 (comp ZE251)	RAF, stored St Athan

Serial	Type (other identity) [code]	Owner/operator, location or fate	Notes
ZD937	Panavia Tornado F2 (comp ZE736)	RAF St Athan Fire Section	
ZD938	Panavia Tornado F2 (comp ZE295)	RAF, stored Shawbury	
ZD939	Panavia Tornado F2 (comp ZE292)	RAF, stored St Athan	
ZD940	Panavia Tornado F2 (comp ZE288)	RAF, stored St Athan	
ZD941	Panavia Tornado F2 (comp ZE254)	RAF St Athan, Fire Section	
ZD948	Lockheed TriStar KC1 (G-BFCA)	RAF No 216 Sqn, Brize Norton	
ZD949	Lockheed TriStar KC1 (G-BFCB)	RAF No 216 Sqn, Brize Norton	
ZD950	Lockheed TriStar KC1 (G-BFCC)	RAF No 216 Sqn, Brize Norton	
ZD951	Lockheed TriStar K1 (G-BFCD)	RAF No 216 Sqn, Brize Norton	
ZD952	Lockheed TriStar KC1 (G-BFCE)	RAF No 216 Sqn, Brize Norton	
ZD953	Lockheed TriStar KC1 (G-BFCF)	RAF No 216 Sqn, Brize Norton	
ZD974	Schempp-Hirth Kestrel TX1 [SY]	Currently not known	
ZD975	Schempp-Hirth Kestrel TX1 [SZ]	Currently not known	
ZD980	B-V Chinook HC2 (N37082) [EA]	DARA, RNAY Fleetlands	
ZD981	B-V Chinook HC2 (N37083) [BH]	RAF No 18 Sqn, Odiham	
ZD982	B-V Chinook HC2 (N37085) [BI]	RAF No 18 Sqn, Odiham	
ZD983	B-V Chinook HC2 (N37086) [EI]	RAF No 27 Sqn, Odiham	
ZD984	B-V Chinook HC2 (N37088) [BJ]	RAF No 18 Sqn, Odiham	
ZD990	BAe Harrier T8 [721/VL]	RN No 899 Sqn, Yeovilton	
ZD991	BAe Harrier T8 (9228M) [722/VL]	RAF, stored St Athan (damaged)	
ZD992	BAe Harrier T8 [724/VL]	Crashed 16 November 2000, Yeovilton	
ZD993	BAe Harrier T8 [723/VL]	RN No 899 Sqn, Yeovilton	
ZD996	Panavia Tornado GR4A [I]	DPA/BAE Systems, Warton (conversion)	
ZE116	Panavia Tornado GR4A [X]	RAF No 13 Sqn, Marham	
ZE154	Panavia Tornado F3 (comp ZD901)	RAF No 43 Sqn, Leuchars	
ZE155	Panavia Tornado F3	DPA/BAE Systems, Warton	
ZE156	Panavia Tornado F3 [E]	RAF No 111 Sqn, Leuchars	
ZE157	Panavia Tornado F3 [GK]	RAF No 25 Sqn, Leeming	
ZE158	Panavia Tornado F3 [Z]	RAF No 25 Sqn, Leeming	
ZE159	Panavia Tornado F3 [R]	RAF No 111 Sqn, Leuchars	
ZE160	Panavia Tornado F3 [DV]	RAF No 11 Sqn, Leeming	
ZE161	Panavia Tornado F3 [GR]	RAF No 43 Sqn, Leuchars	
ZE162	Panavia Tornado F3 [FK]	RAF No 25 Sqn, Leeming	
ZE163	Panavia Tornado F3 (comp ZG753)	DARA, RAF St Athan	
ZE164	Panavia Tornado F3 [DA]	RAF No 11 Sqn, Leeming	
ZE165	Panavia Tornado F3 [Q]	RAF No 111 Sqn, Leuchars	
ZE168	Panavia Tornado F3 [FN]	RAF No 25 Sqn, Leeming	
ZE199	Panavia Tornado F3 [FL]	RAF No 43 Sqn, Leuchars	
ZE200	Panavia Tornado F3 [DB]	RAF No 25 Sqn, Leeming	
ZE201	Panavia Tornado F3 [GA]	RAF No 43 Sqn, Leuchars	
ZE203	Panavia Tornado F3 [FI]	RAF ASF, Leeming	
ZE204	Panavia Tornado F3 [DD]	RAF No 11 Sqn, Leeming	
ZE206	Panavia Tornado F3 [FH]	RAF No 25 Sqn, Leeming	
ZE207	Panavia Tornado F3 [GC]	RAF No 43 Sqn, Leuchars	
ZE209	Panavia Tornado F3 [AX]	RAF F3 OCU/No 56(R) Sqn, Coningsby	
ZE210	Panavia Tornado F3 (fuselage)	RAF St Athan, Fire Section	
ZE250	Panavia Tornado F3 [AM]	RAF F3 OCU/No 56(R) Sqn, Coningsby	
ZE251	Panavia Tornado F3 (comp ZD936) [C]	RAF No 1435 Flt, Mount Pleasant, FI	
ZE253	Panavia Tornado F3 [AC]	RAF F3 OCU/No 56(R) Sqn, Coningsby	
ZE254	Panavia Tornado F3 (comp ZD941) [AW]	RAF No 25 Sqn, Leeming	
ZE255	Panavia Tornado F3 (comp ZD932) [Y]	RAF No 5 Sqn, Coningsby	
ZE256	Panavia Tornado F3 [AO]	RAF F3 OCU/No 56(R) Sqn, Coningsby	
ZE257	Panavia Tornado F3	RAF AWC/F3 OEU, Coningsby	
ZE258	Panavia Tornado F3 (comp ZD905) [AQ]	RAF F3 OCU/No 56(R) Sqn, Coningsby	
ZE287	Panavia Tornado F3 [AF]	RAF F3 OCU/No 56(R) Sqn, Coningsby	
ZE288	Panavia Tornado F3 (comp ZD940) [AT]	RAF No 25 Sqn, Leeming	
ZE289	Panavia Tornado F3 [GB]	RAF No 43 Sqn, Leuchars	
ZE290	Panavia Tornado F3 [AG]	RAF F3 OCU/No 56(R) Sqn, Coningsby	
ZE291	Panavia Tornado F3 [GQ]	RAF No 43 Sqn, Leuchars	
ZE292	Panavia Tornado F3 (comp ZD939) [AZ]	RAF F3 OCU/No 56(R) Sqn, Coningsby	
ZE293	Panavia Tornado F3 [HT]	RAF AWC/F3 OEU, Coningsby	
ZE294	Panavia Tornado F3 (comp ZD906) [AS]	RAF No 25 Sqn, Leeming	
ZE295	Panavia Tornado F3 (comp ZD938) [CA]	RAF No 5 Sqn, Coningsby	
ZE296	Panavia Tornado F3 [AD]	RAF F3 OCU/No 56(R) Sqn, Coningsby	

Notes	Serial	Type (other identity) [code]	Owner/operator, location or fate
	ZE338	Panavia Tornado F3 [G]	RAF No 111 Sqn, Leuchars
	ZE339	Panavia Tornado F3	RAF, stored St Athan
	ZE340	Panavia Tornado F3 [AE]	RAF F3 OCU/No 56(R) Sqn, Coningsby
	ZE341	Panavia Tornado F3 [AT]	RAF F3 OCU/No 56(R) Sqn, Coningsby
	ZE342	Panavia Tornado F3	RAF No 111 Sqn, Leuchars
	ZE343	Panavia Tornado F3 (comp ZD900) [AA]	RAF F3 OCU/No 56(R) Sqn, Coningsby
	ZE353	McD F-4J(UK) Phantom (9083M) [E]	MoD FSCTE, Manston
	ZE354	McD F-4J(UK) Phantom (9084M) [R]	RAF Coningsby Fire Section
	ZE356	McD F-4J(UK) Phantom (9060M) [Q]	RAF Waddington, BDRT
	ZE360	McD F-4J(UK) Phantom (9059M) [O]	MoD FSCTE, Manston
	ZE361	McD F-4J(UK) Phantom (9057M) [P]	RAF Honington Fire Section
	ZE368	WS61 Sea King HAR3	RAF No 203(R) Sqn, St Mawgan
	ZE369	WS61 Sea King HAR3	RAF HMF, St Mawgan
	ZE370	WS61 Sea King HAR3	RAF HMF, St Mawgan
	ZE375	WS Lynx AH9 [2,9]	AAC No 659 Sqn/4 Regt, Wattisham
	ZE376	WS Lynx AH9	AAC No 659 Sqn/4 Regt, Wattisham
	ZE378	WS Lynx AH7	AAC No 654 Sqn/4 Regt, Wattisham
	ZE379	WS Lynx AH7	AAC No 655 Sqn/5 Regt, Aldergrove
	ZE380	WS Lynx AH9 [3]	AAC No 659 Sqn/4 Regt, Wattisham
	ZE381	WS Lynx AH7	AAC No 655 Sqn/5 Regt, Aldergrove
	ZE382	WS Lynx AH9	AAC No 659 Sqn/4 Regt, Wattisham
	ZE395	BAe 125 CC3	RAF No 32(The Royal) Sqn, Northolt
	ZE396	BAe 125 CC3	RAF No 32(The Royal) Sqn, Northolt
	ZE410	Agusta A109A (AE-334)	AAC No 8 Flt, Credenhill
	ZE411	Agusta A109A (AE-331)	AAC No 8 Flt, Credenhill
	ZE412	Agusta A109A	AAC No 8 Flt, Credenhill
	ZE413	Agusta A109A	AAC No 8 Flt, Credenhill
	ZE418	WS61 Sea King AEW2 [182/CU]	RN No 849 Sqn, HQ Flt, Culdrose
	ZE420	WS61 Sea King AEW2 [183/L]	RN No 849 Sqn, B Flt, Culdrose
	ZE422	WS61 Sea King HAS6 [703/PW]	RN No 819 Sqn, Prestwick
	ZE425	WS61 Sea King HC4 [VJ]	RN No 846 Sqn, Yeovilton
	ZE426	WS61 Sea King HC4 [ZW]	RN AMG, Yeovilton
	ZE427	WS61 Sea King HC4 [B]	RN No 845 Sqn, Yeovilton
	ZE428	WS61 Sea King HC4 [VS]	RN No 846 Sqn, Yeovilton
	ZE432	BAC 1-11/479FU (DQ-FBV)	DPA/AFD/ETPS, DERA Boscombe Down
	ZE433	BAC 1-11/479FU (DQ-FBQ)	DPA/GEC-Ferranti, Edinburgh
	ZE438	BAe Jetstream T3 [76]	RN FONA/Heron Flight, Yeovilton
	ZE439	BAe Jetstream T3 [77]	RN, stored Shawbury
	ZE440	BAe Jetstream T3 [78]	RN FONA/Heron Flight, Yeovilton
	ZE441	BAe Jetstream T3 [79]	RN FONA/Heron Flight, Yeovilton
	ZE449	SA330L Puma HC1 (9017M/PA-12)	DPA/GKN Westland, Weston-super-Mare
	ZE477	WS Lynx 3	The Helicopter Museum, Weston-super-Mare
	ZE495	Grob G103 Viking T1 (BGA3000) [VA]	RAF No 622 VGS, Upavon
	ZE496	Grob G103 Viking T1 (BGA3001) [VB]	RAF No 634 VGS, St Athan
	ZE498	Grob G103 Viking T1 (BGA3003) [VC]	RAF CGMF, Syerston
	ZE499	Grob G103 Viking T1 (BGA3004) [VD]	RAF No 615 VGS, Kenley
	ZE501	Grob G103 Viking T1 (BGA3006) [VE]	RAF No 636 VGS, Aberporth
	ZE502	Grob G103 Viking T1 (BGA3007) [VF]	RAF No 614 VGS, Wethersfield
	ZE503	Grob G103 Viking T1 (BGA3008) [VG]	RAF No 645 VGS, Catterick
	ZE504	Grob G103 Viking T1 (BGA3009) [VH]	RAF No 634 VGS, St Athan
	ZE520	Grob G103 Viking T1 (BGA3010) [VJ]	RAF No 636 VGS, Aberporth
	ZE521	Grob G103 Viking T1 (BGA3011) [VK]	RAF No 626 VGS, Predannack
	ZE522	Grob G103 Viking T1 (BGA3012) [VL]	RAF No 634 VGS, St Athan
	ZE524	Grob G103 Viking T1 (BGA3014) [VM]	RAF No 645 VGS, Catterick

Serial	Type (other identity) [code]	Owner/operator, location or fate	Notes
ZE526	Grob G103 Viking T1 (BGA3016) [VN]	RAF No 636 VGS, Aberporth	
ZE527	Grob G103 Viking T1 (BGA3017) [VP]	RAF CGMF, Syerston	
ZE528	Grob G103 Viking T1 (BGA3018) [VQ]	RAF No 614 VGS, Wethersfield	
ZE529	Grob G103 Viking T1 (BGA3019) (comp ZE655) [VR]	RAF ACCGS, Syerston	
ZE530	Grob G103 Viking T1 (BGA3020) [VS]	RAF No 611 VGS, Watton	
ZE531	Grob G103 Viking T1 (BGA3021) [VT]	RAF No 615 VGS, Kenley	
ZE532	Grob G103 Viking T1 (BGA3022) [VU]	RAF No 614 VGS, Wethersfield	
ZE533	Grob G103 Viking T1 (BGA3023) [VV]	RAF No 622 VGS, Upavon	
ZE534	Grob G103 Viking T1 (BGA3024) [VW]	RAF No 614 VGS, Wethersfield	
ZE550	Grob G103 Viking T1 (BGA3025) [VX]	RAF ACCGS, Syerston	
ZE551	Grob G103 Viking T1 (BGA3026) [VY]	RAF No 614 VGS, Wethersfield	
ZE552	Grob G103 Viking T1 (BGA3027) [VZ]	RAF No 661 VGS, Kirknewton	
ZE553	Grob G103 Viking T1 (BGA3028) [WA]	RAF No 611 VGS, Watton	
ZE554	Grob G103 Viking T1 (BGA3029) [WB]	RAF No 611 VGS, Watton	
ZE555	Grob G103 Viking T1 (BGA3030) [WC]	RAF No 645 VGS, Catterick	
ZE556	Grob G103 Viking T1 (BGA3031) [WD]	RAF No 662 VGS, Arbroath	
ZE557	Grob G103 Viking T1 (BGA3032) [WE]	RAF No 622 VGS, Upavon	
ZE558	Grob G103 Viking T1 (BGA3033) [WF]	RAF No 615 VGS, Kenley	
ZE559	Grob G103 Viking T1 (BGA3034) [WG]	RAF No 631 VGS, Sealand	
ZE560	Grob G103 Viking T1 (BGA3035) [WH]	RAF No 661 VGS, Kirknewton	
ZE561	Grob G103 Viking T1 (BGA3036) [WJ]	RAF No 621 VGS, Hullavington	
ZE562	Grob G103 Viking T1 (BGA3037) [WK]	RAF No 626 VGS, Predannack	
ZE563	Grob G103 Viking T1 (BGA3038) [WL]	RAF No 631 VGS, Sealand	
ZE564	Grob G103 Viking T1 (BGA3039) [WN]	RAF No 625 VGS, Hullavington	
ZE584	Grob G103 Viking T1 (BGA3040) [WP]	RAF No 631 VGS, Sealand	
ZE585	Grob G103 Viking T1 (BGA3041) [WQ]	RAF ACCGS, Syerston	
ZE586	Grob G103 Viking T1 (BGA3042) [WR]	RAF No 631 VGS, Sealand	
ZE587	Grob G103 Viking T1 (BGA3043) [WS]	RAF No 611 VGS, Watton	
ZE589	Grob G103 Viking T1 (BGA3045) (wreck)	RAFGSA, stored Bicester	
ZE590	Grob G103 Viking T1 (BGA3046) [WT]	RAF No 661 VGS, Kirknewton	
ZE591	Grob G103 Viking T1 (BGA3047) [WU]	RAF No 631 VGS, Sealand	
ZE592	Grob G103 Viking T1 (BGA3048) [WV]	RAF No 626 VGS, Predannack	
ZE593	Grob G103 Viking T1 (BGA3049) [WW]	RAF No 621 VGS, Hullavington	
ZE594	Grob G103 Viking T1 (BGA3050) [WX]	RAF No 615 VGS, Kenley	
ZE595	Grob G103 Viking T1 (BGA3051) [WY]	RAF No 622 VGS, Upavon	
ZE600	Grob G103 Viking T1 (BGA3052) [WZ]	RAF No 622 VGS, Upavon	

ZE601 – ZE679

Notes	Serial	Type (other identity) [code]	Owner/operator, location or fate
	ZE601	Grob G103 Viking T1 (BGA3053) [XA]	RAF No 611 VGS, Watton
	ZE602	Grob G103 Viking T1 (BGA3054) [XB]	RAF No 645 VGS, Catterick
	ZE603	Grob G103 Viking T1 (BGA3055) [XC]	RAF No 636 VGS, Aberporth
	ZE604	Grob G103 Viking T1 (BGA3056) [XD]	RAF No 615 VGS, Kenley
	ZE605	Grob G103 Viking T1 (BGA3057) [XE]	RAF No 662 VGS, Arbroath
	ZE606	Grob G103 Viking T1 (BGA3058) [XF]	RAF No 625 VGS, Hullavington
	ZE607	Grob G103 Viking T1 (BGA3059) [XG]	RAF No 625 VGS, Hullavington
	ZE608	Grob G103 Viking T1 (BGA3060) [XH]	RAF No 621 VGS, Hullavington
	ZE609	Grob G103 Viking T1 (BGA3061) [XJ]	RAF ACCGS, Syerston
	ZE610	Grob G103 Viking T1 (BGA3062) [XK]	RAF No 626 VGS, Predannack
	ZE611	Grob G103 Viking T1 (BGA3063) [XL]	RAF No 611 VGS, Watton
	ZE613	Grob G103 Viking T1 (BGA3065) [XM]	RAF No 625 VGS, Hullavington
	ZE614	Grob G103 Viking T1 (BGA3066) [XN]	RAF No 631 VGS, Sealand
	ZE625	Grob G103 Viking T1 (BGA3067) [XP]	RAF CGMF, Syerston
	ZE626	Grob G103 Viking T1 (BGA3068) [XQ]	RAF No 626 VGS, Predannack
	ZE627	Grob G103 Viking T1 (BGA3069) [XR]	RAF No 634 VGS, St Athan
	ZE628	Grob G103 Viking T1 (BGA3070) [XS]	RAF ACCGS, Syerston
	ZE629	Grob G103 Viking T1 (BGA3071) [XT]	RAF No 662 VGS, Arbroath
	ZE630	Grob G103 Viking T1 (BGA3072) [XU]	RAF No 662 VGS, Arbroath
	ZE631	Grob G103 Viking T1 (BGA3073) [XV]	RAF No 662 VGS, Arbroath
	ZE632	Grob G103 Viking T1 (BGA3074) [XW]	RAF No 645 VGS, Catterick
	ZE633	Grob G103 Viking T1 (BGA3075) [XX]	RAF No 614 VGS, Wethersfield
	ZE635	Grob G103 Viking T1 (BGA3077) [XY]	RAF No 625 VGS, Hullavington
	ZE636	Grob G103 Viking T1 (BGA3078) [XZ]	RAF CGMF, Syerston
	ZE637	Grob G103 Viking T1 (BGA3079) [YA]	RAF No 622 VGS, Upavon
	ZE650	Grob G103 Viking T1 (BGA3080) [YB]	RAF ACCGS, Syerston
	ZE651	Grob G103 Viking T1 (BGA3081) [YC]	RAF No 661 VGS, Kirknewton
	ZE652	Grob G103 Viking T1 (BGA3082) [YD]	RAF ACCGS, Syerston
	ZE653	Grob G103 Viking T1 (BGA3083) [YE]	RAF No 661 VGS, Kirknewton
	ZE656	Grob G103 Viking T1 (BGA3086) [YH]	RAF CGMF, Syerston
	ZE657	Grob G103 Viking T1 (BGA3087) [YJ]	RAF No 615 VGS, Kenley
	ZE658	Grob G103 Viking T1 (BGA3088) [YK]	RAF No 621 VGS, Hullavington
	ZE659	Grob G103 Viking T1 (BGA3089) [YL]	RAF CGMF, Syerston (on repair)
	ZE677	Grob G103 Viking T1 (BGA3090) [YM]	RAF No 645 VGS, Catterick
	ZE678	Grob G103 Viking T1 (BGA3091) [YN]	RAF No 621 VGS, Hullavington
	ZE679	Grob G103 Viking T1 (BGA3092) [YP]	RAF No 622 VGS, Upavon

Serial	Type (other identity) [code]	Owner/operator, location or fate	Notes
ZE680	Grob G103 Viking T1 (BGA3093) [YQ]	RAF No 662 VGS, Arbroath	
ZE681	Grob G103 Viking T1 (BGA3094) [YR]	RAF No 615 VGS, Kenley	
ZE682	Grob G103 Viking T1 (BGA3095) [YS]	RAF No 662 VGS, Arbroath	
ZE683	Grob G103 Viking T1 (BGA3096) [YT]	RAF No 661 VGS, Kirknewton	
ZE684	Grob G103 Viking T1 (BGA3097) [YU]	RAF No 621 VGS, Hullavington	
ZE685	Grob G103 Viking T1 (BGA3098) [YV]	RAF No 631 VGS, Sealand	
ZE686	Grob G103 Viking T1 (BGA3099)	DPA/Slingsby Kirkbymoorside	
ZE690	BAe Sea Harrier FA2 [005]	RN No 801 Sqn, Yeovilton	
ZE691	BAe Sea Harrier FA2 [710/VL]	RN, stored St Athan (damaged)	
ZE692	BAe Sea Harrier FA2	DPA/BAE Systems, Warton	
ZE693	BAe Sea Harrier FA2 [731]	RN No 899 Sqn, Yeovilton	
ZE694	BAe Sea Harrier FA2 [006/L]	DPA/BAE Systems, Warton	
ZE695	BAe Sea Harrier FA2 [718]	RN FSAIU, Yeovilton	
ZE696	BAe Sea Harrier FA2 [715]	RN No 899 Sqn, Yeovilton	
ZE697	BAe Sea Harrier FA2 [122]	DPA/BAE Systems, Warton	
ZE698	BAe Sea Harrier FA2 [127]	DPA/BAE Systems, Warton	
ZE700	BAe 146 CC2 (G-6-021)	RAF No 32(The Royal) Sqn, Northolt	
ZE701	BAe 146 CC2 (G-6-029)	RAF No 32(The Royal) Sqn, Northolt	
ZE702	BAe 146 CC2 (G-6-124)	RAF No 32(The Royal) Sqn, Northolt	
ZE704	Lockheed TriStar C2 (N508PA)	RAF No 216 Sqn, Brize Norton	
ZE705	Lockheed TriStar C2 (N509PA)	RAF No 216 Sqn, Brize Norton	
ZE706	Lockheed TriStar C2A (N503PA)	RAF No 216 Sqn, Brize Norton	
ZE728	Panavia Tornado F3 (comp ZD903) [AH]	RAF F3 OCU/No 56(R) Sqn, Coningsby	
ZE729	Panavia Tornado F3 (comp ZD933) [D]	RAF No 1435 Flt, Mount Pleasant, FI	
ZE731	Panavia Tornado F3 [GF]	RAF No 43 Sqn, Leuchars	
ZE734	Panavia Tornado F3 [GB]	RAF No 43 Sqn, Leuchars	
ZE735	Panavia Tornado F3 [AL]	RAF F3 OCU/No 56(R) Sqn, Coningsby	
ZE736	Panavia Tornado F3 (comp ZD937) [AX]	RAF No 11 Sqn, Leeming	
ZE737	Panavia Tornado F3	RAF No 11 Sqn, Leeming	
ZE755	Panavia Tornado F3 [GJ]	RAF No 43 Sqn, Leuchars	
ZE756	Panavia Tornado F3	RAF, stored St Athan	
ZE757	Panavia Tornado F3 [AR]	RAF F3 OCU/No 56(R) Sqn, Coningsby	
ZE758	Panavia Tornado F3 [GO]	RAF No 43 Sqn, Leuchars	
ZE763	Panavia Tornado F3 [DG]	RAF No 11 Sqn, Leeming	
ZE764	Panavia Tornado F3 [DH]	RAF No 11 Sqn, Leeming	
ZE785	Panavia Tornado F3	RAF AWC/F3 OEU, Coningsby	
ZE786	Panavia Tornado F3 (comp ZD934) [AN]	RAF No 25 Sqn, Leeming	
ZE788	Panavia Tornado F3 [DF]	RAF No 25 Sqn, Leeming	
ZE790	Panavia Tornado F3 [GD]	RAF No 43 Sqn, Leuchars	
ZE791	Panavia Tornado F3 [N]	RAF No 111 Sqn, Leuchars	
ZE793	Panavia Tornado F3 (comp ZD935) [AI]	RAF F3 OCU/No 56(R) Sqn, Coningsby	
ZE794	Panavia Tornado F3	RAF No 5 Sqn, Coningsby	
ZE808	Panavia Tornado F3 [FA]	RAF No 25 Sqn, Leeming	
ZE810	Panavia Tornado F3 [P]	RAF No 111 Sqn, Leuchars	
ZE812	Panavia Tornado F3 [AV]	RAF F3 OCU/No 56(R) Sqn, Coningsby	
ZE831	Panavia Tornado F3 [GG]	RAF No 43 Sqn, Leuchars	
ZE834	Panavia Tornado F3 [CX]	RAF No 5 Sqn, Coningsby	
ZE838	Panavia Tornado F3 [GH]	RAF No 43 Sqn, Leuchars	
ZE839	Panavia Tornado F3 [CH]	RAF No 5 Sqn, Coningsby	
ZE887	Panavia Tornado F3 [DJ]	RAF No 11 Sqn, Leeming	
ZE888	Panavia Tornado F3 [T]	RAF No 111 Sqn, Leuchars	
ZE889	Panavia Tornado F3 [H]	RAF F3 OCU/No 56(R) Sqn, Coningsby	
ZE907	Panavia Tornado F3 [FM]	RAF No 11 Sqn, Leeming	
ZE908	Panavia Tornado F3 [HV]	RAF No 25 Sqn, Leeming	
ZE934	Panavia Tornado F3 [AP]	RAF F3 OCU/No 56(R) Sqn, Coningsby	
ZE936	Panavia Tornado F3 [DL]	RAF No 11 Sqn, Leeming	
ZE941·	Panavia Tornado F3 [FE]	RAF No 25 Sqn, Leeming	
ZE942	Panavia Tornado F3 [CM]	RAF No 5 Sqn, Coningsby	
ZE961	Panavia Tornado F3 [FD]	RAF AWC/F3 OEU, Coningsby	
ZE962	Panavia Tornado F3 [FJ]	RAF No 25 Sqn, Leeming	
ZE963	Panavia Tornado F3 [GE]	RAF No 111 Sqn, Leuchars	
ZE964	Panavia Tornado F3 [GN]	RAF No 43 Sqn, Leuchars	

Notes	Serial	Type (other identity) [code]	Owner/operator, location or fate
	ZE965	Panavia Tornado F3 [GM]	RAF No 43 Sqn, Leuchars
	ZE966	Panavia Tornado F3 [DXI]	RAF No 11 Sqn, Leeming
	ZE967	Panavia Tornado F3	RAF No 111 Sqn, Leuchars
	ZE968	Panavia Tornado F3 [DM]	RAF No 5 Sqn, Coningsby
	ZE969	Panavia Tornado F3 [F]	RAF No 1435 Flt, Mount Pleasant, FI
	ZE982	Panavia Tornado F3 [CP]	RAF No 5 Sqn, Coningsby
	ZE983	Panavia Tornado F3 [DN]	RAF No 11 Sqn, Leeming
	ZF115	WS61 Sea King HC4	DPA/AFD, DERA Boscombe Down
	ZF116	WS61 Sea King HC4 [ZP]	RN No 848 Sqn, Yeovilton
	ZF117	WS61 Sea King HC4 [VQ]	RN No 846 Sqn, Yeovilton
	ZF118	WS61 Sea King HC4 [VP]	RN No 846 Sqn, Yeovilton
	ZF119	WS61 Sea King HC4 [VW]	RN AMG, Yeovilton
	ZF120	WS61 Sea King HC4 [K]	RN No 845 Sqn, Yeovilton
	ZF121	WS61 Sea King HC4 [VT]	RN No 846 Sqn, Yeovilton
	ZF122	WS61 Sea King HC4 [VU]	RN No 846 Sqn, Yeovilton
	ZF123	WS61 Sea King HC4 [VY]	RN No 846 Sqn, Yeovilton
	ZF124	WS61 Sea King HC4 [L]	RN No 845 Sqn, Yeovilton
	ZF130	BAe 125-600B (G-BLUW)	Cranfield University
	ZF135	Shorts Tucano T1	RAF No 1 FTS, Linton-on-Ouse
	ZF136	Shorts Tucano T1	RAF No 1 FTS, Linton-on-Ouse
	ZF137	Shorts Tucano T1	RAF No 1 FTS, Linton-on-Ouse
	ZF138	Shorts Tucano T1	RAF No 1 FTS, Linton-on-Ouse
	ZF139	Shorts Tucano T1	RAF No 1 FTS, Linton-on-Ouse
	ZF140	Shorts Tucano T1	RAF No 1 FTS, Linton-on-Ouse
	ZF141	Shorts Tucano T1	RAF, stored Shawbury
	ZF142	Shorts Tucano T1	RAF No 1 FTS, Linton-on-Ouse
	ZF143	Shorts Tucano T1	RAF No 1 FTS, Linton-on-Ouse
	ZF144	Shorts Tucano T1	RAF No 1 FTS, Linton-on-Ouse
	ZF145	Shorts Tucano T1	RAF No 1 FTS, Linton-on-Ouse
	ZF160	Shorts Tucano T1	RAF No 1 FTS, Linton-on-Ouse
	ZF161	Shorts Tucano T1	RAF No 1 FTS, Linton-on-Ouse
	ZF162	Shorts Tucano T1	RAF No 1 FTS, Linton-on-Ouse
	ZF163	Shorts Tucano T1	RAF No 1 FTS, Linton-on-Ouse
	ZF164	Shorts Tucano T1	RAF, stored Shawbury
	ZF165	Shorts Tucano T1	RAF, stored Shawbury
	ZF166	Shorts Tucano T1	RAF No 1 FTS, Linton-on-Ouse
	ZF167	Shorts Tucano T1	RAF, stored Shawbury
	ZF168	Shorts Tucano T1	RAF No 1 FTS, Linton-on-Ouse
	ZF169	Shorts Tucano T1	RAF No 1 FTS, Linton-on-Ouse
	ZF170	Shorts Tucano T1	RAF No 1 FTS, Linton-on-Ouse
	ZF171	Shorts Tucano T1	RAF, stored Shawbury
	ZF172	Shorts Tucano T1	RAF, stored Shawbury
	ZF200	Shorts Tucano T1	RAF, stored Shawbury
	ZF201	Shorts Tucano T1	RAF, stored Shawbury
	ZF202	Shorts Tucano T1	RAF, stored Shawbury
	ZF203	Shorts Tucano T1	RAF No 1 FTS, Linton-on-Ouse
	ZF204	Shorts Tucano T1	RAF, stored Shawbury
	ZF205	Shorts Tucano T1	RAF, stored Shawbury
	ZF206	Shorts Tucano T1	RAF No 1 FTS, Linton-on-Ouse
	ZF207	Shorts Tucano T1	RAF No 1 FTS, Linton-on-Ouse
	ZF208	Shorts Tucano T1	RAF No 1 FTS, Linton-on-Ouse
	ZF209	Shorts Tucano T1	RAF, stored Shawbury
	ZF210	Shorts Tucano T1	RAF No 1 FTS, Linton-on-Ouse
	ZF211	Shorts Tucano T1	RAF No 1 FTS, Linton-on-Ouse
	ZF212	Shorts Tucano T1	RAF No 1 FTS, Linton-on-Ouse
	ZF238	Shorts Tucano T1	RAF No 1 FTS, Linton-on-Ouse
	ZF239	Shorts Tucano T1	RAF, stored Shawbury
	ZF240	Shorts Tucano T1	RAF, stored Shawbury
	ZF241	Shorts Tucano T1	RAF No 1 FTS, Linton-on-Ouse
	ZF242	Shorts Tucano T1	RAF No 1 FTS, Linton-on-Ouse
	ZF243	Shorts Tucano T1	RAF, stored Shawbury
	ZF244	Shorts Tucano T1	RAF No 1 FTS, Linton-on-Ouse
	ZF245	Shorts Tucano T1	RAF, stored Shawbury
	ZF263	Shorts Tucano T1	RAF No 1 FTS, Linton-on-Ouse
	ZF264	Shorts Tucano T1	RAF, stored Shawbury
	ZF265	Shorts Tucano T1	RAF, stored Shawbury
	ZF266	Shorts Tucano T1	RAF No 1 FTS, Linton-on-Ouse
	ZF267	Shorts Tucano T1	RAF, stored Shawbury
	ZF268	Shorts Tucano T1	RAF No 1 FTS, Linton-on-Ouse
	ZF269	Shorts Tucano T1	RAF, stored Shawbury
	ZF284	Shorts Tucano T1	RAF, stored Shawbury
	ZF285	Shorts Tucano T1	RAF, stored Shawbury

Serial	Type (other identity) [code]	Owner/operator, location or fate	Notes
ZF286	Shorts Tucano T1	RAF No 1 FTS, Linton-on-Ouse	
ZF287	Shorts Tucano T1	RAF, stored Shawbury	
ZF288	Shorts Tucano T1	RAF No 1 FTS, Linton-on-Ouse	
ZF289	Shorts Tucano T1	RAF No 1 FTS, Linton-on-Ouse	
ZF290	Shorts Tucano T1	RAF No 1 FTS, Linton-on-Ouse	
ZF291	Shorts Tucano T1	RAF No 1 FTS, Linton-on-Ouse	
ZF292	Shorts Tucano T1	RAF No 1 FTS, Linton-on-Ouse	
ZF293	Shorts Tucano T1	RAF No 1 FTS, Linton-on-Ouse	
ZF294	Shorts Tucano T1	RAF No 1 FTS, Linton-on-Ouse	
ZF295	Shorts Tucano T1	RAF No 1 FTS, Linton-on-Ouse	
ZF315	Shorts Tucano T1	RAF No 1 FTS, Linton-on-Ouse	
ZF317	Shorts Tucano T1	RAF, stored Shawbury	
ZF318	Shorts Tucano T1	RAF No 1 FTS, Linton-on-Ouse	
ZF319	Shorts Tucano T1	RAF No 1 FTS, Linton-on-Ouse	
ZF320	Shorts Tucano T1	RAF No 1 FTS, Linton-on-Ouse	
ZF338	Shorts Tucano T1	RAF, stored Shawbury	
ZF339	Shorts Tucano T1	RAF No 1 FTS, Linton-on-Ouse	
ZF340	Shorts Tucano T1	RAF, stored Shawbury	
ZF341	Shorts Tucano T1	RAF No 1 FTS, Linton-on-Ouse	
ZF342	Shorts Tucano T1	RAF No 1 FTS, Linton-on-Ouse	
ZF343	Shorts Tucano T1	RAF, stored Shawbury	
ZF344	Shorts Tucano T1	RAF, stored Shawbury	
ZF345	Shorts Tucano T1	RAF No 1 FTS, Linton-on-Ouse	
ZF346	Shorts Tucano T1	RAF No 1 FTS, Linton-on-Ouse	
ZF347	Shorts Tucano T1	RAF No 1 FTS, Linton-on-Ouse	
ZF348	Shorts Tucano T1	RAF No 1 FTS, Linton-on-Ouse	
ZF349	Shorts Tucano T1	RAF, stored Shawbury	
ZF350	Shorts Tucano T1	RAF No 1 FTS, Linton-on-Ouse	
ZF372	Shorts Tucano T1	RAF, stored Shawbury	
ZF373	Shorts Tucano T1	RAF, stored Shawbury	
ZF374	Shorts Tucano T1	RAF, stored Shawbury	
ZF375	Shorts Tucano T1	RAF No 1 FTS, Linton-on-Ouse	
ZF376	Shorts Tucano T1	RAF No 1 FTS, Linton-on-Ouse	
ZF377	Shorts Tucano T1	RAF, stored Shawbury	
ZF378	Shorts Tucano T1	RAF, stored Shawbury	
ZF379	Shorts Tucano T1	RAF No 1 FTS, Linton-on-Ouse	
ZF380	Shorts Tucano T1	RAF No 1 FTS, Linton-on-Ouse	
ZF405	Shorts Tucano T1	RAF No 1 FTS, Linton-on-Ouse	
ZF406	Shorts Tucano T1	RAF No 1 FTS, Linton-on-Ouse	
ZF407	Shorts Tucano T1	RAF No 1 FTS, Linton-on-Ouse	
ZF408	Shorts Tucano T1	RAF No 1 FTS, Linton-on-Ouse	
ZF409	Shorts Tucano T1	RAF, stored Shawbury	
ZF410	Shorts Tucano T1	RAF No 1 FTS, Linton-on-Ouse	
ZF411	Shorts Tucano T1	RAF, stored Shawbury	
ZF412	Shorts Tucano T1	RAF, stored Shawbury	
ZF413	Shorts Tucano T1	RAF No 1 FTS, Linton-on-Ouse	
ZF414	Shorts Tucano T1	RAF, stored Shawbury	
ZF415	Shorts Tucano T1	RAF, stored Shawbury	
ZF416	Shorts Tucano T1	RAF No 1 FTS, Linton-on-Ouse	
ZF417	Shorts Tucano T1	RAF No 1 FTS, Linton-on-Ouse	
ZF418	Shorts Tucano T1	RAF No 1 FTS, Linton-on-Ouse	
ZF445	Shorts Tucano T1	RAF No 1 FTS, Linton-on-Ouse	
ZF446	Shorts Tucano T1	RAF No 1 FTS, Linton-on-Ouse	
ZF447	Shorts Tucano T1	RAF No 1 FTS, Linton-on-Ouse	
ZF448	Shorts Tucano T1	RAF No 1 FTS, Linton-on-Ouse	
ZF449	Shorts Tucano T1	RAF No 1 FTS, Linton-on-Ouse	
ZF450	Shorts Tucano T1	RAF, stored Shawbury	
ZF483	Shorts Tucano T1	RAF No 1 FTS, Linton-on-Ouse	
ZF484	Shorts Tucano T1	RAF No 1 FTS, Linton-on-Ouse	
ZF485	Shorts Tucano T1 (G-BULU)	RAF No 1 FTS, Linton-on-Ouse	
ZF486	Shorts Tucano T1	RAF No 1 FTS, Linton-on-Ouse	
ZF487	Shorts Tucano T1	RAF No 1 FTS, Linton-on-Ouse	
ZF488	Shorts Tucano T1	RAF, stored Shawbury	
ZF489	Shorts Tucano T1	RAF No 1 FTS, Linton-on-Ouse	
ZF490	Shorts Tucano T1	RAF No 1 FTS, Linton-on-Ouse	
ZF491	Shorts Tucano T1	RAF No 1 FTS, Linton-on-Ouse	
ZF492	Shorts Tucano T1	RAF No 1 FTS, Linton-on-Ouse	
ZF510	Shorts Tucano T1	DPA/AFD, DERA Boscombe Down	
ZF511	Shorts Tucano T1	DPA/AFD, DERA Boscombe Down	
ZF512	Shorts Tucano T1	RAF No 1 FTS, Linton-on-Ouse	
ZF513	Shorts Tucano T1	RAF No 1 FTS, Linton-on-Ouse	
ZF514	Shorts Tucano T1	RAF No 1 FTS, Linton-on-Ouse	
ZF515	Shorts Tucano T1	RAF No 1 FTS, Linton-on-Ouse	

Notes	Serial	Type (other identity) [code]	Owner/operator, location or fate
	ZF516	Shorts Tucano T1	RAF, stored Shawbury
	ZF534	BAe EAP	Loughborough University
	ZF537	WS Lynx AH9	AAC No 659 Sqn/4 Regt, Wattisham
	ZF538	WS Lynx AH9	AAC No 659 Sqn/4 Regt, Wattisham
	ZF539	WS Lynx AH9	AAC No 653 Sqn/3 Regt, Wattisham
	ZF540	WS Lynx AH9	AAC, stored RNAY Fleetlands
	ZF557	WS Lynx HMA8 [407/YK]	DARA, RNAY Fleetlands
	ZF558	WS Lynx HMA8 [348/CM]	RN No 815 Sqn, Chatham Flt, Yeovilton
	ZF560	WS Lynx HMA8 [365/AY]	DARA, RNAY Fleetlands
	ZF562	WS Lynx HMA8 [336/CV]	DARA, RNAY Fleetlands
	ZF563	WS Lynx HMA8 [702]	RN No 815 Sqn, Yeovilton
	ZF573	PBN 2T Islander CC2A (G-SRAY)	RAF Northolt Station Flight
	ZF578	BAC Lightning F53	Privately owned, Quedgeley, Glos
	ZF579	BAC Lightning F53	Gatwick Aviation Museum, Charlwood
	ZF580	BAC Lightning F53	BAE Systems Samlesbury, at main gate
	ZF581	BAC Lightning F53	Privately owned, Portsmouth
	ZF582	BAC Lightning F53 <ff>	Privately owned, Reading
	ZF583	BAC Lightning F53	Solway Aviation Society, Carlisle
	ZF584	BAC Lightning F53	Ferranti Ltd, South Gyle, Edinburgh
	ZF587	BAC Lightning F53 <ff>	Privately owned, Stowmarket
	ZF588	BAC Lightning F53 [L]	East Midlands Airport Aeropark
	ZF592	BAC Lightning F53	Privately owned, Portsmouth
	ZF594	BAC Lightning F53	North-East Aircraft Museum, Usworth
	ZF595	BAC Lightning T55 <ff>	Privately owned, Bruntingthorpe
	ZF596	BAC Lightning T55 <ff>	BAe North-West Heritage Group Warton
	ZF622	Piper PA-31 Navajo Chieftain 350 (N3548Y)	DPA/AFD, DERA Boscombe Down
	ZF641	EHI-101 [PP1]	SFDO, RNAS Culdrose
	ZF649	EHI-101 Merlin [PP5]	RN, stored HMS Sultan, Gosportl
	ZG101	EHI-101 (mock-up) [GB]	GKN Westland/Agusta, Yeovil
	ZG471	BAe Harrier GR7 [61]	RAF No 1 Sqn, Cottesmore
	ZG472	BAe Harrier GR7 [62]	RAF No 1 Sqn, Cottesmore
	ZG474	BAe Harrier GR7 [64]	RAF No 4 Sqn, Cottesmore
	ZG477	BAe Harrier GR7 [67]	RAF No 1 Sqn, Cottesmore
	ZG478	BAe Harrier GR7 [68]	RAF No 4 Sqn, Cottesmore
	ZG479	BAe Harrier GR7 [69]	RAF HOCU/No 20(R) Sqn, Wittering
	ZG480	BAe Harrier GR7 [70]	RAF No 1 Sqn, Cottesmore
	ZG500	BAe Harrier GR7 [71]	RAF No 3 Sqn, Cottesmore
	ZG501	BAe Harrier GR7 [72]	RAF No 3 Sqn, Cottesmore
	ZG502	BAe Harrier GR7 [73]	RAF HOCU/No 20(R) Sqn, Wittering
	ZG503	BAe Harrier GR7 [74]	RAF No 3 Sqn, Cottesmore
	ZG504	BAe Harrier GR7 [75]	RAF No 3 Sqn, Cottesmore
	ZG505	BAe Harrier GR7 [76]	RAF No 3 Sqn, Cottesmore
	ZG506	BAe Harrier GR7 [77]	RAF HOCU/No 20(R) Sqn, Wittering
	ZG507	BAe Harrier GR7 [78]	RAF No 3 Sqn, Cottesmore
	ZG508	BAe Harrier GR7 [79]	RAF No 1 Sqn, Cottesmore
	ZG509	BAe Harrier GR7 [80]	RAF No 1 Sqn, Cottesmore
	ZG510	BAe Harrier GR7 [81]	RAF No 1 Sqn, Cottesmore
	ZG511	BAe Harrier GR7 [82]	RAF No 4 Sqn, Cottesmore
	ZG512	BAe Harrier GR7 [83]	RAF No 3 Sqn, Cottesmore
	ZG530	BAe Harrier GR7 [84]	RAF No 3 Sqn, Cottesmore
	ZG531	BAe Harrier GR7 [85]	RAF No 4 Sqn, Cottesmore
	ZG705	Panavia Tornado GR4A [J]	DPA/BAE Systems, Warton (conversion)
	ZG706	Panavia Tornado GR1A [E]	RAF, stored St Athan
	ZG707	Panavia Tornado GR4A [B]	RAF No 13 Sqn, Marham
	ZG709	Panavia Tornado GR4A [V]	RAF No 13 Sqn, Marham
	ZG710	Panavia Tornado GR4A [D]	RAF No 13 Sqn, Marham
	ZG711	Panavia Tornado GR4A [O]	RAF No 2 Sqn, Marham
	ZG712	Panavia Tornado GR4A [F]	RAF No 13 Sqn, Marham
	ZG713	Panavia Tornado GR4A	RAF No 2 Sqn, Marham
	ZG714	Panavia Tornado GR4A [Q]	RAF No 2 Sqn, Marham
	ZG726	Panavia Tornado GR4A [K]	RAF No 13 Sqn, Marham
	ZG727	Panavia Tornado GR1A [L]	RAF No 2 Sqn, Marham
	ZG729	Panavia Tornado GR4A [M]	RAF No 13 Sqn, Marham
	ZG731	Panavia Tornado F3	RAF AWC/F3 OEU, Coningsby
	ZG750	Panavia Tornado GR4 [DY]	RAF No 31 Sqn, Brüggen
	ZG751	Panavia Tornado F3 [CO]	RAF No 111 Sqn, Leuchars
	ZG752	Panavia Tornado GR1 [TO]	RAF No 15(R) Sqn, Lossiemouth
	ZG753	Panavia Tornado F3 (fuselage)	RAF, stored St Athan
	ZG754	Panavia Tornado GR4 [TQ]	DPA/BAE Systems, Warton (conversion)
	ZG755	Panavia Tornado F3 [CD]	RAF No 11 Sqn, Leeming
	ZG756	Panavia Tornado GR4 [BX]	DPA/BAE Systems, Warton (conversion)

Serial	Type (other identity) [code]	Owner/operator, location or fate	Notes
ZG757	Panavia Tornado F3 [U]	RAF No 25 Sqn, Leeming	
ZG769	Panavia Tornado GR4 [TN]	DPA/BAE Systems, Warton (conversion)	
ZG770	Panavia Tornado F3 [CC]	RAF No 5 Sqn, Coningsby	
ZG771	Panavia Tornado GR4 [AZ]	RAF No 9 Sqn, Brüggen	
ZG772	Panavia Tornado F3 [AU]	RAF No 111 Sqn, Leuchars	
ZG773	Panavia Tornado GR4	DPA/BAE Systems, Warton	
ZG774	Panavia Tornado F3 [D]	RAF, St Athan	
ZG775	Panavia Tornado GR4 [FB]	RAF No 12 Sqn, Lossiemouth	
ZG776	Panavia Tornado F3 [F]	RAF, St Athan	
ZG777	Panavia Tornado GR4 [BS]	DPA/BAE Systems, Warton (conversion)	
ZG778	Panavia Tornado F3 [BG]	RAF F3 OCU/No 56(R) Sqn, Coningsby	
ZG779	Panavia Tornado GR4 [DK]	RAF No 12 Sqn, Lossiemouth	
ZG780	Panavia Tornado F3 [CJ]	RAF No 25 Sqn, Leeming	
ZG791	Panavia Tornado GR4 [BI]	RAF No 14 Sqn, Lossiemouth	
ZG792	Panavia Tornado GR4 [AJ-G]	RAF No 617 Sqn, Lossiemouth	
ZG793	Panavia Tornado F3 [CY]	RAF No 5 Sqn, Coningsby	
ZG794	Panavia Tornado GR4 [BP]	DPA/BAE Systems, Warton (conversion)	
ZG795	Panavia Tornado F3 [H]	RAF No 1435 Flt, Mount Pleasant, FI	
ZG796	Panavia Tornado F3 [CS]	RAF No 5 Sqn, Coningsby	
ZG797	Panavia Tornado F3 [GI]	RAF No 43 Sqn, Leuchars	
ZG798	Panavia Tornado F3 [AP]	RAF F3 OCU/No 56(R) Sqn, Coningsby	
ZG799	Panavia Tornado F3 [GP]	RAF No 43 Sqn, Leuchars	
ZG816	WS61 Sea King HAS6 [701/PW]	DARA, RNAY Fleetlands	
ZG817	WS61 Sea King HAS6 [702/PW]	RN No 819 Sqn, Prestwick	
ZG818	WS61 Sea King HAS6	RN, stored, HMS Sultan, Gosport	
ZG819	WS61 Sea King HAS6 [265/N]	RN, stored, HMS Sultan, Gosport	
ZG820	WS61 Sea King HC4 [A]	RN No 845 Sqn, Yeovilton	
ZG821	WS61 Sea King HC4 [D]	RN No 845 Sqn, Yeovilton	
ZG822	WS61 Sea King HC4 [VN]	RN No 846 Sqn, Yeovilton	
ZG844	PBN 2T Islander AL1 (G-BLNE)	AAC AFWF, Middle Wallop	
ZG845	PBN 2T Islander AL1 (G-BLNT)	AAC AFWF, Middle Wallop	
ZG846	PBN 2T Islander AL1 (G-BLNU)	AAC AFWF, Middle Wallop	
ZG847	PBN 2T Islander AL1 (G-BLNV)	AAC No 1 Flt, Aldergrove	
ZG848	PBN 2T Islander AL1 (G-BLNY)	AAC No 1 Flt, Aldergrove	
ZG857	BAe Harrier GR7 [89]	RAF No 3 Sqn, Cottesmore	
ZG858	BAe Harrier GR7	RAF AWC/SAOEU, DERA Boscombe Down	
ZG859	BAe Harrier GR7 [91]	RAF HOCU/No 20(R) Sqn, Wittering	
ZG860	BAe Harrier GR7 [92]	DPA/BAE Systems, Warton	
ZG862	BAe Harrier GR7 [94]	RAF No 1 Sqn, Cottesmore	
ZG875	WS61 Sea King HAS6 [013/L]	RN, stored HMS Sultan, Gosport (damaged)	
ZG879	Powerchute Raider Mk 1	DPA/Powerchute, Hereford	
ZG884	WS Lynx AH9	DPA/GKN Westland, Yeovil	
ZG885	WS Lynx AH9 [7]	AAC No 653 Sqn/3 Regt, Wattisham	
ZG886	WS Lynx AH9	DARA, RNAY Fleetlands	
ZG887	WS Lynx AH9	AAC No 653 Sqn/3 Regt, Wattisham	
ZG888	WS Lynx AH9	AAC No 653 Sqn/3 Regt, Wattisham	
ZG889	WS Lynx AH9	AAC No 653 Sqn/3 Regt, Wattisham	
ZG914	WS Lynx AH9	AAC, stored RNAY Fleetlands	
ZG915	WS Lynx AH9 [7]	DARA, RNAY Fleetlands	
ZG916	WS Lynx AH9 [8]	DARA, RNAY Fleetlands	
ZG917	WS Lynx AH9 [2,9]	AAC No 659 Sqn/4 Regt, Wattisham	
ZG918	WS Lynx AH9	AAC No 659 Sqn/4 Regt, Wattisham	
ZG919	WS Lynx AH9	AAC, stored RNAY Fleetlands	
ZG920	WS Lynx AH9	AAC No 653 Sqn/3 Regt, Wattisham	
ZG921	WS Lynx AH9	AAC No 659 Sqn/4 Regt, Wattisham	
ZG922	WS Lynx AH9	DARA, RNAY Fleetlands	
ZG923	WS Lynx AH9	AAC No 653 Sqn/3 Regt, Wattisham	
ZG969	Pilatus PC-9 (HB-HQE)	BAE Systems Warton	
ZG989	PBN 2T Islander ASTOR (G-DLRA)	DPA/PBN, Bembridge	
ZG993	PBN 2T Islander AL1 (G-BOMD)	AAC No 1 Flight, Aldergrove	
ZG994	PBN 2T Islander AL1 (G-BPLN)	AAC, stored St Athan (wreck)	
ZH101	Boeing E-3D Sentry AEW1	RAF No 8 Sqn/No 23 Sqn, Waddington	
ZH102	Boeing E-3D Sentry AEW1	RAF No 8 Sqn/No 23 Sqn, Waddington	
ZH103	Boeing E-3D Sentry AEW1	RAF No 8 Sqn/No 23 Sqn, Waddington	
ZH104	Boeing E-3D Sentry AEW1	RAF No 8 Sqn/No 23 Sqn, Waddington	
ZH105	Boeing E-3D Sentry AEW1	RAF No 8 Sqn/No 23 Sqn, Waddington	
ZH106	Boeing E-3D Sentry AEW1	RAF No 8 Sqn/No 23 Sqn, Waddington	
ZH107	Boeing E-3D Sentry AEW1	RAF No 8 Sqn/No 23 Sqn, Waddington	
ZH115	Grob G109B Vigilant T1 [TA]	RAF No 616 VGS, Henlow	
ZH116	Grob G109B Vigilant T1 [TB]	RAF No 664 VGS, Belfast City Airport	

Notes	Serial	Type (other identity) [code]	Owner/operator, location or fate
	ZH117	Grob G109B Vigilant T1 [TC]	RAF No 642 VGS, Linton-on-Ouse
	ZH118	Grob G109B Vigilant T1 [TD]	RAF No 612 VGS, Chivenor RMB
	ZH119	Grob G109B Vigilant T1 [TE]	RAF No 637 VGS, Little Rissington
	ZH120	Grob G109B Vigilant T1 [TF]	RAF ACCGS/No 644 VGS, Syerston
	ZH121	Grob G109B Vigilant T1 [TG]	RAF No 633 VGS, Cosford
	ZH122	Grob G109B Vigilant T1 [TH]	RAF No 635 VGS, Samlesbury
	ZH123	Grob G109B Vigilant T1 [TJ]	RAF No 637 VGS, Little Rissington
	ZH124	Grob G109B Vigilant T1 [TK]	RAF No 642 VGS, Linton-on-Ouse
	ZH125	Grob G109B Vigilant T1 [TL]	RAF No 633 VGS, Cosford
	ZH126	Grob G109B Vigilant T1 [TM]	RAF No 637 VGS, Little Rissington
	ZH127	Grob G109B Vigilant T1 [TN]	RAF No 642 VGS, Linton-on-Ouse
	ZH128	Grob G109B Vigilant T1 [TP]	RAF No 624 VGS, Chivenor RMB
	ZH129	Grob G109B Vigilant T1 [TQ]	RAF No 635 VGS, Samlesbury
	ZH139	BAe Harrier GR7 <R> (BAPC 191/ ZD472)	RAF EPTT, St Athan
	ZH141	AS355F-1 Twin Squirrel HCC1 (G-OILX)	RAF No 32(The Royal) Sqn, Northolt
	ZH144	Grob G109B Vigilant T1 [TR]	RAF No 616 VGS, Henlow
	ZH145	Grob G109B Vigilant T1 [TS]	RAF No 618 VGS, Odiham
	ZH146	Grob G109B Vigilant T1 [TT]	RAF CGMF, Syerston (damaged)
	ZH147	Grob G109B Vigilant T1 [TU]	RAF No 632 VGS, Ternhill
	ZH148	Grob G109B Vigilant T1 [TV]	RAF No 612 VGS, Abingdon
	ZH184	Grob G109B Vigilant T1 [TW]	RAF ACCGS/No 644 VGS, Syerston
	ZH185	Grob G109B Vigilant T1 [TX]	RAF No 642 VGS, Linton-on-Ouse
	ZH186	Grob G109B Vigilant T1 [TY]	RAF No 613 VGS, Halton
	ZH187	Grob G109B Vigilant T1 [TZ]	RAF No 633 VGS, Cosford
	ZH188	Grob G109B Vigilant T1 [UA]	RAF No 612 VGS, Abingdon
	ZH189	Grob G109B Vigilant T1 [UB]	RAF No 635 VGS, Samlesbury
	ZH190	Grob G109B Vigilant T1 [UC]	RAF No 663 VGS, Kinloss
	ZH191	Grob G109B Vigilant T1 [UD]	RAF No 616 VGS, Henlow
	ZH192	Grob G109B Vigilant T1 [UE]	RAF No 635 VGS, Samlesbury
	ZH193	Grob G109B Vigilant T1 [UF]	RAF No 612 VGS, Abingdon
	ZH194	Grob G109B Vigilant T1 [UG]	RAF No 624 VGS, Chivenor RMB
	ZH195	Grob G109B Vigilant T1 [UH]	RAF ACCGS/No 644 VGS, Syerston
	ZH196	Grob G109B Vigilant T1 [UJ]	RAF CGMF, Syerston
	ZH197	Grob G109B Vigilant T1 [UK]	RAF No 633 VGS, Cosford
	ZH200	BAe Hawk 200	DPA, stored BAE Systems Warton
	ZH205	Grob G109B Vigilant T1 [UL]	RAF No 613 VGS, Halton
	ZH206	Grob G109B Vigilant T1 [UM]	RAF No 633 VGS, Cosford
	ZH207	Grob G109B Vigilant T1 [UN]	RAF No 632 VGS, Ternhill
	ZH208	Grob G109B Vigilant T1 [UP]	RAF No 618 VGS, Odiham
	ZH209	Grob G109B Vigilant T1 [UQ]	RAF No 664 VGS, Belfast City Airport
	ZH211	Grob G109B Vigilant T1 [UR]	RAF No 618 VGS, Odiham
	ZH247	Grob G109B Vigilant T1 [US]	RAF ACCGS/No 644 VGS, Syerston
	ZH248	Grob G109B Vigilant T1	RAF ACCGS/No 644 VGS, Syerston
	ZH249	Grob G109B Vigilant T1	RAF ACCGS/No 644 VGS, Syerston
	ZH257	B-V CH-47C Chinook (AE-520/ 9217M)	DARA, RNAY Fleetlands
	ZH263	Grob G109B Vigilant T1 [UV]	RAF No 632 VGS, Ternhill
	ZH264	Grob G109B Vigilant T1 [UW]	RAF No 616 VGS, Henlow
	ZH265	Grob G109B Vigilant T1 [UX]	RAF No 663 VGS, Kinloss
	ZH266	Grob G109B Vigilant T1 [UY]	RAF No 635 VGS, Samlesbury
	ZH267	Grob G109B Vigilant T1 [UZ]	RAF No 637 VGS, Little Rissington
	ZH268	Grob G109B Vigilant T1 [SA]	RAF No 613 VGS, Halton
	ZH269	Grob G109B Vigilant T1 [SB]	RAF No 642 VGS, Linton-on-Ouse
	ZH270	Grob G109B Vigilant T1 [SC]	RAF No 616 VGS, Henlow
	ZH271	Grob G109B Vigilant T1 [SD]	RAF No 613 VGS, Halton
	ZH536	PBN 2T Islander CC2 (G-BSAH)	RAF Northolt Station Flight
	ZH540	WS61 Sea King HAR3A	RAF No 22 Sqn, B Flt, Wattisham
	ZH541	WS61 Sea King HAR3A	RAF No 22 Sqn, B Flt, Wattisham
	ZH542	WS61 Sea King HAR3A	RAF No 22 Sqn, B Flt, Wattisham
	ZH543	WS61 Sea King HAR3A	RAF No 22 Sqn, A Flt, Chivenor RMB
	ZH544	WS61 Sea King HAR3A	RAF No 22 Sqn, A Flt, Chivenor RMB
	ZH545	WS61 Sea King HAR3A	RAF No 22 Sqn, A Flt, Chivenor RMB
	ZH552	Panavia Tornado F3 [AQ]	RAF F3 OCU/No 56(R) Sqn, Coningsby
	ZH553	Panavia Tornado F3 [AB]	RAF No 11 Sqn, Leeming
	ZH554	Panavia Tornado F3	RAF AWC/F3 OEU, Coningsby
	ZH555	Panavia Tornado F3 [CV]	RAF F3 OCU/No 56(R) Sqn, Coningsby
	ZH556	Panavia Tornado F3 [AK]	RAF F3 OCU/No 56(R) Sqn, Coningsby
	ZH557	Panavia Tornado F3 [CT]	RAF No 5 Sqn, Coningsby
	ZH559	Panavia Tornado F3 [AJ]	RAF F3 OCU/No 56(R) Sqn, Coningsby
	ZH588	Eurofighter Typhoon (DA2)	DPA/BAE Systems, Warton
	ZH590	Eurofighter Typhoon (DA4)	DPA/BAE Systems, Warton

Serial	Type (other identity) [code]	Owner/operator, location or fate	Notes
ZH653	BAe Harrier T10	DPA/AFD, DERA Boscombe Down	
ZH654	BAe Harrier T10	Crashed 24 August 2000, Boscombe Down	
ZH655	BAe Harrier T10 [Q]	RAF, stored St Athan (damaged)	
ZH656	BAe Harrier T10 [104]	RAF No 1 Sqn, Cottesmore	
ZH657	BAe Harrier T10 [XX]	DPA/BAE Systems, Warton	
ZH658	BAe Harrier T10 [106]	RAF HOCU/No 20(R) Sqn, Wittering	
ZH659	BAe Harrier T10 [107]	RAF HOCU/No 20(R) Sqn, Wittering	
ZH660	BAe Harrier T10 [108]	DPA/BAE Systems, Warton	
ZH661	BAe Harrier T10 [109]	RAF HOCU/No 20(R) Sqn, Wittering	
ZH662	BAe Harrier T10 [110]	RAF HOCU/No 20(R) Sqn, Wittering	
ZH663	BAe Harrier T10 [111]	RAF HOCU/No 20(R) Sqn, Wittering	
ZH664	BAe Harrier T10 [112]	RAF No 4 Sqn, Cottesmore	
ZH665	BAe Harrier T10 [113]	RAF HOCU/No 20(R) Sqn, Wittering	
ZH762	Westinghouse Skyship 500 (G-SKSC)	Westinghouse, stored Cardington	
ZH763	BAC 1-11/539GL (G-BGKE)	DPA/AFD, DERA Boscombe Down	
ZH775	B-V Chinook HC2 (N7424J) [NS]	RAF No 7 Sqn, Odiham	
ZH776	B-V Chinook HC2 (N7424L) [BF]	RAF No 18 Sqn, Odiham	
ZH777	B-V Chinook HC2 (N7424M) [NY]	RAF No 27 Sqn, Odiham	
ZH796	BAe Sea Harrier FA2 [716/VL]	RN, St Athan	
ZH797	BAe Sea Harrier FA2 [002]	RN No 801 Sqn, Yeovilton	
ZH798	BAe Sea Harrier FA2 [718]	RN No 899 Sqn, Yeovilton	
ZH799	BAe Sea Harrier FA2 [730]	RN No 899 Sqn, Yeovilton	
ZH800	BAe Sea Harrier FA2 [716]	RN No 899 Sqn, Yeovilton	
ZH801	BAe Sea Harrier FA2 [731]	DPA/BAE Systems, Warton	
ZH802	BAe Sea Harrier FA2 [718]	RN AMG, Yeovilton	
ZH803	BAe Sea Harrier FA2 [128/N]	RN No 800 Sqn, Yeovilton	
ZH804	BAe Sea Harrier FA2 [125]	RN No 800 Sqn, Yeovilton	
ZH805	BAe Sea Harrier FA2 [730]	RN No 899 Sqn, Yeovilton	
ZH806	BAe Sea Harrier FA2 [717]	RN No 899 Sqn, Yeovilton	
ZH807	BAe Sea Harrier FA2 [719/VL]	RN No 899 Sqn, Yeovilton	
ZH808	BAe Sea Harrier FA2 [712]	RN No 899 Sqn, Yeovilton	
ZH809	BAe Sea Harrier FA2 [123]	RN No 800 Sqn, Yeovilton	
ZH810	BAe Sea Harrier FA2 [004/L]	RN No 801 Sqn, Yeovilton	
ZH811	BAe Sea Harrier FA2 [714]	RN No 899 Sqn, Yeovilton	
ZH812	BAe Sea Harrier FA2 [006]	RN No 801 Sqn, Yeovilton	
ZH813	BAe Sea Harrier FA2 [000]	RN No 801 Sqn, Yeovilton	
ZH814	Bell 212 (G-BGMH)	AAC No 7 Flt, Brunei	
ZH815	Bell 212 (G-BGCZ)	AAC No 7 Flt, Brunei	
ZH816	Bell 212 (G-BGMG)	AAC No 7 Flt, Brunei	
ZH821	EHI-101 Merlin HM1	DPA/GKN Westland, Yeovil	
ZH822	EHI-101 Merlin HM1	DPA/GKN Westland, Yeovil	
ZH823	EHI-101 Merlin HM1	DPA/GKN Westland, Yeovil	
ZH824	EHI-101 Merlin HM1	DPA/AFD, DERA Boscombe Down	
ZH825	EHI-101 Merlin HM1 [535/CU]	RN No 824 Sqn, Culdrose	
ZH826	EHI-101 Merlin HM1 [536/CU]	RN No 700M Sqn, Culdrose	
ZH827	EHI-101 Merlin HM1 [537/CU]	RN No 700M Sqn, Culdrose	
ZH828	EHI-101 Merlin HM1 [583/CU]	RN No 824 Sqn, Culdrose	
ZH829	EHI-101 Merlin HM1	DPA/GKN Westland, Yeovil	
ZH830	EHI-101 Merlin HM1	DPA/AFD, DERA Boscombe Down	
ZH831	EHI-101 Merlin HM1	RN No 700M Sqn, Culdrose	
ZH832	EHI-101 Merlin HM1	DPA/AFD, DERA Boscombe Down	
ZH833	EHI-101 Merlin HM1 [580/CU]	RN No 824 Sqn, Culdrose	
ZH834	EHI-101 Merlin HM1	GKN Westland, Yeovil	
ZH835	EHI-101 Merlin HM1 [581/CU]	RN No 824 Sqn, Culdrose	
ZH836	EHI-101 Merlin HM1 [582/CU]	RN No 824 Sqn, Culdrose	
ZH837	EHI-101 Merlin HM1 [540]	RN No 700M Sqn, Culdrose	
ZH838	EHI-101 Merlin HM1 [584]	RN No 824 Sqn, Culdrose	
ZH839	EHI-101 Merlin HM1 [539/CU]	RN No 700M Sqn, Culdrose	
ZH840	EHI-101 Merlin HM1	DPA/GKN Westland, Yeovil	
ZH841	EHI-101 Merlin HM1	DPA/GKN Westland, Yeovil	
ZH842	EHI-101 Merlin HM1 [585/CU]	RN No 824 Sqn, Culdrose	
ZH843	EHI-101 Merlin HM1	RN No 700M Sqn, Culdrose	
ZH844	EHI-101 Merlin HM1	RN FSAIU, Yeovilton (wreck)	
ZH845	EHI-101 Merlin HM1	RN AMG, Culdrose	
ZH846	EHI-101 Merlin HM1	RN AMG, Culdrose	
ZH847	EHI-101 Merlin HM1	DPA/GKN Westland, Yeovil	
ZH848	EHI-101 Merlin HM1	DPA/GKN Westland, Yeovil	
ZH849	EHI-101 Merlin HM1	GKN Westland, Yeovil, for RN	
ZH850	EHI-101 Merlin HM1	GKN Westland, Yeovil, for RN	
ZH851	EHI-101 Merlin HM1	GKN Westland, Yeovil, for RN	
ZH852	EHI-101 Merlin HM1	GKN Westland, Yeovil, for RN	

Notes	Serial	Type (other identity) [code]	Owner/operator, location or fate
	ZH853	EHI-101 Merlin HM1	GKN Westland, Yeovil, for RN
	ZH854	EHI-101 Merlin HM1	GKN Westland, Yeovil, for RN
	ZH855	EHI-101 Merlin HM1	GKN Westland, Yeovil, for RN
	ZH856	EHI-101 Merlin HM1	GKN Westland, Yeovil, for RN
	ZH857	EHI-101 Merlin HM1	GKN Westland, Yeovil, for RN
	ZH858	EHI-101 Merlin HM1	GKN Westland, Yeovil, for RN
	ZH859	EHI-101 Merlin HM1	GKN Westland, Yeovil, for RN
	ZH860	EHI-101 Merlin HM1	GKN Westland, Yeovil, for RN
	ZH861	EHI-101 Merlin HM1	GKN Westland, Yeovil, for RN
	ZH862	EHI-101 Merlin HM1	GKN Westland, Yeovil, for RN
	ZH863	EHI-101 Merlin HM1	GKN Westland, Yeovil, for RN
	ZH864	EHI-101 Merlin HM1	GKN Westland, Yeovil, for RN
	ZH865	Lockheed C-130J-30 Hercules C4 (N130JA)	DPA/Lockheed-Martin, Marietta
	ZH866	Lockheed C-130J-30 Hercules C4 (N130JE)	RAF Lyneham Transport Wing
	ZH867	Lockheed C-130J-30 Hercules C4 (N130JJ)	RAF Lyneham Transport Wing
	ZH868	Lockheed C-130J-30 Hercules C4 (N130JN)	LMASC/Marshall Aerospace, Cambridge
	ZH869	Lockheed C-130J-30 Hercules C4 (N130JV)	RAF Lyneham Transport Wing
	ZH870	Lockheed C-130J-30 Hercules C4 (N73235/N78235)	RAF Lyneham Transport Wing
	ZH871	Lockheed C-130J-30 Hercules C4 (N73238)	DPA/AFD, DERA Boscombe Down
	ZH872	Lockheed C-130J-30 Hercules C4 (N4249Y)	RAF Lyneham Transport Wing
	ZH873	Lockheed C-130J-30 Hercules C4 (N4242N)	RAF Lyneham Transport Wing
	ZH874	Lockheed C-130J-30 Hercules C4 (N41030)	RAF Lyneham Transport Wing
	ZH875	Lockheed C-130J-30 Hercules C4 (N4099R)	RAF Lyneham Transport Wing
	ZH876	Lockheed C-130J-30 Hercules C4 (N4080M)	RAF Lyneham Transport Wing
	ZH877	Lockheed C-130J-30 Hercules C4 (N4081M)	RAF Lyneham Transport Wing
	ZH878	Lockheed C-130J-30 Hercules C4 (N73232)	RAF Lyneham Transport Wing
	ZH879	Lockheed C-130J-30 Hercules C4 (N4080M)	RAF Lyneham Transport Wing
	ZH880	Lockheed C-130J Hercules C5 (N73238)	DPA/AFD, DERA Boscombe Down
	ZH881	Lockheed C-130J Hercules C5 (N4081M)	RAF Lyneham Transport Wing
	ZH882	Lockheed C-130J Hercules C5 (N4099R)	RAF Lyneham Transport Wing
	ZH883	Lockheed C-130J Hercules C5 (N4242N)	LMASC/Marshall Aerospace, Cambridge
	ZH884	Lockheed C-130J Hercules C5 (N4249Y)	LMASC/Marshall Aerospace, Cambridge
	ZH885	Lockheed C-130J Hercules C5 (N41030)	LMASC/Marshall Aerospace, Cambridge
	ZH886	Lockheed C-130J Hercules C5 (N73235)	LMASC/Marshall Aerospace, Cambridge
	ZH887	Lockheed C-130J Hercules C5 (N4187W)	LMASC/Marshall Aerospace, Cambridge
	ZH888	Lockheed C-130J Hercules C5 (N4187)	RAF Lyneham Transport Wing
	ZH889	Lockheed C-130J Hercules C5 (N4099R)	RAF Lyneham Transport Wing
	ZH890	Grob G109B Vigilant T1 [SE]	RAF ACCGS/No 644 VGS, Syerston
	ZH891	B-V Chinook HC2A (N20075)	DPA/AFD, DERA Boscombe Down
	ZH892	B-V Chinook HC2A (N2019V) [BL]	RAF No 18 Sqn, Odiham
	ZH893	B-V Chinook HC2A (N2025L)	DPA/AFD, DERA Boscombe Down
	ZH894	B-V Chinook HC2A (N2026E) [BO]	RAF No 18 Sqn, Odiham
	ZH895	B-V Chinook HC2A (N2034K) [BP]	RAF No 18 Sqn, Odiham
	ZH896	B-V Chinook HC2A (N2038G)	DPA/AFD, DERA Boscombe Down
	ZH897	B-V Chinook HC3 (N2045G)	Boeing, Philadelphia, for RAF
	ZH898	B-V Chinook HC3 (N2057Q)	Boeing, Philadelphia, for RAF
	ZH899	B-V Chinook HC3 (N2057R)	Boeing, Philadelphia, for RAF
	ZH900	B-V Chinook HC3 (N2060H)	Boeing, Philadelphia, for RAF

Serial	Type (other identity) [code]	Owner/operator, location or fate	Notes
ZH901	B-V Chinook HC3 (N2060M)	Boeing, Philadelphia, for RAF	
ZH902	B-V Chinook HC3 (N2064W)	Boeing, Philadelphia, for RAF	
ZH903	B-V Chinook HC3 (N20671)	Boeing, Philadelphia, for RAF	
ZH904	B-V Chinook HC3 (N2083K)	Boeing, Philadelphia, for RAF	
ZJ100	BAe Hawk 102D	BAE Systems Warton	
ZJ116	EHI-101 (G-OIOI) (PP8)	DPA/GKN Westland, Yeovil	
ZJ117	EHI-101 Merlin HC3	DPA/AFD, DERA Boscombe Down	
ZJ118	EHI-101 Merlin HC3	DPA/AFD, DERA Boscombe Down	
ZJ119	EHI-101 Merlin HC3 [C]	DPA/GKN Westland, Yeovil	
ZJ120	EHI-101 Merlin HC3	DPA/AFD, DERA Boscombe Down	
ZJ121	EHI-101 Merlin HC3 [E]	DPA/AFD, DERA Boscombe Down	
ZJ122	EHI-101 Merlin HC3 [F]	RAF No 28 Sqn, Benson	
ZJ123	EHI-101 Merlin HC3 [G]	DPA/GKN Westland, Yeovil	
ZJ124	EHI-101 Merlin HC3 [H]	RAF No 28 Sqn,Benson	
ZJ125	EHI-101 Merlin HC3	GKN Westland, Yeovil, for RAF	
ZJ126	EHI-101 Merlin HC3	GKN Westland, Yeovil, for RAF	
ZJ127	EHI-101 Merlin HC3	GKN Westland, Yeovil, for RAF	
ZJ128	EHI-101 Merlin HC3	GKN Westland, Yeovil, for RAF	
ZJ129	EHI-101 Merlin HC3	GKN Westland, Yeovil, for RAF	
ZJ130	EHI-101 Merlin HC3	GKN Westland, Yeovil, for RAF	
ZJ131	EHI-101 Merlin HC3	GKN Westland, Yeovil, for RAF	
ZJ132	EHI-101 Merlin HC3	GKN Westland, Yeovil, for RAF	
ZJ133	EHI-101 Merlin HC3	GKN Westland, Yeovil, for RAF	
ZJ134	EHI-101 Merlin HC3	GKN Westland, Yeovil, for RAF	
ZJ135	EHI-101 Merlin HC3	GKN Westland, Yeovil, for RAF	
ZJ136	EHI-101 Merlin HC3	GKN Westland, Yeovil, for RAF	
ZJ137	EHI-101 Merlin HC3	GKN Westland, Yeovil, for RAF	
ZJ138	EHI-101 Merlin HC3	GKN Westland, Yeovil, for RAF	
ZJ139	AS355F-1 Twin Squirrel HCC1 (G-NUTZ)	RAF No 32(The Royal) Sqn, Northolt	
ZJ140	AS355F-1 Twin Squirrel HCC1 (G-FFHI)	RAF No 32(The Royal) Sqn, Northolt	
ZJ164	AS365N-2 Dauphin 2 (G-BTLC)	RN/Bond Helicopters, Plymouth	
ZJ165	AS365N-2 Dauphin 2 (G-NTOO)	RN/Bond Helicopters, Plymouth	
ZJ166	WAH-64 Apache Longbow AH1 (N9219G)	Boeing Helicopters, Mesa, for AAC	
ZJ167	WAH-64 Apache Longbow AH1 (N3266B)	AAC No 651 Sqn, Middle Wallop	
ZJ168	WAH-64 Apache Longbow AH1 (N3123T)	AAC No 651 Sqn, Middle Wallop	
ZJ169	WAH-64 Apache Longbow AH1 (N3114H)	AAC No 651 Sqn, Middle Wallop	
ZJ170	WAH-64 Apache Longbow AH1 (N3065U)	Boeing Helicopters, Mesa, for AAC	
ZJ171	WAH-64 Apache Longbow AH1 (N3266T)	DPA/GKN Westland, Yeovil	
ZJ172	WAH-64 Apache Longbow AH1	AAC No 651 Sqn, Middle Wallop	
ZJ173	WAH-64 Apache Longbow AH1 (N3267A)	DPA/GKN Westland, Yeovil	
ZJ174	WAH-64 Apache Longbow AH1	DPA/GKN Westland, Yeovil	
ZJ175	WAH-64 Apache Longbow AH1 (N3218V)	AAC No 651 Sqn, Middle Wallop	
ZJ176	WAH-64 Apache Longbow AH1	DPA/GKN Westland, Yeovil	
ZJ177	WAH-64 Apache Longbow AH1	DPA/GKN Westland, Yeovil	
ZJ178	WAH-64 Apache Longbow AH1	DPA/GKN Westland, Yeovil	
ZJ179	WAH-64 Apache Longbow AH1	GKN Westland, for AAC	
ZJ180	WAH-64 Apache Longbow AH1	GKN Westland, for AAC	
ZJ181	WAH-64 Apache Longbow AH1	DPA/GKN Westland, Yeovil	
ZJ182	WAH-64 Apache Longbow AH1	DPA/GKN Westland, Yeovil	
ZJ183	WAH-64 Apache Longbow AH1	GKN Westland, for AAC	
ZJ184	WAH-64 Apache Longbow AH1	GKN Westland, for AAC	
ZJ185	WAH-64 Apache Longbow AH1	GKN Westland, for AAC	
ZJ186	WAH-64 Apache Longbow AH1	GKN Westland, for AAC	
ZJ187	WAH-64 Apache Longbow AH1	GKN Westland, for AAC	
ZJ188	WAH-64 Apache Longbow AH1	GKN Westland, for AAC	
ZJ189	WAH-64 Apache Longbow AH1	GKN Westland, for AAC	
ZJ190	WAH-64 Apache Longbow AH1	GKN Westland, for AAC	
ZJ191	WAH-64 Apache Longbow AH1	GKN Westland, for AAC	
ZJ192	WAH-64 Apache Longbow AH1	GKN Westland, for AAC	
ZJ193	WAH-64 Apache Longbow AH1	GKN Westland, for AAC	
ZJ194	WAH-64 Apache Longbow AH1	GKN Westland, for AAC	
ZJ195	WAH-64 Apache Longbow AH1	GKN Westland, for AAC	

Notes	Serial	Type (other identity) [code]	Owner/operator, location or fate
	ZJ196	WAH-64 Apache Longbow AH1	GKN Westland, for AAC
	ZJ197	WAH-64 Apache Longbow AH1	GKN Westland, for AAC
	ZJ198	WAH-64 Apache Longbow AH1	GKN Westland, for AAC
	ZJ199	WAH-64 Apache Longbow AH1	GKN Westland, for AAC
	ZJ200	WAH-64 Apache Longbow AH1	GKN Westland, for AAC
	ZJ202	WAH-64 Apache Longbow AH1	GKN Westland, for AAC
	ZJ203	WAH-64 Apache Longbow AH1	GKN Westland, for AAC
	ZJ204	WAH-64 Apache Longbow AH1	GKN Westland, for AAC
	ZJ205	WAH-64 Apache Longbow AH1	GKN Westland, for AAC
	ZJ206	WAH-64 Apache Longbow AH1	GKN Westland, for AAC
	ZJ207	WAH-64 Apache Longbow AH1	GKN Westland, for AAC
	ZJ208	WAH-64 Apache Longbow AH1	GKN Westland, for AAC
	ZJ209	WAH-64 Apache Longbow AH1	GKN Westland, for AAC
	ZJ210	WAH-64 Apache Longbow AH1	GKN Westland, for AAC
	ZJ211	WAH-64 Apache Longbow AH1	GKN Westland, for AAC
	ZJ212	WAH-64 Apache Longbow AH1	GKN Westland, for AAC
	ZJ213	WAH-64 Apache Longbow AH1	GKN Westland, for AAC
	ZJ214	WAH-64 Apache Longbow AH1	GKN Westland, for AAC
	ZJ215	WAH-64 Apache Longbow AH1	GKN Westland, for AAC
	ZJ216	WAH-64 Apache Longbow AH1	GKN Westland, for AAC
	ZJ217	WAH-64 Apache Longbow AH1	GKN Westland, for AAC
	ZJ218	WAH-64 Apache Longbow AH1	GKN Westland, for AAC
	ZJ219	WAH-64 Apache Longbow AH1	GKN Westland, for AAC
	ZJ220	WAH-64 Apache Longbow AH1	GKN Westland, for AAC
	ZJ221	WAH-64 Apache Longbow AH1	GKN Westland, for AAC
	ZJ222	WAH-64 Apache Longbow AH1	GKN Westland, for AAC
	ZJ223	WAH-64 Apache Longbow AH1	GKN Westland, for AAC
	ZJ224	WAH-64 Apache Longbow AH1	GKN Westland, for AAC
	ZJ225	WAH-64 Apache Longbow AH1	GKN Westland, for AAC
	ZJ226	WAH-64 Apache Longbow AH1	GKN Westland, for AAC
	ZJ227	WAH-64 Apache Longbow AH1	GKN Westland, for AAC
	ZJ228	WAH-64 Apache Longbow AH1	GKN Westland, for AAC
	ZJ229	WAH-64 Apache Longbow AH1	GKN Westland, for AAC
	ZJ230	WAH-64 Apache Longbow AH1	GKN Westland, for AAC
	ZJ231	WAH-64 Apache Longbow AH1	GKN Westland, for AAC
	ZJ232	WAH-64 Apache Longbow AH1	GKN Westland, for AAC
	ZJ233	WAH-64 Apache Longbow AH1	GKN Westland, for AAC
	ZJ234	Bell 412EP Griffin HT1 (G-BWZR) [S]	DHFS No 60(R) Sqn, RAF Shawbury
	ZJ235	Bell 412EP Griffin HT1 (G-BXBF) [I]	DHFS No 60(R) Sqn, RAF Shawbury
	ZJ236	Bell 412EP Griffin HT1 (G-BXBE) [X]	DHFS No 60(R) Sqn, RAF Shawbury
	ZJ237	Bell 412EP Griffin HT1 (G-BXFF) [T]	DHFS No 60(R) Sqn, RAF Shawbury
	ZJ238	Bell 412EP Griffin HT1 (G-BXHC) [Y]	DHFS No 60(R) Sqn, RAF Shawbury
	ZJ239	Bell 412EP Griffin HT1 (G-BXFH) [R]	DHFS No 60(R) Sqn, RAF Shawbury
	ZJ240	Bell 412EP Griffin HT1 (G-BXIR) [U]	DHFS No 60(R) Sqn/SARTU, RAF Valley
	ZJ241	Bell 412EP Griffin HT1 (G-BXIS) [L]	DHFS No 60(R) Sqn/SARTU, RAF Valley
	ZJ242	Bell 412EP Griffin HT1 (G-BXDK) [E]	DHFS No 60(R) Sqn/SARTU, RAF Valley
	ZJ243	AS350BA Squirrel HT2 (G-BWZS)	School of Army Aviation/No 670 Sqn, Middle Wallop
	ZJ244	AS350BA Squirrel HT2 (G-BXMD)	School of Army Aviation/No 670 Sqn, Middle Wallop
	ZJ245	AS350BA Squirrel HT2 (G-BXME)	School of Army Aviation/No 670 Sqn, Middle Wallop
	ZJ246	AS350BA Squirrel HT2 (G-BXMJ)	School of Army Aviation/No 670 Sqn, Middle Wallop
	ZJ247	AS350BA Squirrel HT2 (G-BXNB)	School of Army Aviation/No 670 Sqn, Middle Wallop
	ZJ248	AS350BA Squirrel HT2 (G-BXNE)	School of Army Aviation/No 670 Sqn, Middle Wallop
	ZJ249	AS350BA Squirrel HT2 (G-BXNJ)	School of Army Aviation/No 670 Sqn, Middle Wallop
	ZJ250	AS350BA Squirrel HT2 (G-BXNY)	School of Army Aviation/No 670 Sqn, Middle Wallop
	ZJ251	AS350BA Squirrel HT2 (G-BXOG)	School of Army Aviation/No 670 Sqn, Middle Wallop

Serial	Type (other identity) [code]	Owner/operator, location or fate	Notes
ZJ252	AS350BA Squirrel HT2 (G-BXOK)	School of Army Aviation/No 670 Sqn, Middle Wallop	
ZJ253	AS350BA Squirrel HT2 (G-BXPG)	School of Army Aviation/No 670 Sqn, Middle Wallop	
ZJ254	AS350BA Squirrel HT2 (G-BXPJ)	School of Army Aviation/No 670 Sqn, Middle Wallop	
ZJ255	AS350BB Squirrel HT1 (G-BXAG)	DHFS, RAF Shawbury	
ZJ256	AS350BB Squirrel HT1 (G-BXCE)	DHFS, RAF Shawbury	
ZJ257	AS350BB Squirrel HT1 (G-BXDJ)	DHFS, RAF Shawbury	
ZJ258	AS350BB Squirrel HT1 (G-BXEO)	DHFS, RAF Shawbury	
ZJ259	AS350BB Squirrel HT1 (G-BXFJ)	DHFS, RAF Shawbury	
ZJ260	AS350BB Squirrel HT1 (G-BXGB)	DHFS, RAF Shawbury	
ZJ261	AS350BB Squirrel HT1 (G-BXGJ)	DHFS, RAF Shawbury	
ZJ262	AS350BB Squirrel HT1 (G-BXHB)	DHFS, RAF Shawbury	
ZJ263	AS350BB Squirrel HT1 (G-BXHK)	DHFS, RAF Shawbury	
ZJ264	AS350BB Squirrel HT1 (G-BXHW)	DHFS, RAF Shawbury	
ZJ265	AS350BB Squirrel HT1 (G-BXHX)	DHFS, RAF Shawbury	
ZJ266	AS350BB Squirrel HT1 (G-BXIL)	DHFS, RAF Shawbury	
ZJ267	AS350BB Squirrel HT1 (G-BXIP)	DHFS, RAF Shawbury	
ZJ268	AS350BB Squirrel HT1 (G-BXJE)	DHFS, RAF Shawbury	
ZJ269	AS350BB Squirrel HT1 (G-BXJN)	DHFS, RAF Shawbury	
ZJ270	AS350BB Squirrel HT1 (G-BXJR)	DHFS, RAF Shawbury	
ZJ271	AS350BB Squirrel HT1 (G-BXKE)	DHFS, RAF Shawbury	
ZJ272	AS350BB Squirrel HT1 (G-BXKN)	DHFS, RAF Shawbury	
ZJ273	AS350BB Squirrel HT1 (G-BXKP)	DHFS, RAF Shawbury	
ZJ274	AS350BB Squirrel HT1 (G-BXKR)	DHFS, RAF Shawbury	
ZJ275	AS350BB Squirrel HT1 (G-BXLB)	DHFS, RAF Shawbury	
ZJ276	AS350BB Squirrel HT1 (G-BXLE)	DHFS, RAF Shawbury	
ZJ277	AS350BB Squirrel HT1 (G-BXLH)	DHFS, RAF Shawbury	
ZJ278	AS350BB Squirrel HT1 (G-BXMB)	DHFS, RAF Shawbury	
ZJ279	AS350BB Squirrel HT1 (G-BXMC)	DHFS, RAF Shawbury	
ZJ280	AS350BB Squirrel HT1 (G-BXMI)	DHFS, RAF Shawbury	
ZJ514	BAE Systems Nimrod MRA4 (XV251) [PA-4]	DPA/BAE Systems, Woodford (conversion)	
ZJ515	BAE Systems Nimrod MRA4 (XV258) [PA-5]	DPA/BAE Systems, Woodford (conversion)	
ZJ516	BAE Systems Nimrod MRA4 (XV247) [PA-1]	DPA/BAE Systems, Woodford (conversion)	
ZJ517	BAE Systems Nimrod MRA4 (XV242) [PA-3]	DPA/BAE Systems, Woodford (conversion)	
ZJ518	BAE Systems Nimrod MRA4 (XV234) [PA-2]	DPA/BAE Systems, Woodford (conversion)	
ZJ519	BAE Systems Nimrod MRA4 (XZ284) [PA-6]	DPA/BAE Systems, Woodford (conversion)	
ZJ520	BAE Systems Nimrod MRA4 (XV233) [PA-7]	DPA/BAE Systems, Woodford (conversion)	
ZJ521	BAE Systems Nimrod MRA4	BAE Systems, for RAF	
ZJ522	BAE Systems Nimrod MRA4	BAE Systems, for RAF	
ZJ523	BAE Systems Nimrod MRA4	BAE Systems, for RAF	
ZJ524	BAE Systems Nimrod MRA4	BAE Systems, for RAF	
ZJ525	BAE Systems Nimrod MRA4	BAE Systems, for RAF	
ZJ526	BAE Systems Nimrod MRA4	BAE Systems, for RAF	
ZJ527	BAE Systems Nimrod MRA4	BAE Systems, for RAF	
ZJ528	BAE Systems Nimrod MRA4	BAE Systems, for RAF	
ZJ529	BAE Systems Nimrod MRA4	BAE Systems, for RAF	
ZJ530	BAE Systems Nimrod MRA4	BAE Systems, for RAF	
ZJ531	BAE Systems Nimrod MRA4	BAE Systems, for RAF	
ZJ532	BAE Systems Nimrod MRA4	BAE Systems, for RAF	
ZJ533	BAE Systems Nimrod MRA4	BAE Systems, for RAF	
ZJ534	BAE Systems Nimrod MRA4	BAE Systems, for RAF	
ZJ535	WS Super Lynx Mk 88A	To German Navy as 83+20	
ZJ536	WS Super Lynx Mk 88A	To German Navy as 83+21	
ZJ537	WS Super Lynx Mk 88A	To German Navy as 83+22	
ZJ538	WS Super Lynx Mk 88A	To German Navy as 83+23	
ZJ539	WS Super Lynx Mk 88A	To German Navy as 83+24, 6 April 2000	
ZJ540	WS Super Lynx Mk 88A	To German Navy as 83+25	
ZJ541	WS Super Lynx Mk 88A	To German Navy as 83+26	
ZJ543	WS Super Lynx Mk 99	To S Korean Navy as 99-0722, 8 November 1999	
ZJ544	WS Super Lynx Mk 99	To S Korean Navy as 99-0723, 8 November 1999	
ZJ545	WS Super Lynx Mk 99	To S Korean Navy as 99-0725, 7 December 1999	

Notes	Serial	Type (other identity) [code]	Owner/operator, location or fate
	ZJ546	WS Super Lynx Mk 99	*To S Korean Navy as 99-0726, 3 January 2000*
	ZJ547	WS Super Lynx Mk 99	*To S Korean Navy as 00-0727*
	ZJ548	WS Super Lynx Mk 99	*To S Korean Navy as 00-0728*
	ZJ549	WS Super Lynx Mk 99	*To S Korean Navy as 00-0729*
	ZJ550	WS Super Lynx Mk 99	*To S Korean Navy as 00-0730*
	ZJ551	WS Super Lynx Mk 99	*To S Korean Navy as 00-0731*
	ZJ552	WS Super Lynx Mk 99	*To S Korean Navy as 00-0732*
	ZJ553	WS Super Lynx Mk 99	*To S Korean Navy as 00-0733*
	ZJ554	WS Super Lynx Mk 99	*To S Korean Navy as 00-0734*
	ZJ565	BAe Hawk 209	*To Indonesian AF as TT-0227, March 2000*
	ZJ566	BAe Hawk 209	*To Indonesian AF as TT-0228, March 2000*
	ZJ567	BAe Hawk 209	*To Indonesian AF as TT-0229, March 2000*
	ZJ568	BAe Hawk 209	*To Indonesian AF as TT-0230,*
	ZJ569	BAe Hawk 209	*To Indonesian AF as TT-0231*
	ZJ570	BAe Hawk 209	*To Indonesian AF as TT-0232*
	ZJ571 to ZJ579	Lockheed C-130J <Sim>	*DPA/LMASC, for RAF*
	ZJ619	Eurofighter Typhoon <Sim>	*RAF No 1 SoTT, Cosford*
	ZJ620 to ZJ626	EHI-101 <Sim>	*For RN*
	ZJ627 to ZJ631	A.3 Cranfield Observer UAV	*For Army*
	ZJ632	BAE Systems Hawk 127	BAE Systems Warton, for R.Australian AF as A27-01
	ZJ633	BAE Systems Hawk 127	*To R.Australian AF as A27-02, 23 September 2000*
	ZJ634	BAE Systems Hawk 127	*To R Australian AF as A27-03, 24 August 2000*
	ZJ635	AS355F-1 Twin Squirrel (G-NEXT)	*DPA/AFD/ETPS, DERA Boscombe Down*
	ZJ636	BAE Systems Hawk 127	*To R.Australian AF as A27-04, 24 August 2000*
	ZJ637	BAE Systems Hawk 127	*To R.Australian AF as A27-05, 3 September 2000*
	ZJ638	BAE Systems Hawk 127	*To R.Australian AF as A27-06, 3 September 2000*
	ZJ639	BAE Systems Hawk 127	*To R.Australian AF as A27-07 8 December 2000*
	ZJ640	BAE Systems Hawk 127	*To R.Australian AF as A27-08, 23 September 2000*
	ZJ641	BAE Systems Hawk 127	*To R.Australian AF as A27-09 8 December 2000*
	ZJ642	BAE Systems Hawk 127	BAE Systems Warton, for R.Australian AF as A27-11
	ZJ643	BAE Systems Hawk 127	BAE Systems Warton, for R.Australian AF as A27-13
	ZJ644	BAE Systems Hawk 127	BAE Systems Warton, for R.Australian AF as A27-15
	ZJ645	D-BD Alpha Jet (98+62)	DPA, DERA Llanbedr
	ZJ646	D-BD Alpha Jet (98+55)	DPA/AFD, DERA Boscombe Down
	ZJ647	D-BD Alpha Jet (98+71)	DPA, DERA Llanbedr
	ZJ648	D-BD Alpha Jet (98+09)	DPA/AFD, DERA Boscombe Down
	ZJ649	D-BD Alpha Jet (98+73)	DPA/AFD, DERA Boscombe Down
	ZJ650	D-BD Alpha Jet (98+35)	Dornier, for DERA
	ZJ651	D-BD Alpha Jet (41+42)	DERA Boscombe Down, spares use
	ZJ652	D-BD Alpha Jet (41+09)	DERA Boscombe Down, spares use
	ZJ653	D-BD Alpha Jet (40+22)	DERA Boscombe Down, spares use
	ZJ654	D-BD Alpha Jet (41+02)	DERA Boscombe Down, spares use
	ZJ655	D-BD Alpha Jet (41+19)	DERA Boscombe Down, spares use
	ZJ656	D-BD Alpha Jet (41+40)	DERA Boscombe Down, spares use
	ZJ669	BAE Systems Hawk 115	*To Canada as 155201, 3 July 2000*
	ZJ670	BAE Systems Hawk 115	*To Canada as 155202, 13 July 2000*
	ZJ671	BAE Systems Hawk 115	*To Canada as 155203, 6 September 2000*
	ZJ672	BAE Systems Hawk 115	*To Canada as 155204, 27 September 2000*
	ZJ673	BAE Systems Hawk 115	*To Canada as 155205, 20 October 2000*
	ZJ674	BAE Systems Hawk 115	*To Canada as 155206, 25 November 2000*

Serial	Type (other identity) [code]	Owner/operator, location or fate	Notes
ZJ675	BAE Systems Hawk 115	*To Canada as 155207 25 November 2000*	
ZJ676	BAE Systems Hawk 115	*To Canada as 155208, 25 November 2000*	
ZJ677	BAE Systems Hawk 115	BAE Systems Warton, for Canada as 155209	
ZJ678	BAE Systems Hawk 115	BAE Systems Warton, for Canada as 155210	
ZJ679	BAE Systems Hawk 115	BAE Systems Warton, for Canada as 155211	
ZJ680	BAE Systems Hawk 115	BAE Systems Warton, for Canada as 155212	
ZJ681	BAE Systems Hawk 115	BAE Systems Warton, for Canada as 155213	
ZJ682	BAE Systems Hawk 115	BAE Systems Warton, for Canada as 155214	
ZJ683	BAE Systems Hawk 115	BAE Systems Warton, for Canada as 155215	
ZJ684	BAE Systems Hawk 115	BAE Systems Warton, for Canada as 155216	
ZJ685	BAE Systems Hawk 115	BAE Systems Warton, for Canada as 155217	
ZJ686	BAE Systems Hawk 115	BAE Systems Warton, for Canada as 155218	
ZJ901	WS Lynx Mk 90B	*To Danish Navy as S-191, 1 November 2000*	
ZJ902	WS Lynx Mk 90B	GKN Westland, for Danish Navy as S-170	
ZK101	EHI-101 (I-HIOI) (PP7)	*Repainted as I-RAIA, 2000*	
ZT800	WS Super Lynx Mk 300	DPA/GKN Westland, Yeovil	
ZZ171	Boeing C-17A Globemaster (00-0201)	Boeing, Long Beach, for RAF	
ZZ172	Boeing C-17A Globemaster (00-0202)	Boeing, Long Beach, for RAF	
ZZ173	Boeing C-17A Globemaster (00-0203)	Boeing, Long Beach, for RAF	
ZZ174	Boeing C-17A Globemaster (00-0204)	Boeing, Long Beach, for RAF	

Jaguar GR3 XZ118 (FF) in No 41 Squadron colours with XZ111 that crashed on 27 October 2000 behind. *PRM*

Shuttleworth's Avro 504K H5199 and Sopwith Pup N6181. *Daniel March*

Homebuilt Issacs Fury K8303. *PRM*

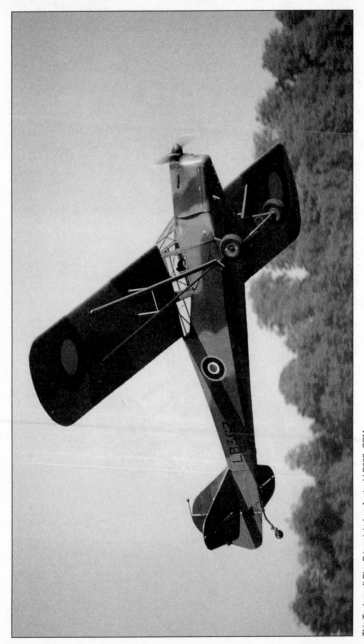

This Taylorcraft Plus D is painted as Auster I LB367. *PRM*

The Battle of Britain Memorial Flight's Lancaster PA474. *PRM*

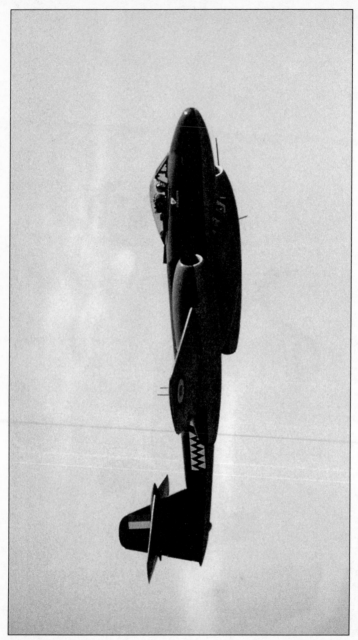

Kennet Aviation at Cranfield operates Meteor F8 VZ467, the only airworthy example of this mark in the UK. *PRM*

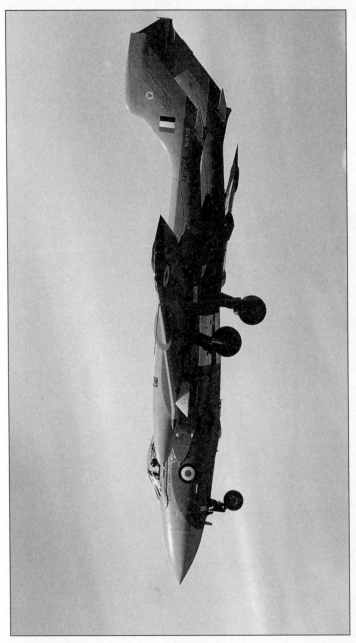

Sea Vixen XP924 (G-CVIX) of de Havilland Aviation (at Bournemouth) climbing out of Swansea on 29 May 2000. *PRM*

No 84 Squadron in Cyprus still flies Wessex HC2 XT680. *PRM*

Nimrod MR2 XV232 from RAF Kinloss with No 20 Squadron Harrier GR7 and an 899 Naval Air Squadron Sea Harrier FA2. *Daniel March*

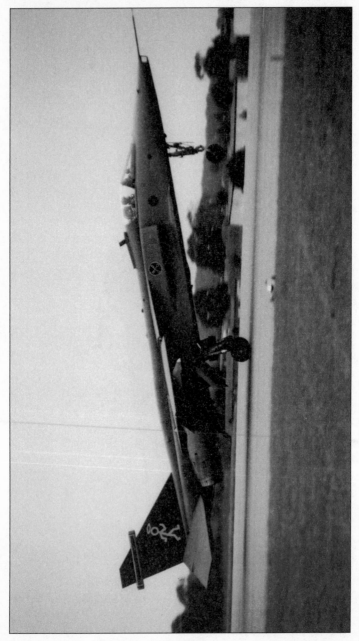

Jaguar GR3A XX752 of No 16(R) Squadron based at RAF Coltishall. *PRM*

Civil Registered Aircraft in UK Military Service

Serial	Type (other identity) [code]	Owner/operator, location or fate	Notes
G-BLVI	Slingsby T.67M Firefly 2	Hunting Aircraft Ltd, Newton/Cranwell	
G-BNSO	Slingsby T.67M Firefly 2	Hunting Aircraft Ltd/JEFTS, Barkston Heath	
G-BNSP	Slingsby T.67M Firefly 2	Hunting Aircraft Ltd/CFS, Cranwell	
G-BNSR	Slingsby T.67M Firefly 2	Hunting Aircraft Ltd/CFS, Cranwell	
G-BUUA	Slingsby T.67M Firefly 2	Hunting Aircraft Ltd/JEFTS, Middle Wallop	
G-BUUB	Slingsby T.67M Firefly 2	Hunting Aircraft Ltd/JEFTS, Middle Wallop	
G-BUUC	Slingsby T.67M Firefly 2	Hunting Aircraft Ltd/JEFTS, Middle Wallop	
G-BUUD	Slingsby T.67M Firefly 2	Hunting Aircraft Ltd/JEFTS, Middle Wallop	
G-BUUE	Slingsby T.67M Firefly 2	Hunting Aircraft Ltd/JEFTS, Middle Wallop	
G-BUUF	Slingsby T.67M Firefly 2	Hunting Aircraft Ltd/JEFTS, Middle Wallop	
G-BUUG	Slingsby T.67M Firefly 2	Hunting Aircraft Ltd/JEFTS, Middle Wallop	
G-BUUI	Slingsby T.67M Firefly 2	Hunting Aircraft Ltd/JEFTS, Middle Wallop	
G-BUUJ	Slingsby T.67M Firefly 2	Hunting Aircraft Ltd/JEFTS, Middle Wallop	
G-BUUK	Slingsby T.67M Firefly 2	Hunting Aircraft Ltd/JEFTS, Middle Wallop	
G-BUUL	Slingsby T.67M Firefly 2	Hunting Aircraft Ltd/JEFTS, Barkston Heath	
G-BVHC	Grob G.115D-2 Heron	Shorts Bros/NFGF, Plymouth	
G-BVHD	Grob G.115D-2 Heron	Shorts Bros/NFGF, Plymouth	
G-BVHE	Grob G.115D-2 Heron	Shorts Bros/NFGF, Plymouth	
G-BVHF	Grob G.115D-2 Heron	Shorts Bros/NFGF, Plymouth	
G-BVHG	Grob G.115D-2 Heron	Shorts Bros/NFGF, Plymouth	
G-BWXA	Slingsby T.67M Firefly 260	Hunting Aircraft Ltd/JEFTS, Barkston Heath	
G-BWXB	Slingsby T.67M Firefly 260	Hunting Aircraft Ltd/JEFTS, Barkston Heath	
G-BWXC	Slingsby T.67M Firefly 260	Hunting Aircraft Ltd/JEFTS, Barkston Heath	
G-BWXD	Slingsby T.67M Firefly 260	Hunting Aircraft Ltd/JEFTS, Barkston Heath	
G-BWXE	Slingsby T.67M Firefly 260	Hunting Aircraft Ltd/JEFTS, Barkston Heath	
G-BWXF	Slingsby T.67M Firefly 260	Hunting Aircraft Ltd/JEFTS, Barkston Heath	
G-BWXG	Slingsby T.67M Firefly 260	Hunting Aircraft Ltd/JEFTS, Barkston Heath	
G-BWXH	Slingsby T.67M Firefly 260	Hunting Aircraft Ltd/JEFTS, Barkston Heath	
G-BWXI	Slingsby T.67M Firefly 260	Hunting Aircraft Ltd/JEFTS, Barkston Heath	
G-BWXJ	Slingsby T.67M Firefly 260	Hunting Aircraft Ltd/JEFTS, Barkston Heath	
G-BWXK	Slingsby T.67M Firefly 260	Hunting Aircraft Ltd/JEFTS, Barkston Heath	
G-BWXL	Slingsby T.67M Firefly 260	Hunting Aircraft Ltd/JEFTS, Barkston Heath	
G-BWXM	Slingsby T.67M Firefly 260	Hunting Aircraft Ltd/JEFTS, Barkston Heath	
G-BWXN	Slingsby T.67M Firefly 260	Hunting Aircraft Ltd/JEFTS, Barkston Heath	
G-BWXO	Slingsby T.67M Firefly 260	Hunting Aircraft Ltd/JEFTS, Barkston Heath	
G-BWXP	Slingsby T.67M Firefly 260	Hunting Aircraft Ltd/JEFTS, Barkston Heath	
G-BWXR	Slingsby T.67M Firefly 260	Hunting Aircraft Ltd/JEFTS, Barkston Heath	
G-BWXS	Slingsby T.67M Firefly 260 [6]	Hunting Aircraft Ltd/JEFTS, Barkston Heath	
G-BWXT	Slingsby T.67M Firefly 260	Hunting Aircraft Ltd/JEFTS, Barkston Heath	
G-BWXU	Slingsby T.67M Firefly 260	Hunting Aircraft Ltd/JEFTS, Barkston Heath	
G-BWXV	Slingsby T.67M Firefly 260	Hunting Aircraft Ltd/JEFTS, Barkston Heath	
G-BWXW	Slingsby T.67M Firefly 260	Hunting Aircraft Ltd/JEFTS, Barkston Heath	

Civil Registered Aircraft in UK Military Service

Notes	Serial	Type (other identity) [code]	Owner/operator, location or fate
	G-BWXX	Slingsby T.67M Firefly 260	Hunting Aircraft Ltd/JEFTS, Barkston Heath
	G-BWXY	Slingsby T.67M Firefly 260	Hunting Aircraft Ltd/JEFTS, Barkston Heath
	G-BWXZ	Slingsby T.67M Firefly 260	Hunting Aircraft Ltd/JEFTS, Barkston Heath
	G-BYOA	Slingsby T.67M Firefly 260	Hunting Aircraft Ltd/JEFTS, Barkston Heath
	G-BYOB	Slingsby T.67M Firefly 260	Hunting Aircraft Ltd/JEFTS, Barkston Heath
	G-BYUA	Grob G.115E Tutor	Bombardier/Cambridge UAS/No 5 AEF, Wyton
	G-BYUB	Grob G.115E Tutor	Bombardier/University of Wales AS, St Athan
	G-BYUC	Grob G.115E Tutor	Bombardier/CFS, Cranwell
	G-BYUD	Grob G.115E Tutor	Bombardier/Yorkshire Universities AS/No 9 AEF, Church Fenton
	G-BYUE	Grob G.115E Tutor	Bombardier/CFS, Cranwell
	G-BYUF	Grob G.115E Tutor	Bombardier/Cambridge UAS/No 5 AEF/University of London AS, Wyton
	G-BYUG	Grob G.115E Tutor	Bombardier/Universities of Glasgow & Strathclyde AS, Glasgow
	G-BYUH	Grob G.115E Tutor	Bombardier/Bristol UAS/No 3 AEF, Colerne
	G-BYUI	Grob G.115E Tutor	Bombardier/Cambridge UAS/No 5 AEF/University of London AS, Wyton
	G-BYUJ	Grob G.115E Tutor	Bombardier/Yorkshire Universities AS/No 9 AEF, Church Fenton
	G-BYUK	Grob G.115E Tutor	Bombardier/Cambridge UAS/No 5 AEF, Wyton
	G-BYUL	Grob G.115E Tutor	Bombardier/University of London AS, Wyton
	G-BYUM	Grob G.115E Tutor	Bombardier/Cambridge UAS/No 5 AEF/University of London AS, Wyton
	G-BYUN	Grob G.115E Tutor	Bombardier/Cambridge UAS/No 5 AEF/University of London AS, Wyton
	G-BYUO	Grob G.115E Tutor	Bombardier/University of London AS, Wyton
	G-BYUP	Grob G.115E Tutor	Bombardier/East Lowlands UAS/Aberdeen, Dundee & St Andrews UAS/No 12 AEF, Leuchars
	G-BYUR	Grob G.115E Tutor	Bombardier/Universities of Glasgow & Strathclyde AS, Glasgow
	G-BYUS	Grob G.115E Tutor	Bombardier/Oxford UAS/No 6 AEF, Benson
	G-BYUT	Grob G.115E Tutor	Bombardier/Oxford UAS/No 6 AEF, Benson
	G-BYUU	Grob G.115E Tutor	Bombardier/Universities of Glasgow & Strathclyde AS, Glasgow
	G-BYUV	Grob G.115E Tutor	Bombardier/Oxford UAS/No 6 AEF, Benson
	G-BYUW	Grob G.115E Tutor	Bombardier/East Lowlands UAS/Aberdeen, Dundee & St Andrews UAS/No 12 AEF, Leuchars
	G-BYUX	Grob G.115E Tutor	Bombardier/Cambridge UAS/No 5 AEF/University of London AS, Wyton
	G-BYUY	Grob G.115E Tutor	Bombardier/East Lowlands UAS/Aberdeen, Dundee & St Andrews UAS/No 12 AEF, Leuchars
	G-BYUZ	Grob G.115E Tutor	Bombardier/Cambridge UAS/No 5 AEF/University of London AS, Wyton
	G-BYVA	Grob G.115E Tutor	Bombardier/CFS, Cranwell
	G-BYVB	Grob G.115E Tutor	Bombardier/Universities of Glasgow & Strathclyde AS, Glasgow
	G-BYVC	Grob G.115E Tutor	Bombardier/Bristol UAS/No 3 AEF, Colerne
	G-BYVD	Grob G.115E Tutor	Bombardier/Cambridge UAS/No 5 AEF/University of London AS, Wyton
	G-BYVE	Grob G.115E Tutor	Bombardier/Cambridge UAS/No 5 AEF/University of London AS, Wyton
	G-BYVF	Grob G.115E Tutor	Bombardier/Universities of Glasgow & Strathclyde AS, Glasgow
	G-BYVG	Grob G.115E Tutor	Bombardier/Yorkshire Universities AS/No 9 AEF, Church Fenton

Serial	Type (other identity) [code]	Owner/operator, location or fate	Notes
G-BYVH	Grob G.115E Tutor	Bombardier/East Lowlands UAS/Aberdeen, Dundee & St Andrews UAS/No 12 AEF, Leuchars	
G-BYVI	Grob G.115E Tutor	Bombardier/Universities of Glasgow & Strathclyde AS, Glasgow	
G-BYVJ	Grob G.115E Tutor	Bombardier/Cambridge UAS/No 5 AEF/ University of London AS, Wyton	
G-BYVK	Grob G.115E Tutor	Bombardier/East Lowlands UAS/Aberdeen, Dundee & St Andrews UAS/No 12 AEF, Leuchars	
G-BYVL	Grob G.115E Tutor	Bombardier/University of Wales AS, St Athan	
G-BYVM	Grob G.115E Tutor	Bombardier/East Lowlands UAS/Aberdeen, Dundee & St Andrews UAS/No 12 AEF, Leuchars	
G-BYVN	Grob G.115E Tutor	Bombardier/Bristol UAS/No 3 AEF, Colerne	
G-BYVO	Grob G.115E Tutor	Bombardier/University of Wales AS, St Athan	
G-BYVP	Grob G.115E Tutor	Bombardier/Oxford UAS/No 6 AEF, Benson	
G-BYVR	Grob G.115E Tutor	Bombardier/Oxford UAS/No 6 AEF, Benson	
G-BYVS	Grob G.115E Tutor	Bombardier/Cambridge UAS/No 5 AEF/ University of London AS, Wyton	
G-BYVT	Grob G.115E Tutor	Bombardier/Cambridge UAS/No 5 AEF/ University of London AS, Wyton	
G-BYVU	Grob G.115E Tutor	Bombardier/Oxford UAS/No 6 AEF, Benson	
G-BYVV	Grob G.115E Tutor	Bombardier/Yorkshire Universities AS/ No 9 AEF, Church Fenton	
G-BYVW	Grob G.115E Tutor	Bombardier/Yorkshire Universities AS/ No 9 AEF, Church Fenton	
G-BYVX	Grob G.115E Tutor	Bombardier/Yorkshire Universities AS/ No 9 AEF, Church Fenton	
G-BYVY	Grob G.115E Tutor	Bombardier/Yorkshire Universities AS/ No 9 AEF, Church Fenton	
G-BYVZ	Grob G.115E Tutor	Bombardier/Yorkshire Universities AS/ No 9 AEF, Church Fenton	
G-BYWA	Grob G.115E Tutor	Bombardier/University of Wales AS, St Athan	
G-BYWB	Grob G.115E Tutor	Bombardier/Bristol UAS/No 3 AEF, Colerne	
G-BYWC	Grob G.115E Tutor	Bombardier/Bristol UAS/No 3 AEF, Colerne	
G-BYWD	Grob G.115E Tutor	Bombardier/CFS, Cranwell	
G-BYWE	Grob G.115E Tutor	Bombardier/Bristol UAS/No 3 AEF, Colerne	
G-BYWF	Grob G.115E Tutor	Bombardier/CFS, Cranwell	
G-BYWG	Grob G.115E Tutor	Bombardier/Bristol UAS/No 3 AEF, Colerne	
G-BYWH	Grob G.115E Tutor	Bombardier/CFS, Cranwell	
G-BYWI	Grob G.115E Tutor	Bombardier/Bristol UAS/No 3 AEF, Colerne	
G-BYWJ	Grob G.115E Tutor	Bombardier/CFS, Cranwell	
G-BYWK	Grob G.115E Tutor	Bombardier/CFS, Cranwell	
G-BYWL	Grob G.115E Tutor	Bombardier/CFS, Cranwell	
G-BYWM	Grob G.115E Tutor	Bombardier/CFS, Cranwell	
G-BYWN	Grob G.115E Tutor	Bombardier/CFS, Cranwell	
G-BYWO	Grob G.115E Tutor	Grob/Bombardier for RAF	
G-BYWP	Grob G.115E Tutor	Grob/Bombardier for RAF	
G-BYWR	Grob G.115E Tutor	Grob/Bombardier for RAF	
G-BYWS	Grob G.115E Tutor	Grob/Bombardier for RAF	
G-BYWT	Grob G.115E Tutor	Grob/Bombardier for RAF	
G-BYWU	Grob G.115E Tutor	Grob/Bombardier for RAF	
G-BYWV	Grob G.115E Tutor	Grob/Bombardier for RAF	
G-BYWW	Grob G.115E Tutor	Grob/Bombardier for RAF	
G-BYWX	Grob G.115E Tutor	Grob/Bombardier for RAF	
G-BYWY	Grob G.115E Tutor	Grob/Bombardier for RAF	
G-BYWZ	Grob G.115E Tutor	Grob/Bombardier for RAF	
G-BYXA	Grob G.115E Tutor	Grob/Bombardier for RAF	
G-BYXB	Grob G.115E Tutor	Grob/Bombardier for RAF	
G-BYXC	Grob G.115E Tutor	Grob/Bombardier for RAF	
G-BYXD	Grob G.115E Tutor	Grob/Bombardier for RAF	
G-BYXE	Grob G.115E Tutor	Grob/Bombardier for RAF	
G-BYXF	Grob G.115E Tutor	Grob/Bombardier for RAF	
G-BYXG	Grob G.115E Tutor	Grob/Bombardier for RAF	
G-BYXH	Grob G.115E Tutor	Grob/Bombardier for RAF	
G-BYXI	Grob G.115E Tutor	Grob/Bombardier for RAF	
G-BYXJ	Grob G.115E Tutor	Grob/Bombardier for RAF	
G-BYXK	Grob G.115E Tutor	Grob/Bombardier for RAF	
G-BYXL	Grob G.115E Tutor	Grob/Bombardier for RAF	

Civil Registered Aircraft in UK Military Service

Notes	Serial	Type (other identity) [code]	Owner/operator, location or fate
	G-BYXM	Grob G.115E Tutor	Grob/Bombardier for RAF
	G-BYXN	Grob G.115E Tutor	Grob/Bombardier for RAF
	G-BYXO	Grob G.115E Tutor	Grob/Bombardier for RAF
	G-BYXP	Grob G.115E Tutor	Grob/Bombardier for RAF
	G-BYXR	Grob G.115E Tutor	Grob/Bombardier for RAF
	G-BYXS	Grob G.115E Tutor	Grob/Bombardier for RAF
	G-BYXT	Grob G.115E Tutor	Grob/Bombardier for RAF
	G-BYXX	Grob G.115E Tutor	Grob/Bombardier for RAF
	G-BYXY	Grob G.115E Tutor	Grob/Bombardier for RAF
	G-BYXZ	Grob G.115E Tutor	Grob/Bombardier for RAF
	G-BYYA	Grob G.115E Tutor	Grob/Bombardier for RAF
	G-BYYB	Grob G.115E Tutor	Grob/Bombardier for RAF
	G-FFRA	Dassault Falcon 20DC (N902FR)	FR Aviation, Tees-side
	G-FRAD	Dassault Falcon 20E (G-BCYF)	FR Aviation, Bournemouth
	G-FRAE	Dassault Falcon 20E (N910FR)	FR Aviation, Bournemouth
	G-FRAF	Dassault Falcon 20E (N911FR)	FR Aviation, Bournemouth
	G-FRAH	Dassault Falcon 20DC (N900FR)	FR Aviation, Tees-side
	G-FRAI	Dassault Falcon 20E (N901FR)	FR Aviation, Tees-side
	G-FRAJ	Dassault Falcon 20E (N903FR)	FR Aviation, Tees-side
	G-FRAL	Dassault Falcon 20DC (N904FR)	FR Aviation, Tees-side
	G-FRAM	Dassault Falcon 20DC (N907FR)	FR Aviation, Bournemouth
	G-FRAO	Dassault Falcon 20DC (N906FR)	FR Aviation, Bournemouth
	G-FRAP	Dassault Falcon 20DC (N908FR)	FR Aviation, Bournemouth
	G-FRAR	Dassault Falcon 20DC (N909FR)	FR Aviation, Bournemouth
	G-FRAS	Dassault Falcon 20C (117501)	FR Aviation, Tees-side
	G-FRAT	Dassault Falcon 20C (117502)	FR Aviation, Tees-side
	G-FRAU	Dassault Falcon 20C (117504)	FR Aviation, Tees-side
	G-FRAW	Dassault Falcon 20ECM (117507)	FR Aviation, Tees-side
	G-FRBA	Dassault Falcon 20C	FR Aviation, Bournemouth
	G-HONG	Slingsby T.67M Firefly 2	Hunting Aircraft Ltd/JEFTS, Middle Wallop
	G-KONG	Slingsby T.67M Firefly 2	Hunting Aircraft Ltd/JEFTS, Middle Wallop
	G-XXEA	Sikorsky S-76C+	Air Hanson/The Royal Flight, Blackbushe

G-BWXY, one of the fleet of Slingsby Fireflies used by the JEFTS at Barkston Heath. *PRM*

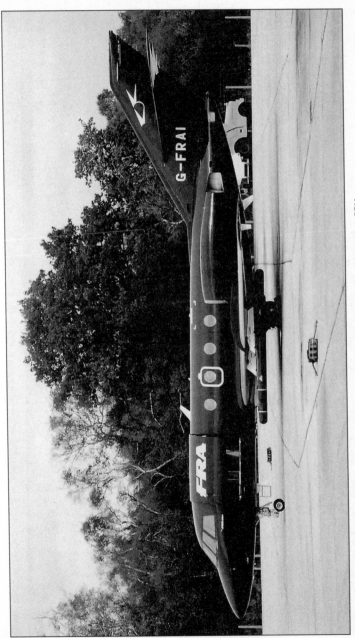

Revealing its new high visibility blue paint scheme, this Falcon 20 (G-FRAI) is flown by FRA for RAF and RN training. *PRM*

Tornado F3 ZE296 of No 56(R) Squadron, the F3 OCU, about to refuel from a VC10 in November 2000. *PRM*

RAF Maintenance Command/ Support Command/Logistics Command 'M' number Cross-reference

1764M/K4972	7525M/WT619	7840M/XK482	8018M/XN344
2015M/K5600	7530M/WT648	7841M/WV783	8019M/WZ869
2292M/K8203	7532M/WT651	7851M/WZ706	8021M/XL824
2361M/K6035	7533M/WT680	7852M/XG506	8022M/XN341
3118M/H5199/(BK892)	7544M/WN904	7854M/XM191	8023M/XD463
3858M/X7688	7548M/PS915	7855M/XK416	8027M/XM555
4354M/BL614	7555M/AR614	7859M/XP283	8032M/XH837
4552M/T5298	7556M/WK584	7860M/XL738	8033M/XD382
5377M/EP120	7564M/XE982	7862M/XR246	8034M/XL703
5378M/AR614	7570M/XD674	7863M/*XP248*	8041M/XF690
5405M/LF738	7582M/WP190	7864M/XP244	8043M/XF836
5466M/*BN230*/(LF751)	7583M/WP185	7865M/TX226	8046M/XL770
5690M/MK356	7602M/WE600	7866M/XH278	8049M/WE168
5718M/BM597	7605M/WS692	7868M/WZ736	8050M/XG329
5758M/DG202	7606M/WV562	7869M/WK935	8052M/WH166
6457M/ML427	7607M/TJ138	7872M/*WZ826*/(XD826)	8054AM/XM410
6490M/LA255	7615M/WV679	7882M/XD525	8054BM/XM417
6640M/RM694	7616M/WW388	7883M/XT150	8055AM/XM402
6850M/TE184	7618M/WW442	7886M/XR985	8055BM/XM404
6946M/RW388	7622M/WV606	7891M/XM693	8056M/XG337
6948M/DE673	7631M/VX185	7894M/XD818	8057M/XR243
6960M/MT847	7641M/XA634	7895M/WF784	8063M/WT536
7008M/EE549	7645M/WD293	7898M/XP854	8070M/EP120
7014M/N6720	7646M/VX461	7900M/WA576	8072M/PK624
7015M/NL985	7648M/XF785	7906M/WH132	8073M/TB252
7035M/*K2567*/(DE306)	7673M/WV332	7917M/WA591	8078M/XM351
7060M/VF301	7688M/WW421	7920M/WL360	8079M/XN492
7090M/EE531	7693M/WV483	7923M/XT133	8080M/XM480
7118M/LA198	7696M/WV493	7928M/XE849	8081M/XM468
7119M/LA226	7698M/WV499	7930M/WH301	8082M/XM409
7150M/PK683	7704M/TW536	7931M/RD253	8086M/TB752
7154M/WB188	7705M/WL505	7932M/WZ744	8092M/WK654
7174M/VX272	7706M/WB584	7933M/XR220	8094M/WT520
7175M/VV106	7709M/WT933	7937M/WS843	8101M/WH984
7200M/VT812	7711M/PS915	7938M/XH903	8102M/WT486
7241M/*MK178*(TE311)	7712M/WK281	7939M/XD596	8103M/WR985
7243M/TE462	7715M/XK724	7940M/XL764	8106M/WR982
7244M/*MK673*(TB382)	7716M/WS776	7955M/XH767	8108M/WV703
7246M/TD248	7718M/WA577	7957M/XF545	8114M/WL798
7256M/TB752	7719M/WK277	7959M/WS774	8117M/WR974
7257M/TB252	7728M/WZ458	7960M/WS726	8118M/WZ549
7279M/TB752	7729M/WB758	7961M/WS739	8119M/WR971
7281M/TB252	7734M/XD536	7964M/WS760	8121M/XM474
7288M/PK724	7737M/XD602	7965M/WS792	8124M/XD614
7293M/RW393	7741M/VZ477	7967M/WS788	8128M/WH775
7323M/VV217	7750M/*WP864*/(WL168)	7970M/WP907	8131M/WT507
7325M/R5868	7751M/WL131	7971M/XK699	8140M/XJ571
7326M/VN485	7755M/WG760	7973M/WS807	8142M/XJ560
7362M/475081/(VP546)	7758M/PM651	7976M/XK418	8143M/XN691
7416M/WN907	7759M/PK664	7979M/XM529	8147M/XR526
7421M/WT660	7761M/XH318	7980M/XM561	8151M/WV795
7422M/WT684	7762M/XE670	7982M/XH892	8153M/WV903
7428M/WK198	7764M/XH318	7983M/XD506	8154M/WV908
7432M/WZ724	7770M/WT746	7984M/XN597	8155M/WV797
7438M/*18671*/(WP905)	7793M/XG523	7986M/WG777	8156M/XE339
7443M/WX853	7796M/WJ676	7988M/XL149	8158M/XE369
7458M/WX905	7798M/XH783	7990M/XD452	8159M/XD528
7464M/XA564	7806M/TA639	7997M/XG452	8160M/XD622
7467M/WP978	7809M/XA699	7998M/*XM515*/(XD515)	8161M/XE993
7470M/XA553	7816M/WG763	8005M/WG768	8162M/WM913
7473M/XE946	7817M/TX214	8009M/XG518	8163M/XP919
7491M/WT569	7825M/WK991	8010M/XG547	8164M/*WN105*/(WF299)
7496M/WT612	7827M/XA917	8012M/VS562	8165M/WH791
7499M/WT555	7829M/XH992	8016M/XT677	8169M/WH364
7510M/WT694	7839M/WV781	8017M/XL762	8173M/XN685

RAF Maintenance Cross-reference

8176M/WH791	8407M/XP585	8576M/XP502	8724M/XW923
8177M/*WM311*/(WM224)	8408M/XS186	8578M/XR534	8726M/XP299
8179M/XN928	8409M/XS209	8582M/XE874	8727M/XR486
8183M/*XN972*/(XN962)	8410M/XR662	8583M/BAPC 94	8728M/WT532
8184M/WT520	8413M/XM192	8584M/WH903	8729M/WJ815
8185M/WH946	8414M/XM173	8585M/XE670	8733M/XL318
8186M/WR977	8417M/XM144	8586M/XE643	8736M/XF375
8187M/WH791	8422M/XM169	8587M/XP677	8738M/*XF519*/(XJ695)
8189M/*WD615*	8427M/XM172	8588M/XR681	8739M/XH170
8190M/XJ918	8429M/XM592	8589M/XR700	8740M/WE173
8192M/XR658	8434M/XM411	8590M/XM191	8741M/XW329
8196M/XE920	8436M/XN554	8591M/XA813	8743M/WD790
8198M/WT339	8437M/WG362	8595M/XH278	8746M/XH171
8203M/XD377	8439M/WZ846	8598M/WP270	8749M/XH537
8205M/XN819	8440M/WD935	8600M/XX761	8751M/XT255
8206M/WG419	8442M/XP411	8602M/*PF179*/(XR541)	8753M/WL795
8207M/WD318	8447M/XP359	8606M/XP530	8762M/WH740
8208M/WG303	8453M/XP745	8608M/XP540	8763M/WH665
8209M/WG418	8457M/XS871	8610M/XL502	8764M/XP344
8210M/WG471	8458M/XP672	8611M/WF128	8767M/XX635
8211M/WK570	8459M/XR650	8617M/XM709	8768M/A-522
8213M/WK626	8460M/XP680	8618M/*XM693*/(XP504)	8769M/A-528
8216M/WP927	8462M/XX477	8620M/XP534	8770M/XL623
8217M/WZ866	8463M/XP355	8624M/*XR991*/(XS102)	8771M/XM602
8218M/WB645	8464M/XJ758	8627M/XP558	8772M/WR960
8229M/XM355	8465M/W1048	8628M/XJ380	8777M/XX914
8230M/XM362	8466M/L-866	8630M/WG362	8778M/XM598
8231M/XM375	8467M/WP912	8631M/XR574	8779M/XM607
8234M/XN458	8468M/MM5701/(BT474)	8633M/3W-17/MK732	8780M/WK102
8235M/XN549	8470M/584219	8634M/WP314	8781M/WE982
8236M/XP573	8471M/701152	8638M/XS101	8782M/XH136
8237M/XS179	8472M/120227/(VN679)	8640M/XR977	8783M/XW272
8238M/XS180	8473M/WP190	8642M/XR537	8785M/XS642
8344M/WH960	8474M/494083	8645M/XD163	8789M/XK970
8350M/WH840	8475M/360043/(PJ876)	8648M/XK526	8791M/XP329
8352M/XN632	8476M/24	8653M/XS120	8792M/XP345
8355M/*KG374*/(KN645)	8477M/4101/(DG200)	8655M/XN126	8793M/XP346
8357M/WK576	8478M/10639	8656M/XP405	8794M/XP398
8359M/WF825	8479M/730301	8657M/VZ634	8796M/XK943
8361M/WB670	8481M/191614	8661M/XJ727	8797M/XX947
8362M/WG477	8482M/112372/(VK893)	8662M/XR458	8799M/WV787
8364M/WG464	8483M/420430	8664M/WJ603	8800M/XG226
8365M/XK421	8484M/5439	8666M/XE793	8805M/XT772
8366M/XG454	8485M/997	8668M/WJ821	8807M/XL587
8367M/XG474	8486M/BAPC 99	8671M/XJ435	8810M/XJ825
8368M/XF926	8487M/J-1172	8672M/XP351	8814M/XM927
8369M/WE139	8488M/WL627	8673M/XD165	8816M/XX734
8370M/N1671	8491M/WJ880	8674M/XP395	8818M/XK527
8371M/XA847	8492M/WJ872	8676M/XL577	8819M/XS479
8372M/K8042	8493M/XR571	8677M/*XF519*/(XJ695)	8820M/VP952
8373M/P2617	8494M/XP557	8679M/XF526	8821M/XX115
8375M/NX611	8495M/XR672	8680M/XF527	8822M/VP957
8376M/RF398	8501M/XP640	8681M/XG164	8828M/XS587
8377M/R9125	8502M/XP686	8682M/XP404	8830M/XF515
8378M/*T9707*	8507M/XS215	8685M/XF516	8831M/XG160
8379M/DG590	8508M/XS218	8687M/XJ639	8832M/XG172
8380M/Z7197	8509M/XT141	8693M/WH863	8833M/XL569
8382M/VR930	8513M/XN724	8696M/WH773	8834M/*XL571*
8383M/K9942	8514M/XS176	8700M/ZD234	8836M/XL592
8384M/X4590	8535M/XN776	8702M/XG196	8838M/*34037*/(429356)
8385M/N5912	8538M/XN781	8703M/VW453	8839M/*69*/(XG194)
8386M/NV778	8545M/XN726	8706M/XF383	8840M/XG252
8387M/T6296	8546M/XN728	8708M/XF509	8841M/XE606
8388M/XL993	8548M/WT507	8709M/XG209	8844M/XJ676
8389M/VX573	8549M/WT534	8710M/XG274	8847M/XX344
8392M/SL674	8554M/TG511	8711M/XG290	8848M/XZ135
8394M/WG422	8560M/XR569	8713M/XG225	8851M/XT595
8395M/WF408	8561M/XS100	8714M/XK149	8852M/XV337
8396M/XK740	8565M/*WT720*/(E-408)	8718M/XX396	8853M/XT277
8399M/WR539	8566M/XV279	8719M/XT257	8855M/XT284
8401M/XP686	8570M/XR954	8720M/XP353	8857M/XW544
8402M/XN769	8573M/XM708	8722M/WJ640	8860M/XW549
8406M/XP831	8575M/XP542	8723M/XL567	8861M/XW528

8863M/XG154	8972M/XR754	9076M/XV808	9181M/XW358
8867M/XK532	8973M/XS922	9078M/XV752	9183M/*XF519*/(XJ695)
8868M/WH775	8974M/XM473	9079M/XZ130	9185M/XZ987
8869M/WH957	8975M/XW917	9083M/ZE353	9187M/XW405
8870M/WH964	8976M/XZ630	9084M/ZE354	9188M/XW364
8871M/WJ565	8978M/XX837	9087M/XX753	9189M/ZD350
8873M/XR453	8983M/XM478	9090M/XW353	9190M/XW318
8875M/XE624	8984M/XN551	9091M/XW434	9191M/XW416
8876M/*VM791*/(XA312)	8985M/WK127	9092M/XH669	9192M/XW361
8877M/XP159	8986M/XV261	9093M/WK124	9193M/XW367
8879M/XX948	8987M/XM358	9095M/XW547	9194M/XW420
8880M/XF435	8988M/XN593	9096M/WV322	9195M/XW330
8881M/XG254	8990M/XM419	9097M/XW366	9196M/XW370
8883M/XX946	8995M/XM425	9098M/XV406	9197M/*XX530*/(XX637)
8884M/VX275	8996M/XM414	9100M/XL188	9198M/XS641
8885M/XW922	8997M/XX669	9103M/XV411	9199M/XW290
8886M/XA243	8998M/XT864	9109M/XW312	9200M/XW425
8888M/XA231	9002M/XW763	9110M/XX736	9201M/ZD667
8889M/XN239	9003M/XZ390	9111M/XW421	9203M/*3066*
8890M/WT532	9004M/XZ370	9113M/*XV498*	9205M/*E449*
8892M/XL618	9005M/XZ374	9115M/XV863	9206M/F6314
8895M/XX746	9006M/XX967	9117M/XV161	9207M/8417/18
8896M/XX821	9007M/XX968	9118M/XV253	9208M/F938
8897M/XX969	9009M/XX763	9119M/XW303	9210M/MF628
8898M/XX119	9010M/XX764	9120M/XW419	9211M/733682
8899M/XX756	9011M/XM412	9122M/XZ997	9212M/*KL216*/
8900M/XZ368	9012M/XN494	9123M/XT773	(45-49295)
8901M/XZ383	9014M/XN584	9124M/XW427	9213M/N5182
8902M/XX739	9015M/XW320	9125M/XW410	9215M/XL164
8903M/XX747	9017M/ZE449	9126M/XW413	9216M/XL190
8904M/XX966	9018M/XW365	9127M/XW432	9217M/ZH257
8905M/XX975	9019M/XX824	9128M/XW292	9218M/XL563
8906M/XX976	9020M/XX825	9129M/XW294	9219M/XZ971
8907M/XZ371	9021M/XX826	9130M/XW327	9220M/XZ995
8908M/XZ382	9022M/XX958	9131M/*DD931*	9221M/XZ966
8909M/XV784	9026M/XP629	9132M/XX977	9222M/XZ968
8910M/XL160	9027M/XP556	9133M/*413573*	9224M/XL568
8911M/XH673	9028M/XP563	9134M/XT288	9225M/XX885
8917M/XM372	9029M/XS217	9136M/XT891	9226M/XV865
8918M/XX109	9031M/XP688	9137M/XN579	9227M/XB812
8920M/XT469	9032M/XR673	9139M/XV863	9228M/ZD991
8921M/XT466	9033M/XS181	9140M/XZ287	9229M/ZA678
8922M/XT467	9034M/XP638	9141M/XV118	9230M/ZA676
8923M/XX819	9036M/XM350	9143M/XN589	9231M
8924M/XP701	9038M/XV810	9144M/XV353	9232M/XV332
8925M/XP706	9039M/XN586	9145M/XV863	9234M/XV864
8931M/XV779	9040M/XZ138	9146M/XW299	9236M
8932M/XR718	9041M/XW763	9147M/XW301	9238M/ZA717
8934M/XR749	9042M/XL954	9148M/XW436	9239M/7198/18
8935M/XR713	9044M/XS177	9149M/XW375	9241M
8937M/XX751	9045M/XN636	9150M/*FX760*	9242M
8938M/WV746	9046M/XM349	9151M/XT907	9243M/XX163
8941M/XT456	9047M/XW409	9152M/XV424	9244M
8942M/XN185	9048M/XM403	9153M/XW360	9245M
8943M/XE799	9049M/XW404	9154M/XW321	9246M/XS714
8944M/WZ791	9050M/XG577	9155M/WL679	9247M/XV420
8945M/XX818	9052M/WJ717	9159M/XV468	9248M/WB627
8946M/XZ389	9054M/XT766	9162M/XZ991	9249M/WV396
8947M/XX726	9055M/XT770	9163M/XV415	9250M/162068
8948M/XX757	9056M/XS488	9165M/XW408	9251M
8949M/XX743	9057M/ZE361	9166M/XW323	9252M
8950M/XX956	9059M/ZE360	9167M/XV744	9253M
8951M/XX727	9060M/ZE356	9168M/XZ132	9254M
8952M/XX730	9061M/XW335	9169M/XW547	9255M/XZ375
8953M/XX959	9062M/XW351	9170M/XZ994	9256M/XX839
8954M/XZ384	9064M/XT867	9172M/XW304	9257M
8955M/XX110	9065M/XV577	9173M/XW418	9258M
8956M/XN577	9066M/XV582	9174M/XZ131	9259M/XS710
8957M/XN582	9067M/XV586	9175M/P1344	9260M/XS734
8958M/XN501	9070M/XV581	9176M/XW430	9261M
8961M/XS925	9072M/XW768	9177M/XW328	9262M
8967M/XV263	9073M/XW924	9179M/XW309	9263M
8969M/XR753	9075M/XV753	9180M/XW311	9264M

RAF Maintenance Cross-reference

9265M	9273M/XS726	9280M/XV804	9287M
9266M	9274M/XS738	9281M/XZ146	9288M
9267M	9275M/XS729	9282M/XZ101	9289M
9268M	9276M/XS733	9283M/XZ322	9290M
9269M	9277M/XT601	9284M	
9270M	9278M/XS643	9285M	
9272M/XS486	9279M/XT681	9286M	

Tornado GR4 ZD811 of No 14 Squadron, RAF Lossiemouth. *PRM*

This Tucano T1 ZF242 is operated by No 1FTS at RAF Linton-on-Ouse. *PRM*

RN Landing Platform and Shore Station Code-letters

Code	Deck Letters	Vessel Name & Pennant No	Vessel Type & Unit
—	AS	RFA *Argus* (A135)	Aviation Training ship
365/6	AY	HMS *Argyll* (F231)	Type 23 (815 Sqn)
—	BD	RFA *Sir Bedivere* (L3004)	Landing ship
—	BV	RFA *Black Rover* (A273)	Fleet tanker
335	CF	HMS *Cardiff* (D108)	Type 42 (815 Sqn)
350/1	CL	HMS *Cumberland* (F85)	Type 22 (815 Sqn)
-	CM	HMS *Chatham* (F87)	Type 22
515	CT	HMS *Campbeltown* (F86)	Type 22 (810 Sqn)
—	CU	RNAS Culdrose (HMS *Seahawk*)	
336/7	CV	HMS *Coventry* (F98)	Type 22 (815 Sqn)
412/3	CW	HMS *Cornwall* (F99)	Type 22 (815 Sqn)
—	DC	HMS *Dumbarton Castle* (P265)	Fishery protection
—	DG	RFA *Diligence* (A132)	Maintenance
411	EB	HMS *Edinburgh* (D97)	Type 42 (815 Sqn)
434/5	EE	HMS *Endurance* (A171)	Ice Patrol (815 Sqn)
420	EX	HMS *Exeter* (D89)	Type 42 (815 Sqn)
—	FA	RFA *Fort Austin* (A386)	Support ship
—	FG	RFA *Fort Rosalie* (A385)	Support ship
—	FL	RNAY Fleetlands	
—	FS	HMS *Fearless* (L10)	Assault
410	GC	HMS *Gloucester* (D96)	Type 42 (815 Sqn)
—	GD	RFA *Sir Galahad* (L3005)	Landing ship
—	GR	RFA *Sir Geraint* (L3027)	Landing ship
437	GT	HMS *Grafton* (F80)	Type 23 (815 Sqn)
—	GV	RFA *Gold Rover* (A271)	Fleet tanker
344	GW	HMS *Glasgow* (D88)	Type 42 (815 Sqn)
—	GY	RFA *Grey Rover* (A269)	Fleet tanker
—	HR	HMS *Herald* (H138)	Survey ship
—	ID	HMS *Intrepid* (L11)	Assault
404	IR	HMS *Iron Duke* (F234)	Type 23 (815 Sqn)
—	L	HMS *Illustrious* (R06)	Carrier
457	LA	HMS *Lancaster* (F229)	Type 23 (815 Sqn)
—	LC	HMS *Leeds Castle* (P258)	Fishery protection
332	LP	HMS *Liverpool* (D92)	Type 42 (815 Sqn)
363/4	MA	HMS *Marlborough* (F233)	Type 23 (815 Sqn)
360	MC	HMS *Manchester* (D95)	Type 42 (815 Sqn)
415	MM	HMS *Monmouth* (F235)	Type 23 (815 Sqn)
444	MR	HMS *Montrose* (F236)	Type 23 (815 Sqn)
—	N	HMS *Invincible* (R05)	Carrier
345	NC	HMS *Newcastle* (D87)	Type 42 (815 Sqn)
361/2	NF	HMS *Norfolk* (F230)	Type 23 (815 Sqn)
372	NL	HMS *Northumberland* (F238)	Type 23 (815 Sqn)
417	NM	HMS *Nottingham* (D91)	Type 42 (815 Sqn)
—	O	HMS *Ocean* (L12)	Helicopter carrier
—	ON	RFA *Olna* (A123)	Fleet tanker
—	OW	RFA *Olwen* (A122)	Fleet tanker
—	PO	RNAS Portland (HMS *Osprey*)	
—	PV	RFA *Sir Percivale* (L3036)	Landing ship
—	PW	Prestwick Airport (HMS *Gannet*)	
—	R	HMS *Ark Royal* (R07)	Carrier
474	RM	HMS *Richmond* (F239)	Type 23 (815 Sqn)
352/3	SD	HMS *Sheffield* (F96)	Type 22 (815 Sqn)
355	SM	HMS *Somerset* (F82)	Type 23 (815 Sqn)
334	SN	HMS *Southampton* (D90)	Type 42 (815 Sqn)
422	SU	HMS *Sutherland* (F81)	Type 23 (815 Sqn)
—	TM	RFA *Sir Tristram* (L3055)	Landing ship
—	VL	RNAS Yeovilton (HMS *Heron*)	
462	WM	HMS *Westminster* (F237)	Type 23 (815 Sqn)
407	YK	HMS *York* (D98)	Type 42 (815 Sqn)
—	—	HMS *Albion* (L14)	Assault
—	—	HMS *Bulwark* (L15)	Assault
—	—	RFA *Fort Victoria* (A387)	Auxiliary Oiler

RN Landing Platforms

Code	Deck Letters	Vessel Name & Pennant No	Vessel Type & Unit
—	—	RFA *Fort George* (A388)	Auxiliary Oiler
—	—	HMS *Kent* (F78)	Type 23
—	—	HMS *Portland* (F79)	Type 23
—	—	HMS *St Albans* (F83)	Type 23
—	—	RFA *Wave Knight* (A389)	Auxiliary Oiler
—	—	RFA *Wave Ruler* (A390)	Fleet tanker

Flown by 824 NAS from RNAS Culdrose, this Merlin HM1, ZH836, was one of the first in service. *PRM*

The aptly named de Havilland Aviation operates this Vampire T11 XE920. *PRM*

Ships' Numeric Code – Deck Letters Analysis

	0	1	2	3	4	5	6	7	8	9
33			LP		SN	CF	CV	CV		
34					GW	NC				
35	CL	CL	SD	SD		SM				
36	MC	NF	NF	MA	MA	AY	AY			
37			NL							
40					IR			YK		
41	GC	EB	CW	CW		MM		NM		
42	EX		SU							
43					EE	EE		GT		
44					MR					
45								LA		
46			WM							
47					RM					

RN Code – Squadron – Base – Aircraft Cross-check

Deck/Base Code Numbers	Letters	Unit	Location	Aircraft Type(s)
000 — 006	L	801 Sqn	Yeovilton	Sea Harrier FA2
010 — 020	L	820 Sqn	Culdrose	Sea King HAS6
122 — 129	N	800 Sqn	Yeovilton	Sea Harrier FA2
180 — 182, 189	CU	849 Sqn HQ Flt	Culdrose	Sea King AEW2/HU5
183 — 185	L	849 Sqn B Flt	Culdrose	Sea King AEW2
186 — 188	N	849 Sqn A Flt	Culdrose	Sea King AEW2
300 — 308	PO	815 Sqn	Yeovilton	Lynx HAS3/HMA8
318 — 319	PO	815 Sqn OEU	Yeovilton	Lynx HMA8
332 — 479	*	815 Sqn	Yeovilton	Lynx HAS3/HMA8
500 — 515	CT/CU/CW	810 Sqn	Culdrose	Sea King HAS6
535 — 541	CU	700M Sqn	Culdrose	Merlin HM1
560 — 573	CU	750 Sqn	Culdrose	Jetstream T2
576 — 579	-	FONA	Yeovilton	Jetstream T3
580 — 585	CU	824 Sqn	Culdrose	Merlin HM1
630 — 648	PO	702 Sqn	Yeovilton	Lynx HAS3
670 — 676	PO	702 Sqn	Yeovilton	Lynx HMA8
700 — 709	PW	819 Sqn	Prestwick	Sea King HAS6
710 — 719	VL	899 Sqn	Yeovilton	Sea Harrier FA2
720 — 724	VL	899 Sqn	Yeovilton	Harrier T8
730 — 731	VL	899 Sqn	Yeovilton	Sea Harrier FA2
820 — 827	CU	771 Sqn	Culdrose	Sea King HU5

*See foregoing separate ships' Deck Letter Analysis

Note that only the 'last two' digits of the Code are worn by some aircraft types, especially helicopters.

Royal Air Force Squadron Markings

This table gives brief details of the markings worn by aircraft of RAF squadrons. While this may help to identify the operator of a particular machine, it may not always give the true picture. For example, from time to time aircraft are loaned to other units while others (such as those with No 4 FTS at Valley) wear squadron marks but are actually operated on a pool basis. Squadron badges are usually located on the front fuselage.

Squadron	Type(s) operated	Base(s)	Distinguishing marks & other comments
No 1 Sqn	Harrier GR7/T10	RAF Cottesmore	Badge: A red & white winged number 1 on a white diamond. Tail fin has a red stripe with the badge repeated on it.
No 2 Sqn	Tornado GR1/GR1A/GR4A	RAF Marham	Badge: A wake knot on a white circular background flanked on either side by black and white triangles. Tail fin has a black stripe with white triangles and the badge repeated on it. Codes are single letters inside a white triangle on the tail.
No 3 Sqn	Harrier GR7/T10	RAF Cottesmore	Badge: A blue cockatrice on a white circular background flanked by two green bars edged with yellow. Tail fin has a green stripe edged with yellow.
No 4 Sqn	Harrier GR7/T10	RAF Cottesmore	Badge: A yellow lightning flash inside a red and black circle flanked by bars on either side repeating this design. Tail fin has a yellow lightning flash on a red and black stripe.
No 5 Sqn	Tornado F3	RAF Coningsby	Tail fin has a red stripe with a green maple leaf in the middle. Aircraft are coded C*.
No 6 Sqn	Jaguar GR1A/GR3/T2A	RAF Coltishall	Badge: A red winged can opener inside a circle edged in red. Tail has a light blue bar with red diagonal lines. Aircraft are coded E*.
No 7 Sqn	Chinook HC2/ Gazelle HT3	RAF Odiham	Badge (on tail): A blue badge containing the seven stars of Ursa Major ('The Plough') in yellow. Aircraft are coded E*. Aircraft pooled with No 18 Sqn and No 27 Sqn.
No 8 Sqn	Sentry AEW1	RAF Waddington	Badge (on tail): A grey, sheathed, Arabian dagger. Aircraft pooled with No 23 Sqn.
No 9 Sqn	Tornado GR4	RAF Brüggen	Badge: A green bat on a black circular background, flanked by yellow and green horizontal stripes. The green bat also appears on the tail, edged in yellow. Aircraft are coded A*.
No 10 Sqn	VC10 C1K	RAF Brize Norton	Badge (on tail): A yellow arrow with red wings.
No 11 Sqn	Tornado F3	RAF Leeming	Roundel is superimposed over a yellow diamond on a black background. Badge (on tail): Two black eagles in flight. Aircraft are coded D*.
No 12 Sqn	Tornado GR1/GR1B/GR4	RAF Lossiemouth	Roundel is superimposed on a green chevron. Tail fin has a black & white horizontal stripe with the squadron badge, a fox's head on a white circle, in the middle. Aircraft are coded F*.

RAF Squadron Markings

Squadron	Type(s) operated	Base(s)	Distinguishing marks & other comments
No 13 Sqn	Tornado GR4/GR4A	RAF Marham	A yellow lightning flash on a green and blue background on the nose. Badge (on tail): A lynx's head over a dagger on a white shield.
No 14 Sqn	Tornado GR1/GR4	RAF Lossiemouth	Badge: A red cross on a white circle, with wings either side, flanked by blue diamonds on a white background. The blue diamonds are repeated horizontally across the tail. Aircraft are coded B*.
No 15(R) Sqn	Tornado GR1/GR1B/GR4	RAF Lossiemouth	Roman numerals XV appear in white on the tail. Aircraft are either coded T* or TA*.
No 16(R) Sqn	Jaguar GR3/T2A/T4	RAF Coltishall	Badge: Two keys crossed on a black circle. On the tail is a black circle containing the 'Saint' emblem from the 60's TV series.
No 18 Sqn	Chinook HC2	RAF Odiham	Badge (on tail): A red winged horse on a black circle. Aircraft are coded B*. Aircraft pooled with No 7 Sqn and No 27 Sqn.
No 19(R) Sqn	Hawk T1/T1A/T1W	RAF Valley	Badge (on tail): A fish flanked by two wings on a yellow circle. Aircraft pooled with No 208(R) Sqn; part of No 4 FTS.
No 20(R) Sqn [HOCU]	Harrier GR7/T10	RAF Wittering	Badge: An eagle in a white circle flanked by a white stripe on a blue background. On the tail is a stripe made up of black, yellow, green and red triangles.
No 22 Sqn	Sea King HAR3/HAR3A	A Flt: RMB Chivenor B Flt: Wattisham C Flt: RAF Valley	Badge: A black π in front of a white Maltese cross on a red circle.
No 23 Sqn	Sentry AEW1	RAF Waddington	Badge (on tail): A red eagle preying on a yellow falcon. Aircraft pooled with No 8 Sqn.
No 24 Sqn	Hercules C1/C3/C4/C5	RAF Lyneham	No squadron markings carried. Aircraft pooled with No 30 Sqn, No 47 Sqn, No 57(R) Sqn and No 70 Sqn.
No 25 Sqn	Tornado F3	RAF Leeming	Badge (on tail): A hawk on a gauntlet. Aircraft are coded F*.
No 27 Sqn	Chinook HC2	RAF Odiham	Badge (on tail): An dark green elephant on a green circle, flanked by green and dark green stripes. Aircraft pooled with No 7 Sqn and No 18 Sqn.
No 28 Sqn	Merlin HC3	RAF Benson	Badge: A winged horse above white two crosses on a red shield.
No 30 Sqn	Hercules C1/C3/C4/C5	RAF Lyneham	No squadron markings carried. Aircraft pooled with No 24 Sqn, No 47 Sqn, No 57(R) Sqn and No 70 Sqn.
No 31 Sqn	Tornado GR4	RAF Brüggen	Badge: A gold, five-pointed star on a yellow circle flanked by yellow and green checks. The star is repeated on the tail. Aircraft are coded D*.

RAF Squadron Markings

Squadron	Type(s) operated	Base(s)	Distinguishing marks & other comments
No 32 (The Royal) Sqn	125 CC3/146 CC2/ Twin Squirrel HCC1	RAF Northolt	No squadron markings carried but aircraft carry a distinctive livery with a blue flash along the middle of the fuselage and a red tail.
No 33 Sqn	Puma HC1	RAF Benson	Badge: A stag's head.
No 39 (1PRU) Sqn	Canberra PR9/T4	RAF Marham	Badge (on tail): A winged bomb on a light blue circle. Aircraft are coded A*.
No 41 Sqn	Jaguar GR3/T4	RAF Coltishall	Badge: A red, double armed cross, flanked by red and white horizontal stipes. Stripes repeated on tail. Aircraft are coded F*.
No 42(R) Sqn	Nimrod MR2	RAF Kinloss	No squadron markings usually carried. Aircraft pooled with No 120 Sqn, No 201 Sqn and No 206 Sqn.
No 43 Sqn	Tornado F3	RAF Leuchars	Badge (on tail): A black and red gamecock. Aircraft are usually coded G*.
No 45(R) Sqn	Jetstream T1	RAF Cranwell	No squadron markings usually carried. Part of No 3 FTS.
No 47 Sqn	Hercules C1/C3/C4/C5	RAF Lyneham	No squadron markings usually carried. Aircraft pooled with No 24 Sqn, 30 Sqn, No 57(R) Sqn and No 70 Sqn.
No 51 Sqn	Nimrod R1	RAF Waddington	Badge (on tail): A red goose in flight.
No 54 Sqn	Jaguar GR3/GR3A/T2/T4	RAF Coltishall	Badge: A blue lion on a yellow shield, flanked by blue and yellow checks. A stripe of blue and yellow checks also appears on the tail. Aircraft are coded G*.
No 55(R) Sqn	Dominie T1	RAF Cranwell	No squadron markings usually carried. Part of No 3 FTS.
No 56(R) Sqn [F3OCU]	Tornado F3	RAF Coningsby	Badge (on tail): A gold phoenix rising from red flames. The tail fin has a stripe made up of red and white checks. Aircraft are usually coded A*.
No 57(R) Sqn	Hercules C1/C3/C4/C5	RAF Lyneham	No squadron markings usually carried. Aircraft pooled with No 24 Sqn, No 30 Sqn, No 47 Sqn and No 70 Sqn.
No 60(R) Sqn	Griffin HT1	RAF Shawbury [DHFS] & RAF Valley [SARTU]	No squadron markings usually carried.
No 70 Sqn	Hercules C1/C3	RAF Lyneham	No squadron markings usually carried. Aircraft pooled with No 24 Sqn, No 30 Sqn, No 47 Sqn and No 57(R) Sqn.
No 72 Sqn	Wessex HC2/Puma HC1	RAF Aldergrove	Badge: A blue swift in flight on a red circle, flanked by red bars. The badge appears on the tail of the Wessex and by the cockpit on the Puma. Aircraft are sometimes coded A*.
No 78 Sqn	Chinook HC2/ Sea King HAR3	RAF Mount Pleasant	Badge: A yellow, heraldic tiger with two tails, on a black circle. The badge appears on the tail of the Chinook and by the cockpit on the Sea King.

Squadron	Type(s) operated	Base(s)	Distinguishing marks & other comments
No 84 Sqn	Wessex HC2	RAF Akrotiri	Badge (on tail): A scorpion on a playing card symbol (diamonds, clubs etc.). Aircraft carry a vertical blue stripe through the roundel on the fuselage.
No 99 Sqn	Globemaster	RAF Brize Norton	Badge (on tail): A leaping black puma
No 100 Sqn	Hawk T1/T1A	RAF Leeming	Badge (on tail): A skull in front of two bones crossed. Aircraft are usually coded C*.
No 101 Sqn	VC10 K3/K4	RAF Brize Norton	Badge (on tail): A lion behind a castle turret.
No 111 Sqn	Tornado F3	RAF Leuchars	Badge (on tail): A cross in front of crossed swords on a light grey circle, flanked by a stripe of darker grey.
No 120 Sqn	Nimrod MR2	RAF Kinloss	No squadron markings usually carried. Aircraft pooled with No 42(R) Sqn, No 201 Sqn and No 206 Sqn.
No 201 Sqn	Nimrod MR2	RAF Kinloss	No squadron markings usually carried. Aircraft pooled with No 42(R) Sqn, No 120 Sqn and No 206 Sqn.
No 202 Sqn	Sea King HAR3	A Flt: RAF Boulmer D Flt: RAF Lossiemouth E Flt: RAF Leconfield	Badge: A mallard alighting on a white circle.
No 203(R) Sqn	Sea King HAR3	RAF St Mawgan	Badge: A green sea horse on a white circle.
No 206 Sqn	Nimrod MR2	RAF Kinloss	No squadron markings usually carried. Aircraft pooled with No 42(R) Sqn, No 120 Sqn and No 201 Sqn.
No 208(R) Sqn	Hawk T1/T1A/T1W	RAF Valley	Badge (on tail): A Sphinx inside a white circle, flanked by flashes of yellow. Aircraft pooled with No 19(R) Sqn, part of No 4 FTS.
No 216 Sqn	TriStar K1/KC1/C2/C2A	RAF Brize Norton	Badge (on tail): An eagle in flight with a bomb in its claws.
No 230 Sqn	Puma HC1	RAF Aldergrove	Badge: A tiger in front of a palm tree on a black pentagon.
No 617 Sqn	Tornado GR1/GR1B/GR4	RAF Lossiemouth	Badge: Dam breached, flanked on either side by red lightning flashes on a black background. Tail fin is black with a red lightning flash. Aircraft are coded AJ-*.
No 1435 Flt	Tornado F3	RAF Mount Pleasant	Badge (on tail): Red Maltese cross on a white circle, flanked by red and white bars

Historic Aircraft in Overseas Markings

Some *historic, classic and warbird* aircraft carry the markings of overseas air arms and can be seen in the UK, mainly preserved in museums and collections or taking part in air shows.

Notes	Serial	Type (other identity)	Owner/operator, location
	ARGENTINA		
	0729	Beech T-34C Turbo Mentor	FAA Museum, stored RNAS Yeovilton
	0767	Aermacchi MB339AA	Rolls-Royce Heritage Trust, Filton
	A-515	FMA IA58 Pucara (ZD485)	RAF Museum, Cosford
	A-517	FMA IA58 Pucara (G-BLRP)	Privately owned, Channel Islands
	A-522	FMA IA58 Pucara (8768M)	FAA Museum, at NE Aircraft Museum, Usworth
	A-528	FMA IA58 Pucara (8769M)	Norfolk & Suffolk Avn Museum, Flixton
	A-533	FMA IA58 Pucara (ZD486) <ff>	Boscombe Down Museum
	A-549	FMA IA58 Pucara (ZD487)	Imperial War Museum, Duxford
	AE-409	Bell UH-1H Iroquois [656]	Museum of Army Flying, Middle Wallop
	AE-422	Bell UH-1H Iroquois	FAA Museum, stored RNAS Yeovilton
	AUSTRALIA		
	A2-4	Supermarine Seagull V (VH-ALB)	RAF Museum, Hendon
	A16-199	Lockheed Hudson IIIA (G-BEOX) [SF-R]	RAF Museum, Hendon
	A17-48	DH82A Tiger Moth (G-BPHR)	Privately owned, Swindon
	A19-144	Bristol 156 Beaufighter XIc (JM135/A8-324)	The Fighter Collection, Duxford
	A92-480	GAF Jindivik 4A (A92-LLAN-1)	DERA Llanbedr, on display
	A92-664	GAF Jindivik 4A	Maes Artro Craft Village, Llanbedr
	A92-708	GAF Jindivik 4A	Bristol Aero Collection, stored Kemble
	N6-766	DH115 Sea Vampire T22 (XG766/G-SPDR)	De Havilland Aviation, Swansea
	WH588	Hawker Sea Fury FB11 (N588/G-EEMV) [114/NW]	Privately owned, Sywell
	BELGIUM		
	FT-36	Lockheed T-33A	Dumfries & Galloway Avn Mus, Dumfries
	H-50	Noorduyn AT-16 Harvard IIB (OO-DAF)	Privately owned, Brasschaat, Belgium
	HD-75	Hanriot HD1 (G-AFDX)	RAF Museum, Hendon
	IF-68	Hawker Hunter F6 <ff>	Privately owned, Welshpool
	K-16	Douglas C-53D Skytrooper (OT-CWG/N49G)	Air Dakota, Brussels, Belgium
	L-44	Piper L-18C Super Cub (OO-SPQ)	Privately owned, Belgium
	L-47	Piper L-18C Super Cub (OO-SPG)	Privately owned, Belgium
	L-57	Piper L-18C Super Cub (OO-GDH)	Privately owned, Belgium
	L-156	Piper L-18C Super Cub (OO-LGB)	Privately owned, Belgium
	SG-3	VS379 Spitfire FR XIV (RN201/ SG-31/G-BSKP)	Privately owned, Catfield
	V-18	Stampe SV-4B (OO-GWD)	Antwerp Stampe Centre, Antwerp-Deurne, Belgium
	V-29	Stampe SV-4B (OO-GWB)	Antwerp Stampe Centre, Antwerp-Deurne, Belgium
	BOLIVIA		
	FAB184	SIAI-Marchetti SF.260W (F-GVAB)	Privately owned, Booker
	BOTSWANA		
	OJ1	BAC Strikemaster 83 (ZG805/ G-BXFU)	Global Aviation, Humberside
	OJ4	BAC Strikemaster 87 (G-AYHR/ G-UNNY) [Z2]	The Aircraft Restoration Company, Duxford
	OJ10	BAC Strikemaster 87 (G-BXFS)	Privately owned, North Weald
	BRAZIL		
	1317	Embraer T-27 Tucano	Shorts, Belfast (engine test bed)
	BURKINA FASO		
	BF-8431	SIAI-Marchetti SF.260W (G-NRRA) [31]	Privately owned, Elstree

Serial	Type (other identity)	Owner/operator, location	Notes
CANADA			
622	Piasecki HUP-3 Retriever (51-16622/N6699D)	The Helicopter Museum, Weston-super-Mare	
920	VS Stranraer (CF-BXO) [Q-N]	RAF Museum, Hendon	
3349	NA64 Yale (G-BYNF)	Privately owned, Duxford	
5450	Hawker Hurricane XII (G-TDTW)	Hawker Restorations Ltd, Milden	
9754	Consolidated PBY-5A Catalina (VP-BPS) [P]	Privately owned, Lasham	
9893	Bristol 149 Bolingbroke IVT	Imperial War Museum store, Duxford	
9940	Bristol 149 Bolingbroke IVT	Royal Scottish Mus'm of Flight, E Fortune	
15195	Fairchild PT-19A Cornell	RAF Museum, stored Wyton	
16693	Auster J/1N Alpha (G-BLPG) [693]	Privately owned, Headcorn	
18013	DHC1 Chipmunk 22 (G-TRIC) [013]	The Shuttleworth Collection, Old Warden	
18393	Avro Canada CF-100 Canuck 4B (G-BCYK)	Imperial War Museum, Duxford	
18671	DHC1 Chipmunk 22 (WP905/ 7438M/G-BNZC) [671]	Privately owned, Wombleton	
20310	CCF T-6J Harvard IV (G-BSBG) [310]	Privately owned, Liverpool	
21417	Canadair CT-133 Silver Star	Yorkshire Air Museum, Elvington	
23140	Canadair CL-13 Sabre [AX] <rf> (fuselage)	Midland Air Museum, Coventry	
23380	Canadair CL-13 Sabre <rf>	RAF Millom Museum, Haverigg	
FJ777	Boeing-Stearman PT-13D Kaydet (42-17786/G-BRTK)	Privately owned, Swanton Morley	
CHINA			
1532008	Nanchang CJ-6A Chujiao (G-BVFX) [08]	Privately owned, Breighton	
2632016	Nanchang CJ-6A Chujiao (G-BXZB) (also wears 2632019)	Privately owned, Hibaldstow	
CZECH REPUBLIC			
3677	Letov S-102 (MiG-15) (613677)	Royal Scottish Museum of Flight, E Fortune	
3794	Letov S-102 (MiG-15) (623794)	Imperial War Museum, stored Duxford	
9147	Mil Mi-4	The Helicopter Museum, Weston-super-Mare	
DENMARK			
A-011	SAAB A.35XD Draken	Privately owned, Grainthorpe, Lincs	
AR-107	SAAB S-35XD Draken	Newark Air Museum, Winthorpe	
E-402	Hawker Hunter F51	Bournemouth Aviation Museum	
E-409	Hawker Hunter F51 (XF383)	City of Norwich Aviation Museum	
E-419	Hawker Hunter F51	North-East Aircraft Museum, Usworth	
E-420	Hawker Hunter F51 (G-9-442)	Privately owned, Walton-on-Thames	
E-421	Hawker Hunter F51	Brooklands Museum, Weybridge	
E-423	Hawker Hunter F51 (G-9-444)	SWWAPS, Lasham	
E-424	Hawker Hunter F51 (G-9-445)	Aeroventure, Doncaster	
ET-272	Hawker Hunter T7 <ff>	Boulton Paul Association, Wolverhampton	
ET-273	Hawker Hunter T7 <ff>	South Yorkshire Avn Museum, Firbeck	
K-682	Douglas C-47A Skytrain (OY-BPB)	Foreningen For Flyvende Mus, Vaerløse, Denmark	
L-866	Consolidated PBY-6A Catalina (8466M)	RAF Museum, Cosford	
R-756	Lockheed F-104G Starfighter	Midland Air Museum, Coventry	
S-881	Sikorsky S-55C	The Helicopter Museum, Weston-super-Mare	
S-882	Sikorsky S-55C	The Helicopter Museum, Weston-super-Mare	
S-886	Sikorsky S-55C	The Helicopter Museum, Weston-super-Mare	
S-887	Sikorsky S-55C	The Helicopter Museum, Weston-super-Mare	
EGYPT			
0446	Mikoyan MiG-21UM <ff>	Thameside Aviation Museum, Tilbury	
7907	Sukhoi Su-7 <ff>	Robertsbridge Aviation Society, Mayfield	
FINLAND			
VI-3	Valtion Viima 2 (OO-EBL)	Privately owned, Wevelgem, Belgium	
FRANCE			
3	Mudry/CAARP CAP-10B (G-BXRA)	Privately owned, Sedlescombe, Sussex	

Historic Aircraft

Notes	Serial	Type (other identity)	Owner/operator, location
	06	Dewoitine D27 (290/F-AZJD)	The Old Flying Machine Company, Duxford
	20	MH1521C1 Broussard (G-BWGG) [315-SQ]	Privately owned, Rednal
	37	Nord 3400 (G-ZARA) [MAB]	Privately owned, Boston
	57	Dassault Mystère IVA [8-MT]	Imperial War Museum, Duxford
	67	SNCAN 1101 Noralpha (F-GMCY) [CY]	Privately owned, la Ferté-Alais, France
	68	Nord 3400 [MHA]	*Current location not known*
	70	Dassault Mystère IVA	Midland Air Museum, Coventry
	78	Nord 3202 (G-BIZK)	Privately owned, Swanton Morley
	79	Dassault Mystère IVA [2-EG]	Norfolk & Suffolk Avn Museum, Flixton
	83	Dassault Mystère IVA [8-MS]	Newark Air Museum, Winthorpe
	84	Dassault Mystère IVA [8-NF]	Lashenden Air Warfare Museum, Headcorn
	85	Dassault Mystère IVA [8-MV]	British Aviation Heritage, Bruntingthorpe
	100	Mudry/CAARP CAP-10B (G-BXRB)	Privately owned, Sedlescombe, Sussex
	101	Dassault Mystère IVA [8-MN]	Bomber County Aviation Museum, Hemswell
	104	MH1521M Broussard (F-GHFG) [307-FG]	Privately owned, France
	105	Nord N2501F Noratlas (F-AZVM) [62-SI]	Le Noratlas de Provence, Aix-les-Milles, France
	FR108	SO1221 Djinn [CDL]	The Helicopter Museum, Weston-super-Mare
	120	SNCAN Stampe SV4C (G-AZGC)	Privately owned, Reading
	121	Dassault Mystère IVA	City of Norwich Aviation Museum
	134	Mudry/CAARP CAP-10B (G-BXRC)	Privately owned, Sedlescombe, Sussex
	135	Mudry/CAARP CAP-10B (G-BXFE)	Privately owned, Sedlescombe, Sussex
	143	Morane-Saulnier MS733 Alcyon (G-MSAL)	The Squadron, North Weald
	FR145	SO1221 Djinn [CDL]	Privately owned, Luton
	146	Dassault Mystère IVA [8-MC]	North-East Aircraft Museum, Usworth
	185	MH1521M Broussard (G-BWLR)	Privately owned, Longhope
	282	Dassault MD311 Flamant (F-AZFX) [316-KY]	Memorial Flt Association, la Ferté-Alais, France
	316	MH1521M Broussard (F-GGKR) [315-SN]	The Old Flying Machine Company, Duxford
	318	Dassault Mystère IVA [8-NY]	Dumfries & Galloway Avn Mus, Dumfries
	319	Dassault Mystère IVA [8-ND]	Rebel Air Museum, Andrewsfield
	348	SO4050 Vautour IIN (F-AZHP)	Privately owned, Bretigny, France
	396	Stampe SV4A (G-BWRE)	Privately owned, stored Sandown
	538	Dassault Mirage IIIE [3-QH]	Yorkshire Air Museum, Elvington
	1417	SA.341G Gazelle I (G-BXJK)	Privately owned, Stapleford Tawney
	17473	Lockheed T-33A	Midland Air Museum, Coventry
	42157	NA F-100D Super Sabre [11-ML]	North-East Aviation Museum, Usworth
	63938	NA F-100F Super Sabre [11-MU]	Lashenden Air Warfare Museum, Headcorn
	121748	Grumman F8F-2 Bearcat (F-AZRJ) [P]	Privately owned, Anemasse, France
	125716	Douglas AD-4N Skyraider (F-AZFN) [22-DG]	Privately owned, Etampes, France
	126965	Douglas AD-4NA Skyraider (OO-FOR)	Privately owned, Braaschaat, Belgium
	517545	NA T-28S Fennec (N14113) [CD-113]	The Aircraft Restoration Company, Duxford
	517692	NA T-28S Fennec (F-AZFV/ G-TROY) [142]	The Old Flying Machine Company, Duxford
	56-5395	Piper L-18C Super Cub (52-2436/ G-CUBJ) [CDG]	Privately owned, Oaksey Park
	C850	Salmson 2A2 <R>	Barton Aviation Heritage Society, Barton
	MS824	Morane-Saulnier Type N <R> (G-AWBU)	Privately owned, Booker
	TE184	VS361 Spitfire LF XVIE (6850M/ G-MXVI) [D]	De Cadanet Motor Racing, North Weald

GERMANY

	-	Fieseler Fi103R-IV (V-1) (BAPC 91)	Lashenden Air Warfare Museum, Headcorn
	-	Focke-Achgelis Fa330A-1 (8469M)	RAF Museum, Cosford
	-	Fokker Dr1 Dreidekker <R> (BAPC 88)	FAA Museum, RNAS Yeovilton
	-	Fokker Dr1 Dreidekker <R> (G-BVGZ)	Museum of Army Flying, Middle Wallop

Serial	Type (other identity)	Owner/operator, location	Notes
2	Messerschmitt Bf109G-10 (151591/D-HDME)	Privately owned, Mannheim, Germany	
3	SNCAN 1101 Noralpha (G-BAYV)	Barton Aviation Heritage Society, Barton	
6	Messerschmitt Bf109G-2/Trop (10639/8478M/G-USTV)	RAF/Imperial War Museum, Duxford	
8	Focke Wulf Fw190 <R> (G-WULF)	The Real Aeroplane Company, Breighton	
14	Fiat G46-3B (G-BBII)	Privately owned, stored Staverton	
14	Messerschmitt Bf109 <R> (BAPC 67)	Kent Battle of Britain Museum, Hawkinge	
14	SNCAN 1101 Noralpha (G-BSMD)	Privately owned, North Weald	
152/17	Fokker Dr1 Dreidekker <R> (G-ATJM)	Privately owned, North Weald	
210/16	Fokker EIII (BAPC 56)	Science Museum, South Kensington	
214	Yak C-11 (G-DYAK)	Privately owned, Berlin	
422/15	Fokker EIII <R> (G-AVJO)	Privately owned, Booker	
425/17	Fokker Dr1 Dreidekker <R> (BAPC 133)	Kent Battle of Britain Museum, Hawkinge	
626/8	Fokker DVII <R> (N6268)	Blue Max Movie Aircraft Museum, Booker	
959	Mikoyan MiG-21SPS	The Old Flying Machine Company, Duxford	
1190	Messerschmitt Bf109E-3 [4]	Imperial War Museum, Duxford	
1227	Focke-Wulf Fw190A-5 (G-FOKW) [DG+HO]	Privately owned, Milden	
1480	Messerschmitt Bf109 <R> (BAPC 66) [6]	Kent Battle of Britain Museum, Hawkinge	
2100	Focke-Wulf Fw189A-1 (G-BZKY) [V7+1H]	Privately owned, W Sussex	
4101	Messerschmitt Bf109E-3 (DG200/ 8477M) [12]	RAF Museum, Hendon	
6357	Messerschmitt Bf109 <R> (BAPC 74) [6]	Kent Battle of Britain Museum, Hawkinge	
7198/18	LVG CVI (G-AANJ/9239M)	The Air Historical Branch, at RAF Museum, Hendon	
8147	Messerschmitt Bf109F-4	Charleston Aviation Services, Colchester	
8417/18	Fokker DVII (9207M)	RAF Museum, Hendon	
12802	Antonov An-2T (D-FOFM)	Privately owned, Lahr, Germany	
100143	Focke-Achgelis Fa330A-1	Imperial War Museum, Duxford	
100502	Focke-Achgelis Fa330A-1	The Real Aeroplane Company, Breighton	
100509	Focke-Achgelis Fa330A-1	Science Museum, stored Wroughton	
100545	Focke-Achgelis Fa330A-1	Fleet Air Arm Museum, stored RNAS Yeovilton	
100549	Focke-Achgelis Fa330A-1	Lashenden Air Warfare Museum, Headcorn	
112372	Messerschmitt Me262A-2a (AM.51/VK893/8482M) [9K+XK]	RAF Museum, Cosford	
120227	Heinkel He162A-2 Salamander (VH513/8472M) [2]	RAF Museum, Hendon	
120235	Heinkel He162A-1 Salamander (AM.68)	Imperial War Museum, Lambeth	
191316	Messerschmitt Me163B Komet	Science Museum, South Kensington	
191614	Messerschmitt Me163B Komet (8481M)	RAF Museum, Cosford	
191659	Messerschmitt Me163B Komet (8480M) [15]	Royal Scottish Mus'm of Flight, E Fortune	
191660	Messerschmitt Me163B Komet (AM.214) [3]	Imperial War Museum, Duxford	
280020	Flettner Fl282/B-V20 Kolibri (frame only)	Midland Air Museum, Coventry	
360043	Junkers Ju88R-1 (PJ876/8475M) [D5+EV]	RAF Museum, Hendon	
420430	Messerschmitt Me410A-1/U2 (AM.72/8483M) [3U+CC]	RAF Museum, Cosford	
475081	Fieseler Fi156C-7 Storch (VP546/ AM.101/7362M)[GM+AK]	RAF Museum, Cosford	
494083	Junkers Ju87D-3 (8474M) [RI+JK]	RAF Museum, Hendon	
584219	Focke Wulf Fw190F-8/U1 (AM.29/8470M) [38]	RAF Museum, Hendon	
701152	Heinkel He111H-23 (8471M) [NT+SL]	RAF Museum, Hendon	
730301	Messerschmitt Bf110G-4 (AM.34/ 8479M) [D5+RL]	RAF Museum, Hendon	
733682	Focke Wulf Fw190A-8/R7 (AM.75/ 9211M)	Imperial War Museum, Lambeth	
1Z-NK	Amiot AAC1/Ju52 (Port.AF 6316)	Imperial War Museum, Duxford	

Historic Aircraft

Notes	Serial	Type (other identity)	Owner/operator, location
	2+1	Focke Wulf Fw190 <R> (G-SYFW) [7334]	Privately owned, Guernsey, CI
	2E+RA	Fieseler Fi-156C-2 Storch (NX436FS)	Privately owned, North Weald
	4+1	Focke Wulf Fw190 <R> (G-BSLX)	Privately owned, Riseley
	6J+PR	CASA 2.111D (G-AWHB)	Privately owned, North Weald
	22+35	Lockheed F-104G Starfighter	SWWAPS, Lasham
	22+57	Lockheed F-104G Starfighter	Privately owned, Grainthorpe, Lincs
	96+21	Mil Mi-24D (406)	Imperial War Museum, Duxford
	96+26	Mil Mi-24D (429)	The Helicopter Museum, Weston-super-Mare
	97+04	Putzer Elster B (G-APVF)	Privately owned, Tadlow
	98+14	Sukhoi Su-22M-4	The Old Flying Machine Company, stored Scampton
	99+24	NA OV-10B Bronco (F-AZKM)	Privately owned, Montelimar, France
	99+26	NA OV-10B Bronco (G-BZGL)	Privately owned, Fassberg, Germany
	99+32	NA OV-10B Bronco (G-BZGK)	Privately owned, Fassberg, Germany
	BU+CC	CASA 1.131E Jungmann (G-BUCC)	Privately owned, Goodwood
	BU+CK	CASA 1.131E Jungmann (G-BUCK)	Privately owned, White Waltham
	CC+43	Pilatus P-2 (G-CJCI)	Privately owned, Norwich
	CF+HF	Morane-Saulnier MS502 (EI-AUY)	Imperial War Museum, Duxford
	D5397/17	Albatros DVA <R> (G-BFXL)	FAA Museum, RNAS Yeovilton
	FI+S	Morane-Saulnier MS505 (G-BIRW)	Royal Scottish Mus'm of Flight, E Fortune
	FM+BB	Messerschmitt Bf109G-6 (D-FMBB)	Daimler-Benz Aerospace, Manching, Germany
	JA+120	Canadair CL-13 Sabre 4 (MM19607)	Privately owned
	KG+EM	Nord 1002 (G-ETME)	Privately owned, Booker
	LG+01	Bücker Bü133C Jungmeister (G-AYSJ)	The Fighter Collection, Duxford
	LG+03	Bücker Bü133C Jungmeister (G-AEZX)	Privately owned, Milden
	NJ+C11	Nord 1002 (G-ATBG)	Privately owned, Sutton Bridge
	S4+A07	CASA 1.131E Jungmann (G-BWHP)	Privately owned, Yarcombe, Devon
	S5+B06	CASA 1.131E Jungmann 2000 (G-BSFB)	Privately owned, Stretton, Cheshire
	TA+RC	Morane-Saulnier MS505 (G-BPHZ)	The Aircraft Restoration Co, Duxford

GHANA

Notes	Serial	Type (other identity)	Owner/operator, location
	G-102	SA122 Bulldog	Privately owned, Bourne Park, Hants
	G-108	SA122 Bulldog (G-BCUP)	Privately owned, Bourne Park, Hants

GREECE

Notes	Serial	Type (other identity)	Owner/operator, location
	51-6171	NA F-86D Sabre	North-East Aircraft Museum, Usworth
	52-6541	Republic F-84F Thunderflash [541]	North-East Aircraft Museum, Usworth

HONG KONG

Notes	Serial	Type (other identity)	Owner/operator, location
	HKG-5	SA128 Bulldog (G-BULL)	Privately owned, Slinfold
	HKG-6	SA128 Bulldog (G-BPCL)	Privately owned, Elstree
	HKG-11	Slingsby T.7M Firefly 200 (VR-HZQ)	Slingsby, stored Kirkbymoorside
	HKG-13	Slingsby T.7M Firefly 200 (G-BXKW)	Slingsby, stored Kirkbymoorside

HUNGARY

Notes	Serial	Type (other identity)	Owner/operator, location
	501	Mikoyan MiG-21PF	Imperial War Museum, Duxford

INDIA

Notes	Serial	Type (other identity)	Owner/operator, location
	Q497	EE Canberra T4 (WE191) (fuselage)	BAE Systems Warton Fire Service

INDONESIA

Notes	Serial	Type (other identity)	Owner/operator, location
	LL-5306	BAe Hawk T53	BAE Systems, stored Bournemouth
	LL-5313	BAe Hawk T53	BAE Systems, stored Bournemouth
	LL-5315	BAe Hawk T53	BAE Systems, stored Bournemouth
	LL-5317	BAe Hawk T53	BAE Systems, stored Bournemouth
	LL-5319	BAe Hawk T53	BAE Systems, stored Bournemouth
	LL-5320	BAe Hawk T53	BAE Systems, stored Bournemouth

IRAQ

Notes	Serial	Type (other identity)	Owner/operator, location
	333	DH115 Vampire T55 <ff>	Military Aircraft Pres'n Grp, Barton

Historic Aircraft

Serial	Type (other identity)	Owner/operator, location	Notes
ISRAEL			
41	NA P-51D Mustang (G-LYNE)	Privately owned, Tees-side	
ITALY			
MM5701	Fiat CR42 (BT474/8468M) [13-95]	RAF Museum, Hendon	
MM53211	Fiat G46-4 (BAPC 79) [ZI-4]	The Aircraft Restoration Co, stored Duxford	
MM53432	NA T-6D Texan [RM-11]	Privately owned, South Wales	
MM53692	CCF T-6G Texan	RAeS Medway Branch, Rochester	
MM53774	Fiat G59-4B (I-MRSV) [181]	Privately owned, Parma, Italy	
MM54099	NA T-6G Texan (G-BRBC) [RR-56]	Privately owned, Chigwell	
MM54-2372	Piper L-21B Super Cub	Privately owned, Kesgrave, Suffolk	
W7	Avia FL3 (G-AGFT)	Privately owned, Leicester	
JAPAN			
-	Yokosuka MXY 7 Ohka II (BAPC 159)	Defence School, Chattenden	
24	Kawasaki Ki100-1B (8476M/BAPC 83)	RAF Museum, Cosford	
3685	Mitsubishi A6M3-2 Zero	Imperial War Museum, Duxford	
5439	Mitsubishi Ki46-III (8484M/BAPC 84)	RAF Museum, Cosford	
15-1585	Yokosuka MXY 7 Ohka II (BAPC 58)	Science Museum, at FAA Museum, RNAS Yeovilton	
997	Yokosuka MXY 7 Ohka II (8485M/BAPC 98)	Gr Manchester Mus of Science & Industry	
I-13	Yokosuka MXY 7 Ohka II (8486M/BAPC 99)	RAF Museum, Cosford	
MYANMAR			
UB441	VS361 Spitfire IX (ML119)	Privately owned, Sandown	
NETHERLANDS			
204	Lockheed SP-2H Neptune [V]	RAF Museum, Cosford	
361	Hawker Fury FB10 (N36SF)	Privately owned, Kemble	
3W-17	VS 361 Spitfire LF IXC (MK732/8633M/PH-OUQ)	KLu Historic Flight, Lelystad, The Netherlands	
A-12	DH82A Tiger Moth (PH-TYG)	Privately owned, Gilze-Rijen, The Netherlands	
B-64	Noorduyn AT-16 Harvard IIB (PH-LSK)	Privately owned, Gilze-Rijen, The Netherlands	
B-71	Noorduyn AT-16 Harvard IIB (PH-MLM)	Privately owned, Gilze-Rijen, The Netherlands	
B-118	Noorduyn AT-16 Harvard IIB (PH-IIB)	Privately owned, Gilze-Rijen, The Netherlands	
E-14	Fokker S-11 Instructor (PH-AFS)	Privately owned, Lelystad, The Netherlands	
E-15	Fokker S-11 Instructor (G-BIYU)	Privately owned, White Waltham	
E-18	Fokker S-11 Instructor (PH-HTC)	Dukes of Brabant AF, Eindhoven, The Netherlands	
E-20	Fokker S-11 Instructor (PH-GRB)	Privately owned, Gilze-Rijen, The Netherlands	
E-27	Fokker S-11 Instructor (PH-HOL)	Privately owned, Lelystad, The Netherlands	
E-31	Fokker S-11 Instructor (G-BEPV)	Privately owned, Elstree	
E-32	Fokker S-11 Instructor (PH-HOI)	Privately owned, Gilze-Rijen, The Netherlands	
E-36	Fokker S-11 Instructor (PH-ACG)	Privately owned, Lelystad, The Netherlands	
E-39	Fokker S-11 Instructor (PH-HOG)	Privately owned, Lelystad, The Netherlands	
G-29	Beech D18S (N5369X)	KLu Historic Flt, Gilze-Rijen, The Netherlands	
N-202	Hawker Hunter F6 [10] <ff>	Privately owned, Eaglescott	
N-250	Hawker Hunter F6 (G-9-185) <ff>	Imperial War Museum, Duxford	
N-268	Hawker Hunter FGA78 (Qatar QA-10)	Yorkshire Air Museum, Elvington	
N-315	Hawker Hunter T7 (XM121)	Jet Avn Preservation Grp, Long Marston	
N5-149	NA B-25J Mitchell (44-29507/HD346/N320SQ) [232511]	Duke of Brabant AF, Eindhoven, The Netherlands	
R-109	Piper L-21B Super Cub (54-2337/PH-GAZ)	Privately owned, Gilze-Rijen, The Netherlands	
R-122	Piper L-21B Super Cub (54-2412/PH-PPW)	Privately owned, Gilze-Rijen, The Netherlands	

Historic Aircraft

Notes	Serial	Type (other identity)	Owner/operator, location
	R-137	Piper L-21B Super Cub (54-2427/ PH-PSC)	Privately owned, Gilze-Rijen, The Netherlands
	R-151	Piper L-21B Super Cub (54-2441/ G-BIYR)	Privately owned, Dunkeswell
	R-163	Piper L-21B Super Cub (54-2453/ G-BIRH)	Privately owned, Lee-on-Solent
	R-167	Piper L-21B Super Cub (54-2457/ G-LION)	Privately owned, Turweston, Bucks
	R-177	Piper L-21B Super Cub (54-2467/ PH-KNR)	Privately owned, Gilze-Rijen, The Netherlands
	R-181	Piper L-21B Super Cub (54-2471/ PH-GAU)	Privately owned, Gilze-Rijen, The Netherlands
	R-345	Piper J-3C Cub (PH-UCS)	Privately owned, The Netherlands
	S-9	DHC2 L-20A Beaver (PH-DHC)	KLu Historic Flt, Gilze-Rijen, The Netherlands
	Y-74	Consolidated PBY-5A Catalina (PH-PBY)	Cat Air, Lelystad, The Netherlands

NEW ZEALAND

Notes	Serial	Type (other identity)	Owner/operator, location
	NZ3009	Curtiss P-40E Kittyhawk (ZK-RMH)	The Old Flying Machine Company, Duxford
	NZ3905	WS Wasp HAS1 (XT787)	Kennet Aviation, Cranfield
	NZ3907	WS Wasp HAS1 (XT435/G-RIMM)	Privately owned, Cranfield
	NZ3909	WS Wasp HAS1 (XT782)	Kennet Aviation, Cranfield, spares use
	NZ5648	Goodyear FG-1D Corsair (G-BXUL) [648]	The Old Flying Machine Company, Duxford
	NZ6361	BAC Strikemaster 87 (OJ5/ G-BXFP)	Privately owned, Chalgrove

NORTH KOREA

Notes	Serial	Type (other identity)	Owner/operator, location
	-	WSK Lim-2 (MiG-15) (01420/ G-BMZF)	FAA Museum, RNAS Yeovilton
	1211	WSK Lim-5 (MiG-17F) (G-BWUF)	The Old Flying Machine Company, Duxford

NORWAY

Notes	Serial	Type (other identity)	Owner/operator, location
	423/427	Gloster Gladiator I (L8032/ G-AMRK/*N2308*)	The Shuttleworth Collection, Old Warden
	848	Piper L-18C Super Cub (LN-ACL) [FA-N]	Privately owned, Norway
	56321	SAAB S91B Safir (G-BKPY) [U-AB]	Newark Air Museum, Winthorpe

POLAND

Notes	Serial	Type (other identity)	Owner/operator, location
	05	WSK SM-2 (Mi-2) (1005)	The Helicopter Museum, Weston-super-Mare
	309	WSK SBLim-2A (MiG-15UTI) <ff>	Royal Scottish Museum of Flight, E Fortune
	408	WSK-PZL Mielec TS-11 Iskra (1H-0408)	The Old Flying Machine Company, Scampton
	1018	WSK-PZL Mielec TS-11 Iskra (1H-1018/G-ISKA)	Privately owned, Bruntingthorpe
	1120	WSK Lim-2 (MiG-15bis)	RAF Museum, Hendon
	09008	WSK SBLim-2A (MiG-15UTI) (G-BZMN)	Privately owned, Sproughton

PORTUGAL

Notes	Serial	Type (other identity)	Owner/operator, location
	85	Isaacs Fury II (G-BTPZ)	Privately owned, Ormskirk
	1372	OGMA/DHC1 Chipmunk T20 (HB-TUM)	Privately owned, Switzerland
	1377	DHC1 Chipmunk 22 (G-BARS)	Privately owned, Yeovilton
	1741	CCF Harvard IV (G-HRVD)	Air Atlantique Historic Flight, Coventry
	1747	CCF T-6J Harvard IV (*20385*/ G-BGPB)	The Aircraft Restoration Co, Duxford

QATAR

Notes	Serial	Type (other identity)	Owner/operator, location
	QA12	Hawker Hunter FGA78 <ff>	The Planets Leisure Centre, Woking
	QP30	WS Lynx Mk 28 (G-BFDV/TD 013)	Army SEAE, Arborfield
	QP31	WS Lynx Mk 28	RNAY Fleetlands Apprentice School
	QP32	WS Lynx Mk 28 (TAD 016)	AAC Stockwell Hall, Middle Wallop

RUSSIA (& FORMER SOVIET UNION)

Notes	Serial	Type (other identity)	Owner/operator, location
	-	Mil Mi-24V (3532424810853)	Privately owned, Hawarden
	2	Yakovlev Yak-52 (9311708/ G-YAKS)	Privately owned, North Weald

Serial	Type (other identity)	Owner/operator, location	Notes
03	Mil Mi-24D (3532461715415)	Privately owned, Hawarden	
03	Yakovlev Yak-3UA (0470403/ F-AZYJ)	Privately owned, Dijon, France	
04	Mikoyan MiG-23ML (024003607)	Privately owned, Hawarden	
04	Yakovlev Yak-52 (9211612/ RA-22521)	Privately owned, Wellesbourne Mountford	
05	Yakovlev Yak-50 (832507/ YL-CBH)	Privately owned, Strathallan	
06	Mil Mi-24D (3532464505029)	Privately owned, Hawarden	
07	WSK SM-1 (Mi-1)	The Helicopter Museum, Weston-super-Mare	
07	Yakovlev Yak-18M (G-BMJY)	Privately owned, North Weald	
09	Yakovlev Yak-52 (9411809/ G-BVMU)	Privately owned, Sandy, Beds	
10	Yakovlev Yak-52 (9110580)	Privately owned, White Waltham	
11	SPP Yak C-11 (G-YCII)	Privately owned, North Weald	
11	SPP Yak C-11 (G-BZMY)	Privately owned, North Weald	
12	LET L-29 Delfin (194555/ ES-YLM/G-DELF)	Privately owned, Manston	
14	Yakovlev Yak-52 (899404/ G-CCCP)	Privately owned, North Weald	
15	Yakovlev Yak-52 (866915/LY-ABQ)	Privately owned, Leicester	
18	LET L-29S Delfin (591771/YL-PAF)	Privately owned, Hawarden	
19	Yakovlev Yak-52 (811202/YL-CBI)	Privately owned, Cumbernauld	
20	Lavochkin La-11	The Fighter Collection, Duxford	
20	Yakovlev Yak-52 (790404/YL-CBJ)	Privately owned, Strathallan	
23	Mikoyan MiG-27D (83712515040)	Privately owned, Hawarden	
26	Yakovlev Yak-52 (9111306/ G-BVXK)	Privately owned, White Waltham	
27	SPP Yak C-11 (G-OYAK)	Privately owned, North Weald	
27	Yakovlev Yak-52 (9111307/ G-YAKX)	Privately owned, Old Sarum	
31	Yakovlev Yak-52 (9111311/ RA-02209)	Privately owned, Rendcomb	
35	Sukhoi Su-17M-3 (25102)	Privately owned, Hawarden	
35	Yakovlev Yak-52 (9010508/ RA-02080)	Privately owned, White Waltham	
36	LET/Yak C-11 (G-KYAK)	Privately owned, North Weald	
36	SPP Yak C-11 (G-IYAK)	Privately owned, Earls Colne	
40	Yakovlev Yak-55M (920506/ RA-01333/G-YAKM)	Privately owned,	
42	Yakovlev Yak-52 (833901/LY-AMU)	Privately owned, North Weald	
48	Yakovlev Yak-52 (RA-44514)	Privately owned, White Waltham	
49	Yakovlev Yak-55M (880606/ RA-44526)	Privately owned, White Waltham	
50	Mikoyan MiG-23MF (023003508)	Privately owned, Hawarden	
50	Yakovlev Yak-50 (812003/G-BWJT)	Privately owned, Little Gransden	
50	Yakovlev Yak-50 (822305/G-BXNO)	Privately owned, Denham	
50	Yakovlev Yak-52 (9111415/ RA-44464)	Privately owned, White Waltham	
51	Curtiss P-40E Warhawk (41-13570)	Privately owned, stored Sandown	
51	LET L-29S Delfin (491273/YL-PAG)	Privately owned, Hawarden	
52	Yakovlev Yak-52 (878202/G-BWVR)	Privately owned, Barton	
52	Yakovlev Yak-52 (800708/LY-AMP)	Privately owned, Breighton	
54	Sukhoi Su-17M (69004)	Privately owned, Hawarden	
55	Yakovlev Yak-52 (9111505/ G-BVOK)	Intrepid Aviation, North Weald	
56	Yakovlev Yak-52 (811504/LY-AKW)	Privately owned, Hawarden	
56	Yakovlev Yak-52 (9111506/ RA-44516)	Privately owned, White Waltham	
69	Hawker Hunter FGA9 (8839M/ XG194)	RAF North Luffenham Training Area	
69	Yakovlev Yak-50 (801810/G-BTZB)	Privately owned, Audley End	
69	Yakovlev Yak-52 (855509/LY-ALS)	Privately owned, North Weald	
71	Mikoyan MiG-27M (61912507006)	Privately owned, Hawarden	
72	Yakovlev Yak-52 (9111608/ G-BXAV)	Privately owned, North Weald	
74	Yakovlev Yak-52 (877404/LY-AOK)	Privately owned, Tollerton	
74	Yakovlev Yak-52 (888802/G-BXID)	Privately owned, Wellesbourne Mountford	
96	Yakovlev Yak-55 (901103/ RA-44525)	Privately owned, White Waltham	
98	Yakovlev Yak-52 (888911/ RA-02042)	Privately owned, White Waltham	
100	Yakovlev Yak-52 (866904/G-YAKI)	Privately owned, Popham	

Historic Aircraft

Notes	Serial	Type (other identity)	Owner/operator, location
	101	Yakovlev Yak-52 (888914/ RA-02075)	Privately owned, White Waltham
	107	Yakovlev Yak-50 (822210/LY-AGG)	Privately owned, Old Sarum
111	Aero L-39ZO Albatros (*28+02*/ G-OTAF)	The Old Flying Machine Company, Duxford
	112	Yakovlev Yak-52 (822610/LY-AFB)	Privately owned, Little Gransden
	114	Yakovlev Yak-52 (8890012/ LY-ALM)	Privately owned, Compton Abbas
	139	Yakovlev Yak-52 (833810/ G-BWOD)	Privately owned, Sywell
503	Mikoyan MiG-21SMT (G-BRAM)	Bournemouth Aviation Museum
	1342	Yakovlev Yak-1 (G-BTZD)	Privately owned, Milden
1-12	Yakovlev Yak-52 (9011013/ RA-02293)	Privately owned, Halfpenny Green
	BH328	Hawker Hurricane IIb	Privately owned, Isle of Wight
	PT879	VS361 Spitfire LF IX (G-BYDE)	Privately owned, Isle of Wight
	(RK858)	VS361 Spitfire LF IX	The Fighter Collection, Duxford
	(SM639)	VS361 Spitfire LF IX	Privately owned, Catfield

SAUDI ARABIA

Notes	Serial	Type (other identity)	Owner/operator, location
	405	Agusta-Bell AB.212	Privately owned, Margate
	420	Agusta-Bell AB.212	Privately owned, Margate
	1102	BAC Strikemaster 80 (G-AWOR)	Global Aviation, Humberside
	1104	BAC Strikemaster 80	Global Aviation, Humberside
	1105	BAC Strikemaster 80	Global Aviation, Humberside
	1107	BAC Strikemaster 80	Global Aviation, Humberside
	1108	BAC Strikemaster 80	Global Aviation, Humberside
	1112	BAC Strikemaster 80	Global Aviation, Humberside
	1114	BAC Strikemaster 80A	Global Aviation, Humberside
	1115	BAC Strikemaster 80A	Global Aviation, Humberside
	1120	BAC Strikemaster 80A	Global Aviation, Humberside
	1121	BAC Strikemaster 80A	Global Aviation, Humberside
	1125	BAC Strikemaster 80A	Global Aviation, Humberside
	1129	BAC Strikemaster 80A	Global Aviation, Humberside
	1130	BAC Strikemaster 80A	Global Aviation, Humberside
	1133	BAC Strikemaster 80A (G-BESY)	Imperial War Museum, Duxford
	55-713	BAC Lightning T55 (ZF598)	Midland Air Museum, Coventry

SLOVAKIA

Notes	Serial	Type (other identity)	Owner/operator, location
	7708	Mikoyan MiG-21MF	Boscombe Down Museum

SOUTH AFRICA

Notes	Serial	Type (other identity)	Owner/operator, location
	92	Westland Wasp HAS1 (G-BYCX)	Privately owned, Thruxton
	6130	Lockheed Ventura II (AJ469)	RAF Museum, Cosford
	7429	NA AT-6D Harvard III	Privately owned, Germany

SOUTH VIETNAM

Notes	Serial	Type (other identity)	Owner/operator, location
24550	Cessna L-19E Bird Dog (G-PDOG) [GP]	Privately owned, Lincs

SPAIN

Notes	Serial	Type (other identity)	Owner/operator, location
B.2I-27	CASA 2.111B (He111H-16) (B.2I-103)	Imperial War Museum, Duxford
	C.4E-88	Messerschmitt Bf109E	Privately owned, Hungerford
	C.4K-102	Hispano HA 1.112M1L Buchon (G-BWUE)	Privately owned, Sandown
	E.1-9	CASA 1.133L Jungmeister (G-BVXJ)	The Real Aeroplane Company, Breighton
	E.3B-114	CASA 1.131E Jungmann (G-BJAL)	Privately owned, Breighton
	E.3B-143	CASA 1.131E Jungmann (G-JUNG)	Privately owned, White Waltham
	E.3B-153	CASA 1.131E Jungmann (G-BPTS) [781-75]	The Old Flying Machine Company, Duxford
	E.3B-336	CASA 1.131E Jungmann (G-BUTA)	Privately owned, Breighton
	E.3B-350	CASA 1.131E Jungmann (G-BHPL) [05-97]	Privately owned, Kemble
	(E.3B-369)	CASA 1.131E Jungmann (G-BPDM) [781-32]	Privately owned, Chilbolton
	E.3B-521	CASA 1.131E Jungmann [781-3]	RAF Museum, stored Wyton
EM-01	DH60G Moth (G-AAOR)	Privately owned, Rendcomb
	ES.1-16	CASA 1.133L Jungmeister	Privately owned, Stretton, Cheshire

SWEDEN

Notes	Serial	Type (other identity)	Owner/operator, location
081	CFM 01 Tummelisa <R> (SE-XIL)	Privately owned, Karlstad, Sweden
	05108	DH60 Moth	Privately owned, Langham

Serial	Type (other identity)	Owner/operator, location	Notes
17239	SAAB B-17A (SE-BYH) [7-J]	Flygvapenmuseum, Linköping, Sweden	
28693	DH100 Vampire FB6 (J-1184/ SE-DXY) [9-G]	Scandinavian Historic Flight, North Weald	
29640	SAAB J-29F [20-08]	Midland Air Museum, Coventry	
29670	SAAB J-29F (SE-DXB) [10-R]	Flygvapenmuseum/F10 Wing, Angelholm, Sweden	
32028	SAAB 32A Lansen (G-BMSG)	Privately owned, Cranfield	
34066	Hawker Hunter F58 (J-4089/ SE-DXA) [9-G]	Scandinavian Historic Flight, North Weald	
35075	SAAB J-35J Draken [40]	Imperial War Museum, Duxford	
A14	Thulin A/Bleriot XI (SE-XMC)	Privately owned, Karlstad, Sweden	
N3-615	NA P-51D Mustang (26158/ SE-BKG)	Privately owned, Hässlo, Sweden	

SWITZERLAND

Serial	Type (other identity)	Owner/operator, location	Notes
A-10	CASA 1.131E Jungmann (G-BECW)	Privately owned, Denham	
A-57	CASA 1.131E Jungmann (G-BECT)	Privately owned, Shoreham	
A-701	Junkers Ju52/3m (HB-HOS)	Ju-Air, Dubendorf, Switzerland	
A-702	Junkers Ju52/3m (HB-HOT)	Ju-Air, Dubendorf, Switzerland	
A-703	Junkers Ju52/3m (HB-HOP)	Ju-Air, Dubendorf, Switzerland	
A-806	Pilatus P3-03 (G-BTLL)	Privately owned, stored Headcorn	
C-552	EKW C-3605 (G-DORN)	Privately owned, Bournemouth	
C-558	EKW C-3605	Privately owned, Catfield	
J-1008	DH100 Vampire FB6	Mosquito Aircraft Museum, London Colney	
J-1149	DH100 Vampire FB6 (G-SWIS)	Privately owned, Bournemouth	
J-1172	DH100 Vampire FB6 (8487M)	RAF Museum, stored Wyton	
J-1573	DH112 Venom FB50 (G-VICI)	Source Classic Jet Flight, Bournemouth	
J-1605	DH112 Venom FB50 (G-BLID)	Gatwick Aviation Museum, Charlwood, Surrey	
J-1614	DH112 Venom FB50 (G-VENM)	Kennet Aviation, Cranfield	
J-1629	DH112 Venom FB50	Source Classic Jet Flight, Bournemouth	
J-1632	DH112 Venom FB50 (G-VNOM)	Kennet Aviation, Cranfield	
J-1649	DH112 Venom FB50	Source Classic Jet Flight, Bournemouth	
J-1704	DH112 Venom FB54	RAF Museum, Cosford	
J-1712	DH112 Venom FB54 <ff>	Botany Bay Village, Chroley, Lancs	
J-1758	DH112 Venom FB54 (N203DM)	Privately owned, stored North Weald	
J-4021	Hawker Hunter F58 (G-BWIU)	Historic Flying Ltd/OFMC, Scampton	
J-4031	Hawker Hunter F58 (G-BWFR)	The Old Flying Machine Company, Scampton	
J-4058	Hawker Hunter F58 (G-BWFS)	The Old Flying Machine Company, Scampton	
J-4066	Hawker Hunter F58 (G-BXNZ)	The Old Flying Machine Company, Scampton	
J-4072	Hawker Hunter F58	Privately owned, Scampton	
J-4081	Hawker Hunter F58 (G-BWKB)	The Old Flying Machine Company, Scampton	
J-4083	Hawker Hunter F58 (G-EGHH)	Privately owned, Bournemouth	
J-4090	Hawker Hunter F58 (G-SIAL)	The Old Flying Machine Company, Duxford	
J-4091	Hawker Hunter F58	British Aviation Heritage, Bruntingthorpe	
U-80	Bücker Bü133D Jungmeister (G-BUKK)	Privately owned, White Waltham	
U-99	Bücker Bü133C Jungmeister (G-AXMT)	Privately owned, Breighton	
U-110	Pilatus P-2 (G-PTWO)	Privately owned, Earls Colne	
U-125	Pilatus P-2 (G-BLKZ)	Privately owned, North Weald	
U-142	Pilatus P-2 (G-BONE)	Privately owned, Hibaldstow	
U-1234	DH115 Vampire T55 (G-DHAV)	De Havilland Aviation, Swansea	
V-54	SE3130 Alouette II (G-BVSD)	Privately owned, Staverton	

USA

Serial	Type (other identity)	Owner/operator, location	Notes
-	Noorduyn AT-16 Harvard IIB (KLu B-168)	American Air Museum, Duxford	
1	Spad XIII <R> (G-BFYO/S3398)	American Air Museum, Duxford	
2	Boeing-Stearman N2S-5 Kaydet (G-AZLE)	Privately owned, Tongham	
5	Boeing P-26A Peashooter <R> (G-BEEW)	Privately owned, Barton	
14	Boeing-Stearman A75N-1 Kaydet (G-ISDN)	Privately owned, Rendcomb	
23	Fairchild PT-23 (N49272)	Privately owned, Halfpenny Green	

Historic Aircraft

Notes	Serial	Type (other identity)	Owner/operator, location
	26	Boeing-Stearman A75N-1 Kaydet (G-BAVO)	Privately owned, Old Buckenham
	27	NA SNJ-7 Texan (90678/G-BRVG)	Intrepid Aviation, North Weald
33-K	PA-18 Super Cub 95 (51-15541/ G-BJLH)	Privately owned, Felthorpe
	43	Noorduyn AT-16 Harvard IIB (43-13064/G-AZSC) [SC]	Privately owned, Duxford
	44	Boeing-Stearman D75N-1 Kaydet (42-15852/G-RJAH)	Privately owned, Rendcomb
	44	Piper L-21B Super Cub (54-2405/ G-BWHH)	Privately owned, Felthorpe
	49	Curtiss P-40M Kittyhawk (43-5802/ G-KITT/P8196)	The Fighter Collection, Duxford
	57	WS55 Whirlwind HAS7 (XG592)	Task Force Adventure Park, Cowbridge, S Glam
	85	WAR P-47 Thunderbolt <R> (G-BTBI)	Privately owned, Carlisle
	112	Boeing-Stearman PT-13D Kaydet (42-17397/G-BSWC)	Privately owned, Old Sarum
	118	Boeing-Stearman PT-13A Kaydet (38-470/G-BSDS)	Privately owned, Swanton Morley
	243	Boeing-Stearman A75N-1 Kaydet (41-25243/G-BUKE)	Privately owned, Goodwood
	379	Boeing-Stearman PT-13D Kaydet (42-14865/G-ILLE)	Privately owned, Compton Abbas
	441	Boeing-Stearman N2S-4 Kaydet (30010/G-BTFG)	Privately owned, Bunns Bank, Norfolk
	540	Piper L-4H Grasshopper (43-29877/G-BCNX)	Privately owned, Monewden
	578	Boeing-Stearman N2S-5 Kaydet (N1364V)	Privately owned, North Weald
	628	Beech D17S (44-67761/N18V)	Privately owned, stored North Weald
	744	Boeing-Stearman A75N-1 Kaydet (42-16532/OO-USN)	Privately owned, Wevelghem, Belgium
	854	Ryan PT-22 Recruit (42-17378/ G-BTBH)	Privately owned, Wellesbourne Mountford
	855	Ryan PT-22 Recruit (41-15510/ N56421)	Privately owned, Halfpenny Green
	897	Aeronca 11AC Chief (G-BJEV) [E]	Privately owned, English Bicknor, Glos
	1164	Beech D18S (G-BKGL)	The Aircraft Restoration Co, Duxford
	1180	Boeing-Stearman N2S-3 Kaydet (3403/G-BRSK)	Privately owned, Tibenham
	2525	Curtiss JN-4D Jenny (G-ECAB)	Aerosuperbatics, Rendcomb
	2807	NA T-6G Texan (49-3072/ G-BHTH) [V-103]	Northbrook College, Shoreham
	5547	Lockheed T-33A (51-9036)	Newark Air Museum, Winthorpe
	6136	Boeing-Stearman A75N-1 Kaydet (42-16136/G-BRUJ) [205]	Privately owned, Liverpool
	6771	Republic F-84F Thunderstreak (BAF FU-6)	RAF Museum, stored Cosford
	7797	Aeronca L-16A (47-0797/G-BFAF)	Privately owned, Finmere
	8178	NA F-86A Sabre (48-0178/ G-SABR) [FU-178]	Golden Apple Operations/OFMC, Duxford
	8242	NA F-86A Sabre (48-0242) [FU-242]	American Air Museum, Duxford
	01532	Northrop F-5E Tiger II <R>	RAF Alconbury on display
	02538	Fairchild PT-19B Cornell (N33870)	Privately owned, Priory Farm, Norfolk
	07539	Boeing-Stearman N2S-3 Kaydet (N63590) [143]	Privately owned, Tibenham
	14286	Lockheed T-33A (51-4286)	American Air Museum, Duxford
	O-14419	Lockheed T-33A (51-4419)	Midland Air Museum, Coventry
	14863	NA AT-6D Harvard III (41-33908/ G-BGOR)	Privately owned, Goudhurst, Kent
	15154	Bell OH-58A Kiowa (70-15154)	R. Military College of Science, Shrivenham
	16445	Bell AH-1F Hueycobra (69-16445)	R. Military College of Science, Shrivenham
	16506	Hughes OH-6A Cayuse (67-16506)	The Helicopter Museum, Weston-super-Mare
	16579	Bell UH-1H Iroquois (66-16579)	The Helicopter Museum, Weston-super-Mare
	16718	Lockheed T-33A (51-6718)	City of Norwich Aviation Museum
	18263	Boeing-Stearman PT-17 Kaydet (41-8263/N38940) [822]	Privately owned, Tibenham
	19252	Lockheed T-33A (51-9252)	Tangmere Military Aviation Museum

Serial	Type (other identity)	Owner/operator, location	Notes
20249	Noorduyn AT-16 Harvard IIB (PH-KLU) [XS-249]	Privately owned, Lelystad, The Netherlands	
21605	Bell UH-1H Iroquois (72-21605)	American Air Museum, Duxford	
21714	Grumman F8F-2P Bearcat (121714/G-RUMM) [201-B]	The Fighter Collection, Duxford	
24538	Kaman HH-43F Huskie (62-4538)	Midland Air Museum, Coventry	
28521	CCF Harvard IV (G-TVIJ) [TA-521]	Privately owned, Woodchurch, Kent	
30861	NA TB-25J Mitchell (44-30861/ N9089Z)	Privately owned, North Weald	
31145	Piper L-4B Grasshopper (43-1145/ G-BBLH) [26-G]	Privately owned, Biggin Hill	
31171	NA B-25J Mitchell (44-31171/ N7614C)	American Air Museum, Duxford	
31952	Aeronca O-58B Defender (43-1952/G-BRPR)	Privately owned, Earls Colne	
34037	NA TB-25N Mitchell (44-29366/ N9115Z/8838M)	RAF Museum, Hendon	
37414	McD F-4C Phantom (63-7414)	Midland Air Museum, Coventry	
38674	Thomas-Morse S4 Scout <R> (G-MTKM)	Privately owned, Rugby	
39624	Wag Aero Sport Trainer (G-BVMH) [39-D]	Privately owned, Lincoln	
40467	Grumman F6F-5K Hellcat (80141/ G-BTCC) [19]	The Fighter Collection, Duxford	
41386	Thomas-Morse S4 Scout <R> (G-MJTD)	Privately owned, Hitchin	
42163	NA F-100D Super Sabre (54-2163) [HE]	Dumfries & Galloway Avn Mus, Dumfries	
42165	NA F-100D Super Sabre (54-2165) [VM]	American Air Museum, Duxford	
42174	NA F-100D Super Sabre (54-2174) [UH]	Midland Air Museum, Coventry	
43578	Boeing-Stearman N2S-3 Kaydet (N1364V) [578]	Privately owned, North Weald	
46214	Grumman TBM-3E Avenger (69327/CF-KCG) [X-3]	American Air Museum, Duxford	
46867	Grumman FM-2 Wildcat (N909WJ)	Flying A Services, North Weald	
48846	Boeing B-17E Fortress (44-8846/ F-AZDX) [DS-M]	Assoc Fortresse Toujours Volant, Rouen, France	
53319	Grumman TBM-3R Avenger (G-BTDP) [319-RB]	Privately owned, North Weald	
54137	CCF Harvard IV (MM54137/ G-CTKL) [69]	Privately owned, North Weald	
54433	Lockheed T-33A (55-4433)	Norfolk & Suffolk Avn Museum, Flixton	
54439	Lockheed T-33A (55-4439)	North-East Aircraft Museum, Usworth	
58811	NA B-25J Mitchell (45-8811/ F-AZID) [HD]	Privately owned, Athens, Greece	
60312	McD F-101F Voodoo (56-0312)	Midland Air Museum, Coventry	
60689	Boeing B-52D Stratofortress (56-0689)	American Air Museum, Duxford	
63000	NA F-100D Super Sabre (54-2212) [FW-000]	USAF Croughton, Oxon, at gate	
63319	NA F-100D Super Sabre (54-2269) [FW-319]	RAF Lakenheath, on display	
63428	Republic F-105G Thunderchief (62-4428)	USAF Croughton, Oxon, at gate	
66692	Lockheed U-2CT (56-6692)	American Air Museum, Duxford	
70270	McD F-101B Voodoo (57-270) (fuselage)	Midland Air Museum, Coventry	
79863	Grumman F6F-5K Hellcat (N79863)	Flying A Services, North Weald	
80425	Grumman F7F-3P Tigercat (N7235C/G-RUMT) [WT-14]	The Fighter Collection, Duxford	
82062	DHC U-6A Beaver (58-2062)	Midland Air Museum, Coventry	
85869	Grumman TBM-3E Avenger (F-AZJA) [401-AK]	Privately owned, Etampes, France	
91007	Lockheed T-33A (51-8566/ G-NASA) [TR-007]	De Havilland Aviation, Swansea	
92399	CV F4U-1 Corsair (G-CCMV) [17]	Privately owned, Sywell	
93542	CCF Harvard IV (G-BRLV) [LTA-542]	Privately owned, North Weald	
96995	CV F4U-4 Corsair (OE-EAS) [BR-37]	Tyrolean Jet Services, Innsbruck, Austria	
97264	CV F4U-4 Corsair (F-AZVJ) [403]	Flying Legend, Dijon, France	

Historic Aircraft

Notes	Serial	Type (other identity)	Owner/operator, location
	111836	NA AT-6C Harvard IIA (41-33262/ G-TSIX) [JZ-6]	The Real Aeroplane Company, Breighton
	111989	Cessna L-19A Bird Dog (51-11989/ N33600)	Museum of Army Flying, Middle Wallop
	115042	NA T-6G Texan (51-15042/ G-BGHU) [TA-042]	Privately owned, Headcorn
	115302	Piper L-18C Super Cub (51-15302/ G-BJTP) [TP]	Privately owned, Bidford
	115684	Piper L-21A Super Cub (51-15684/ G-BKVM) [DC]	Privately owned, Woodhall Spa
	122351	Beech C-45G (51-11665/G-BKRG)	Privately owned, Bruntingthorpe
	124143	Douglas AD-4NA Skyraider (F-AZDP) [205-RM]	Amicale J-B Salis, la Ferté-Alais, France
	124485	Boeing B-17G Fortress (44-85784/ G-BEDF) [DF-A]	B-17 Preservation Ltd, Duxford
	124724	CV F4U-5NL Corsair (F-AZEG) [22]	Amicale J-B Salis, la Ferté-Alais, France
	126922	Douglas AD-4NA Skyraider (G-RAID) [402-AK]	The Fighter Collection, Duxford
	126956	Douglas AD-4NA Skyraider (F-AZDQ) [3-RM]	Aéro Retro, St Rambert d'Albon, France
	127002	Douglas AD-4NA Skyraider (F-AZHK) [618-G]	Privately owned, le Castellet, France
	138179	NA T-28A Trojan (OE-ESA) [BA]	Tyrolean Jet Services, Innsbruck, Austria
	140547	NA T-28C Trojan (N2800Q)	Privately owned
	146289	NA T-28C Trojan (N99153) [2W]	Norfolk & Suffolk Aviation Museum, Flixton
	150225	WS58 Wessex 60 (G-AWOX) [123]	Privately owned, Lulsgate
	151632	NA TB-25N Mitchell (44-30925/ G-BWGR)	Privately owned, Sandtoft
	155529	McD F-4S Phantom (ZE359) [AJ-114]	American Air Museum, Duxford
	155848	McD F-4S Phantom [WT-11]	Royal Scottish Mus'm of Flight, E Fortune
	159233	HS AV-8A Harrier [CG-33]	FAA Museum, stored RNAS Yeovilton
	162068	McD AV-8B Harrier II (9250M) (fuselage)	RAF Cottesmore BDRT
	162071	McD AV-8B Harrier II (fuselage)	Rolls-Royce, Filton
	211072	Boeing-Stearman PT-17 Kaydet (N50755)	Privately owned, Swanton Morley
	217786	Boeing-Stearman PT-17 Kaydet (41-8169/CF-EQS) [25]	American Air Museum, Duxford
	219993	Bell P-39Q Airacobra (42-19993/ N139DP)	The Fighter Collection
	226413	Republic P-47D Thunderbolt (45-49192/N47DD) [ZU-N]	American Air Museum, Duxford
	226671	Republic P-47M Thunderbolt (G-THUN) [LH-X,MX-X]	The Fighter Collection, Duxford
	231983	Boeing B-17G Fortress (44-83735/ F-BDRS) [IY-G]	American Air Museum, Duxford
	234539	Fairchild PT-19B Cornell (42-34539/N50429) [63]	Privately owned, Dunkeswell
	237123	Waco CG-4A Hadrian (BAPC 157) (fuselage)	Yorkshire Air Museum, Elvington
	238410	Piper L-4A Grasshopper (42-38410/G-BHPK) [44-A]	Privately owned, Tibenham
	243809	Waco CG-4A Hadrian (BAPC 185)	Museum of Army Flying, Middle Wallop
	252983	Schweizer TG-3A (42-52983/ N66630)	American Air Museum, Duxford
	269097	Bell P-63A Kingcobra (42-69097/ G-BTWR)	The Fighter Collection, Duxford
	290321	Douglas C-53C Skytrooper (43-2022/N32MS)	Bevrijdende Vleugels, Eindhoven, The Netherlands
	292912	Douglas C-47A Skytrain (42-23838/N47FK) [L4-S]	Privately owned, North Weald
	314887	Fairchild Argus III (43-14887/ G-AJPI)	Privately owned, Swanton Morley
	315211	Douglas C-47A (43-15211/ N1944A) [J8-Z]	Privately owned, Booker
	315509	Douglas C-47A (43-15509/ G-BHUB) [W7-S]	American Air Museum, Duxford
	329405	Piper L-4H Grasshopper (43-29405/G-BCOB) [23-A]	Privately owned, South Walsham
	329417	Piper L-4A Grasshopper (42-38400/G-BDHK)	Privately owned, Coleford
	329471	Piper L-4H Grasshopper (43-29471/G-BGXA) [44-F]	Privately owned, Martley, Worcs

Serial	Type (other identity)	Owner/operator, location	Notes
329601	Piper L-4H Grasshopper (43-29601/G-AXHR) [44-D]	Privately owned, Nayland	
329854	Piper L-4H Grasshopper (43-29854/G-BMKC) [44-R]	Privately owned, St Just	
329934	Piper L-4H Grasshopper (43-29934/G-BCPH) [72-B]	Privately owned, White Waltham	
330238	Piper L-4H Grasshopper (43-30238/G-LIVH) [24-A]	Privately owned, Barton	
330485	Piper L-4H Grasshopper (43-30485/G-AJES) [44-C]	Privately owned, Shifnal	
343251	Boeing-Stearman N2S-5 Kaydet (43517/G-NZSS) [27]	Privately owned, Swanton Morley	
413573	NA P-51D Mustang (44-73415/ 9133M/N6526D) [B6-V]	RAF Museum, Hendon	
414151	NA P-51D Mustang (44-73140/ NL314BG) [HO-M]	Flying A Services, North Weald	
434602	Douglas A-26B Invader (44-34602/ N167B) [S]	Scandinavian Historic Flight, North Weald	
435710	Douglas A-26C Invader (44-35710/ N7705C)	Historic Invader Avn, Schiphol, The Netherlands	
436021	Piper J-3C Cub 65 (G-BWEZ)	Privately owned, Cumbernauld	
442268	Noorduyn AT-16 Harvard IIB (KF568/LN-TEX) [TA-268]	Scandinavian Historic Flight, Oslo, Norway	
454467	Piper L-4J Grasshopper (45-4467/ G-BILI) [44-J]	Privately owned, White Waltham	
454537	Piper L-4J Grasshopper (45-4537/ G-BFDL) [04-J]	Privately owned, Pontefract	
461748	Boeing B-29A Superfortress (44-61748/G-BHDK) [Y]	American Air Museum, Duxford	
463209	NA P-51D Mustang <R> (BAPC 255) [WZ-S]	American Air Museum, Duxford	
463221	NA P-51D Mustang (44-73149/ G-BTCD) [E2-Z]	The Old Flying Machine Company, Duxford	
472035	NA P-51D Mustang (44-72035/ F-AZMU)	Aéro Retro, St Rambert d'Albon, France	
472216	NA P-51D Mustang (44-72216/ G-BIXL) [AJ-L]	Privately owned, North Weald	
472218	CAC-18 Mustang 22 (A68-192/ G-HAEC) [WZ-I]	Privately owned, Woodchurch, Kent	
472258	NA P-51D Mustang (44-73979) [WZ-I]	Imperial War Museum, Lambeth	
472773	NA P-51D Mustang (44-72773/ G-SUSY) [QP-M]	Privately owned, Sywell	
473877	NA P-51D Mustang (44-73877/ N167F) [E2-D]	Scandinavian Historic Flight, North Weald	
474008	NA P-51D Mustang (44-73339/ G-SIRR) [VF-R]	Intrepid Aviation, North Weald	
474425	NA P-51D Mustang (44-74425/ NL11T) [OC-G]	Dutch Mustang Flt, Lelystad, The Netherlands	
474832	NA P-51D Mustang (44-74506/ F-AZJJ) [GA-N]	Air B Aviation, Marmaz, France	
474923	NA P-51D Mustang (44-74923/ N6395)	Privately owned, Lelystad, The Netherlands	
479744	Piper L-4H Grasshopper (44-79744/G-BGPD) [49-M]	Privately owned, Marsh, Bucks	
479766	Piper L-4H Grasshopper (44-79766/G-BKHG) [63-D]	Privately owned, Goldcliff, Gwent	
480015	Piper L-4H Grasshopper (44-80015/G-AKIB) [44-M]	Privately owned, Bodmin	
480133	Piper L-4J Grasshopper (44-80133/G-BDCD) [44-B]	Privately owned, Slinfold	
480321	Piper L-4J Grasshopper (44-80321/G-FRAN) [44-H]	Privately owned, Rayne, Essex	
480480	Piper L-4J Grasshopper (44-80480/G-BECN) [44-E]	Privately owned, Kersey, Suffolk	
480551	Piper L-4J Grasshopper (44-80551/LN-KLT) [43-S]	Scandinavian Historic Flight, Oslo, Norway	
480636	Piper L-4J Grasshopper (44-80636/G-AXHP) [58-A]	Privately owned, Southend	
480752	Piper L-4J Grasshopper (44-80752/G-BCXJ) [39-E]	Privately owned, Old Sarum	
483868	Boeing B-17G Fortress (44-83868/N5237V) [A-N]	RAF Museum, Hendon	
486893	NA B-25J Mitchell (N6123C)	Tyrolean Jet Services, Innsbruck, Austria	

Historic Aircraft

Notes	Serial	Type (other identity)	Owner/operator, location
	493209	NA T-6G Texan (49-3209/ G-DDMV/41)	Privately owned, Sywell
	511701A	Beech C-45H (51-11701/G-BSZC) [AF258]	Privately owned, Bryngwyn Bach
	607327	PA-18 Super Cub 95 (G-ARAO) [09-L]	Privately owned, Denham
	2106449	NA P-51C Mustang (43-25147/ N51PR/G-PSIC) [HO-W]	The Fighter Collection, Duxford
	2-134	NA T-6G Texan (114700)	Privately owned, North Weald
	3-1923	Aeronca O-58B Defender (43-1923/G-BRHP)	Privately owned, Chiseldon
	18-2001	Piper L-18C Super Cub (52-2401/ G-BIZV)	Privately owned, Oxenhope
	39-139	Beech YC-43 Traveler (N295BS)	Dukes of Brabant AF, Eindhoven, The Netherlands
	40-1766	Boeing-Stearman PT-17 Kaydet	Privately owned, Swanton Morley
	41-33275	NA AT-6C Texan (G-BICE) [CE]	Privately owned, Ipswich
	42-40557	Consolidated B-24D Liberator <ff>	American Air Museum, Duxford
	42-58678	Taylorcraft DF-65 (G-BRIY) [IY]	Privately owned, North Weald
	42-78044	Aeronca 11AC Chief (G-BRXL)	Privately owned, High Cross, Herts
	42-84555	NA AT-6D Harvard III (FAP.1662/ G-ELMH) [EP-H]	Privately owned, Hardwick, Norfolk
	42-93510	Douglas C-47A Skytrain [CM] <ff>	Privately owned, Kew
	43-9628	Douglas A-20G Havoc <ff>	Privately owned, Hinckley, Leics
	44-14291	NA P-51D Mustang	Classic Warbirds, Norwich
	44-14574	NA P-51D Mustang (fuselage)	East Essex Aviation Museum, Clacton
	44-51228	Consolidated B-24M Liberator [RE-N]	American Air Museum, Duxford
	44-79609	Piper L-4H Grasshopper (G-BHXY) [PR]	Privately owned, Bodmin
	44-80594	Piper L-4J Grasshopper (G-BEDJ)	Privately owned, White Waltham
	44-83184	Fairchild UC-61K Argus III (G-RGUS)	Privately owned, Lincs
	49-1217	NA F-86A Sabre (G-BZNL)	The Fighter Collection, Duxford
	51-14526	NA T-6G Texan (G-BRWB)	Monafield Ltd, Audley End
	51-15227	NA T-6G Texan (G-BKRA) [10]	Privately owned, Shoreham
	52-8543	CCF T-6J Harvard IV (G-BUKY) [66]	Privately owned, Breighton
	54-223	NA F-100D Super Sabre (54-2223)	Newark Air Museum, Winthorpe
	54-2447	Piper L-21B Super Cub (G-SCUB)	Privately owned, Anwick
	54-21261	Lockheed T-33A-N Silver Star (N33VC/G-TBRD)	Golden Apple Operations/OFMC, Duxford
	63-699	McD F-4C Phantom (63-7699) [CG]	Midland Air Museum, Coventry
	64-17657	Douglas A-26A Invader (N99218) <ff>	Tower Museum, Ludham, Norfolk
	65-777	McD F-4C Phantom (63-7419) [LN]	RAF Lakenheath, on display
	67-120	GD F-111E Aardvark [UH]	American Air Museum, Duxford
	68-0060	GD F-111E Aardvark <ff>	Dumfries & Galloway Avn Mus, Dumfries
	72-1447	GD F-111F Aardvark <ff>	American Air Museum, Duxford
	72-448	GD F-111E Aardvark (68-0011) [LN]	RAF Lakenheath, on display
	76-124	McD F-15B Eagle [LN]	RAF Lakenheath, instructional use
	77-259	Fairchild A-10A Thunderbolt [AR]	American Air Museum, Duxford
	80-219	Fairchild GA-10A Thunderbolt [AR]	RAF Alconbury, on display
	92-048	McD F-15A Eagle (74-0131) [LN]	RAF Lakenheath, on display
	146-11042	Wolf WII <R> (G-BMZX) [7]	Privately owned, Haverfordwest
	146-11083	Wolf WII <R> (G-BNAI) [5]	Privately owned, Haverfordwest
	998-8888	Bell UH-1H Iroquois (Arg. AE-406)	Museum of Army Flying, Middle Wallop
	H-57	Piper L-4A Grasshopper (42-36375/G-AKAZ)	Privately owned, Duxford

YUGOSLAVIA

	23170	Soko G-2A Galeb (YU-YAB)	Privately owned, Biggin Hill
	23187	Soko G-2A Galeb (YU-YAD)	Privately owned, Biggin Hill
	23194	Soko G-2A Galeb (YU-YAG)	Privately owned, Biggin Hill
	23196	Soko G-2A Galeb (YU-YAC)	Privately owned, Biggin Hill
	30139	Soko P-2 Kraguj [139]	Privately owned, Biggin Hill
	30140	Soko P-2 Kraguj (G-RADA) [140]	Privately owned, Biggin Hill
	30146	Soko P-2 Kraguj (G-BSXD) [146]	Privately owned, Elstree
	30149	Soko P-2 Kraguj (G-SOKO) [149]	Privately owned, Liverpool
	30151	Soko P-2 Kraguj [151]	Privately owned, Bournemouth
	51182	UTVA-66 (YU-DMN)	Privately owned, Biggin Hill
	51183	UTVA-66 (YU-DMT)	Privately owned, Biggin Hill

Fokker Dr.1 Triplane and RAF SE5a replicas, part of the Great Warbirds Display team. *PRM*

Famous B-17 Flying Fortress 'Sally B' escorted by a pair of P-51D Mustangs over Duxford. *Daniel March*

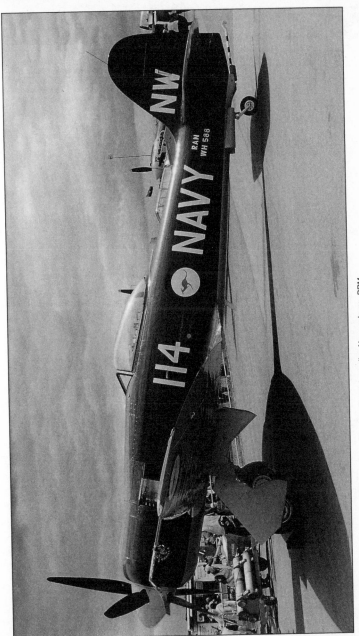

Paul Morgan's immaculate Sea Fury FB11 WH588 is painted in Royal Australian Navy colours. *PRM*

Irish Military Aircraft Markings

Notes	Serial	Type (other identity)	Owner/operator, location
	34	Miles M14A Magister (N5392)	IAC Engineering Wing stored, Baldonnel
	141	Avro 652A Anson C19	IAC Engineering Wing stored, Baldonnel
	164	DHC1 Chipmunk T20	IAC Engineering Wing stored, Baldonnel
	168	DHC1 Chipmunk T20	IAC No 2 Support Wing, Gormanston
	172	DHC1 Chipmunk T20	IAC Training Wing stored, Gormanston
	176	DH104 Dove 4 (VP-YKF)	Privately owned,
	177	Percival P56 Provost T51 (G-BLIW)	Privately owned, Shoreham
	183	Percival P56 Provost T51	IAC Engineering Wing stored, Baldonnel
	184	Percival P56 Provost T51	South East Aviation Enthusiasts, Waterford
	187	DH115 Vampire T55	Av'n Society of Ireland, stored, Waterford
	189	Percival P56 Provost T51 (comp XF846)	IAC Baldonnel Fire Section
	191	DH115 Vampire T55	IAC Museum, Baldonnel
	192	DH115 Vampire T55	South East Aviation Enthusiasts, Waterford
	193	DH115 Vampire T55 <ff>	IAC Baldonnel Fire Section
	195	Sud SA316 Alouette III	IAC No 3 Support Wing, Baldonnel
	196	Sud SA316 Alouette III	IAC No 3 Support Wing, Baldonnel
	197	Sud SA316 Alouette III	IAC No 3 Support Wing, Baldonnel
	198	DH115 Vampire T11 (XE977)	IAC Engineering Wing stored, Baldonnel
	199	DHC1 Chipmunk T22	IAC Training Wing store, Gormanston (spares)
	202	Sud SA316 Alouette III	IAC No 3 Support Wing, Baldonnel (under repair)
	203	Reims-Cessna FR172H	IAC No 2 Support Wing, Gormanston
	205	Reims-Cessna FR172H	IAC No 2 Support Wing, Gormanston
	206	Reims-Cessna FR172H	IAC No 2 Support Wing, Gormanston
	207	Reims-Cessna FR172H	IAC Engineering Wing, stored, Waterford
	208	Reims-Cessna FR172H	IAC No 2 Support Wing, Gormanston
	209	Reims-Cessna FR172H	IAC No 2 Support Wing, Gormanston, wfu
	210	Reims-Cessna FR172H	IAC No 2 Support Wing, Gormanston
	211	Sud SA316 Alouette III	IAC No 3 Support Wing, Baldonnel
	212	Sud SA316 Alouette III	IAC No 3 Support Wing, Baldonnel
	213	Sud SA316 Alouette III	IAC No 3 Support Wing, Baldonnel
	214	Sud SA316 Alouette III	IAC No 3 Support Wing, Baldonnel
	215	Fouga CM170 Super Magister	IAC, stored Baldonnel
	216	Fouga CM170 Super Magister	IAC Engineering Wing, Baldonnel
	217	Fouga CM170 Super Magister	IAC, stored Baldonnel
	218	Fouga CM170 Super Magister	IAC, stored Baldonnel
	219	Fouga CM170 Super Magister	IAC, stored Baldonnel
	220	Fouga CM170 Super Magister	IAC, stored Baldonnel
	222	SIAI SF-260WE Warrior	IAC Training Wing, Baldonnel
	225	SIAI SF-260WE Warrior	IAC Training Wing, Baldonnel
	226	SIAI SF-260WE Warrior	IAC Training Wing, Baldonnel
	227	SIAI SF-260WE Warrior	IAC Training Wing, Baldonnel
	229	SIAI SF-260WE Warrior	IAC Training Wing, Baldonnel
	230	SIAI SF-260WE Warrior	IAC Training Wing, Baldonnel
	231	SIAI SF-260WE Warrior	IAC Training Wing, Baldonnel
	237	Aérospatiale SA342L Gazelle	IAC No 3 Support Wing, Baldonnel
	240	Beech Super King Air 200MR	IAC No 1 Support Wing, Baldonnel
	241	Aérospatiale SA342L Gazelle	IAC No 3 Support Wing, Baldonnel
	243	Reims-Cessna FR172K	IAC No 2 Support Wing, Gormanston
	244	Aérospatiale SA365F Dauphin II	IAC No 3 Support Wing, Baldonnel
	245	Aérospatiale SA365F Dauphin II	IAC No 3 Support Wing, Baldonnel
	246	Aérospatiale SA365F Dauphin II	IAC No 3 Support Wing, Baldonnel
	247	Aérospatiale SA365F Dauphin II	IAC No 3 Support Wing, Baldonnel
	251	Grumman G1159C Gulfstream IV	IAC No 1 Support Wing, Baldonnel
	252	Airtech CN.235 MPA Persuader	IAC No 1 Support Wing, Baldonnel
	253	Airtech CN.235 MPA Persuader	IAC No 1 Support Wing, Baldonnel
	254	PBN-2T Defender 4000 (G-BWPN)	Garda Air Support Unit, Baldonnel
	255	AS355N Twin Squirrel (G-BXEV)	Garda Air Support Unit, Baldonnel

Overseas Military Aircraft Markings

Aircraft included in this section are a selection of those likely to be seen visiting UK civil and military airfields on transport flights, exchange visits, exercises and for air shows. It is not a comprehensive list of *all* aircraft operated by the air arms concerned.

ALGERIA
Force Aérienne Algérienne/
Al Quwwat al Jawwiya al
Jaza'eriya
Lockheed C-130H
Hercules
7T-WHE	(4935)
7T-WHF	(4934)
7T-WHI	(4930)
7T-WHJ	(4928)
7T-WHQ	(4926)
7T-WHR	(4924)
7T-WHS	(4912)
7T-WHT	(4911)
7T-WHY	(4913)
7T-WHZ	(4914)

Lockheed C-130H-30
Hercules
7T-WHA	(4997)
7T-WHB	(5224)
7T-WHD	(4987)
7T-WHL	(4989)
7T-WHM	(4919)
7T-WHN	(4894)
7T-WHO	(4897)
7T-WHP	(4921)

Algerian Govt
Dassault Falcon 900
Ministry of Defence, Boufarik
7T-VPA	(81)
7T-VPB	(82)

Grumman G.1159A
Gulfstream III
Ministry of Defence, Boufarik
7T-VRD	(399)

Grumman G.1159C
Gulfstream IVSP
Ministry of Defence, Boufarik
7T-VPR	(1288)
7T-VPS	(1291)

AUSTRALIA
Royal Australian Air Force
Boeing 707-338C/368C*
33 Sqn, Amberley
A20-261*
A20-623
A20-624
A20-627
A20-629

Lockheed C-130H
Hercules
36 Sqn, Richmond, NSW
A97-001
A97-002
A97-003

A97-004
A97-005
A97-006
A97-007
A97-008
A97-009
A97-010
A97-011
A97-012

Lockheed C-130J-30
Hercules
37 Sqn, Richmond, NSW
A97-440
A97-441
A97-442
A97-447
A97-448
A97-449
A97-450
A97-464
A97-465
A97-466
A97-467
A97-468

Lockheed P-3C Orion
10/11 Sqns, Maritime Patrol
  Group, Edinburgh, NSW
A9-656	10 Sqn
A9-657	11 Sqn
A9-658	10 Sqn
A9-659	11 Sqn
A9-660	10 Sqn
A9-661	10 Sqn
A9-662	11 Sqn
A9-663	11 Sqn
A9-664	11 Sqn
A9-665	10 Sqn
A9-751	11 Sqn
A9-752	10 Sqn
A9-753	10 Sqn
A9-755	11 Sqn
A9-756	11 Sqn
A9-757	10 Sqn
A9-758	10 Sqn
A9-759	10 Sqn
A9-760	10 Sqn

AUSTRIA
Öesterreichische
Luftstreitkräfte
Airtech CN.235-300
Fliegerregiment I
Flachenstaffel, Tulln
6T-AA

SAAB 35ÖE Draken
Fliegerregiment II
  1 Staffel/Uberwg, Zeltweg;
  2 Staffel/Uberwg, Graz
01	(351401)	1 Staffel
02	(351402)	1 Staffel
03	(351403)	1 Staffel
04	(351404)	1 Staffel
05	(351405)	1 Staffel
06	(351406)	1 Staffel
07	(351407)	1 Staffel
08	(351408)	1 Staffel
09	(351409)	1 Staffel
10	(351410)	1 Staffel
11	(351411)	1 Staffel
12	(351412)	1 Staffel
13	(351413)	2 Staffel
14	(351414)	2 Staffel
15	(351415)	2 Staffel
16	(351416)	2 Staffel
18	(351418)	2 Staffel
19	(351419)	2 Staffel
20	(351420)	2 Staffel
21	(351421)	2 Staffel
22	(351422)	2 Staffel
23	(351423)	2 Staffel
24	(351424)	2 Staffel

SAAB 105ÖE
Dusenstastaffel, Linz
(yellow)
B	(105402)
D	(105404)
E	(105405)
F	(105406)
G	(105407)
I	(105409)
J	(105410)

(green)
A	(105411)
B	(105412)
D	(105414)
GF-16	(105416)
GG-17	(105417)

(red)
B	(105422)
C	(105423)
D	(105424)
E	(105425)
F	(105426)
G	(105427)
H	(105428)
I	(105429)
J	(105430)

(blue)
A	(105431)
B	(105432)
C	(105433)
D	(105434)
E	(105435)
F	(105436)
G	(105437)
I	(105439)
J	(105440)

Short SC7 Skyvan 3M
Fliegerregiment I
Flachenstaffel, Tulln
5S-TA
5S-TB

BAHRAIN
Boeing 727-2M7
Govt of Bahrain
A9C-BA

Boeing 747SP-21
Bahrain Amiri Flt
A9C-HHH

Grumman
G.1159 Gulfstream IITT
G.1159C Gulfstream IV
Govt of Bahrain
A9C-BAH Gulfstream IV
A9C-BG Gulfstream IITT

BELGIUM
Force Aérienne Belge/
Belgische Luchtmacht
D-BD Alpha Jet E
7/11 Smaldeel (1 Wg),
Bevekom
AT-01
AT-03
AT-05
AT-06
AT-08
AT-10
AT-11
AT-12
AT-13
AT-14
AT-15
AT-17
AT-18
AT-19
AT-20
AT-21
AT-22
AT-23
AT-24
AT-25
AT-26
AT-27
AT-28
AT-29
AT-30
AT-31
AT-32
AT-33

Airbus A.310-322
21 Smaldeel (15 Wg),
Melsbroek
CA-01
CA-02

Dassault Falcon 900B
21 Smaldeel (15 Wg),
Melsbroek
CD-01

Swearingen Merlin IIIA
21 Smaldeel (15 Wg),
Melsbroek
CF-01
CF-02

CF-04
CF-05
CF-06

Lockheed C-130H Hercules
20 Smaldeel (15 Wg),
Melsbroek
CH-01
CH-02
CH-03
CH-04
CH-05
CH-07
CH-08
CH-09
CH-10
CH-11
CH-12

Dassault Falcon 20E
21 Smaldeel (15 Wg),
Melsbroek
CM-01
CM-02

Hawker-Siddeley
HS748 Srs 2A
21 Smaldeel (15 Wg),
Melsbroek
CS-01
CS-02
CS-03

General Dynamics F-16
(MLU aircraft are marked
with a *)
1,2,350 Smaldeel (2 Wg),
Florennes [FS];
23,31,349 Smaldeel, OCU
(10 Wg), Kleine-Brogel
[BL]

FA-27	F-16A(R)	2 Wg
FA-46	F-16A	2 Wg
FA-47	F-16A	2 Wg
FA-48	F-16A*	2 Wg
FA-49	F-16A(R)	2 Wg
FA-50	F-16A	2 Wg
FA-53	F-16A(R)	10 Wg
FA-55	F-16A	2 Wg
FA-56	F-16A*	10 Wg
FA-57	F-16A*	10 Wg
FA-58	F-16A*	2 Wg
FA-60	F-16A*	10 Wg
FA-61	F-16A*	10 Wg
FA-65	F-16A*	10 Wg
FA-66	F-16A	10 Wg
FA-67	F-16A*	2 Wg
FA-68	F-16A	2 Sm
FA-69	F-16A	31 Sm
FA-70	F-16A*	10 Wg
FA-71	F-16A*	2 Wg
FA-72	F-16A	2 Wg
FA-73	F-16A*	10 Wg
FA-74	F-16A*	10 Wg
FA-75	F-16A*	2 Wg
FA-76	F-16A*	10 Wg
FA-77	F-16A*	10 Wg
FA-78	F-16A*	10 Wg
FA-81	F-16A*	10 Wg
FA-82	F-16A*	10 Wg
FA-83	F-16A*	10 Wg
FA-84	F-16A	10 Wg
FA-86	F-16A*	10 Wg
FA-87	F-16A	2 Wg
FA-88	F-16A	2 Wg
FA-89	F-16A	10 Wg
FA-90	F-16A*	10 Wg
FA-91	F-16A*	10 Wg
FA-92	F-16A(R)	10 Wg
FA-93	F-16A*	10 Wg
FA-94	F-16A*	2 Wg
FA-95	F-16A	10 Wg
FA-96	F-16A	10 Wg
FA-97	F-16A*	10 Wg
FA-98	F-16A*	10 Wg
FA-99	F-16A*	10 Wg
FA-100	F-16A*	10 Wg
FA-101	F-16A*	10 Wg
FA-102	F-16A*	10 Wg
FA-103	F-16A*	349 Sm
FA-104	F-16A*	2 Wg
FA-106	F-16A	2 Wg
FA-107	F-16A	2 Wg
FA-108	F-16A*	2 Wg
FA-109	F-16A	2 Wg
FA-110	F-16A	2 Wg
FA-111	F-16A	10 Wg
FA-112	F-16A*	10 Wg
FA-114	F-16A	10 Wg
FA-115	F-16A*	2 Wg
FA-116	F-16A	2 Wg
FA-117	F-16A	2 Wg
FA-118	F-16A	2 Sm
FA-119	F-16A	2 Wg
FA-120	F-16A*	10 Wg
FA-121	F-16A	2 Wg
FA-122	F-16A*	10 Wg
FA-123	F-16A	2 Wg
FA-124	F-16A	10 Wg
FA-125	F-16A	2 Wg
FA-126	F-16A*	10 Wg
FA-127	F-16A	2 Wg
FA-128	F-16A	2 Wg
FA-129	F-16A	2 Wg
FA-130	F-16A	2 Wg
FA-131	F-16A(R)	2 Wg
FA-132	F-16A	2 Wg
FA-133	F-16A	2 Wg
FA-134	F-16A	2 Wg
FA-135	F-16A	2 Wg
FA-136	F-16A	10 Wg
FB-01	F-16B	2 Wg
FB-02	F-16B	OCU
FB-04	F-16B*	OCU
FB-05	F-16B	2 Wg
FB-07	F-16B	2 Wg
FB-08	F-16B	OCU
FB-09	F-16B	OCU
FB-10	F-16B	10 Wg
FB-12	F-16B	2 Wg
FB-14	F-16B*	10 Wg
FB-15	F-16B*	OCU
FB-17	F-16B*	OCU
FB-18	F-16B*	2 Wg
FB-19	F-16B	10 Wg
FB-20	F-16B	2 Wg
FB-21	F-16B*	10 Wg
FB-22	F-16B*	OCU
FB-23	F-16B	10 Wg
FB-24	F-16B	OCU

Fouga CM170 Magister
Fouga Flight/7 Smaldeel
(1 Wg), Bevekom
MT-04
MT-13
MT-14
MT-26

MT-34
MT-35
MT-40
MT-44
MT-48

**Westland Sea King
Mk48/48A***
40 Smaldeel, Koksijde
RS-01
RS-02
RS-03*
RS-04
RS-05

**SIAI Marchetti
SF260MB/SF260D***
Ecole de Pilotage
Elementaire (5 Sm/1 Wg),
Bevekom
ST-02
ST-03
ST-04
ST-06
ST-12
ST-15
ST-16
ST-17
ST-18
ST-19
ST-20
ST-22
ST-23
ST-24
ST-25
ST-26
ST-27
ST-31
ST-32
ST-34
ST-35
ST-36
ST-40*
ST-41*
ST-42*
ST-43*
ST-44*
ST-45*
ST-46*
ST-47*
ST-48*

**Aviation Légère de la
Force Terrestre/
Belgische Landmacht
Sud SA318C/SE3130*
Alouette II**
16 BnHLn, Bierset;
SLV, Brasschaat
A-22* 16 BnHLn
A-37* 16 BnHLn
A-40 SLV
A-41 SLV
A-42 16 BnHLn
A-43 16 BnHLn
A-44 SLV
A-46 16 BnHLn
A-47 16 BnHLn
A-49 16 BnHLn
A-50 16 BnHLn
A-53 16 BnHLn
A-54 SLV
A-55 SLV
A-57 SLV

A-59 16 BnHLn
A-61 SLV
A-62 16 BnHLn
A-64 SLV
A-65 SLV
A-66 SLV
A-68 16 BnHLn
A-69 16 BnHLn
A-70 SLV
A-72 SLV
A-73 16 BnHLn
A-74 SLV
A-75 16 BnHLn
A-77 16 BnHLn
A-78 16 BnHLn
A-79 SLV
A-80 16 BnHLn

**Britten-Norman
BN-2A/BN-2B-21* Islander**
16 BnHLn, Bierset;
SLV, Brasschaat
B-01 LA SLV
B-02* LB SLV
B-03* LC 16 BnHLn
B-04* LD SLV
B-07* LG 16 BnHLn
B-08* LH 16 BnHLn
B-09* LI 16 BnHLn
B-10* LJ 16 BnHLn
B-11* LK 16 BnHLn
B-12 LL SLV

Agusta A109HA/HO*
17 BnHATk, Bierset;
18 BnHATk, Bierset;
SLV, Brasschaat
H-01* SLV
H-02* SLV
H-03* SLV
H-04* 17 BnHATk
H-05* 17 BnHATk
H-06* 17 BnHATk
H-07* 17 BnHATk
H-08* 18 BnHATk
H-09* 18 BnHATk
H-10* 18 BnHATk
H-11* SLV
H-12* SLV
H-13* SLV
H-14* SLV
H-15* SLV
H-16* 18 BnHATk
H-17* 17 BnHATk
H-18* 18 BnHATk
H-20 18 BnHATk
H-21 18 BnHATk
H-22 17 BnHATk
H-23 18 BnHATk
H-24 17 BnHATk
H-25 18 BnHATk
H-26 18 BnHATk
H-27 18 BnHATk
H-28 18 BnHATk
H-29 18 BnHATk
H-30 18 BnHATk
H-31 18 BnHATk
H-32 18 BnHATk
H-33 18 BnHATk
H-34 17 BnHATk
H-35 18 BnHATk
H-36 17 BnHATk
H-37 17 BnHATk
H-38 17 BnHATk

H-39 18 BnHATk
H-40 SLV
H-41 17 BnHATk
H-42 17 BnHATk
H-43 17 BnHATk
H-44 17 BnHATk
H-45 17 BnHATk
H-46 17 BnHATk

**Force Navale Belge/Belgische
Zeemacht
Sud SA316B Alouette III**
Koksijde Heli Flight
M-1 (OT-ZPA)
M-2 (OT-ZPB)
M-3 (OT-ZPC)

**Gendarmerie/Rijkswacht
Britten-Norman PBN-2T
Islander**
Luchtsteundetachment,
Melsbroek
G-05 (OT-GLA)

Cessna 182 Skylane
Luchtsteundetachment,
Melsbroek
G-01 C.182Q
G-03 C.182R
G-04 C.182R

MDH MD.520N
Luchtsteundetachment,
Melsbroek
G-14
G-15

MDH MD.900 Explorer
Luchtsteundetachment,
Melsbroek
G-10
G-11

Sud Alouette II
Luchtsteundetachment,
Melsbroek
G-93
G-94

**BOTSWANA
Botswana Defence Force
Grumman G.1159C
Gulfstream IV**
OK-1

Lockheed C-130B Hercules
OM-1
OM-2
OM-3

**BRAZIL
Força Aérea Brasileira
Boeing KC-137**
2° GT 2° Esq, Galeão
2401
2402
2403
2404

Lockheed C-130E Hercules
1° GT, 1° Esq, Galeão;
1° GTT, 1° Esq, Afonsos
2451 C-130E 1° GTT
2453 C-130E 1° GTT

2454	C-130E	1° GTT
2455	C-130E	1° GTT
2456	C-130E	1° GTT
2458	SC-130E	1° GT
2459	SC-130E	1° GT
2461	KC-130H	1° GT
2462	KC-130H	1° GT
2463	C-130H	1° GT
2464	C-130H	1° GT
2465	C-130H	1° GT
2467	C-130H	1° GT

BRUNEI
Airbus A.340
Brunei Govt, Bandar Seri
  Bergawan
V8-BKH   A.340-212
V8-JBB   A.340-213

Boeing 747-430
Brunei Govt, Bandar Seri
  Bergawan
V8-AL1

Boeing 767-27GER
Brunei Govt, Bandar Seri
  Bergawan
V8-MHB

Gulfstream Aerospace
Gulfstream V
Brunei Govt, Bandar Seri
  Bergawan
V8-007

BULGARIA
Bulgarsky Voenno-
Vazdushni Sily
  Antonov An-30
  16 TAP, Sofia/Dobroslavtzi
  055

Bulgarian Govt
Dassault Falcon 50
Bulgarian Govt, Sofia
LZ-011

Tupolev Tu-154M
Bulgarian Govt, Sofia
LZ-BTQ

BURKINA FASO
Boeing 727-14
Govt of Burkina Faso,
  Ouagadougou
XT-BBE

CAMEROON
Grumman G.1159A
Gulfstream III
Govt of Cameroon, Yaounde
TJ-AAW

CANADA
Canadian Forces
Lockheed CC-130/
CC-130E/CC-130E(SAR)*
Hercules
413 Sqn, Greenwood (SAR)
  (14 Wing);
424 Sqn, Trenton (SAR)
  (8 Wing);
426 Sqn, Trenton (8 Wing);

429 Sqn, Trenton (8 Wing);
435 Sqn, Winnipeg
  (17 Wing);
436 Sqn, Trenton (8 Wing)

130305*	8 Wing
130306*	14 Wing
130307	8 Wing
130308*	8 Wing
130310*	14 Wing
130311*	14 Wing
130313	8 Wing
130314*	14 Wing
130315*	14 Wing
130316	8 Wing
130317	8 Wing
130319	8 Wing
130320	8 Wing
130323	8 Wing
130324*	8 Wing
130325	8 Wing
130326	8 Wing
130327	8 Wing
130328	8 Wing

CC-130H/CC-130H(T)*

130332	17 Wing
130333	17 Wing
130334	8 Wing
130335	8 Wing
130336	17 Wing
130337	8 Wing
130338*	17 Wing
130339*	17 Wing
130340*	17 Wing
130341*	17 Wing
130342*	17 Wing

CC-130H-30

130343	8 Wing
130344	8 Wing

Lockheed CP-140 Aurora/
CP-140A Arcturus*
404/405/415 Sqns,
  Greenwood (14 Wing);
407 Sqn, Comox (19 Wing)

140101		14 Wing
140102		14 Wing
140103		407 Sqn
140104		14 Wing
140105	[LQ-Y]	14 Wing
140106		407 Sqn
140107		407 Sqn
140108		14 Wing
140109		14 Wing
140110		14 Wing
140111		14 Wing
140112		407 Sqn
140113		14 Wing
140114	[GX-N]	14 Wing
140115		407 Sqn
140116		407 Sqn
140117		14 Wing
140118		407 Sqn
140119*		14 Wing
140120*		14 Wing
140121*		14 Wing

De Havilland Canada
CC-142
402 Sqn, Winnipeg
  (17 Wing)

142801	CC-142
142802	CC-142
142803	CT-142
142804	CT-142
142805	CT-142
142806	CT-142

Canadair CC-144
Challenger
412 Sqn, Ottawa (8 Wing)

144601	CC-144A
144602	CC-144A
144604	CC-144A
144614	CC-144B
144615	CC-144B
144616	CC-144B

Airbus CC-150 Polaris
(A310-304/A310-304F*)
437 Sqn, Trenton (8 Wing)

15001	216
15002*	212
15003*	202
15004*	205
15005*	204

CHILE
Fuerza Aérea de Chile
Boeing 707
Grupo 10, Santiago

902	707-351C
903	707-330B
904	707-358C

Extra EA-300
Los Halcones

021	[6]
022	[7]
024	[2]
025	[3]
027	[4]
028	[5]
029	[1]

Lockheed C-130B/H
Hercules
Grupo 10, Santiago

994	C-130H
995	C-130H
996	C-130H
997	C-130B
998	C-130B

CROATIA
Canadair CL.601
Challenger
Croatian Govt, Zagreb
9A-CRO
9A-CRT

CZECH REPUBLIC
Ceske Vojenske Letectvo
Aero L-39/L-59 Albatros
42 slt/4 zTL, Cáslav;
321 tpzlt & 322 tlt/32 zTL,
  Náměšt;
341 vlt/34 zSL, Pardubice;
LZú, Praha/Kbely

0001	L-39MS	LZO
0004	L-39MS	LZO
0005	L-39MS	LZO
0103	L-39C	341 vlt/34 zSL
0105	L-39C	341 vlt/34 zSL
0106	L-39C	341 vlt/34 zSL
0107	L-39C	341 vlt/34 zSL
0108	L-39C	341 vlt/34 zSL
0113	L-39C	341 vlt/34 zSL
0115	L-39C	341 vlt/34 zSL

0440	L-39C	341 vlt/34 zSL
0441	L-39C	341 vlt/34 zSL
0441	L-39C	341 vlt/34 zSL
0444	L-39C	341 vlt/34 zSL
0445	L-39C	341 vlt/34 zSL
0448	L-39C	341 vlt/34 zSL
2341	L-39ZA	42 slt/4 zTL
2344	L-39ZA	42 slt/4 zTL
2347	L-39ZA	42 slt/4 zTL
2350	L-39ZA	42 slt/4 zTL
2415	L-39ZA	42 slt/4 zTL
2418	L-39ZA	42 slt/4 zTL
2421	L-39ZA	42 slt/4 zTL
2424	L-39ZA	32 zTL
2427	L-39ZA	42 slt/4 zTL
2430	L-39ZA	42 slt/4 zTL
2433	L-39ZA	42 slt/4 zTL
2436	L-39ZA	42 slt/4 zTL
3903	L-39ZA	32 zTL
4605	L-39C	341 vlt/34 zSL
4606	L-39C	341 vlt/34 zSL
5013	L-39ZA	32 zTL
5015	L-39ZA	32 zTL
5017	L-39ZA	32 zTL
5019	L-39ZA	32 zTL

Aero L-159 ALCA/L-159T*
4 zTL, Cáslav;
LZO, Praha/Kbely
5831*	LZO
5832	LZO
6001	4 zTL
6002	4 zTL
6003	4 zTL

Antonov An-24V
1 dlt/6 zDL, Praha/Kbely
7109
7110

**Antonov An-26/
An-26Z-1M***
1 dlt/6 zDL, Praha/Kbely
2408	
2409	
2507	
3209*	
4201	

Antonov An-30FG
344 pzdlt/34 zSL, Pardubice
1107

**Canadair CL.601-3A
Challenger**
1 dlt/6 zDL, Praha/Kbely
5105

Let 410 Turbolet
1 dlt/6 zDL, Praha/Kbely;
344 pzdlt/34 zSL, Pardubice
0503	L-410MA	
		344 pzdlt/34 zSL
0712	L-410UVP-S	
		344 pzdlt/34 zSL
0731	L-410UVP	
		1 dlt/6 zDL
0926	L-410UVP-T	
		1 dlt/6 zDL [4]
0928	L-410UVP-T	
		1 dlt/6 zDL
0929	L-410UVP-T	
		1 dlt/6 zDL [2]

1132	L-410UVP-T	
		1 dlt/6 zDL [3]
1134	L-410UVP	
		1 dlt/6 zDL
1504	L-410UVP	
		1 dlt/6 zDL
1523	L-410FG	
		344 pzdlt/34 zSL
1525	L-410FG	
		344 pzdlt/34 zSL
1526	L-410FG	
		344 pzdlt/34 zSL
2312	L-410UVP-E	
		1 dlt/6 zDL
2601	L-410UVP-E	
		1 dlt/6 zDL
2602	L-410UVP-E	
		1 dlt/6 zDL
2710	L-410UVP-E	
		1 dlt/6 zDL

Let 610M
1 dlt/6 zDL, Praha/Kbely;
LZO, Praha/Kbely
0003	1 dlt/6 zDL
0005	LZO

**Mikoyan MiG-21MF/
MiG-21UM***
42 slt/4 zTL, Cáslav;
LZO, Ceske Budejovice
2205	42 slt/4 zTL
2500	42 slt/4 zTL
2614	42 slt/4 zTL
3186*	42 slt/4 zTL
3746*	42 slt/4 zTL
4017	42 slt/4 zTL
4175	42 slt/4 zTL
4307	LZO
5031*	42 slt/4 zTL
5201	42 slt/4 zTL
5203	LZO
5210	42 slt/4 zTL
5212	42 slt/4 zTL
5213	42 slt/4 zTL
5214	42 slt/4 zTL
5301	42 slt/4 zTL
5302	42 slt/4 zTL
5303	42 slt/4 zTL
5304	42 slt/4 zTL
5305	42 slt/4 zTL
5508	42 slt/4 zTL
5512	42 slt/4 zTL
5581	42 slt/4 zTL
5603	42 slt/4 zTL
7701	42 slt/4 zTL
7802	42 slt/4 zTL
9011*	42 slt/4 zTL
9332*	42 slt/4 zTL
9333*	42 slt/4 zTL
9341*	42 slt/4 zTL
9399*	42 slt/4 zTL
9410	42 slt/4 zTL
9414	42 slt/4 zTL
9707	42 slt/4 zTL
9711	42 slt/4 zTL
9801	42 slt/4 zTL
9802	LZO
9804	42 slt/4 zTL
9805	42 slt/4 zTL

**Mikoyan MiG-23ML/
MiG-23UB***
41 slt/4 zTL, Cáslav
2402	
2406	
2409	
2410	
2422	
2423	
2425	
3303	
3304	
3307	
4641	
4645	
4850	
4855	
4860	
8107*	
8109*	
8327*	

Mil Mi-24
331 ltBVr/33 zVrL, Přerov
0103	Mi-24D
0140	Mi-24D
0142	Mi-24D
0146	Mi-24D
0151	Mi-24D
0214	Mi-24D
0216	Mi-24D
0217	Mi-24D
0218	Mi-24D
0219	Mi-24D
0220	Mi-24D
0701	Mi-24V1
0702	Mi-24V1
0703	Mi-24V1
0705	Mi-24V1
0709	Mi-24V1
0710	Mi-24V1
0788	Mi-24V1
0789	Mi-24V1
0790	Mi-24V1
0812	Mi-24V1
0815	Mi-24V1
0816	Mi-24V1
0834	Mi-24V2
0835	Mi-24V2
0836	Mi-24V2
0837	Mi-24V2
0838	Mi-24V2
0839	Mi-24V2
4010	Mi-24D
4011	Mi-24D
6050	Mi-24DU

**Sukhoi Su-22M-4K/
Su-22UM-3K***
321 tpzlt/32 zTL, Náměšt
2217	01	
2218	18	
2619	34	NA-2D
2620	35	NA-2D
2701	36	
3402	05	
3701	02	NA-1A
3703	43	NA-1D
3704	44	NA-1D
3705	51	
3706	52	NA-1E
3802	26	NA-2B
3803	27	NA-2B
4005	30	NA-2C

Czech Republic - Denmark

4006	31	NA-2C
4008	29	NA-2B
4010	28	NA-2B
4011	22	NA-2A
4208	53	NA-1E
4209	54	NA-1E
6602	55*	
7103	03	NA-1A*
7104	40	NA-2C*
7309	41	NA-2D*
7310	25	NA-2A*

Sukhoi Su-25K/
Su-25UBK*
322 tlt/32 zTL, Náměšt
1002
1004
1005
3348*
5007
5039
5040
8076
8077
8078
8079
8080
8081
9013
9014
9093
9094
9098
9099

Tupolev Tu-154
1 dlt/6 zDL, Praha/Kbely
0601	Tu-154B-2
1003	Tu-154M
1016	Tu-154M

Yakovlev Yak-40
1 dlt/6 zDL, Praha/Kbely
0260	Yak-40
1257	Yak-40K

DENMARK
Flyvevåbnet

Lockheed C-130H Hercules
Eskadrille 721, Vaerløse
B-678
B-679
B-680

Canadair CL.604
Challenger
Eskadrille 721, Vaerløse
C-080
C-168

General Dynamics F-16
(MLU aircraft are marked
with a *)
Eskadrille 723, Aalborg;
Eskadrille 726, Aalborg;
Eskadrille 727, Skrydstrup;
Eskadrille 730, Skrydstrup

E-004	F-16A*	Esk 726
E-005	F-16A	Esk 723
E-006	F-16A	Esk 726
E-007	F-16A*	Esk 726
E-008	F-16A*	Esk 723
E-011	F-16A	Esk 730
E-016	F-16A*	Esk 726
E-017	F-16A	Esk 726
E-018	F-16A*	Esk 726
E-024	F-16A	Esk 730
E-070	F-16A	
E-074	F-16A	Esk 730
E-075	F-16A	Esk 730
E-107	F-16A	Esk 730
E-174	F-16A	Esk 727
E-176	F-16A	Esk 726
E-177	F-16A*	Esk 726
E-178	F-16A	Esk 730
E-180	F-16A	Esk 730
E-181	F-16A	Esk 730
E-182	F-16A	Esk 730
E-183	F-16A	Esk 730
E-184	F-16A	Esk 727
E-187	F-16A	Esk 727
E-188	F-16A	Esk 723
E-189	F-16A	Esk 730
E-190	F-16A*	Esk 726
E-191	F-16A	Esk 730
E-192	F-16A*	Esk 727
E-193	F-16A	Esk 727
E-194	F-16A	Esk 730
E-195	F-16A	Esk 730
E-196	F-16A	Esk 727
E-197	F-16A	Esk 727
E-198	F-16A	Esk 730
E-199	F-16A	Esk 727
E-200	F-16A	Esk 727
E-202	F-16A	Esk 730
E-203	F-16A	Esk 730
E-596	F-16A*	Esk 723
E-597	F-16A*	Esk 723
E-598	F-16A*	Esk 723
E-599	F-16A*	Esk 726
E-600	F-16A*	Esk 723
E-601	F-16A	Esk 727
E-602	F-16A	Esk 730
E-603	F-16A	Esk 726
E-604	F-16A*	Esk 723
E-605	F-16A*	Esk 723
E-606	F-16A*	Esk 723
E-607	F-16A*	Esk 723
E-608	F-16A*	Esk 723
E-609	F-16A*	Esk 726
E-610	F-16A*	Esk 726
E-611	F-16A	Esk 727
ET-022	F-16B	Esk 727
ET-197	F-16B	Esk 727
ET-198	F-16B	Esk 726
ET-199	F-16B	Esk 726
ET-204	F-16B*	
ET-206	F-16B	Esk 730
ET-207	F-16B*	Esk 726
ET-208	F-16B	Esk 730
ET-210	F-16B	Esk 727
ET-612	F-16B*	Esk 726
ET-613	F-16B*	Esk 723
ET-614	F-16B*	Esk 723
ET-615	F-16B*	Esk 727
ET-626	F-16B	Esk 727

Grumman G.1159A
Gulfstream III
Eskadrille 721, Vaerløse
F-249
F-313

SAAB T-17 Supporter
Eskadrille 721, Vaerløse;
Flyveskolen, Karup (FLSK)
T-401	FLSK
T-402	FLSK
T-403	FLSK
T-404	FLSK
T-405	FLSK
T-407	Esk 721
T-408	FLSK
T-409	FLSK
T-410	FLSK
T-411	FLSK
T-412	FLSK
T-413	FLSK
T-414	FLSK
T-415	FLSK
T-417	FLSK
T-418	Esk 721
T-419	FLSK
T-420	Esk 721
T-421	FLSK
T-423	FLSK
T-425	FLSK
T-426	FLSK
T-427	FLSK
T-428	FLSK
T-429	FLSK
T-430	FLSK
T-431	Esk 721
T-432	FLSK

Sikorsky S-61A Sea King
Eskadrille 722, Vaerløse
U-240
U-275
U-276
U-277
U-278
U-279
U-280
U-481

Søvaernets Flyvetjaeneste
(Navy)
Westland Lynx
Mk 80/90/90B
Eskadrille 722, Vaerløse
S-134	Mk 80
S-142	Mk 80
S-170	Mk 90B
S-175	Mk 80
S-181	Mk 80
S-191	Mk 90B
S-249	Mk 90
S-256	Mk 90

Haerens Flyvetjaeneste
(Army)
Hughes 500M
OVH Kmp, Vandel;
PVH Kmp, Vandel
H-201
H-202
H-203
H-205
H-206
H-207
H-209
H-211
H-213
H-244
H-245
H-246

Aérospatiale AS.550C-2
Fennec
PVH Kmp, Vandel

P-090		**FRANCE**		69	315-WL	
P-234		**Armée de l'Air**		70	315-WM	
P-254		**Aérospatiale SN601 Corvette**		72	315-WO	
P-275		CEV, Bretigny		73	315-WP	
P-276		1	MV	74	315-WQ	
P-287		2	MW	75	315-WR	
P-288		10	MX	76	315-WS	
P-319				77	315-WT	
P-320		**Aérospatiale TB-30 Epsilon**		78	315-WU	
P-339		*Cartouche Dorée*,		79	315-WV	
P-352		(EPAA 00.315) Cognac;		80	315-WW	
P-369		EPAA 00.315, Cognac;		81	315-WX	
		SOCATA, Tarbes		82	315-WY	
EGYPT		1	315-UA	83	315-WZ	
Al Quwwat al-Jawwiya ilMisriya		2	315-UB	84	315-XA	
Lockheed C-130H/		3	FZ SOCATA	85	315-XB	
C-130H-30* Hercules		4	315-UC	86	315-XC	
16 Sqn, Cairo West		5	315-UD	87	315-XD	
1271/SU-BAB		6	315-UE	88	315-XE	
1272/SU-BAC		7	315-UF	89	315-XF	
1273/SU-BAD		8	315-UG	90	315-XG	
1274/SU-BAE		9	315-UH	91	315-XH	
1275/SU-BAF		10	315-UI	92	F-SEXI [1]*	
1277/SU-BAI		12	315-UK	93	315-XJ	
1278/SU-BAJ		13	315-UL	94	315-XK	
1279/SU-BAK		14	315-UM	95	315-XL	
1280/SU-BAL		15	315-UN	96	315-XM	
1281/SU-BAM		16	315-UO	97	315-XN	
1282/SU-BAN		17	315-UP	98	315-XO	
1283/SU-BAP		18	315-UQ	99	315-XP	
1284/SU-BAQ		19	315-UR	100	F-SEXQ [2]*	
1285/SU-BAR		20	315-US	101	315-XR	
1286/SU-BAS		21	315-UT	102	315-XS	
1287/SU-BAT		23	315-UV	103	315-XT	
1288/SU-BAU		24	315-UW	104	315-XU	
1289/SU-BAV		25	315-UX	105	F-SEXV [4]*	
1290/SU-BAW		26	315-UY	106	315-XW	
1291/SU-BAX		27	315-UZ	107	315-XX	
1292/SU-BAY		28	315-VA	108	315-XY	
1293/SU-BKS*		29	315-VB	109	315-XZ	
1294/SU-BKT*		30	315-VC	110	315-YA	
1295/SU-BKU*		31	315-VD	111	315-YB	
		32	315-VE	112	315-YC	
Egyptian Govt		33	315-VF	113	315-YD	
Airbus A.340-211		34	315-VG	114	315-YE	
Egyptian Govt, Cairo		35	315-VH	115	315-YF	
SU-GGG		36	315-VI	116	315-YG	
		37	315-VJ	117	F-SEYH [3]*	
Boeing 707-366C		38	315-VK	118	315-YI	
Egyptian Govt, Cairo		39	315-VL	119	315-YJ	
SU-AXJ		40	315-VM	120	315-YK	
		41	315-VN	121	315-YL	
Grumman		42	315-VO	122	315-YM	
G.1159A Gulfstream III/		43	315-VP	123	315-YN	
G.1159C Gulfstream IV		44	315-VQ	124	315-YO	
Egyptian Air Force/Govt,		45	315-VR	125	315-YP	
Cairo		46	315-VS	126	315-YQ	
SU-BGM Gulfstream IV		47	315-VT	127	315-YR	
SU-BGU Gulfstream III		48	315-VU	128	315-YS	
SU-BGV Gulfstream III		49	315-VV	129	315-YT	
SU-BNC Gulfstream IV		50	315-VW	130	315-YU	
SU-BND Gulfstream IV		52	315-VX	131	315-YV	
		53	315-VY	132	315-YW	
FINLAND		54	315-VZ	133	315-YX	
Suomen Ilmavoimat		56	315-WA	134	315-YY	
Fokker F.27 Friendship		57	F-ZVLB	135	315-YZ	
Tukilentolaivue,		61	315-WD	136	315-ZA	
Jyväskylä/Tikkakoski		62	315-WE	137	315-ZB	
FF-1 F.27-100		63	315-WF	138	315-ZC	
FF-2 F.27-100		64	315-WG	139	315-ZD	
FF-3 F.27-400M		65	315-WH	140	315-ZE	
		66	315-WI	141	315-ZF	
		67	315-WJ	142	315-ZG	
		68	315-WK	143	315-ZH	

144	315-ZI
145	315-ZJ
146	315-ZK
149	315-ZM
150	315-ZN
152	315-ZO
153	315-ZP
154	315-ZQ
155	315-ZR
158	315-ZS
159	315-ZT

Airbus A.300B2-103
CEV, Bretigny

03	(F-BUAD)

Airbus A.310-304
ET 03.060 *Esterel*,
  Paris/Charles de Gaulle

418	F-RADC
421	F-RADA
422	F-RADB

Airtech CN-235M-200
ETL 01.062 *Vercours*, Creil;
ETOM 00.052 *La Tontouta*,
  Noumea;
ETOM 00.082 *Maine*,
  Faaa-Tahiti

043	62-IA	01.062
045	62-IB	01.062
065	82-IC	00.082
066	52-ID	00.052
071	62-IE	01.062
072	82-IF	00.082
105	62-IG	01.062
107	52-IH	00.052
111	62-II	01.062
114	62-IJ	01.062
123	62-IM	01.062
128	62-IK	01.062
129	62-IL	01.062
137	62-IN	01.062
141	62-IO	01.062

Boeing C-135 Stratotanker
ERV 00.093 *Bretagne*, Istres

470	C-135FR	93-CA
471	C-135FR	93-CB
472	C-135FR	93-CC
474	C-135FR	93-CE
475	C-135FR	93-CF
497	KC-135R	93-CM
525	KC-135R	93-CN
574	KC-135R	93-CP
735	C-135FR	93-CG
736	C-135FR	93-CH
737	C-135FR	93-CI
738	C-135FR	93-CJ
739	C-135FR	93-CK
740	C-135FR	93-CL

Boeing E-3F Sentry
EDCA 00.036, Avord

201	36-CA
202	36-CB
203	36-CC
204	36-CD

CASA 212-300 Aviocar
CEV, Bretigny

377	MO
378	MP
386	MQ
387	MR
388	MS

Cessna 310
CEV, Bretigny, Cazaux,
  Istres & Melun

046	310L	AV
185	310N	AU
187	310N	BJ
188	310N	BK
190	310N	BL
192	310N	BM
193	310N	BG
194	310N	BH
242	310K	AW
244	310K	AX
513	310N	BE
693	310N	BI
820	310Q	CL
981	310Q	BF

D-BD Alpha Jet
AMD-BA, Istres;
CEAM (EC 05.330),
  Mont-de-Marsan;
CEV, Bretigny;
EAC 00.314, Tours;
EC 01.002 *Cicogne*, Dijon;
EC 02.007 *Argonne*,
  St Dizier;
EPNER, Istres;
ERS 01.091 *Gascogne*,
  Mont-de-Marsan;
ETO 01.008 *Saintonge* &
  ETO 02.008 *Nice*, Cazaux;
GI 00.312, Salon de
  Provence;
Patrouille de France (PDF)
  (EPAA 20.300),
  Salon de Provence

01	F-ZJTS	CEV
E1		CEV
E3	314-LV	00.314
E4		CEV
E5	7-PE	02.007
E7	314-LJ	00.314
E8		CEV
E9	8-MJ	01.008
E10	314-LK	00.314
E11	8-MW	01.008
E12		CEV
E13	8-NM	02.008
E14	2-EI	01.002
E15	8-NO	02.008
E17		
E18	8-NN	02.008
E19	330-AL	CEAM
E20	2-EF	01.002
E21	330-AL	CEAM
E22	314-TG	00.314
E23	8-MQ	01.008
E24	314-TW	00.314
E25	314-UK	00.314
E26	F-TERO	PDF [4]
E28	8-NK	02.008
E29	314-TM	00.314
E30	8-NR	02.008
E31		
E32	8-NQ	02.008
E33		
E34	8-MF	01.008
E35	314-UF	00.314
E36	314-LT	00.314
E37	8-NI	02.008
E38	314-TY	00.314
E41	F-TERA	*PDF*
E42	7-PX	02.007
E43	314-LI	00.314
E44		CEV
E45	330-AK	CEAM
E46		CEV
E47	7-PJ	02.007
E48	314-TD	00.314
E49	314-TA	00.314
E51	314-TH	00.314
E52		
E53		
E55	314-UC	00.314
E58	314-LF	00.314
E59	314-LY	00.314
E60		EPNER
E61	314-TR	00.314
E63	314-LN	00.314
E64	314-TL	00.314
E65	8-MD	01.008
E66	8-ME	01.008
E67	314-TB	00.314
E68	2-EL	01.002
E69	314-RS	00.314
E72	314-LA	00.314
E73	314-TV	00.314
E74	8-MS	01.008
E75	2-EM	01.002
E76	8-MR	01.008
E79	8-MI	01.008
E80		CEV
E81	F-TERI	*PDF* [9]
E82	8-NB	02.008
E83	2-EI	01.002
E84	8-MH	01.008
E85	314-LF	00.314
E86	8-NS	02.008
E87	314-LU	00.314
E88	314-TF	00.314
E89	314-TQ	00.314
E90		
E91	8-NL	02.008
E92	314-UE	00.314
E93	314-LD	00.314
E94	314-TE	00.314
E95	314-UA	00.314
E96	8-MT	01.008
E97	314-UN	00.314
E98	314-TT	00.314
E99	314-LW	00.314
E100		EPNER
E101	314-LX	00.314
E102		
E103		
E104	F-TERB	*PDF* [6]
E105	314-LE	00.314
E106	8-NA	02.008
E107	312-RT	00.312
E108	8-NF	02.008
E109	8-NJ	02.008
E110	8-NG	02.008
E112	DA	01.091
E113	312-RU	00.312
E114	314-TU	00.314
E115	8-NW	02.008
E116	8-MG	01.008
E117		
E118	314-LM	00.314
E119	7-PZ	02.007
E120	F-TERG	*PDF* [3]
E121	F-TERK	*PDF*
E122		
E123	8-ML	01.008

E124	312-RS	00.312		238	F-RAEE	00.065		206	33-FN	03.033

E124	312-RS	00.312
E125	314-LP	00.314
E126	314-LI	00.314
E127	8-MB	01.008
E128	F-TERN	PDF [2]
E129	314-TO	00.314
E130	314-LQ	00.314
E131	312-RV	00.312
E132	314-UJ	00.314
E133	8-NE	02.008
E134		
E135	8-ND	02.008
E136	314-TN	00.314
E137	314-LB	00.314
E138	F-TERM	PDF [0]
E139	330-AH	CEAM
E140	314-UH	00.314
E141	314-LC	00.314
E142	8-NV	02.008
E143	8-MM	01.008
E144		
E145	314-LZ	00.314
E146	8-MC	01.008
E147	8-NH	02.008
E148	8-NP	02.008
E149	8-MO	01.008
E150	8-NC	02.008
E151	F-TERJ	PDF
E152	8-MP	01.008
E153	F-TERH	PDF [1]
E154	8-NT	02.008
E155	314-TP	00.314
E156	314-TI	00.314
E157	314-LG	00.314
E158	F-TERG	PDF [2]
E159	7-PP	02.007
E160		
E161	8-MK	01.008
E162	314-TZ	00.314
E163	314-UM	00.314
E164		
E165	F-TER.	PDF [5]
E166	314-TX	00.314
E167	314-LL	00.314
E168	314-TS	00.314
E169	F-TERQ	PDF [6]
E170	2-EO	01.002
E171		
E173	314-LH	00.314
E175	F-TERL	PDF
E176	8-MA	01.008

Dassault Falcon 20
CEV, Bretigny[1], Cazaux[2],
Istres[3] & Melun[4];
CITac 00.339 Aquitaine,
Luxeuil;
EAM 09.120, Cazaux;
ETEC 00.065, Villacoublay

22	CS	CEV[3]
49	120-FA	09.120
79	CT	CEV[1]
86	CG	CEV[2]
93	F-RAED	00.065
96	CB	CEV[1]
104	CW	CEV[1]
115	339-JG	00.339
124	CC	CEV[1]
131	CD	CEV[1]
138	CR	CEV[2]
145	CU	CEV[1]
167	(F-RAEB)	00.065
182	339-JA	00.339
188	CX	CEV[4]

238	F-RAEE	00.065
252	CA	CEV[1]
260	F-RAEA	00.065
263	CY	CEV[1]
268	F-RAEF	00.065
288	CV	CEV[1]
291	65-EG	00.065
342	F-RAEC	00.065
375	CZ	CEV[1]
422	65-EH	00.065
451	339-JC	00.339
483	339-JI	00.339

Dassault Falcon 50
ETEC 00.065, Villacoublay

5	F-RAFI	
27	(F-RAFK)	
34	(F-RAFL)	
78	F-RAFJ	

Dassault Falcon 900
ETEC 00.065, Villacoublay

2	(F-RAFP)	
4	(F-RAFQ)	

Dassault Mirage IVP
ERS 01.091 Gascogne,
Mont-de-Marsan

25	AX	
36	BI	
53	BZ	
59	CF	
61	CH	

**Dassault
Mirage F.1**
CEAM (EC 05.330),
Mont-de-Marsan;
CEV, Bretigny & Istres;
EC 01.030 Alsace &
EC 02.030 Normandie
Niemen, Colmar;
ER 01.033 Belfort,
ER 02.033 Savoie
& EC 03.033 Lorraine,
Reims;
EC 04.033 Vexin, Djibouti

Mirage F.1C/F.1CT*

5	33-FV	03.033
24	33-FC	03.033
31	330-AC	CEAM
32	33-FR	03.033
33		
52	33-FB	03.033
62	33-FD	03.033
64	33-FK	03.033
74		
76	33-FQ	03.033
77	33-FF	03.033
80	33-FT	03.033
81	33-LJ	04.033
82		
83		
84		
85		
87	33-FS	03.033
90	33-LD	04.033
100	33-LA	04.033
103	33-FU	03.033
201	33-FJ	03.033
202	33-FN	03.033
203	33-FE	03.033
205	33-LB	04.033

206	33-FN	03.033
207*	330-AO	CEAM
210	33-LC	04.033
211	33-FP	03.033
213	33-LF	04.033
214	33-FO	03.033
218	33-LC	04.033
219*	30-QV	02.030
220*	30-QM	02.030
221*	30-SY	01.030
223*		
224	33-LG	04.033
225*	30-QE	02.030
226*	30-QU	02.030
227*	330-AP	CEAM
228*	30-SN	01.030
229*	30-QC	02.030
230*	30-SP	01.030
231*	30-SA	01.030
232*	30-QW	02.030
233*	30-QG	02.030
234*	30-SI	01.030
235*	30-SK	01.030
236*	30-SB	01.030
237*	30-SM	01.030
238*	30-QN	02.030
239*	30-QD	02.030
241*	30-QA	02.030
242*	30-SG	01.030
243*	30-QJ	02.030
244*	30-QH	02.030
245*	30-SX	01.030
246*	30-ST	01.030
247*	30-QP	02.030
248*	30-SQ	01.030
251*	330-AI	CEAM
252*	30-QO	02.030
253*		
254*	30-QV	02.030
255*	30-QI	02.030
256*	30-QK	02.030
257*	30-SD	01.030
258*	30-SZ	01.030
259*		
260*	30-SO	01.030
261*	30-SL	01.030
262*	30-SE	01.030
264*	30-SW	01.030
265*	30-SH	01.030
267*	30-QB	02.030
268*	30-SR	01.030
271*	30-QQ	02.030
272*		
273*	30-QL	02.030
274*	30-QT	02.030
275*	30-QM	02.030
278*		
279*	30-SC	01.030
280*		
281*	30-QF	02.030
283*	30-SV	01.030

Mirage F.1B

501		
502	33-FX	03.033
503	33-FG	03.033
504	33-FJ	03.033
505		
507	33-FA	03.033
509	330-AD	CEAM
510	33-FI	03.033
511	33-FT	03.033
512	33-FL	03.033
513	33-FY	03.033

514	33-FZ	03.033	502	5-OH	02.005	42*	2-FH	02.002
516	33-FH	03.033	504*	BOB	CEV	43*	2-FB	02.002
517			505	5-NW	01.005	44*	2-EQ	01.002
518	33-FF	03.033	506	5-OY	02.005	45*	2-ES	01.002
519	33-FM	03.033	507	5-OX	02.005	46*	2-EN	01.002
520			508	5-OT	02.005	47*	2-EP	01.002
			509	5-OP	02.005	48*	2-ER	01.002

Mirage F.1CR

602		CEV	510	5-OQ	02.005	49*	2-FF	02.002
603	33-CB	01.033	511	5-OR	02.005	51*	330-AS	CEAM
604	33-NU	01.033	512	5-OU	02.005	52*	2-FC	02.002
605	33-NS	02.033	513	5-OI	02.005	53*	2-FA	02.002
606	33-NP	02.033	514	5-OE	02.005	54*	2-EA	01.002
607	33-CE	01.033	515	5-OG	02.005	55*	2-FW	02.002
608	33-NG	02.033	516	5-OL	02.005	56*	2-FK	02.002
610	33-NQ	02.033	518	5-OM	02.005	57*	2-FL	02.002
611	33-NN	02.033	519	5-OW	02.005	58*	2-FO	02.002
612	33-NJ	02.033	520	5-OS	02.005	59*	2-EV	01.002
613	33-NK	02.033	521	5-ON	02.005	61*	2-FM	02.002
614	33-NF	02.033	522	5-OV	02.005	62*	2-FZ	02.002
615	33-CU	01.033	523	12-YS	01.012	63*	2-FQ	02.002
616	33-NM	02.033	524	330-AZ	CEAM	64	330-AQ	CEAM
617	33-NO	02.033	525	2-FV	02.002	65*	2-EC	01.002
620	33-CT	01.033	526	12-KM	02.012	66*	2-FN	02.002
622	33-NH	02.033	527	12-KJ	02.012	67*	2-ED	01.002
623	33-CM	01.033	528	330-AN	CEAM	68*	2-FP	02.002
624			529			69*	2-EG	01.002
627	33-CFI	01.033	530	12-YA	01.012	70*	2-FD	02.002
628	33-NB	02.033				71*	2-EH	01.002
629	33-NN	02.033	**Dassault Mirage 2000C/**			72*	2-FR	02.002
630	33-NL	02.033	**2000-5***			73*	2-EB	01.002
631	33-CR	01.033	CEAM (EC 05.330),			74*	2-FT	02.002
632	33-NE	02.033	Mont-de-Marsan;			76*	2-EK	01.002
634	33-CK	01.033	CEV, Istres;			77*	330-AX	CEAM
635	33-NX	02.033	EC 01.002 *Cicogne* &			78*	2-FS	02.002
636	33-CG	01.033	EC 02.002 *Côte d'Or*,			79	12-KL	02.012
637	33-CP	01.033	Dijon;			80	12-YJ	01.012
638	33-CI	01.033	EC 01.005 *Vendée* &			81	12-YI	01.012
640	33-CH	01.033	EC 02.005 *Ile de France*,			82		
641	33-CD	01.033	Orange;			83		
642	33-NC	02.033	EC 01.012 *Cambrésis* &			85	12-YE	01.012
643	33-NR	02.033	EC 02.012 *Picardie*,			86	12-KH	02.012
645	33-CC	01.033	Cambrai			87	12-YQ	01.012
646	33-NW	02.033	1			88	12-YR	01.012
647			2		CEV	89	12-KU	02.012
648	33-NT	02.033	3	5-NP	01.005	90	12-KO	02.012
649	33-CZ	01.033	4	5-OD	02.005	91	12-YO	01.012
650	33-CJ	01.033	5	5-OO	02.005	92	330-AW	CEAM
651	33-NB	02.033	8	5-OA	02.005	93	12-KF	02.012
653	33-NV	01.033	9	5-OJ	02.005	94	12-KA	02.012
654	33-CL	01.033	11	5-NJ	01.005	95	12-YF	01.012
655	330-AT	CEAM	12	5-NN	01.005	96	12-KK	02.012
656	33-CS	01.033	13	5-NM	01.005	97	12-YV	01.012
657	33-CV	01.033	14	5-NK	01.005	98	12-YB	01.012
658	33-CW	01.033	15	5-NA	01.005	99	12-KP	02.012
659	33-CA	01.033	16	5-NE	01.005	100	12-KG	02.012
660	33-CY	01.033	17	5-NR	01.005	101	2-FB	02.002
661	33-CX	01.033	18	5-OF	01.005	102	2-FE	02.002
662	33-NA	02.033	19	5-OB	02.005	103	12-YN	01.012
			20	5-NB	01.005	104	12-YK	01.012
Dassault Mirage 2000B/			21	5-NG	01.005	105	12-YL	01.012
2000-5*			22	5-ND	01.005	106	2-FP	02.002
AMD-BA, Istres;			25	5-NU	01.005	107	12-KQ	02.012
CEAM (EC 05.330),			27	5-NT	01.005	108	12-KE	02.012
Mont-de-Marsan;			28	5-OK	02.005	109	12-YT	01.012
CEV, Bretigny;			29	5-NO	01.005	111	12-KI	02.012
EC 02.002 *Côte d'Or*, Dijon;			30	5-OZ	02.005	112	12-YC	01.012
EC 01.005 *Vendée* &			32	5-NQ	01.005	113	12-KN	02.012
EC 02.005 *Ile de France*,			34	5-NH	01.005	114	12-KS	02.012
Orange;			35	5-NL	01.005	115	12-KC	02.012
EC 01.012 *Cambrésis* &			36	5-OC	02.005	116		
EC 02.012 *Picardie*,			37	5-NF	01.005	117		
Cambrai			38*	2-EU	01.002	118	12-YG	01.012
501*	(BX1)	CEV	40*	2-FG	02.002	119	12-KD	02.012
			41*	2-EJ	01.002	120	12-YM	01.012

121	12-YD	01.012
122	12-YU	01.012
123	12-KR	02.012
124	12-KB	02.012

Dassault Mirage 2000D
AMD-BA, Istres;
CEAM (EC 05.330),
    Mont-de-Marsan;
CEV, Istres;
EC 01.003 *Navarre*,
    EC 02.003 *Champagne* &
    EC 03.003 *Ardennes*,
    Nancy

601	3-IA	01.003
602	3-JR	02.003
603	3-IC	01.003
604		
605	3-IE	01.003
606	3-XL	03.003
607		CEV
609	3-XD	03.003
610	3-II	01.003
611	3-XS	03.003
612	3-IL	01.003
613	3-IF	01.003
614	330-A.	CEAM
615	3-JA	02.003
616	3-IJ	01.003
617	3-XA	03.003
618	3-JF	02003
619	3-JE	02.003
620	3-IM	01.003
621	3-XC	03.003
622		
623	3-IB	01.003
624	3-XF	03.003
625	3-IK	01.003
626	3-XH	03.003
627	3-JG	02.003
628	330-AE	CEAM
629	3-XJ	03.003
630	3-JI	02.003
631	3-XI	03.003
632	3-XM	03.003
634		
635	3-XP	03.003
636	3-JJ	02.003
637	3-JH	02.003
638	3-IQ	01.003
639	3-XQ	03.003
640	3-IR	01.003
641	3-XG	03.003
642	3-JB	02.003
643	3-JC	02.003
644	3-JD	02.003
645	3-JO	02.003
646	3-JP	02.003
647	3-IU	01.003
648	3-XT	03.003
649	3-IS	01.003
650	3-IN	01.003
651	3-IH	01.003
652	3-XN	03.003
653	3-JK	02.003
654	3-IT	01.003
655	3-XE	03.003
656	3-JL	02.003
657	3-JM	02.003
658	3-JN	02.003
659	3-XR	03.003
660	3-IO	01.003
661	3-JS	02.003
662	3-XU	03.003
663	3-IP	01.003
664	3-JU	02.003
665	3-XV	03.003
666	3-IK	01.003
667	3-JX	02.003
668	3-XU	03.003
669	3-ID	01.003
670	3-JV	02.003
671	3-XK	03.003
672	3-JQ	02.003
673	3-XA	03.003
674	3-XL	03.003
675		
676		
677		
678		
679		
680		
681		
682		
683		
684		
685		
686		

Dassault Mirage 2000N
CEAM (EC 05.330),
    Mont-de-Marsan;
CEV, Istres;
EC 01.004 *Dauphiné* &
    EC 02.004 *Lafayette*,
    Luxeuil;
EC 03.004 *Limousin*, Istres

301		CEV
303	4-CL	03.004
304	4-CK	03.004
305	4-CS	03.004
306	4-BL	02.004
307	4-CH	03.004
309	4-AO	01.004
310	4-CE	03.004
311	4-BT	02.004
312	4-CN	03.004
313	4-CV	03.004
314	4-AX	01.004
315	4-BF	02.004
316	4-BH	02.004
317	4-CR	03.004
318	4-BP	02.004
319	4-AC	01.004
320		
322		
323		
325	4-CC	03.004
326	4-CM	03.004
327	4-CJ	03.004
329	4-AU	01.004
330	4-AT	01.004
331	4-BT	02.004
332	4-BN	02.004
333	4-AB	01.004
334	330-AV	CEAM
335	4-BJ	02.004
336		
337	4-CB	03.004
338	4-CI	03.004
339	4-AD	01.004
340	4-AA	01.004
341	4-AF	01.004
342	4-AG	01.004
343	4-AH	01.004
344	4-AJ	01.004
345	4-AK	01.004
348	4-AL	01.004
349	4-BA	02.004
350	4-BQ	02.004
351	4-BL	02.004
353		
354		
355	4-AE	01.004
356	4-AN	01.004
357	4-BD	02.004
358	4-AM	01.004
359	4-BG	02.004
360	4-AI	01.004
361	4-AP	01.004
362	4-BM	02.004
363	4-BK	02.004
364	4-BB	02.004
365	4-BE	02.004
366	4-BO	02.004
367	4-AS	01.004
368	4-AR	01.004
369		
370	4-CA	03.004
371	4-AV	01.004
372	4-BR	02.004
373	4-CF	03.004
374	4-BS	02.004
375	4-BC	02.004

Dassault Rafale-B
AMD-BA, Istres;
CEV, Istres

B01		CEV
B1		AMD-BA
301		AMD-BA

Dassault Rafale-C
AMD-BA, Istres

C01	

DHC-6 Twin Otter 200/300*
ET 00.042 *Ventoux*,
    Mont-de-Marsan;
GAM 00.056 *Vaucluse*,
    Evreux

292	CC	00.056
298	CD	00.056
300	CE	00.056
730*	CA	00.042
742*	CB	00.042
745*	CV	00.042
786*	CT	00.042
790*	CW	00.042

Douglas DC-8-53/72CF*
CEV, Istres;
EE 00.051 *Aubrac*, Evreux;
ET 03.060 *Esterel*,
    Paris/Charles de Gaulle

45570	F-ZVMT	00.051
46013*	F-RAFG	03.060
46043*	F-ZWMT	CEV
46130*	F-RAFF	03.060

Embraer
EMB.121AA/AN* Xingu
EAT 00.319, Avord

054	YX
055*	
064	YY
066*	
069*	
070*	
072	YA
073	YB
075	YC

076	YD
077*	
078	YE
080	YF
082	YG
083*	ZE
084	YH
086	YI
089	YJ
090*	ZF
091	YK
092	YL
095	YM
096	YN
098	YO
099	YP
101	YR
102	YS
103	YT
105	YU
107	YV
108	YW
111	YQ

Embraer EMB.312F Tucano
GI 00.312, Salon de Provence

438	312-UW
439	312-UY
456	312-JA
457	312-JB
458	312-JC
459	312-JD
460	312-JE
461	312-JF
462	312-JG
463	312-JH
464	312-JI
466	312-JK
467	312-JL
468	312-JM
469	312-JN
470	312-JO
471	312-JP
472	312-JQ
473	312-JR
474	312-JS
475	312-JT
477	312-JU
478	312-JV
479	312-JX
480	312-JY
481	312-JZ
483	312-UB
484	312-UC
485	312-UD
486	312-UE
487	312-UF
488	312-UG
489	312-UH
490	312-UI
491	312-UJ
492	312-UK
493	312-UL
494	312-UM
495	312-UN
496	312-UO
497	312-UP
498	312-UQ
499	312-UR
500	312-US
501	312-UT
502	312-UU
503	312-UV
504	312-UX

Eurocopter AS.332 Super Puma/AS.532 Cougar
EH 03.067 Parisis, Villacoublay;
EH 05.067 Alpilles, Aix-en-Provence;
ETOM 00.082 Maine, Faaa-Tahiti;
GAM 00.056 Vaucluse, Evreux

2014	AS.332C	PN	05.067
2057	AS.332C	PO	00.082
2093	AS.332L	F-ZKCM	
2233	AS.332L-1	67-FY	03.067
2235	AS.332L-1	67-FZ	03.067
2244	AS.332C	PM	00.082
2342	AS.532UL	FX	00.056
2369	AS.532UL	FW	00.056
2375	AS.532UL	FV	00.056
2377	AS.332L-1	67-FU	03.067

Lockheed C-130H/C-130H-30* Hercules
ET 02.061 Franche-Comté, Orléans

4588	61-PM
4589	61-PN
5114	61-PA
5116	61-PB
5119	61-PC
5140	61-PD
5142*	61-PE
5144*	61-PF
5150*	61-PG
5151*	61-PH
5152*	61-PI
5153*	61-PJ
5226*	61-PK
5227*	61-PL

Morane Saulnier MS.760 Paris
CEV, Bretigny & Istres;
EAC 00.314, Tours;
EAM 09.115, Orange;
EAM 09.116, Luxeuil;
EAM 09.128, Metz

27	316-DQ	
30		
34	115-MH	09.115
44	116-CB	09.116
54	115-MG	09.115
57	316-DJ	
61	316-DI	
65	314-DD	00.314
68	NB	CEV
71	316-DO	
93	316-DS	
94	115-MF	09.115
115	OV	CEV
116	ON	CEV
118	NQ	CEV
119	NL	CEV

Nord 262A/262D* Frégate
CEV, Istres;
EPNER, Istres;
ETE 00.041 Verdun, Metz;
ET 00.042 Ventoux, Mont-de-Marsan;
ETE 00.043 Médoc, Bordeaux;
ETE 00.044 Mistral, Villacoublay;
ETEC 00.065, Villacoublay

58	MJ	EPNER
64*	AA	00.065
66*	AB	00.065
67	MI	CEV
68*	AC	00.065
77*	AK	00.044
80*	AW	00.065
81*	AH	00.041
88*	AL	00.042
89*	AZ	00.041
91*	AT	00.042
93*	AP	00.065
94*	AU	00.065
95*	AR	00.065
105*	AE	00.065
106*	AY	00.041
107*	AX	00.065
108*	AG	00.041
109*	AM	00.043
110*	AS	00.041

SEPECAT Jaguar
CEV, Bretigny & Istres;
CEAM (EC 05.330), Mont-de-Marsan;
CITac 00.339 Aquitaine, Luxeuil;
EC 01.007 Provence, EC 02.007 Argonne & EC 03.007 Languedoc, St Dizier
Jaguar A

A1		
A17	7-HN	01.007
A25		
A28		
A43		
A47		
A53	7-PB	02.007
A55	7-PA	02.007
A58	7-HE	01.007
A61	7-IQ	03.007
A66		
A67	7-PV	02.007
A75	7-PW	02.007
A84	7-PY	02.007
A87	7-PF	02.007
A88	7-PR	02.007
A89	7-HF	01.007
A90	7-HN	01.007
A92		
A93	7-PN	02.007
A94	7-IG	03.007
A96	7-HD	01.007
A98		
A99	7-IR	03.007
A100	7-HR	01.007
A101	7-HB	01.007
A103	7-IE	03.007
A104	7-HM	01.007
A107	7-HC	01.007

A108	7-HQ	01.007
A112	7-HS	01.007
A113	7-II	03.007
A115	7-HO	01.007
A117	7-HA	01.007
A118	7-HE	01.007
A120	7-IJ	03.007
A122	7-IM	03.007
A123	7-IO	03.007
A12	7-IN	03.007
A126	7-HJ	03.007
A127	7-IP	03.007
A128	7-IC	03.007
A129	7-IL	03.007
A130	7-PW	02.007
A133	7-HF	01.007
A135	7-IU	01.007
A137	7-HQ	01.007
A138	7-HV	01.007
A139	7-HU	01.007
A140	7-HI	01.007
A141	7-IS	03.007
A144	7-IF	03.007
A145	7-HG	01.007
A148	7-IK	03.007
A149	7-HP	01.007
A150	7-IT	03.007
A151		
A153	7-ID	03.007
A154	7-IS	03.007
A157	7-HH	01.007
A158	7-HK	01.007
A159	7-HL	01.007
A160	7-IH	03.007

Jaguar E

E2	7-PT	02.007
E3	7-HL	01.007
E4	7-PG	02.007
E5	339-WH	00.339
E6		
E7	7-PL	02.007
E8	7-PQ	02.007
E9		
E10	339-WL	00.339
E12	339-WI	00.339
E15		
E18		
E19	339-WG	00.339
E20		
E21	339-WM	00.339
E22	7-PU	02.007
E23		
E24	7-PH	02.007
E25		
E27		
E29	339-WJ	00.339
E30		
E32	7-PD	02.007
E35	7-PU	02.007
E36	7-PK	02.007
E37	7-PM	02.007
E39	339-WN	00.339
E40	7-PI	02.007

SOCATA TBM 700
CEV, Bordeaux;
ETE 00.041 *Verdun*, Metz;
ETE 00.043 *Médoc*, Bordeaux;
ETE 00.044 *Mistral*, Villacoublay;
ETEC 00.065, Villacoublay;
EdC 00.070, Chateaudun

33	43-XA	00.043

35	65-XB	00.065
70	43-XC	00.043
77	XD	00.065
78	65-XE	00.044
80	41-XF	00.041
93	XL	00.043
94	65-XG	00.070
95	65-XH	00.065
103	41-XI	00.041
104	XJ	00.070
105	XK	00.065
106	MN	CEV
110	XP	00.041
111	65-XM	00.065
117	XN	00.044
125	65-XO	00.065
131	XQ	
146	XR	00.065
147	XS	00.065

Transall C-160A/C-160F/ C-160H/C-160NG/C-160NG GABRIEL*/C-160R
CEAM (EET 06.330), Mont-de-Marsan;
CEV, Bretigny;
EA 01.059 *Bigorre*, Evreux;
EET 01.054 *Dunkerque*, Metz;
ET 01.061 *Touraine* & ET 03.061 *Poitou*, Orléans;
ET 01.064 *Bearn* & ET 02.064 *Anjou*, Evreux;
ETOM 00.050 *Réunion*, St Denis;
ETOM 00.055 *Ouessant*, Dakar;
ETOM 00.058 *Guadeloupe*, Pointe-à-Pitre;
ETOM 00.088 *Larzac*, Djibouti

RA02	C-160R	61-MI	01.061
RA04	C-160R	61-MS	01.061
RA06	C-160R	61-ZB	03.061
R1	C-160R	61-MA	01.061
R2	C-160R	61-MB	01.061
R3	C-160R	61-MC	00.058
R4	C-160R	61-MD	01.061
R5	C-160R	61-ME	01.061
R11	C-160R	61-MF	01.061
R12	C-160R	61-MG	01.061
R13	C-160R	61-MH	00.050
R15	C-160R	61-MJ	01.061
R17	C-160R	61-ML	01.061
R18	C-160R	61-MM	01.061
R42	C-160R	61-MN	01.061

R43	C-160R	61-MO	01.061
R44	C-160R	61-MP	01.061
R45	C-160R	61-MQ	01.061
R46	C-160R	61-MR	01.061
R48	C-160R	61-MT	01.061
R49	C-160R	59-MU	01.059
R51	C-160R	61-MW	01.061
R52	C-160R	61-MX	01.061
R53	C-160R	61-MY	01.061
R54	C-160R	61-MZ	01.061
R55	C-160R	61-ZC	03.061
R86	C-160R	61-ZD	03.061
R87	C-160R	61-ZE	00.050
R88	C-160R	61-ZF	03.061
R89	C-160R	61-ZG	03.061
R90	C-160R	61-ZH	03.061
R91	C-160R	61-ZI	03.061
R92	C-160R	61-ZJ	03.061
R93	C-160R	61-ZK	03.061
R94	C-160R	61-ZL	03.061
R95	C-160R	61-ZM	03.061
R96	C-160R	61-ZN	03.061
R97	C-160R	61-ZO	03.061
R98	C-160R	61-ZP	03.061
R99	C-160R	61-ZQ	03.061
R100	C-160R	61-ZR	03.061
R153	C-160R	61-ZS	03.061
R154	C-160R	61-ZT	03.061
R157	C-160R	61-ZW	03.061
R158	C-160R	61-ZX	03.061
R159	C-160R	61-ZY	03.061
R160	C-160R	61-ZZ	03.061
R201	C-160R	64-GA	01.064
R202	C-160R	64-GB	02.064
R203	C-160R	64-GC	01.064
R204	C-160R	64-GD	02.064
R205	C-160R	64-GE	01.064

R206	C-160R	64-GF
		02.064
R207	C-160R	64-GG
		01.064
R208	C-160R	64-GH
		02.064
R210	C-160R	64-GJ
		02.064
R211	C-160R	64-GK
		01.064
R212	C-160R	64-GL
		02.064
R213	C-160R	64-GM
		01.064
R214	C-160R	64-GN
		02.064
R215	C-160R	64-GO
		01.064
F216	C-160NG*	54-GT
		01.054
R217	C-160R	64-GQ
		01.064
F218	C-160NG	64-GR
		02.064
F221	C-160NG*	61-GS
		01.061
F223	C-160NG	64-GW
		01.064
R224	C-160R	64-GX
		02.064
R225	C-160R	64-GY
		01.064
R226	C-160R	64-GZ
		02.064
H01	C-160H	59-BA
		01.059
H02	C-160H	59-BB
		01.059
H03	C-160H	59-BC
		01.059
H04	C-160H	59-BD
		01.059

Aéronavale/Marine
Aérospatiale SA.321G
Super Frelon
32 Flottille, Lanvéoc/
 Poulmic;
35 Flottille, St Mandrier

101	32F
102	32F
106	32F
118	32F
120	32F
134	32F
137	32F
144	32F
148	32F
150	32F
160	32F
162	32F
163	35F
164	32F
165	

Dassault-Breguet
Atlantique 2
21 Flottille,
 Nimes/Garons;
23 Flottille,
 Lorient/Lann Bihoué

1	21F
2	21F
3	23F

4	23F
5	23F
6	21F
7	23F
8	23F
9	21F
10	23F
11	23F
12	23F
13	21F
14	21F
15	23F
16	21F
17	23F
18	23F
19	23F
20	23F
21	21F
22	21F
23	21F
24	21F
25	21F
26	21F
27	23F
28	23F
29	
30	

Dassault Falcon 10(MER)
ES 57, Landivisiau

32	
101	
129	
133	
143	
185	

Dassault Falcon 20G
Guardian
ES 9 Tontouta;
ES 12 Papeete

48	12S
65	9S
72	12S
77	9S
80	

Dassault Falcon 50
SURMAR
24 Flottille, Lorient/
 Lann Bihoué

30	
36	

Dassault Rafale-M
AMD-BA, Istres
CEV, Istres

M01	AMD-BA
M02	AMD-BA
1	CEV

Dassault Super Etendard
11 Flottille, Landivisiau;
17 Flottille, Landivisiau;
CEV, Bretigny & Istres

1	11F
2	11F
3	17F
6	11F
8	17F
10	11F
11	17F
12	17F

13	17F
14	17F
15	
16	11F
17	11F
18	11F
19	11F
23	11F
24	11F
25	17F
26	17F
28	17F
30	11F
31	11F
32	11F
33	17F
35	CEV
37	11F
38	11F
39	17F
41	11F
43	17F
44	17F
45	11F
46	7F
47	17F
48	17F
49	11F
50	17F
51	17F
52	11F
55	17F
57	11F
59	11F
60	11F
61	17F
62	11F
64	11F
65	11F
66	11F
68	CEV
69	11F
71	17F

Embraer EMB.121AN
Xingu
24 Flottille, Lorient/
 Lann Bihoué
28 Flottille, Hyères;
ES 2, Lorient/Lann Bihoué

30	2S
47	2S
65	2S
67	2S
68	2S
71	28F
74	24F
79	2S
81	2S
85	28F
87	2S

Eurocopter SA.365/AS.565
Panther
32 Flottille, Lanvéoc/Poulmic
 (with detachments at
 Cherbourg, La Rochelle &
 Le Touquet)
35 Flottille, St Mandrier;
36 Flottille, St Mandrier

17	SA.365N	32F
19	SA.365N	32F
24	SA.365N	32F
81	SA.365N	32F

152

91	SA.365N	32F
313	SA.365F1	35F
316	AS.565MA	35F
318	SA.365F1	35F
319	AS.565MA	32F
322	SA.365F1	35F
355	AS.565MA	36F
362	AS.565MA	32F
436	AS.565MA	36F
452	AS.565MA	36F
453	AS.565MA	32F
466	AS.565MA	36F
482	AS.565MA	32F
486	AS.565SA	36F
503	AS.565MA	36F
505	AS.565MA	35F
506	AS.565MA	36F
507	AS.565SA	36F
511	AS.565SA	
519	AS.565SA	36F
522	AS.565SA	36F

Nord 262E Frégate
28 Flottille, Hyères;
ERCE, Hyères;
ES 2, Lorient/Lann Bihoué;
ES 55, Aspretto;
ES 56, Nimes/Garons

45	56S
46	56S
51	2S
52	56S
53	2S
60	
63	28F
69	56S
70	56S
71	56S
72	56S
73	56S
75	56S
79	28F
100	2S

Northrop Grumman E-2C Hawkeye
4 Flottille, Lorient/
Lann Bihoué

1	(165455)
2	(165456)

Westland Lynx HAS2(FN)/ HAS4(FN)*
31 Flottille, St Mandrier;
34 Flottille, Lanvéoc/Poulmic

260	
262	34F
263	31F
264	34F
265	34F
266	34F
267	31F
268	
269	31F
270	31F
271	34F
272	31F
273	
274	34F
275	31F
276	34F
620	34F
621	34F
622	34F

623	34F
624	31F
625	34F
627	34F
801*	34F
802*	34F
804*	34F
806*	34F
807*	34F
808*	34F
810*	34F
811*	34F
812*	31F
813*	34F
814*	31F

Aviation Legère de l'Armée de Terre (ALAT)
Cessna F.406 Caravan II
EAAT, Rennes

0008	ABM
0010	ABN

SOCATA TBM 700
EAAT, Rennes

99	ABO
100	ABP
115	ABQ
136	ABR
139	ABS
156	ABT
159	ABU
160	ABV

French Govt
Aérospatiale AS.355F-1 Twin Ecureuil
Douanes Francaises

F-ZBAC	(5026)
F-ZBEF	(5236)
F-ZBEJ	(5003)
F-ZBEK	(5298)
F-ZBEL	(5299)

Aérospatiale ATR-42-320
CNET, Rennes

F-SEBK	(264)

Cessna 404 Titan
Douanes Francaises

F-ZBDY	(0815)

Cessna F.406 Caravan II
Douanes Francaises

F-ZBAB	(0025)
F-ZBBB	(0039)
F-ZBCE	(0042)
F-ZBCF	(0077)
F-ZBCG	(0066)
F-ZBCH	(0075)
F-ZBCI	(0070)
F-ZBCJ	(0074)
F-ZBEP	(0006)
F-ZBES	(0017)
F-ZBFA	(0001)
F-ZBGA	(0086)

Dassault Falcon 20
AVDEF, Nimes/Garons

F-GPAA	Falcon 20ECM
F-GPAB	Falcon 20E

Fokker F-27-600
Sécurité Civile

F-ZBFF	71	(10432)
F-ZBFG	72	(10440)

GERMANY
Luftwaffe, Marineflieger
Airbus A.310-304/MRTT*
1/FBS, Köln-Bonn

10+21
10+22
10+23
10+24*
10+25*
10+26*
10+27*

Canadair CL601-1A Challenger
1/FBS, Köln-Bonn

12+02
12+03
12+04
12+05
12+06
12+07

Mikoyan MiG-29G/ MiG-29GT*
JG-73 *Steinhoff*, Laage

29+01
29+02
29+03
29+04
29+05
29+06
29+07
29+08
29+10
29+11
29+12
29+14
29+15
29+16
29+17
29+18
29+19
29+20
29+21
29+22*
29+23*
29+24*
29+25*

McD F-4F Phantom
JG-71 *Richthoven*,
   Wittmundhaven;
JG-72 *Westfalen*, Hopsten;
JG-73 *Steinhoff*, Laage;
JG-74 *Molders*,
   Neuburg/Donau;
TsLw-1, Kaufbeuren;
WTD-61, Ingolstadt

37+01	JG-74
37+03	JG-71
37+04	TsLw-1
37+06	JG-72
37+07	JG-72
37+08	JG-74
37+09	JG-72
37+10	JG-72
37+11	JG-73
37+12	JG-72
37+13	JG-74
37+14	TsLw-1
37+15	WTD-61

Germany

37+16	WTD-61	38+26	JG-74	43+22[1]	JbG-38
37+17	JG-74	38+27	JG-72	43+23[1]	JbG-38
37+22	JG-71	38+28	JG-74	43+25	JbG-31
37+26	JG-73	38+29	JG-74	43+27	JbG-34
37+28	JG-71	38+30	JG-71	43+29[1]	JbG-31
37+29	JG-74	38+31	JG-72	43+31[1]	JbG-31
37+31	JG-72	38+32	JG-71	43+32	JbG-31
37+32	JG-71	38+33	JG-73	43+33[1]	JbG-38
37+33	JG-72	38+34	JG-72	43+34	TsLw-1
37+34	JG-72	38+36	JG-71	43+35[1]	JbG-38
37+35	JG-72	38+37	JG-72	43+37[1]	JbG-32
37+36	JG-72	38+39	JG-74	43+38	JbG-33
37+37	JG-72	38+40	JG-71	43+40	JbG-33
37+38	JG-71	38+42	JG-71	43+41	JbG-31
37+39	JG-71	38+43	JG-72	43+43[1]	JbG-38
37+42	JG-72	38+44	JG-71	43+46	AkG-51
37+43	JG-72	38+45	JG-71	43+47	AkG-51
37+44	JG-72	38+46	JG-71	43+48	AkG-51
37+45	JG-72	38+48	JG-74	43+50	AkG-51
37+47	JG-72	38+49	JG-71	43+52	JbG-38
37+48	JG-74	38+50	JG-72	43+53	JbG-34
37+49	JG-71	38+53	JG-74	43+54	JbG-34
37+50	JG-74	38+54	JG-73	43+55	MFG-2
37+52	JG-72	38+55	JG-71	43+58	JbG-34
37+54	JG-74	38+56	JG-73	43+59	TsLw-1
37+55	JG-71	38+57	JG-74	43+60	JbG-34
37+58	JG-72	38+58	JG-73	43+61	TsLw-1
37+61	JG-74	38+60	JG-74	43+62	JbG-34
37+63	JG-71	38+61	JG-72	43+63	JbG-34
37+64	JG-72	38+62	JG-74	43+64	JbG-33
37+65	JG-71	38+64	JG-72	43+65	JbG-38
37+66	JG-71	38+66	JG-73	43+67	JbG-34
37+67	JG-74	38+67	JG-73	43+68	JbG-34
37+71	JG-74	38+68	JG-74	43+69	JbG-38
37+75	JG-73	38+69	JG-74	43+70	JbG-33
37+76	JG-71	38+70	JG-74	43+71	JbG-38
37+77	JG-74	38+73	JG-72	43+72	JbG-38
37+78	JG-71	38+74	JG-74	43+73	AkG-51
37+79	JG-71	38+75	JG-71	43+75	JbG-34
37+81	JG-72	99+91	WTD-61	43+76	JbG-38
37+82	JG-71			43+77	JbG-34
37+83	JG-71	**Panavia Tornado Strike/**		43+78	JbG-34
37+84	JG-74	**Trainer[1]/ECR[2]**		43+79	AkG-51
37+85	JG-71	AkG-51 *Immelmann,*		43+80	AkG-51
37+86	JG-71	Schleswig/Jagel;		43+81	AkG-51
37+88	JG-74	EADS, Manching;		43+82	AkG-51
37+89	JG-73	JbG-31 *Boelcke,*		43+85	JbG-38
37+90		Nörvenich;		43+86	JbG-34
37+92	JG-74	JbG-32, Lechfeld;		43+87	MFG-2
37+93	JG-72	JbG-33, Büchel;		43+90[1]	JbG-31
37+94	JG-72	JbG-34 *Algau,*		43+92[1]	JbG-31
37+96	JG-72	Memmingen;		43+94[1]	JbG-34
37+97	JG-74	JbG-38 *Ostfriesland,*		43+96	AkG-51
37+98	JG-71	Jever;		43+98	AkG-51
38+00	JG-74	MFG-2, Eggebek;		44+00	JbG-31
38+01	JG-73	TsLw-1, Kaufbeuren;		44+04	AkG-51
38+02	JG-73	WTD-61, Ingolstadt		44+06	JbG-34
38+03	JG-72	43+01[1]	JbG-38	44+07	JbG-31
38+04	JG-72	43+02[1]	JbG-38	44+08	JbG-31
38+05	JG-73	43+03[1]	JbG-38	44+09	JbG-33
38+06	JG-74	43+04[1]	JbG-32	44+10[1]	JbG-38
38+07	JG-71	43+05[1]	JbG-38	44+11	JbG-34
38+09	JG-74	43+06[1]	JbG-38	44+13	TsLw-1
38+10	JG-74	43+07[1]	JbG-38	44+14	JbG-31
38+11		43+08[1]	JbG-32	44+15	JbG-38
38+12	JG-71	43+09[1]	JbG-38	44+16[1]	JbG-31
38+13	WTD-61	43+10[1]	JbG-38	44+17	AkG-51
38+14	JG-71	43+11[1]	JbG-38	44+19	JbG-31
38+16	JG-74	43+13	EADS	44+21	JbG-31
38+17	JG-74	43+15[1]	JbG-38	44+23	JbG-33
38+18	JG-74	43+16[1]	JbG-38	44+24	AkG-51
38+20	JG-72	43+17[1]	JbG-38	44+25[1]	JbG-38
38+24	JG-74	43+18	JbG-31	44+26	JbG-31
38+25	JG-74	43+20	JbG-34		

Reg	Unit	Reg	Unit	Reg	Unit
44+27	JbG-33	45+23	JbG-31	46+15	MFG-2
44+29	JbG-31	45+24	JbG-33	46+18	MFG-2
44+30	JbG-31	45+25	AkG-51	46+19	MFG-2
44+31	JbG-31	45+27	MFG-2	46+20	MFG-2
44+32	JbG-38	45+28	MFG-2	46+21	MFG-2
44+33	JbG-33	45+29	WTD-61	46+22	MFG-2
44+34	JbG-33	45+30	MFG-2	46+23[2]	JbG-32
44+35	JbG-31	45+31	MFG-2	46+24[2]	JbG-32
44+37[1]	JbG-34	45+33	MFG-2	46+25[2]	JbG-32
44+40	JbG-33	45+34	MFG-2	46+26[2]	JbG-32
44+41	JbG-31	45+35	MFG-2	46+27[2]	JbG-32
44+42	AkG-51	45+36	MFG-2	46+28[2]	JbG-32
44+43	JbG-34	45+37	MFG-2	46+29[2]	JbG-32
44+44	JbG-31	45+38	MFG-2	46+30[2]	JbG-32
44+46	JbG-34	45+39	MFG-2	46+31[2]	JbG-32
44+48	JbG-33	45+40	MFG-2	46+32[2]	JbG-32
44+49	JbG-31	45+41	MFG-2	46+33[2]	JbG-32
44+50	AkG-51	45+42	MFG-2	46+34[2]	JbG-32
44+51	JbG-31	45+43	MFG-2	46+35[2]	JbG-32
44+52	JbG-34	45+44	MFG-2	46+36[2]	JbG-32
44+54	JbG-33	45+45	MFG-2	46+37[2]	JbG-32
44+55	JbG-38	45+46	MFG-2	46+38[2]	JbG-32
44+56	JbG-34	45+47	MFG-2	46+39[2]	JbG-32
44+57	JbG-31	45+49	MFG-2	46+40[2]	JbG-32
44+58	JbG-31	45+50	MFG-2	46+41[2]	JbG-32
44+61	AkG-51	45+51	AkG-51	46+42[2]	JbG-32
44+62	JbG-33	45+52	MFG-2	46+43[2]	JbG-32
44+63	JbG-33	45+53	MFG-2	46+44[2]	JbG-32
44+64	AkG-51	45+54	MFG-2	46+45[2]	JbG-32
44+65	AkG-51	45+55	MFG-2	46+46[2]	JbG-32
44+66	JbG-31	45+56	MFG-2	46+47[2]	JbG-32
44+68	AkG-51	45+57	JbG-34	46+48[2]	JbG-32
44+69	AkG-51	45+59	MFG-2	46+49[2]	JbG-32
44+70	JbG-31	45+64	TsLw-1	46+50[2]	JbG-32
44+71	JbG-31	45+66	MFG-2	46+51[2]	JbG-32
44+72[1]	JbG-33	45+67	AkG-51	46+52[2]	JbG-32
44+75[1]	JbG-33	45+68	MFG-2	46+53[2]	JbG-32
44+76	JbG-34	45+69	MFG-2	46+54[2]	JbG-32
44+78	JbG-31	45+70[1]	JbG-33	46+55[2]	JbG-32
44+79	JbG-33	45+71	MFG-2	46+56[2]	JbG-32
44+80	JbG-33	45+72	MFG-2	46+57[2]	JbG-32
44+83	JbG-33	45+73[1]	JbG-31	98+03[2]	WTD-61
44+84	JbG-33	45+74	MFG-2	98+59	WTD-61
44+85	JbG-33	45+76	JbG-38	98+60	WTD-61
44+86	AkG-51	45+77[1]	JbG-33	98+79[2]	WTD-61
44+87	AkG-51	45+78	JbG-33		
44+88	AkG-51	45+79	JbG-31	**Transall C-160D**	
44+89	JbG-33	45+81	JbG-34	LTG-61, Landsberg;	
44+90	JbG-33	45+82	JbG-31	LTG-62, Wunstorf;	
44+91	JbG-33	45+84	AkG-51	LTG-63, Hohn;	
44+92	JbG-38	45+85	AkG-51	WTD-61, Ingolstadt	
44+94	JbG-33	45+86	JbG-33	50+06	LTG-63
44+95	JbG-38	45+87	JbG-34	50+07	LTG-61
44+96	JbG-31	45+88	JbG-33	50+08	LTG-63
44+97	JbG-38	45+89	JbG-34	50+09	LTG-62
44+98	JbG-34	45+90	JbG-31	50+10	LTG-62
45+00	JbG-33	45+91	AkG-51	50+17	LTG-62
45+02	JbG-34	45+93	AkG-51	50+29	LTG-62
45+03	JbG-34	45+94	JbG-33	50+33	LTG-62
45+04	JbG-33	45+95	JbG-34	50+34	LTG-63
45+06	AkG-51	45+98	AkG-51	50+35	LTG-62
45+07	JbG-33	45+99[1]	AkG-51	50+36	LTG-62
45+08	JbG-33	46+00	JbG-34	50+37	LTG-62
45+12[1]	MFG-2	46+01	JbG-34	50+38	LTG-62
45+13[1]	MFG-2	46+02	JbG-33	50+40	LTG-61
45+14[1]	JbG-38	46+04[1]	JbG-32	50+41	LTG-62
45+15[1]	MFG-2	46+05[1]	MFG-2	50+42	LTG-63
45+16[1]	MFG-2	46+07[1]	JbG-34	50+44	LTG-62
45+17	JbG-33	46+08[1]	AkG-51	50+45	LTG-63
45+18	JbG-33	46+10	WTD-61	50+46	LTG-62
45+19	JbG-33	46+11	MFG-2	50+47	LTG-61
45+20	AkG-51	46+12	MFG-2	50+48	LTG-61
45+21	JbG-33	46+13	JbG-34	50+49	LTG-63
45+22	JbG-33	46+14	JbG-34	50+50	LTG-62

Germany

<table>
<tr><td>50+51</td><td>LTG-61</td></tr>
<tr><td>50+52</td><td>LTG-62</td></tr>
<tr><td>50+53</td><td>LTG-61</td></tr>
<tr><td>50+54</td><td>LTG-63</td></tr>
<tr><td>50+55</td><td>LTG-62</td></tr>
<tr><td>50+56</td><td>LTG-63</td></tr>
<tr><td>50+57</td><td>WTD-61</td></tr>
<tr><td>50+58</td><td>LTG-62</td></tr>
<tr><td>50+59</td><td>LTG-63</td></tr>
<tr><td>50+60</td><td>LTG-62</td></tr>
<tr><td>50+61</td><td>LTG-63</td></tr>
<tr><td>50+62</td><td>LTG-62</td></tr>
<tr><td>50+64</td><td>LTG-61</td></tr>
<tr><td>50+65</td><td>LTG-62</td></tr>
<tr><td>50+66</td><td>LTG-61</td></tr>
<tr><td>50+67</td><td>LTG-63</td></tr>
<tr><td>50+68</td><td>LTG-61</td></tr>
<tr><td>50+69</td><td>LTG-63</td></tr>
<tr><td>50+70</td><td>LTG-63</td></tr>
<tr><td>50+71</td><td>LTG-63</td></tr>
<tr><td>50+72</td><td>LTG-63</td></tr>
<tr><td>50+73</td><td>LTG-63</td></tr>
<tr><td>50+74</td><td>LTG-61</td></tr>
<tr><td>50+75</td><td>LTG-63</td></tr>
<tr><td>50+76</td><td>LTG-63</td></tr>
<tr><td>50+77</td><td>LTG-63</td></tr>
<tr><td>50+78</td><td>LTG-62</td></tr>
<tr><td>50+79</td><td>LTG-63</td></tr>
<tr><td>50+81</td><td>LTG-62</td></tr>
<tr><td>50+82</td><td>LTG-63</td></tr>
<tr><td>50+83</td><td>LTG-62</td></tr>
<tr><td>50+84</td><td>LTG-61</td></tr>
<tr><td>50+85</td><td>LTG-63</td></tr>
<tr><td>50+86</td><td>LTG-61</td></tr>
<tr><td>50+87</td><td>LTG-63</td></tr>
<tr><td>50+88</td><td>LTG-61</td></tr>
<tr><td>50+89</td><td>LTG-62</td></tr>
<tr><td>50+90</td><td>LTG-62</td></tr>
<tr><td>50+91</td><td>LTG-62</td></tr>
<tr><td>50+92</td><td>LTG-61</td></tr>
<tr><td>50+93</td><td>LTG-61</td></tr>
<tr><td>50+94</td><td>LTG-61</td></tr>
<tr><td>50+95</td><td>LTG-63</td></tr>
<tr><td>50+96</td><td>LTG-61</td></tr>
<tr><td>50+97</td><td>LTG-62</td></tr>
<tr><td>50+98</td><td>LTG-61</td></tr>
<tr><td>50+99</td><td>LTG-61</td></tr>
<tr><td>51+00</td><td>LTG-62</td></tr>
<tr><td>51+01</td><td>LTG-62</td></tr>
<tr><td>51+02</td><td>LTG-63</td></tr>
<tr><td>51+03</td><td>LTG-62</td></tr>
<tr><td>51+04</td><td>LTG-61</td></tr>
<tr><td>51+05</td><td>LTG-62</td></tr>
<tr><td>51+06</td><td>LTG-63</td></tr>
<tr><td>51+07</td><td>LTG-62</td></tr>
<tr><td>51+08</td><td>WTD-61</td></tr>
<tr><td>51+09</td><td>LTG-63</td></tr>
<tr><td>51+10</td><td>LTG-61</td></tr>
<tr><td>51+11</td><td>LTG-62</td></tr>
<tr><td>51+12</td><td>LTG-63</td></tr>
<tr><td>51+13</td><td>LTG-61</td></tr>
<tr><td>51+14</td><td>LTG-63</td></tr>
<tr><td>51+15</td><td>LTG-61</td></tr>
</table>

Dornier Do.228/Do.228LM*
MFG-3, Nordholz;
WTD-61, Ingolstadt

<table>
<tr><td>57+01*</td><td>MFG-3</td></tr>
<tr><td>57+02*</td><td>MFG-3</td></tr>
<tr><td>57+03</td><td>MFG-3</td></tr>
<tr><td>57+04*</td><td>MFG-3</td></tr>
<tr><td>98+78</td><td>WTD-61</td></tr>
</table>

Breguet Br.1150 Atlantic *Elint
MFG-3, Nordholz

61+03*
61+04
61+05
61+06*
61+08
61+09
61+10
61+11
61+12
61+13
61+14
61+15
61+16
61+17
61+18*
61+19*
61+20

Eurocopter AS.532U-2 Cougar
3/FBS, Berlin-Tegel

82+01
82+02
82+03

Westland Lynx Mk88/ Super Lynx Mk88A*
MFG-3, Nordholz

83+02
83+03
83+04
83+05
83+06
83+07
83+09
83+10
83+11
83+12
83+13
83+17
83+18
83+19
83+20*
83+21*
83+22*
83+23*
83+24*
83+25*
83+26*

Westland Sea King HAS41
MFG-5, Kiel-Holtenau

89+50
89+51
89+52
89+53
89+54
89+55
89+56
89+57
89+58
89+60
89+61
89+62
89+63
89+64
89+65
89+66
89+67
89+68
89+69
89+70
89+71

Eurofighter Typhoon
WTD-61, Ingolstadt

98+29 WTD-61
98+30 WTD-61

NH Industries NH.90
98+90

Heeresfliegertruppe
Eurocopter EC.135P-1
HFWS, Bückeburg

82+51
82+52
82+53
82+54
82+55
82+56
82+57
82+58
82+59
82+60
82+61
82+62
82+63
82+64
82+65

MBB Bo.105
HFlgRgt-15, Rheine-
  Bentlage;
HFlgRgt-16, Celle;
HFlgRgt-25, Laupheim;
HFlgRgt-26, Roth;
HFlgRgt-35, Mendig;
HFlgRgt-36, Fritzlar;
HFS-400, Cottbus;
HFVS-910, Bückeburg;
HFWS, Bückeburg;
TsLw-3, Fassberg;
WTD-61, Ingolstadt

<table>
<tr><td>80+01</td><td>Bo.105M</td><td>HFR-35</td></tr>
<tr><td>80+02</td><td>Bo.105M</td><td>HFWS</td></tr>
<tr><td>80+03</td><td>Bo.105M</td><td>HFWS</td></tr>
<tr><td>80+04</td><td>Bo.105M</td><td>HFWS</td></tr>
<tr><td>80+05</td><td>Bo.105M</td><td>HFR-35</td></tr>
<tr><td>80+06</td><td>Bo.105M</td><td>HFWS</td></tr>
<tr><td>80+07</td><td>Bo.105M</td><td>HFWS</td></tr>
<tr><td>80+08</td><td>Bo.105M</td><td>HFR-25</td></tr>
<tr><td>80+09</td><td>Bo.105M</td><td>HFR-35</td></tr>
<tr><td>80+10</td><td>Bo.105M</td><td>HFR-25</td></tr>
<tr><td>80+11</td><td>Bo.105M</td><td>HFWS</td></tr>
<tr><td>80+12</td><td>Bo.105M</td><td>HFWS</td></tr>
<tr><td>80+13</td><td>Bo.105M</td><td>HFR-15</td></tr>
<tr><td>80+14</td><td>Bo.105M</td><td>TsLw-3</td></tr>
<tr><td>80+15</td><td>Bo.105M</td><td>HFR-15</td></tr>
<tr><td>80+16</td><td>Bo.105M</td><td>HFR-15</td></tr>
<tr><td>80+17</td><td>Bo.105M</td><td>HFS-400</td></tr>
<tr><td>80+18</td><td>Bo.105M</td><td>HFR-15</td></tr>
<tr><td>80+19</td><td>Bo.105M</td><td>HFR-15</td></tr>
<tr><td>80+20</td><td>Bo.105M</td><td>HFS-400</td></tr>
<tr><td>80+21</td><td>Bo.105M</td><td>HFR-15</td></tr>
<tr><td>80+22</td><td>Bo.105M</td><td>HFS-400</td></tr>
<tr><td>80+23</td><td>Bo.105M</td><td>HFR-15</td></tr>
<tr><td>80+24</td><td>Bo.105M</td><td>HFR-15</td></tr>
<tr><td>80+25</td><td>Bo.105M</td><td>HFR-35</td></tr>
<tr><td>80+26</td><td>Bo.105M</td><td>HFR-35</td></tr>
<tr><td>80+27</td><td>Bo.105M</td><td>HFR-35</td></tr>
<tr><td>80+28</td><td>Bo.105M</td><td>TsLw-3</td></tr>
<tr><td>80+29</td><td>Bo.105M</td><td>HFR-35</td></tr>
<tr><td>80+30</td><td>Bo.105M</td><td>HFR-35</td></tr>
</table>

80+31	Bo.105M	HFR-35	86+08	Bo.105P	HFWS	86+85	Bo.105P	HFR-16
80+32	Bo.105M	HFR-35	86+09	Bo.105P	HFWS	86+86	Bo.105P	HFR-16
80+33	Bo.105M	HFR-35	86+10	Bo.105P	HFR-16	86+87	Bo.105P	HFR-16
80+34	Bo.105M	HFR-25	86+11	Bo.105P	HFWS	86+88	Bo.105P	HFR-16
80+35	Bo.105M	HFS-400	86+12	Bo.105P	HFWS	86+89	Bo.105P	TsLw-3
80+36	Bo.105M	HFR-25	86+13	Bo.105P	HFWS	86+90	Bo.105P	HFR-26
80+37	Bo.105M	HFS-400	86+14	Bo.105P	HFR-16	86+91	Bo.105P	HFR-26
80+38	Bo.105M	HFR-25	86+15	Bo.105P	HFR-16	86+92	Bo.105P	HFR-36
80+39	Bo.105M	HFR-25	86+16	Bo.105P	HFWS	86+93	Bo.105P	HFVS-910
80+40	Bo.105M	HFR-25	86+17	Bo.105P	HFVS-910	86+94	Bo.105P	HFWS
80+41	Bo.105M	HFR-25	86+18	Bo.105P	HFR-26	86+95	Bo.105P	HFR-16
80+42	Bo.105M	HFR-25	86+19	Bo.105P	HFR-26	86+96	Bo.105P	HFR-26
80+43	Bo.105M	HFR-25	86+20	Bo.105P	HFWS	86+97	Bo.105P	HFR-36
80+44	Bo.105M	HFR-25	86+21	Bo.105P	HFR-36	86+98	Bo.105P	HFR-16
80+46	Bo.105M	TsLw-3	86+22	Bo.105P	HFWS	86+99	Bo.105P	HFR-26
80+47	Bo.105M	HFR-25	86+23	Bo.105P	HFWS	87+00	Bo.105P	HFR-26
80+48	Bo.105M	HFR-25	86+24	Bo.105P	HFVS-910	87+01	Bo.105P	HFR-26
80+49	Bo.105M	HFS-400	86+25	Bo.105P	HFR-16	87+02	Bo.105P	HFR-26
80+50	Bo.105M	HFS-400	86+26	Bo.105P	HFR-36	87+03	Bo.105P	HFR-26
80+51	Bo.105M	HFR-15	86+27	Bo.105P	HFR-26	87+04	Bo.105P	HFR-26
80+52	Bo.105M	HFR-15	86+28	Bo.105P	HFR-16	87+05	Bo.105P	HFR-26
80+53	Bo.105M	HFS-400	86+29	Bo.105P	HFR-16	87+06	Bo.105P	HFR-36
80+54	Bo.105M	HFR-15	86+30	Bo.105P	HFR-26	87+07	Bo.105P	HFR-26
80+55	Bo.105M	HFS-400	86+31	Bo.105P	HFR-16	87+08	Bo.105P	HFR-16
80+56	Bo.105M	HFS-400	86+32	Bo.105P	HFR-26	87+09	Bo.105P	HFR-36
80+57	Bo.105M	HFR-35	86+33	Bo.105P	HFR-26	87+10	Bo.105P	HFR-26
80+58	Bo.105M	HFR-35	86+34	Bo.105P	HFR-26	87+11	Bo.105P	HFR-36
80+59	Bo.105M	HFR-35	86+35	Bo.105P	HFR-26	87+12	Bo.105P	HFR-36
80+60	Bo.105M	HFR-35	86+36	Bo.105P	HFR-36	87+13	Bo.105P	HFR-36
80+61	Bo.105M	HFS-400	86+37	Bo.105P	HFR-16	87+14	Bo.105P	HFR-36
80+62	Bo.105M	HFR-35	86+38	Bo.105P	HFR-36	87+15	Bo.105P	HFR-36
80+64	Bo.105M	HFR-35	86+39	Bo.105P	HFR-16	87+16	Bo.105P	HFR-36
80+65	Bo.105M	HFR-15	86+41	Bo.105P	HFR-16	87+17	Bo.105P	HFR-26
80+66	Bo.105M	HFR-15	86+42	Bo.105P	HFR-26	87+18	Bo.105P	HFR-36
80+67	Bo.105M	HFR-15	86+43	Bo.105P	HFR-16	87+19	Bo.105P	HFR-36
80+68	Bo.105M	HFR-15	86+44	Bo.105P	HFR-26	87+20	Bo.105P	HFR-26
80+69	Bo.105M	HFR-15	86+45	Bo.105P	HFVS-910	87+21	Bo.105P	HFWS
80+70	Bo.105M	HFR-15	86+46	Bo.105P	HFR-26	87+22	Bo.105P	HFR-16
80+71	Bo.105M	HFR-15	86+47	Bo.105P	HFR-16	87+23	Bo.105P	HFR-36
80+72	Bo.105M	HFR-15	86+48	Bo.105P	HFR-16	87+24	Bo.105P	HFR-16
80+73	Bo.105M	HFR-15	86+49	Bo.105P	HFR-26	87+25	Bo.105P	HFR-26
80+74	Bo.105M	HFR-15	86+50	Bo.105P	HFR-16	87+26	Bo.105P	HFR-16
80+76	Bo.105M	HFR-15	86+51	Bo.105P	HFR-36	87+27	Bo.105P	HFR-16
80+77	Bo.105M	HFR-35	86+52	Bo.105P	HFR-16	87+28	Bo.105P	HFR-16
80+78	Bo.105M	HFR-35	86+53	Bo.105P	HFR-26	87+29	Bo.105P	HFR-26
80+79	Bo.105M	HFR-35	86+54	Bo.105P	HFR-16	87+30	Bo.105P	HFWS
80+80	Bo.105M	HFR-35	86+55	Bo.105P	HFR-16	87+31	Bo.105P	HFR-16
80+81	Bo.105M	HFR-25	86+56	Bo.105P	HFR-36	87+32	Bo.105P	HFVS-910
80+82	Bo.105M	HFR-25	86+57	Bo.105P	HFR-16	87+33	Bo.105P	HFR-26
80+83	Bo.105M	HFR-25	86+58	Bo.105P	HFR-36	87+34	Bo.105P	HFR-26
80+84	Bo.105M	HFR-25	86+59	Bo.105P	HFR-16	87+35	Bo.105P	HFR-26
80+85	Bo.105M	HFR-25	86+60	Bo.105P	HFR-16	87+36	Bo.105P	HFR-26
80+86	Bo.105M	HFS-400	86+61	Bo.105P	HFR-26	87+37	Bo.105P	HFR-26
80+87	Bo.105M	HFS-25	86+62	Bo.105P	HFVS-910	87+38	Bo.105P	HFR-36
80+88	Bo.105M	HFS-400	86+63	Bo.105P	HFVS-910	87+39	Bo.105P	HFR-36
80+89	Bo.105M	HFS-400	86+64	Bo.105P	HFR-26	87+41	Bo.105P	HFR-16
80+90	Bo.105M	HFS-400	86+65	Bo.105P	HFR-26	87+42	Bo.105P	HFR-36
80+91	Bo.105M	HFR-35	86+66	Bo.105P	HFVS-910	87+43	Bo.105P	HFR-36
80+92	Bo.105M	HFR-35	86+67	Bo.105P	HFR-26	87+44	Bo.105P	HFR-36
80+93	Bo.105M	HFR-35	86+68	Bo.105P	HFR-36	87+45	Bo.105P	TsLw-3
80+94	Bo.105M	HFR-25	86+69	Bo.105P	HFR-26	87+46	Bo.105P	HFR-16
80+95	Bo.105M	HFS-400	86+70	Bo.105P	HFR-16	87+47	Bo.105P	HFR-16
80+96	Bo.105M	HFR-25	86+71	Bo.105P	HFR-36	87+48	Bo.105P	HFR-16
80+97	Bo.105M	HFR-35	86+72	Bo.105P	HFR-36	87+49	Bo.105P	HFR-16
80+98	Bo.105M	HFR-25	86+73	Bo.105P	HFWS	87+50	Bo.105P	HFR-26
80+99	Bo.105M	HFR-25	86+74	Bo.105P	HFR-16	87+51	Bo.105P	HFR-16
81+00	Bo.105M	HFR-25	86+75	Bo.105P	HFR-36	87+52	Bo.105P	HFR-16
86+01	Bo.105P	HFWS	86+76	Bo.105P	HFR-26	87+53	Bo.105P	HFR-26
86+02	Bo.105P	HFWS	86+77	Bo.105P	HFR-16	87+55	Bo.105P	HFVS-910
86+03	Bo.105P	HFWS	86+78	Bo.105P	HFR-26	87+56	Bo.105P	HFR-26
86+04	Bo.105P	HFR-36	86+80	Bo.105P	HFR-16	87+57	Bo.105P	HFR-26
86+05	Bo.105P	HFWS	86+81	Bo.105P	HFR-16	87+58	Bo.105P	HFR-26
86+06	Bo.105P	HFWS	86+83	Bo.105P	HFR-16	87+59	Bo.105P	HFR-36
86+07	Bo.105P	HFWS	86+84	Bo.105P	HFR-16	87+60	Bo.105P	HFR-36

87+61	Bo.105P	HFR-35
87+62	Bo.105P	HFR-36
87+63	Bo.105P	TsLw-3
87+64	Bo.105P	HFR-36
87+65	Bo.105P	HFR-36
87+66	Bo.105P	TsLw-3
87+67	Bo.105P	HFWS
87+68	Bo.105P	HFR-16
87+69	Bo.105P	HFR-26
87+70	Bo.105P	HFR-16
87+71	Bo.105P	HFR-26
87+72	Bo.105P	HFR-16
87+73	Bo.105P	HFR-16
87+74	Bo.105P	HFVS-910
87+75	Bo.105P	HFR-16
87+76	Bo.105P	HFR-16
87+77	Bo.105P	HFR-16
87+78	Bo.105P	HFR-16
87+79	Bo.105P	HFR-16
87+80	Bo.105P	HFR-16
87+81	Bo.105P	HFR-16
87+82	Bo.105P	HFR-16
87+83	Bo.105P	HFR-16
87+84	Bo.105P	HFVS-910
87+85	Bo.105P	HFR-26
87+86	Bo.105P	HFR-26
87+87	Bo.105P	HFVS-910
87+88	Bo.105P	HFR-26
87+89	Bo.105P	HFR-26
87+90	Bo.105P	HFWS
87+91	Bo.105P	HFR-26
87+92	Bo.105P	HFR-26
87+93	Bo.105P	HFR-26
87+94	Bo.105P	HFR-26
87+95	Bo.105P	HFR-26
87+96	Bo.105P	HFR-26
87+97	Bo.105P	HFR-36
87+98	Bo.105P	HFR-26
87+99	Bo.105P	HFR-36
88+01	Bo.105P	HFR-26
88+02	Bo.105P	HFR-36
88+03	Bo.105P	HFR-36
88+04	Bo.105P	HFR-16
88+05	Bo.105P	HFVS-910
88+06	Bo.105P	HFR-36
88+07	Bo.105P	HFR-36
88+08	Bo.105P	HFR-36
88+09	Bo.105P	HFR-36
88+10	Bo.105P	HFWS
88+11	Bo.105P	HFR-36
88+12	Bo.105P	HFR-36
98+28	Bo.105C	WTD-61

Sikorsky/VFW CH-53G/CH-53GS*
HFlgRgt-15, Rheine-Bentlage;
HFlgRgt-25, Laupheim;
HFlgRgt-35, Mendig;
HFWS, Bückeburg;
TsLw-3, Fassberg;
WTD-61, Ingolstadt

84+01*	WTD-61
84+02	WTD-61
84+03	HFR-15
84+04	HFWS
84+05	HFR-35
84+06	HFR-15
84+07	HFWS
84+08*	HFWS
84+09	HFR-25
84+10	HFWS
84+11	HFWS
84+12	HFR-15

84+13	HFWS
84+14	HFWS
84+15*	HFR-25
84+16	HFWS
84+17	HFR-25
84+18	HFWS
84+19	HFWS
84+20	HFR-35
84+21	HFWS
84+22	HFR-15
84+23	HFR-35
84+24	HFR-35
84+25	HFR-35
84+26	HFR-35
84+27	HFR-35
84+28	HFR-25
84+29	HFR-35
84+30	HFR-35
84+31	HFR-35
84+32	HFR-35
84+33	HFR-35
84+34	HFR-35
84+35	HFR-35
84+36	HFR-35
84+37	HFWS
84+38	HFR-35
84+39	HFR-35
84+40	HFR-25
84+41	HFWS
84+42	HFR-25
84+43	HFR-25
84+44	HFR-25
84+45	HFR-25
84+46	HFR-35
84+4	HFR-25
84+48	HFR-25
84+49	HFWS
84+50	HFR-25
84+51	HFR-25
84+52*	HFR-25
84+53	HFR-25
84+54	HFR-25
84+55	HFR-25
84+56	HFR-35
84+57	HFR-25
84+58	HFR-25
84+59	HFR-25
84+60	HFR-25
84+62	HFR-25
84+63	HFR-25
84+64	HFR-35
84+65	HFR-35
84+66	HFR-35
84+67	HFR-35
84+68	HFWS
84+69	HFR-15
84+70	HFR-15
84+71	HFR-15
84+72	HFR-15
84+73	HFR-15
84+74	HFR-15
84+75	HFR-15
84+76	HFR-15
84+77	HFR-15
84+78	HFR-15
84+79*	HFR-15
84+80	HFR-15
84+82	HFR-35
84+83	HFR-15
84+84	TsLw-3
84+85	HFR-15
84+86	HFR-15
84+87	HFR-15
84+88	HFR-15

84+89	HFR-15
84+90	HFR-15
84+91	HFR-15
84+93	HFR-35
84+94	HFR-35
84+95	HFR-25
84+96	HFR-25
84+97	HFR-25
84+98	HFWS
84+99	HFR-15
85+00*	HFWS
85+01	HFR-35
85+02	HFR-35
85+03	HFR-35
85+04	HFR-25
85+05	HFR-25
85+06	HFR-25
85+07	HFR-15
85+08	HFR-15
85+09	HFR-15
85+10	HFR-35
85+11	HFR-25
85+12*	HFWS

Eurocopter AS.665 Tiger
WTD-61, Ingolstadt
98+23
98+25

GHANA
Ghana Air Force
Fokker F-28 Fellowship 3000
VIP Flight, Accra
G-530

Grumman G.1159A Gulfstream III
VIP Flight, Accra
G-540

GREECE
Ellinikí Polemikí Aeroporía
Embraer ERJ.135LR
356 MTM/112 PM, Elefsís
209

Lockheed C-130H Hercules
356 MTM/112 PM, Elefsís
*ECM
741*
742
743
744
745
746
747*
749
751
752

Lockheed F-16C/F-16D* Fighting Falcon
330 Mira/111 PM, Nea Ankhialos;
341 Mira/111 PM, Nea Ankhialos;
346 MAPK/110 PM, Larissa;
347 Mira/111 PM, Nea Ankhialos

045	347 Mira
046	341 Mira
047	347 Mira
048	341 Mira

049	347 Mira
050	341 Mira
051	347 Mira
052	341 Mira
053	347 Mira
054	341 Mira
055	347 Mira
056	341 Mira
057	347 Mira
058	341 Mira
059	347 Mira
060	347 Mira
061	347 Mira
062	341 Mira
063	347 Mira
064	341 Mira
065	347 Mira
066	341 Mira
067	347 Mira
068	341 Mira
069	347 Mira
070	341 Mira
071	347 Mira
072	341 Mira
073	347 Mira
074	341 Mira
075	341 Mira
076	347 Mira
077*	347 Mira
078*	341 Mira
079*	347 Mira
080*	341 Mira
081*	347 Mira
082*	341 Mira
083*	347 Mira
084*	341 Mira
110	330 Mira
111	330 Mira
112	346 MAPK
113	330 Mira
114	346 MAPK
115	330 Mira
116	330 Mira
117	330 Mira
118	346 MAPK
119	330 Mira
120	330 Mira
121	330 Mira
122	346 MAPK
123	330 Mira
124	330 Mira
125	330 Mira
126	346 MAPK
127	330 Mira
128	346 MAPK
129	330 Mira
130	346 MAPK
132	346 MAPK
133	330 Mira
134	346 MAPK
136	346 MAPK
138	346 MAPK
139	330 Mira
140	346 MAPK
141	330 Mira
143	330 Mira
144*	330 Mira
145*	330 Mira
146*	346 MAPK
147*	330 Mira
148*	346 MAPK
149*	330 Mira

Greek Govt
Dassault Falcon 900
Greek Govt/Olympic
  Airways, Athens
SX-ECH

Piaggio P-180AM Avanti
Greek Govt/Olympic
  Airways, Athens
SX-BNC
SX-BND

HUNGARY
Magyar Honvédseg Repülö
  Csapatai
Antonov An-26
89 VSD, Szolnok

405	(03405)	
406	(03406)	
407	(03407)	
603	(03603)	

ISRAEL
Heyl ha'Avir
Boeing 707
120 Sqn, Tel Aviv

120	RC-707
128	RC-707
137	RC-707
140	KC-707
242	VC-707
248	KC-707
250	KC-707
255	EC-707
258	EC-707
260	KC-707
264	RC-707
272	VC-707
290	VC-707

Lockheed C-130 Hercules
103 Sqn & 131 Sqn, Tel Aviv

102	C-130H
106	C-130H
302	C-130E
305	C-130E
307	C-130E
309	C-130H
310	C-130E
311	C-130E
312	C-130E
313	C-130E
314	C-130E
316	C-130E
420	C-130H
423	C-130H
427	C-130H
428	C-130H
435	C-130H
436	KC-130H
448	C-130H
522	KC-130H
545	KC-130H

Israeli Govt
Hawker 800XP
Israeli Govt, Tel Aviv
4X-COV

ITALY
Aeronautica Militare Italiana
Aeritalia G222
9ª Brigata Aerea,
  Pratica di Mare:
    8° Gruppo & 71° Gruppo;
46ª Brigata Aerea, Pisa:
    2° Gruppo & 98° Gruppo;
RSV, Pratica di Mare
G222AAA
CSX62144
G222TCM

MM62104	46-91	98
MM62109	46-96	98
MM62111	46-83	98
MM62115	46-22	2
MM62117	46-25	2
MM62119	46-21	2
MM62120	46-90	98
MM62124	46-88	98
MM62125	14-24	8
MM62126	46-26	2
MM62133	46-93	98
MM62135	46-94	98
MM62136	46-97	98
MM62137	46-95	98
MM62152	RS-45	RSV
MM62153X	RS-46	RSV

G222VS

MM62107		71

G222RM

MM62139	14-20	8
MM62140	14-21	8
MM62141	14-22	8
MM62142	14-23	8

Aeritalia-EMB AMX/AMX-T*
2° Stormo, Rivolto:
  14° Gruppo;
32° Stormo, Amendola:
  13° Gruppo &
  101° Gruppo;
51° Stormo, Istrana:
  103° Gruppo &
  132° Gruppo;
RSV, Pratica di Mare

MMX595		Alenia
MMX596		Alenia
MMX597		Alenia
MMX599		Alenia
MM7089		
MM7090	2-14	14
MM7091	32-64	101
MM7092	RS-14	RSV
MM7093		
MM7094	3-37	
MM7095		103
MM7096		
MM7097	3-36	
MM7098	3-35	
MM7099		
MM7100	32-66	101
MM7101	51-25	103
MM7102	2-03	14
MM7103		
MM7104	51-26	103
MM7105	32-20	13
MM7106	3-25	
MM7107		
MM7110		
MM7111	51-50	132
MM7112		
MM7114	32-15	13
MM7115	2-12	14

MM7116	32-11	13
MM7117	3-34	
MM7118	2-11	14
MM7119		
MM7120	51-52	132
MM7122	3-32	
MM7123		
MM7124	51-53	132
MM7125	RS-11	RSV
MM7126	32-12	13
MM7127	3-24	
MM7128		
MM7129	2-03	14
MM7130	32-02	13
MM7131	2-19	14
MM7132	51-14	103
MM7133	2-18	14
MM7134	51-15	103
MM7135		
MM7138		
MM7139	51-16	103
MM7140	51-40	132
MM7141		
MM7142	51-37	132
MM7143	51-20	103
MM7144	51-41	132
MM7145	51-21	103
MM7146	51-42	132
MM7147	32-04	13
MM7148	51-51	132
MM7149		
MM7150	32-65	101
MM7151		
MM7152		
MM7153	2-20	14
MM7154	51-54	132
MM7155	32-05	13
MM7156	32-10	13
MM7157	32-06	13
CSX7158	RS-12	RSV
MM7159		
MM7160	32-14	13
MM7161	2-21	14
MM7162	51-01	103
MM7163	51-63	132
MM7164	51-30	132
MM7165	51-31	132
MM7166		
MM7167	2-01	14
MM7168	2-04	14
MM7169	2-06	14
MM7170	2-23	14
MM7171	2-15	14
MM7172	2-07	14
MM7173	2-16	14
MM7174		
MM7175	51-43	132
MM7176	2-20	14
MM7177	2-22	14
MM7178	2-24	14
MM7179	51-11	103
MM7180		
MM7181	51-32	132
MM7182	51-04	103
MM7183	32-01	13
MM7184	51-33	132
MM7185	51-35	132
MM7186	51-05	103
MM7187	32-16	13
MM7188	51-36	132
MM7189	51-03	103
MM7190	32-17	13
MM7191		

MM7192	51-06	103
MM7193	51-07	103
MM7194	32-07	13
MM7195	51-37	132
MM7196	32-13	13
MM7197	32-21	13
MM7198	32-03	13
MM55024*	15	RSV
MM55025*	RS-16	RSV
MM55026*	32-43	101
MM55027*		
MM55028*	3-26	
MM55029*	3-55	
MM55030*	32-41	101
MM55031*	32-40	101
MM55034*	18	RSV
MM55035*	32-50	101
MM55036*	32-51	101
MM55037*	51-55	132
MM55038*	32-53	101
MM55039*	32-54	101
MM55040*	32-52	101
MM55041*	32-55	101
MM55042*	32-56	101
MM55043*	51-10	103
MM55044*	32-57	101
MM55045*	2-10	14
MM55046*	32-47	101
MM55047*	32-45	101
MM55048*	32-44	101
MM55049*	32-46	101
MM55050*		
MM55051*	32-42	101

Aermacchi MB339A/MB339CD*
61° Stormo, Lecce:
212° Gruppo &
213° Gruppo;
Aermacchi, Venegono;
Frecce Tricolori [FT]
(313° Gruppo), Rivolto
(MB339A/PAN);
RSV, Pratica di Mare

MMX606*		RSV
MM54438	61-93	
MM54440	61-00	
MM54441	RS-28	RSV
MM54442	61-95	
MM54443	61-50	
MM54445	61-25	
MM54446	61-01	
MM54447	61-02	
MM54449	61-04	
MM54450	61-94	
MM54451	61-86	
MM54452		
MM54453	61-05	
MM54454	61-06	
MM54455	61-07	
MM54456	61-10	
MM54457	61-11	
MM54458	61-12	
MM54459	61-13	
MM54460	61-14	
MM54461		
MM54462	61-16	
MM54463	61-17	
MM54467	61-23	
MM54468	61-24	
MM54471	61-27	
MM54472	61-30	
MM54473	8	[FT]

MM54475	1	[FT]
MM54478		[FT]
MM54479	12	[FT]
MM54480	7	[FT]
MM54482	13	[FT]
MM54483		[FT]
MM54484		[FT]
MM54485	9	[FT]
MM54486		[FT]
MM54487	61-31	
MM54488	61-32	
MM54489	61-33	
MM54490	61-34	
MM54491	61-35	
MM54492	61-36	
MM54493	61-37	
MM54494	61-40	
MM54496	61-42	
MM54497	61-43	
MM54498	61-44	
MM54499	61-45	
MM54500	4	[FT]
MM54503	61-51	
MM54504	61-52	
MM54505	61-53	
MM54506	61-54	
MM54507	61-55	
MM54508	61-56	
MM54509	61-57	
MM54510	61-60	
MM54511	61-61	
MM54512	61-62	
MM54513	61-63	
MM54514	61-64	
MM54515	61-65	
MM54516	61-66	
MM54517	3	[FT]
MM54518	61-70	
MM54532	61-71	
MM54533	61-72	
MM54534	61-73	
MM54535	61-74	
MM54536	5	[FT]
MM54537		
MM54538	61-75	
MM54539	61-76	
MM54541	61-80	
MM54542	10	[FT]
MM54543	6	[FT]
MM54544*	Aermacchi	
MM54545	61-84	
MM54546	2	[FT]
MM54547	0	[FT]
MM54548	61-90	
MM54549	61-107	
MM54550	61-110	
MM54551		[FT]
MM55052	61-96	
MM55053	61-97	
MM55054	61-15	
MM55055	61-20	
MM55058	61-41	
MM55059	61-26	
MM55062*	RS-26	RSV
MM55063*	RS-27	RSV
MM55064*	61-130	
MM55065*	61-131	
MM55066*	61-132	
MM55067*	61-133	
MM55068*	61-134	
MM55069*	61-135	
MM55070*	61-136	
MM55072*	61-140	

MM55073* 61-141
MM55074* 61-142
MM55075* 61-143
MM55076* 61-144

Airbus A.319CJ-115
31° Stormo,
  Roma-Ciampino:
  93° Gruppo
MM62173
MM62174

Boeing 707-328B/-3F5C*
9ª Brigata Aerea,
  Pratica di Mare:
  8° Gruppo;
MM62148 14-01
MM62149 14-02
MM62150* 14-03
MM62151* 14-04

Breguet Br.1150 Atlantic
30° Stormo, Cagliari:
  86° Gruppo;
41° Stormo, Catania:
  88° Gruppo
MM40108 41-70
MM40109 30-71
MM40110 41-72
MM40111 41-73
MM40112 30-74
MM40113 30-75
MM40114 41-76
MM40115 41-77
MM40116 30-01
MM40117 41-02
MM40118 30-03
MM40119 30-04
MM40120 41-05
MM40121 41-06
MM40122 30-07
MM40123 30-10
MM40124 41-11
MM40125 30-12

Dassault Falcon 50
31° Stormo,
  Roma-Ciampino:
  93° Gruppo
MM62020
MM62021
MM62026
MM62029

Dassault Falcon 900EX
31° Stormo,
  Roma-Ciampino:
  93° Gruppo
MM62171
MM62172

Eurofighter Typhoon
Aeritalia, Torino/Caselle;
RSV, Pratica di Mare
MMX602 RS-01 RSV
MMX603 (Aeritalia)

Grumman G.1159A Gulfstream III
31° Stormo,
  Roma-Ciampino:
  306° Gruppo
MM62022
MM62025

Lockheed F-104 Starfighter
4° Stormo, Grosseto:
  9° Gruppo & 20° Gruppo;
5° Stormo, Cervia:
  23° Gruppo;
9° Stormo, Grazzanise:
  10° Gruppo;
37° Stormo, Trapani:
  18° Gruppo;
RSV, Pratica di Mare
F-104S-ASA/F104ASA-M*
CMX611* RS-06 RSV
MM6701 4-16 9
MM6704 4-7 9
MM6705 4-5 9
MM6710
MM6713 4-2 9
MM6714 4-11 9
MM6716* 9-31 10
MM6717* 5-44 23
MM6719* 9-52 10
MM6720* 9-51 10
MM6721 4-12 9
MM6722* 5-31 23
MM6726
MM6731* 37-03 18
MM6732* 37-04 18
MM6733* 9-33 10
MM6734* 5-37 23
MM6735* 9-50 10
MM6736
MM6737* 5-46 23
MM6739* 5-47 23
MM6740* 37-31 18
MM6748
MM6756* 5-42 23
MM6759* 37-20 18
MM6760
MM6761
MM6762* 37-02 18
MM6763* 4-58 20
MM6764*
MM6767 37-05 18
MM6769 4-53 20
MM6770* 9-35 10
MM6771* 5-35 23
MM6772 37-11 18
MM6773
MM6774 4-1 9
MM6775 37-10 18
MM6776* 9-46 10
MM6781
MM6786
MM6787* 9-32 10
MM6795 4-56 20
MM6796
MM6797
MM6805 4-10 9
MM6807
MM6809
MM6810
MM6816 4-6 9
MM6817 4-55 20
MM6818
MM6821
MM6822 4-51 20
MM6823
MM6824 4-3 9
MM6825
MM6826
MM6827 RSV
MM6830 4-42 20
MM6831 4-22 20
MM6833 5-22

MM6838* 4-57 20
MM6839
MM6841
MM6842 4-54 20
MM6845 5-11
MM6847
MM6848*
MM6849* 5-32 23
MM6850
MM6870* 5-45 23
MM6872* 37-23 18
MM6873 4-52 20
MM6875 4-14 9
MM6876* 37-21 18
MM6879 4-15 9
MM6880*
MM6881* 5-41 23
MM6886 5-02
MM6887* 5-33 23
MM6909
MM6912
MM6913
MM6914* 37-01 18
MM6915 5-15
MM6918
MM6920
MM6923* 9-30 10
MM6924
MM6925 37-15 18
MM6926
MM6929* 9-43 10
MM6930* 9-53 10
MM6932* 5-40 23
MM6934 RS-07 RSV
MM6935* 5-30 23
MM6936 5-36 23
MM6939* 37-22 18
MM6940 4-50 20
MM6941 4-4 9
MM6942
MM6943 4-20 9
MM6944
MM6946 37-06 18
TF-104G/TF-104G-M*
MM54226* 4-23 20
MM54228 4-26 20
MM54232 4-29 20
MM54237* 4-32 20
MM54250* 4-33 20
MM54251* 4-34 20
MM54253 4-35 20
MM54254* 4-36 20
MM54255 4-37 20
MM54256 4-38 20
MM54258 4-40 20
MM54260 4-41 20
MM54261* 4-42 20
MM54553* 4-44 20
MM54554* 4-48 20
MM54555* 4-45 20
MM54556* 4-47 20

Lockheed C-130H Hercules
46ª Brigata Aerea, Pisa:
  50° Gruppo
MM61988 46-02
MM61989 46-03
MM61990 46-04
MM61991 46-05
MM61992 46-06
MM61993 46-07
MM61994 46-08
MM61995 46-09
MM61997 46-11

MM61998	46-12
MM61999	46-13
MM62001	46-15

Lockheed C-130J Hercules II
46ª Brigata Aerea, Pisa:
2° Gruppo

MM62175	46-40
MM62176	46-41
MM62177	46-42
MM62178	46-43
MM62179	46-44
MM62180	46-45

McDonnell Douglas DC-9-32
31° Stormo,
Roma-Ciampino:
306° Gruppo

| MM62012 | |

Panavia Tornado ADV/Trainer[1]
36° Stormo, Gioia del Colle:
12° Gruppo

MM7202	36-33	(ZE832)
MM7203	36-02	(ZE761)
MM7204	36-05	(ZE730)
MM7205	36-06	(ZE787)
MM7206	36-26	(ZE760)
MM7207	36-27	(ZE762)
MM7208	36-32	(ZE811)
MM7209	36-25	(ZE835)
MM7210	36-14	(ZE836)
MM7211	36-16	(ZE792)
MM7225	36-04	(ZE252)
MM7226	36-21	(ZE911)
MM7227	36-22	(ZG732)
MM7228		(ZG733)
MM7229	36-31	(ZG728)
MM7230	36-11	(ZG730)
MM7231	36-12	(ZG734)
MM7232	36-10	(ZG735)
MM7233	36-23	(ZG768)
MM7234	36-24	(ZE167)
MM55056[1]	36-01	(ZE202)
MM55057[1]	36-03	(ZE837)
MM55060[1]	36-30	(ZE208)
MM55061[1]	36-21	(ZE205)

Panavia Tornado Strike/Trainer[1]/ECR[2]
6° Stormo, Ghedi:
102° Gruppo &
154° Gruppo;
50° Stormo, Piacenza:
155° Gruppo;
156° Gruppo Autonomo,
Gioia del Colle:
RSV, Pratica di Mare

MM7002	6-10	154
MM7003	6-23	154
MM7004	50-52	155
MM7005	6-05	154
MM7006	6-16	154
MM7007	36-37	156
MM7008		
MM7009	50-50	155
MM7010	36-..	156
MM7011	6-33	102
MM7013	36-40	156
MM7014		
MM7015	50-53	155
MM7016	RS-01	RSV
MM7018	6-18	154
MM7019[2]	50-05	155
MM7020[2]	50-41	155
MM7021[2]	50-01	155
MM7022	50-51	155
MM7023	36-31	156
MM7025	6-43	102
MM7026	6-26	154
MM7027	6-47	102
MM7028	6-18	154
MM7029	6-19	154
MM7030		
MM7031	6-21	154
MM7033	6-11	154
MM7034	6-30	154
MM7035	36-47	156
MM7036[2]	50-..	155
MM7037	6-07	154
MM7038	36-41	156
MM7039	50-03	155
CMX7040	36-35	156
MM7041		
MM7042	6-31	102
MM7043	6-13	154
MM7044	6-20	154
MM7046[2]	50-46	155
MM7047	50-43	155
MM7048	36-54	Alenia
MM7049	6-34	102
MM7050	36-44	156
MM7051	50-45	155
MM7052		
MM7053[2]	50-07	155
MM7054[2]	50-40	155
MM7055	50-42	155
MM7056	50-47	155
MM7057	6-12	154
MM7058	6-36	102
MM7059	50-47	155
MM7060	6-32	102
MM7061	6-01	154
MM7062[2]	50-44	155
MM7063	36-42	156
MM7064	6-24	154
MM7065	6-25	154
MM7066	6-44	102
MM7067	67	154
MM7068[2]		Alenia
MM7070	50-06	155
MM7071	6-35	102
MM7072	6-36	102
MM7073	36-43	156
MM7075	50-05	155
MM7078	50-02	155
CMX7079[2]		Alenia
MM7080	6-41	102
MM7081	6-02	154
MM7082[2]	6-14	154
MM7083	6-37	102
CMX7085	36-50	Alenia
MM7086	6-04	154
MM7087	36-35	156
MM7088	6-18	154
MM55000[1]	6-51	102
MM55001[1]	6-42	102
MM55002[1]		
MM55003[1]	6-..	154
MM55004[1]	6-15	154
MM55005[1]	6-40	102
MM55006[1]	6-44	102
MM55007[1]	36-55	156
MM55008[1]	6-45	102
MM55009[1]	36-56	156
MM55010[1]	6-42	102
MM55011[1]	50-50	155

Piaggio P-180AM Avanti
14° Stormo, Guidonia:
303° Gruppo;
36° Stormo, Gioia del Colle:
636ª SC;
RSV, Pratica di Mare

MM62159		636
MM62160	54	RSV
MM62161		303
MM62162		303
MM62163		303
CSX62164		RSV

Piaggio-Douglas PD-808-GE/PD-808-RM/PD-808-TA
9ª Brigata Aerea,
Pratica di Mare:
8° Gruppo &
71° Gruppo;
RSV, Pratica di Mare

MM61952	GE	71
MM61954	TA	71
MM61955	GE	71
MM61960	GE	71
MM61961	GE	71
MM61962	GE	71
MM62014	RM	8

Guardia di Finanza Aérospatiale ATR.42-400MP
2° Gruppo EM,
Pratica di Mare

| MM62165 | GF-13 |
| MM62166 | GF-14 |

Marina Militare Italiana McDonnell Douglas AV-8B/TAV-8B Harrier II+
Gruppo Aerei Imbarcati,
Taranto/Grottaglie

AV-8B

MM7199	1-03
MM7200	1-04
MM7201	1-05
MM7212	1-06
MM7213	1-07
MM7214	1-08
MM7215	1-09
MM7216	1-10
MM7217	1-11
MM7218	1-12
MM7219	1-13
MM7220	1-14
MM7221	1-15
MM7222	1-16
MM7223	1-17
MM7224	1-18

TAV-8B

| MM55032 | 1-01 |
| MM55033 | 1-02 |

Italian Govt Dassault Falcon 50
Italian Govt/Soc. CAI,
Roma/Ciampino
I-SAME

Dassault Falcon 200
Italian Govt/Soc. CAI,
Roma/Ciampino
I-CNEF
I-SOBE

Dassault Falcon 900
Italian Govt/Soc. CAI,
Roma/Ciampino
I-DIES
I-FICV
I-NUMI

IVORY COAST
Fokker 100
Ivory Coast Govt, Abidjan
TU-VAA

JAPAN
Japan Air Self Defence Force
Boeing 747-47C
701st Flight Sqn, Chitose
20-1101
20-1102

JORDAN
Al Quwwat al Jawwiya
al Malakiya al Urduniya
Extra EA-300S
Royal Jordanian Falcons,
Amman
JY-RNA
JY-RNC
JY-RND
JY-RNE
JY-RNG

Lockheed C-130H Hercules
3 Sqn, Al Matar AB/Amman
344
345
346
347

Jordanian Govt
Airbus A.340-211
Jordanian Govt, Amman
JY-ABH

Canadair CL.604
Challenger
Jordanian Govt, Amman
JY-ONE
JY-TWO

Lockheed L.1011
TriStar 500
Jordanian Govt, Amman
JY-HKJ

KAZAKHSTAN
Boeing 757-2M6
Govt of Kazakhstan, Almaty
P4-NSN

Tupolev Tu-134A-3
Govt of Kazakhstan, Almaty
UN-65799

KENYA
Kenyan Air Force
Fokker 70ER
308

KUWAIT
Al Quwwat al Jawwiya
al Kuwaitiya
Lockheed
L100-30 Hercules
41 Sqn, Kuwait International
KAF 323
KAF 324
KAF 325

Kuwaiti Govt
Airbus A.310-308
Kuwaiti Govt,
Safat
9K-ALD

Grumman G.1159C
Gulfstream IV
Kuwaiti Govt/Kuwait
Airways, Safat
9K-AJA
9K-AJB

Gulfstream Aerospace
Gulfstream V
Kuwaiti Govt/Kuwait
Airways, Safat
9K-AJD
9K-AJE
9K-AJF

KYRGYZSTAN
Tupolev Tu-134A-3
Govt of Kyrgyzstan, Bishkek
EX-65119

Tupolev Tu-134B/Tu-154M
Govt of Kyrgyzstan, Bishkek
EX-85294 Tu-154B
EX-85718 Tu-154M
EX-85762 Tu-154M

LITHUANIA
Karines Oro Pajegos
Let 410 Turbolet
I Transporto Eskadrile,
Zokniai
01
02

Lithuanian Govt
Lockheed L.1329
Jetstar 731
Lithuanian Govt, Vilnius
LY-AMB

LUXEMBOURG
NATO
Boeing 707-307C/329C*
NAEWF, Geilenkirchen
LX-N19996*
LX-N19997
LX-N19999
LX-N20000
LX-N20199*

Boeing E-3A
NAEWF, Geilenkirchen
LX-N90442
LX-N90443
LX-N90444
LX-N90445
LX-N90446
LX-N90447

LX-N90448
LX-N90449
LX-N90450
LX-N90451
LX-N90452
LX-N90453
LX-N90454
LX-N90455
LX-N90456
LX-N90458
LX-N90459

MALAYSIA
Royal Malaysian Air Force/
Tentera Udara Diraja
Malaysia
Bombardier BD.700-1A10
Global Express
2 Sqn, Simpang
M48-01

Lockheed C-130 Hercules
4 Sqn, Subang;
14 Sqn, Labuan;
20 Sqn, Subang
M30-01	C-130H(MP)	4 Sqn
M30-02	C-130H	14 Sqn
M30-03	C-130H	14 Sqn
M30-04	C-130H	14 Sqn
M30-05	C-130H	14 Sqn
M30-06	C-130H	14 Sqn
M30-07	C-130T	4 Sqn
M30-08	C-130H(MP)	20 Sqn
M30-09	C-130H(MP)	20 Sqn
M30-10	C-130H-30	20 Sqn
M30-11	C-130H-30	20 Sqn
M30-12	C-130H-30	20 Sqn
M30-14	C-130H-30	20 Sqn
M30-15	C-130H-30	20 Sqn
M30-16	C-130H-30	20 Sqn

MEXICO
Fuerza Aérea Mexicana
Boeing 757-225
8° Grupo Aéreo, Mexico City
TP-01 (XC-UJM)

MOROCCO
Force Aérienne Royaume
Marocaine/ Al Quwwat al
Jawwiya al Malakiya
Marakishiya
Airtech CN.235M-100
Escadrille de Transport,
Rabat
023	CNA-MA
024	CNA-MB
025	CNA-MC
026	CNA-MD
027	CNA-ME
028	CNA-MF
031	CNA-MG

CAP-230
Marche Verte
04	CN-ABD
05	CN-ABF
06	CN-ABI
07	CN-ABJ
08	CN-ABK
09	CN-ABL
22	CN-ABM
23	CN-ABN
24	CN-ABO

Morocco - Netherlands

Lockheed C-130H Hercules
Escadrille de Transport,
Rabat

4535	CN-AOA
4551	CN-AOC
4575	CN-AOD
4581	CN-AOE
4583	CN-AOF
4713	CN-AOG
4717	CN-AOH
4733	CN-AOI
4738	CN-AOJ
4739	CN-AOK
4742	CN-AOL
4875	CN-AOM
4876	CN-AON
4877	CN-AOO
4888	CN-AOP
4892	CN-AOQ
4907	CN-AOR
4909	CN-AOS
4940	CN-AOT

Govt of Morocco
Boeing 707-138B
Govt of Morocco, Rabat
CNA-NS

Dassault Falcon 100
Govt of Morocco, Rabat
CN-TNA

Grumman
G.1159 Gulfstream IITT/
G.1159A Gulfstream III
Govt of Morocco, Rabat

CNA-NL	Gulfstream IITT
CNA-NU	Gulfstream III
CNA-NV	Gulfstream III

NAMIBIA
Dassault Falcon 900B
Namibian Govt, Windhoek
V5-NAM

NETHERLANDS
Koninklijke Luchtmacht
Agusta-Bell AB.412SP
303 Sqn, Leeuwarden
R-01
R-02
R-03

Boeing-Vertol CH-47D
Chinook
298 Sqn, Soesterberg
D-101
D-102
D-103
D-104
D-105
D-106
D-661
D-662
D-663
D-664
D-665
D-666
D-667

Eurocopter AS.532U-2
Cougar
300 Sqn, Gilze-Rijen
S-400

S-419
S-433
S-438
S-440
S-441
S-442
S-444
S-445
S-447
S-450
S-453
S-454
S-456
S-457
S-458
S-459

Fokker 50
334 Sqn, Eindhoven
U-05
U-06

Fokker 60UTA-N
334 Sqn, Eindhoven
U-01
U-02
U-03
U-04

General Dynamics F-16
(MLU aircraft are marked
with a *)
TGp/306/311/312 Sqns,
Volkel;
313/315 Sqns, Twenthe;
322/323 Sqns, Leeuwarden

J-001	F-16A*	322 Sqn
J-002	F-16A*	323 Sqn
J-003	F-16A*	322 Sqn
J-004	F-16A*	322 Sqn
J-005	F-16A*	322 Sqn
J-006	F-16A*	322 Sqn
J-008	F-16A*	322 Sqn
J-009	F-16A*	322 Sqn
J-010	F-16A*	323 Sqn
J-011	F-16A*	322 Sqn
J-013	F-16A*	322 Sqn
J-014	F-16A*	322 Sqn
J-015	F-16A*	312 Sqn
J-016	F-16A*	323 Sqn
J-017	F-16A*	311 Sqn
J-018	F-16A*	322 Sqn
J-019	F-16A*	323 Sqn
J-020	F-16A*	315 Sqn
J-021	F-16A*	311 Sqn
J-055	F-16A*	322 Sqn
J-057	F-16A*	323 Sqn
J-058	F-16A*	315 Sqn
J-060	F-16A*	315 Sqn
J-061	F-16A*	322 Sqn
J-062	F-16A*	322 Sqn
J-063	F-16A*	322 Sqn
J-064	F-16B*	322 Sqn
J-065	F-16B*	313 Sqn
J-066	F-16B*	323 Sqn
J-067	F-16B*	315 Sqn
J-068	F-16B*	322 Sqn
J-135	F-16A*	311 Sqn
J-136	F-16A*	315 Sqn
J-137	F-16A*	322 Sqn
J-138	F-16A*	315 Sqn
J-139	F-16A	312 Sqn
J-141	F-16A*	315 Sqn
J-142	F-16A*	323 Sqn
J-143	F-16A*	315 Sqn
J-144	F-16A*	315 Sqn
J-145	F-16A*	315 Sqn
J-146	F-16A*	323 Sqn
J-192	F-16A*	315 Sqn
J-193	F-16A*	311 Sqn
J-194	F-16A*	322 Sqn
J-196	F-16A	312 Sqn
J-197	F-16A	312 Sqn
J-198	F-16A	312 Sqn
J-199	F-16A	312 Sqn
J-201	F-16A	312 Sqn
J-202	F-16A	315 Sqn
J-203	F-16A*	311 Sqn
J-204	F-16A*	323 Sqn
J-205	F-16A*	322 Sqn
J-206	F-16A*	311 Sqn
J-207	F-16A	311 Sqn
J-208	F-16B*	311 Sqn
J-209	F-16B*	315 Sqn
J-210	F-16B*	312 Sqn
J-211	F-16B*	322 Sqn
J-220	F-16A	306 Sqn
J-230	F-16A	306 Sqn
J-231	F-16A	306 Sqn
J-232	F-16A	306 Sqn
J-235	F-16A	306 Sqn
J-236	F-16A	306 Sqn
J-240	F-16A	312 Sqn
J-241	F-16A	312 Sqn
J-243	F-16A	306 Sqn
J-248	F-16A	306 Sqn
J-249	F-16A	306 Sqn
J-251	F-16A*	322 Sqn
J-253	F-16A	312 Sqn
J-254	F-16A*	313 Sqn
J-255	F-16A	312 Sqn
J-256	F-16A	312 Sqn
J-257	F-16A	312 Sqn
J-261	F-16B	306 Sqn
J-264	F-16B	312 Sqn
J-265	F-16B	312 Sqn
J-266	F-16B	312 Sqn
J-267	F-16B*	323 Sqn
J-268	F-16B	312 Sqn
J-269	F-16B	306 Sqn
J-270	F-16B	306 Sqn
J-360	F-16A*	323 Sqn
J-362	F-16A*	315 Sqn
J-363	F-16A*	323 Sqn
J-364	F-16A	312 Sqn
J-365	F-16A*	315 Sqn
J-366	F-16A*	315 Sqn
J-367	F-16A*	323 Sqn
J-368	F-16B*	315 Sqn
J-369	F-16B*	315 Sqn
J-508	F-16A*	315 Sqn
J-509	F-16A*	315 Sqn
J-510	F-16A*	323 Sqn
J-511	F-16A*	315 Sqn
J-512	F-16A*	311 Sqn
J-513	F-16A*	323 Sqn
J-514	F-16A*	315 Sqn
J-515	F-16A*	323 Sqn
J-516	F-16A*	311 Sqn
J-616	F-16A	312 Sqn
J-617	F-16A	312 Sqn
J-619	F-16A	312 Sqn
J-620	F-16A*	315 Sqn
J-622	F-16A*	323 Sqn
J-623	F-16A	312 Sqn
J-624	F-16A*	313 Sqn
J-627	F-16A(R)	306 Sqn
J-628	F-16A(R)	306 Sqn

J-630	F-16A*	311 Sqn
J-631	F-16A*	311 Sqn
J-632	F-16A*	
J-633	F-16A(R)	306 Sqn
J-635	F-16A*	311 Sqn
J-636	F-16A*	311 Sqn
J-637	F-16A(R)	306 Sqn
J-638	F-16A*	
J-640	F-16A(R)	306 Sqn
J-641	F-16A*	311 Sqn
J-642	F-16A(R)	306 Sqn
J-643	F-16A(R)	306 Sqn
J-644	F-16A(R)	306 Sqn
J-646	F-16A*	311 Sqn
J-647	F-16A*	311 Sqn
J-648	F-16A*	311 Sqn
J-649	F-16B	312 Sqn
J-650	F-16B*	313 Sqn
J-651	F-16B	312 Sqn
J-652	F-16B*	313 Sqn
J-653	F-16B	306 Sqn
J-654	F-16B*	311 Sqn
J-655	F-16B	306 Sqn
J-656	F-16B*	311 Sqn
J-657	F-16B*	313 Sqn
J-864	F-16A(R)	306 Sqn
J-866	F-16A(R)	306 Sqn
J-867	F-16A(R)	306 Sqn
J-868	F-16A*	311 Sqn
J-869	F-16A	312 Sqn
J-870	F-16A	312 Sqn
J-871	F-16A	312 Sqn
J-872	F-16A*	311 Sqn
J-873	F-16A	306 Sqn
J-874	F-16A*	311 Sqn
J-875	F-16A*	323 Sqn
J-876	F-16A*	311 Sqn
J-877	F-16A	312 Sqn
J-878	F-16A	311 Sqn
J-879	F-16A*	313 Sqn
J-881	F-16A*	323 Sqn
J-882	F-16B	306 Sqn
J-884	F-16B*	311 Sqn
J-885	F-16B*	323 Sqn

Grumman G-1159C
Gulfstream IV
334 Sqn, Eindhoven
V-11

Lockheed C-130H-30
Hercules
334 Sqn, Eindhoven
G-273
G-275

MBB Bo.105CB/
Bo.105CB-4*
299 Sqn, Gilze-Rijen
B-39*
B-40*
B-41*
B-43
B-44
B-47
B-64
B-66
B-68
B-69
B-70
B-74
B-75
B-76
B-77

B-78*
B-79
B-80

MDH AH-64A Apache/
NAH-64D Apache Longbow
301 Sqn, Gilze-Rijen;
302 Sqn, Gilze-Rijen
AH-64A
25474	301 Sqn
25480	301 Sqn
25482	301 Sqn
25485	301 Sqn
68970	301 Sqn
69029	301 Sqn
NAH-64D
Q-01	302 Sqn
Q-02	302 Sqn
Q-03	302 Sqn
Q-04	302 Sqn
Q-05	302 Sqn
Q-06	302 Sqn
Q-07	302 Sqn
Q-08	302 Sqn
Q-09	302 Sqn
Q-10	302 Sqn

McDonnell Douglas
KDC-10
334 Sqn, Eindhoven
T-235
T-264

Pilatus PC-7
131 EMVO Sqn,
   Woensdrecht
L-01
L-02
L-03
L-04
L-05
L-06
L-07
L-08
L-09
L-10
L-11
L-12
L-13

Sud Alouette III
300 Sqn, Soesterberg
A-247
A-275
A-292
A-301

Marine Luchtvaart Dienst
Beechcraft Super King
Air 200
OVALK, Valkenburg
PH-SBK

Lockheed P-3C Orion
MARPAT (320 Sqn &
   321 Sqn), Valkenburg
   and Keflavik
300
301
302
303
304
305
306

307
308
309
310
311
312

Westland SH-14D Lynx
HELIGRP (7 Sqn &
   860 Sqn), De Kooij
   (7 Sqn operates
   860 Sqn aircraft on loan)
260
261
262
264
265
266
267
268
269
270
271
272
273
274
276
277
278
279
280
281
283

Netherlands Govt
Fokker 70
Dutch Royal Flight, Schiphol
PH-KBX

NEW ZEALAND
Royal New Zealand Air Force
Boeing 727-22C
40 Sqn, Whenuapai
NZ7271
NZ7272

Lockheed
C-130H Hercules
40 Sqn, Whenuapai
NZ7001
NZ7002
NZ7003
NZ7004
NZ7005

Lockheed
P-3K Orion
5 Sqn, Whenuapai
NZ4201
NZ4202
NZ4203
NZ4204
NZ4205
NZ4206

NIGERIA
Federal Nigerian Air Force
Lockheed C-130H Hercules
NAF-910
NAF-912
NAF-913
NAF-915
NAF-917
NAF-918

Nigerian Govt
Dassault Falcon 900
Federal Govt of Nigeria,
Lagos
5N-FGE
5N-FGO

Grumman
G.1159 Gulfstream II/
G.1159A Gulfstream III
Federal Govt of Nigeria,
Lagos
5N-AGV Gulfstream II
5N-FGP Gulfstream III

NORWAY
Kongelige Norske
Luftforsvaret
Bell 412SP
339 Skv, Bardufoss;
720 Skv, Rygge

139	339 Skv
140	339 Skv
141	720 Skv
142	339 Skv
143	339 Skv
144	339 Skv
145	720 Skv
146	339 Skv
147	720 Skv
148	339 Skv
149	339 Skv
161	339 Skv
162	339 Skv
163	720 Skv
164	720 Skv
165	720 Skv
166	720 Skv
167	720 Skv
194	720 Skv

Dassault Falcon 20 ECM
717 Skv, Rygge
041
053
0125

DHC-6 Twin Otter
719 Skv, Bodø
057
184
7062

General Dynamics F-16
(MLU aircraft are marked
with a *)
331 Skv, Bodø (r/w/bl);
332 Skv, Rygge (y/bk);
334 Skv, Bodø (r/w);
338 Skv, Ørland

272	F-16A*	332 Skv
273	F-16A	332 Skv
275	F-16A*	332 Skv
276	F-16A	338 Skv
277	F-16A*	332 Skv
279	F-16A	338 Skv
281	F-16A	332 Skv
282	F-16A	338 Skv
284	F-16A*	332 Skv
285	F-16A	338 Skv
286	F-16A	338 Skv
288	F-16A	338 Skv
289	F-16A	338 Skv
291	F-16A	338 Skv
292	F-16A	338 Skv
293	F-16A	338 Skv
295	F-16A*	338 Skv
297	F-16A*	332 Skv
298	F-16A	338 Skv
299	F-16A*	338 Skv
302	F-16B*	332 Skv
304	F-16B*	332 Skv
305	F-16B*	332 Skv
306	F-16B*	332 Skv
658	F-16A	334 Skv
659	F-16A*	334 Skv
660	F-16A	334 Skv
661	F-16A*	334 Skv
662	F-16A*	334 Skv
663	F-16A	334 Skv
664	F-16A	331 Skv
665	F-16A	334 Skv
666	F-16A*	334 Skv
667	F-16A	334 Skv
668	F-16A*	334 Skv
669	F-16A*	334 Skv
670	F-16A	332 Skv
671	F-16A	338 Skv
672	F-16A	334 Skv
673	F-16A*	332 Skv
674	F-16A	332 Skv
675	F-16A	331 Skv
677	F-16A	331 Skv
678	F-16A	331 Skv
680	F-16A*	338 Skv
681	F-16A*	331 Skv
682	F-16A*	338 Skv
683	F-16A	334 Skv
686	F-16A	331 Skv
687	F-16A	338 Skv
688	F-16A	331 Skv
689	F-16B	338 Skv
690	F-16B	338 Skv
691	F-16B	334 Skv
692	F-16B	334 Skv
693	F-16B*	332 Skv
711	F-16B*	332 Skv
712	F-16B	334 Skv

Lockheed C-130H Hercules
335 Skv, Gardermoen
952
953
954
955
956
957

Lockheed P-3C Orion
333 Skv, Andøya
3296
3297
3298
3299

Lockheed P-3N Orion
333 Skv, Andøya
4576
6603

Northrop F-5A
Eye of the Tiger Project,
Rygge
128
130
131
133
134
896
902

Northrop F-5B
Eye of the Tiger Project,
Rygge
136
243
244
387
906
907
908
909

Westland Sea King Mk 43/
Mk 43A/Mk 43B
330 Skv:
A Flt, Bodø;
B Flt, Banak;
C Flt, Ørland;
D Flt, Sola

060	Mk 43
062	Mk 43
066	Mk 43
069	Mk 43
070	Mk 43
071	Mk 43B
072	Mk 43
073	Mk 43
074	Mk 43
189	Mk 43A
322	Mk 43B
329	Mk 43B
330	Mk 43B

Kystvakt (Coast Guard)
Westland Lynx Mk86
337 Skv, Bardufoss
207
216
228
232
237
350

OMAN
Royal Air Force of Oman
BAC 1-11/485GD
4 Sqn, Seeb
551
552
553

Lockheed C-130H Hercules
4 Sqn, Seeb
501
502
503

Short Skyvan 3M/
Seavan 3M*
2 Sqn, Seeb
902
903
904
905
907
908
910*
911
912
914
915*

916*

Omani Govt
Boeing 747SP-27
Govt of Oman, Seeb
A4O-SO
A4O-SP

Grumman G.1159C
Gulfstream IV
Govt of Oman, Seeb
A4O-AB
A4O-AC

PAKISTAN
Pakistan Fiza'ya
Boeing 707-340C
68-19866   12 Sqn
69-19635   12 Sqn

Pakistani Govt
Boeing 737-33A
Govt of Pakistan, Karachi
AP-BEH

PERU
Fuerza Aérea Peruana
Douglas DC-8-62AF
370   (OB-1372)
371   (OB-1373)

POLAND
Polskie Wojska Lotnicze
Antonov An-26
13 PLT, Krakow/Balice
1307
1310
1402
1403
1406
1407
1508
1509
1602
1603
1604

Mikoyan MiG-29A/UB*
1 ELT, Minsk/Mazowiecki
15*
28*
29
38
40
42*
54
56
59
64*
65
66
67
70
77
83
89
92
105
108
111
114
115

Tupolev Tu-154M
36 SPLT, Warszawa
101
102

Yakovlev Yak-40
36 SPLT, Warszawa
032
034
036
037
038
039
040
041
042
043
044
045
047
048

PORTUGAL
Força Aérea Portuguesa
Aérospatiale SA.330C
Puma
Esq 711, Lajes;
Esq 751, Montijo
19502   Esq 751
19503   Esq 751
19504   Esq 751
19505   Esq 751
19506   Esq 711
19508   Esq 711
19509   Esq 751
19511   Esq 711
19512   Esq 751
19513   Esq 711

CASA 212A/212ECM*
Aviocar
Esq 401, Sintra;
Esq 501, Sintra;
Esq 502, Sintra;
Esq 711, Lajes
16501*   Esq 501
16502*   Esq 501
16503   Esq 501
16504   Esq 501
16505   Esq 502
16506   Esq 502
16507   Esq 502
16508   Esq 502
16509   Esq 501
16510   Esq 401
16511   Esq 502
16512   Esq 401
16513   Esq 711
16514   Esq 711
16515   Esq 711
16517   Esq 711
16519   Esq 401
16520   Esq 711
16521*   Esq 401
16522*   Esq 401
16523*   Esq 401
16524*   Esq 401

CASA 212-300 Aviocar
Esq 401, Sintra
17201
17202

D-BD Alpha Jet
Esq 103, Beja;
Esq 301, Beja
15201
15202
15204
15205
15206
15208
15209
15210
15211
15213
15214
15215
15216
15217
15218
15219
15220
15221
15222
15223
15224
15225
15226
15227
15228
15229
15230
15231
15232
15233
15234
15235
15236
15237
15238
15239
15240
15241
15242
15243
15244
15246
15247
15248
15249
15250

Dassault Falcon 20DC
Esq 504, Lisbon/Montijo
17103

Dassault Falcon 50
Esq 504, Lisbon/Montijo
17401
17402
17403

Lockheed C-130H/
C-130H-30* Hercules
Esq 501, Lisbon/Montijo
16801*
16802*
16803
16804
16805
16806*

Lockheed (GD)
F-16A/F-16B*
Esq 201, Monte Real
15101

15102
15103
15104
15105
15106
15107
15108
15109
15110
15111
15112
15113
15114
15115
15116
15117
15118*
15119*
15120*

Lockheed P-3P Orion
Esq 601, Lisbon/Montijo
14801
14802
14803
14804
14805
14806

Marinha
Westland Super Lynx
Mk 95
Esq de Helicopteros,
Lisbon/Montijo
19201
19202
19203
19204
19205

QATAR
Airbus A.310-304
Qatari Govt, Doha
A7-AAF

Airbus A.320-232
Qatari Govt, Doha
A7-AAG

Airbus A.340-211
Qatari Govt, Doha
A7-HHK

Dassault Falcon 900
Qatari Govt, Doha
A7-AAE

ROMANIA
Fortele Aeriene Romania
Lockheed C-130B Hercules
19 FMT, Bucharest/Otapeni
5927
6150
6166

RUSSIA
Voenno-Vozdushniye Sily
Rossioki Federatsii (Russian
Air Force)
Sukhoi Su-27
TsAGI, Gromov Flight
Institute, Zhukovsky
595 Su-27P
597 Su-30

598 Su-27P

Russian Govt
Ilyushin Il-62M
Russian Govt, Moscow
RA-86466
RA-86467
RA-86468
RA-86536
RA-86537
RA-86540
RA-86553
RA-86554
RA-86559
RA-86561
RA-86710
RA-86711
RA-86712

Ilyushin Il-96-300
Russian Govt, Moscow
RA-96012

Tupolev Tu-134A
Russian Govt, Moscow
RA-65904

Tupolev Tu-154B-2
Russian Govt, Moscow
RA-85426

Tupolev Tu-154M
Russian Govt, Moscow;
Open Skies*
RA-85629
RA-85630
RA-85631
RA-85645
RA-85651
RA-85653
RA-85655*
RA-85658
RA-85659
RA-85666
RA-85675
RA-85676

SAUDI ARABIA
Al Quwwat al Jawwiya
as Sa'udiya
BAe 125-800/-800B*
1 Sqn, Riyadh
HZ-105
HZ-109*
110*

Boeing E-3A/KE-3A*
Sentry
18 Sqn, Riyadh;
19 Sqn, Riyadh
1801
1802
1803
1804
1805
1811*
1812*
1813*
1814*
1815*
1816*
1818*
1901*

Grumman
G.1159A Gulfstream III/
G.1159C Gulfstream IV
1 Sqn, Riyadh
HZ-103   Gulfstream IV
HZ-108   Gulfstream III

Lockheed C-130/L.100
Hercules
1 Sqn, Riyadh;
4 Sqn, Jeddah;
16 Sqn, Jeddah;
32 Sqn, Jeddah

No.	Type	Sqn
111	VC-130H	1 Sqn
112	VC-130H	1 Sqn
451	C-130E	4 Sqn
452	C-130H	4 Sqn
455	C-130E	4 Sqn
461	C-130H	4 Sqn
462	C-130H	4 Sqn
463	C-130H	4 Sqn
464	C-130H	4 Sqn
465	C-130H	4 Sqn
466	C-130H	4 Sqn
467	C-130H	4 Sqn
468	C-130H	4 Sqn
471	C-130H-30	4 Sqn
472	C-130H	4 Sqn
473	C-130H	4 Sqn
474	C-130H	4 Sqn
475	C-130H	4 Sqn
476	C-130H	4 Sqn
477	C-130H	4 Sqn
478	C-130H	4 Sqn
479	C-130H	4 Sqn
1601	C-130H	16 Sqn
1602	C-130H	16 Sqn
1603	C-130H	16 Sqn
1604	C-130H	16 Sqn
1605	C-130H	16 Sqn
1606	C-130E	16 Sqn
1607	C-130E	16 Sqn
1608	C-130E	16 Sqn
1609	C-130E	16 Sqn
1610	C-130E	16 Sqn
1611	C-130E	16 Sqn
1612	C-130H	16 Sqn
1613	C-130H	16 Sqn
1614	C-130H	16 Sqn
1615	C-130H	16 Sqn
1618	C-130H	16 Sqn
1619	C-130H	16 Sqn
1622	C-130H-30	16 Sqn
1623	C-130H-30	16 Sqn
1624	C-130H	16 Sqn
1625	C-130H	16 Sqn
1626	C-130H	16 Sqn
3201	KC-130H	32 Sqn
3202	KC-130H	32 Sqn
3203	KC-130H	32 Sqn
3204	KC-130H	32 Sqn
3205	KC-130H	32 Sqn
3206	C-130H	32 Sqn
3207	KC-130H	32 Sqn
3208	KC-130H	32 Sqn
HZ-114	VC-130H	1 Sqn
HZ-115	VC-130H	1 Sqn
HZ-116	VC-130H	1 Sqn
HZ-117	L.100-30	1 Sqn
HZ-128	L.100-30	1 Sqn
HZ-129	L.100-30	1 Sqn

Saudi Govt

Airbus A.340-211
Royal Embassy of Saudi
Arabia, Riyadh
HZ-124

Boeing 737-268
Saudi Royal Flight, Jeddah
HZ-HM4

Boeing 747-3G1
Saudi Royal Flight, Jeddah
HZ-HM1A

Boeing 747SP-68
Saudi Govt, Jeddah;
Saudi Royal Flight, Jeddah
HZ-AIF   Govt
HZ-AIJ   Royal Flight
HZ-HM1B   Royal Flight

Boeing MD-11
Saudi Royal Flight, Jeddah
HZ-HM7
HZ-HM8

**Canadair
CL.604 Challenger**
Saudi Royal Flight, Jeddah
HZ-AFA2

Dassault Falcon 900
Saudi Govt, Jeddah
HZ-AFT
HZ-AFZ

**Grumman
G.1159A Gulfstream III**
Armed Forces Medical
Services, Riyadh;
Saudi Govt, Jeddah
HZ-AFN   Govt
HZ-AFR   Govt
HZ-MS3   AFMS

**Grumman
G.1159C Gulfstream IV**
Armed Forces Medical
Services, Riyadh;
Saudi Govt, Jeddah
HZ-AFU   Govt
HZ-AFV   Govt
HZ-AFW   Govt
HZ-AFX   Govt
HZ-AFY   Govt
HZ-MS4   AFMS

**Gulfstream Aerospace
Gulfstream V**
Armed Forces Medical
Services, Riyadh
HZ-MS5

**Lockheed C-130H/L.100
Hercules**
Armed Forces Medical
Services, Riyadh
HZ-MS6   L.100-30
HZ-MS7   C-130H
HZ-MS8   C-130H-30
HZ-MS09   L.100-30
HZ-MS019 C-130H

**Lockheed L.1011
TriStar 500**
Saudi Royal Flight, Jeddah
HZ-HM5
HZ-HM6

SINGAPORE
**Republic of Singapore Air Force
Boeing KC-135R
Stratotanker**
750
751
752
753

Lockheed C-130 Hercules
122 Sqn, Paya Labar
720   KC-130B
721   KC-130B
724   KC-130B
725   KC-130B
730   C-130H
731   C-130H
732   C-130H
733   C-130H
734   KC-130H
735   C-130H

SLOVAKIA
**Slovenské Vojenske Letectvo
Aero L-39/L-59 (L-39MS)
Albatros**
31 SLK/3 Letka, Sliač [SL];
VSL, Košice;
White Albatroses,
Košice (*WA*)

0002	L-39MS	VSL
0003	L-39MS	VSL
0101	L-39C	WA [4]
0102	L-39C	WA [6]
0103	L-39C	VSL
0111	L-39C	WA [5]
0112	L-39C	WA [1]
0442	L-39C	WA [2]
0443	L-39C	WA [7]
0730	L-39V	VSL
0745	L-39V	VSL
1701	L-39ZA	31 SLK
1725	L-39ZA	31 SLK
1730	L-39ZA	31 SLK
3905	L-39ZA	31 SLK
4355	L-39C	WA [3]
4701	L-39ZA	31 SLK
4703	L-39ZA	31 SLK
4705	L-39ZA	31 SLK
4707	L-39ZA	31 SLK
4711	L-39ZA	31 SLK

Antonov An-24V
32 ZmDK/1 Letka, Piešťany
2903
5605

Antonov An-26
32 ZmDK/1 Letka, Piešťany
2506
3208

LET 410 Turbolet
31 SLK/4 Letka, Sliač [SL];
32 ZmDK/1 Letka, Piešťany;
VSL, Košice

0730	L-410UVP	32 ZmDK
0927	L-410T	31 SLK
0930	L-410T	32 ZmDK
1133	L-410T	VSL
1203	L-410FG	32 ZmDK
1521	L-410FG	32 ZmDK
2311	L-410UVP	32 ZmDK

Mikoyan MiG-29A/UB*
31 SLK/1 & 2 Letka,
Sliač [SL]
0619
0820
0921
1303*
2022
2123
3709
3911
4401*
5113
5304*
5515
5817
6124
6425
6526
6627
6728
6829
6930
7501
8003
8605
9308

Sukhoi Su-25K/UBK*
33 SBoLK/2 Letka, Malacky
1006
1007
1008
1027
3237*
5033
5036
6017
6018
8072
8073
8074
8075

**Slovak Govt
Tupolev Tu-154M**
Slovak Govt,
Bratislava/Ivanka
OM-BYO
OM-BYR

Yakovlev Yak-40
Slovak Govt,
Bratislava/Ivanka
OM-BYE
OM-BYL

SLOVENIA
**Slovene Army
Let 410UVP-E**
15 Brigada, Ljubljana
L4-01

Pilatus PC-9
15 Brigada, Ljubljana
L9-51
L9-52
L9-53

L9-54
L9-55
L9-56
L9-57
L9-58
L9-59
L9-60
L9-61
L9-62
L9-63
L9-64
L9-65
L9-66
L9-67
L9-68
L9-69

Slovenian Govt
Gates LearJet
Slovenian Govt, Ljubljana
S5-BAA LearJet 35A
S5-BAB LearJet 24D

SOUTH AFRICA
South African Air Force/
Suid Afrikaanse Lugmag
Boeing 707
60 Sqn, Waterkloof

1415	328C
1417	328C
1419	328C
1423	344C

Dassault Falcon 900
21 Sqn, Waterkloof
ZS-NAN

Lockheed C-130B Hercules
28 Sqn, Waterkloof
401
402
403
404
405
406
407
408
409

SPAIN
Ejército del Aire Airtech
CN.235M-10 (T.19A)/
CN.235M-100 (T.19B)
Ala 35, Getafe

T.19A-01	35-60
T.19A-02	35-61
T.19B-03	35-21
T.19B-04	35-22
T.19B-05	35-23
T.19B-06	35-24
T.19B-07	35-25
T.19B-08	35-26
T.19B-09	35-27
T.19B-10	35-28
T.19B-11	35-29
T.19B-12	35-30
T.19B-13	35-31
T.19B-14	35-32
T.19B-15	35-33
T.19B-16	35-34
T.19B-17	35-35
T.19B-18	35-36
T.19B-19	35-37
T.19B-20	35-38

Boeing 707
408 Esc, Torrejón;
Grupo 45, Torrejón

T.17-1	331B	45-10
T.17-2	331B	45-11
T.17-3	368C	45-12
TM.17-4	351C	408-21

CASA 101EB Aviojet
Grupo 54, Torrejón;
Grupo de Escuelas de
  Matacán (74);
AGA, San Javier (79);
Patrulla Aguila, San Javier*

E.25-01	79-01	[5]*
E.25-05	79-05	
E.25-06	79-06	[1]*
E.25-07	79-07	
E.25-08	79-08	
E.25-09	79-09	
E.25-10	79-10	
E.25-11	79-11	
E.25-12	79-12	
E.25-13	79-13	[7]*
E.25-14	79-14	[8]*
E.25-15	79-15	
E.25-16	79-16	
E.25-17	74-40	
E.25-18	74-42	
E.25-19	79-19	
E.25-20	79-20	
E.25-21	79-21	[4]*
E.25-22	79-22	
E.25-23	79-23	
E.25-24	79-24	
E.25-25	79-25	[3]*
E.25-26	79-26	
E.25-27	79-27	
E.25-28	79-28	[2]*
E.25-29		
E.25-31	79-31	
E.25-33	74-02	
E.25-34	79-34	
E.25-35	54-20	
E.25-37	74-04	
E.25-38	79-38	
E.25-40	79-40	
E.25-41	74-41	
E.25-43	74-43	
E.25-44	79-44	
E.25-45	79-45	
E.25-46	79-46	
E.25-47	79-47	
E.25-48	79-48	
E.25-49	79-49	
E.25-50	79-33	
E.25-51	74-07	
E.25-52	79-34	
E.25-53	411-07	
E.25-54	79-35	
E.25-55	44-05	
E.25-56	74-11	
E.25-57	74-12	
E.25-59	74-13	
E.25-61	54-22	
E.25-62	74-16	
E.25-63	74-17	
E.25-64	74-18	
E.25-65	79-95	
E.25-66	74-20	
E.25-67	74-21	
E.25-68	74-22	
E.25-69	79-97	
E.25-71	74-25	
E.25-72	74-26	
E.25-73	79-98	
E.25-74	74-28	
E.25-75	74-29	
E.25-76	74-30	
E.25-78	79-02	
E.25-79	74-32	
E.25-80	79-03	
E.25-81	74-34	
E.25-83	74-35	
E.25-84	79-04	
E.25-86	79-32	[6]*
E.25-87	79-29	
E.25-88	74-39	

CASA 212 Aviocar
212 (XT.12)/
212A (T.12B)/
212B (TR.12A)/
212D (TE.12B)/
212DE (TM.12D)/
212E (T.12C)/
212S (D.3A)/
212S1 (D.3B)/
212-200 (T.12D)/
212-200 (TR.12D)
Ala 22, Morón;
Ala 37, Villanubla;
Ala 46, Gando, Las Palmas;
CLAEX, Torrejón (54);
Grupo 72, Alcantarilla;
Grupo Esc, Matacán (74);
AGA (Ala 79), San Javier;
403 Esc, Getafe;
408 Esc, Torrejón;
801 Esc, Palma/
  Son San Juan;
803 Esc, Cuatro Vientos;
INTA, Torrejón

D.3A-1	(801 Esc)
D.3A-2	(803 Esc)
D.3B-3	(803 Esc)
D.3B-4	(801 Esc)
D.3B-5	(801 Esc)
D.3B-6	(801 Esc)
D.3B-7	(803 Esc)
D.3B-8	(801 Esc)
XT.12A-1	54-10
TR.12A-4	403-02
TR.12A-5	403-03
TR.12A-6	403-04
TR.12A-8	403-06
T.12B-9	74-83
TE.12B-10	79-92
T.12B-12	74-82
T.12B-13	74-70
T.12B-14	37-01
T.12B-15	37-02
T.12B-16	74-71
T.12B-17	37-03
T.12B-18	46-31
T.12B-19	46-32
T.12B-20	37-04
T.12B-21	37-05
T.12B-22	37-06
T.12B-23	72-01
T.12B-24	37-07
T.12B-25	74-72
T.12B-26	72-02
T.12B-27	46-33
T.12B-28	72-03
T.12B-29	37-08
T.12B-30	74-73
T.12B-31	46-34

T.12B-33	72-04
T.12B-34	74-74
T.12B-35	37-09
T.12B-36	37-10
T.12B-37	72-05
T.12B-39	74-75
TE.12B-40	79-93
TE.12B-41	79-94
T.12C-43	46-50
T.12C-44	37-50
T.12B-46	74-76
T.12B-47	72-06
T.12B-48	37-11
T.12B-49	72-07
T.12B-50	74-77
T.12B-51	74-78
T.12B-52	46-35
T.12B-53	46-36
T.12B-54	46-37
T.12B-55	46-38
T.12B-56	74-79
T.12B-57	72-08
T.12B-58	46-39
T.12C-59	37-51
T.12C-60	37-52
T.12C-61	37-53
T.12B-63	37-14
T.12B-64	46-40
T.12B-65	74-80
T.12B-66	72-09
T.12B-67	74-81
T.12B-68	37-15
T.12B-69	37-16
T.12B-70	37-17
T.12B-71	37-18
TM.12D-72	408-01
TM.12D-74	54-11
T.12D-75	403-07
TR.12D-76	37-60
TR.12D-77	37-61
TR.12D-78	37-62
TR.12D-79	37-63
TR.12D-80	37-64
TR.12D-81	37-65

Cessna 560 Citation VI
403 Esc, Getafe

TR.20-01	403-11
TR.20-02	403-12

Dassault Falcon 20D/E/F
Grupo 45, Torrejón;
408 Esc, Torrejón

T.11-1	20E	45-02
TM.11-2	20D	45-03
TM.11-3	20D	408-11
TM.11-4	20E	408-12
T.11-5	20F	45-05

Dassault Falcon 50
Grupo 45, Torrejón

T.16-1	45-20

Dassault Falcon 900
Grupo 45, Torrejón

T.18-1	45-40
T.18-2	45-41

Eurofighter Typhoon
CASA, Getafe
XCE.16-01

Fokker F.27M Friendship 400MPA
802 Esc, Gando, Las Palmas

D.2-01	802-10
D.2-02	802-11
D.2-03	802-12

Lockheed C-130H/C-130H-30/KC-130H Hercules
311 Esc/312 Esc (Ala 31), Zaragoza

TL.10-01	C-130H-30	31-01
T.10-02	C-130H	31-02
T.10-03	C-130H	31-03
T.10-04	C-130H	31-04
TK.10-5	KC-130H	31-50
TK.10-6	KC-130H	31-51
TK.10-7	KC-130H	31-52
T.10-8	C-130H	31-05
T.10-9	C-130H	31-06
T.10-10	C-130H	31-07
TK.10-11	KC-130H	31-53
TK.10-12	KC-130H	31-54

Lockheed P-3A/P-3B* Orion
Grupo 22, Morón

P.3-01	22-21
P.3-03	22-22
P.3-08	22-31*
P.3-09	22-32*
P.3-10	22-33*
P.3-11	22-34*
P.3-12	22-35*

McDonnell Douglas F-18 Hornet
Ala 11, Morón;
Ala 12, Torrejón;
Ala 15, Zaragoza
EF-18A/EF-18B* Hornet

CE.15-1	15-70*
CE.15-2	15-71*
CE.15-3	15-72*
CE.15-4	15-73*
CE.15-5	15-74*
CE.15-6	15-75*
CE.15-7	15-76*
CE.15-8	12-71*
CE.15-9	15-77*
CE.15-10	12-73*
CE.15-11	12-74*
CE.15-12	12-75*
C.15-13	12-01
C.15-14	15-01
C.15-15	15-02
C.15-16	15-03
C.15-18	15-05
C.15-20	15-07
C.15-21	15-08
C.15-22	15-09
C.15-23	15-10
C.15-24	15-11
C.15-25	15-12
C.15-26	15-13
C.15-27	15-14
C.15-28	15-15
C.15-29	15-16
C.15-30	15-17
C.15-31	15-18
C.15-32	15-19
C.15-33	15-20
C.15-34	15-21
C.15-35	15-22
C.15-36	15-23
C.15-37	15-24
C.15-38	15-25
C.15-39	15-26
C.15-40	15-27
C.15-41	15-28
C.15-43	15-30
C.15-44	12-02
C.15-45	12-03
C.15-46	12-04
C.15-47	15-31
C.15-48	12-06
C.15-49	12-07
C.15-50	12-08
C.15-51	12-09
C.15-52	12-10
C.15-53	12-11
C.15-54	12-12
C.15-55	12-13
C.15-56	12-14
C.15-57	12-15
C.15-58	12-16
C.15-59	12-17
C.15-60	12-18
C.15-61	12-19
C.15-62	12-20
C.15-64	12-22
C.15-65	12-23
C.15-66	12-24
C.15-67	15-33
C.15-68	12-26
C.15-69	12-27
C.15-70	12-28
C.15-72	12-30

F/A-18A Hornet

C.15-73	11-01
C.15-74	21-02
C.15-75	11-03
C.15-76	21-04
C.15-77	21-05
C.15-78	11-06
C.15-79	11-07
C.15-80	21-08
C.15-81	11-09
C.15-82	11-10
C.15-83	21-11
C.15-84	21-12
C.15-85	21-13
C.15-86	11-14
C.15-87	11-15
C.15-88	11-16
C.15-89	21-17
C.15-90	11-18
C.15-91	21-19
C.15-92	21-20
C.15-93	21-21
C.15-94	21-22
C.15-95	21-23
C.15-96	21-24

Arma Aérea de l'Armada Española
BAe/McDonnell Douglas EAV-8B/EAV-8B+/TAV-8B+ Harrier II
Esc 009, Rota
EAV-8B

VA.2-3	01-903
VA.2-4	01-904
VA.2-5	01-905
VA.2-6	01-906
VA.2-7	01-907

VA.2-9	01-909
VA.2-10	01-910
VA.2-11	01-911
VA.2-12	01-912
EAV-8B+	
VA.2-14	01-914
VA.2-15	01-915
VA.2-16	01-916
VA.2-17	01-917
VA.2-18	01-918
VA.2-19	01-919
VA.2-20	01-920
VA.2-21	01-921
VA.2-22	01-922
TAV-8B+	
VA.2-23	01-923

Cessna 550 Citation 2
Esc 004, Rota

U.20-1	01-405
U.20-2	01-406
U.20-3	01-407

SWEDEN
Svenska Flygvapnet
Beechcraft Super King Air (Tp.101)
Flottiljer 7, Såtenäs;
Flottiljer 17, Ronneby/Kallinge;
Flottiljer 21, Luleå/Kallax

101002	012	F21
101003	013	F17
101004	014	F7

Cessna 550 Citation 2 (Tp.103)
Flottiljer 17, Ronneby/Kallinge

103002	

Grumman G.1159C Gulfstream 4 (Tp.102A/S.102B Korpen*)
Flottiljer 16, Uppsala;
Flottiljer 16M, Stockholm/Bromma

102001	021	F16M
102002*	022	F16
102003*	023	F16
102004	024	F16

Lockheed C-130 Hercules (Tp.84)
Flottiljer 7, Såtenäs

84001	841	C-130E
84002	842	C-130E
84003	843	C-130H
84004	844	C-130H
84005	845	C-130H
84006	846	C-130H
84007	847	C-130H
84008	848	C-130H

Rockwell Sabreliner-40 (Tp.86)
FMV, Malmslätt

86001	861
86002	862

SAAB 37 Viggen
Flottiljer 4, Östersund/Frösön;
Flottiljer 16, Uppsala;
Flottiljer 17, Ronneby/Kallinge;
Flottiljer 21, Luleå/Kallax;
FMV, Malmslätt

JA 37/JA 37D/JA 37DI

37304	01	F17
37305	05	F4
37311	03	F21
37313	53	F16
37316	16	F17
37317	06	F21
37318	58	F16
37319	59	F16
37320	60	F16
37322	62	F16
37323	73	F16
37325	25	F4
37326I	26	FMV
37327	08	F4
37328	68	F16
37329	29	F4
37330	30	F16
37331	31	F4
37332	12	F16
37335	75	F16
37336	04	F21
37337	05	F21
37339	07	F21
37341	41	F4
37343	43	F4
37345	45	F17
37347D	47	F16
37350	50	F21
37351	51	F17
37352	40	F16
37353	33	F21
37354	42	F17
37355	43	F17
37356	76	F16
37357	57	F4
37358	46	F16
37359	29	F17
37362	09	F21
37363	10	F21
37364	11	F21
37365	30	F21
37366	13	F21
37367	14	F21
37368	15	F16
37369	16	F21
37370	17	F21
37371	18	F21
37374	74	F16
37375	25	F17
37376	36	F4
37377	37	F4
37379	15	F21
37380	50	F4
37382	52	F4
37383	53	F4
37385	55	F4
37386D	46	F17
37388	58	F4
37389D	59	F17
37390	60	F4
37393	63	F4
37394	47	F17
37395	65	F4
37397I	20	F17
37398I	08	F17
37399	69	F4
37400	50	F16
37401I	01	F17
37402D	02	F17
37403	23	F21
37404D	24	F17
37405	25	F21
37406	26	F21
37407	27	F21
37408	28	F21
37409	29	F21
37410	10	F16
37411	11	F16
37412D	12	F17
37413D	13	F17
37414I	14	F17
37415I	15	F17
37416D	36	F17
37417	17	F17
37418	18	F17
37419	19	F16
37420	20	F16
37421I	21	F17
37422D	22	F17
37423	23	F16
37424D	24	F17
37426I	26	F16
37427D	27	F17
37428D	28	F17
37429D	29	F17
37431D	31	F17
37432	32	F16
37433	33	F16
37434	34	F16
37435D	35	F17
37436I	32	F17
37437I	37	F17
37438D	38	F17
37439	01	F4
37440I	40	F17
37441D	41	F17
37442	52	F17
37443D	43	F17
37444D	04	F17
37445D	45	F17
37446I	06	F17
37447	35	F21
37448	04	F4
37449D	49	F17

Sk 37/Sk 37E*

37801	80	F4
37802	81	F4
37804	83	F4
37807*	70	F4
37808*	71	F4
37809*	72	F4
37811*	74	F4
37813	56	F4
37814*	76	F4
37815*	77	F4
37816*	78	F4
37817	52	F4

AJSH 37

37901		
37903		
37905	53	F21
37910	57	F21
37911	33	F21
37913		
37914	61	F21
37915	69	F21
37916		

37918	71	F21
37922		
AJSF 37		
37950	48	F21
37951	50	F21
37952	52	F21
37954	30	F21
37957	58	F21
37958	48	F21
37960		
37971	62	F21
37976		

SAAB JAS 39 Gripen
Flottiljer 7, Såtenäs [G];
Flottiljer 10, Angelholm;
FMV, Malmslätt

JAS 39

39-2	52	FMV
39-3	53	FMV
39-4	54	SAAB
39-5	55	SAAB
JAS 39A		
39101	51	FMV
39103	03	FMV
39104	04	F7
39105	105	F7
39106	106	F7
39107	07	F7
39108	08	F7
39109	09	F7
39110	10	F7
39111	11	F7
39112	12	F7
39113	13	F7
39114	14	F7
39115	15	F7
39116	16	F7
39117	17	F7
39118	18	SAAB
39119	19	F7
39120	20	F7
39121	21	F7
39122	22	F7
39123	23	F7
39124	24	F7
39125	25	F7
39126	26	F7
39127	27	F7
39128	28	F7
39129	29	F7
39130	30	F7
39131	31	F7
39132	32	F7
39133	33	F7
39134	134	F10
39135	35	F10
39136	36	F7
39137	37	F10
39138	38	F7
39139	139	F7
39140	40	F7
39141	41	F7
39142	42	F7
39143	43	F10
39144	44	F10
39145	45	F10
39146	46	F10
39147	47	F10
39148	48	F10
39149	49	F7
39150	50	F7
39151	51	F7
39152	52	F7

39153	53	F7
39154	54	F7
39155	55	F7
39157	57	F7
39158	58	F7
39159	59	F7
39160	60	F7
39161	61	F7
39162	62	F7
39163	63	F7
39164	64	F10
39165	65	F10
39166	66	F7
39167	67	F10
39168	168	F10
39169	169	F10
39170	170	F10
39171	171	F10
39172	172	F7
39173	173	F10
39174	174	F10
39175	175	F10
39176	176	F10
39177		FMV
39178	178	F7
39179		
39180		
39181	181	F7
39182		
39183	183	F10
39184	184	F10
39185	185	F7
39186		
39187	187	FMV
39188		
39189		
39190		
39191		
39192		
39193		
39194		
39195		
39196		
39197		
39198		
39199		
39200		
39200		
39200		
39201		
39202		
39203		
39204		
39205		
39206		
39207		
39208		
39209		
39210		
39211		
39212		
39213		
39214		
39215		
39216		
39217		
39218		
39219		
39220		
39221		
39222		
39223		
39224		
39225		

39226		
JAS 39B		
39800	58	FMV
39801	70	F7
39802	802	FMV
39803	803	F7
39804	804	F7
39805	805	FMV
39806		
39807		
39808		
39809		
39810		
39811		
39812		
39813		

SAAB SF.340B (Tp.100A)/
SF.340AEW&C (S.100B)
Argus*
Flottiljer 16, Uppsala;
Flottiljer 16M,
Stockholm/Bromma

100001	001	F16M
100002*	002	F16
100005*	005	F16
100006*	006	F16
100007*	007	F16

Förvarsmaktens
Helikopterflottilj
Aérospatiale
AS.332M-1 Super Puma
(Hkp.10)
1.HkpBat/
 Flygräddningsgrupp F4,
 Östersund/Frösön;
1.HkpBat/
 Flygräddningsgrupp F21,
 Luleå/Kallax;
2.HkpBat/
 Flygräddningsgrupp F16,
 Uppsala;
3.HkpBat/
 Flygräddningsgrupp F7,
 Såtenäs;
3.HkpBat/
 Flygräddningsgrupp F17,
 Ronneby/Kallinge;

10401	91	F7
10402	92	F7
10403	93	F21
10405	95	F17
10406	96	
10407	97	F17
10408	98	F16
10409	99	F17
10410	90	F17
10411	88	F21
10412	89	

Agusta-Bell AB.412
(Hkp.11)
1.HkpBat/Armeflyget 1
 (AF1), Boden

11331	31
11332	32
11333	33
11334	34
11335	35
11336	36
11337	37
11338	38
11339	39

11340	40	
11341	41	
11342	42	

MBB Bo.105CB (Hkp.9A)
1.HkpBat/Armeflyget 1
  (AF1), Boden;
4.HkpBat/Armeflyget 2
  (AF2), Malmslätt;
FMV (Flygvapnet),
  Malmslätt

09201	01	AF1
09202	02	AF1
09203	03	AF2
09204	04	AF2
09205	05	AF1
09206	06	AF1
09207	07	AF1
09208	08	AF1
09209	09	AF2
09210	10	AF1
09211	11	AF1
09212	12	AF1
09213	13	AF2
09214	14	AF2
09215	15	AF2
09216	16	AF2
09217	17	AF2
09218	18	AF1
09219	19	AF1
09220	20	AF2
09221	90	FMV

Vertol/Kawasaki-Vertol 107
2.HkpBat/11
  11 Helikopterdivison,
  Berga;
3.HkpBat/
  12 Helikopterdivision,
  Goteborg/Säve;
3.HkpBat/
  13 Helikopterdivison,
  Ronneby/Kallinge;
FMV (Flygvapnet),
  Malmslätt

Vertol 107-II-15 (Hkp.4B)

04061	61	11 Hkp Div
04063	63	11 Hkp Div
04064	64	11 Hkp Div

**Kawasaki-Vertol
KV.107-II-16 (Hkp.4C)**

04065	65	12 Hkp Div
04067	67	12 Hkp Div
04068	68	12 Hkp Div
04069	69	12 Hkp Div
04070	70	11 Hkp Div
04071	71	12 Hkp Div
04072	72	FMV

Vertol 107-II-15 (Hkp.4A)

04073	73	11 Hkp Div
04074	74	13 Hkp Div
04075	75	13 Hkp Div
04076	76	13 Hkp Div

SWITZERLAND
Schweizerische Flugwaffe
  (Most aircraft are pooled
  centrally. Some carry unit
  badges but these rarely
  indicate actual operators.)
**Aérospatiale
AS.332M-1 Super Puma**
Leichte Flieger Staffel 5
  (LtSt 5), Interlaken;

Leichte Flieger Staffel 6
  (LtSt 6), Alpnach;
Leichte Flieger Staffel 8
  (LtSt 8), Ulrichen
Detachments at Alpnach,
  Emmen, Meiringen,
  Payerne & Sion
T-311
T-312
T-313
T-314
T-315
T-316
T-317
T-318
T-319
T-320
T-321
T-322
T-323
T-324
T-325

**Beechcraft Super King
Air 350C**
Flugswaffenbrigade 31,
  Dübendorf
HB-GII

Dassault Falcon 50
VIP Flight, Dübendorf
T-783

Dassault Mirage III
Flieger Staffel 3 (FlSt 3),
  Sion;
Flieger Staffel 4 (FlSt 4),
  Payerne;
Flieger Staffel 10 (FlSt 10),
  Buochs;
Gruppe fur Rustungdienste
  (GRD), Emmen;
Instrumentation Flieger
  Staffel 14 (InstruFlSt 14),
  Payerne

Mirage IIIBS

J-2001	InstruFlSt 14
U-2004	InstruFlSt 14

Mirage IIIUDS

J-2011	InstruFlSt 14
J-2012	InstruFlSt 14

Mirage IIIRS
R-2102
R-2103
R-2104
R-2105
R-2106
R-2107
R-2108
R-2109
R-2110
R-2111
R-2112
R-2113
R-2114
R-2115
R-2116
R-2117
R-2118

Gates Learjet 35A
VIP Flight, Dübendorf
T-781

**McDonnell Douglas
F/A-18 Hornet**
Flieger Staffel 11 (FlSt 11),
  Meiringen;
Flieger Staffel 17 (FlSt 17),
  Payerne;
Flieger Staffel 18 (FlSt 18),
  Payerne

F/A-18C
J-5001
J-5002
J-5003
J-5004
J-5005
J-5006
J-5007
J-5008
J-5009
J-5010
J-5011
J-5012
J-5013
J-5014
J-5015
J-5016
J-5017
J-5018
J-5019
J-5020
J-5021
J-5022
J-5023
J-5024
J-5025
J-5026

F/A-18D
J-5232
J-5233
J-5234
J-5235
J-5236
J-5237
J-5238

Northrop F-5 Tiger II
Flieger Staffel 1 (FlSt 1),
  Turtman;
Flieger Staffel 6 (FlSt 6),
  Sion;
Flieger Staffel 8 (FlSt 8),
  Meiringen;
Flieger Staffel 11 (FlSt 11),
  Meiringen;
Flieger Staffel 13 (FlSt 13),
  Meiringen;
Flieger Staffel 18 (FlSt 18),
  Payerne;
Flieger Staffel 19 (FlSt 19),
  Mollis;
Gruppe fur Rustunggdienste
  (GRD), Emmen;
Instrumentation Flieger
  Staffel 14 (InstruFlSt 14),
  Dübendorf;
Patrouille Suisse, Emmen
(P. Suisse)

F-5E
J-3001
J-3002
J-3004
J-3005
J-3006
J-3007

J-3008	InstruFlSt 14

J-3009		
J-3010		
J-3011		
J-3014		
J-3015		
J-3016		
J-3024		
J-3025		
J-3027		
J-3029		
J-3030		
J-3033		
J-3034		
J-3036		
J-3037		
J-3038		
J-3041		
J-3043		
J-3044		
J-3046		
J-3047		
J-3049		
J-3051		
J-3052		
J-3053		
J-3054		
J-3055		
J-3056		
J-3057		
J-3058		
J-3060		
J-3061		
J-3062		
J-3063		
J-3065		
J-3066		
J-3067		
J-3068		
J-3069		
J-3070		
J-3072		
J-3073		
J-3074		
J-3075		
J-3076		
J-3077		
J-3079		
J-3080		
J-3081	P. Suisse	
J-3082		
J-3083	P. Suisse	
J-3084	P. Suisse [4]	
J-3085	P. Suisse [3]	
J-3086	P. Suisse [6]	
J-3087	P. Suisse	
J-3088	P. Suisse [5]	
J-3089		
J-3090	P. Suisse [2]	
J-3091	P. Suisse [1]	
J-3092		
J-3093		
J-3094		
J-3095		
J-3096		
J-3097	GRD	
J-3098		
F-5F		
J-3201		
J-3202		
J-3203		
J-3204	GRD	
J-3205		
J-3206		
J-3207		

J-3208	
J-3209	
J-3210	
J-3211	
J-3212	

SYRIA
Tupolev Tu-134A
Govt of Syria, Damascus
YK-AYA

TURKEY
Türk Hava Kuvvetleri
Boeing KC-135R
Stratotanker
101 Filo, Incirlik

00325	
00326	
23539	
23563	
23567	
72609	
80110	

Cessna 650 Citation VII
224 Filo, Ankara/Etimeşgut

93-7024	ETI-024
93-7026	ETI-026

Grumman G.1159C
Gulfstream 4
224 Filo, Ankara/Etimeşgut
003

Lockheed C-130B Hercules
222 Filo, Erkilet

3496 (23496)	
10960	
10963	
70527	
80736	
91527	

Lockheed C-130E Hercules
222 Filo, Erkilet

00991	
01468	12-468
01947	
13186	12-186
13187	12-187
13188	
13189	

Transall C-160D
221 Filo, Erkilet

019	
020	
021	
022	
023	
024	
025	12-025
69-026	
027	
69-028	12-028
029	
031	
032	
033	
034	
035	
036	
037	12-037
038	

039	
040	12-040

TUSAS-GD F-16C/F-16D*
Fighting Falcon
4 AJÜ, Mürted:
   141 Filo & Öncel Filo;
5 AJÜ, Merzifon:
   151 Filo & 152 Filo;
6 AJÜ, Bandirma:
   161 Filo & 162 Filo;
8 AJÜ, Diyarbakir:
   181 Filo & 182 Filo;
9 AJÜ, Balikesir:
   191 Filo & 192 Filo

86-0066	Öncel Filo
86-0068	Öncel Filo
86-0069	Öncel Filo
86-0070	Öncel Filo
86-0071	Öncel Filo
86-0072	Öncel Filo
86-0191*	Öncel Filo
86-0192*	Öncel Filo
86-0193*	Öncel Filo
86-0194*	Öncel Filo
86-0195*	Öncel Filo
86-0196*	Öncel Filo
87-0002*	Öncel Filo
87-0003*	Öncel Filo
87-0009	Öncel Filo
87-0010	Öncel Filo
87-0011	Öncel Filo
87-0013	Öncel Filo
87-0014	Öncel Filo
87-0015	Öncel Filo
87-0016	Öncel Filo
87-0017	Öncel Filo
87-0018	Öncel Filo
87-0019	Öncel Filo
87-0020	Öncel Filo
87-0021	Öncel Filo
88-0013*	Öncel Filo
88-0014*	141 Filo
88-0015*	141 Filo
88-0019	Öncel Filo
88-0020	Öncel Filo
88-0021	Öncel Filo
88-0024	Öncel Filo
88-0025	141 Filo
88-0026	Öncel Filo
88-0027	Öncel Filo
88-0028	191 Filo
88-0029	Öncel Filo
88-0030	191 Filo
88-0031	Öncel Filo
88-0032	Öncel Filo
88-0033	141 Filo
88-0034	141 Filo
88-0035	141 Filo
88-0036	141 Filo
88-0037	141 Filo
89-0022	141 Filo
89-0023	141 Filo
89-0024	141 Filo
89-0025	141 Filo
89-0026	141 Filo
89-0027	141 Filo
89-0028	141 Filo
89-0030	141 Filo
89-0031	141 Filo
89-0032	141 Filo
89-0034	162 Filo
89-0035	162 Filo
89-0036	162 Filo

89-0037	162 Filo	92-0023*	191 Filo	94-0089	
89-0038	162 Filo	92-0024*	161 Filo	94-0090	
89-0039	162 Filo	93-0001	181 Filo	94-0091	152 Filo
89-0040	162 Filo	93-0002	181 Filo	94-0092	
89-0041	162 Filo	93-0003	181 Filo	94-0093	
89-0042*	141 Filo	93-0004	181 Filo	94-0094	Öncel Filo
89-0043*	162 Filo	93-0005	181 Filo	94-0095	
89-0044*	162 Filo	93-0006	181 Filo	94-0096	
89-0045*	141 Filo	93-0007		94-0105*	191 Filo
90-0001	162 Filo	93-0008	181 Filo	94-0106*	191 Filo
90-0004	162 Filo	93-0009	182 Filo	94-0107*	191 Filo
90-0005	162 Filo	93-0010	181 Filo	94-0108*	151 Filo
90-0006	162 Filo	93-0011	182 Filo	94-0109*	
90-0007	162 Filo	93-0012	181 Filo	94-0110*	
90-0008	162 Filo	93-0013	181 Filo	94-1557*	
90-0009	162 Filo	93-0014	181 Filo	94-1558*	Öncel Filo
90-0010	162 Filo	93-0657	141 Filo	94-1559*	152 Filo
90-0011	162 Filo	93-0658		94-1560*	151 Filo
90-0012	161 Filo	93-0659		94-1561*	
90-0013	161 Filo	93-0660	151 Filo	94-1562*	192 Filo
90-0014	161 Filo	93-0661		94-1563*	192 Filo
90-0015	161 Filo	93-0662	151 Filo	94-1564*	
90-0016	161 Filo	93-0663			
90-0017	161 Filo	93-0664		**Turkish Govt**	
90-0018	161 Filo	93-0665		**Grumman G.1159C**	
90-0019	161 Filo	93-0666		**Gulfstream IV**	
90-0020	162 Filo	93-0667		Govt of Turkey, Istanbul	
90-0021	161 Filo	93-0668		TC-ATA	
90-0022*	161 Filo	93-0669	152 Filo	TC-GAP	
90-0023*	161 Filo	93-0670			
90-0024*	161 Filo	93-0671		**TURKMENISTAN**	
91-0001	161 Filo	93-0672	152 Filo	**BAe 1000B**	
91-0002	161 Filo	93-0673	Öncel Filo	Govt of Turkmenistan,	
91-0003	161 Filo	93-0674	192 Filo	Ashkhabad	
91-0004	161 Filo	93-0675	192 Filo	EZ-B021	
91-0005	162 Filo	93-0676	192 Filo		
91-0006	161 Filo	93-0677	192 Filo	**UGANDA**	
91-0007	161 Filo	93-0678	192 Filo	**Grumman G.1159C**	
91-0008	141 Filo	93-0679	192 Filo	**Gulfstream IV**	
91-0010	141 Filo	93-0680	192 Filo	Govt of Uganda,	
91-0011	141 Filo	93-0681	192 Filo	Entebbe	
91-0012	141 Filo	93-0682		5X-UEF	
91-0013	192 Filo	93-0683	192 Filo		
91-0014	141 Filo	93-0684	192 Filo	**UKRAINE**	
91-0015	182 Filo	93-0685	192 Filo	**Ukrainian Air Force**	
91-0016	192 Filo	93-0686	192 Filo	**Ilyushin Il-76MD**	
91-0017	182 Filo	93-0687	192 Filo	321 TAP, Uzin	
91-0018	182 Filo	93-0688	192 Filo	UR-76413	
91-0019	192 Filo	93-0689	Öncel Filo	UR-76537	
91-0020	182 Filo	93-0690	192 Filo	UR-76624	
91-0022*	141 Filo	93-0691*		UR-76677	
91-0024*	141 Filo	93-0692*	152 Filo	UR-76687	
92-0001	191 Filo	93-0693*	Öncel Filo	UR-76697	
92-0002	192 Filo	93-0694*		UR-76699	
92-0003	182 Filo	93-0695*	192 Filo	UR-78820	
92-0004	191 Filo	93-0696*	192 Filo		
92-0005	191 Filo	94-0071	192 Filo	**UNITED ARAB EMIRATES**	
92-0006	182 Filo	94-0072	192 Filo	**United Arab Emirates Air Force**	
92-0007	182 Filo	94-0073		*Abu Dhabi*	
92-0008	191 Filo	94-0074	191 Filo	**Lockheed C-130H Hercules**	
92-0009	191 Filo	94-0075		1211	
92-0010		94-0076		1212	
92-0011	182 Filo	94-0077		1213	
92-0012	191 Filo	94-0078		1214	
92-0013	191 Filo	94-0079			
92-0014	191 Filo	94-0080		*Dubai*	
92-0015	182 Filo	94-0081		**Lockheed**	
92-0016	191 Filo	94-0082	191 Filo	**L.100-30 Hercules**	
92-0017	191 Filo	94-0083	191 Filo	311	
92-0018	191 Filo	94-0084	191 Filo	312	
92-0019		94-0085	191 Filo		
92-0020		94-0086		**UAE Govt**	
92-0021	181 Filo	94-0087	191 Filo	**Airbus A.300B4-620**	
92-0022*	181 Filo	94-0088		Govt of Abu Dhabi	

A6-PFD
A6-SHZ

Boeing 737-2W8
Govt of Sharjah
A6-ESH

Boeing 737-7F0/7Z5*
Govt of Abu Dhabi;
Govt Of Dubai

A6-AIN*	Abu Dhabi
A6-DAS*	Abu Dhabi
A6-HRS	Dubai
A6-LIW*	Dubai
A6-SIR*	Dubai

**Boeing
747SP-31/
747SP-Z5***
Govt of Dubai
A6-SMM

A6-SMR
A6-ZSN*

Boeing 747-4F6
Govt of Abu Dhabi
A6-YAS

Boeing 767-341ER
Govt of Abu Dhabi
A6-SUL

Dassault Falcon 900
Govt of Abu Dhabi
A6-AUH
A6-UAE
A6-ZKM

**Grumman G.1159C
Gulfstream IV**
Dubai Air Wing
A6-HHH

YUGOSLAVIA

Dassault Falcon 50
Govt of Yugoslavia,
Belgrade

| YU-BNA | (72102) |
| YU-BPZ | (72101) |

**Gates LearJet 25B/
LearJet 25D***
Govt of Yugoslavia,
Belgrade
YU-BJG
YU-BKR*

Colourful Saab Draken flown by 1 Staffel from Zeltweg, Austria. *PRM*

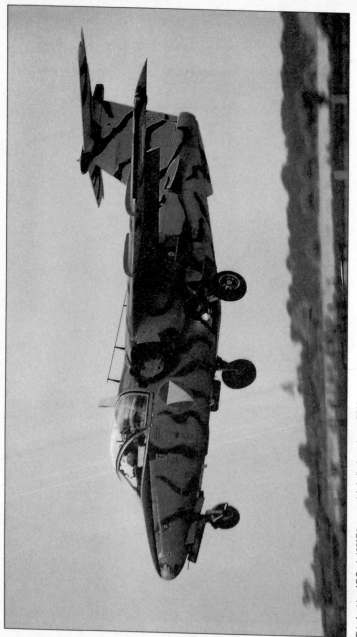

This Austrian AF Saab 1050E has special air display colours. *PRM*

178

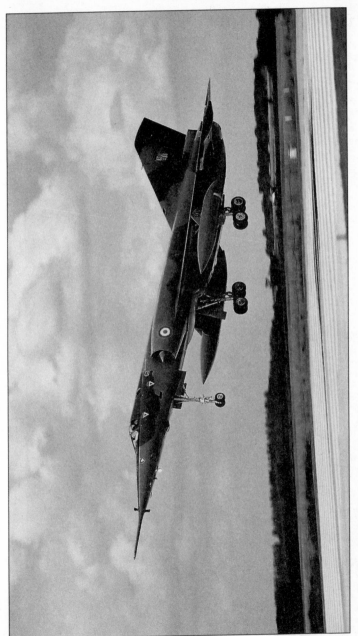

One of five Mirage IVs, based at Mont-de-Marsan, France. *PRM*

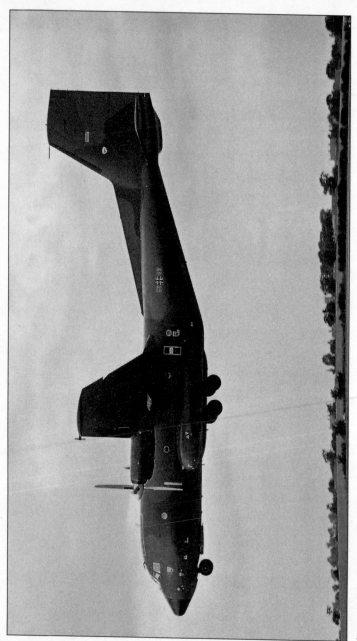

German Air Force Transall 51+09. *PRM*

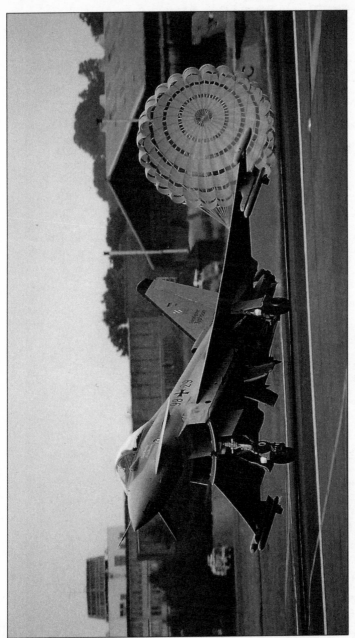

The first Eurofighter Typhoon 98+29 (DA1) touching down at Farnborough. *Daniel March*

Brightly painted AMX, of 103° Gruppo, 51° Stormo of the Italian Air Force, based at Istrana *PRM*

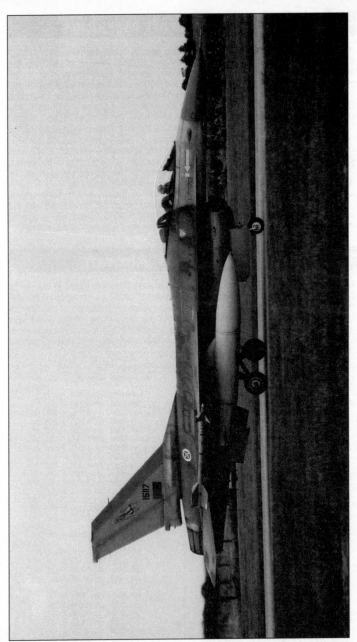

Portuguese AF F-16A (15117) operated by 201 Esq at Monte Real. *PRM*

US Military Aircraft Markings

All USAF aircraft have been allocated a fiscal year (FY) number since 1921. Individual aircraft are given a serial according to the fiscal year in which they are ordered. The numbers commence at 0001 and are prefixed with the year of allocation. For example F-15C Eagle 84-001 (84-0001) was the first aircraft ordered in 1984. The fiscal year (FY) serial is carried on the technical data block which is usually stencilled on the left-hand side of the aircraft just below the cockpit. The number displayed on the fin is a corruption of the FY serial. Most tactical aircraft carry the fiscal year in small figures followed by the last three or four digits of the serial in large figures. For example Aviano-based F-16C Fighting Falcon 89-2009 carries 89-009/AV on its tail. Large transport and tanker aircraft such as C-130s and KC-135s sometimes display a five-figure number commencing with the last digit of the appropriate fiscal year and four figures of the production number. An example of this is KC-135R 58-0128 which displays 80128 on its fin.

USN serials follow a straightforward numerical sequence which commenced, for the present series, with the allocation of 00001 to an SB2C Helldiver by the Bureau of Aeronautics in 1940. Numbers in the 165000 series are presently being issued. They are usually carried in full on the rear fuselage of the aircraft.

UK-based USAF Aircraft

The following aircraft are normally based in the UK. They are listed in numerical order of type with individual aircraft in serial number order, as depicted on the aircraft. The number in brackets is either the alternative presentation of the five-figure number commencing with the last digit of the fiscal year, or the fiscal year where a five-figure serial is presented on the aircraft. Where it is possible to identify the allocation of aircraft to individual squadrons by means of colours carried on fin or cockpit edge, this is also provided.

Notes	Type				Notes	Type			
	McDonnell Douglas F-15C Eagle/					86-0180	(86-0180)	F-15C	y
	F-15D Eagle/F-15E Strike Eagle								[48th OG]
	LN: 48th FW, RAF Lakenheath:					86-0182	(86-0182)	F-15D	y
	492nd FS blue/white					91-0300	(91-0300)	F-15E	r
	493rd FS black/yellow					91-0301	(91-0301)	F-15E	bl
	494th FS red/white					91-0302	(91-0302)	F-15E	bl
	84-0001	(84-0001)	F-15C	y		91-0303	(91-0303)	F-15E	bl
	84-0009	(84-0009)	F-15C	y		91-0304	(91-0304)	F-15E	r
	84-0010	(84-0010)	F-15C	y		91-0305	(91-0305)	F-15E	bl
	84-0014	(84-0014)	F-15C	y		91-0306	(91-0306)	F-15E	r
	84-0015	(84-0015)	F-15C	y		91-0307	(91-0307)	F-15E	bl
	84-0019	(84-0019)	F-15C	y		91-0308	(91-0308)	F-15E	bl
	84-0044	(84-0044)	F-15D	y		91-0309	(91-0309)	F-15E	bl
	86-0147	(86-0147)	F-15C	y		91-0310	(91-0310)	F-15E	r
	86-0154	(86-0154)	F-15C	y		91-0311	(91-0311)	F-15E	bl
	86-0156	(86-0156)	F-15C	y		91-0312	(91-0312)	F-15E	bl
	86-0159	(86-0159)	F-15C	y		91-0313	(91-0313)	F-15E	m
	86-0160	(86-0160)	F-15C	y					[3rd AF]
	86-0163	(86-0163)	F-15C	y		91-0314	(91-0314)	F-15E	r
	86-0164	(86-0164)	F-15C	y					[494th FS]
				[493rd FS]		91-0315	(91-0315)	F-15E	r
	86-0165	(86-0165)	F-15C	y		91-0316	(91-0316)	F-15E	r
	86-0166	(86-0166)	F-15C	y		91-0317	(91-0317)	F-15E	r
	86-0167	(86-0167)	F-15C	y		91-0318	(91-0318)	F-15E	r
	86-0169	(86-0169)	F-15C	y		91-0319	(91-0319)	F-15E	r
	86-0171	(86-0171)	F-15C	y		91-0320	(91-0320)	F-15E	r
	86-0172	(86-0172)	F-15C	y		91-0321	(91-0321)	F-15E	r
	86-0174	(86-0174)	F-15C	y		91-0322	(91-0322)	F-15E	r
	86-0175	(86-0175)	F-15C	y		91-0323	(91-0323)	F-15E	r
	86-0176	(86-0176)	F-15C	y		91-0324	(91-0324)	F-15E	r
	86-0178	(86-0178)	F-15C	y		91-0326	(91-0326)	F-15E	bl

Type			Notes	Type		Notes
91-0328	(91-0328)	F-15E	r	95796	(FY69)	
91-0329	(91-0329)	F-15E	bl			
91-0330	(91-0330)	F-15E	r	**Lockheed C-130 Hercules**		
91-0331	(91-0331)	F-15E	r	352nd SOG, RAF Mildenhall:		
91-0332	(91-0332)	F-15E	bl	7th SOS* & 67th SOS,		
91-0333	(91-0333)	F-15E	r	37814	(FY63)	C-130E
91-0334	(91-0334)	F-15E	r	40476	(FY84)	MC-130H*
91-0335	(91-0335)	F-15E	r	61699	(FY86)	MC-130H*
91-0601	(91-0601)	F-15E	r	70023	(FY87)	MC-130H*
91-0602	(91-0602)	F-15E	r	80193	(FY88)	MC-130H*
91-0603	(91-0603)	F-15E	r	80194	(FY88)	MC-130H*
91-0604	(91-0604)	F-15E	r	95823	(FY69)	MC-130P
91-0605	(91-0605)	F-15E	r	95826	(FY69)	MC-130P
92-0364	(92-0364)	F-15E	r	95828	(FY69)	MC-130P
96-0201	(96-0201)	F-15E	bl	95831	(FY69)	MC-130P
96-0202	(96-0202)	F-15E	bl	95832	(FY69)	MC-130P
96-0204	(96-0204)	F-15E	bl			
96-0205	(96-0205)	F-15E	bl	**Boeing KC-135R Stratotanker**		
97-0217	(97-0217)	F-15E	bl	351st ARS/100th ARW,		
97-0218	(97-0218)	F-15E	m	RAF Mildenhall [D] (r/w/bl)		
			[48th FW]	00360	(FY60)	
97-0219	(97-0219)	F-15E	bl	10288	(FY61)	
97-0220	(97-0220)	F-15E	bl	10312	(FY61)	
97-0221	(97-0221)	F-15E	bl	14838	(FY64)	
			[492nd FS]	23498	(FY62)	
97-0222	(97-0222)	F-15E	bl	23517	(FY62)	
98-0131	(98-0131)	F-15E	bl	23528	(FY62)	
98-0132	(98-0132)	F-15E	bl	23538	(FY62)	
98-0133	(98-0133)	F-15E	bl	23561	(FY62)	
98-0134	(98-0134)	F-15E	bl	23564	(FY62)	
98-0135	(98-0135)	F-15E	bl	23578	(FY62)	
				37979	(FY63)	
Sikorsky MH-53M				38017	(FY63)	
21st SOS/352nd SOG,				38874	(FY63)	
RAF Mildenhall				38887	(FY63)	
01625	(FY70)			71474	(FY57)	
01630	(FY70)					
14994	(FY67)					
31649	(FY73)					
31652	(FY73)					
95784	(FY69)					
95795	(FY69)					

UK-based US Navy Aircraft

Beech UC 12M Super King Air
Naval Air Facility, Mildenhall
3836 (163836)
3843 (163843)

European-based USAF Aircraft

These aircraft are normally based in Western Europe with the USAFE. They are shown in numerical order of type designation, with individual aircraft in serial number order as carried on the aircraft. An alternative five-figure presentation of the serial is shown in brackets where appropriate. Fiscal year (FY) details are also provided if necessary. The unit allocation and operating bases are given for most aircraft.

Notes	Type				Notes	Type			
	Lockheed U-2S					**Lockheed (GD) F-16C/F-16D***			
	OL-FR/9th RW, Istres, France [BB]					**AV:** 31st FW, Aviano, Italy:			
	01081	(FY80)				510th FS purple/white			
	01082	(FY80)				555th FS green/yellow			
	01083	(FY80)				**SP:** 52nd FW, Spangdahlem,			
						Germany:			
	McDonnell Douglas					22nd FS red/white			
	C-9A Nightingale					23rd FS blue/white			
	86th AW, Ramstein,					87-350	(87-0350)	AV gn	
	Germany:					87-351	(87-0351)	AV m [31st OSS]	
	75th AS & 76th AS[1]					87-355	(87-0355)	AV pr	
	FY71					87-359	(87-0359)	AV gn	
	10876[1] (VIP)					88-413	(88-0413)	AV pr [510th FS]	
	10879					88-425	(88-0425)	AV gn	
	10880					88-435	(88-0435)	AV gn	
	10881					88-443	(88-0443)	AV pr	
	10882					88-444	(88-0444)	AV pr	
	FY67					88-446	(88-0446)	AV pr	
	22585					88-491	(88-0491)	AV pr	
	FY68					88-525	(88-0525)	AV pr	
	88934					88-526	(88-0526)	AV gn	
						88-529	(88-0529)	AV pr	
	Fairchild A-10A Thunderbolt II					88-532	(88-0532)	AV gn [31st OG]	
	SP: 52nd FW, Spangdahlem,					88-535	(88-0535)	AV gn [555th FS]	
	Germany:					88-541	(88-0541)	AV pr	
	81st FS black/yellow					89-001	(89-2001)	AV m [31st FW]	
	80-171	(80-0171)	bk			89-009	(89-2009)	AV gn	
	80-276	(80-0276)	bk			89-011	(89-2011)	AV gn	
	81-951	(81-0951)	bk			89-016	(89-2016)	AV gn [16th AF]	
	81-952	(81-0952)	m	[52nd FW]		89-018	(89-2018)	AV gn	
	81-954	(81-0954)	bk	[81st FS]		89-023	(89-2023)	AV gn	
	81-956	(81-0956)	bk			89-024	(89-2024)	AV gn	
	81-962	(81-0962)	bk			89-026	(89-2026)	AV gn	
	81-963	(81-0963)	bk			89-029	(89-2029)	AV pr	
	81-966	(81-0966)	bk			89-030	(89-2030)	AV pr	
	81-976	(81-0976)	bk			89-035	(89-2035)	AV gn [555th FS]	
	81-978	(81-0978)	bk			89-038	(89-2038)	AV gn	
	81-980	(81-0980)	bk			89-039	(89-2039)	AV gn	
	81-983	(81-0983)	bk			89-044	(89-2044)	AV gn	
	81-984	(81-0984)	bk			89-046	(89-2046)	AV pr	
	81-985	(81-0985)	bk			89-047	(89-2047)	AV pr	
	81-988	(81-0988)	bk			89-049	(89-2049)	AV pr	
	81-991	(81-0991)	bk			89-050	(89-2050)	AV pr	
	81-992	(81-0992)	m	[52nd OG]		89-057	(89-2057)	AV pr	
	82-649	(82-0649)	bk			89-137	(89-2137)	AV pr [31st OG]	
	82-650	(82-0650)	bk			89-178	(89-2178)*	AV pr	
	82-654	(82-0654)	bk			90-709	(90-0709)	AV pr	
	82-655	(82-0655)	bk			90-795	(90-0795)*	AV pr	
	82-656	(82-0656)	bk			90-796	(90-0796)*	AV pr	
						90-800	(90-0800)*	AV gn	
	Beech C-12C/C-12D/C-12F					90-813	(90-0813)	SP r	
	JUSMG, Ankara, Turkey;					90-818	(90-0818)	SP r	
	US Embassy Flight, Budapest,					90-827	(90-0827)	SP r	
	Hungary					90-828	(90-0828)	SP r	
	FY83					90-829	(90-0829)	SP r	[22nd FS]
	30495	C-12D	Budapest			90-831	(90-0831)	SP r	
	FY73					90-833	(90-0833)	SP r	
	31216	C-12C	Ankara			90-843	(90-0843)*	SP r	
						90-846	(90-0846)*	SP bl	

Type			Notes
91-336	(91-0336)	SP *r*	
91-337	(91-0337)	SP *r*	
91-338	(91-0338)	SP *r*	
91-339	(91-0339)	SP *r*	
91-340	(91-0340)	SP *r*	
91-341	(91-0341)	SP *r*	
91-342	(91-0342)	SP *r*	
91-343	(91-0343)	SP *r*	
91-344	(91-0344)	SP *r*	
91-351	(91-0351)	SP *r*	
91-352	(91-0352)	SP *m*	[52nd FW]
91-391	(91-0391)	SP bl	
91-402	(91-0402)	SP *bl*	
91-403	(91-0403)	SP *bl*	[23rd FS]
91-405	(91-0405)	SP *bl*	
91-406	(91-0406)	SP *bl*	[23rd FS]
91-407	(91-0407)	SP *bl*	
91-408	(91-0408)	SP *bl*	
91-409	(91-0409)	SP *bl*	
91-410	(91-0410)	SP *bl*	
91-412	(91-0412)	SP *bl*	
91-414	(91-0414)	SP *bl*	
91-415	(91-0415)	SP *bl*	
91-416	(91-0416)	SP *bl*	
91-417	(91-0417)	SP *bl*	
91-418	(91-0418)	SP *bl*	
91-419	(91-0419)	SP *bl*	
91-420	(91-0420)	SP *bl*	
91-421	(91-0421)	SP *bl*	
91-464	(91-0464)*	SP *r*	
91-472	(91-0472)*	SP *bl*	
91-474	(91-0474)*	SP *bl*	
92-915	(92-3915)	SP *bl*	
92-918	(92-3918)	SP *bl*	
96-080	(96-0080)	SP *bl*	[23rd FS]
96-081	(96-0081)	SP *bl*	
96-082	(96-0082)	SP *m*	[52nd FW]
96-083	(96-0083)	SP *bl*	

Grumman C-20A Gulfstream III
76th AS/86th AW, Ramstein,
  Germany
FY83
30500
30501
30502

Gates C-21A Learjet
76th AS/86th AW, Ramstein,
  Germany;
*7005th ABS/HQ USEUCOM,
  Stuttgart, Germany
FY84
40068*
40081*

Type		Notes
40082*		
40083*		
40084		
40085		
40086		
40087		
40108		
40109		
40110		
40111		
40112		

**Gulfstream Aerospace
C-37A Gulfstream V**
Det 1, 86th OG/SHAPE, Chievres,
  Belgium
FY99
90402

Sikorsky HH-60G Blackhawk
56th RQS/85th Wing, Keflavik,
  Iceland [IS]

26109	(FY88)	
26205	(FY89)	
26206	(FY89)	
26208	(FY89)	
26212	(FY89)	

Lockheed C-130E Hercules
37th AS/86th AW, Ramstein,
  Germany [RS] (*bl/w*)

01260	(FY70)	
01264	(FY70)	[86th AW]
01271	(FY70)	
01274	(FY70)	
10935	(FY68)	
10938	(FY68)	
10943	(FY68)	[86th OG]
10947	(FY68)	
17681	(FY64)	
18240	(FY64)	
37885	(FY63)	
37887	(FY63)	
40502	(FY64)	
40527	(FY64)	
40533	(FY64)	
40550	(FY64)	
96566	(FY69)	[37th AS]
96582	(FY69)	
96583	(FY69)	

European-based US Navy Aircraft

Notes	Type	Notes	Type
	Lockheed P-3 Orion		
	CinCUSNFE, NAF Sigonella, Italy;		**Fairchild C-26D**
	NAF Keflavik, Iceland;		NAF Naples, Italy;
	VQ-2, NAF Rota, Spain		NAF Sigonella, Italy
	150495 UP-3A NAF Keflavik		900528 Sigonella
	150496 VP-3A CinCUSNFE		900530 Sigonella
	156519 [21] EP-3E VQ-2		900531 Sigonella
	156520 [10] P-3C VQ-2		910502 Naples
	156525 [11] P-3C VQ-2		
	156529 [24] EP-3E VQ-2		**Sikorsky MH-53E Sea Stallion**
	157316 [23] EP-3E VQ-2		HC-4, NAF Sigonella, Italy
	157325 [25] EP-3E VQ-2		162504 [HC-47]
	157326 [22] EP-3E VQ-2		162509 [HC-49]
	159512 [512] P-3C VQ-2		162516 [HC-46]
	161121 [15] P-3C VQ-2		163053 [HC-44]
	161414 [14] P-3C VQ-2		163055 [HC-45]
			163057 [HC-41]
	Beech UC-12M Super King Air		163065 [HC-43]
	NAF Rota, Spain		163068 [HC-42]
	3839 (163839) Rota		164864 [HC-48]
	3842 (163842) Rota		

European-based US Army Aircraft

Notes	Type	Notes	Type
	Bell UH-1H Iroquois		
	LANDSOUTHEAST, Cigli, Turkey;		**Beech C-12 Super King Air**
	'B' Co, 2nd Btn, 502nd Avn Reg't,		214th Avn, Heidelberg;
	Coleman Barracks;		'A' Co, 2nd Btn, 228th Avn Reg't,
	7th Army Training		Heidelberg;
	Center, Grafenwöhr;		'B' Co, 2nd Btn, 228th Avn Reg't,
	Combat Manoeuvre Training Centre,		Heidelberg;
	Hohenfels;		LANDSOUTHEAST, Izmir, Turkey;
	HQ/USEUCOM, Stuttgart;		HQ/USEUCOM, Stuttgart;
	6th Avn Co, Vicenza, Italy		6th Avn Co, Vicenza, Italy;
	FY69		1st Military Intelligence Btn,
	15605 HQ/USEUCOM		Wiesbaden
	15606 HQ/USEUCOM		*FY84*
	FY68		40144 C-12F 214th Avn
	16341 LANDSOUTHEAST		40152 C-12F 214th Avn
	16662 LANDSOUTHEAST		40153 C-12F 1st MIB
	FY72		40155 C-12F 214th Avn
	21569 CMTC		40156 C-12F 214th Avn
	21632 CMTC		40157 C-12F 214th Avn
	21636 CMTC		40158 C-12F HQ/USEUCOM
	FY73		40160 C-12F HQ/USEUCOM
	21668 CMTC		40161 C-12F 6th Avn Co
	21786 CMTC		40162 C-12F 6th Avn Co
	21806 LANDSOUTHEAST		40164 C-12F LANDSOUTHEAST
	21824 7th ATC		40165 C-12F LANDSOUTHEAST
	22127 B/2-502nd Avn		*FY94*
	FY74		40315 C-12R A/2-228th Avn
	22303 CMTC		40316 C-12R A/2-228th Avn
	22318 6th Avn Co		40317 C-12R A/2-228th Avn
	22330 CMTC		40318 C-12R A/2-228th Avn
	22347 CMTC		40319 C-12R A/2-228th Avn
	22355 CMTC		*FY95*
	22368 HQ/USEUCOM		50088 C-12R B/2-228th Avn
	22370 CMTC		*FY85*
	22410 CMTC		50147 RC-12K 1st MIB
	22448 CMTC		50148 RC-12K 1st MIB
	22465 CMTC		50149 RC-12K 1st MIB
	22504 7th ATC		50150 RC-12K 1st MIB
	22513 HQ/USEUCOM		50152 RC-12K 1st MIB
	22514 HQ/USEUCOM		50153 RC-12K 1st MIB

Type	Notes	Type	Notes
50154 RC-12K 1st MIB		40174 1-4th Cav	
50155 RC-12K 1st MIB		40175 1-1st Cav	
		40176 1-4th Cav	
Beech C-12J		40178 1-1st Cav	
HQ/USEUCOM, Stuttgart		40179 1-1st Cav	
FY86		40180 1-1st Cav	
60079		*FY89*	
		90114 1-1st Cav	
Cessna UC-35A Citation V		90116 1-1st Cav	
214th Avn Reg't, Heidelberg		90117 1-1st Cav	
FY95			
50123		**Sikorsky H-60 Black Hawk**	
50124		2nd Btn, 1st Avn Reg't, Ansbach;	
FY97		45th Medical Co, Ansbach;	
70101		'B' Co, 5th Btn, 158th Avn Reg't,	
70102		Aviano;	
		'A' Co, 127th Divisional Avn	
		Support Btn, Bad Kreuznach;	
Boeing-Vertol CH-47D Chinook		357th Avn Det/SHAPE, Chievres;	
'F' Co, 159th Avn Reg't Giebelstadt		'B' Co, 70th Transportation Reg't,	
FY87		Coleman Barracks;	
70072		'A' Co, 5th Btn, 158th Avn Reg't,	
70073		Giebelstadt;	
FY88		'C' Co, 5th Btn, 158th Avn Reg't,	
80098		Giebelstadt;	
80099		'C' Co, 158th Avn Reg't, Giebelstadt;	
80100		'D' Co, 158th Avn Reg't, Giebelstadt;	
80101		2nd Btn, 501st Avn Reg't, Hanau;	
80102		214th Avn, Heidelberg;	
80103		'B' Co, 7th Btn, 159th AVIM, Illesheim;	
80104		236th Medical Co (HA), Landstuhl;	
80106		6th Avn Co, Vicenza, Italy;	
FY89		159th Medical Co, Wiesbaden	
90138		*FY82*	
90139		223675 UH-60A 45th Med Co	
90140		23685 UH-60A 159th Med Co	
90141		23692 UH-60A C/158th Avn	
90142		23693 UH-60A 45th Med Co	
90143		23727 UH-60A 159th Med Co	
90144		23729 UH-60A 45th Med Co	
90145		23735 UH-60A 236th Med Co	
		23736 UH-60A 236th Med Co	
Bell OH-58D(I) Kiowa Warrior		23737 UH-60A 236th Med Co	
1st Btn, 1st Cavalry Reg't, Budingen;		23738 UH-60A 159th Med Co	
1st Btn, 4th Cavalry Reg't,		23745 UH-60A 236th Med Co	
Schweinfurt		23749 UH-60A 236th Med Co	
FY90		23750 UH-60A 159th Med Co	
00348 1-1st Cav		23751 UH-60A 45th Med Co	
00371 1-1st Cav		23752 UH-60A 236th Med Co	
00373 1-4th Cav		23753 UH-60A 159th Med Co	
FY91		23754 UH-60A 45th Med Co	
10540 1-1st Cav		23755 UH-60A 45th Med Co	
10544 1-1st Cav		23756 UH-60A 236th Med Co	
10564 1-1st Cav		23757 UH-60A 214th Avn	
FY92		23761 UH-60A 2-501st Avn	
20520 1-1st Cav		*FY83*	
20529 1-1st Cav		23854 UH-60A 357th Avn Det	
20545 1-1st Cav		23855 UH-60A 214th Avn	
FY93		23868 UH-60A 214th Avn	
30971 1-4th Cav		23869 UH-60A 214th Avn	
30996 1-4th Cav		*FY84*	
30998 1-4th Cav		23951 UH-60A 45th Med Co	
31002 1-4th Cav		23970 UH-60A C/5-158th Avn	
31005 1-4th Cav		23975 UH-60A C/5-158th Avn	
31006 1-4th Cav		24019 EH-60A 2-1st Avn	
31007 1-4th Cav		*FY85*	
31008 1-4th Cav		24391 UH-60A 45th Med Co	
FY94		24467 EH-60A 2-1st Avn	
40149 1-4th Cav		24475 EH-60A 2-1st Avn	
40150 1-4th Cav		24478 EH-60A 2-1st Avn	
40151 1-4th Cav		*FY86*	
40152 1-1st Cav		24498 UH-60A 2-501st Avn	
40153 1-4th Cav		24530 UH-60A 2-501st Avn	
40154 1-4th Cav			

US Army Europe

Notes	Type			Notes	Type		
	24531	UH-60A	45th Med Co		26146	UH-60A	159th Med Co
	24532	UH-60A	45th Med Co		26153	UH-60A	B/5-158th Avn
	24538	UH-60A	214th Avn		26155	UH-60A	2-1st Avn
	24550	UH-60A	236th Med Co		26164	UH-60A	C/5-158th Avn
	24551	UH-60A	236th Med Co		26165	UH-60A	214th Avn
	24552	UH-60A	159th Med Co		*FY95*		
	24554	UH-60A	C/5-158th Avn		26621	UH-60L	2-1st Avn
	24555	UH-60A	159th Med Co		26628	UH-60L	2-1st Avn
	24566	EH-60C	2-501st Avn		26629	UH-60L	2-1st Avn
	FY87				26630	UH-60L	2-1st Avn
	24579	UH-60A	A/5-158th Avn		26631	UH-60L	2-1st Avn
	24581	UH-60A	159th Med Co		26632	UH-60L	2-1st Avn
	24583	UH-60A	357th Avn Det		26633	UH-60L	2-1st Avn
	24584	UH-60A	357th Avn Det		26635	UH-60L	2-1st Avn
	24589	UH-60A	214th Avn		26636	UH-60L	2-1st Avn
	24621	UH-60A	214th Avn		26637	UH-60L	2-1st Avn
	24628	UH-60A	2-1st Avn		26638	UH-60L	2-1st Avn
	24634	UH-60A	159th Med Co		26639	UH-60L	2-1st Avn
	24642	UH-60A	214th Avn		26640	UH-60L	D/158th Avn
	24643	UH-60A	2-1st Avn		26641	UH-60L	D/158th Avn
	24644	UH-60A	45th Med Co		26642	UH-60L	D/158th Avn
	24645	UH-60A	45th Med Co		26643	UH-60L	D/158th Avn
	24646	UH-60A	2-1st Avn		26644	UH-60L	2-1st Avn
	24647	UH-60A	214th Avn		26645	UH-60L	D/158th Avn
	24650	UH-60A	159th Med Co		26646	UH-60L	2-1st Avn
	24656	UH-60A	159th Med Co		26647	UH-60L	2-1st Avn
	24660	EH-60C	2-501st Avn		26648	UH-60L	2-1st Avn
	24664	EH-60A	2-501st Avn		26649	UH-60L	D/158th Avn
	24667	EH-60A	2-501st Avn		26650	UH-60L	D/158th Avn
	26001	UH-60A	45th Med Co		26651	UH-60L	C/158th Avn
	26002	UH-60A	159th Med Co		26652	UH-60L	C/158th Avn
	26003	UH-60A	B/5-158th Avn		26653	UH-60L	C/158th Avn
	26004	UH-60A	2-1st Avn		26654	UH-60L	C/158th Avn
	FY88				26655	UH-60L	C/158th Avn
	26019	UH-60A	214th Avn		*FY96*		
	26020	UH-60A	236th Med Co		26674	UH-60L	D/158th Avn
	26023	UH-60A	236th Med Co		26675	UH-60L	D/158th Avn
	26025	UH-60A	214th Avn		26676	UH-60L	D/158th Avn
	26026	UH-60A	B/5-158th Avn		26677	UH-60L	D/158th Avn
	26027	UH-60A	214th Avn		26678	UH-60L	D/158th Avn
	26028	UH-60A	C/5-158th Avn		26679	UH-60L	D/158th Avn
	26031	UH-60A	2-1st Avn		26680	UH-60L	D/158th Avn
	26034	UH-60A	236th Med Co		26681	UH-60L	D/158th Avn
	26037	UH-60A	B/7-159th AVIM		26682	UH-60L	D/158th Avn
	26038	UH-60A	A/5-158th Avn		26683	UH-60L	C/158th Avn
	26039	UH-60A	45th Med Co		26684	UH-60L	C/158th Avn
	26040	UH-60A	2-1st Avn		26685	UH-60L	C/158th Avn
	26041	UH-60A	A/5-158th Avn		26686	UH-60L	C/158th Avn
	26042	UH-60A	A/5-158th Avn		26687	UH-60L	C/158th Avn
	26045	UH-60A	45th Med Co		26688	UH-60L	C/158th Avn
	26050	UH-60A	159th Med Co		26689	UH-60L	C/158th Avn
	26051	UH-60A	A/5-158th Avn		26690	UH-60L	C/158th Avn
	26052	UH-60A	B/5-158th Avn		26691	UH-60L	C/158th Avn
	26053	UH-60A	A/5-158th Avn		26692	UH-60L	C/158th Avn
	26054	UH-60A	236th Med Co		*FY97*		
	26055	UH-60A	236th Med Co		26762	UH-60L	2-501st Avn
	26056	UH-60A	A/5-158th Avn		26763	UH-60L	2-501st Avn
	26058	UH-60A	159th Med Co		26764	UH-60L	2-501st Avn
	26063	UH-60A	B/5-158th Avn		26765	UH-60L	2-501st Avn
	26067	UH-60A	B/5-158th Avn		26766	UH-60L	2-501st Avn
	26068	UH-60A	2-501st Avn		26767	UH-60L	2-501st Avn
	26071	UH-60A	2-501st Avn		*FY98*		
	26072	UH-60A	236th Med Co		26795	UH-60L	2-501st Avn
	26075	UH-60A	2-501st Avn		26796	UH-60L	2-501st Avn
	26077	UH-60A	C/5-158th Avn		26797	UH-60L	2-501st Avn
	26080	UH-60A	236th Med Co		26798	UH-60L	2-501st Avn
	26083	UH-60A	B/5-158th Avn		26799	UH-60L	2-501st Avn
	26085	UH-60A	2-501st Avn		26800	UH-60L	2-501st Avn
	26086	UH-60A	2-501st Avn		26801	UH-60L	2-501st Avn
	FY89				26802	UH-60L	2-501st Avn
	26138	UH-60A	2-1st Avn		26813	UH-60L	2-501st Avn
	26142	UH-60A	B/7-159th AVIM		26814	UH-60L	2-501st Avn
	26145	UH-60A	B/5-158th Avn				

Type	Notes	Type		Notes
MDH AH-64A Apache		70437	1-1st Avn	
1st Btn, 1st Avn Reg't, Ansbach;		70438	1-501st Avn	
127th ASB, Hanau;		70439	1-1st Avn	
1st Btn, 501st Avn Reg't, Hanau;		70440	1-501st Avn	
2nd Btn, 6th Cavalry Reg't, Illesheim;		70441	2-6th Cav	
6th Btn, 6th Cavalry Reg't, Illesheim;		70442	1-1st Avn	
'A' Co, 7th Btn, 159th Avn Reg't,		70443	2-6th Cav	
Illesheim		70444	1-501st Avn	
FY86		70445	1-501st Avn	
68940	2-6th Cav	70446	1-501st Avn	
68941	6-6th Cav	70447	1-501st Avn	
68942	2-6th Cav	70449	1-501st Avn	
68943	2-6th Cav	70451	1-501st Avn	
68946	2-6th Cav	70454		
68947	6-6th Cav	70455	1-501st Avn	
68948	2-6th Cav	70457	1-1st Avn	
68949	2-6th Cav	70465		
68950	6-6th Cav	70470	1-1st Avn	
68951	2-6th Cav	70471	1-1st Avn	
68952	2-6th Cav	70474	1-1st Avn	
68955	2-6th Cav	70475	1-1st Avn	
68956	2-6th Cav	70476	1-1st Avn	
68957	2-6th Cav	70477	1-1st Avn	
68959	2-6th Cav	70478	1-1st Avn	
68960	2-6th Cav	70481	1-1st Avn	
68961	2-6th Cav	70487	1-501st Avn	
68981	2-6th Cav	70496	1-501st Avn	
69010	2-6th Cav	70503	1-501st Avn	
69011	2-6th Cav	70504	1-501st Avn	
69019	2-6th Cav	70505	1-501st Avn	
69026	2-6th Cav	70506	1-501st Avn	
69030	2-6th Cav	*FY88*		
69032	2-6th Cav	80197	1-501st Avn	
69037	2-6th Cav	80198	1-501st Avn	
69039	2-6th Cav	80203	6-6th Cav	
69041	1-501st Avn	80212	6-6th Cav	
69048	2-6th Cav	80213	6-6th Cav	
FY87		80214	6-6th Cav	
70409	1-1st Avn	80215	6-6th Cav	
70410	1-501st Avn	80216	6-6th Cav	
70411	6-6th Cav	80217	6-6th Cav	
70412	1-1st Avn	80219	6-6th Cav	
70413	1-1st Avn	80222	6-6th Cav	
70415	1-501st Avn	80225	6-6th Cav	
70417	1-1st Avn	80228	6-6th Cav	
70418	1-501st Avn	80229	6-6th Cav	
70420	1-1st Avn	80232	6-6th Cav	
70428	1-1st Avn	80233	6-6th Cav	
70431	6-6th Cav	80234	6-6th Cav	
70432	1-1st Avn	80236	6-6th Cav	
70435	1-501st Avn	80243	6-6th Cav	
70436	1-1st Avn	80246	6-6th Cav	

US-based USAF Aircraft

The following aircraft are normally based in the USA but are likely to be seen visiting the UK from time to time. The presentation is in numerical order of the type, commencing with the B-1B and concluding with the C-141. The aircraft are listed in numerical progression by the serial actually carried externally. Fiscal year information is provided, together with details of mark variations and in some cases operating units. Where base-code letter information is carried on the aircrafts' tails, this is detailed with the squadron/base data; for example the 7th Wing's B-1B 30069 carries the letters DY on its tail, thus identifying the Wing's home base as Dyess AFB, Texas.

Notes	Type			Notes	Type		
	Rockwell B-1B Lancer				50082	412th TW	
	7th BW, Dyess AFB, Texas [DY]:				50083	28th BW	*bl*
	9th BS (*bk*), 13th BS				50084	28th BW	*pr/y*
	& 28th BS (*bl/w*);				50085	28th BW	*pr/y*
	28th BW, Ellsworth AFB,				50086	28th BW	*pr/y*
	South Dakota [EL]:				50087	28th BW	*pr/y*
	13th BS (*bl/br*), 37th BS (*bl*)				50088	127th BS	*r/w*
	& 77th BS (*pr/y*);				50089	128th BS	
	127th BS/184th BW, Kansas ANG,				50090	28th BW	*pr/y*
	McConnell AFB, Kansas (*r/w*);				50091	28th BW	*bl*
	128th BS/116th BW, Georgia ANG,				50092	128th BS	
	Robins AFB, Georgia [GA];				*FY86*		
	34th BS/366th Wg, Mountain				60093	28th BW	*pr/y*
	Home AFB, Idaho [MO] (*r/bk*);				60094	28th BW	*pr/y*
	419th FLTS/412th TW, Edwards AFB,				60095	127th BS	*r/w*
	California [ED]				60096	28th BW	*pr/y*
	FY83				60097	28th BW	*pr/y*
	30065	7th BW	*bk*		60098	128th BS	
	30066	7th BW	*bl/w*		60099	28th BW	*pr/y*
	30067	7th BW	*bk*		60100	7th BW	*bl/w*
	30068	7th BW	*bl/w*		60101	7th BW	*bl/w*
	30069	7th BW	*bl/w*		60102	28th BW	*pr/y*
	30070	7th BW	*bl/w*		60103	7th BW	*bk*
	30071	7th BW	*bk*		60104	28th BW	*pr/y*
	FY84				60105	7th BW	*bl/w*
	40049	412th TW			60107	128th BS	
	40050	7th BW	*bl/w*		60108	7th BW	*bl/w*
	40051	7th BW	*bk*		60109	7th BW	*bl/w*
	40053	7th BW			60110	7th BW	*bl/w*
	40054	7th BW	*bl/w*		60111	28th BW	*pr/y*
	40055	7th BW	*bl/w*		60112	7th BW	*bk*
	40056	7th BW	*bl/w*		60113	28th BW	*pr/y*
	40058	7th BW	*bk*		60114	28th BW	*pr/y*
	FY85				60115	127th BS	*r/w*
	50059	128th BS			60116	366th Wg	*r/bk*
	50060	127th BS	*r/w*		60117	7th BW	*bl/w*
	50061	128th BS			60118	366th Wg	*r/bk*
	50062	7th BW	*bk*		60119	7th BW	*bl/w*
	50064	127th BS	*r/w*		60120	7th BW	*bk*
	50065	7th BW	*bk*		60121	366th Wg	*r/bk*
	50066	28th BW	*pr/y*		60122	7th BW	*bl/w*
	50067	7th BW	*bl/w*		60123	7th BW	*bk*
	50068	412th TW			60124	128th BS	
	50069	127th BS	*r/w*		60125	366th Wg	*r/bk*
	50070	127th BS	*r/w*		60126	127th BS	*r/w*
	50071	128th BS			60127	128th BS	
	50072	28th BW	*bk*		60128	28th BW	*pr/y*
	50073	28th BW	*pr/y*		60129	28th BW	*pr/y*
	50074	28th BW			60130	7th BW	*bl/w*
	50075	28th BW	*pr/y*		60131	366th Wg	*r/bk*
	50077	28th BW	*pr/y*		60132	7th BW	*bl/w*
	50079	7th BW	*bk*		60133	128th BS	
	50080	127th BS	*r/w*		60134	366th Wg	*r/bk*
	50081	127th BS	*r/w*		60135	7th BW	*bk*

Type			Notes
60136	127th BS	r/w	
60137	7th BW	bl/w	
60138	366th Wg	r/bk	
60139	366th Wg	r/bk	
60140	7th BW	bk	

Northrop B-2 Spirit
419th FLTS/412th TW, Edwards AFB,
  California [ED];
509th BW, Whiteman AFB,
  Missouri [WM]:
    325th BS, 393rd BS & 715th BS
(Names are given where known.
Each begins *Spirit of ...*)

FY90			
00040	509th BW	Alaska	
00041	509th BW	Hawaii	
FY92			
20700	509th BW	Florida	
FY82			
21066	509th BW	America	
21067	509th BW	Arizona	
21068	412th TW	New York	
21069	509th BW	Indiana	
21070	Northrop	Ohio	
21071	509th BW	Mississippi	
FY93			
31085	509th BW	Oklahoma	
31086	509th BW	Kitty Hawk	
31087	509th BW	Pennsylvania	
31088	509th BW	Louisiana	
FY88			
80328	509th BW	Texas	
80329	509th BW	Missouri	
80330	509th BW	California	
80331	509th BW	South Carolina	
80332	509th BW	Washington	
FY89			
90127	509th BW	Kansas	
90128	509th BW	Nebraska	
90129	509th BW	Georgia	

Boeing E-3 Sentry
552nd ACW, Tinker AFB,
  Oklahoma [OK]:
    963rd AACS (*bk*), 964th AACS (*r*)
    965th AACS (*y*) & 966th AACS (*bl*)
961st AACS/18th Wg, Kadena AB,
  Japan [ZZ] (*or*);
962nd AACS/3rd Wg, Elmendorf AFB,
  Alaska [AK] (*gn*);

FY80			
00137	E-3C	bk	
00138	E-3C	y	
00139	E-3C	bl	
FY81			
10004	E-3C	bk	
10005	E-3C	or	
FY71			
11407	E-3B	or	
11408	E-3B	bk	
FY82			
20006	E-3C	y	
20007	E-3C	m	
FY83			
30008	E-3C	or	
30009	E-3C	bk	
FY73			
31674	JE-3C	Boeing	
31675	E-3B	gn	
FY75			
50556	E-3B	r	
50557	E-3B	gn	

Type			Notes
50558	E-3B	y	
50559	E-3B	m	
50560	E-3B	bk	
FY76			
61604	E-3B	r	
61605	E-3B	gn	
61606	E-3B	gn	
61607	E-3B	bl	
FY77			
70351	E-3B	y	
70352	E-3B	r	
70353	E-3B	y	
70355	E-3B	r	
70356	E-3B	y	
FY78			
80576	E-3B	or	
80577	E-3B	r	
80578	E-3B	gn	
FY79			
90001	E-3B	r	
90002	E-3B	y	
90003	E-3B	gn	

Boeing E-4B
1st ACCS/55th Wg, Offutt AFB,
  Nebraska [OF]

31676	(FY73)	
31677	(FY73)	
40787	(FY74)	
50125	(FY75)	

Lockheed C-5 Galaxy
60th AMW, Travis AFB, California:
  21st AS (*bk/gd*) & 22nd AS (*bk/bl*);
56th AS/97th AMW, Altus AFB,
  Oklahoma (*r/y*);
137th AS/105th AW, Stewart AFB,
  New York (*bl*);
68th AS/433rd AW AFRC, Kelly AFB,
  Texas;
436th AW, Dover AFB, Delaware:
  3rd AS & 9th AS (*y/r* & *y/bl*);
337th AS/439th AW AFRC, Westover
  ARB, Massachusetts (*bl/r*)

FY70				
00445	C-5A	433rd AW		
00446	C-5A	433rd AW		
00447	C-5A	436th AW	y	
00448	C-5A	439th AW	bl/r	
00449	C-5A	60th AMW	bk/gd	
00450	C-5A	60th AMW	bk/gd	
00451	C-5A	97th AMW	r/y	
00452	C-5A	97th AMW	r/y	
00453	C-5A	436th AW	y/r	
00454	C-5A	97th AMW	r/y	
00455	C-5A	97th AMW	r/y	
00456	C-5A	60th AMW	bk/gd	
00457	C-5A	60th AMW	bk/gd	
00458	C-5A	433rd AW		
00459	C-5A	60th AMW	bk/gd	
00460	C-5A	105th AW	bl	
00461	C-5A	436th AW	y	
00462	C-5A	60th AMW		
00463	C-5A	436th AW	y	
00464	C-5A	60th AMW	bk/bl	
00465	C-5A	436th AW		
00466	C-5A	436th AW		
00467	C-5A	97th AMW	r/y	
FY83				
31285	C-5B	436th AW	y/r	
FY84				
40059	C-5B	436th AW		
40060	C-5B	60th AMW	bk/bl	

Notes	Type			
	40061	C-5B	436th AW	y
	40062	C-5B	60th AMW	bk/gd
FY85				
	50001	C-5B	436th AW	m
	50002	C-5B	60th AMW	bk/bl
	50003	C-5B	436th AW	y
	50004	C-5B	60th AMW	bk/bl
	50005	C-5B	436th AW	y
	50006	C-5B	60th AMW	bk/gd
	50007	C-5B	436th AW	y/bl
	50008	C-5B	60th AMW	bk/gd
	50009	C-5B	436th AW	y
	50010	C-5B	60th AMW	bk/gd
FY86				
	60011	C-5B	436th AW	y/bl
	60012	C-5B	60th AMW	bk/bl
	60013	C-5B	436th AW	y
	60014	C-5B	60th AMW	bk/bl
	60015	C-5B	436th AW	y/r
	60016	C-5B	60th AMW	bk/bl
	60017	C-5B	436th AW	y
	60018	C-5B	60th AMW	bk/gd
	60019	C-5B	436th AW	y
	60020	C-5B	436th AW	y
	60021	C-5B	60th AMW	bk/gd
	60022	C-5B	60th AMW	bk/bl
	60023	C-5B	436th AW	y
	60024	C-5B	60th AMW	bk/bl
	60025	C-5B	436th AW	y
	60026	C-5B	60th AMW	bk/gd
FY66				
	68304	C-5A	439th AW	bl/r
	68305	C-5A	433rd AW	
	68306	C-5A	433rd AW	
	68307	C-5A	433rd AW	
FY87				
	70027	C-5B	436th AW	y/bl
	70028	C-5B	60th AMW	bk/bl
	70029	C-5B	436th AW	y
	70030	C-5B	60th AMW	bk/bl
	70031	C-5B	436th AW	
	70032	C-5B	60th AMW	bk/bl
	70033	C-5B	436th AW	y
	70034	C-5B	60th AMW	bk/gd
	70035	C-5B	436th AW	y
	70036	C-5B	60th AMW	bk/gd
	70037	C-5B	436th AW	y
	70038	C-5B	60th AMW	bk/bl
	70039	C-5B	436th AW	
	70040	C-5B	60th AMW	bk/gd
	70041	C-5B	436th AW	y
	70042	C-5B	60th AMW	bk/gd
	70043	C-5B	436th AW	y/bl
	70044	C-5B	60th AMW	bk/gd
	70045	C-5B	436th AW	y
FY67				
	70167	C-5A	439th AW	bl/r
	70168	C-5A	433rd AW	
	70169	C-5A	105th AW	bl
	70170	C-5A	105th AW	bl
	70171	C-5A	433rd AW	
	70173	C-5A	105th AW	bl
	70174	C-5A	105th AW	bl
FY68				
	80211	C-5A	439th AW	bl/r
	80212	C-5A	105th AW	bl
	80213	C-5C	60th AMW	bk/bl
	80214	C-5A	436th AW	
	80215	C-5A	439th AW	bl/r
	80216	C-5C	60th AMW	bk/bl
	80217	C-5A	436th AW	y
	80219	C-5A	439th AW	bl/r
	80220	C-5A	433rd AW	

Notes	Type			
	80221	C-5A	433rd AW	
	80222	C-5A	439th AW	bl/r
	80223	C-5A	433rd AW	
	80224	C-5A	105th AW	bl
	80225	C-5A	439th AW	bl/r
	80226	C-5A	105th AW	bl
FY69				
	90001	C-5A	97th AMW	r/y
	90002	C-5A	433rd AW	
	90003	C-5A	439th AW	bl/r
	90004	C-5A	433rd AW	
	90005	C-5A	439th AW	bl/r
	90006	C-5A	433rd AW	
	90007	C-5A	433rd AW	
	90008	C-5A	105th AW	bl
	90009	C-5A	105th AW	bl
	90010	C-5A	60th AMW	bk/gd
	90011	C-5A	439th AW	bl/r
	90012	C-5A	105th AW	bl
	90013	C-5A	439th AW	bl/r
	90014	C-5A	97th AMW	r/y
	90015	C-5A	105th AW	bl
	90016	C-5A	433rd AW	
	90017	C-5A	439th AW	bl/r
	90018	C-5A	97th AMW	r/y
	90019	C-5A	439th AW	bl/r
	90020	C-5A	439th AW	bl/r
	90021	C-5A	105th AW	bl
	90022	C-5A	439th AW	bl/r
	90023	C-5A	60th AMW	bk/bl
	90024	C-5A	97th AMW	r/y
	90025	C-5A	97th AMW	r/y
	90026	C-5A	60th AMW	bk/gd
	90027	C-5A	436th AW	y

Boeing E-8 J-STARS

Grumman, Melbourne, Florida;
12th ACCS/93rd ACW, Robins AFB,
Georgia [WR] (gn)

	Type			
FY90				
	00175	E-8A	Grumman	
	02000	E-8C	93rd ACW	
FY92				
	23289	E-8C	93rd ACW	
	23290	E-8C	93rd ACW	
FY93				
	30597	E-8C	93rd ACW	
	31097	E-8C	93rd ACW	
FY94				
	40284	E-8C	93rd ACW	
	40285	E-8C		
FY95				
	50121	E-8C	93rd ACW	
	50122	E-8C	93rd ACW	
	50123	E-8C		
FY96				
	60042	E-8C	93rd ACW	
	60043	E-8C		
FY86				
	60417	TE-8A	93rd ACW	
FY97				
	70100	E-8C		
	70200	E-8C		
	70201	E-8C		
FY99				
	90006	E-8C		

McDonnell Douglas C-9 Nightingale

86th AW, Ramstein, Germany:
75th AS & 76th AS;
99th AS/89th AW, Andrews AFB,
Maryland;

Type			Notes
30th AS/374th AW, Yokota AB, Japan;			
11th AS/375th AW, Scott AFB, Illinois			
FY71			
10874	C-9A	374th AW	
10875	C-9A	374th AW	
10876	C-9A	76th AS	
10877	C-9A	374th AW	
10878	C-9A	375th AW	
10879	C-9A	75th AS	
10880	C-9A	75th AS	
10881	C-9A	75th AS	
10882	C-9A	75th AS	
FY68			
10958	C-9A	375th AW	
10959	C-9A	375th AW	
10960	C-9A	375th AW	
10961	C-9A	375th AW	
FY67			
22583	C-9A	374th AW	
22584	C-9A	375th AW	
22585	C-9A	75th AS	
FY73			
31681	C-9C	89th AW	
31682	C-9C	89th AW	
31683	C-9C	89th AW	
FY68			
88932	C-9A	375th AW	
88933	C-9A	375th AW	
88934	C-9A	374th AW	
88935	C-9A	375th AW	

McDonnell Douglas KC-10A Extender

60th AMW, Travis AFB, California: 6th ARS (*bk/r*) & 9th ARS (*bk/bl*);
305th AMW, McGuire AFB, New Jersey: 2nd ARS (*bl/r*) & 32nd ARS (*bl*)

Type			Notes
FY82			
20191	60th AMW	*bk/bl*	
20192	60th AMW	*bk/r*	
20193	60th AMW	*bk/bl*	
FY83			
30075	60th AMW	*bk/r*	
30076	60th AMW	*bk/bl*	
30077	60th AMW	*bk/r*	
30078	60th AMW	*bk/bl*	
30079	305th AMW	*bl/r*	
30080	60th AMW	*bk/bl*	
30081	305th AMW	*bl*	
30082	305th AMW	*bl*	
FY84			
40185	60th AMW	*bk/bl*	
40186	305th AMW	*bl/r*	
40187	60th AMW	*bk/bl*	
40188	305th AMW	*bl/r*	
40189	305th AMW	*bl*	
40190	305th AMW	*bl/r*	
40191	60th AMW	*bk/bl*	
40192	305th AMW	*bl/r*	
FY85			
50027	305th AMW	*bl/r*	
50028	305th AMW	*bl/r*	
50029	60th AMW	*bk/r*	
50030	305th AMW	*bl/r*	
50031	305th AMW	*bl/r*	
50032	305th AMW	*bl/r*	
50033	305th AMW	*bl*	
50034	305th AMW	*bl/r*	
FY86			
60027	305th AMW	*bl*	

Type			Notes
60028	305th AMW	*bl/r*	
60029	60th AMW	*bk/r*	
60030	305th AMW	*bl/r*	
60031	60th AMW	*bk/r*	
60032	60th AMW	*bk/r*	
60033	60th AMW	*bk/r*	
60034	60th AMW	*bk/r*	
60035	305th AMW	*bl*	
60036	305th AMW	*bl*	
60037	60th AMW	*bk/r*	
60038	60th AMW	*bk/r*	
FY87			
70117	60th AMW	*bk/r*	
70118	60th AMW	*bk/bl*	
70119	60th AMW	*bk/r*	
70120	305th AMW	*bl*	
70121	305th AMW	*bl*	
70122	305th AMW	*bl/r*	
70123	305th AMW	*bl*	
70124	305th AMW	*bl/r*	
FY79			
90433	305th AMW	*bl*	
90434	305th AMW	*bl/r*	
91710	305th AMW	*bl/r*	
91711	305th AMW	*bl*	
91712	305th AMW	*bl/r*	
91713	305th AMW	*bl*	
91946	60th AMW	*bk/r*	
91947	305th AMW	*bl*	
91948	60th AMW	*bk/bl*	
91949	305th AMW	*bl/r*	
91950	60th AMW	*bk/bl*	
91951	60th AMW	*bk/bl*	

Boeing C-17 Globemaster III

7th AS/62nd AW, McChord AFB, Washington
58th AS/97th AMW, Altus AFB, Oklahoma (*r/y*);
417th FLTS/412th TW, Edwards AFB, California [ED];
437th AW, Charleston AFB, South Carolina (*y/bl*): 14th AS, 15th AS & 17th AS

Type			Notes
FY00			
00171	C-17A		
00172	C-17A		
00173	C-17A		
00174	C-17A		
00175	C-17A		
00176	C-17A		
00177	C-17A		
00178	C-17A		
00179	C-17A		
00180	C-17A		
00181	C-17A		
00182	C-17A		
00183	C-17A		
00184	C-17A		
00185	C-17A		
FY90			
00532	C-17A	437th AW	*y/bl*
00533	C-17A	97th AMW	*r/y*
00534	C-17A	437th AW	*y/bl*
00535	C-17A	437th AW	*y/bl*
FY92			
23291	C-17A	97th AMW	*r/y*
23292	C-17A	437th AW	*y/bl*
23293	C-17A	437th AW	*y/bl*
23294	C-17A	437th AW	*y/bl*
FY93			
30599	C-17A	437th AW	*y/bl*
30600	C-17A	97th AMW	*r/y*

Notes	Type			
	30601	C-17A	437th AW	y/bl
	30602	C-17A	97th AMW	r/y
	30603	C-17A	437th AW	y/bl
	30604	C-17A	437th AW	y/bl
	FY94			
	40065	C-17A	437th AW	y/bl
	40066	C-17A	437th AW	y/bl
	40067	C-17A	437th AW	y/bl
	40068	C-17A	437th AW	y/bl
	40069	C-17A	437th AW	y/bl
	40070	C-17A	437th AW	y/bl
	FY95			
	50102	C-17A	437th AW	y/bl
	50103	C-17A	97th AMW	r/y
	50104	C-17A	437th AW	y/bl
	50105	C-17A	97th AMW	r/y
	50106	C-17A	437th AW	y/bl
	50107	C-17A	437th AW	y/bl
	FY96			
	60001	C-17A	437th AW	y/bl
	60002	C-17A	437th AW	y/bl
	60003	C-17A	437th AW	y/bl
	60004	C-17A	97th AMW	r/y
	60005	C-17A	437th AW	y/bl
	60006	C-17A	437th AW	y/bl
	60007	C-17A	437th AW	y/bl
	60008	C-17A	437th AW	y/bl
	FY87			
	70025	C-17A	412th TW	
	FY97			
	70041	C-17A	437th AW	y/bl
	70042	C-17A	437th AW	y/bl
	70043	C-17A	437th AW	y/bl
	70044	C-17A	437th AW	y/bl
	70045	C-17A	437th AW	y/bl
	70046	C-17A	437th AW	y/bl
	70047	C-17A	437th AW	y/bl
	70048	C-17A	437th AW	y/bl
	FY98			
	80049	C-17A	437th AW	y/bl
	80050	C-17A	437th AW	y/bl
	80051	C-17A	62nd AW	
	80052	C-17A	62nd AW	
	80053	C-17A	62nd AW	
	80054	C-17A	62nd AW	
	80055	C-17A	62nd AW	
	80056	C-17A	62nd AW	
	80057	C-17A	62nd AW	
	FY88			
	80265	C-17A	437th AW	y/bl
	80266	C-17A	97th AMW	r/y
	FY99			
	90058	C-17A	62nd AW	
	90059	C-17A	62nd AW	
	90060	C-17A	62nd AW	
	90061	C-17A	62nd AW	
	90062	C-17A	62nd AW	
	90063	C-17A	62nd AW	
	90064	C-17A	62nd AW	
	90165	C-17A	62nd AW	
	90166	C-17A	62nd AW	
	90167	C-17A	62nd AW	
	90168	C-17A	62nd AW	
	90169	C-17A	62nd AW	
	90170	C-17A	62nd AW	
	FY89			
	91189	C-17A	437th AW	y/bl
	91190	C-17A	97th AMW	r/y
	91191	C-17A	437th AW	y/bl
	91192	C-17A	437th AW	y/bl

Notes	Type	
	Boeing EC-18B	
	412th TW, Edwards AFB,	
	California [ED]:	
	452nd FLTS;	
	552nd ACW, Tinker AFB,	
	Oklahoma [OK]:	
	966th AACS (*bl*)	
	FY81	
	10891	EC-18B 412th TW
	10892	EC-18B 412th TW
	10893	TC-18E 552nd ACW
	10894	EC-18B 412th TW
	10898	TC-18E 552nd ACW
	Grumman	
	C-20 Gulfstream III/IV	
	99th AS/89th AW, Andrews AFB,	
	Maryland;	
	OSAC/PAT, US Army, Andrews AFB,	
	Maryland;	
	Pacific Flight Detachment,	
	Hickam AFB, Hawaii	
	C-20B Gulfstream III	
	FY86	
	60201	89th AW
	60202	89th AW
	60203	89th AW
	60204	89th AW
	60206	89th AW
	60403	89th AW
	C-20C Gulfstream III	
	FY85	
	50049	89th AW
	50050	89th AW
	C-20E Gulfstream III	
	FY87	
	70139	Pacific Flt Det
	70140	OSAC/PAT
	C-20F Gulfstream IV	
	FY91	
	10108	OSAC/PAT
	C-20H Gulfstream IV	
	FY90	
	00300	89th AW
	FY92	
	20375	89th AW
	Boeing C-22B/C-22C*	
	88th ABW, Wright-Patterson AFB,	
	Ohio;	
	201st AS/113th FW, DC ANG,	
	Andrews AFB, Maryland	
	FY83	
	34610	201st AS
	34615	201st AS
	34616	201st AS
	34618*	88th ABW
	Boeing VC-25A	
	89th AW, Andrews AFB, Maryland	
	FY82	
	28000	
	FY92	
	29000	
	Boeing C-32A	
	1st AS/89th AW, Andrews AFB,	
	Maryland	
	FY98	
	80001	
	80002	

Type			Notes
FY99			
90003			
90004			
Gulfstream Aerospace C-37A			
Gulfstream V			
99th AS/89th AW, Andrews AFB,			
Maryland;			
OSAC/PAT, US Army, Andrews AFB,			
Maryland			
FY97			
70049	OSAC/PAT		
70400	89th AW		
70401	89th AW		
FY99			
90402	89th AW		
IAI C-38A Astra			
201st AS/113th FW, DC ANG,			
Andrews AFB, Maryland			
FY94			
41569			
41570			
Boeing T-43A/CT-43A*			
562nd FTS/12th FTW, Randolph			
AFB, Texas [RA] (bk/y)			
FY71			
11403	12th FTW	bk/y	
11404	12th FTW	bk/y	
11405	12th FTW	bk/y	
FY72			
20283*			
20288	12th FTW	bk/y	
FY73			
31150	12th FTW	bk/y	
31151	12th FTW	bk/y	
31152	12th FTW	bk/y	
31153	12th FTW	bk/y	
31154	12th FTW	bk/y	
31156	12th FTW	bk/y	
Boeing B-52H Stratofortress			
2nd BW, Barksdale AFB,			
Louisiana [LA]:			
11th BS (gd), 20th BS (bl)			
& 96th BS (r);			
23rd BS/5th BW, Minot AFB,			
North Dakota [MT] (r/y);			
93rd BS/917th Wg AFRC,			
Barksdale AFB,			
Louisiana [BD] (y/bl);			
419th FLTS/412th TW Edwards AFB,			
California [ED]			
FY60			
00001	2nd BW	bl	
00002	2nd BW	gd	
00003	93rd BS	y/bl	
00004	5th BW	r/y	
00005	5th BW	r/y	
00007	5th BW	r/y	
00008	2nd BW	r	
00009	5th BW	r/y	
00010	2nd BW	r	
00011	2nd BW	gd	
00012	2nd BW	r	
00013	2nd BW	r	
00014	2nd BW	bl	
00015	5th BW	r/y	
00016	2nd BW	r	
00017	2nd BW	gd	
00018	5th BW	r/y	
00019	2nd BW	r	

Type			Notes
00020	2nd BW	bl	
00022	2nd BW	r	
00023	5th BW	r/y	
00024	5th BW	r/y	
00025	2nd BW	bl	
00026	2nd BW	r	
00028	2nd BW	r	
00029	5th BW	r/y	
00030	2nd BW	bl	
00031	2nd BW	bl	
00032	2nd BW	gd	
00033	5th BW	r/y	
00034	5th BW	r/y	
00035	2nd BW	gd	
00036	5th BW	r/y	
00037	2nd BW	r	
00038	2nd BW	gd	
00041	93rd BS	y/bl	
00042	93rd BS	y/bl	
00043	2nd BW	bl	
00044	5th BW	r/y	
00045	93rd BS	y/bl	
00046	2nd BW	bl	
00048	2nd BW	gd	
00049	2nd BW	bl	
00050	412th TW		
00051	5th BW	r/y	
00052	2nd BW	r	
00053	2nd BW	r	
00054	2nd BW	r	
00055	5th BW	r/y	
00056	5th BW	r/y	
00057	2nd BW	bl	
00058	2nd BW	gd	
00059	2nd BW	r	
00060	5th BW	r/y	
00061	2nd BW	gd	
00062	2nd BW	bl	
FY61			
10001	5th BW	r/y	
10002	2nd BW	bl	
10003	2nd BW	gd	
10004	2nd BW	bl	
10005	5th BW	r/y	
10006	2nd BW	gd	
10007	5th BW	r/y	
10008	93rd BS	y/bl	
10009	2nd BW	r	
10010	2nd BW	bl	
10011	2nd BW	gd	
10012	2nd BW	gd	
10013	2nd BW	r	
10014	5th BW	r/y	
10015	2nd BW	gd	
10016	2nd BW	r	
10017	93rd BS	y/bl	
10018	5th BW	r/y	
10019	2nd BW	r	
10020	2nd BW	r	
10021	93rd BS	y/bl	
10022	93rd BS	y/bl	
10023	2nd BW	bl	
10024	2nd BW	r	
10025	2nd BW	gd	
10027	5th BW	r/y	
10028	2nd BW	gd	
10029	93rd BS	y/bl	
10031	2nd BW	gd	
10032	93rd BS	y/bl	
10034	5th BW	r/y	
10035	5th BW	r/y	
10036	5th BW	r/y	
10038	2nd BW	gd	

Notes	Type		Notes	Type
	10039	2nd BW gd		4th SOS/16th SOW, Hurlburt Field,
	10040	5th BW r/y		Florida;
				7th SOS/352nd SOG,
	Lockheed F-117A Nighthawk			RAF Mildenhall, UK;
	49th FW, Holloman AFB, New Mexico			8th SOS/16th SOW, Duke Field,
	[HO]:			Florida;
	7th FS (si), 8th FS (y) & 9th FS (r)			9th SOS/16th OG, Eglin AFB, Florida;
	53rd Wg, Nellis AFB, Nevada [OT]			15th SOS/16th SOW, Hurlburt Field,
	(gy/w);			Florida;
	445th FLTS/412th TW, Edwards AFB,			16th SOS/16th SOW, Hurlburt Field,
	California [ED]			Florida;
	79-783 (79-10783) ED			17th SOS/353rd SOG, Kadena AB,
	79-784 (79-10784) ED			Japan;
	80-786 (80-0786) HO r			37th AS/86th AW, Ramstein AB,
	80-787 (80-0787) HO si			Germany [RS] (bl/w);
	80-788 (80-0788) HO si			39th RQS/939th RQW AFRC,
	80-789 (80-0789) HO r			Patrick AFB, Florida [FL];
	80-790 (80-0790) HO r			41st ECS/355th Wg, Davis-Monthan
	80-791 (80-0791) HO y			AFB, Arizona [DM] (bl);
	81-794 (81-10794) HO r			42nd ACCS/355th Wg,
	81-795 (81-10795) HO y			Davis-Monthan AFB, Arizona [DM]
	81-796 (81-10796) HO si			(w);
	81-797 (81-10797) HO r			43rd AW, Pope AFB,
	81-798 (81-10798) HO r			North Carolina [FT]:
	82-799 (82-0799) HO y			2nd AS (gn/bl) & 41st AS (gn/or);
	82-800 (82-0800) HO y			43rd ECS/355th Wg, Davis-Monthan
	82-801 (82-0801) HO			AFB, Arizona [DM] (r);
	82-802 (82-0802) HO y			53rd WRS/403rd AW AFRC,
	82-803 (82-0803) HO y			Keesler AFB, Mississippi
	82-804 (82-0804) HO y			58th SOW, Kirtland AFB,
	82-805 (82-0805) HO si			New Mexico:
	83-807 (83-0807) HO r			550th SOS;
	83-808 (83-0808) HO si			67th SOS/352nd SOG,
	84-809 (84-0809) HO r [9th FS]			RAF Mildenhall, UK;
	84-810 (84-0810) HO r			71st RQS/347th Wg, Moody AFB,
	84-811 (84-0811) HO si			Georgia [MY] (bl);
	84-812 (84-0812) HO r [49th OG]			95th AS/440th AW AFRC,
	84-824 (84-0824) HO r			General Mitchell ARS,
	84-826 (84-0826) HO r			Wisconsin (w/r);
	84-827 (84-0827) HO y			96th AS/934th AW AFRC,
	84-828 (84-0828) HO r			Minneapolis/St Paul,
	85-813 (85-0813) HO y			Minnesota (pr);
	85-814 (85-0814) HO y			102nd RQS/106th RQW, Suffolk
	85-816 (85-0816) HO y [49th FW]			Field, New York ANG [LI];
	85-817 (85-0817) HO y			105th AS/118th AW, Nashville,
	85-818 (85-0818) HO y			Tennessee ANG (r);
	85-819 (85-0819) HO y [8th FS]			109th AS/133rd AW,
	85-820 (85-0820) HO r			Minneapolis/St Paul,
	85-829 (85-0829) HO y			Minnesota ANG [MN] (gn/bl);
	85-830 (85-0830) HO r			115th AS/146th AW,
	85-831 (85-0831) ED			Channel Island ANGS,
	85-832 (85-0832) HO y			California [CI] (gn);
	85-833 (85-0833) HO si [49th OG]			122nd FS/159th FW,
	85-834 (85-0834) HO y			NAS New Orleans,
	85-835 (85-0835) HO r			Louisiana [JZ];
	85-836 (85-0836) HO y			129th RQS/129th RQW, Moffet Field,
	86-821 (86-0821) HO r			California ANG [CA] (bl);
	86-822 (86-0822) HO			130th AW/130th AW, Yeager Int'l
	86-823 (86-0823) HO r			Airport, Charleston
	86-837 (86-0837) HO y			West Virginia ANG [WV] (pr/y);
	86-838 (86-0838) HO y [8th FS]			135th AS/135th AW, Martin State
	86-839 (86-0839) HO r			Airport, Maryland ANG [MD] (bk/y);
	86-840 (86-0840) HO y			139th AS/109th AW, Schenectady,
	88-841 (88-0841) HO r [9th FS]			New York ANG [NY];
	88-842 (88-0842) HO y			142nd AS/166th AW,
	88-843 (88-0843) HO si [49th FW]			New Castle County Airport,
				Delaware ANG [DE] (bl);
	Lockheed C-130 Hercules			143rd AS/143rd AW, Quonset,
	1st SOS/353rd SOG, Kadena AB,			Rhode Island ANG [RI] (r);
	Japan;			144th AS/176th CW, Kulis ANGB,
	3rd Wg, Elmendorf AFB,			Alaska ANG (bk/y);
	Alaska [AK]:			154th TS/189th AW, Little Rock,
	517th AS (w);			Arkansas ANG (r);

Type	Notes
156th AS/145th AW, Charlotte, North Carolina ANG [NC] (*bl*);	
157th FS/169th FW, McEntire ANGS, South Carolina ANG [SC];	
158th AS/165th AW, Savannah, Georgia ANG (*r*);	
159th FS/125th FW, Jacksonville, Florida ANG;	
164th AS/179th AW, Mansfield, Ohio ANG [OH] (*bl*);	
165th AS/123rd AW, Standiford Field, Kentucky ANG [KY];	
167th AS/167th AW, Martinsburg, West Virginia ANG [WV] (*r*);	
169th AS/182nd AW, Peoria, Illinois ANG [IL];	
171st AS/191st AW, Selfridge ANGB, Michigan ANG (*y/bk*);	
180th AS/139th AW, Rosencrans Memorial Airport, Missouri ANG [XP];	
181st AS/136th AW, NAS Dallas, Texas ANG [bl/w];	
185th AS/137th AW, Will Rogers World Airport, Oklahoma ANG [OK] (*bl*);	
187th AS/153rd AW, Cheyenne, Wyoming ANG [WY];	
189th AS/124th Wg, Boise, Idaho ANG [ID];	
192nd AS/152nd AW, Reno, Nevada ANG [NV] (*w*);	
193rd SOS/193rd SOW, Harrisburg, Pennsylvania ANG [PA];	
198th AS/156th AW, San Juan, Puerto Rico ANG;	
204th AS/154th Wg, Hickam AFB, Hawaii ANG;	
210th RQS/176th CW, Kulis ANGB, Alaska ANG [AK];	
303rd RQS/939th RQW AFRC, Portland, Oregon [PD] (*y*);	
314th AW, Little Rock AFB, Arkansas:	
53rd AS (*bk*) & 62nd AS (*bl*);	
317th AG, Dyess AFB, Texas:	
39th AS (*r*) & 40th AS (*bl*);	
327th AS/913th AW AFRC, NAS Willow Grove, Pennsylvania (*bk*);	
328th AS/914th AW AFRC, Niagara Falls, New York [NF] (*bl*);	
357th AS/908th AW AFRC, Maxwell AFB, Alabama (*bl*);	
36th AS/374th AW, Yokota AB, Japan [YJ] (*r*);	
412th TW Edwards AFB, California:	
452nd FLTS [ED];	
463rd AG Little Rock AFB, Arkansas [LK]:	
50th AS (*r*) & 61st AS (*gn*);	
645th Materiel Sqn, Palmdale, California [D4];	
700th AS/94th AW AFRC, Dobbins ARB, Georgia [DB] (*bl*);	
711th SOS/919th SOW AFRC, Duke Field, Florida;	
731st AS/302nd AW AFRC, Peterson AFB, Colorado (*pr/w*);	
757th AS/910th AW AFRC, Youngstown ARS, Ohio [YO] (*bl*);	
758th AS/911th AW AFRC,	

Type	Notes
Pittsburgh ARS, Pennsylvania (*bk/y*);	
773rd AS/910th AW AFRC, Youngstown ARS, Ohio [YO] (*r*);	
815th AS/403rd AW AFRC, Keesler AFB, Mississippi [KT] (*r*);	
LMTAS, Marietta, Georgia	

Type			Notes
FY90			
00161	MC-130H	15th SOS	
00162	MC-130H	15th SOS	
00163	AC-130U	4th SOS	
00164	AC-130U	4th SOS	
00165	AC-130U	4th SOS	
00166	AC-130U	4th SOS	
00167	AC-130U	4th SOS	
FY80			
00320	C-130H	158th AS	r
00321	C-130H	158th AS	r
00322	C-130H	158th AS	r
00323	C-130H	158th AS	r
00324	C-130H	158th AS	r
00325	C-130H	158th AS	r
00326	C-130H	158th AS	r
00332	C-130H	158th AS	r
FY90			
01057	C-130H	181st AS	bl/w
01058	C-130H	130th AS	prl/y
FY70			
01259	C-130E	43rd AW	gn/or
01260	C-130E	37th AS	bl/w
01261	C-130E	43rd AW	gn/bl
01262	C-130E	43rd AW	gn/or
01263	C-130E	43rd AW	gn/or
01264	C-130E	37th AS	bl/w
01265	C-130E	43rd AW	gn/bl
01266	C-130E	43rd AW	gn/or
01267	C-130E	43rd AW	gn/or
01268	C-130E	43rd AW	gn/bl
01270	C-130E	43rd AW	gn/bl
01271	C-130E	37th AS	bl/w
01272	C-130E	43rd AW	gn/bl
01273	C-130E	43rd AW	gn/bl
01274	C-130E	37th AS	bl/w
01275	C-130E	43rd AW	gn/bl
01276	C-130E	43rd AW	gn/bl
FY90			
01791	C-130H	164th AS	bl
01792	C-130H	164th AS	bl
01793	C-130H	164th AS	bl
01794	C-130H	164th AS	bl
01795	C-130H	164th AS	bl
01796	C-130H	164th AS	bl
01797	C-130H	164th AS	bl
01798	C-130N	164th AS	bl
02103	HC-130N	210th RQS	
09107	C-130H	757th AS	bl
09108	C-130H	757th AS	bl
FY81			
10626	C-130H	700th AS	bl
10627	C-130H	700th AS	bl
10628	C-130H	700th AS	bl
10629	C-130H	700th AS	bl
10630	C-130H	700th AS	bl
10631	C-130H	700th AS	bl
FY68			
10934	C-130E	43rd AW	gn/bl
10935	C-130E	37th AS	bl/w
10937	C-130E	43rd AW	gn/or
10938	C-130E	37th AS	bl/w
10939	C-130E	43rd AW	gn/bl
10940	C-130E	43rd AW	gn/or
10941	C-130E	43rd AW	gn/bl
10942	C-130E	43rd AW	gn/bl

C-130

Notes	Type				Notes	Type			
	10943	C-130E	37th AS	bl/w		21292	C-130E	463rd AG	gn
	10947	C-130E	37th AS	bl/w		21293	C-130E	463rd AG	gn
	10948	C-130E	463rd AG	gn		21294	C-130E	463rd AG	gn
	FY91					21295	C-130E	314th AW	bl
	11231	C-130H	165th AS			21296	C-130E	314th AW	bk
	11232	C-130H	165th AS			21299	C-130E	374th AW	r
	11233	C-130H	165th AS			*FY92*			
	11234	C-130H	165th AS			21451	C-130H	156th AS	bl
	11235	C-130H	165th AS			21452	C-130H	156th AS	bl
	11236	C-130H	165th AS			21453	C-130H	156th AS	bl
	11237	C-130H	165th AS	..		21454	C-130H	156th AS	bl
	11238	C-130H	165th AS			21531	C-130H	187th AS	
	11239	C-130H	165th AS			21532	C-130H	187th AS	
	11651	C-130H	165th AS			21533	C-130H	187th AS	
	11652	C-130H	165th AS			21534	C-130H	187th AS	
	11653	C-130H	165th AS			21535	C-130H	187th AS	
	FY61					21536	C-130H	187th AS	
	12358	C-130E	171st AS	y/bk		21537	C-130H	187th AS	
	12359	C-130E	115th AS	gn		21538	C-130H	187th AS	
	12361	C-130E	192nd AS	w		*FY62*			
	12367	C-130E	115th AS	gn		21784	C-130E	154th TS	r
	12369	C-130E	198th AS			21786	C-130E	189th AS	
	12370	C-130E	171st AS	y/bk		21787	C-130E	154th TS	r
	12371	C-130E	171st AS	y/bk		21788	C-130E	154th TS	r
	12372	C-130E	115th AS	gn		21789	C-130E	314th AW	bk
	FY64					21790	C-130E	154th TS	r
	14852	HC-130P	71st RQS	bl		21791	EC-130E	42nd ACCS	w
	14853	HC-130P	71st RQS	bl		21792	C-130E	463rd AG	gn
	14854	MC-130P	9th SOS			21793	C-130E	115th AS	gn
	14855	HC-130P	303rd RQS	y		21795	C-130E	154th TS	r
	14858	MC-130P	58th SOW			21798	C-130E	314th AW	bk
	14859	C-130E	16th SOW			21799	C-130E	115th AS	gn
	14860	HC-130P	303rd RQS	y		21801	C-130E	115th AS	gn
	14861	WC-130H	53rd WRS			21804	C-130E	154th TS	r
	14862	EC-130H	645th MS			21806	C-130E	96th AS	pr
	14863	HC-130P	71st RQS	bl		21808	C-130E	314th AW	bk
	14864	HC-130P	39th RQS	bl		21810	C-130E	314th AW	bl
	14865	HC-130P	71st RQS	bl		21811	C-130E	115th AS	gn
	14866	WC-130H	53rd WRS			21812	C-130E	115th AS	gn
	17680	C-130E	314th AW	bk		21816	C-130E	314th AW	bl
	17681	C-130E	37th AS	bl/w		21817	C-130E	189th AS	
	18240	C-130E	37th AS	bl/w		21818	EC-130E	42nd ACCS	w
	FY91					21820	C-130E	171st AS	y/bk
	19141	C-130H	773rd AS	r		21823	C-130E	96th AS	pr
	19142	C-130H	773rd AS	r		21824	C-130E	154th TS	r
	19143	C-130H	773rd AS	r		21825	EC-130E	42nd ACCS	w
	19144	C-130H	773rd AS	r		21826	C-130E	115th AS	gn
	FY82					21829	C-130E	171st AS	y/bk
	20054	C-130H	144th AS	bk/y		21832	EC-130E	42nd ACCS	w
	20055	C-130H	144th AS	bk/y		21833	C-130E	115th AS	gn
	20056	C-130H	144th AS	bk/y		21834	C-130E	374th AW	r
	20057	C-130H	144th AS	bk/y		21835	C-130E	96th AS	pr
	20058	C-130H	144th AS	bk/y		21836	EC-130E	42nd ACCS	w
	20059	C-130H	144th AS	bk/y		21837	C-130E	189th AS	
	20060	C-130H	144th AS	bk/y		21839	C-130E	96th AS	pr
	20061	C-130H	144th AS	bk/y		21842	C-130E	171st AS	y/bk
	FY92					21843	MC-130E	711th SOS	
	20253	AC-130U	4th SOS			21844	C-130E	96th AS	pr
	20547	C-130H	463rd AG	r		21846	C-130E	189th AS	
	20548	C-130H	463rd AG	r		21847	C-130E	96th AS	pr
	20549	C-130H	463rd AG	r		21848	C-130E	96th AS	pr
	20550	C-130H	463rd AG	r		21849	C-130E	463rd AG	gn
	20551	C-130H	463rd AG	r		21850	C-130E	314th AW	bk
	20552	C-130H	463rd AG	r		21851	C-130E	115th AS	gn
	20553	C-130H	463rd AG	r		21852	C-130E	96th AS	pr
	20554	C-130H	463rd AG	r		21855	C-130E	374th AW	r
	21094	LC-130H	139th AS			21856	C-130E	143rd AS	r
	21095	LC-130H	139th AS			21857	EC-130E	42nd ACCS	w
	FY72					21858	C-130E	192nd AS	w
	21288	C-130E	374th AW	r		21859	C-130E	122nd FS	
	21289	C-130E	374th AW	r		21862	C-130E	115th AS	gn
	21290	C-130E	374th AW	r		21863	EC-130E	42nd ACCS	w
	21291	C-130E	314th AW	bk		21864	C-130E	189th AS	

Type			Notes		Type			Notes
21866	C-130E	314th AW	bk		37769	C-130E	327th AS	bk
FY92					37770	C-130E	96th AS	pr
23021	C-130H	773rd AS	r		37773	EC-130E	193rd SOS	
23022	C-130H	773rd AS	r		37776	C-130E	327th AS	bk
23023	C-130H	773rd AS	r		37777	C-130E	198th AS	
23024	C-130H	773rd AS	r		37778	C-130E	314th AW	bk
23281	C-130H	328th AS	bl		37781	C-130E	463rd AG	gn
23282	C-130H	328th AS	bl		37782	C-130E	143rd AS	r
23283	C-130H	328th AS	bl		37783	EC-130E	193rd SOS	
23284	C-130H	328th AS	bl		37784	C-130E	314th AW	bl
23285	C-130H	328th AS	bl		37785	MC-130E	711th SOS	
23286	C-130H	328th AS	bl		37786	C-130E	171st AS	y/bk
23287	C-130H	328th AS	bl		37788	C-130E	143rd AS	r
23288	C-130H	328th AS	bl		37790	C-130E	374th AW	r
FY83					37791	C-130E	314th AW	bl
30486	C-130H	139th AS			37792	C-130E	169th AS	
30487	C-130H	139th AS			37796	C-130E	314th AW	bk
30488	C-130H	139th AS			37799	C-130E	314th AW	bl
30489	C-130H	139th AS			37800	C-130E	169th AS	
30490	LC-130H	139th AS			37804	C-130E	314th AW	bl
30491	LC-130H	139th AS			37805	C-130E	171st AS	y/bk
30492	LC-130H	139th AS			37808	C-130E	463rd AG	gn
30493	LC-130H	139th AS			37809	C-130E	463rd AG	gn
FY93					37811	C-130E	143rd AS	r
31036	C-130H	463rd AG	r		37812	C-130E	169th AS	
31037	C-130H	463rd AG	r		37814	C-130E	67th AS	
31038	C-130H	463rd AG	r		37815	C-130E	193rd SOS	
31039	C-130H	463rd AG	r		37816	C-130E	193rd SOS	
31040	C-130H	463rd AG	r		37817	C-130E	314th AW	
31041	C-130H	463rd AG	r		37818	C-130E	169th AS	
31096	LC-130H	139th AS			37819	C-130E	374th AW	r
FY83					37821	C-130E	374th AW	r
31212	MC-130H	15th SOS			37822	C-130E	96th AS	pr
FY93					37823	C-130E	327th AS	bk
31455	C-130H	156th AS	bl		37824	C-130E	143rd AS	r
31456	C-130H	156th AS	bl		37825	C-130E	169th AS	
31457	C-130H	156th AS	bl		37826	C-130E	327th AS	bk
31458	C-130H	156th AS	bl		37828	EC-130E	193rd SOS	
31459	C-130H	156th AS	bl		37829	C-130E	463rd AG	gn
31561	C-130H	156th AS	bl		37830	C-130E	314th AW	bk
31562	C-130H	156th AS	bl		37831	C-130E		
31563	C-130H	156th AS	bl		37832	C-130E	327th AS	bk
FY73					37833	C-130E	327th AS	bk
31580	EC-130H	43rd ECS	r		37834	C-130E	327th AS	bk
31581	EC-130H	43rd ECS	r		37835	C-130E	314th AW	bk
31582	C-130H	317th AG	r		37837	C-130E	374th AW	r
31583	EC-130H	43rd ECS	r		37838	C-130E	314th AW	bl
31584	EC-130H	43rd ECS	r		37839	C-130E	463rd AG	gn
31585	EC-130H	41st ECS	bl		37840	C-130E	143rd AS	r
31586	EC-130H	41st ECS	bl		37841	C-130E	198th AS	
31587	EC-130H	41st ECS	bl		37842	C-130E	303rd RQS	y
31588	EC-130H	41st ECS	bl		37845	C-130E	463rd AG	
31590	EC-130H	43rd ECS	r		37846	C-130E	314th AW	
31592	EC-130H	41st ECS	bl		37847	C-130E	154th TS	r
31594	EC-130H	41st ECS	bl		37848	C-130E	327th AS	bk
31595	EC-130H	43rd ECS	r		37849	C-130E	314th AW	bl
31597	C-130H	317th AG	r		37850	C-130E	374th AW	r
31598	C-130H	317th AG	r		37851	C-130E	192nd AS	w
FY93					37852	C-130E	463rd AG	
32041	C-130H	204th AS			37853	C-130E	327th AS	bk
32042	C-130H	204th AS			37856	C-130E	815th AS	r
32104	HC-130N	210th RQS			37857	C-130E	463rd AG	gn
32105	HC-130N	210th RQS			37858	C-130E	169th AS	
32106	HC-130N	210th RQS			37859	C-130E	143rd AS	r
37311	C-130H	731st AS	pr/w		37860	C-130E	314th AW	bl
37312	C-130H	731st AS	pr/w		37861	C-130E	129th RQS	bl
37313	C-130H	731st AS	pr/w		37864	C-130E	314th AW	bl
37314	C-130H	731st AS	pr/w		37865	C-130E	374th AW	r
FY63					37866	C-130E	314th AW	bk
37764	C-130E	463rd AG	gn		37867	C-130E	327th AS	bk
37765	C-130E	314th AW	bl		37868	C-130E	143rd AS	r
37767	C-130E	314th AW	bl		37869	EC-130E	193rd SOS	
37768	C-130E	314th AW	bl		37871	C-130E	374th AW	r

C-130

Notes	Type				Notes	Type			
	37872	C-130E	169th AS			40551	MC-130E	711th SOS	
	37874	C-130E	314th AW	bk		40555	MC-130E	711th SOS	
	37876	C-130E	463rd AG	gn		40559	MC-130E	8th SOS	
	37877	C-130E	169th AS			40561	MC-130E	711th SOS	
	37879	C-130E	374th AW	r		40562	MC-130E	711th SOS	
	37880	C-130E	314th AW	bl		40565	MC-130E	711th SOS	
	37882	C-130E	314th AW	bk		40566	MC-130E	8th SOS	
	37883	C-130E	327th AS	bk		40567	MC-130E	8th SOS	
	37884	C-130E	463rd AG	gn		40568	MC-130E	8th SOS	
	37885	C-130E	37th AS	bl/w		40569	C-130E	314th AW	bl
	37887	C-130E	37th AS	bl/w		40570	C-130E	43rd AW	gn/or
	37888	C-130E	463rd AG	gn		40571	MC-130E	711th SOS	
	37889	C-130E	143rd AS	r		40572	MC-130E	8th SOS	
	37890	C-130E	314th AW	bl		*FY74*			
	37892	C-130E	327th AS	bk		41658	C-130H	3rd Wg	w
	37893	C-130E	314th AW	bk		41659	C-130H	3rd Wg	w
	37894	C-130E	463rd AG	gn		41660	C-130H	3rd Wg	w
	37895	C-130E	171st AS	y/bk		41661	C-130H	3rd Wg	w
	37896	C-130E	314th AW			41663	C-130H	317th AG	bl
	37897	C-130E	169th AS	or		41664	C-130H	3rd Wg	w
	37898	C-130E	8th SOS			41665	C-130H	317th AG	bl
	37899	C-130E	314th AW	bl		41666	C-130H	317th AG	bl
	39810	C-130E	71st RQS	bl		41667	C-130H	317th AG	r
	39812	C-130E	314th AW	bk		41668	C-130H	3rd Wg	w
	39813	C-130E	171st AS	y/bk		41669	C-130H	317th AG	bl
	39814	C-130E	314th AW	bl		41670	C-130H	317th AG	r
	39815	C-130E	198th AS			41671	C-130H	317th AG	bl
	39816	EC-130E	193rd SOS			41673	C-130H	317th AG	bl
	39817	EC-130E	193rd SOS			41674	C-130H	317th AG	r
	FY84					41675	C-130H	317th AG	r
	40204	C-130H	700th AS	bl		41676	C-130H	3rd Wg	m
	40205	C-130H	700th AS	bl		41677	C-130H	317th AG	bl
	40206	C-130H	142nd AS	bl		41679	C-130H	317th AG	bl
	40207	C-130H	142nd AS	bl		41680	C-130H	317th AG	r
	40208	C-130H	142nd AS	bl		41682	C-130H	3rd Wg	w
	40209	C-130H	142nd AS	bl		41684	C-130H	3rd Wg	w
	40210	C-130H	142nd AS	bl		41685	C-130H	3rd Wg	w
	40211	C-130H	142nd AS	bl		41687	C-130H	317th AG	r
	40212	C-130H	142nd AS	bl		41688	C-130H	317th AG	bl
	40213	C-130H	142nd AS	bl		41689	C-130H	317th AG	bl
	40475	MC-130H	15th SOS			41690	C-130H	3rd Wg	w
	40476	MC-130H	7th SOS			41691	C-130H	317th AG	r
	FY64					41692	C-130H	3rd Wg	w
	40495	C-130E	43rd AW	gn/or		42061	C-130H	317th AG	r
	40496	C-130E	43rd AW	gn/bl		42062	C-130H	3rd Wg	w
	40498	C-130E	43rd AW	gn/bl		42063	C-130H	317th AG	bl
	40499	C-130E	43rd AW	gn/bl		42065	C-130H	317th AG	bl
	40502	C-130E	37th AS	bl/w		42066	C-130H	3rd Wg	w
	40504	C-130E	43rd AW	gn/bl		42067	C-130H	317th AG	r
	40510	C-130E	198th AS			42069	C-130H	317th AG	r
	40512	C-130E	154th TS	r		42070	C-130H	3rd Wg	w
	40514	C-130E	154th TS	r		42071	C-130H	3rd Wg	w
	40515	C-130E	198th AS			42072	C-130H	317th AG	bl
	40517	C-130E	43rd AW	gn/bl		42130	C-130H	317th AG	r
	40518	C-130E	463rd AG	gn		42131	C-130H	3rd Wg	w
	40519	C-130E	314th AW	bl		42132	C-130H	317th AG	r
	40520	C-130E	157th FS			42133	C-130H	3rd Wg	w
	40521	C-130E	159th FS			42134	C-130H	317th AG	r
	40523	MC-130E	8th SOS			*FY94*			
	40525	C-130E	43rd AW	gn/bl		46701	C-130H	167th AS	r .
	40526	C-130E	154th TS	r		46702	C-130H	167th AS	r
	40527	C-130E	37th AS	bl/w		46703	C-130H	167th AS	r
	40529	C-130E	43rd AW	gn/or		46704	C-130H	167th AS	r
	40531	C-130E	43rd AW	gn/bl		46705	C-130H	167th AS	r
	40533	C-130E	37th AS	bl/w		46706	C-130H	167th AS	r
	40537	C-130E	43rd AW	gn/or		46707	C-130H	167th AS	r
	40538	C-130E	314th AW	bk		46708	C-130H	167th AS	r
	40539	C-130E	43rd AW	gn/or		47310	C-130H	731st AS	pr/w
	40540	C-130E	43rd AW	gn/bl		47315	C-130H	731st AS	pr/w
	40541	C-130E	314th AW	bk		47316	C-130H	731st AS	pr/w
	40542	C-130E	314th AW	bk		47317	C-130H	731st AS	pr/w
	40544	C-130E	198th AS			47318	C-130H	731st AS	pr/w
	40550	C-130E	37th AS	bl/w		47319	C-130H	731st AS	pr/w

C-130

Type			Notes
47320	C-130H	731st AS	pr/w
47321	C-130H	731st AS	pr/w
48151	C-130J	LMTAS	
48152	C-130J	412th TW	
FY85			
50011	MC-130H	58th SOW	
50012	MC-130H	15th SOS	
50035	C-130H	357th AS	bl
50036	C-130H	357th AS	bl
50037	C-130H	357th AS	bl
50038	C-130H	357th AS	bl
50039	C-130H	357th AS	bl
50040	C-130H	357th AS	bl
50041	C-130H	357th AS	bl
50042	C-130H	357th AS	bl
FY65			
50962	EC-130H	42nd ACCS	w
50963	WC-130H	53rd WRS	
50964	MC-130P		
50966	WC-130H	53rd WRS	
50967	WC-130H	53rd WRS	
50968	WC-130H	53rd WRS	
50970	HC-130P	303rd RQS	y
50971	MC-130P	58th SOW	
50973	HC-130P	71st RQS	bl
50974	HC-130P	102nd RQS	
50975	MC-130P	58th SOW	
50976	HC-130P		
50977	WC-130H	53rd WRS	
50978	HC-130P	102nd RQS	
50979	NC-130H	412th TW	
50980	WC-130H	53rd WRS	
50981	HC-130P	71st RQS	bl
50982	HC-130P	71st RQS	bl
50983	MC-130P	71st RQS	bl
50984	WC-130H	53rd WRS	
50985	WC-130H	53rd WRS	
50986	HC-130P	71st RQS	bl
50987	HC-130P	71st RQS	bl
50988	HC-130P	71st RQS	bl
50989	EC-130H	41st ECS	bl
50991	MC-130P	9th SOS	
50992	MC-130P	17th SOS	
50993	MC-130P	17th SOS	
50994	MC-130P	17th SOS	
FY95			
51001	C-130H	109th AS	gn/bl
51002	C-130H	109th AS	gn/bl
FY85			
51361	C-130H	181st AS	bl/w
51362	C-130H	181st AS	bl/w
51363	C-130H	181st AS	bl/w
51364	C-130H	181st AS	bl/w
51365	C-130H	181st AS	bl/w
51366	C-130H	181st AS	bl/w
51367	C-130H	181st AS	bl/w
51368	C-130H	181st AS	bl/w
FY95			
56709	C-130H	167th AS	r
56710	C-130H	167th AS	r
56711	C-130H	167th AS	r
56712	C-130H	167th AS	r
FY66			
60212	HC-130P	129th RQS	bl
60213	MC-130P	9th SOS	
60215	MC-130P	17th SOS	
60216	HC-130P	129th RQS	bl
60217	MC-130P	9th SOS	
60219	HC-130P	129th RQS	bl
60220	MC-130P	17th SOS	
60221	HC-130P	129th RQS	bl
60222	HC-130P	102nd RQS	
60223	MC-130P	9th SOS	

Type			Notes
60224	HC-130P	39th RQS	
60225	MC-130P	9th SOS	
FY86			
60410	C-130H	758th AS	bk/y
60411	C-130H	758th AS	bk/y
60412	C-130H	758th AS	bk/y
60413	C-130H	758th AS	bk/y
60414	C-130H	758th AS	bk/y
60415	C-130H	758th AS	bk/y
60418	C-130H	758th AS	bk/y
60419	C-130H	758th AS	bk/y
FY96			
61003	C-130H	109th AS	gn/bl
61004	C-130H	109th AS	gn/bl
61005	C-130H	109th AS	gn/bl
61006	C-130H	109th AS	gn/bl
61007	C-130H	109th AS	gn/bl
61008	C-130H	109th AS	gn/bl
FY86			
61391	C-130H	180th AS	
61392	C-130H	180th AS	
61393	C-130H	180th AS	
61394	C-130H	180th AS	
61395	C-130H	180th AS	
61396	C-130H	180th AS	
61397	C-130H	180th AS	
61398	C-130H	180th AS	
61699	MC-130H	7th SOS	
FY76			
63300	LC-130R	139th AS	
63301	LC-130R	139th AS	
63302	LC-130R	139th AS	
FY96			
65300	WC-130J	53rd WRS	
65301	WC-130J	53rd WRS	
65302	WC-130J	53rd WRS	
67322	C-130H	731st AS	pr/w
67323	C-130H	731st AS	pr/w
67324	C-130H	731st AS	pr/w
67325	C-130H	731st AS	pr/w
68153	C-130J	815th AS	r
68154	C-130J	815th AS	r
FY87			
70023	MC-130H	7th SOS	
70024	MC-130H	15th SOS	
70125	MC-130H	58th SOW	
70126	MC-130H	58th SOW	
70127	MC-130H	58th SOW	
70128	AC-130U	4th SOS	
FY97			
71351	C-130J	135th AS	bk/y
71352	C-130J	135th AS	bk/y
71353	C-130J	135th AS	bk/y
71354	C-130J	135th AS	bk/y
71931	EC-130J	LMTAS	
75303	WC-130J	53rd WRS	
75304	WC-130J	53rd WRS	
75305	WC-130J	53rd WRS	
75306	WC-130J	53rd WRS	
FY87			
79281	C-130H	95th AS	w/r
79282	C-130H	95th AS	w/r
79283	C-130H	95th AS	w/r
79284	C-130H	700th AS	bl
79285	C-130H	95th AS	w/r
79286	C-130H	357th AS	bl
79287	C-130H	95th AS	w/r
79288	C-130H	758th AS	bk/y
FY88			
80191	MC-130H	1st SOS	
80192	MC-130H	1st SOS	
80193	MC-130H	7th SOS	
80194	MC-130H	7th SOS	

203

Notes	Type			
	80195	MC-130H	1st SOS	
	80264	MC-130H	1st SOS	
	FY78			
	80806	C-130H	185th AS	*bl*
	80807	C-130H	185th AS	*bl*
	80808	C-130H	185th AS	*bl*
	80809	C-130H	185th AS	*bl*
	80810	C-130H	185th AS	*bl*
	80811	C-130H	185th AS	*bl*
	80812	C-130H	185th AS	*bl*
	80813	C-130H	185th AS	*bl*
	FY88			
	81301	C-130H	130th AS	*pr/y*
	81302	C-130H	130th AS	*pr/y*
	81303	C-130H	130th AS	*pr/y*
	81304	C-130H	130th AS	*pr/y*
	81305	C-130H	130th AS	*pr/y*
	81306	C-130H	130th AS	*pr/y*
	81307	C-130H	130th AS	*pr/y*
	81308	C-130H	130th AS	*pr/y*
	FY98			
	81355	C-130J	135th AS	*bk/y*
	81356	C-130J	135th AS	*bk/y*
	81357	C-130J	135th AS	*bk/y*
	81358	C-130J	135th AS	*bk/y*
	FY88			
	81803	MC-130H	1st SOS	
	FY98			
	81932	EC-130J	LMTAS	
	FY88			
	82101	HC-130N	102nd RQS	
	82102	HC-130N	102nd RQS	
	84401	C-130H	95th AS	*w/r*
	84402	C-130H	95th AS	*w/r*
	84403	C-130H	95th AS	*w/r*
	84404	C-130H	95th AS	*w/r*
	84405	C-130H	95th AS	*w/r*
	84406	C-130H	95th AS	*w/r*
	84407	C-130H	95th AS	*w/r*
	FY98			
	85307	WC-130J	53rd WRS	
	85308	WC-130J	53rd WRS	
	FY89			
	90280	MC-130H	15th SOS	
	90281	MC-130H	15th SOS	
	90282	MC-130H	15th SOS	
	90283	MC-130H	15th SOS	
	FY79			
	90473	C-130H	192nd AS	*w*
	90474	C-130H	192nd AS	*w*
	90475	C-130H	192nd AS	*w*
	90476	C-130H	192nd AS	*w*
	90477	C-130H	192nd AS	*w*
	90478	C-130H	192nd AS	*w*
	90479	C-130H	192nd AS	*w*
	90480	C-130H	192nd AS	*w*
	FY89			
	90509	AC-130U	4th SOS	
	90510	AC-130U	4th SOS	
	90511	AC-130U	4th SOS	
	90512	AC-130U	4th SOS	
	90513	AC-130U	4th SOS	
	90514	AC-130U	4th SOS	
	91051	C-130H	105th AS	*r*
	91052	C-130H	105th AS	*r*
	91053	C-130H	105th AS	*r*
	91054	C-130H	105th AS	*r*
	91055	C-130H	142nd AS	*bl*
	91056	C-130H	180th AS	
	91181	C-130H	105th AS	*r*
	91182	C-130H	105th AS	*r*
	91183	C-130H	105th AS	*r*
	91184	C-130H	105th AS	*r*

Notes	Type			
	91185	C-130H	105th AS	*r*
	91186	C-130H	105th AS	*r*
	91187	C-130H	105th AS	*r*
	91188	C-130H	105th AS	*r*
	FY99			
	91431	C-130J-30	LMTAS	
	91432	C-130J-30	LMTAS	
	91433	C-130J-30	LMTAS	
	91933	EC-130J	LMTAS	
	95309	WC-130J	53rd WRS	
	FY69			
	95819	MC-130P	9th SOS	
	95820	MC-130P	9th SOS	
	95821	MC-130P	58th SOW	
	95822	MC-130P	9th SOS	
	95823	MC-130P	67th SOS	
	95825	MC-130P	9th SOS	
	95826	MC-130P	67th SOS	
	95827	MC-130P	9th SOS	
	95828	MC-130P	67th SOS	
	95829	HC-130N	39th RQS	
	95830	HC-130N	39th RQS	
	95831	MC-130P	67th SOS	
	95832	MC-130P	67th SOS	
	95833	HC-130N	39th RQS	
	96566	C-130E	37th AS	*bl/w*
	96568	AC-130H	16th SOS	
	96569	AC-130H	16th SOS	
	96570	AC-130H	16th SOS	
	96572	AC-130H	16th SOS	
	96573	AC-130H	16th SOS	
	96574	AC-130H	16th SOS	
	96575	AC-130H	16th SOS	
	96577	AC-130H	16th SOS	
	96580	C-130E	43rd AW	*gn/or*
	96582	C-130E	37th AS	*bl/w*
	96583	C-130E	37th AS	*bl/w*
	FY89			
	99101	C-130H	757th AS	*bl*
	99102	C-130H	757th AS	*bl*
	99103	C-130H	757th AS	*bl*
	99104	C-130H	757th AS	*bl*
	99105	C-130H	757th AS	*bl*
	99106	C-130H	757th AS	*bl*

Boeing C-135/C-137

6th ARW, MacDill AFB, Florida:
  91st ARS (*y/bl*);
15th ABW, Hickam AFB, Hawaii:
  65th AS;
18th Wg, Kadena AB, Japan [ZZ]:
  909th ARS (*w*);
19th ARG, Robins AFB, Georgia:
  99th ARS (*y/bl*);
22nd ARW, McConnell AFB, Kansas:
  344th ARS (*y/bk*), 349th ARS (*y/bl*)
  350th ARS (*y/r*) & 384th ARS (*y/pr*);
55th Wg, Offutt AFB, Nebraska [OF]:
  38th RS (*gn*) & 45th RS (*bk*);
88th ABW, Wright-Patterson AFB,
  Ohio;
89th AW, Andrews AFB, Maryland:
  1st AS;
92nd ARW, Fairchild AFB,
  Washington:
  92nd ARS (*bk*), 93rd ARS (*bl*),
  96th ARS (*gn*), 97th ARS (*y*) &
  98th ARS (*r*);
97th AMW, Altus AFB, Oklahoma:
  55th ARS (*y/r*);
100th ARW, RAF Mildenhall, UK [D]:
  351st ARS (*r/w/bl*);

Type	Notes
106th ARS/117th ARW, Birmingham, Alabama ANG (w/r);	
108th ARS/126th ARW, Scott AFB, Illinois ANG (w/bl);	
108th ARW, McGuire AFB, New Jersey ANG:	
141st ARS & 150th ARS (bl);	
116th ARS/141st ARW, Fairchild AFB, Washington ANG (gn/w);	
117th ARS/190th ARW, Forbes Field, Kansas ANG (bl/y);	
121st ARW, Rickenbacker ANGB, Ohio ANG:	
145th ARS & 166th ARS (bl);	
126th ARS/128th ARW, Mitchell Field, Wisconsin ANG (w/bl);	
132nd ARS/101st ARW, Bangor, Maine ANG (w/gn);	
133rd ARS/157th ARW, Pease ANGB, New Hampshire ANG (bl);	
136th ARS/107th ARW, Niagara Falls, New York ANG (bl);	
151st ARS/134th ARW, Knoxville, Tennessee ANG (w/or);	
153rd ARS/186th ARW, Meridian, Mississippi ANG (bk/gd);	
168th ARS/168th ARW, Eielson AFB, Alaska ANG (bl/y);	
171st ARW, Greater Pittsburgh, Pennsylvania ANG:	
146th ARS (y/bk) & 147th ARS (bk/y);	
173rd ARS/155th ARW, Lincoln, Nebraska ANG (r/w);	
191st ARS/151st ARW, Salt Lake City, Utah ANG (bl/bk);	
196th ARS/163rd ARW, March ARB, California ANG (bl/w);	
197th ARS/161st ARW, Phoenix, Arizona ANG;	
203rd ARS/154th Wg, Hickam AFB, Hawaii ANG [HH] (y/bk);	
319th ARW, Grand Forks AFB, North Dakota:	
905th ARS (bl), 906th ARS (y), 911th ARS (r) & 912th ARS (w);	
366th Wg, Mountain Home AFB, Idaho [MO]:	
22nd ARS (y/gn);	
412th TW, Edwards AFB, California [ED]:	
452nd FLTS (bl);	
434th ARW AFRC, Grissom AFB, Indiana:	
72nd ARS (bl) & 74th ARS (r/w);	
452nd AMW AFRC, March ARB, California:	
336th ARS (y);	
507th ARW AFRC, Tinker AFB, Oklahoma:	
465th ARS (bl/y);	
645th Materiel Sqn, Greenville, Texas;	
916th ARW AFRC, Seymour Johnson AFB, North Carolina:	
77th ARS (gn);	
927th ARW AFRC, Selfridge ANGB, Michigan:	
63rd ARS (pr/w);	
940th ARW AFRC, McClellan AFB, California:	
314th ARS (or/bk);	

Type			Notes
CinC CentCom (CinC CC)/6th ARW, MacDill AFB, Florida			
FY60			
00313	KC-135R	22nd ARW	
00314	KC-135R	434th ARW	r/w
00315	KC-135R	126th ARS	w/bl
00316	KC-135E	116th ARS	gn/w
00318	KC-135R	203rd ARS	y/bk
00319	KC-135R	319th ARW	
00320	KC-135R	319th ARW	w
00321	KC-135R	97th AMW	y/r
00322	KC-135R	434th ARW	bl
00323	KC-135R	203rd ARS	y/bk
00324	KC-135R	18th Wg	w
00327	KC-135E	191st ARS	bl/bk
00328	KC-135R	18th Wg	w
00329	KC-135R	203rd ARS	y/bk
00331	KC-135R	97th AMW	y/r
00332	KC-135R	6th ARW	y/bl
00333	KC-135R	97th AMW	y/r
00334	KC-135R	168th ARS	bl/y
00335	KC-135T	22nd ARW	y/bk
00336	KC-135T	92nd ARW	gn
00337	KC-135T	92nd ARW	m
00339	KC-135T	92nd ARW	bl
00341	KC-135R	121st ARW	bl
00342	KC-135T	319th ARW	y
00343	KC-135T	319th ARW	w
00344	KC-135T	22nd ARW	y/bk
00345	KC-135T	92nd ARW	y
00346	KC-135T	92nd ARW	bk
00347	KC-135R	121st ARW	bl
00348	KC-135R	319th ARW	r
00349	KC-135R	916th ARW	gn
00350	KC-135R	22nd ARW	y/bk
00351	KC-135R	18th Wg	w
00353	KC-135R	18th Wg	w
00355	KC-135R	319th ARW	y
00356	KC-135R	22nd ARW	y/bl
00357	KC-135R	22nd ARW	y/bk
00358	KC-135R	136th ARS	bl
00359	KC-135R	434th ARW	r/w
00360	KC-135R	100th ARW	r/w/bl
00362	KC-135R	22nd ARW	y/r
00363	KC-135R	434th ARW	bl
00364	KC-135R	434th ARW	r/w
00365	KC-135R	19th ARG	y/bl
00366	KC-135R	19th ARG	y/bl
00367	KC-135R	121st ARW	bl
00372	C-135E	412th TW	bl
00375	C-135E	412th TW	bl
00376	C-135E	15th ABW	
FY61			
10264	KC-135R	121st ARW	bl
10266	KC-135R	173rd ARS	r/w
10267	KC-135R		
10268	KC-135E	940th ARW	or/bk
10270	KC-135E	927th ARW	pr/w
10271	KC-135E	927th ARW	pr/w
10272	KC-135R	434th ARW	r/w
10275	KC-135R	6th ARW	y/bl
10276	KC-135R	173rd ARS	r/w
10277	KC-135R	366th Wg	y/gn
10280	KC-135R	452nd AMW	y
10281	KC-135R	197th ARS	
10284	KC-135R		
10288	KC-135R	100th ARW	r/w/bl
10290	KC-135R	203rd ARS	y/bk
10292	KC-135R	22nd ARW	y/pr
10293	KC-135R	22nd ARW	y/r
10294	KC-135R	92nd ARW	y
10295	KC-135R	6th ARW	y/bl
10298	KC-135R	126th ARS	w/bl

C-135

Type			
10299	KC-135R	92nd ARW	y
10300	KC-135R	19th ARG	y/bl
10302	KC-135R	319th ARW	w
10303	KC-135E	452nd AMW	y
10304	KC-135R	6th ARW	y/bl
10305	KC-135R	18th Wg	w
10306	KC-135R	18th Wg	w
10307	KC-135R	434th ARW	r/w
10308	KC-135R	97th AMW	y/r
10309	KC-135R	126th ARS	w/bl
10310	KC-135R	133rd ARS	bl
10311	KC-135R	22nd ARW	y
10312	KC-135R	100th ARW	r/w/bl
10313	KC-135R	916th ARW	gn
10314	KC-135R	97th AMW	y/r
10315	KC-135R	97th AMW	y/r
10317	KC-135R	18th Wg	w
10318	KC-135R	6th ARW	y/bl
10320	KC-135R	412th TW	
10321	KC-135R	92nd ARW	bl
10323	KC-135R	6th ARW	y/bl
10324	KC-135R	452nd AMW	y
10327	EC-135N	CinC CC	
10330	EC-135E	412th TW	bl
12662	RC-135S	55th Wg	bk
12663	RC-135S	55th Wg	bk
12666	WC-135W	645th MS	
12669	C-135C	412th TW	bl
12670	OC-135B	55th Wg	
12672	OC-135B	55th Wg	
FY64			
14828	KC-135R	22nd ARW	y/pr
14829	KC-135R	22nd ARW	
14830	KC-135R	6th ARW	y/bl
14831	KC-135R	18th Wg	w
14832	KC-135R	203rd ARS	y/bk
14833	KC-135R	6th ARW	y/bl
14834	KC-135R	434th ARW	r/w
14835	KC-135R	22nd ARW	y/bk
14836	KC-135R	319th ARW	r
14837	KC-135R	6th ARW	y/bl
14838	KC-135R	100th ARW	r/w/bl
14839	KC-135R	136th ARS	w
14840	KC-135R	121st ARW	bl
14841	RC-135V	55th Wg	gn
14842	RC-135V	55th Wg	gn
14843	RC-135V	55th Wg	gn
14844	RC-135V	55th Wg	gn
14845	RC-135V	55th Wg	gn
14846	RC-135V	55th Wg	gn
14847	RC-135U	55th Wg	gn
14848	RC-135V	55th Wg	gn
14849	RC-135U	55th Wg	gn
FY67			
19417	EC-137D	6th ARW	
FY62			
23498	KC-135R	100th ARW	r/w/bl
23499	KC-135R	22nd ARW	y/pr
23500	KC-135R	126th ARS	w/bl
23502	KC-135R	319th ARW	y
23503	KC-135R	18th Wg	w
23504	KC-135R	319th ARW	bl
23505	KC-135R	6th ARW	y/bl
23506	KC-135R	133rd ARS	bl
23507	KC-135R	22nd ARW	
23508	KC-135R	19th ARG	y/bl
23509	KC-135R	916th ARW	gn
23510	KC-135R	434th ARW	r/w
23511	KC-135R	121st ARW	bl
23512	KC-135R	126th ARS	w/bl
23513	KC-135R	366th Wg	y/gn
23514	KC-135R	203rd ARS	y/bk
23515	KC-135R	133rd ARS	bl

Type			
23516	KC-135R	22nd ARW	
23517	KC-135R	100th ARW	r/w/bl
23518	KC-135R	434th ARW	bl
23519	KC-135R	319th ARW	r
23520	KC-135R	319th ARW	w
23521	KC-135R	434th ARW	r/w
23523	KC-135R	19th ARG	y/bl
23524	KC-135R	106th ARS	w/r
23526	KC-135R	173rd ARS	r/w
23527	KC-135E	108th ARW	bl
23528	KC-135R	100th ARW	r/w/bl
23529	KC-135R	97th AMW	y/r
23530	KC-135R	434th ARW	bl
23531	KC-135R	121st ARW	bl
23533	KC-135R		
23534	KC-135R	19th ARG	y/bl
23537	KC-135R	22nd ARW	
23538	KC-135R	100th ARW	r/w/bl
23540	KC-135R	18th Wg	w
23541	KC-135R	22nd ARW	
23542	KC-135R	916th ARW	gn
23543	KC-135R	434th ARW	bl
23544	KC-135R	319th ARW	r
23545	KC-135R	319th ARW	r
23546	KC-135R	97th AMW	y/r
23547	KC-135R	133rd ARS	bl
23548	KC-135R	18th Wg	w
23549	KC-135R	97th AMW	y/r
23550	KC-135R	97th AMW	y/r
23551	KC-135R	97th AMW	y/r
23552	KC-135R	6th ARW	y/bl
23553	KC-135R	22nd ARW	y/r
23554	KC-135R	19th ARG	y/bl
23556	KC-135R	916th ARW	gn
23557	KC-135R	18th Wg	w
23558	KC-135R	22nd ARW	y/bk
23559	KC-135R	22nd ARW	y/pr
23561	KC-135R	100th ARW	r/w/bl
23562	KC-135R	319th ARW	w
23564	KC-135R	100th ARW	r/w/bl
23565	KC-135R	97th AMW	y/r
23566	KC-135E	153rd ARS	bk/gd
23568	KC-135R	319th ARW	w
23569	KC-135R	19th ARG	y/bl
23571	KC-135R	168th ARS	bl/y
23572	KC-135R	366th Wg	y/gn
23573	KC-135R	6th ARW	y/bl
23575	KC-135R	22nd ARW	
23576	KC-135R	133rd ARS	bl
23577	KC-135R	916th ARW	gn
23578	KC-135R	100th ARW	r/w/bl
23580	KC-135R	97th AMW	y/r
23582	WC-135C	55th Wg	bk
24125	RC-135W	55th Wg	gn
24126	C-135B	108th ARW	bk/y
24127	RC-135W	55th Wg	
24128	RC-135S	55th Wg	
24129	TC-135W	55th Wg	gn
24130	RC-135W	55th Wg	gn
24131	RC-135W	55th Wg	gn
24132	RC-135W	55th Wg	gn
24133	TC-135S	55th Wg	bk
24134	RC-135W	55th Wg	gn
24135	RC-135W	55th Wg	gn
24138	RC-135W	55th Wg	gn
24139	RC-135W	55th Wg	gn
FY72			
27000	C-137C	89th AW	
FY63			
37976	KC-135R	319th ARW	bl
37977	KC-135R	6th ARW	y/bl
37978	KC-135R	22nd ARW	

Type			Notes	Type			Notes
37979	KC-135R	100th ARW	r/w/bl	38885	KC-135R	319th ARW	y
37980	KC-135R	22nd ARW		38886	KC-135R	97th AMW	y/r
37981	KC-135R	136th ARS	bl	38887	KC-135R	100th ARW	r/w/bl
37982	KC-135R	319th ARW	y	38888	KC-135R	319th ARW	bl
37984	KC-135R	106th ARS	w/r	39792	RC-135V	55th Wg	gn
37985	KC-135R	507th ARW	bl/y	FY55			
37987	KC-135R	319th ARW	bl	53132	NKC-135E	412th TW	bl
37988	KC-135R	173rd ARS	r/w	53135	NKC-135E	412th TW	bl
37991	KC-135R	173rd ARS	r/w	53141	KC-135E	116th ARW	gn/w
37992	KC-135R	121st ARW	bl	53143	KC-135E	197th ARS	
37993	KC-135R	121st ARW	m	53145	KC-135E	940th ARW	or/bk
37995	KC-135R	22nd ARW	y/bl	53146	KC-135E	108th ARW	bk/y
37996	KC-135R	434th ARW	bl	FY56			
37997	KC-135R	18th Wg	w	63593	KC-135E	08th ARW	bk/y
37999	KC-135R	97th AMW	y/r	63604	KC-135E	108th ARW	bk/y
38000	KC-135R	19th ARW	y/bl	63606	KC-135E	132nd ARS	w/gn
38002	KC-135R	22nd ARW		63607	KC-135E	151st ARS	w/or
38003	KC-135R	18th Wg	w	63609	KC-135E	151st ARS	w/or
38004	KC-135R	366th Wg	y/gn	63611	KC-135E	171st ARW	y/bk
38006	KC-135R	19th ARG	y/bl	63612	KC-135E	171st ARS	y/bk
38007	KC-135R	106th ARS	w/r	63622	KC-135E	132nd ARS	w/gn
38008	KC-135R	22nd ARW	y/r	63626	KC-135E	171st ARW	y/bk
38011	KC-135R	6th ARW	y/bl	63630	KC-135E	171st ARW	y/bk
38012	KC-135R	319th ARW	bl	63631	KC-135E	191st ARS	bl/bk
38013	KC-135R	121st ARW	bl	63638	KC-135E	197th ARS	
38014	KC-135R	18th Wg	w	63640	KC-135E	132nd ARS	w/gn
38015	KC-135R	168th ARS	bl/y	63641	KC-135E	117th ARS	bl/y
38017	KC-135R	100th ARW	r/w/bl	63643	KC-135E	151st ARS	w/or
38018	KC-135R	173rd ARS	r/w	63648	KC-135E	171st ARW	y/bk
38019	KC-135R	22nd ARW	y/pr	63650	KC-135E	116th ARS	gn/w
38020	KC-135R	97th AMW	y/r	63654	KC-135E	132nd ARS	w/gn
38021	KC-135R	319th ARW	bl	63658	KC-135E	117th ARS	bl/y
38022	KC-135R	22nd ARW	m	FY57			
38023	KC-135R	97th AMW	y/r	71418	KC-135R	153rd ARS	bk/gd
38024	KC-135R	452nd AMW	y	71419	KC-135R	18th Wg	w
38025	KC-135R	319th ARW	bl	71421	KC-135E	116th ARS	w/bl
38026	KC-135R	319th ARW	y	71422	KC-135E	927th ARW	pr/w
38027	KC-135R	92nd ARW	gn	71423	KC-135E	171st ARW	bk/y
38028	KC-135R	168th ARS	bl/y	71425	KC-135E	151st ARS	w/or
38029	KC-135R	126th ARS	w/bl	71426	KC-135E	197th ARS	
38030	KC-135R	203rd ARS	y/bk	71427	KC-135R	121st ARW	bl
38031	KC-135R	19th ARG	y/bl	71428	KC-135E	196th ARS	bl/w
38032	KC-135R	434th ARW	bl	71429	KC-135E	117th ARS	bl/y
38033	KC-135R	92nd ARW	bl	71430	KC-135E	133rd ARS	bl
38034	KC-135R	97th AMW	y/r	71431	KC-135E	108th ARW	bk/y
38035	KC-135R	106th ARS	w/r	71432	KC-135E	106th ARS	w/r
38036	KC-135R	136th ARS	bl	71433	KC-135E	197th ARS	
38037	KC-135R	97th AMW	y/r	71434	KC-135E	116th ARS	gn/w
38038	KC-135R	133rd ARS	bl	71435	KC-135R	18th Wg	w
38039	KC-135R	507th ARW	bl/y	71436	KC-135E	196th ARS	bl/w
38040	KC-135R	18th Wg	w	71437	KC-135R	916th ARW	gn
38041	KC-135R	434th ARW	bl	71438	KC-135R	927th ARW	pr/w
38043	KC-135R	168th ARS	bl/y	71439	KC-135E	92nd ARW	y
38044	KC-135R	18th Wg	w	71440	KC-135R	319th ARW	r
38045	KC-135R	97th AMW	y/r	71441	KC-135E	108th ARS	w/bl
38050	NKC-135B	412th TW	bl	71443	KC-135E	132nd ARS	w/gn
38058	KC-135D	117th ARS	bl/y	71445	KC-135E	108th ARW	bk/y
38059	KC-135D	117th ARS	bl/y	71447	KC-135E	171st ARW	y/bk
38060	KC-135D	117th ARS	bl/y	71448	KC-135E	132nd ARS	w/gn
38061	KC-135D	117th ARS	bl/y	71450	KC-135E	132nd ARS	w/gn
38871	KC-135R	18th Wg	w	71451	KC-135E	196th ARS	bl/w
38872	KC-135R	136th ARS	bl	71452	KC-135E	197th ARS	
38873	KC-135R	6th ARW	y/bl	71453	KC-135E	106th ARS	w/r
38874	KC-135R	100th ARW	r/w/bl	71454	KC-135R	319th ARW	y
38875	KC-135R	366th Wg	y/gn	71455	KC-135E	151st ARS	w/or
38876	KC-135R	168th ARS	bl/y	71456	KC-135E	18th Wg	w
38877	KC-135R	22nd ARW		71458	KC-135E	108th ARS	w/bl
38878	KC-135R	97th AMW	y/r	71459	KC-135E	196th ARS	bl/w
38879	KC-135R	319th ARW		71460	KC-135E	117th ARS	bl/y
38880	KC-135R	507th ARW	bl/y	71461	KC-135E	173rd ARS	r/w
38881	KC-135R	97th AMW	y/r	71462	KC-135R	121st ARW	bl
38883	KC-135R	319th ARW	w	71463	KC-135E	117th ARS	bl/y
38884	KC-135R	22nd ARW	y/r	71464	KC-135E	108th ARW	bk/y

C-135

Notes	Type				Notes	Type			
	71465	KC-135E	151st ARS	w/or		80023	KC-135R	136th ARS	bl
	71468	KC-135E	452nd AMW	y		80024	KC-135E	171st ARW	y/bk
	71469	KC-135R	121st ARW	bl		80027	KC-135R	22nd ARW	y/bl
	71471	KC-135E	132nd ARS	w/gn		80030	KC-135R	106th ARW	w/r
	71472	KC-135R	434th ARW	bl		80032	KC-135E	108th ARW	bl
	71473	KC-135R	319th ARW			80034	KC-135R	319th ARW	bl
	71474	KC-135R	100th ARW	r/w/bl		80035	KC-135R	22nd ARW	y/bl
	71475	KC-135E	197th ARS			80036	KC-135R	319th ARW	
	71479	KC-135E	452nd AMW	y		80037	KC-135E	171st ARW	bk/y
	71480	KC-135E	108th ARS	w/bl		80038	KC-135R	916th ARW	gn
	71482	KC-135E	108th ARS	w/bl		80040	KC-135E	108th ARW	bl
	71483	KC-135R	319th ARW	w		80041	KC-135E	927th ARW	pr/w
	71484	KC-135E	197th ARS			80042	KC-135T	319th ARW	y
	71485	KC-135E	151st ARS	w/or		80043	KC-135E	191st ARS	bl/bk
	71486	KC-135R	92nd ARW	bk		80044	KC-135E	108th ARW	bk/y
	71487	KC-135R	434th ARW	bl		80045	KC-135T	92nd ARW	bl
	71488	KC-135R	319th ARW	w		80046	KC-135T	92nd ARW	r
	71491	KC-135E	132nd ARS	w/gn		80047	KC-135T	319th ARW	w
	71492	KC-135E	151st ARS	w/or		80049	KC-135T	92nd ARW	y
	71493	KC-135R	22nd ARW			80050	KC-135T	92nd ARW	bk
	71494	KC-135E	108th ARS	w/bl		80051	KC-135R	507th ARW	bl/y
	71495	KC-135E	197th ARS			80052	KC-135E	452nd AMW	y
	71496	KC-135E	197th ARS			80053	KC-135E	927th ARW	pr/w
	71497	KC-135E	191st ARS	bl/bk		80054	KC-135T	92nd ARW	gn
	71499	KC-135R	92nd ARW	gn		80055	KC-135T	92nd ARW	bk
	71501	KC-135E	116th ARS	gn/w		80056	KC-135R	153rd ARS	bk/gd
	71502	KC-135R	97th ARW	y/r		80057	KC-135E	108th ARS	w/bl
	71503	KC-135E	151st ARS	w/or		80058	KC-135R	940th ARW	or/bk
	71504	KC-135E	927th ARW	pr/w		80059	KC-135R	153rd ARS	bk/gd
	71505	KC-135E	132nd ARS	w/gn		80060	KC-135T	92nd ARW	gn
	71506	KC-135R	319th ARW	w		80061	KC-135T	319th ARW	r
	71507	KC-135E	108th ARW	bk/y		80062	KC-135T	92nd ARW	gn
	71508	KC-135R	203rd ARS	y/bk		80063	KC-135R	507th ARW	bl/y
	71509	KC-135E	171st ARW	bk/y		80064	KC-135E	940th ARW	or/bk
	71510	KC-135E	191st ARS	bl/bk		80065	KC-135T	319th ARW	bl
	71511	KC-135E	940th ARW	or/bk		80066	KC-135R	507th ARW	bl/y
	71512	KC-135R	452nd AMW	y		80067	KC-135E	108th ARS	w/bl
	71514	KC-135R	126th ARS	w/bl		80068	KC-135E	108th ARS	w/bl
	72589	KC-135E	15th ABW			80069	KC-135T	92nd ARW	y
	72593	KC-135R	121st ARW	bl		80071	KC-135T	22nd ARW	y/bk
	72594	KC-135E	108th ARS	w/bl		80072	KC-135T	92nd ARW	gn
	72595	KC-135R	171st ARW	bk/y		80073	KC-135R	106th ARW	w/r
	72597	KC-135R	153rd ARS	bk/gd		80074	KC-135T	92nd ARW	bl
	72598	KC-135R	452nd AMW	y		80075	KC-135R	434th ARW	bl
	72599	KC-135R	916th ARW	gn		80076	KC-135R	434th ARW	r/w
	72600	KC-135E	116th ARS	gn/w		80077	KC-135T	92nd ARW	bk
	72601	KC-135E	151st ARS	w/or		80078	KC-135E	108th ARW	bl
	72602	KC-135E	108th ARW	bl		80079	KC-135R	507th ARW	bl/y
	72603	KC-135E	927th ARW	pr/w		80080	KC-135E	191st ARS	bl/bk
	72604	KC-135E	171st ARW	y/bk		80082	KC-135E	116th ARS	gn/w
	72605	KC-135R	22nd ARW			80083	KC-135E	121st ARW	bl
	72606	KC-135E	108th ARW	bl		80084	KC-135T	92nd ARW	r
	72607	KC-135E	171st ARW	bk/y		80085	KC-135E	452nd AMW	y
	72608	KC-135E	171st ARW	bk/y		80086	KC-135T	92nd ARW	gn
	FY58					80087	KC-135E	108th ARW	bl
	80001	KC-135R	6th ARW	y/bl		80088	KC-135T	22nd ARW	y/bk
	80003	KC-135E	108th ARS	w/bl		80089	KC-135T	319th ARW	w
	80004	KC-135R	153rd ARS	bk/gd		80090	KC-135E	940th ARW	or/bk
	80005	KC-135E	117th ARS	bl/y		80092	KC-135R	133rd ARS	bl
	80006	KC-135E	191st ARS	bl/bk		80093	KC-135R	319th ARW	r
	80008	KC-135R	133rd ARS	bl		80094	KC-135T	92nd ARW	bk
	80009	KC-135R	126th ARS	w/bl		80095	KC-135T	22nd ARW	y/bk
	80010	KC-135R	153rd ARS	bk/gd		80096	KC-135E	940th ARW	or/bk
	80011	KC-135R	22nd ARW	y/bl		80098	KC-135R	133rd ARS	bl
	80012	KC-135E	191st ARS	bl/bk		80099	KC-135T	92nd ARW	bl
	80013	KC-135E	927th ARW	pr/w		80100	KC-135R	22nd ARW	
	80014	KC-135E	108th ARS	w/bl		80102	KC-135R	434th ARW	r/w
	80015	KC-135R	434th ARW	r/w		80103	KC-135T	92nd ARW	gn
	80016	KC-135R	18th Wg	w		80104	KC-135R	136th ARS	bl
	80017	KC-135E	171st ARW	y/bk		80106	KC-135R	106th ARW	w/r
	80018	KC-135R	22nd ARW	y/pr		80107	KC-135E	191st ARS	bl/bk
	80020	KC-135E	116th ARS	gn/w		80108	KC-135E	940th ARW	or/bk
	80021	KC-135R	126th ARS	w/bl		80109	KC-135R	153rd ARS	bk/gd

Type			Notes		Type			Notes
80111	KC-135E	108th ARW	bk/y		91501	KC-135R	319th ARW	
80112	KC-135E	92nd ARW	bl		91502	KC-135R		
80113	KC-135R	319th ARW	r		91503	KC-135E	108th ARW	bk/y
80114	KC-135R	319th ARW	r		91504	KC-135T	92nd ARW	y
80115	KC-135E	108th ARW	bl		91505	KC-135R	196th ARS	bl/w
80116	KC-135E	197th ARS			91506	KC-135E	171st ARW	bk/y
80117	KC-135T	92nd ARW	r		91507	KC-135R	22nd ARW	y/bl
80118	KC-135R	18th Wg	w		91508	KC-135R	319th ARW	r
80119	KC-135R	319th ARW	bl		91509	KC-135R	196th ARS	bl/w
80120	KC-135R	319th ARW	y		91510	KC-135T	22nd ARW	y/bk
80121	KC-135R	507th ARW	bl/y		91511	KC-135R	319th ARW	w
80122	KC-135R	168th ARS	bl/y		91512	KC-135T	92nd ARW	gn
80123	KC-135R	22nd ARW			91513	KC-135T	92nd ARW	bl
80124	KC-135R	22nd ARW	y/bl		91515	KC-135R	18th Wg	w
80125	KC-135T	92nd ARW	bl		91516	KC-135R	196th ARS	bl/w
80126	KC-135R	22nd ARW	y/bl		91517	KC-135R	97th AMW	y/r
80128	KC-135R	6th ARW	y/bl		91518	C-135K	15th ABW	
80129	KC-135T	92nd ARW	bl		91519	KC-135E	171st ARW	y/bk
80130	KC-135R	126th ARS	w/bl		91520	KC-135T	92nd ARW	bl
FY88					91521	KC-135R	168th ARS	bl/y
86005	EC-137D	88th ABW			91522	KC-135R	136th ARS	bl
86008	EC-137D	88th ABW			91523	KC-135T	92nd ARW	bk
FY59								
91444	KC-135R	121st ARW	bl					
91445	KC-135E	116th ARS	gn/w					

Lockheed C-141 Starlifter
62nd AW, McChord AFB,
  Washington (gn):
  4th AS & 8th AS;
164th AW, Memphis, Tennessee ANG:
  155th AS (r);
172nd AW, Jackson Int'l
  Airport, Mississippi ANG:
  183rd AS (bl/gd);
305th AMW, McGuire AFB,
  New Jersey (bl):
  6th AS, 13th AS & 18th AS;
445th AW AFRC, Wright-
  Patterson AFB, Ohio (si):
  89th AS & 356th AS;
452nd AMW AFRC, March ARB,
  California (or/y):
  729th AS & 730th AS;
756th AS/459th AW, AFRC,
  Andrews AFB, Maryland (y/bk)
C-141B/C-141C*

91446	KC-135R	153rd ARS	bk/gd
91447	KC-135E	927th ARW	pr/w
91448	KC-135R	196th ARS	bl/w
91450	KC-135R	196th ARS	bl/w
91451	KC-135E	927th ARW	pr/w
91453	KC-135R	121st ARW	bl
91455	KC-135R	153rd ARS	bk/gd
91456	KC-135E	108th ARW	bk/y
91457	KC-135E	171st ARW	bk/y
91458	KC-135R	121st ARW	bl
91459	KC-135R	97th AMW	y/r
91460	KC-135T	92nd ARW	gn
91461	KC-135T	168th ARS	bl/y
91462	KC-135T	22nd ARW	y/bl
91463	KC-135R	173rd ARS	r/w
91464	KC-135T	92nd ARW	bk
91466	KC-135R	136th ARS	bl
91467	KC-135T	92nd ARW	bl
91468	KC-135T	92nd ARW	bl
91469	KC-135R	916th ARW	gn
91470	KC-135T	92nd ARW	y
91471	KC-135T	92nd ARW	r
91472	KC-135R	203rd ARS	y/bk
91473	KC-135E	191st ARS	bl/bk
91474	KC-135T	92nd ARW	y
91475	KC-135R	97th AMW	y/r
91476	KC-135R	319th ARW	
91477	KC-135E	927th ARW	pr/w
91478	KC-135R	153rd ARS	bk/gd
91479	KC-135E	171st ARW	y/bk
91480	KC-135T	92nd ARW	bl
91482	KC-135R	319th ARW	bl
91483	KC-135R	121st ARW	bl
91484	KC-135E	171st ARW	bk/y
91485	KC-135E	108th ARW	bl
91486	KC-135R	22nd ARW	y/bl
91487	KC-135E	108th ARS	w/bl
91488	KC-135E	22nd ARW	y/r
91489	KC-135E	191st ARS	bl/bk
91490	KC-135T	92nd ARW	bk
91492	KC-135R	319th ARW	r
91493	KC-135E	132nd ARS	w/gn
91495	KC-135R	173rd ARS	r/w
91496	KC-135E	171st ARW	y/bk
91497	KC-135E	108th ARW	bl
91498	KC-135R	366th Wg	y/gn
91499	KC-135R	196th ARS	bl/w
91500	KC-135R	22nd ARW	

FY61			
12778*	164th AW	r	
FY63			
38076	62nd AW	gn	
38080*	164th AW	r	
38082	62nd AW	gn	
38084*	452nd AMW	or/y	
38085*	452nd AMW	or/y	
38088			
FY64			
40611	62nd AW	gn	
40614*	172nd AW	bl/gd	
40618	62nd AW	gn	
40619	305th AMW	bl	
40620*	459th AW	y/bk	
40622*	172nd AW	bl/gd	
40627*	164th AW	r	
40631	62nd AW	gn	
40632*	172nd AW	bl/gd	
40633	62nd AW	gn	
40637*	459th AW	y/bk	
40638	62nd AW	gn	
40640*	172nd AW	bl/gd	
40645*	459th AW	y/bk	
FY65			
50216*	445th AW		
50217			
50218	62nd AW	gn	
50219			

Notes	Type			Notes	Type		
	50220	305th AMW	bl		60163	305th AMW	bl
	50221	62nd AW	gn		60164*	172nd AW	bl/gd
	50222*	164th AW	r		60165	62nd AW	gn
	50224	305th AMW	bl		60166	62nd AW	gn
	50225*	452nd AMW	or/y		60167*	452nd AMW	or/y
	50226*	459th AW	y/bk		60168	305th AMW	bl
	50229*	452nd AMW	or/y		60169	305th AMW	bl
	50231	62nd AW	gn		60171	62nd AW	gn
	50232*	445th AW	si		60174*	459th AW	y/bk
	50235	62nd AW	gn		60175	62nd AW	gn
	50237*	445th AW	si		60177*	445th AW	si
	50240	62nd AW	gn		60181*	452nd AMW	or/y
	50245*	452nd AMW	or/y		60182*	452nd AMW	or/y
	50248*	452nd AMW	or/y		60183	62nd AW	gn
	50249*	445th AW	si		60184	62nd AW	gn
	50250*	445th AW	si		60185*	172nd AW	bl/gd
	50251	62nd AW	gn		60190*	172nd AW	bl/gd
	50256*	445th AW	si		60191*	172nd AW	bl/gd
	50258	445th AW	si		60192	305th AMW	bl
	50259	62nd AW	gn		60193*	445th AW	si
	50261*	445th AW	si		60196	305th AMW	bl
	50267	62nd AW	gn		60197	62nd AW	gn
	50271*	459th AW	y/bk		60201*	452nd AMW	or/y
	50273	305th AMW	bl		60206	62nd AW	gn
	50279	305th AMW	bl		67944	62nd AW	gn
	59401	305th AMW	bl		67947	305th AMW	bl
	59408	305th AMW	bl		67948	305th AMW	bl
	59409*	445th AW	si		67950*	445th AW	si
	59411	62nd AW	gn		67952*	452nd AMW	or/y
	59412*	445th AW	si		67953*	445th AW	si
	59413	305th AMW	bl		67954*	445th AW	si
	59414*	452nd AMW	or/y		67955	62nd AW	gn
	FY66				67956	62nd AW	gn
	60130*	172nd AW	bl/gd		67957*	452nd AMW	or/y
	60131	305th AMW	bl		67959	445th AW	si
	60132*	445th AW	si		FY67		
	60133	305th AMW	bl		70002	62nd AW	gn
	60134*	445th AW	si		70003	305th AMW	bl
	60136*	452nd AMW	or/y		70004	305th AMW	bl
	60137	62nd AW	m		70010	305th AMW	bl
	60139*	164th AW	r		70011	305th AMW	bl
	60140	62nd AW	gn		70012	305th AMW	bl
	60144	62nd AW			70014	305th AMW	bl
	60147	62nd AW	gn		70015*	452nd AMW	or/y
	60148*	445th AW	si		70016	62nd AW	gn
	60149	62nd AW	gn		70018	62nd AW	gn
	60151*	452nd AMW	or/y		70019	62nd AW	gn
	60152*	452nd AMW	or/y		70021*	164th AW	r
	60155	305th AMW	bl		70024*	164th AW	r
	60156				70027*	459th AW	y/bk
	60157*	164th AW	r		70028	62nd AW	gn
	60158	62nd AW	gn		70029*	164th AW	r
	60160	62nd AW	gn		70031*	445th AW	si
	60161				70165	305th AMW	bl
	60162	305th AMW	bl		70166	305th AMW	(VIP)

US-based USN/USMC Aircraft

Lockheed P-3 Orion
CinCLANT/VP-30, NAS Jacksonville, Florida;
CinCPAC/ETD, MCBH Kaneohe Bay, Hawaii;
CinCUSNFE, NAF Sigonella, Italy;
CNO/VP-30, NAS Jacksonville, Florida;
NAF Keflavik, Iceland;
NASC, Point Mugu, California;
NAWC 23, Dallas/Love Field, Texas;
Navy Research Lab, Patuxent River, Maryland;
NFATS, Patuxent River, Maryland;
NWTSPM, NAS Point Mugu, California;
USNTPS, NAS Point Mugu, California;
VP-1, NAS Whidbey Island, Washington [YB];
VP-4, MCBH Kaneohe Bay, Hawaii [YD];
VP-5, NAS Jacksonville, Florida [LA];
VP-8, NAS Brunswick, Maine [LC];
VP-9, MCBH Kaneohe Bay, Hawaii [PD];
VP-10, NAS Brunswick, Maine [LD];
VP-16, NAS Jacksonville, Florida [LF];
VP-26, NAS Brunswick, Maine [LK];
VP-30, NAS Jacksonville, Florida [LL];
VP-40, NAS Whidbey Island, Washington [QE];
VP-45, NAS Jacksonville, Florida [LN];
VP-46, NAS Whidbey Island, Washington [RC];
VP-47, MCBH Kaneohe Bay, Hawaii [RD];
VP-62, NAS Jacksonville, Florida [LT];
VP-64, NAS Willow Grove, Pennsylvania [LU];
VP-65, NAS Point Mugu, California [PG];
VP-66, NAS Willow Grove, Pennsylvania [LV];
VP-69, NAS Whidbey Island, Washington [PJ];
VP-92, NAS Brunswick, Maine [LY];
VP-94, NAS New Orleans, Louisiana [PZ];
VPU-1, NAS Brunswick, Maine;
VPU-2, MCBH Kaneohe Bay, Hawaii;
VQ-1, NAS Whidbey Island, Washington [PR];
VQ-2, NAF Rota, Spain;
VX-1, NAS Patuxent River, Maryland

148883		NP-3D	NFATS
148889		UP-3A	VPU-2
149674		NP-3D	NRL
149675		VP-3A	CinCPAC
149676		UP-3A	CNO
150495		UP-3A	NAF Keflavik
150496		VP-3A	CinCUSNFE
150499	[337]	NP-3D	NWTSPM
150511		VP-3A	
150515		VP-3A	VP-30
150521	[341]	NP-3D	NWTSPM
150522	[340]	NP-3D	NWTSPM
150524	[335]	NP-3D	NWTSPM
150525	[336]	NP-3D	NWTSPM
150526		UP-3A	
151392		TP-3A	VP-47
152150		NP-3D	NFATS
152739		NP-3B	NASC-FS
153442		NP-3D	NRL
153443		NP-3D	USNTPS
154587		NP-3D	NRL
154589		NP-3D	NRL
156507	[PR-31]	EP-3E	VQ-1
156509		P-3C	VP-8
156510	[LL-510]	P-3C	VP-30
156511	[PR-32]	EP-3E	VQ-1
156514	[PR-33]	EP-3E	VQ-1
156515	[LY-515]	P-3C	VP-92
156516	[LL-38]	P-3C	VP-30
156517	[PR-34]	EP-3E	VQ-1
156518	[LL-518]	P-3C	VP-30
156519	[21]	EP-3E	VQ-2
156520	[10]	P-3C	VQ-2
156521	[LY-521]	P-3C	VP-92
156522	[LL-522]	P-3C	VP-30
156523	[LL-523]	P-3C	VP-30
156525	[11]	P-3C	VQ-2
156527		P-3C	
156528	[PR-36]	EP-3E	VQ-1
156529	[24]	EP-3E	VQ-2
156530	[LL-530]	P-3C	VP-30
157310	[LL-310]	P-3C	VP-30
157311		P-3C	VP-45
157312		P-3C	
157313	[LC-313]	P-3C	VP-8
157314	[314]	P-3C	VP-10
157315		P-3C	VP-16
157316	[23]	EP-3E	VQ-2
157317		P-3C	VP-1
157318	[PR-35]	EP-3E	VQ-1
157319	[LD-319]	P-3C	VP-10
157321	[LK-321]	P-3C	VP-26
157322	[322]	P-3C	VP-1
157323		P-3C	VP-62
157324	[PD-324]	P-3C	VP-9
157325	[25]	EP-3E	VQ-2
157326	[22]	EP-3E	VQ-2
157327	[LD-327]	P-3C	VP-10
157328	[LL-328]	P-3C	VP-30
157329	[RD-329]	P-3C	VP-47
157330	[LC-330]	P-3C	VP-8
157331	[LL-331]	P-3C	VP-30
158204	[204]	P-3C	NFATS
158205	[QE-205]	P-3C	VP-40
158206	[JA-03]	P-3C	VX-1
158207	[LC-207]	P-3C	VP-8
158208	[RD-208]	P-3C	VP-47
158209	[YD-209]	P-3C	VP-4
158210	[LD-210]	P-3C	VP-10
158211	[211]	P-3C	VP-1
158212	[RD-212]	P-3C	VP-47
158214	[LL-214]	P-3C	VP-30
158215	[YD-215]	P-3C	VP-4
158216		P-3C	
158218	[YD-218]	P-3C	VP-4
158219	[LN-219]	P-3C	VP-45
158220	[YD-220]	P-3C	VP-4
158221	[RC-221]	P-3C	VP-46
158222	[QE-222]	P-3C	VP-40
158223	[PD-223]	P-3C	VP-9
158224	[LD-224]	P-3C	VP-10
158225	[225]	P-3C	VP-9
158226	[226]	P-3C	VP-47
158227	[227]	NP-3D	NRL
158563	[LD-563]	P-3C	VP-10
158564	[LK-564]	P-3C	VP-26
158565	[LD-565]	P-3C	VP-10
158566	[LN-566]	P-3C	VP-45
158567	[LF-567]	P-3C	VP-16
158568	[LC-568]	P-3C	VP-8
158569	[569]	P-3C	VP-16
158570	[LN-570]	P-3C	VP-45
158571	[LA-571]	P-3C	VP-5
158572	[LA-572]	P-3C	VP-5
158573	[LD-573]	P-3C	VP-10
158574		P-3C	NASC
158912		P-3C	NFATS
158913	[QE-913]	P-3C	VP-40
158914	RC-914]	P-3C	VP-46
158915	[915]	P-3C	VP-40
158916	[LL-916]	P-3C	VP-30
158917	[LC-917]	P-3C	VP-8
158918	[YD-918]	P-3C	VP-4
158919	[LD-919]	P-3C	VP-10
158920	[LF-920]	P-3C	VP-16

158921	[YD-921]	P-3C	VP-4	161014	[LV-014]	P-3C	VP-66
158922	[RD-922]	P-3C	VP-47	161121	[15]	P-3C	VQ-2
158923	[923]	P-3C	VP-4	161122	[224]	P-3C	VPU-1
158924	[LN-924]	P-3C	VP-45	161123	[LU-123]	P-3C	VP-64
158925	[LC-925]	P-3C	VP-8	161124	[LA-124]	P-3C	VP-5
158926	[LD-926]	P-3C	VP-10	161125	[LV-125]	P-3C	VP-66
158927	[927]	P-3C	VP-5	161126	[PR-50]	P-3C	VQ-1
158929	[LD-929]	P-3C	VP-10	161127	[127]	P-3C	VP-62
158931	[LN-931]	P-3C	VP-45	161128	[128]	P-3C	VP-5
158932	[LN-932]	P-3C	VP-45	161129	[LV-129]	P-3C	VP-66
158933	[LN-933]	P-3C	VP-45	161130	[130]	P-3C	VP-1
158934	[QE-934]	P-3C	VP-40	161131	[LU-131]	P-3C	VP-64
158935	[LL-43]	P-3C	VP-30	161132	[PD-132]	P-3C	VP-9
159318	[LA-318]	P-3C	VP-5	161329	[PG-329]	P-3C	VP-65
159319	[LA-319]	P-3C	VP-5	161330	[YB-330]	P-3C	VP-1
159320	[LC-320]	P-3C	VP-8	161331	[LY-331]	P-3C	VP-92
159321	[RC-321]	P-3C	VP-46	161332	[PG-332]	P-3C	VP-65
159322	[322]	P-3C	VP-16	161333	[PG-333]	P-3C	VP-65
159323	[RC-323]	P-3C	VP-46	161334	[PG-334]	P-3C	VP-65
159324	[YD-324]	P-3C	VP-4	161335	[PZ-335]	P-3C	VP-94
159326	[PD-326]	P-3C	VP-9	161336		P-3C	
159327	[PD-327]	P-3C	VP-9	161337	[PZ-337]	P-3C	VP-92
159328	[RC-328]	P-3C	VP-46	161338		P-3C	VP-16
159329	[RC-329]	P-3C	VP-46	161339	[YD-339]	P-3C	VP-4
159503	[LN-503]	P-3C	VP-45	161340	[LC-340]	P-3C	VP-8
159504		P-3C	VPU-2	161404	[LL-404]	P-3C	VP-30
159506	[568]	P-3C	VPU-1	161405	[RD-405]	P-3C	VP-47
159507	[RC-507]	P-3C	VP-46	161406	[PG-406]	P-3C	VP-65
159512	[512]	P-3C	VQ-2	161407	[PG-407]	P-3C	VP-65
159513	[LL-18]	P-3C	VP-30	161408	[PZ-408]	P-3C	VP-94
159514	[LL-514]	P-3C	VP-30	161409	[PZ-409]	P-3C	VP-94
159884	[LL-14]	P-3C	VP-30	161410		P-3C	NAWC 23
159885	[885]	P-3C	VP-9	161411	[LL-411]	P-3C	VP-30
159886	[LL-886]	P-3C	VP-30	161412	[PG-412]	P-3C	VP-65
159887		P-3C	NASC	161413	[LL-39]	P-3C	VP-30
159889	[889]	P-3C	VX-1	161414	[14]	P-3C	VQ-2
159891	[LN-891]	P-3C	VP-45	161415	[LL-415]	P-3C	VP-30
159894	[LL-40]	P-3C	VP-30	161585		P-3C	VPU-1
160283	[PD-283]	P-3C	VP-9	161586	[LL-586]	P-3C	VP-30
160284	[LK-284]	P-3C	VP-26	161587	[YD-587]	P-3C	VP-4
160286	[286]	P-3C	VP-26	161588		P-3C	VP-30
160287	[LC-287]	P-3C	VP-8	161589	[589]	P-3C	VP-9
160288		P-3C	NASC	161590	[LL-590]	P-3C	VP-30
160290	[290]	P-3C	NFATS	161591	[PZ-591]	P-3C	VP-94
160291	[JA-05]	P-3C	VX-1	161592	[PZ-592]	P-3C	VP-94
160292		P-3C	VPU-2	161593		P-3C	VP-30
160293	[293]	P-3C	VPU-2	161594	[LL-594]	P-3C	VP-30
160610	[RC-610]	P-3C	VP-46	161595	[PZ-595]	P-3C	VP-94
160611	[LU-611]	P-3C	VP-64	161596		P-3C	VP-30
160612	[LV-612]	P-3C	VP-66	161763	[763]	P-3C	VP-47
160761	[LU-761]	P-3C	VP-64	161764	[YD-764]	P-3C	VP-4
160762	[LV-762]	P-3C	VP-66	161765	[PG-765]	P-3C	VP-65
160763	[LT-763]	P-3C	VP-62	161766	[PJ-766]	P-3C	VP-69
160764	[764]	P-3C	NRL	161767	[PD-767]	P-3C	VP-9
160765	[LC-765]	P-3C	VP-8	162314	[LY-314]	P-3C	VP-92
160766	[766]	P-3C	VPU-2	162315	[YD-315]	P-3C	VP-1
160767	[767]	P-3C	VP-66	162316		P-3C	VP-92
160768		P-3C	VQ-1	162317	[YD-317]	P-3C	VP-4
160769	[LK-769]	P-3C	VP-26	162318	[PJ-318]	P-3C	VP-69
160770		P-3C	VP-8	162770		P-3C	NFATS
160999	[LL-999]	P-3C	VP-30	162771	[YD-771]	P-3C	VP-4
161000	[LF-000]	P-3C	VP-16	162772	[772]	P-3C	VP-1
161001	[LU-001]	P-3C	VP-64	162773	[773]	P-3C	VP-40
161002	[LF-002]	P-3C	VP-16	162774	[RD-04]	P-3C	NFATS
161003	[003]	P-3C	VP-62	162775	[QE-775]	P-3C	VP-40
161004	[LK-004]	P-3C	VP-26	162776	[LA-776]	P-3C	VP-5
161005	[LU-005]	P-3C	VP-64	162777	[RD-777]	P-3C	VP-47
161006	[PG-006]	P-3C	VP-65	162778	[LA-778]	P-3C	VP-5
161007	[LU-007]	P-3C	VP-64	162998	[RD-998]	P-3C	VP-47
161008	[LL-008]	P-3C	VP-30	162999	[PJ-999]	P-3C	VP-69
161009	[LL-50]	P-3C	VP-30	163000	[PJ-000]	P-3C	VP-69
161010	[LL-010]	P-3C	VP-30	163001	[LT-001]	P-3C	VP-62
161011	[LK-011]	P-3C	VP-26	163002	[LT-002]	P-3C	VP-62
161012	[YD-012]	P-3C	VP-4	163003	[PJ-003]	P-3C	VP-69
161013	[LT-013]	P-3C	VP-62	163004	[PG-004]	P-3C	VP-65

163005	[LT-005]	P-3C	VP-62
163006	[JA-06]	P-3C	VX-1
163289	[LT-289]	P-3C	VP-62
163290	[PJ-290]	P-3C	VP-69
163291	[PG-291]	P-3C	VP-65
163292	[LF-292]	P-3C	VP-16
163293	[LF-293]	P-3C	VP-16
163294	[LY-294]	P-3C	VP-92
163295	[LY-295]	P-3C	VP-92

Boeing E-6 Mercury
Boeing, McConnell AFB, Kansas;
VQ-3 & VQ-4, SCW-1, Tinker AFB, Oklahoma

162782	E-6B	VQ-4
162783	E-6B	VQ-3
162784	E-6B	VQ-3
163918	E-6B	VQ-3
163919	E-6B	VQ-3
163920	E-6B	VQ-3
164386	E-6A	VQ-3
164387	E-6B	VQ-3
164388	E-6A	VQ-4
164404	E-6A	VQ-4
164405	E-6A	VQ-4
164406	E-6B	VQ-3
164407	E-6A	VQ-4
164408	E-6A	VQ-4
164409	E-6B	VQ-4
164410	E-6A	VQ-4

McDonnell Douglas C-9B Skytrain II/DC-9-32*
VMR-1, Cherry Point MCAS, North Carolina;
VR-46, Atlanta, Georgia [JS];
VR-52, Willow Grove NAS, Pennsylvania [JT];
VR-56, Norfolk NAS, Virginia [JU];
VR-57, North Island NAS, California [RX];
VR-58, Jacksonville NAS, Florida [JV];
VR-59, NAS Fort Worth JRB, Texas [RY];
VR-61, Whidbey Island NAS, Washington [RS]

159113	[RX]	VR-57
159114	[JS]	VR-46
159115	[RX]	VR-57
159116	[RX]	VR-57
159117	[JU]	VR-56
159118	[JU]	VR-56
159119	[JU]	VR-56
159120	[JU]	VR-56
160046		VMR-1
160047		VMR-1
160048	[JV]	VR-58
160049	[JV]	VR-58
160050	[JV]	VR-58
160051	[JS]	VR-46
161266	[RY]	VR-59
161529	[JS]	VR-46
161530	[RY]	VR-59
162753	[JT]	VR-52
162754	[JT]	VR-52
163036*	[JT]	VR-52
163037*	[JT]	VR-52
163208*	[RY]	VR-59
163511*	[JS]	VR-46
163512*	[RX]	VR-57
163513*	[JV]	VR-58
164605*	[RS]	VR-61
164606*	[RS]	VR-61
164607*	[RS]	VR-61
164608*	[RS]	VR-61

Boeing TC-18F
VQ-7, SCW-1, Tinker AFB, Oklahoma
165342

Grumman C-20D Gulfstream III/
C-20G Gulfstream IV*
VR-1, NAF Washington, Maryland;
VR-48, NAF Washington, Maryland [JR];
VR-51, MCBH Kaneohe Bay, Hawaii [RG]

163691		VR-1
163692		VR-1
165093*	[JR]	VR-48
165094*	[JR]	VR-48
165151*	[RG]	VR-51
165152*	[RG]	VR-51
165153*		

Boeing C-40A Clipper
VR-59, NAS Fort Worth JRB, Texas [RY]

165829	[RY]	VR-59
165830	[RY]	VR-59
165831	[RY]	VR-59
165832		Boeing
165833		Boeing
165834		Boeing
165835		Boeing
165836		Boeing

Lockheed C-130 Hercules
NAWC-AD, NAS Patuxent River, Maryland;
VR-53, NAF Washington,Maryland [WV];
VR-54, New Orleans NAS, Louisiana [CW];
VR-55, Moffett Field, California [RU];
VR-62, Brunswick NAS, Maine [JW];
VMGR-152, Futenma MCAS, Japan [QD];
VMGR-234, NAS Fort Worth, Texas [QH];
VMGR-252, Cherry Point MCAS,
   North Carolina [BH];
VMGRT-253, Cherry Point MCAS,
   North Carolina [GR];
VMGR-352, MCAS Miramar, California [QB];
VMGR-452, Stewart Field, New York [NY]

147572	[QB]	KC-130F	VMGR-352
147573	[QD]	KC-130F	VMGR-152
148246	[GR]	KC-130F	VMGRT-253
148247	[QD]	KC-130F	VMGR-152
148248	[QD]	KC-130F	VMGR-152
148249	[GR]	KC-130F	VMGRT-253
148890	[GR]	KC-130F	VMGRT-253
148891	[BH]	KC-130F	VMGR-252
148893	[QD]	KC-130F	VMGR-152
148894	[BH]	KC-130F	VMGR-252
148895	[BH]	KC-130F	VMGR-252
148896	[BH]	KC-130F	VMGR-252
148897	[BH]	KC-130F	VMGR-252
148898	[BH]	KC-130F	VMGR-252
148899	[BH]	KC-130F	VMGR-252
149788	[BH]	KC-130F	VMGR-252
149789	[BH]	KC-130F	VMGR-252
149791	[QB]	KC-130F	VMGR-352
149792	[QB]	KC-130F	VMGR-352
149795	[QB]	KC-130F	VMGR-352
149796	[QB]	KC-130F	VMGR-352
149798	[QB]	KC-130F	VMGR-352
149799	[QD]	KC-130F	VMGR-152
149800	[QB]	KC-130F	VMGR-352
149803	[GR]	KC-130F	VMGRT-253
149804	[GR]	KC-130F	VMGRT-253
149806		KC-130F	NAWC-AD
149807	[QD]	KC-130F	VMGR-152
149808	[BH]	KC-130F	VMGR-252
149811	[GR]	KC-130F	VMGRT-253
149812	[QD]	KC-130F	VMGR-152
149815	[QB]	KC-130F	VMGR-352
149816	[QD]	KC-130F	VMGR-152
150684	[GR]	KC-130F	VMGRT-253
150686	[BH]	KC-130F	VMGR-252
150687	[GR]	KC-130F	VMGRT-253
150688	[GR]	KC-130F	VMGRT-253

213

150689	[QB]	KC-130F	VMGR-352	164598	[QH]	KC-130T-30	VMGR-234
150690	[QD]	KC-130F	VMGR-152	164762		C-130T	NAWC-AD
151891		TC-130G	*Blue Angels*	164763		C-130T	NAWC-AD
160013	[QD]	KC-130R	VMGR-152	164993	[CW]	C-130T	VR-54
160014	[QD]	KC-130R	VMGR-152	164994	[WV]	C-130T	VR-53
160015	[QB]	KC-130R	VMGR-352	164995	[CW]	C-130T	VR-54
160016	[QB]	KC-130R	VMGR-352	164996	[WV]	C-130T	VR-53
160017	[QB]	KC-130R	VMGR-352	164997	[WV]	C-130T	VR-53
160018	[QD]	KC-130R	VMGR-152	164998	[WV]	C-130T	VR-53
160019	[QD]	KC-130R	VMGR-152	164999	[QH]	KC-130T	VMGR-234
160020	[QD]	KC-130R	VMGR-152	165000	[QH]	KC-130T	VMGR-234
160021	[QB]	KC-130R	VMGR-352	165158	[CW]	C-130T	VR-54
160022	[QB]	KC-130R	VMGR-352	165159	[CW]	C-130T	VR-54
160240	[QB]	KC-130R	VMGR-352	165160	[CW]	C-130T	VR-54
160625	[BH]	KC-130R	VMGR-252	165161	[RU]	C-130T	VR-55
160626	[BH]	KC-130R	VMGR-252	165162	[QH]	KC-130T	VMGR-234
160627	[BH]	KC-130R	VMGR-252	165163	[QH]	KC-130T	VMGR-234
160628	[BH]	KC-130R	VMGR-252	165313	[JW]	C-130T	VR-62
162308	[QH]	KC-130T	VMGR-234	165314	[JW]	C-130T	VR-62
162309	[QH]	KC-130T	VMGR-234	165315	[NY]	KC-130T	VMGR-452
162310	[QH]	KC-130T	VMGR-234	165316	[NY]	KC-130T	VMGR-452
162311	[QH]	KC-130T	VMGR-234	165348	[JW]	C-130T	VR-62
162785	[QH]	KC-130T	VMGR-234	165349	[JW]	C-130T	VR-62
162786	[QH]	KC-130T	VMGR-234	165350	[RU]	C-130T	VR-55
163022	[QH]	KC-130T	VMGR-234	165351	[RU]	C-130T	VR-55
163023	[QH]	KC-130T	VMGR-234	165352	[NY]	KC-130T	VMGR-452
163310	[QH]	KC-130T	VMGR-234	165353	[NY]	KC-130T	VMGR-452
163311	[NY]	KC-130T	VMGR-452	165378	[RU]	C-130T	VR-55
163591	[NY]	KC-130T	VMGR-452	165379	[RU]	C-130T	VR-55
163592	[NY]	KC-130T	VMGR-452	165735	[BH]	KC-130J	VMGR-252
164105	[NY]	KC-130T	VMGR-452	165736	[BH]	KC-130J	VMGR-252
164106	[NY]	KC-130T	VMGR-452	165737	[BH]	KC-130J	VMGR-252
164180	[NY]	KC-130T	VMGR-452	165738	[BH]	KC-130J	VMGR-252
164181	[NY]	KC-130T	VMGR-452	165739		KC-130J	
164441	[NY]	KC-130T	VMGR-452	165809		KC-130J	
164442	[NY]	KC-130T	VMGR-452	165810		KC-130J	
164597	[NY]	KC-130T-30	VMGR-452				

US-based US Coast Guard Aircraft

Grumman C-20B Gulfstream III
USCG, Washington DC
01

Lockheed HC-130H Hercules
USCGS Barbers Point, Hawaii;
USCGS Clearwater, Florida;
USCGS Elizabeth City, North Carolina;
USCGS Kodiak, Alaska;
USCGS Sacramento, California

1500	Elizabeth City
1501	Elizabeth City
1502	Elizabeth City
1503	Elizabeth City
1504	Elizabeth City
1601	Sacramento
1602	Sacramento
1603	Sacramento
1700	Kodiak
1701	Barbers Point
1702	Barbers Point
1703	Clearwater
1704	Clearwater
1705	Sacramento
1706	Kodiak
1707	Kodiak
1708	Kodiak
1709	Kodiak
1710	Clearwater
1711	Barbers Point
1712	Elizabeth City
1713	Clearwater
1714	Elizabeth City
1715	Sacramento
1716	Clearwater
1717	Clearwater
1718	Clearwater
1719	Clearwater
1720	Clearwater
1790	Sacramento

US Government Aircraft

BAe 125-800A (C-29A)
Federal Aviation Administration, Oklahoma

N94	(88-0269)
N95	(88-0270)
N96	(88-0271)
N97	(88-0272)
N98	(88-0273)
N99	(88-0274)

Gates LearJet 35A
Phoenix Aviation/Flight International/
US Navy, Naples
N20DK
N50FN
N88JA
N118FN

Rockwell B-1B Lancer flown by 7th BW at Dyess AFB, Texas. *Daniel March*

Gates C-21A Learjet carries USAFE on the tail as it is based at Ramstein, Germany, with the 86th AW. *PRM*

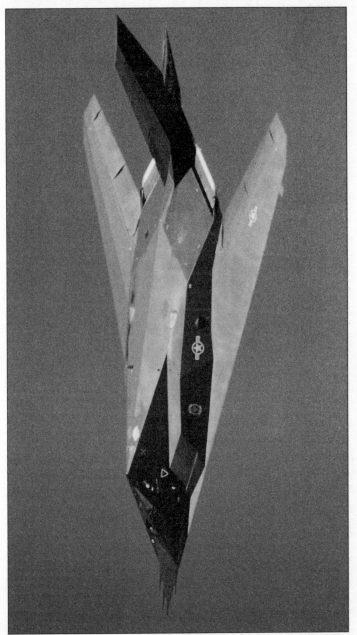

F-117A Nighthawk flown by the 49th FW, Holloman AFB, New Mexico. *PRM*

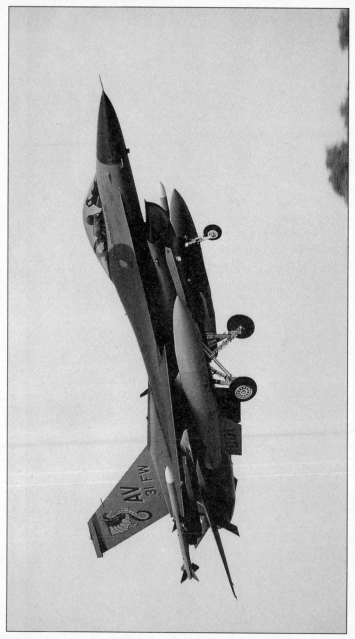

F-16C Fighting Falcon of the 31st FW, Aviano, Italy. *Daniel March*

Military Aviation Sites on the Internet

The list below is not intended to be a complete list of military aviation sites on the Internet. The sites listed cover Museums, Locations, Air Forces, Companies and Organisations that are mentioned elsewhere in *Military Aircraft Markings*. Sites listed are in English or contain sufficient English to be reasonably easily understood. Each site address is believed to be correct at the time of going to press. Additions are welcome, via the usual address found at the front of the book, or via e-mail to hjcurtis@cwcom.net

Name of site	*Internet Dial (all prefixed 'http;//')*
MILITARY SITES – UK	
No 2 Sqn	www.rafmarham.co.uk/organisation/2squadron/2squadron.htm
No 6 Flt	www.rafshawbury.demon.co.uk/6%20flt%20aac.htm
No 8 Sqn	www.users.globalnet.co.uk/~8sqnwad/
No 13 Sqn	www.rafmarham.co.uk/organisation/13squadron/13squadron.htm
No 15 Sqn	www.xvsquadron.f9.co.uk/
No 23 Sqn	www.users.globalnet.co.uk/~23sqnwad/
No 31 Sqn	members.xoom.com/kariba/31main.htm
No 39(1 PRU) Sqn	www.rafmarham.co.uk/organisation/39squadron/39squadron.htm
No 42(R) Sqn	www.kinloss.raf.mod.uk/opswing/ops42r.htm
No 45(R) Sqn	www.cranwell.raf.mod.uk/3fts/45sqn/45sqn.htm
No 47 Sqn	www.secant.co.uk/47sqn/
No 55(R) Sqn	www.cranwell.raf.mod.uk/3fts/55sqn/55sqn.htm
No 56 Sqn	www.56firebirds.raf.mod.uk/
No 120 Sqn	www.kinloss.raf.mod.uk/opswing/ops120.htm
No 201 Sqn	www.kinloss.raf.mod.uk/opswing/ops201.htm
No 206 Sqn	www.kinloss.raf.mod.uk/opswing/ops206.htm
Blue Eagles Home Page	www.deltaweb.co.uk/eagles/
Defence Helicopter Flying School	www.rafshawbury.demon.co.uk/dhfs.htm
DERA	www.dera.gov.uk/dera.htm
Fleet Air Arm	www.royal-navy.mod.uk/today/faa.htm
Manchester & Salford Universities Air Sqn	www.masuas.dial.pipex.com/
Ministry of Defence	www.mod.uk/
Oxford University Air Sqn	users.ox.ac.uk/~ouairsqn/
RAF Brize Norton	www.rafbrizenorton.com/
RAF Church Fenton (unofficial)	users.breathemail.net/churchfenton/
RAF College Cranwell	www.cranwell.raf.mod.uk/
RAF Cosford	www.raf.mod.uk/cosford/
RAF Kinloss	www.kinloss.raf.mod.uk/
RAF Leuchars	www.leuchars.raf.mod.uk/
RAF Lossiemouth	www.raflossiemouth.co.uk/
RAF Lyneham	www.lyneham.raf.mod.uk/
RAF Marham	www.rafmarham.co.uk/
RAF Northolt	www.northolt.com/
RAF Northolt (unofficial)	www.fly.to/Northolt/
RAF St Athan	ourworld.compuserve.com/homepages/st_athan/
RAF Shawbury	www.rafshawbury.demon.co.uk/
RAF Valley	www.ecafe.org/~paul/valley.htm
RAF Waddington	www.sandygordon.freeserve.co.uk/frames.htm
Red Arrows	www.deltaweb.co.uk/reds/
Royal Air Force	www.raf.mod.uk/
Royal Auxiliary Air Force	www.rauxaf.mod.uk/
University of London Air Sqn	www.raf.mod.uk/ulas
MILITARY SITES – US	
86th AW Home Page	www.ramstein.af.mil/org.htm
106th Rescue Wing, New York ANG	www.infoshop.com/106rescue/
Air Combat Command	www.acc.af.mil/
Air Force Flight Test Center (Edwards AFB)	www.edwards.af.mil/
Air Force Reserve Command	www.afrc.af.mil/
Air National Guard	www.ang.af.mil/
AMARC - up to date list of aircraft	www.dm.af.mil/amarc/inventory.htm
Aviano Air Base	www.aviano.af.mil/
Holloman Air Force Base	www.holloman.af.mil/
Hurricane Hunters Home Page (53rd WRS)	www.hurricanehunters.com/
Liberty Wing Home Page (48th FW)	www.lakenheath.af.mil/

Military Aviation Internet

Name of site	Internet Dial (all prefixed 'http://')
NASA	www.nasa.gov/
Nellis Air Force Base	www.nellis.af.mil/
Spangdahlem Air Base	www.spangdahlem.af.mil/
Travis Air Force Base	www.travis.af.mil/
The Thunderbirds	www.nellis.af.mil/thunderbirds/
USAF	www.af.mil/
USAF Europe	www.usafe.af.mil/
USAF World Wide Web Sites	www.af.mil/sites/
US Army	www.army.mil/
US Marine Corps	www.usmc.mil/
US Navy	www.navy.mil/
US Navy Patrol Squadrons (unofficial)	www.vpnavy.com/
Whiteman Air Force Base	www.whiteman.af.mil/

MILITARY SITES – ELSEWHERE

301 Sqn KLu	www.301sqn.com/
315 Sqn KLu	www.geocities.com/Pentagon/Quarters/8440/
Armée de l'Air	www.defense.gouv.fr/air/
Armée de l'Air (unofficial)	www.mygale.org/06/airmil/index.shtml
Aeronautica Militare	www.aeronautica.difesa.it
Austrian Armed Forces (in German)	www.bmlv.gv.at/
Belgian Air Force	www.mil.be/baf/eng/index_e.htm
East European Air Forces (unofficial)	mm.iit.uni-miskolc.hu/Data/Winx/
Finnish Defence Force	www.mil.fi/english/
Forca Aerea Portuguesa	www.emfa.pt/
Frecce Tricolori	users.iol.it/gromeo/
German Marine	www.bundeswehr.de/bundeswehr/marine/index.html
Indian Air Force	www.bharat-rakshak.com/IAF/
Israeli Defence Force/Air Force	www.idf.il/
Japan Air Self Defence Force	www.jda.go.jp/jasdf/indexE.htm
Luftforsvaret	www.mil.no/luftforsvaret/
Luftwaffe	www.bundeswehr.de/bundeswehr/luftwaffe/ index.html
NATO	www.nato.int/
Royal Australian Air Force	www.adfa.oz.au/DOD/RAAF/
Royal Danish Air Force (in Danish)	www.ftk.dk/
Royal Netherlands AF (unofficial)	web.inter.NL.net/hcc/D.vanDolderen/
Royal New Zealand AF	www.airforce.mil.nz/
Royal Thai Air Force	www.rtaf.mi.th
Singapore Air Force	www.mindef.gov.sg/rsaf/
South African AF Site (unofficial)	www.geocities.com/dwingrin/saaf.htm
Spanish Air Force	www.aire.org/
Swedish Air Force	www2.mil.se/
Swedish Military Aviation (unofficial)	www.canit.se/%7Egriffon/aviation/
Swiss Air Force (Unofficial)	www.airpic.ch/
Swiss Armed Forces	www.vbs.admin.ch/internet/e/armee/
Turkish General Staff (Armed Forces)	www.tsk.mil.tr/

AIRCRAFT & AERO ENGINE MANUFACTURERS

Aérospatiale	www.aerospatiale.fr/
BAE Systems	www.BAe.co.uk/
Bell Helicopter Textron	www.bellhelicopter.textron.com/index.html
Boeing	www.boeing.com/
Bombardier	www.bombardier.com/
Britten-Norman	www.britten-norman.com/
CFM International	www.cfm56.com/
Daimler-Benz Aerospace AG	www.dasa.com/
Dassault	www.dassault-aviation.com/
Embraer	www.embraer.com/
Fairchild Dornier	www.fairchilddornier.com/
Fokker	www.fokker.com/
General Electric	www.ge.com/
GKN Westland	www.gkn-whl.co.uk/
Gulfstream Aerospace	www.gulfstreamaircraft.com/
Kaman Aerospace	www.kaman.com/
LET	www.let.cz/
Lockheed Martin	www.lmco.com/
Lockheed Martin Skunk Works	www.skunkworks.net/
Raytheon (Beech, Hawker)	www.raytheon.com/rac/
Rolls-Royce	www.rolls-royce.com/
SAAB	www.saab.se/
Sikorsky	www.sikorsky.com/

Name of site	Internet Dial (all prefixed 'http;//')

UK AVIATION MUSEUMS

Aviation Museums in Great Britain	www.rdg.ac.uk/AcaDepts/sn/wsn1/dept/av/gb.html
Bournemouth Aviation Museum	www.aviation-museum.co.uk/
Brooklands Museum	www.motor-software.co.uk/brooklands/
City of Norwich Aviation Museum	www.mth.uea.ac.uk/~h720/aviation/conam.html
De Havilland Heritage Museum	www.netlink.co.uk/users/aeroflt/mus/mosqmus.htm
Flambards Village Theme Park	www.flambards.co.uk/
Gatwick Aviation Museum	www.gatwick-aviation-museum.co.uk/
Gloucestershire Avn Coll	gac.future.easyspace.com/gac.htm
The Helicopter Museum	www.Geocities.com/CapeCanaveral/Cockpit/2996/
Imperial War Museum, Duxford	www.iwm.org.uk/duxford.htm
Imperial War Museum, Duxford (unofficial)	dspace.dial.pipex.com/town/square/rcy85/
Lincs Aviation Heritage Centre	freespace.virgin.net/nick.tasker/ekirkby.htm
Midland Air Museum	fly.to/midlandairmuseum/
Museum of Berkshire Aviation	fly.to/MuseumofBerkshireAviation/
Museum of Flight, East Fortune	www.nms.ac.uk/flight/main.htm
Museum of Science & Industry, Manchester	www.msim.org.uk/
Newark Air Museum	www.emnet.co.uk/Museums/NewarkAir/
Norfolk and Suffolk Aviation Museum	www.aviationmuseum.net/
North East Aircraft Museum	members.tripod.com/~BDaugherty/neam.html
RAF Manston Spitfire & Hurricane Memorial	www.spitfire-museum.com/
RAF Museum, Cosford	www.rafmuseum.org.uk/flat/cosford/
RAF Museum, Hendon	www.rafmuseum.org.uk/
Science Museum, South Kensington	www.nmsi.ac.uk/on-line/flight/
Yorkshire Air Museum, Elvington	www.yorksairmuseum.freeserve.co.uk/

AVIATION SOCIETIES

Air Britain	www.air-britain.com/
Air Britain Merseyside	members.xoom.com/ABM/
Air North	www.airnorth.demon.co.uk/
Cleveland Aviation Society	members.aol.com/philc2/ctwhome.html
East London Aviation Society	www.westrowops.co.uk/newsletter/elas.htm
Friends of Leeming Aviation Group	www.crakehal.demon.co.uk/aviation/flag.htm
Gatwick Aviation Society	www.totavia.com/hawkeye/
Gilze-Rijen Aviation Society	fly.to/GRAS/
Royal Aeronautical Society	www.raes.org.uk/
St Athan Aviation Group	www.westrowops.co.uk/newsletter/stamu.htm
Scramble (Dutch Aviation Society)	www.scramble.nl/
Solent Aviation Society	www.solent-aviation-society.co.uk/
Spitfire Society	www.spitfiresociety.demon.co.uk/
Ulster Aviation Society	www.d-n-a.net/users/dnetrAzQ/

OPERATORS OF HISTORIC AIRCRAFT

Battle of Britain Memorial Flight	www.raf.mod.uk/on_display/bbmf.html
Catalina Online	www.catalina.org.uk/
Classic Jet Aircraft Company	www.classicjets.co.uk/
Delta Jets	www.deltajets.ik.com/
Kennet Aircraft	www.airplane.demon.co.uk/
Old Flying Machine Company	www.ofmc.co.uk/
The Fighter Collection	www.avnet.co.uk/tfc/
The Real Aeroplane Company	www.realaero.com/
The Vulcan Operating Company	www.tvoc.co.uk/

SITES RELATING TO SPECIFIC TYPES OF MILITARY AIRCRAFT

The 655 Maintenance & Preservation Society	www.jetman.dircon.co.uk/xm655/
The Avro Shackleton Page	www.home.aone.net.au/shack_one/
B-24 Liberator	www.b24bestweb.com/
B-52 Stratofortress Association	www.stratofortress.org/
Blackburn Buccaneer	ourworld.compuserve.com/homepages/andrewbrooks1/
EE Canberra	www.netcomuk.co.uk/~lesb/canberra.html
EE Lightning	homepages.enterprise.net/garry/light.html
The Eurofighter site	www.eurofighter.org/
The ex FRADU Canberra Site	www.fradu-hunters.co.uk/canberra/
The ex FRADU Hunter Site	www.fradu-hunters.co.uk/
F-4 Phantom II Society	www.f4phantom.org/
F-16: The Complete Reference	www.f-16.net/
F-86 Web Page	www.geocities.com/CapeCanaveral/Launchpad/8608/
F-105 Thunderchief	www.geocities.com/Pentagon/7002/
The Gripen	www.gripen.saab.se/
International F-104 Society	home.hetnet.nl/~hluijkx/ifs/ifs.html

Military Aviation Internet

Name of site	Internet Dial (all prefixed 'http://')
K5083 - Home Page (Hawker Hurricane)	www3.mistral.co.uk/k5083/
Lockheed C-130 Hercules	hometown.aol.com/SamC130/
Lockheed SR-71 Blackbird	www.wvi.com/~lelandh/sr-71~1.htm
The MiG-21 Page	www.topedge.com/panels/aircraft/sites/kraft/mig.htm
P-3 Orion Research Group	home.wxs.nl/~p3orin/
P-51 Mustang	www.p51mustang.com/
Scramble on the Web - SAAB Viggen Database	www.scramble.nl/viggen.htm
Swiss F-18 Hornet site (unofficial)	www.geocities.com/CapeCanaveral/Lab/6063/
Thunder & Lightnings (Postwar British Aircraft)	www.thunder-and-lightnings.co.uk/
Vulcan 558 Club	www.vulcan558club.demon.co.uk/
Vulcan Restoration Trust	www.XL426.com

MISCELLANEOUS

Aerodata	dspace.dial.pipex.com/aerodata/
Aeroflight	www.netlink.co.uk/users/aeroflt/
The 'AirNet' Links Site	fly.to/AirNet/
Air-Scene UK	www.f4aviation.co.uk
AirSpeed	www.netmontage.co.uk/airspeed/
The Aviator's Network	www.aviators.net/
Chinese Military Aviation	www.concentric.net/~Jetfight/
David Hastings' Military Aviation Page	users.ox.ac.uk/~daveh/Military/
Dutch Spotters On-line	www.dutchspotters.com/
Farnborough Movements & Photographs	www.geocities.com/CapeCanaveral/Hangar/1937/
Military Aircraft Database	www.csd.uwo.ca/~pettypi/elevon/gustin_military/
Military Aviation	www.crakehal.demon.co.uk/aviation/aviation.htm
Military Aviation Review/MAP	www.mar.co.uk/
Moray Air Net	morayairnet.co.uk/
Polish Aviation Site	aviation.pol.pl/
Russian Aviation Page	aeroweb.lucia.it/~agretch/RAP.html
Scramble on the Web - Air Show Reports	www.scramble.nl/airshows.htm
The Spotter's Nest	www.spotters.it/
UK Military Spotting	www.thunder-and-lightnings.co.uk/spotting/

Chinook HC2 ZA684 of No 7 Squadron, Odiham. *PRM*

VC10 K3 ZA148 of No 101 Squadron, Brize Norton in October 2000. *PRM*

Army Air Corps Gazelle AH1 XZ309, Lynx AH9 and Lynx AH7 at Middle Wallop. *PRM*